Justice in America

Wartyna L. Davis

William Paterson University

Kendall Hunt
p u b l i s h i n g   c o m p a n y

Cover image provided by author.

Kendall Hunt
publishing company

www.kendallhunt.com
Send all inquiries to:
4050 Westmark Drive
Dubuque, IA 52004-1840

Copyright © 2009 by Wartyna L. Davis

ISBN 978-0-7575-6477-2

Printed in the United States of America
10 9 8 7 6 5 4 3 2 1

For my Parents, Warren III and Tyna D. Davis

"If I have seen a little further it is by standing on the shoulders of Giants"
—Sir Isaac Newton

Contents

Section 4
Problems for and Progress Towards a More Perfect Union 297

Section 5
Where Do We Go from Here? The Nexus of Citizenship and Justice   393

Appendicies   431

Contributors

Wartyna L. Davis earned a Ph.D. in Political Science from Florida State University. She is currently Professor and Chair of the Department of Political Science at William Paterson University. Dr. Davis is the author of several works on race and gender politics, as well as, political parties and interest groups in the United States. Professor Davis is a committed educator and scholar whose efforts have been focused on advancing social justice.

*****

Tyna D. Davis earned the doctorate in Education, Policy and Law from Alabama State University. She is a renowned educator having served as a classroom teacher, leader, writer and consultant on many educational issues. Dr. Davis has been a change agent in education and has been intricately involved in education policy decisions at the federal, state, and local levels. She presently serves as the Managing Director of the Education Policy and Professional Practice Division of the Alabama Education Association.

H. Mark Ellis earned his Ph.D. from Northwestern University and is currently an Associate Professor of Sociology at William Paterson University. His research interests include cultural sociology and the social organization of work and occupations. Dr. Ellis' teaching interests are social stratification, race, social problems and inequality.

J.T. Ghim is a doctoral student at the University Massachusetts, Amherst in Political Science and has interests in justice, equity and political philosophy.

Diana M. Judd earned her Ph.D. at Rutgers University in Political Science. She is an Assistant Professor of Political Science at William Paterson University. Dr. Judd has recently published *Questioning Authority and* has teaching and research specialties in political philosophy, and religion and politics.

Kendra A. King earned her Ph.D. in Political Science from The Ohio State University. She is currently an Associate Professor of Political Science at Oglethorpe University. She is also the Assistant Director of the Urban Leadership Program. Dr. King is an international speaker and author on the subject of race and ethnic politics.

Arnold C. Lewis, Jr. earned his Ph.D. in Political Science from Florida State University. He has published several works on legislative affairs and state and urban political economy. He most recently published *American Government: Assessing Behavior & Ideas*. Dr. Lewis is an Assistant Professor in the Department of Political Science at William Paterson University.

Andrew M. Manis is an Associate Professor of History at Macon State College in Georgia and a graduate of the Southern Baptist Theological Seminary. His book, *A Fire You Can't Put Out: The Civil Rights Life of Birmingham's Rev. Fred Shuttlesworth,* won several prizes including the 2000 Lillian Smith Book Award. His most recent book is *Macon Black and White: An Unutterable Separation in the American Century.*

Michael Luis Principe earned his Ph.D. in Political Science from the University of California at Santa Barbara and his J.D. from the University of Washington. He is the author of several books and articles, most recently *Bill of Rights: a Comparative Constitutional Analysis, 2nd ed.* and *American Government, Policy, and Law, 2nd ed.* His research interests are constitutional law, comparative rights, political theory, international human rights & policy.

R. L. Raines is a *cum laude* graduate of Amherst College and majored in American Studies. He received his J.D. from a New York Law School. Professor Raines is a faculty member in the Department of African, African-American and Caribbean Studies. Professor Raines' teaching and research interest is the African American experience in the pre-civil War period.

Dr. Darlene Russell earned her doctorate degree from Columbia University's Teachers College. Her research interests include culturally responsive pedagogy, critical literacies, and effective practices for supervising student teachers. Dr. Russell is the Founder and Director of the Nurturing Culturally Responsive English Equity Teachers (NCREET) Research Project. The Project grooms selected undergraduate English education students to become practitioners of culturally responsive instruction and teachers for social justice in the K-12 classroom.

Arlene Holpp Scala is Professor and Chair of the Department of Women and Gender studies at William Paterson University. She earned her doctorate from Columbia University. Dr. Scala's teaching and research interest are popular culture, LGBT issues, and pedagogy.

Martha Thomas is a doctoral candidate at Pennsylvania State University. Her primary research interests are international affairs and the immigrant experience in the United States.

1

America's Promise

Wartyna L. Davis

> We hold these truths to be self-evident, that all men are created equal, that they are endowed by their Creator with certain unalienable rights, that among these are life, liberty and the pursuit of happiness.
>
> —The Declaration of Independence, 1776

When one reads the magnificent words of the Declaration of Independence and the demand for universal acknowledgement of the fundamental rights of all men, one cannot help but be filled with pride. One imagines an America in which hard work and perseverance are appropriately rewarded. This imagery was constructed and retold as part of the mythology of America.

But that original demand for equality was tragically flawed. It required freedom and liberty for all while the authors devised a system of government that denied equality to an overwhelming majority of the population.

We find ourselves well into the 21st century dealing with tremendous inequity with regards to: education, employment, health care, and the criminal justice system.

- Twenty-six percent of white adults had at least a bachelor's degree, as compared to 14% of black adults and 10% of Latino adults.[1]
- The median income for white households was $50,622. It was $30,939 for black households and $36,278 for Latino households.[2]
- Twenty-six percent of blacks and 22% of Latinos live below the poverty line as compared to 9% of the white population.[3]
- Seventy-five percent of white households own their homes, compared with 46% of black households and 48% of Latino households.[4]
- Eleven percent of white Americans do not have health insurance. Twenty percent of blacks and 33% of Latinos are uninsured.[5]
- Thirty-two percent of blacks do not have a regular doctor, as compared to only 20% of white Americans that do not have a regular doctor.[6]
- Infant mortality rates for blacks are more than twice the rate for whites.[7]

- Life expectancy for whites is 78.3 years and 73.2 years for blacks[8]
- Black males comprise 12% of the male population in the United States but 40% of the incarcerated male population. Latinos make up 13% of the male population but 20% of the incarcerated population.[9]
- The number of Latina women incarcerated has increased 71% from 2000–2008.[10]

Is the American dream available to everyone or are there systematic forces in play that limit the possibilities for some? How do we reconcile the mythology and the current reality? One way to do this is to acknowledge that the United States is in fact a work in progress. We are a promise yet to be fulfilled—a promise that grows closer generation by generation through the commitment of its citizens. We can look to the significant progress that has been made over the last 200 years as evidence of that commitment. It is my hope that this anthology will provoke lively debate on the meaning and application of justice in the United States.

In Section 1, we shall interrogate the concept of justice. This section will provide the reader with literature that demonstrates the complexity in developing a common understanding of the concept. Contributions include classical works as well as more contemporary pieces that illustrate attempts to apply justice.

Section 2 looks at the concept of race and examines how racism impacts the expectation and implementation of justice on abstract and concrete levels. The reader will be given the opportunity to understand the unique evolution and construction of "race" in the United States. The selection includes a survey writings from the last century that address the impact of this unique racial hierarchy.

We then will see, in Section 3, specific examples of how race and justice have interacted in the history of the United States. This section will give the reader a chronology of the often troubled juncture of race and United States courts. These specific examples will highlight the discrepancies between the mythology of American justice and the reality from a historical perspective.

Section 4 addresses the quest for justice. We examine some of the major questions we encounter in our pursuit, such as inequity in education and employment, access to political arenas, the validity of Affirmative Action as a remedy, and the problem of social inequity.

Lastly, Section 5 examines potential directions for accelerating our quest for justice. We visit literature that proposes methods to lessen the divide between the mythology of American justice and our reality.

It is my hope that this text sheds light on the problems of racial inequity from a modern and historical perspective. Through understanding, critical analysis, and honesty with ourselves and others, it is my hope that we can demolish the barriers hindering us from achieving "justice for all." It is then, and only then, that we will finally fulfill America's Promise.

Endnotes

1. *http://factfinder.census.gov/*
2. U.S. Census Bureau, 2005–2007 American Community Survey, *http://www.census.gov/acs/www/index.html*
3. *http://www.census.gov/prod/2007pubs/acs-04.pdf* and *http://www.census.gov/Press-Release/www/releases/archives/income_wealth/005647.html*
4. U.S. Census Bureau, 2005–2007 American Community Survey, *http://www.census.gov/acs/www/index.html*
5. *http://www.census.gov/Press-Release/www/releases/archives/income_wealth/005647.html*
6. "2001 Health Care Quality Survey," The Commonwealth Fund, New York, NY, November 2001, chart 37.
7. *http://www.cdc.gov/nchs/data/hus/hus07.pdf*, p. 159
8. *http://www.cdc.gov/nchs/data/hus/hus07.pdf*, p. 175
9. *http://www.ojp.usdoj.gov/bjs/pub/pdf/pim08st.pdf*, p. 17
10. *http://www.ojp.usdoj.gov/bjs/pub/pdf/pim08st.pdf*, p.17

SECTION 1

Justice—The Evolution of an Idea

2

Defining Justice

Diana M. Judd

What is justice? This question has occupied thinkers since the first stirrings of political philosophy in the West over 2,000 years ago. In this chapter, we will explore some of the more influential conceptions of justice. The central questions driving our investigation will be, first, how may we inquire into the nature of justice, and second, what is the relationship between justice and the law? This chapter is divided into two parts. In Part I we will consider the political philosophy of four thinkers from the ancient and medieval eras: Plato, Aristotle, Cicero, and Aquinas. The readings that follow this part, one each from Aristotle and Thomas Aquinas, serve to illustrate two approaches to our central questions that were unique to this era. In Part II we will consider three political philosophers of the modern era: Hobbes, Rousseau, and Marx. As we will see, modern political thinkers formulated conceptions of justice differently from their ancient and medieval counterparts. The readings that follow Part II, one each from Rousseau and Hobbes, illustrate this difference. Of course, these selections are by no means exhaustive. There are many ways we can conceptualize justice, and each is a crucial step on the road in discovering *how ought we to live:* the principal question driving political thought for over two millennia.

3

Part A:
Ancient and Medieval Foundations of Justice

Diana M. Judd

In terms of political thought, the ancient era is commonly dated from the inception of philosophy proper in Athens, Greece, in the fifth century B.C.E. to the fall of the Roman Empire in the fifth century C.E. We may date the medieval era as beginning at this point, and lasting through the 15th century C.E. During this span of time, political philosophy in general and the approach to the problem of justice in particular underwent significant changes. The works of Plato, Aristotle, Cicero, and Aquinas are representative of these changes, and we will explore how each philosopher approached the problem of justice.

Plato (427–347 B.C.E.) is considered to be the first—and some would claim the greatest—political philosopher. He lived and wrote during the so-called "golden age" of ancient Athens. He approached the question of justice most famously in his masterwork, *The Republic*. The form of this work is a dialogue between several characters, each of whom represents a different aspect of the argument. The "hero" of the dialogue is Socrates, Plato's mentor and friend. In many of Plato's works, Socrates engages an individual of reputation in Athenian society in conversation. Invariably, Socrates demonstrates (publicly) that his interlocutors do not possess any real knowledge, and are relying on opinions they cannot defend, or on rhetoric they cannot escape. In *The Republic*, Socrates engages a small gathering of friends and acquaintances in the *elenchus*, a method involving a series of questions and answers.

Socrates and Plato believed that philosophy was a crucial component in the search for the good life, and a necessary step on the road to happiness, which is the goal of all life. Both considered justice to be vitally important to these concerns. At the beginning of *The Republic*, Plato introduces us to three differing concepts of justice. The first concept is put forth by Cephalus, a respected, older man of considerable wealth. He states that justice consists in giving each what is owed. After being questioned by Socrates, however, it becomes clear that Cephalus cannot defend his answer. He simply relies on authority for his knowledge, specifically the words of famous authors. The next definition of justice is given by Polemarchus, Cephalus's son. After some consideration, he amends his father's answer and claims that justice consists of doing good to friends and harm to enemies. Socrates questions this conception on the grounds of what "good" and "bad" are. For example, are friends always good people and are enemies always bad people? Furthermore, Socrates argues, it can never be just to harm anyone. Polemarchus quickly gives in to Socrates' position.

The most intriguing character of the dialogue enters at this stage. Plato depicts Thrasymachus as impatient with the direction of the conversation, and hostile to Socrates' seemingly childish tactics of questioning everything without ever putting forth his own views. Significantly, Thrasymachus is the only one to remain undeterred from his position throughout. His idea is: Justice is simply the advantage of the stronger. As Thrasymachus explains, in every government a ruling body forms laws on the basis of its own advantage. That way, they can maintain their power by punishing anyone acting against their advantage as a lawbreaker and an unjust man. Thus, Thrasymachus concludes, the essence of justice is everywhere the same: the advantage of the stronger. Although Socrates proceeds to poke holes in this position, Thrasymachus never changes his stance.

We may now ask the first of our two questions. How did Plato inquire into the nature of justice? In *The Republic* he invoked abstract categories such as "good," "bad," "truth," and "knowledge." Indeed, Plato's own definition of justice in *The Republic*—offered by Socrates—makes sense only if we accept the existence of these categories as metaphysical absolutes. According to Plato, justice consists of a well-ordered soul: the intellect must rule and keep our appetites in check. The only proper way to live is in moderation, because moderation is the only route to happiness. Plato illustrates this by having Socrates and his interlocutors speculate about what kind of city would be the most just. They decide that a city in which the leaders are also philosophers ("philosopher-kings"), and in which the population is divided into separate strata according to their job or "excellence" (e.g., medicine, carpentry, defense), will be the most just. Why? Because such a city would be characterized by harmony between its constituent parts and by moderation, and therefore it would be a virtuous city. Recall that this city is an ideal: it is meant to be a metaphor for the soul. Thus Plato's overall point is that each one of us is capable of living a just life if we embrace moderation, the route to happiness.

We can now address the second of our two questions. Are justice and the law the same thing for Plato? The answer to this question must be no. For if we accept Plato's argument that there is an absolute idea of "the good," which is perfect but cannot be achieved in reality, there can be no set of laws in political reality that reflect true justice. The best we can do is discover virtue and the good in ourselves, and help our fellows do the same. Then, perhaps, we may be fortunate enough to live in a just society.

Aristotle (384–322 B.C.E.), Plato's star student and tutor of Alexander the Great, disagreed with certain aspects of his teacher's philosophy. Although he embraced the notions of moderation and the importance of happiness, he rejected Plato's metaphysical idealism. Whereas Plato considered justice to be a virtue of the soul, Aristotle's inquiry into the nature of justice was carried out in terms of the benefits and obligations shared by each member of society. Aristotle's method also parted company from Plato's. Instead of a dialogue between several interlocutors, Aristotle's argument is conveyed in the more familiar format of the treatise.

The Politics contains Aristotle's most direct treatment of justice, citizenship, and the law. How did Aristotle inquire into the nature of justice? He argued that justice, like human beings themselves, cannot exist in isolation. If we are to properly investigate justice, we must do so in terms of the *polis* (the ancient Greek word for city-state and the root of the word "political") and not in terms of the soul. For Aristotle, political association is the highest, most noble form of the good we can attain, and as social animals we can only achieve the good life—and thus happiness—in association with others. Aristotle's notion of justice is *distributive*: it centers on what citizens owe their political society, and in turn what society owes its citizenry (literally, the distribution of benefits and obligations). His two-pronged definition of justice reflects this approach. Justice is the good in the sphere of politics, and justice promotes the common interest.

Are justice and the law the same thing for Aristotle? In strict terms, they are not. Aristotle frames the matter thusly: There are just laws and unjust laws. Just laws are those that support "right constitutions"; unjust laws are those that support "perverted constitutions." A constitution determines the organization of offices in a *polis*, and prescribes "the nature of the end to be pursued by the association and all of its members." Aristotle enumerates "right constitutions" as kingships, aristocracies, and polities. "Perverted constitutions" are tyrannies, oligarchies, and democracies. Aristotle was not alone in considering democracy an unjust form of government. Plato also believed that democracies were run by experts in rhetoric who preyed on the uninformed, instead of those who partook of true knowledge and calm, philosophical reflection.

Aristotle categorizes constitutions into six categories, the best of which is the "polity." A polity is described as consisting of three separate powers: "deliberative," "executive," and "judicial." Although this formulation certainly reflects the structure of the U.S. Constitution, we should not assume that the framers of the latter took their cues directly from Aristotle. Rather, what should be noted is that the link between divided sovereign authority and justice itself has been present in political philosophy since Aristotle.

In the end, Aristotle's inquiries into the nature of justice lead him to a different place than Plato's. The latter's involved metaphysical absolutes and the conclusion that justice is a virtue of the well-ordered soul. Aristotle's approach is less absolute and more dependent upon the type of constitution and the kind of laws present in it. As he himself put it in Book VI of *The Politics*, "to find where truth resides, in these matters of equality and justice, is a very difficult task. Nevertheless, it is an easier task than that of persuading men to act justly, if they have power enough to secure their own selfish interests. The weaker are always anxious for equality and justice. The strong pay no heed to either."

The influence of Plato and Aristotle on subsequent political theory cannot be overstated. Their respective approaches to the concept of justice in particular informed treatments of this idea for millennia. Indeed, we could argue that the history of Western political philosophy itself may be categorized in terms of an alternating embrace or rejection of ancient Greek thought.

For example, the rise of the Roman Empire and the fall of the Greek city-states heralded a rejection of Greek political philosophy. Considered to be the culture of the vanquished, things Greek were either assimilated into the larger Roman framework (which was itself a complex combination of peoples and cultures within its vast borders), or considered outmoded and superfluous, if not suppressed altogether. Greek political theory had centered on the city-state, which had ceased to be a meaningful political unit. Of what use was a philosophy based on the *polis* in the age of empire? Marcus Tullius Cicero (106–43 B.C.E.), a Roman statesman and lawyer, answered this question in the following way: the particular philosophies of the Greeks might no longer be relevant, but their approach to knowledge itself was valuable. Therefore all we need, he argued, is to emulate them only insofar as we need to create a political philosophy for our times, one that addresses Rome's unique political problems.

Cicero's analysis of justice represented a significant shift in Western political thought. A pressing political concern in the Roman Republic was how to maintain stability across an expanding empire encompassing many religions, cultures, and nationalities. Rome's answer was a sophisticated legal system. Cicero's political philosophy reflects a respect for the overarching importance of the law in Roman political life. In *On the Commonwealth*, Cicero inquires into the nature of justice in terms of its relationship to the law.

On the Commonwealth is in the form of a dialogue whose interlocutors investigate the nature of justice by asking such questions as: Does justice consist only in following the laws of a particular constitution? Can justice exist if laws only reflect the self-interest of the rulers? If people obey laws only because they fear punishment, is the concept of justice relevant? If laws vary from country to country, does justice itself also vary in the same way? Cicero brings these questions together by positing the existence of two different kinds of law. The first is written legislation, created by every political society, and which differs from place to place. The second kind of law, however, transcends time and place and is unchanging. This is *natural law*, which may be thought of as morality transcending codified human laws. This unchanging natural law may be broken by the immoral, but that has no effect upon its existence. In other words, Cicero's natural law is *justice itself*. It is universally applicable, discoverable, and no person, nation, or empire can destroy it. The best laws are those that follow its dictates.

Given Cicero's formulation, our question—are justice and the law the same thing?—takes on a new dimension, for the terms of the debate have been changed. Justice itself is now reformulated as law, but a different conception of law than we have seen before. Various forms of natural law theory would be taken up by medieval political philosophers after the fall of the Roman Empire, and it is to one of them that we now turn.

The spread of Christianity and the fall of the Roman Empire signaled the onset of the medieval era in the West. Medieval political philosophy may be defined as the marriage between Greek philosophy (reason) on the one hand, and religious doctrine (faith), on the other. After being rejected for centuries, ancient Greek philosophy was embraced during this era. The works of Plato and Aristotle were rediscovered by Islamic thinkers and their work reflected a unique blending of monotheistic religion and Greek philosophy, which set the stage for Thomas Aquinas (ca. 1225–1274 C.E.), commonly considered to be one of the greatest Christian theologians of all time.

The Crusades brought the works of Aristotle from the Islamic East to the Christian West. Within a few years of the translation of Aristotle's *Politics* into Latin, Aquinas set to work on his magnum opus, the *Summa Theologica* (1266). In this work, Aquinas set down what he considered to be the proper relationship between reason and faith. He covered a dizzying array of topics, including the proof of the existence of the Christian God, ethics, free will, and the world's creation. His work was groundbreaking in that it made the pagan Greek philosophy acceptable in the West, albeit by making it the servant of theology. Aquinas cemented the direction knowledge itself would take until the modern era. One of the major topics he explored in the *Summa Theologica* was the nature of justice.

Like Cicero before him, Aquinas inquired into the nature of justice in terms of natural law. Unlike Cicero, however, Aquinas added a Christian component, which enabled him to develop a tripartite conception of law. Aquinas's method may seem confusing at first glance, but it is systematic throughout. For each of his topics he asks a particular question (i.e., "Whether there is a natural law?"). He then presents three "objections," which are usually the words of Greek philosophers, Roman writers, or other theologians. He then gives a contrary statement to the objections, which is usually a quote from the Bible or from Augustine (354–430 C.E.; a Roman writer and the father of Christian theology). And finally, Aquinas presents his own views with the phrase "I answer that. . . ."

There are three levels of Aquinas's natural law theory: eternal law, natural law, and human law. Eternal law is God's will. Aquinas also refers to this as "Divine Wisdom" and "Divine Reason." Because this is unchanging, it has the nature of an unchanging law which is not subject to time or human action. Natural law is related to eternal law in that it is how humans partake in God's will. Because we can never know exactly what God's will is, the closest approximation we have is natural law. In other words, natural law is morality, a sense of good and evil, given by God to us. It is only through the natural law that humans can discover what justice is. What of human law? Aquinas argues that this is merely the particular determination of certain matters. That is, human law is merely the law on the books, i.e., legislation. What is important to realize is that for Aquinas, because humans are fallible, erring creatures, human law can also be fallible and filled with error. "Divine wisdom," on the other hand, is perfect. Therefore anything that is derived from it is also perfect.

What are the implications of this for justice? If justice itself is an element of natural law, and if natural law is how we partake in God's will (i.e., eternal law), then justice and morality are part and parcel of the same thing. Yet if humans are fallible, error prone creatures, human legislation cannot always be in accordance with either justice or morality. We may well ask ourselves, if human law and justice are in conflict, which should we follow? This question was asked by Martin Luther King, Jr. (1929–1968) in the mid-1960s in his "Letter from Birmingham Jail," and he answered it in terms of Aquinas's conception of natural law. By using Aquinas's categories, King was able to posit the difference between just laws and unjust laws. He argued that just laws are those that partake of a sense of morality that transcends human law—just laws uplift the human personality. Likewise, unjust laws are those that do not partake in morality—they degrade the human personality. In this fashion King was able to make a compelling argument for civil disobedience and protest against segregation laws, and he did so via the idea that justice itself is separate from human legislation.

From the death of Aquinas in the mid-13th century, through the Renaissance, and up to the dawn of the modern era, Greek philosophy was heartily embraced. Indeed, Aristotle's works were disseminated through universities all over Europe, and his words were commented upon and debated in endless tomes. All scholarship and knowledge in the West during this time stemmed from this blending of Aristotle's philosophy with Christian doctrine, which came to be known as Aristotelian Scholasticism. With the dawn of the modern age came a rejection of the intellectual hegemony of this form of Greek thought and philosophy.

4

Politics

Aristotle

The Principles of Oligarchy and Democracy, and the Nature of Distributive Justice

Chapter IX

> The principle of a constitution is its conception of justice; and this is the funda-
> mental ground of difference between oligarchy and democracy. Democrats hold
> that if men are equal by birth, they should in justice have equal rights: oligarchs
> hold that if they are unequal in wealth, they should in justice have unequal rights.
> True justice means that those who have contributed to the end of the state should
> have rights in proportion to their contribution to that end. The end of the state
> is not mere life, nor an alliance for mutual defence; it is the common promotion
> of a good quality of life. We must distinguish between the necessary conditions of
> the state's existence (contiguity, consanguinity, and economic co-operation) and
> its operative aim. The operative aim is always the promotion of a good quality of
> life; and those who contribute most to the realization of that aim should in justice
> have most rights.

§ 1. We must next ascertain [now that we have discovered the social ground on which they
rest] what are the distinctive principles attributed by their advocates to oligarchy and
democracy, and what are the oligarchical and the democratic conceptions of justice.[1] Both
oligarchs and democrats have a hold on a sort of conception of justice; but they both fail
to carry it far enough, and neither of them expresses the true conception of justice in the
whole of its range. In democracies, for example, justice is considered to mean equality [in
the distribution of office]. It does mean equality—but equality for those who are equal, and
not for all. § 2. In oligarchies, again, inequality in the distribution of office is considered to
be just; and indeed it is—but only for those who are unequal, and not for all. The advocates
of oligarchy and democracy both refuse to consider this factor—who are the persons to
whom their principles properly apply—and they both make erroneous judgments. The rea-

son is that they are judging *in their own case*; and most men, as a rule, are bad judges where their own interests are involved. § 3. Justice is relative to persons; and a just distribution is one in which the relative values of the things given correspond to those of the persons receiving—a point which has already been made in the *Ethics*. [It follows that a just distribution of offices among a number of different persons will involve a consideration of the personal values, or merits, of each of those persons.] But the advocates of oligarchy and democracy, while they agree about what constitutes equality in the *thing,* disagree about what constitutes it in *persons.*[2] The main reason for this is the reason just stated—they are judging, and judging erroneously, in their own case; but there is also another reason—they are misled by the fact that they are professing a sort of conception of justice, and professing it up to a point, into thinking that they profess one which is absolute and complete. § 4. The oligarchs think that superiority on one point—in their case wealth—means superiority on all: the democrats believe that equality in one respect—for instance, that of free birth—means equality all round.

§ 5. Both sides, however, fail to mention the really cardinal factor [i.e. the nature of the end for which the state exists]. If property were the end for which men came together and formed an association, men's share [in the offices and honours] of the state would be proportionate to their share of property; and in that case the argument of the oligarchical side—that it is not just for a man who has contributed one pound to share equally in a sum of a hundred pounds (or, for that matter, in the interest accruing upon that sum) with the man who has contributed all the rest—would appear to be a strong argument. § 6. But the end of the state is not mere life; it is, rather, a good quality of life. [If mere life were the end], there might be a state of slaves, or even a state of animals; but in the world as we know it any such state is impossible, because slaves and animals do not share in true felicity[3] and free choice [i.e. the attributes of a good quality of life]. Similarly, it is not the end of the state to provide an alliance for mutual defence against all injury, or to ease exchange and promote economic intercourse. If that had been the end, the Etruscans and the Carthaginians [who are united by such bonds] would be in the position of belonging to a single state; and the same would be true of all peoples who have commercial treaties with one another. § 7. It is true that such peoples have agreements about imports and exports; treaties to ensure just conduct [in the course of trade]; and written terms of alliance for mutual defence. On the other hand they have no common offices of state to deal with these matters: each, on the contrary, has its own offices, confined to itself. Neither of the parties concerns itself to ensure a proper quality of character among the members of the other;[4] neither of them seeks to ensure that all who are included in the scope of the treaties shall be free from injustice[5] and from any form of vice; and neither of them goes beyond the aim of preventing its own members from committing injustice [in the course of trade] against the members of the other. § 8. But it is the cardinal issue of goodness or badness in the life of the polis which always engages the attention of any state that concerns itself to secure a system of good laws well obeyed [*eunomia*]. The conclusion which clearly follows is that any polis which is truly so called, and is not merely one in name, must devote itself to the end of encouraging goodness. Otherwise, a political association sinks into a mere alliance, which only differs in space [i.e. in the contiguity of its members] from other forms of alliance where the members live at a distance from one another. Otherwise, too, law becomes a mere covenant—or (in the phrase of the Sophist Lycophron) 'a guarantor of men's rights against one another'—instead of being, as it should be, a rule of life such as will make the members of a polis good and just.[6]

§ 9. That this is the case [i.e. that a polis is truly a polis only when it makes the encouragement of goodness its end] may be readily proved.[7] If two different sites could be united in one, so that the polis of Megara and that of Corinth were embraced by a single wall, that would not make a single polis. If the citizens of two cities intermarried with one another, that would not make a single polis—even though intermarriage is one of the forms of social life which are characteristic of a polis. § 10. Nor would it make a polis if a number of persons—living at a distance from one another, but not at so great a distance but that they could still associate—had a common system of laws to prevent their injuring one another in the course of exchange. We can imagine, for instance, one being a carpenter, another a farmer, a third a shoemaker, and others producing other goods; and we can imagine a total number of as many as 10,000. But if these people were associated in nothing further than matters such as exchange and alliance, they would still have failed to reach the stage of a polis. § 11. Why should this be the case? It cannot be ascribed to any lack of contiguity in such an association. The members of a group so constituted might come together on a single site; but if that were all—if each still treated his private house as if it were a state, and all of them still confined their mutual assistance to action against aggressors (as if it were only a question of a defensive alliance)—if, in a word, the spirit of their intercourse were still the same after their coming together as it had been when they were living apart—their association, even on its new basis, could not be deemed by any accurate thinker to be a polis. § 12. It is clear, therefore, that a polis is not an association for residence on a common site, or for the sake of preventing mutual injustice and easing exchange. These are indeed conditions which must be present before a polis can exist; but the presence of all these conditions is not enough, in itself, to constitute a polis. What constitutes a polis is an association of households and clans in a good life, for the sake of attaining a perfect and self-sufficing existence.[8] § 13. This consummation, however, will not be reached unless the members inhabit one and the self-same place and practise intermarriage.[9] It was for this reason [i.e. to provide these necessary conditions] that the various institutions of a common social life—marriage-connexions, kin-groups, religious gatherings, and social pastimes generally—arose in cities. But these institutions are the business of friendship [and not the purpose of the polis]. It is friendship [and not a polis] which consists in the pursuit of a common social life. The end and purpose of a polis is the good life, and the institutions of social life are means to that end. § 14. A polis is constituted by the association of families and villages in a perfect and self-sufficing existence; and such an existence, on our definition, consists in a life of true felicity and goodness.

It is therefore for the sake of good actions, and not for the sake of social life, that political associations must be considered to exist. § 15. [This conclusion enables us to attain a proper conception of justice.] Those who contribute most to an association of this character [i.e. who contribute mast to good action] have a greater share in the polis [and should therefore, in justice, receive a larger recognition from it] than those who are equal to them (or even greater) in free birth and descent, but unequal in civic excellence, or than those who surpass them in wealth but are surpassed by them in excellence.[10] From what has been said it is plain that both sides to the dispute about constitutions [i.e. both the democratic and the oligarchical side] profess only a partial conception of justice.

Chapter XII[11]

> Justice is the political good. It involves equality, or the distribution of equal amounts to equal persons. But who are equals, and by what criterion are persons to be reckoned as equals? Many criteria can be applied; but the only proper criterion, in a political society, is that of contribution to the function of that society. Those who are equal *in that respect* should receive equal amounts: those who are superior or inferior should receive superior or inferior amounts, in proportion to the degree of their superiority or inferiority. If all are thus treated proportionately to the contribution they make, all are really receiving equal treatment; for the proportion between contribution and reward is the same in every case. The sort of equality which justice involves is thus proportionate equality; and this is the essence of distributive justice.

§ 1. In all arts and sciences the end in view is some good. In the most sovereign of all the arts and sciences—and this is the art and science of politics—the end in view is the greatest good and the good which is most pursued.[12] The good in the sphere of politics is justice; and justice consists in what tends to promote the common interest. General opinion makes it consist in some sort of equality.[13] Up to a point this general opinion agrees with the philosophical inquiries which contain our conclusions on ethics. In other words, it holds that justice involves two factors—things, and the persons to whom things are assigned—and it considers that persons who are equal should have assigned to them equal things. § 2. But here there arises a question which must not be overlooked. Equals and unequals—yes; but equals and equals *in what?* This is a question which raises difficulties, and involves us in philosophical speculation on politics.[14] It is possible to argue that offices and honours ought to be distributed unequally [i.e. that superior amounts should be assigned to superior persons] on the basis of superiority *in any respect whatsoever*—even though there were similarity, and no shadow of any difference, in every other respect; and it may be urged, in favour of this argument, that where people differ from one another there must be a difference in what is just and proportionate to their merits. § 3. If this argument were accepted, the mere fact of a better complexion, or greater height, or any other such advantage, would establish a claim for a greater share of political rights to be given to its possessor. § 4. But is not the argument obviously wrong? To be clear that it is, we have only to study the analogy of the other arts and sciences. If you were dealing with a number of flute-players who were equal in their art, you would not assign them flutes on the principle that the better born should have a greater amount. Nobody will play the better for being better born; and it is to those who are better at the job that the better supply of tools should be given. If our point is not yet plain, it can be made so if we push it still further. § 5. Let us suppose a man who is superior to others in flute-playing, but far inferior in birth and beauty. Birth and beauty may be greater goods than ability to play the flute, and those who possess them may, upon balance, surpass the flute-player more in these qualities than he surpasses them in his flute-playing; but the fact remains that *he* is the man who ought to get the better supply of flutes. [If it is to be recognized in connexion with a given function], superiority in a quality such as birth— or for that matter wealth—ought to contribute something to the performance of that function; and here these qualities contribute nothing to such performance.

§ 6. There is a further objection. If we accept this argument [that offices and honours should be assigned on the basis of excellence in *any* respect], every quality will have to be commensurable with every other. You will begin by reckoning a given degree of (say) height as superior to a given degree of some other quality, and you will thus be driven to pit height in general against (say) wealth and birth in general. But on this basis—i.e. that, *in a given case*, A is counted as excelling in height to a greater degree than B does in goodness, and that, *in general*, height is counted as excelling to a greater degree than goodness does— qualities are made commensurable. [We are involved in mere arithmetic]; for if amount X of some quality is 'better' than amount Y of some other, some amount which is other than X must clearly be equal to it [i.e. must be *equally* good].[15] § 7. This is impossible [because things that differ in quality cannot be treated in terms of quantity, or regarded as commensurable]. It is therefore clear that in matters political [just as in matters belonging to other arts and sciences] there is no good reason for basing a claim to the exercise of authority on any and every kind of superiority. Some may be swift and others slow; but this is no reason why the one should have more [political rights], and the other less. It is in athletic contests that the superiority of the swift receives its reward. § 8. Claims to political rights must be based on the ground of contribution to the elements which constitute the being of the state.[16] There is thus good ground for the claims to honour and office which are made by persons of good descent, free birth, or wealth. Those who hold office must necessarily be free men and taxpayers: a state could not be composed entirely of men without means, any more than it could be composed entirely of slaves. § 9. But we must add that if wealth and free birth are necessary elements, the temper of justice and a martial habit are also necessary. These too are elements which must be present if men are to live together in a state. The one difference is that the first two elements are necessary to the simple existence of a state, and the last two for its good life.

Endnotes

1. The fact that democracy and oligarchy, as perversions of right constitutions, rest on a social class, is essentially connected with the 'distinctive principle' of each, which leads them to *justify* the predominance of that class. This 'distinctive principle' is thus, in effect, a conception of justice—that is to say, of *distributive* justice, or, in other words, of the justice which distributes the offices of the state among its members on a plan or principle.

2. **The Theory of Distributive Justice**
   Aristotle is here enunciating a theory of distributive justice which goes on the basis of proportionate equality. As A and B have given to the state, in the way of personal merit and personal contribution to its well-being, so A and B should receive from the state, in the way of office and honour. If the personal merit and personal contribution of both are equal, they will receive equal amounts: if they are unequal, they will receive unequal amounts: but in either cue the basis of proportionate equality will be observed, and the proportion between the thing A receives and A's personal merit will be the same as that between the thing B receives and *his* personal merit. The reference to the *Ethics* is to Book V, c. III, §§ 4 and following (1131 a 14 onwards). We may notice especially the phrase in the *Ethics*, 'The same equality will exist between the persons and the things concerned'; . . . 'if they are not equal, they will not have what is equal—but this is the origin of quarrels and complaints'.

3. The Greek word is *eudaimionia*, which means something higher than the mere happiness of pleasure (*hēdonē*), and involves an 'energy of the spirit' impossible to slaves and animals. In Book VII, c. XIII, § 5, Aristotle defines *eudaimonia* as 'the energy and practice of goodness'. See the Introduction lxxv–lxxvi.

4. Aristotle here implies (what he proceeds to make explicit) that a true state does concern itself to secure *excellence* of character and conduct among its members; that its end is essentially a *good* quality of life; and that its laws are intended to make the citizens *good* and just men.

5. I.e. unrighteousness.

6. On the general Greek notion of law (or *nomos*) see the Introduction, IV, § 3, and the references there given.

7. **Aristotle's Method of Determining the State's Purpose**
   The method of proof which follows is a method of exhaustion of possibilities. Aristotle takes various possibilities—(1) contiguity of place, (a) a common scheme of intermarriage, (3) a common scheme for the prevention of mutual injuries—and proves that none of them is sufficient to constitute a polis. It is only a common scheme for the encouragement of a good quality of life which can be the basis of a polis. . . . The same method of exhaustion of possibilities has been followed in the definition of the citizen (c. I. §§ 4–5), and in the discussion of the identity of the state (c. III, §§ 1–9).

We may also note that the same problem which is here discussed—the problem of the true end of the state, which 'constitutes' it and makes it a state—has already been discussed in c. V.I., §§ 3–5. In that passage the problem was discussed as a preliminary to a classification of states. Here it is again discussed, but now as a preliminary to a proper notion of distributive justice. We can only determine properly the principle on which offices and honours should be distributed after we have ascertained the true purpose of the state. It will be contributions to that purpose which must justly be rewarded in the distribution of offices and honours; and that purpose will thus be the standard of distributive justice.

8. See Book I, c. II, § 8 (and note B on p. 7), for the implications of this definition.

9. In other words, contiguity and consanguinity are necessary conditions, or *sine quibus non*; but the essence, and the *causa causans*, is co-operation in a common scheme of good life. Social life (*to suzēn*), arising from the ties of contiguity and consanguinity, is a necessary basis; but the essential structure which arises on this basis is a good life (*to eu zēn*).

10. The conception of distributive justice here enunciated is that the criterion of contribution to the specific and essential end of the state—the performance of good actions—is greater than either the democratic criterion of free birth or the oligarchical criterion of wealth. Those who contribute more to the performance of good actions in and by the association, and who thus show a greater 'civic excellence' (i.e. a higher quality of membership of the association), deserve more from the polis—even if, on the ground of free birth, they are only equal or even inferior, and even if, on the ground of wealth, they are actually inferior.

11. The last three chapters—IX, X, and XI—have all been concerned, in different ways, with the general problem of distributive justice, or, in other words, with an attempt to determine what persons, in view of their contribution to the state, should be specially recognized by it in its distribution of office and honour. The argument of c. XI has appeared to go in favour of the special recognition of the people at large. The argument of the present chapter goes along a somewhat different line, and in favour of the view that all contributions, by all different persons and bodies of persons, should alike be recognized.

12. The argument is the same as that of the first section of the first chapter of the first book.

13. Here the argument repeats that of c.IX, §§ 1–3 of this book, where Aristotle has already raised the issue of equality in reference to justice, and has already referred to the *Ethics*, as he does again here.

14. In all this passage a contrast is implied between 'general opinion' (*doxa*, or the current views of the ordinary man), and 'philosophic inquiry', which does not despise, but is none the less bound to analyse (and by analysing to correct and to elevate) the implications of 'general opinion'. Aristotle has a fundamental respect for general opinion,

and indeed he states, in the *Ethics*, that a general opinion which is universally held is, in ethical matters, the truth—'that which everyone thinks *is* so' (*Ethics*, X, c, II, § 4). But he also believes that general opinion must be analysed, corrected, and elevated by philosophic analysis.

15. The argument is that if you say that 5/8 of a perfect stature is 'better' than $x/8$ of perfect goodness, you are also bound to say that 1/2 of a perfect stature is equal to 1/2 of perfect goodness. But in that case you make stature and goodness commensurable: i.e. you treat either of them as a quantitative mass, without any difference of quality, and on that basis you assume that some fraction of the one is as good as some fraction of the other.

16. The elements which constitute the life of the polis are defined later, in Book IV, c. XIII, § 1 as 'free birth, wealth, culture, and good descent.' Culture may be held to imply, or to be linked with, goodness, as appears in the first section of the next chapter of this book. The Greek word for it is *paideia*, the general 'training' of the human faculties.

5

The Summa Theologica—
Of The Various Kinds of Law (Six Articles)

St. Thomas Aquinas

We must now consider the various kinds of law: under which head there are six points of inquiry:

1. Whether there is an eternal law?
2. Whether there is a natural law?
3. Whether there is a human law?
4. Whether there is a Divine law?
5. Whether there is one Divine law, or several?
6. Whether there is a law of sin?

Article 1: Whether There Is an Eternal Law?

Objection 1: It would seem that there is no eternal law. Because every law is imposed on someone. But there was not someone from eternity on whom a law could be imposed: since God alone was from eternity. Therefore no law is eternal.

Objection 2: Further, promulgation is essential to law. But promulgation could not be from eternity: because there was no one to whom it could be promulgated from eternity. Therefore no law can be eternal.

Objection 3: Further, a law implies order to an end. But nothing ordained to an end is eternal: for the last end alone is eternal. Therefore no law is eternal.

On the contrary, Augustine says (De Lib. Arb. i, 6): "That Law which is the Supreme Reason cannot be understood to be otherwise than unchangeable and eternal."

I answer that, As stated above (Q[90], A[1], ad 2; AA[3],4), a law is nothing else but a dictate of practical reason emanating from the ruler who governs a perfect community. Now it is evident, granted that the world is ruled by Divine Providence, as was stated in the FP,

Q[22], AA[1],2, that the whole community of the universe is governed by Divine Reason. Wherefore the very Idea of the government of things in God the Ruler of the universe, has the nature of a law. And since the Divine Reason's conception of things is not subject to time but is eternal, according to *Prov. 8:23*, therefore it is that this kind of law must be called eternal.

Reply to Objection 1: Those things that are not in themselves, exist with God, inasmuch as they are foreknown and preordained by Him, according to *Rom. 4:17*: "Who calls those things that are not, as those that are." Accordingly the eternal concept of the Divine law bears the character of an eternal law, in so far as it is ordained by God to the government of things foreknown by Him.

Reply to Objection 2: Promulgation is made by word of mouth or in writing; and in both ways the eternal law is promulgated: because both the Divine Word and the writing of the Book of Life are eternal. But the promulgation cannot be from eternity on the part of the creature that hears or reads.

Reply to Objection 3: The law implies order to the end actively, in so far as it directs certain things to the end; but not passively—that is to say, the law itself is not ordained to the end—except accidentally, in a governor whose end is extrinsic to him, and to which end his law must needs be ordained. But the end of the Divine government is God Himself, and His law is not distinct from Himself. Wherefore the eternal law is not ordained to another end.

Article 2: Whether There Is In Us a Natural Law?

Objection 1: It would seem that there is no natural law in us. Because man is governed sufficiently by the eternal law: for Augustine says (De Lib. Arb. i) that "the eternal law is that by which it is right that all things should be most orderly." But nature does not abound in superfluities as neither does she fail in necessaries. Therefore no law is natural to man.

Objection 2: Further, by the law man is directed, in his acts, to the end, as stated above (Q[90], A[2]). But the directing of human acts to their end is not a function of nature, as is the case in irrational creatures, which act for an end solely by their natural appetite; whereas man acts for an end by his reason and will. Therefore no law is natural to man.

Objection 3: Further, the more a man is free, the less is he under the law. But man is freer than all the animals, on account of his free-will, with which he is endowed above all other animals. Since therefore other animals are not subject to a natural law, neither is man subject to a natural law.

On the contrary, A gloss on *Rom. 2:14:* "When the Gentiles, who have not the law, do by nature those things that are of the law," comments as follows: "Although they have no written law, yet they have the natural law, whereby each one knows, and is conscious of, what is good and what is evil."

I answer that, As stated above (Q[90], A[1], ad 1), law, being a rule and measure, can be in a person in two ways: in one way, as in him that rules and measures; in another way, as in that which is ruled and measured, since a thing is ruled and measured, in so far as it partakes of the rule or measure. Wherefore, since all things subject to Divine providence are ruled and measured by the eternal law, as was stated above (A[1]); it is evident that all things partake somewhat of the eternal law, in so far as, namely, from its being imprinted on them, they derive their respective inclinations to their proper acts and ends. Now among all others, the rational creature is subject to Divine providence in the most excellent way, in so far as it partakes of a share of providence, by being provident both for itself and for others. Wherefore it has a share of the Eternal Reason, whereby it has a natural inclination to its proper act and end: and this participation of the eternal law in the rational creature is called the natural law. Hence the Psalmist after saying (*Ps. 4:6*): "Offer up the sacrifice of justice," as though someone asked what the works of justice are, adds: "Many say, Who showeth us good things?" in answer to which question he says: "The light of Thy countenance, O Lord, is signed upon us": thus implying that the light of natural reason, whereby we discern what is good and what is evil, which is the function of the natural law, is nothing else than an imprint on us of the Divine light. It is therefore evident that the natural law is nothing else than the rational creature's participation of the eternal law.

Reply to Objection 1: This argument would hold, if the natural law were something different from the eternal law: whereas it is nothing but a participation thereof, as stated above.

Reply to Objection 2: Every act of reason and will in us is based on that which is according to nature, as stated above (Q[10], A[1]): for every act of reasoning is based on principles that are known naturally, and every act of appetite in respect of the means is derived from the natural appetite in respect of the last end. Accordingly the first direction of our acts to their end must needs be in virtue of the natural law.

Reply to Objection 3: Even irrational animals partake in their own way of the Eternal Reason, just as the rational creature does. But because the rational creature partakes thereof in an intellectual and rational manner, therefore the participation of the eternal law in the rational creature is properly called a law, since a law is something pertaining to reason, as stated above (Q[90], A[1]). Irrational creatures, however, do not partake thereof in a rational manner, wherefore there is no participation of the eternal law in them, except by way of similitude.

Article 3: Whether There Is a Human Law?

Objection 1: It would seem that there is not a human law. For the natural law is a participation of the eternal law, as stated above (A[2]). Now through the eternal law "all things are most orderly," as Augustine states (De Lib. Arb. i, 6). Therefore the natural law suffices for the ordering of all human affairs. Consequently there is no need for a human law.

Objection 2: Further, a law bears the character of a measure, as stated above (Q[90], A[1]). But human reason is not a measure of things, but vice versa, as stated in Metaph. x, text. 5. Therefore no law can emanate from human reason.

Objection 3: Further, a measure should be most certain, as stated in Metaph. x, text. 3. But the dictates of human reason in matters of conduct are uncertain, according to Wis. 9:14: "The thoughts of mortal men are fearful, and our counsels uncertain." Therefore no law can emanate from human reason.

On the contrary, Augustine (De Lib. Arb. i, 6) distinguishes two kinds of law, the one eternal, the other temporal, which he calls human.

I answer that, As stated above (Q[90], A[1], ad 2), a law is a dictate of the practical reason. Now it is to be observed that the same procedure takes place in the practical and in the speculative reason: for each proceeds from principles to conclusions, as stated above (De Lib. Arb. i, 6). Accordingly we conclude that just as, in the speculative reason, from naturally known indemonstrable principles, we draw the conclusions of the various sciences, the knowledge of which is not imparted to us by nature, but acquired by the efforts of reason, so too it is from the precepts of the natural law, as from general and indemonstrable principles, that the human reason needs to proceed to the more particular determination of certain matters. These particular determinations, devised by human reason, are called human laws, provided the other essential conditions of law be observed, as stated above (Q[90], AA[2],3,4). Wherefore Tully says in his Rhetoric (De Invent. Rhet. ii) that "justice has its source in nature; thence certain things came into custom by reason of their utility; afterwards these things which emanated from nature and were approved by custom, were sanctioned by fear and reverence for the law."

Reply to Objection 1: The human reason cannot have a full participation of the dictate of the Divine Reason, but according to its own mode, and imperfectly. Consequently, as on the part of the speculative reason, by a natural participation of Divine Wisdom, there is in us the knowledge of certain general principles, but not proper knowledge of each single truth, such as that contained in the Divine Wisdom; so too, on the part of the practical reason, man has a natural participation of the eternal law, according to certain general principles, but not as regards the particular determinations of individual cases, which are, however, contained in the eternal law. Hence the need for human reason to proceed further to sanction them by law.

Reply to Objection 2: Human reason is not, of itself, the rule of things: but the principles impressed on it by nature, are general rules and measures of all things relating to human conduct, whereof the natural reason is the rule and measure, although it is not the measure of things that are from nature.

Reply to Objection 3: The practical reason is concerned with practical matters, which are singular and contingent: but not with necessary things, with which the speculative reason is concerned. Wherefore human laws cannot have that inerrancy that belongs to the demonstrated conclusions of sciences. Nor is it necessary for every measure to be altogether unerring and certain, but according as it is possible in its own particular genus.

Article 4: Whether There Was Any Need for a Divine Law?

Objection 1: It would seem that there was no need for a Divine law. Because, as stated above (A[2]), the natural law is a participation in us of the eternal law. But the eternal law is a Divine law, as stated above (A[1]). Therefore there was no need for a Divine law in addition to the natural law, and human laws derived therefrom.

Objection 2: Further, it is written (*Ecclus. 15:14*) that "God left man in the hand of his own counsel." Now counsel is an act of reason, as stated above (Q[14], A[1]). Therefore man was left to the direction of his reason. But a dictate of human reason is a human law as stated above (A[3]). Therefore there is no need for man to be governed also by a Divine law.

Objection 3: Further, human nature is more self-sufficing than irrational creatures. But irrational creatures have no Divine law besides the natural inclination impressed on them. Much less, therefore, should the rational creature have a Divine law in addition to the natural law.

On the contrary, David prayed God to set His law before him, saying (*Ps. 118:33*): "Set before me for a law the way of Thy justifications, O Lord."

I answer that, Besides the natural and the human law it was necessary for the directing of human conduct to have a Divine law. And this for four reasons. First, because it is by law that man is directed how to perform his proper acts in view of his last end. And indeed if man were ordained to no other end than that which is proportionate to his natural faculty, there would be no need for man to have any further direction of the part of his reason, besides the natural law and human law which is derived from it. But since man is ordained to an end of eternal happiness which is inproportionate to man's natural faculty, as stated above (Q[5], A[5]), therefore it was necessary that, besides the natural and the human law, man should be directed to his end by a law given by God.

Secondly, because, on account of the uncertainty of human judgment, especially on contingent and particular matters, different people form different judgments on human acts; whence also different and contrary laws result. In order, therefore, that man may know without any doubt what he ought to do and what he ought to avoid, it was necessary for man to be directed in his proper acts by a law given by God, for it is certain that such a law cannot err.

Thirdly, because man can make laws in those matters of which he is competent to judge. But man is not competent to judge of interior movements, that are hidden, but only of exterior acts which appear: and yet for the perfection of virtue it is necessary for man to conduct himself aright in both kinds of acts. Consequently human law could not sufficiently curb and direct interior acts; and it was necessary for this purpose that a Divine law should supervene.

Fourthly, because, as Augustine says (De Lib. Arb. i, 5,6), human law cannot punish or forbid all evil deeds: since while aiming at doing away with all evils, it would do away with many good things, and would hinder the advance of the common good, which is necessary for human intercourse. In order, therefore, that no evil might remain unforbidden and unpunished, it was necessary for the Divine law to supervene, whereby all sins are forbidden.

And these four causes are touched upon in *Ps. 118:8*, where it is said: "The law of the Lord is unspotted," i.e. allowing no foulness of sin; "converting souls," because it directs not only exterior, but also interior acts; "the testimony of the Lord is faithful," because of the certainty of what is true and right; "giving wisdom to little ones," by directing man to an end supernatural and Divine.

Reply to Objection 1: By the natural law the eternal law is participated proportionately to the capacity of human nature. But to his supernatural end man needs to be directed in a yet higher way. Hence the additional law given by God, whereby man shares more perfectly in the eternal law.

Reply to Objection 2: Counsel is a kind of inquiry: hence it must proceed from some principles. Nor is it enough for it to proceed from principles imparted by nature, which are the precepts of the natural law, for the reasons given above: but there is need for certain additional principles, namely, the precepts of the Divine law.

Reply to Objection 3: Irrational creatures are not ordained to an end higher than that which is proportionate to their natural powers: consequently the comparison fails.

6

Part B: Justice in the Modern Era

Diana M. Judd

The modern era may be dated from the early 17th century with the development of modern natural science and the subsequent scientific revolution. This heralded a sea change in philosophical thought, which would have a profound effect on politics. The beginning of the Enlightenment witnessed the rise of many crucial ideas, such as individual liberty, unalienable rights, natural equality, the primacy of political consent, and the radical notion that we are all capable of reason and hence of thinking for ourselves. These ideas all helped shape new ways to inquire into the nature of justice. In this section we will consider the work of three influential political philosophers: Thomas Hobbes, Jean-Jacques Rousseau, and Karl Marx.

Thomas Hobbes (1588–1679) was the first modern political philosopher. *The Leviathan* (1651) represents a definitive break from the ancient and medieval approaches to political thought in general and justice in particular. Hobbes approached the idea of justice by theorizing about the condition in which humans would live in the absence of government. This so-called "state of nature" was an intellectual construct that allowed Hobbes to do several things. First, it allowed him to argue that in the absence of any monarchical or religious authority, humans are essentially equal in both reason and physical strength. Second, it allowed him to posit that we possess certain rights from birth that the state cannot take away—i.e., rights are unalienable. Third, it allowed him to theorize that in the absence of traditional authority, humans would come together to form their own governments based on consent. They would do this via a "social contract." The particulars of Hobbes's social contract are less important for us than the fact of its existence. For it is via this contract that humans consent to construct a governmental power to which they would be equally subject. And it is here that we find Hobbes's conception of justice.

Hobbes's state of nature, the condition that predates government, is described as a place "where every man is enemy to every man." It is anarchical, and in it there can be no peace because human nature is both selfish and violent. As he famously put it in chapter 13, the state of nature is one of "continual feare, and danger of violent death; And the life of man, solitary, poore, nasty, brutish, and short." It is because of this conception that Hobbes is able to argue that in the state of nature the concept of justice itself cannot exist. For if the state of nature is a state of all against all, nothing that happens there can be considered "unjust," for there is no "right" or "wrong." Rather, there are only humans existing according to their nature. There is only one way to maintain peace: law stemming from a recognized power. For "where there is no common Power, there is no Law: Where no Law, no Injustice."

Justice and the law are thus one and the same for Hobbes. It is important to keep in mind that this is *not* a theory of natural law: both Cicero and Aquinas posited the existence of morality and a sense of right and wrong above and beyond human political association. Hobbes, on the other hand, equated justice with legislation. The only way to achieve justice at all is through the institution of government. Or as James Madison (1751–1836) would restate the matter over a century later in *Federalist Paper* 51, "If men were angels no government would be necessary."

Whether or not we agree with Hobbes on his dour view of human nature, it represented a crucial shift away from the ancient and medieval. By rejecting abstract metaphysical and religious concepts of good and evil in his discussion of justice, Hobbes made individual human beings the arbiters of what counts as right and wrong in their own political associations, which they determine by consent. Furthermore, by positing the existence of unalienable rights (i.e., those rights that exist in the state of nature and predate government), Hobbes paved the way for subsequent political philosophers (e.g., John Locke [1632–1704]) to theorize that the only end of government is the protection of our rights. When it ceases to do so, it is no longer a just government, and we have the right to dissolve that government and begin anew. This political tradition became known as *classical liberalism*. Indeed, Thomas Jefferson adopted Locke's argument wholesale in the *Declaration of Independence* (1776).

If the political tradition begun by Hobbes and carried on by Locke was a major inspiration for the American Revolution, the work of Jean-Jacques Rousseau (1712–1778) is widely held to be the inspiration for the French Revolution. *The Social Contract* (1761) contains his views on freedom, legitimate government, and what he conceives to be the proper ends of political association. Rousseau inquires into the nature of justice through the lens of what he termed the *general will*, which is the collective wills of all those who have formed a political association on the basis of consent through a social contract. The general will is the most important component of Rousseau's political association, for it is this that determines justice.

Rousseau argues that any real conception of justice must be reciprocal. That is, it cannot be the case that justice is determined by metaphysical, religious, or any other abstract idea. For it to have any meaning, justice must be determined by people in a society acting in concert with one another. Thus, Rousseau is able to argue that justice is whatever the general will desires. How can Rousseau make this claim?

The general will does not act with regard to specific individuals or actions. It can only act with a view towards what is general and universally applicable. By the same token, laws are by definition the "authentic acts" of the general will. That is, whatever the general will can conceive of as a general rule applicable to all should become law. In this way, law and justice are one and the same. For the general will would never be unjust to itself, and hence would never make unjust laws.

The influence of Rousseau on concepts of justice and in political thought cannot be overstated. Scholars have spent hundreds of years arguing about whether Rousseau's philosophy is the ultimate expression of the individual in community, or whether it amounts to an apology for totalitarianism. Regardless of which is true, directly or indirectly Rousseau influenced generations of European political philosophers who rejected the classical liberal notions of individual liberty and unalienable rights in favor of a more collective idea of justice. Karl Marx (1818–1883) is arguably the most influential of these philosophers.

Marx is considered by many to be the single most influential critic of capitalism. His *Manifesto of the Communist Party* (1848) was hugely influential to subsequent socialist and communist revolutions across Western Europe and Russia. Indeed, it may be argued that Marx's writings helped shape the direction of 20th-century international politics, as they were the main intellectual inspiration behind the formation of the Soviet Union. Marx inquired into the nature of justice via his examination of history. For Marx, the history of the world is the history of class struggle. In every epoch, he argued, there has been a dominant economic class. In the feudal era it was the aristocracy, and in the capitalist era it is the bourgeoisie. Shifts between historical epochs occur when the existing ruling economic class is usurped by a new one, which takes its place. When that happens, the entire society changes. With the new ruling class comes a change in culture, modes of religious worship, tastes in literature, art, even morality. In other words, the class that controls the means of material production also controls the "mental production," and makes all other segments of society subject to it. As Marx put it in *The German Ideology*, "The ideas of the ruling class are in every epoch the ruling ideas; i.e., the class which is the ruling material force of society, is at the same time its ruling *intellectual* force." In this way Marx is able to argue that justice is the expressed self-interest of the ruling economic class. Likewise, because this class controls the state, it determines the law. Hence, justice and the law are the same thing for Marx: both are part of the same "superstructure," the socioeconomic, cultural and political façade placed on the "base" of material relationships. The latter is fundamental, and always determines the former.

Marx could not leave things there, however. In all of his works Marx argued that capitalism would produce the next ruling class, the *proletariat* (working class). But instead of merely taking their place as the next ruling class Marx hoped the proletariat would break the cycle of history and end class struggle permanently. If they could, they could institute an entirely new kind of society that would have no need for laws (because the law was in place to perpetuate the self-interest of an economic ruling class at the expense of all others), and in which the state would slowly lose relevance and "wither away." He called this society *communism*, and believed that only here could humans even begin to think of justice in a new, cooperative way.

Conclusion

Since the birth of philosophy in the West over two millennia ago, the question of justice has played center stage in political thought. As we have seen, the question of justice has been approached in many ways, and there are many ways we can ask what justice is, or should be. In the ancient and medieval eras, political philosophers conceived of justice as something over and above mere legislation. Plato, Aristotle, Cicero, and Aquinas each tended to measure justice in terms of something higher and more absolute, whether an idea of "the good," happiness, or an all-powerful deity such as the Christian God. In the modern era, concepts of justice and the law were informed by notions such as equality and rights, two elements which did not come into play for their ancient and medieval predecessors. As such, Hobbes, Rousseau, and Marx each viewed justice as more of a product of human deliberation (for better or worse), and not as a reflection of metaphysical or religious absolutes. Their conceptions tended to place justice on a par with the law.

It might be tempting to think that such an approach somehow lowered the standards of what justice is or should be. However, by identifying justice with legislation, political philosophers in the modern era waged their own revolution against traditional authority itself. By arguing against the need to adhere to something higher than mankind, these thinkers left open the possibility that humans are capable of determining for our own standards of justice, and how we may uphold them. In our own political associations, we should strive to ask anew the question that has driven political philosophy from the beginning: *How ought we to live?*

7

The Leviathan

Thomas Hobbes

Chapter 13

Of the Natural Condition of Mankind as Concerning their Felicity and Misery

NATURE hath made men so equal in the faculties of body and mind as that, though there be found one man sometimes manifestly stronger in body or of quicker mind than another, yet when all is reckoned together the difference between man and man is not so considerable as that one man can thereupon claim to himself any benefit to which another may not pretend as well as he. For as to the strength of body, the weakest has strength enough to kill the strongest, either by secret machination or by confederacy with others that are in the same danger with himself.

And as to the faculties of the mind, setting aside the arts grounded upon words, and especially that skill of proceeding upon general and infallible rules, called science, which very few have and but in few things, as being not a native faculty born with us, nor attained, as prudence, while we look after somewhat else, I find yet a greater equality amongst men than that of strength. For prudence is but experience, which equal time equally bestows on all men in those things they equally apply themselves unto. That which may perhaps make such equality incredible is but a vain conceit of one's own wisdom, which almost all men think they have in a greater degree than the vulgar; that is, than all men but themselves, and a few others, whom by fame, or for concurring with themselves, they approve. For such is the nature of men that howsoever they may acknowledge many others to be more witty, or more eloquent or more learned, yet they will hardly believe there be many so wise as themselves; for they see their own wit at hand, and other men's at a distance. But this proves rather that men are in that point equal, than unequal. For there is not ordinarily a greater sign of the equal distribution of anything than that every man is contented with his share.

From this equality of ability arises equality of hope in the attaining of our ends. And therefore if any two men desire the same thing, which nevertheless they cannot both enjoy, they become enemies; and in the way to their end (which is principally their own conservation, and sometimes their delectation only) endeavour to destroy or subdue one another.

And from hence it comes to pass that where an invader hath no more to fear than another man's single power, if one plant, sow, build, or possess a convenient seat, others may probably be expected to come prepared with forces united to dispossess and deprive him, not only of the fruit of his labour, but also of his life or liberty. And the invader again is in the like danger of another.

And from this diffidence of one another, there is no way for any man to secure himself so reasonable as anticipation; that is, by force, or wiles, to master the persons of all men he can so long till he see no other power great enough to endanger him: and this is no more than his own conservation requires, and is generally allowed. Also, because there be some that, taking pleasure in contemplating their own power in the acts of conquest, which they pursue farther than their security requires, if others, that otherwise would be glad to be at ease within modest bounds, should not by invasion increase their power, they would not be able, long time, by standing only on their defence, to subsist. And by consequence, such augmentation of dominion over men being necessary to a man's conservation, it ought to be allowed him.

Again, men have no pleasure (but on the contrary a great deal of grief) in keeping company where there is no power able to overawe them all. For every man lookes that his companion should value him at the same rate he sets upon himself, and upon all signs of contempt or undervaluing naturally endeavours, as far as he dares (which amongst them that have no common power to keep them in quiet is far enough to make them destroy each other), to extort a greater value from his contemners, by damage; and from others, by the example.

So that in the nature of man, we find three principal causes of quarrel. First, competition; secondly, diffidence; thirdly, glory.

The first makes men invade for gain; the second, for safety; and the third, for reputation. The first use violence, to make themselves masters of other men's persons, wives, children, and cattle; the second, to defend them; the third, for trifles, as a word, a smile, a different opinion, and any other sign of undervalue, either direct in their persons or by reflection in their kindred, their friends, their nation, their profession, or their name.

Hereby it is manifest that during the time men live without a common power to keep them all in awe, they are in that condition which is called war; and such a war as is of every man against every man. For war consistes not in battle only, or the act of fighting, but in a tract of time, wherein the will to contend by battle is sufficiently known: and therefore the notion of time is to be considered in the nature of war, as it is in the nature of weather. For as the nature of foul weather lies not in a shower or two of rain, but in an inclination thereto of many days together: so the nature of war consistes not in actual fighting, but in the known disposition thereto during all the time there is no assurance to the contrary. All other time is peace.

Whatsoever therefore is consequent to a time of war, where every man is enemy to every man, the same consequent to the time wherein men live without other security than what their own strength and their own invention shall furnish them withal. In such condition there is no place for industry, because the fruit thereof is uncertain: and consequently no culture of the earth; no navigation, nor use of the commodities that may be imported by sea; no commodious building; no instruments of moving and removing such things as require much force; no knowledge of the face of the earth; no account of time; no arts; no letters; no society; and which is worst of all, continual fear, and danger of violent death; and the life of man, solitary, poor, nasty, brutish, and short.

It may seem strange to some man that has not well weighed these things that Nature should thus dissociate and render men apt to invade and destroy one another: and he may therefore, not trusting to this inference, made from the passions, desire perhaps to have the same confirmed by experience. Let him therefore consider with himself: when taking a journey, he arms himself and seeks to go well accompanied; when going to sleep, he locks his doors; when even in his house he locks his chests; and this when he knows there be laws and public officers, armed, to revenge all injuries shall be done him; what opinion he has of his fellow subjects, when he rides armed; of his fellow citizens, when he locks his doors; and of his children, and servants, when he locks his chests. Does he not there as much accuse mankind by his actions as I do by my words? But neither of us accuse man's nature in it. The desires, and other passions of man, are in themselves no sin. No more are the actions that proceed from those passions till they know a law that forbids them; which till laws be made they cannot know, nor can any law be made till they have agreed upon the person that shall make it.

It may peradventure be thought there was never such a time nor condition of war as this; and I believe it was never generally so, over all the world: but there are many places where they live so now. For the savage people in many places of America, except the government of small families, the concord whereof dependeth on natural lust, have no government at all, and live at this day in that brutish manner, as I said before. Howsoever, it may be perceived what manner of life there would be, where there were no common power to fear, by the manner of life which men that have formerly lived under a peaceful government use to degenerate into a civil war.

But though there had never been any time wherein particular men were in a condition of war one against another, yet in all times kings and persons of sovereign authority, because of their independency, are in continual jealousies, and in the state and posture of gladiators, having their weapons pointing, and their eyes fixed on one another; that is, their forts, garrisons, and guns upon the frontiers of their kingdoms, and continual spies upon their neighbours, which is a posture of war. But because they uphold thereby the industry of their subjects, there does not follow from it that misery which accompanies the liberty of particular men.

To this war of every man against every man, this also is consequent; that nothing can be unjust. The notions of right and wrong, justice and injustice, have there no place. Where there is no common power, there is no law; where no law, no injustice. Force and fraud are in war the two cardinal virtues. Justice and injustice are none of the faculties neither of the body nor mind. If they were, they might be in a man that were alone in the world, as well as his senses and passions. They are qualities that relate to men in society, not in solitude. It is consequent also to the same condition that there be no propriety, no dominion, no mine and thine distinct; but only that to be every man's that he can get, and for so long as he can keep it. And thus much for the ill condition which man by mere nature is actually placed in; though with a possibility to come out of it, consisting partly in the passions, partly in his reason.

The passions that incline men to peace are: fear of death; desire of such things as are necessary to commodious living; and a hope by their industry to obtain them. And reason suggesteth convenient articles of peace upon which men may be drawn to agreement. These articles are they which otherwise are called the laws of nature, whereof I shall speak more particularly in the two following chapters.

Chapter XIV

Of The First And Second Natural Laws, and of Contracts

THE right of nature, which writers commonly call *jus naturale*, is the liberty each man hath to use his own power as he will himself for the preservation of his own nature; that is to say, of his own life; and consequently, of doing anything which, in his own judgement and reason, he shall conceive to be the aptest means thereunto.

By liberty is understood, according to the proper signification of the word, the absence of external impediments; which impediments may oft take away part of a man's power to do what he would, but cannot hinder him from using the power left him according as his judgement and reason shall dictate to him.

A law of nature, *lex naturalis*, is a precept, or general rule, found out by reason, by which a man is forbidden to do that which is destructive of his life, or takes away the means of preserving the same, and to omit that by which he thinkes it may be best preserved. For though they that speak of this subject use to confound *jus* and *lex*, right and law, yet they ought to be distinguished, because right consistes in liberty to do, or to forbear; whereas law determines and bindes to one of them: so that law and right differ as much as obligation and liberty, which in one and the same matter are inconsistent.

And because the condition of man (as hath been declared in the precedent chapter) is a condition of war of every one against every one, in which case every one is governed by his own reason, and there is nothing he can make use of that may not be a help unto him in preserving his life against his enemies; it followed that in such a condition every man has a right to every thing, even to one another's body. And therefore, as long as this natural right of every man to every thing endure, there can be no security to any man, how strong or wise soever he be, of living out the time which nature ordinarily allowes men to live. And consequently it is a precept, or general rule of reason: that every man ought to endeavour peace, as far as he has hope of obtaining it; and when he cannot obtain it, that he may seek and use all helps and advantages of war. The first branch of which rule contains the first and fundamental law of nature, which is: to seek peace and follow it. The second, the sum of the right of nature, which is: by all means we can to defend ourselves.

From this fundamental law of nature, by which men are commanded to endeavour peace, is derived this second law: that a man be willing, when others are so too, as far forth as for peace and defence of himself he shall think it necessary, to lay down this right to all things; and be contented with so much liberty against other men as he would allow other men against himself. For as long as every man holds this right, of doing anything he liketh; so long are all men in the condition of war. But if other men will not lay down their right, as well as he, then there is no reason for anyone to divest himself of his: for that were to expose himself to prey, which no man is bound to, rather than to dispose himself to peace. This is that law of the gospel: Whatsoever you require that others should do to you, that do ye to them. And that law of all men, *quod tibi fieri non vis, alteri ne feceris.*

To lay down a man's right to anything is to divest himself of the liberty of hindering another of the benefit of his own right to the same. For he that renounces or passes away his right gives not to any other man a right which he had not before, because there is nothing to which every man had not right by nature, but only stands out of his way that he may enjoy his own original right without hindrance from him, not without hindrance from another. So that the effect which redounds to one man by another man's defect of right is but so much diminution of impediments to the use of his own right original.

Right is laid aside, either by simply renouncing it, or by transferring it to another. By simply renouncing, when he cares not to whom the benefit thereof redounds. By transferring, when he intends the benefit thereof to some certain person or persons. And when a man hath in either manner abandoned or granted away his right, then is he said to be obliged, or bound, not to hinder those to whom such right is granted, or abandoned, from the benefit of it: and that he ought, and it is duty, not to make void that voluntary act of his own: and that such hindrance is injustice, and injury, as being *sine jure*; the right being before renounced or transferred. So that injury or injustice, in the controversies of the world, is somewhat like to that which in the disputations of scholars is called absurdity. For as it is there called an absurdity to contradict what one maintained in the beginning; so in the world it is called injustice, and injury voluntarily to undo that which from the beginning he had voluntarily done. The way by which a man either simply renounces or transferrs his right is a declaration, or signification, by some voluntary and sufficient sign, or signs, that he doth so renounce or transfer, or hath so renounced or transferred the same, to him that accepts it. And these signs are either words only, or actions only; or, as it happeneth most often, both words and actions. And the same are the bonds, by which men are bound and obliged: bonds that have their strength, not from their own nature (for nothing is more easily broken than a man's word), but from fear of some evil consequence upon the rupture.

Whensoever a man transferreth his right, or renounces it, it is either in consideration of some right reciprocally transferred to himself, or for some other good he hopes for thereby. For it is a voluntary act: and of the voluntary acts of every man, the object is some good to himself. And therefore there be some rights which no man can be understood by any words, or other signs, to have abandoned or transferred. As first a man cannot lay down the right of resisting them that assault him by force to take away his life, because he cannot be understood to aim thereby at any good to himself. The same may be said of wounds, and chains, and imprisonment, both because there is no benefit consequent to such patience, as there is to the patience of suffering another to be wounded or imprisoned, as also because a man cannot tell when he seeth men proceed against him by violence whether they intend his death or not. And lastly the motive and end for which this renouncing and transferring of right is introduced is nothing else but the security of a man's person, in his life, and in the means of so preserving life as not to be weary of it. And therefore if a man by words, or other signs, seem to despoil himself of the end for which those signs were intended, he is not to be understood as if he meant it, or that it was his will, but that he was ignorant of how such words and actions were to be interpreted.

The mutual transferring of right is that which men call contract.

There is difference between transferring of right to the thing, the thing, and transferring or tradition, that is, delivery of the thing itself. For the thing may be delivered together with the translation of the right, as in buying and selling with ready money, or exchange of goods or lands, and it may be delivered some time after.

Again, one of the contractors may deliver the thing contracted for on his part, and leave the other to perform his part at some determinate time after, and in the meantime be trusted; and then the contract on his part is called pact, or covenant: or both parts may contract now to perform hereafter, in which cases he that is to perform in time to come, being trusted, his performance is called keeping of promise, or faith, and the failing of performance, if it be voluntary, violation of faith.

[. . .]

If a covenant be made wherein neither of the parties perform presently, but trust one another, in the condition of mere nature (which is a condition of war of every man against every man) upon any reasonable suspicion, it is void: but if there be a common power set over them both, with right and force sufficient to compel performance, it is not void. For he that performs first has no assurance the other will perform after, because the bonds of words are too weak to bridle men's ambition, avarice, anger, and other passions, without the fear of some coercive power; which in the condition of mere nature, where all men are equal, and judges of the justness of their own fears, cannot possibly be supposed. And therefore he which performs first does but betray himself to his enemy, contrary to the right he can never abandon of defending his life and means of living.

But in a civil estate, where there a power set up to constrain those that would otherwise violate their faith, that fear is no more reasonable; and for that cause, he which by the covenant is to perform first is obliged so to do.

The cause of fear, which makes such a covenant invalid, must be always something arising after the covenant made, as some new fact or other sign of the will not to perform, else it cannot make the covenant void. For that which could not hinder a man from promising ought not to be admitted as a hindrance of performing.

He that transfers any right transfers the means of enjoying it, as far as lies in his power. As he that sells land is understood to transfer the herbage and whatsoever grows upon it; nor can he that sells a mill turn away the stream that drives it. And they that give to a man the right of government in sovereignty are understood to give him the right of levying money to maintain soldiers, and of appointing magistrates for the administration of justice.

To make covenants with brute beasts is impossible, because not understanding our speech, they understand not, nor accept of any translation of right, nor can translate any right to another: and without mutual acceptation, there is no covenant.

To make covenant with God is impossible but by mediation of such as God speaks to, either by revelation supernatural or by His lieutenants that govern under Him and in His name: for otherwise we know not whether our covenants be accepted or not. And therefore they that vow anything contrary to any law of nature, vow in vain, as being a thing unjust to pay such vow. And if it be a thing commanded by the law of nature, it is not the vow, but the law that binds them.

The matter or subject of a covenant is always something that falls under deliberation, for to covenant is an act of the will; that is to say, an act, and the last act, of deliberation; and is therefore always understood to be something to come, and which judged possible for him that covenants to perform.

And therefore, to promise that which is known to be impossible is no covenant. But if that prove impossible afterwards, which before was thought possible, the covenant is valid and binds, though not to the thing itself, yet to the value; or, if that also be impossible, to the unfeigned endeavour of performing as much as is possible, for to more no man can be obliged.

Men are freed of their covenants two ways; by performing, or by being forgiven. For performance is the natural end of obligation, and forgiveness the restitution of liberty, as being a retransferring of that right in which the obligation consisted.

Covenants entered into by fear, in the condition of mere nature, are obligatory. For example, if I covenant to pay a ransom, or service for my life, to an enemy, I am bound by it. For it is a contract, wherein one receives the benefit of life; the other is to receive money, or service for it, and consequently, where no other law (as in the condition of mere nature) forbids the performance, the covenant is valid. Therefore prisoners of war, if trusted with the payment of their ransom, are obliged to pay it: and if a weaker prince make a disadvantageous peace with a stronger, for fear, he is bound to keep it; unless (as hath been said before) there arises some new and just cause of fear to renew the war. And even in Commonwealths, if I be forced to redeem myself from a thief by promising him money, I am bound to pay it, till the civil law discharge me. For whatsoever I may lawfully do without obligation, the same I may lawfully covenant to do through fear: and what I lawfully covenant, I cannot lawfully break.

A former covenant makes void a later. For a man that hath passed away his right to one man today hath it not to pass tomorrow to another: and therefore the later promise passes no right, but is null.

A covenant not to defend myself from force, by force, is always void. For (as I have shown before) no man can transfer or lay down his right to save himself from death, wounds, and imprisonment, the avoiding whereof is the only end of laying down any right; and therefore the promise of not resisting force, in no covenant transfers any right, nor is obliging. For though a man may covenant thus, unless I do so, or so, kill me; he cannot covenant thus, unless I do so, or so, I will not resist you when you come to kill me. For man by nature chooses the lesser evil, which is danger of death in resisting, rather than the greater, which is certain and present death in not resisting. And this is granted to be true by all men, in that they lead criminals to execution, and prison, with armed men, notwithstanding that such criminals have consented to the law by which they are condemned.

A covenant to accuse oneself, without assurance of pardon, is likewise invalid. For in the condition of nature where every man is judge, there is no place for accusation: and in the civil state the accusation is followed with punishment, which, being force, a man is not obliged not to resist. The same is also true of the accusation of those by whose condemnation a man falls into misery; as of a father, wife, or benefactor. For the testimony of such an accuser, if it be not willingly given, is presumed to be corrupted by nature, and therefore not to be received: and where a man's testimony is not to be credited, he is not bound to give it. Also accusations upon torture are not to be reputed as testimonies. For torture is to be used but as means of conjecture, and light, in the further examination and search of truth: and what is in that case confessed tends to the ease of him that is tortured, not to the informing of the torturers, and therefore ought not to have the credit of a sufficient testimony: for whether he deliver himself by true or false accusation, he does it by the right of preserving his own life.

The force of words being (as I have formerly noted) too weak to hold men to the performance of their covenants, there are in man's nature but two imaginable helps to strengthen it. And those are either a fear of the consequence of breaking their word, or a glory or pride in appearing not to need to break it. This latter is a generosity too rarely found to be presumed on, especially in the pursuers of wealth, command, or sensual pleasure, which are the greatest part of mankind. The passion to be reckoned upon is fear; whereof there be two very general objects: one, the power of spirits invisible; the other, the power of those men they shall therein offend. Of these two, though the former be the greater power, yet the fear of the latter is commonly the greater fear. The fear of the former is in every man his own religion, which hath place in the nature of man before civil society. The latter hath not so; at least not place enough to keep men to their promises, because in the condition of mere nature, the inequality of power is not discerned, but by the event of battle. So that before the time of civil society, or in the interruption thereof by war, there is nothing can strengthen a covenant of peace agreed on against the temptations of avarice, ambition, lust, or other strong desire, but the fear of that invisible power which they every one worship as God, and fear as a revenger of their perfidy. All therefore that can be done between two men not subject to civil power is to put one another to swear by the God he feareth: which swearing, or oath, is a form of speech, added to a promise, by which he that promises signifies that unless he perform he renounces the mercy of his God, or calls to him for vengeance on himself. Such was the heathen form, Let Jupiter kill me else, as I kill this beast. So is our form, I shall do thus, and thus, so help me God. And this, with the rites and ceremonies which every one useth in his own religion, that the fear of breaking faith might be the greater.

By this it appears that an oath taken according to any other form, or rite, than his that swears is in vain and no oath, and that there is no swearing by anything which the swearer thinks not God. For though men have sometimes used to swear by their kings, for fear, or flattery; yet they would have it thereby understood they attributed to them divine honour. And that swearing unnecessarily by God is but profaning of his name: and swearing by other things, as men do in common discourse, is not swearing, but an impious custom, gotten by too much vehemence of talking.

It appears also that the oath adds nothing to the obligation. For a covenant, if lawful, binds in the sight of God, without the oath, as much as with it; if unlawful, bindeth not at all, though it be confirmed with an oath.

8

The Social Contract

Jean-Jacques Rousseau

Chapter 6

LAW

By the social compact we have given the body politic existence and life; we have now by legislation to give it movement and will. For the original act by which the body is formed and united still in no respect determines what it ought to do for its preservation.

What is well and in conformity with order is so by the nature of things and independently of human conventions. All justice comes from God, who is its sole source; but if we knew how to receive so high an inspiration, we should need neither government nor laws. Doubtless, there is a universal justice emanating from reason alone; but this justice, to be admitted among us, must be mutual. Humanly speaking, in default of natural sanctions, the laws of justice are ineffective among men: they merely make for the good of the wicked and the undoing of the just, when the just man observes them towards everybody and nobody observes them towards him. Conventions and laws are therefore needed to join rights to duties and refer justice to its object. In the state of nature, where everything is common, I owe nothing to him whom I have promised nothing; I recognize as belonging to others only what is of no use to me. In the state of society all rights are fixed by law, and the case becomes different.

But what, after all, is a law? As long as we remain satisfied with attaching purely metaphysical ideas to the word, we shall go on arguing without arriving at an understanding; and when we have defined a law of nature, we shall be no nearer the definition of a law of the State.

I have already said that there can be no general will directed to a particular object. Such an object must be either within or outside the State. If outside, a will which is alien to it cannot be, in relation to it, general; if within, it is part of the State, and in that case there arises a relation between whole and part which makes them two separate beings, of which the part is one, and the whole minus the part the other. But the whole minus a part cannot be the whole; and while this relation persists, there can be no whole, but only two unequal parts; and it follows that the will of one is no longer in any respect general in relation to the other.

But when the whole people decrees for the whole people, it is considering only itself; and if a relation is then formed, it is between two aspects of the entire object, without there being any division of the whole. In that case the matter about which the decree is made is, like the decreeing will, general. This act is what I call a law.

When I say that the object of laws is always general, I mean that law considers subjects *en masse* and actions in the abstract, and never a particular person or action. Thus the law may indeed decree that there shall be privileges, but cannot confer them on anybody by name. It may set up several classes of citizens, and even lay down the qualifications for membership of these classes, but it cannot nominate such and such persons as belonging to them; it may establish a monarchical government and hereditary succession, but it cannot choose a king, or nominate a royal family. In a word, no function which has a particular object belongs to the legislative power.

On this view, we at once see that it can no longer be asked whose business it is to make laws, since they are acts of the general will; nor whether the prince is above the law, since he is a member of the State; nor whether the law can be unjust, since no one is unjust to himself; nor how we can be both free and subject to the laws, since they are but registers of our wills.

We see further that, as the law unites universality of will with universality of object, what a man, whoever he be, commands of his own motion cannot be a law; and even what the Sovereign commands with regard to a particular matter is no nearer being a law, but is a decree, an act, not of sovereignty, but of magistracy.

I therefore give the name "Republic" to every State that is governed by laws, no matter what the form of its administration may be: for only in such a case does the public interest govern, and the *res publica* rank as a *reality*. Every legitimate government is republican;[1] what government is I will explain later on.

Laws are, properly speaking, only the conditions of civil association. The people, being subject to the laws, ought to be their author: the conditions of the society ought to be regulated solely by those who come together to form it. But how are they to regulate them? Is it to be by common agreement, by a sudden inspiration? Has the body politic an organ to declare its will? Who can give it the foresight to formulate and announce its acts in advance? Or how is it to announce them in the hour of need? How can a blind multitude, which often does not know what it wills, because it rarely knows what is good for it, carry out for itself so great and difficult an enterprise as a system of legislation? Of itself the people wills always the good, but of itself it by no means always sees it. The general will is always in the right, but the judgment which guides it is not always enlightened. It must be got to see objects as they are, and sometimes as they ought to appear to it; it must be shown the good road it is in search of, secured from the seductive influences of individual wills, taught to see times and spaces as a series, and made to weigh the attractions of present and sensible advantages against the danger of distant and hidden evils. The individuals see the good they reject; the public wills the good it does not see. All stand equally in need of guidance. The former must be compelled to bring their wills into conformity with their reason; the latter must be taught to know what it wills. If that is done, public enlightenment leads to the union of understanding and will in the social body: the parts are made to work exactly together, and the whole is raised to its highest power. This makes a legislator necessary.

Chapter 7

The Legislator

In order to discover the rules of society best suited to nations, a superior intelligence beholding all the passions of men without experiencing any of them would be needed. This intelligence would have to be wholly unrelated to our nature, while knowing it through and through; its happiness would have to be independent of us, and yet ready to occupy itself with ours; and lastly, it would have, in the march of time, to look forward to a distant glory, and, working in one century, to be able to enjoy in the next.[2] It would take gods to give men laws.

What Caligula argued from the facts, Plato, in the dialogue called the *Politicus*, argued in defining the civil or kingly man, on the basis of right. But if great princes are rare, how much more so are great legislators? The former have only to follow the pattern which the latter have to lay down. The legislator is the engineer who invents the machine, the prince merely the mechanic who sets it up and makes it go. "At the birth of societies," says Montesquieu, "the rulers of Republics establish institutions, and afterwards the institutions mould the rulers."[3]

He who dares to undertake the making of a people's institutions ought to feel himself capable, so to speak, of changing human nature, of transforming each individual, who is by himself a complete and solitary whole, into part of a greater whole from which he in a manner receives his life and being; of altering man's constitution for the purpose of strengthening it; and of substituting a partial and moral existence for the physical and independent existence nature has conferred on us all. He must, in a word, take away from man his own resources and give him instead new ones alien to him, and incapable of being made use of without the help of other men. The more completely these natural resources are annihilated, the greater and the more lasting are those which he acquires, and the more stable and perfect the new institutions; so that if each citizen is nothing and can do nothing without the rest, and the resources acquired by the whole are equal or superior to the aggregate of the resources of all the individuals, it may be said that legislation is at the highest possible point of perfection.

The legislator occupies in every respect an extraordinary position in the State. If he should do so by reason of his genius, he does so no less by reason of his office, which is neither magistracy, nor Sovereignty. This office, which sets up the Republic, nowhere enters into its constitution; it is an individual and superior function, which has nothing in common with human empire; for if he who holds command over men ought not to have command over the laws, he who has command over the laws ought not any more to have it over men; or else his laws would be the ministers of his passions and would often merely serve to perpetuate his injustices: his private aims would inevitably mar the sanctity of his work.

When Lycurgus gave laws to his country, he began by resigning the throne. It was the custom of most Greek towns to entrust the establishment of their laws to foreigners. The Republics of modern Italy in many cases followed this example; Geneva did the same and profited by it.[4] Rome, when it was most prosperous, suffered a revival of all the crimes of tyranny, and was brought to the verge of destruction, because it put the legislative authority and the sovereign power into the same hands.

Nevertheless, the decemvirs themselves never claimed the right to pass any law merely on their own authority. "Nothing we propose to you," they said to the people, "can pass into law without your consent. Romans, be yourselves the authors of the laws which are to make you happy."

He, therefore, who draws up the laws has, or should have, no right of legislation, and the people cannot, even if it wishes, deprive itself of this incommunicable right, because, according to the fundamental compact, only the general will can bind the individuals, and there can be no assurance that a particular will is in conformity with the general will, until it has been put to the free vote of the people. This I have said already; but it is worth while to repeat it.

Thus in the task of legislation we find together two things which appear to be incompatible: an enterprise too difficult for human powers, and, for its execution, an authority that is no authority.

There is a further difficulty that deserves attention. Wise men, if they try to speak their language to the common herd instead of its own, cannot possibly make themselves understood. There are a thousand kinds of ideas which it is impossible to translate into popular language. Conceptions that are too general and objects that are too remote are equally out of its range: each individual, having no taste for any other plan of government than that which suits his particular interest, finds it difficult to realise the advantages he might hope to draw from the continual privations good laws impose. For a young people to be able to relish sound principles of political theory and follow the fundamental rules of statecraft, the effect would have to become the cause; the social spirit, which should be created by these institutions, would have to preside over their very foundation; and men would have to be before law what they should become by means of law. The legislator therefore, being unable to appeal to either force or reason, must have recourse to an authority of a different order, capable of constraining without violence and persuading without convincing.

This is what has, in all ages, compelled the fathers of nations to have recourse to divine intervention and credit the gods with their own wisdom, in order that the peoples, submitting to the laws of the State as to those of nature, and recognising the same power in the formation of the city as in that of man, might obey freely, and bear with docility the yoke of the public happiness.

This sublime reason, far above the range of the common herd, is that whose decisions the legislator puts into the mouth of the immortals, in order to constrain by divine authority those whom human prudence could not move.[5] But it is not anybody who can make the gods speak, or get himself believed when he proclaims himself their interpreter. The great soul of the legislator is the only miracle that can prove his mission. Any man may grave tablets of stone, or buy an oracle, or feign secret intercourse with some divinity, or train a bird to whisper in his ear, or find other vulgar ways of imposing on the people. He whose knowledge goes no further may perhaps gather round him a band of fools; but he will never found an empire, and his extravagances will quickly perish with him. Idle tricks form a passing tie; only wisdom can make it lasting. The Judaic law, which still subsists, and that of the child of Ishmael, which, for ten centuries, has ruled half the world, still proclaim the great men who laid them down; and, while the pride of philosophy or the blind spirit of faction sees in them no more than lucky impostures, the true political theorist admires, in the institutions they set up, the great and powerful genius which presides over things made to endure.

We should not, with Warburton, conclude from this that politics and religion have among us a common object, but that, in the first periods of nations, the one is used as an instrument for the other.

Endnotes

1. I understand by this word, not merely an aristocracy or a democracy, but generally any government directed by the general will, which is the law. To be legitimate, the government must be, not one with the Sovereign, but its minister. In such a case even a monarchy is a Republic. This will be made clearer in the following book.
2. A people becomes famous only when its legislation begins to decline. We do not know for how many centuries the system of Lycurgus made the Spartans happy before the rest of Greece took any notice of it.
3. Montesquieu, *The Greatness and Decadence of the Romans*, ch. i.
4. Those who know Calvin only as a theologian much under-estimate the extent of his genius. The codification of our wise edicts, in which he played a large part, does him no less honour than his *Institute*. Whatever revolution time may bring in our religion, so long as the spirit of patriotism and liberty still lives among us, the memory of this great man will be for ever blessed.
5. "In truth," says Machiavelli, "there has never been, in any country, an extraordinary legislator who has not had recourse to God; for otherwise his laws would not have been accepted: there are, in fact, many useful truths of which a wise man may have knowledge without their having in themselves such clear reasons for their being so as to be able to convince others" (*Discourses on Livy*, Bk. v, ch. xi).

9

Great Society Speech

Lyndon B. Johnson, 1964

President Hatcher, Governor Romney, Senators McNamara and Hart, Congressmen Meader and Staebler, and other members of the fine Michigan delegation, members of the graduating class, my fellow Americans:

It is a great pleasure to be here today. This university has been coeducational since 1870, but I do not believe it was on the basis of your accomplishments that a Detroit high school girl said, "In choosing a college, you first have to decide whether you want a coeducational school or an educational school."

Well, we can find both here at Michigan, although perhaps at different hours.

I came out here today very anxious to meet the Michigan student whose father told a friend of mine that his son's education had been a real value. It stopped his mother from bragging about him.

I have come today from the turmoil of your Capital to the tranquility of your campus to speak about the future of your country.

The purpose of protecting the life of our Nation and preserving the liberty of our citizens is to pursue the happiness of our people. Our success in that pursuit is the test of our success as a Nation.

For a century we labored to settle and to subdue a continent. For half a century we called upon unbounded invention and untiring industry to create an order of plenty for all of our people.

The challenge of the next half century is whether we have the wisdom to use that wealth to enrich and elevate our national life, and to advance the quality of our American civilization.

Your imagination, your initiative, and your indignation will determine whether we build a society where progress is the servant of our needs, or a society where old values and new visions are buried under unbridled growth. For in your time we have the opportunity to move not only toward the rich society and the powerful society, but upward to the Great Society.

The Great Society rests on abundance and liberty for all. It demands an end to poverty and racial injustice, to which we are totally committed in our time. But that is just the beginning.

The Great Society is a place where every child can find knowledge to enrich his mind and to enlarge his talents. It is a place where leisure is a welcome chance to build and reflect, not a feared cause of boredom and restlessness. It is a place where the city of man serves not only the needs of the body and the demands of commerce but the desire for beauty and the hunger for community.

It is a place where man can renew contact with nature. It is a place which honors creation for its own sake and for what is adds to the understanding of the race. It is a place where men are more concerned with the quality of their goals than the quantity of their goods.

But most of all, the Great Society is not a safe harbor, a resting place, a final objective, a finished work. It is a challenge constantly renewed, beckoning us toward a destiny where the meaning of our lives matches the marvelous products of our labor.

So I want to talk to you today about three places where we begin to build the Great Society—in our cities, in our countryside, and in our classrooms.

Many of you will live to see the day, perhaps 50 years from now, when there will be 400 million Americans—four-fifths of them in urban areas. In the remainder of this century urban population will double, city land will double, and we will have to build homes, highways, and facilities equal to all those built since this country was first settled. So in the next 40 years we must re-build the entire urban United States.

Aristotle said: "Men come together in cities in order to live, but they remain together in order to live the good life." It is harder and harder to live the good life in American cities today.

The catalog of ills is long: there is the decay of the centers and the despoiling of the suburbs. There is not enough housing for our people or transportation for our traffic. Open land is vanishing and old landmarks are violated.

Worst of all expansion is eroding the precious and time honored values of community with neighbors and communion with nature. The loss of these values breeds loneliness and boredom and indifference.

Our society will never be great until our cities are great. Today the frontier of imagination and innovation is inside those cities and not beyond their borders.

New experiments are already going on. It will be the task of your generation to make the American city a place where future generations will come, not only to live but to live the good life.

I understand that if I stayed here tonight I would see that Michigan students are really doing their best to live the good life.

This is the place where the Peace Corps was started. It is inspiring to see how all of you, while you are in this country, are trying so hard to live at the level of the people.

A second place where we begin to build the Great Society is in our countryside. We have always prided ourselves on being not only America the strong and America the free, but America the beautiful. Today that beauty is in danger. The water we drink, the food we eat, the very air that we breathe, are threatened with pollution. Our parks are overcrowded, our seashores overburdened. Green fields and dense forests are disappearing.

A few years ago we were greatly concerned about the "Ugly American." Today we must act to prevent an ugly America.

For once the battle is lost, once our natural splendor is destroyed, it can never be recaptured. And once man can no longer walk with beauty or wonder at nature his spirit will wither and his sustenance be wasted.

A third place to build the Great Society is in the classrooms of America. There your children's lives will be shaped. Our society will not be great until every young mind is set free to scan the farthest reaches of thought and imagination. We are still far from that goal.

Today, 8 million adult Americans, more than the entire population of Michigan, have not finished 5 years of school. Nearly 20 million have not finished 8 years of school. Nearly 54 million—more than one quarter of all America—have not even finished high school.

Each year more than 100,000 high school graduates, with proved ability, do not enter college because they cannot afford it. And if we cannot educate today's youth, what will we do in 1970 when elementary school enrollment will be 5 million greater than 1960? And high school enrollment will rise by 5 million. College enrollment will increase by more than 3 million.

In many places, classrooms are overcrowded and curricula are outdated. Most of our qualified teachers are underpaid, and many of our paid teachers are unqualified. So we must give every child a place to sit and a teacher to learn from. Poverty must not be a bar to learning, and learning must offer an escape from poverty.

But more classrooms and more teachers are not enough. We must seek an educational system which grows in excellence as it grows in size. This means better training for our teachers. It means preparing youth to enjoy their hours of leisure as well as their hours of labor. It means exploring new techniques of teaching, to find new ways to stimulate the love of learning and the capacity for creation.

These are three of the central issues of the Great Society. While our Government has many programs directed at those issues, I do not pretend that we have the full answer to those problems.

But I do promise this: We are going to assemble the best thought and the broadest knowledge from all over the world to find those answers for America. I intend to establish working groups to prepare a series of White House conferences and meetings—on the cities, on natural beauty, on the quality of education, and on other emerging challenges. And from these meetings and from this inspiration and from these studies we will begin to set our course toward the Great Society.

The solution to these problems does not rest on a massive program in Washington, nor can it rely solely on the strained resources of local authority. They require us to create new concepts of cooperation, a creative federalism, between the National Capital and the leaders of local communities.

Woodrow Wilson once wrote: "Every man sent out from his university should be a man of his Nation as well as a man of his time."

Within your lifetime powerful forces, already loosed, will take us toward a way of life beyond the realm of our experience, almost beyond the bounds of our imagination.

For better or for worse, your generation has been appointed by history to deal with those problems and to lead America toward a new age. You have the chance never before afforded to any people in any age. You can help build a society where the demands of morality, and the needs of the spirit, can be realized in the life of the Nation.

So, will you join in the battle to give every citizen the full equality which God enjoins and the law requires, whatever his belief, or race, or the color of his skin?

Will you join in the battle to give every citizen an escape from the crushing weight of poverty?

Will you join in the battle to make it possible for all nations to live in enduring peace— as neighbors and not as mortal enemies?

Will you join in the battle to build the Great Society, to prove that our material progress is only the foundation on which we will build a richer life of mind and spirit?

There are those timid souls who say this battle cannot be won; that we are condemned to a soulless wealth. I do not agree. We have the power to shape the civilization that we want. But we need your will, your labor, your hearts, if we are to build that kind of society.

Those who came to this land sought to build more than just a new country. They sought a new world. So I have come here today to your campus to say that you can make their vision our reality. So let us from this moment begin our work so that in the future men will look track and say: It was then, after a long and weary way, that man turned the exploits of his genius to the full enrichment of his life.

Thank you. Good-bye.

10

Universal Declaration of Human Rights

United Nations

Preamble

Whereas recognition of the inherent dignity and of the equal and inalienable rights of all members of the human family is the foundation of freedom, justice and peace in the world,

Whereas disregard and contempt for human rights have resulted in barbarous acts which have outraged the conscience of mankind, and the advent of a world in which human beings shall enjoy freedom of speech and belief and freedom from fear and want has been proclaimed as the highest aspiration of the common people,

Whereas it is essential, if man is not to be compelled to have recourse, as a last resort, to rebellion against tyranny and oppression, that human rights should be protected by the rule of law,

Whereas it is essential to promote the development of friendly relations between nations,

Whereas the peoples of the United Nations have in the Charter reaffirmed their faith in fundamental human rights, in the dignity and worth of the human person and in the equal rights of men and women and have determined to promote social progress and better standards of life in larger freedom,

Whereas Member States have pledged themselves to achieve, in co-operation with the United Nations, the promotion of universal respect for and observance of human rights and fundamental freedoms,

Whereas a common understanding of these rights and freedoms is of the greatest importance for the full realization of this pledge,

Now, therefore,

The General Assembly

Proclaims this Universal Declaration of Human Rights as a common standard of achievement for all peoples and all nations, to the end that every individual and every organ of society, keeping this Declaration constantly in mind, shall strive by teaching and education to promote respect for these rights and freedoms and by progressive measures, national and international, to secure their universal and effective recognition and observance, both among the peoples of Member States themselves and among the peoples of territories under their jurisdiction.

Article 1

All human beings are born free and equal in dignity and rights. They are endowed with reason and conscience and should act towards one another in a spirit of brotherhood.

Article 2

Everyone is entitled to all the rights and freedoms set forth in this Declaration, without distinction of any kind, such as race, colour, sex, language, religion, political or other opinion, national or social origin, property, birth or other status.

Furthermore, no distinction shall be made on the basis of the political, jurisdictional or international status of the country or territory to which a person belongs, whether it be independent, trust, non-self-governing or under any other limitation of sovereignty.

Article 3

Everyone has the right to life, liberty and the security of person.

Article 4

No one shall be held in slavery or servitude; slavery and the slave trade shall be prohibited in all their forms.

Article 5

No one shall be subjected to torture or to cruel, inhuman or degrading treatment or punishment.

Article 6

Everyone has the right to recognition everywhere as a person before the law.

Article 7

All are equal before the law and are entitled without any discrimination to equal protection against any discrimination in violation of this Declaration and against any incitement to such discrimination.

Article 8

Everyone has the right to an effective remedy by the competent national tribunals for acts violating the fundamental rights granted him by the constitution or by law.

Article 9

No one shall be subjected to arbitrary arrest, detention or exile.

Article 10

Everyone is entitled in full equality to a fair, and public hearing by an independent and impartial tribunal, in the determination of his rights and obligations and of any criminal charge against him.

Article 11

1. Everyone charged with a penal offence has the right to be presumed innocent until proven guilty according to law in a public trial at which he has had all the guarantees necessary for his defence.
2. No one shall be held guilty of any penal offence on account of any act or omission which did not constitute a penal offence, under national or international law, at the time when it was committed. Nor shall a heavier penalty be imposed than the one that was applicable at the time the penal offence was committed.

Article 12

No one shall be subjected to arbitrary interference with his privacy, family, home or correspondence, nor to attacks upon his honour and reputation. Everyone has the right to the protection of the law against such interference or attacks.

Article 13

1. Everyone has the right to freedom of movement and residence within the borders of each State.
2. Everyone has the right to leave any country, including his own, and to return to his country.

Article 14

1. Everyone has the right to seek and to enjoy in other countries asylum from persecution.
2. This right may not be invoked in the case of prosecutions genuinely arising from non-political crimes or from acts contrary to the purposes and principles of the United Nations.

Article 15

1. Everyone has the right to a nationality.
2. No one shall be arbitrarily deprived of his nationality nor denied the right to change his nationality.

Article 16

1. Men and women of full age, without any limitation due to race, nationality or religion, have the right to marry and to found a family. They are entitled to equal rights as to marriage, during marriage and at its dissolution.
2. Marriage shall be entered into only with the free and full consent of the intending spouses.
3. The family is the natural and fundamental group unit of society and is entitled to protection by society and the State.

Article 17

1. Everyone has the right to own property alone as well as in association with others.
2. No one shall be arbitrarily deprived of his property.

Article 18

Everyone has the right to freedom of thought, conscience and religion; this right includes freedom to change his religion or belief, and freedom, either alone or in community with others and in public or private, to manifest his religion or belief in teaching, practice, worship and observance.

Article 19

Everyone has the right to freedom of opinion and expression; this right includes freedom to hold opinions without interference and to seek, receive and impart information and ideas through any media and regardless of frontiers.

Article 20

1. Everyone has the right to freedom of peaceful assembly and association.
2. No one may be compelled to belong to an association.

Article 21

1. Everyone has the right to take part in the government of his country, directly or through freely chosen representatives.
2. Everyone has the right of equal access to public service in his country.
3. The will of the people shall be the basis of the authority of government; this will shall be expressed in periodic and genuine elections which shall be by universal and equal suffrage and shall be held by secret vote or by equivalent free voting procedures.

Article 22

Everyone, as a member of society, has the right to social security and is entitled to realization, through national effort and international co-operation and in accordance with the organization and resources of each State, of the economic, social and cultural rights indispensable for his dignity and the free development of his personality.

Article 23

1. Everyone has the right to work, to free choice of employment, to just and favourable conditions of work and to protection against unemployment.
2. Everyone, without any discrimination, has the right to equal pay for equal work.
3. Everyone who works has the right to just and favourable remuneration ensuring for himself and his family an existence worthy of human dignity, and supplemented, if necessary, by other means of social protection.
4. Everyone has the right to form and to join trade unions for the protection of his interests.

Article 24

Everyone has the right to rest and leisure, including reasonable limitation of working hours and periodic holidays with pay.

Article 25

1. Everyone has the right to a standard of living adequate for the health and well-being of himself and of his family, including food, clothing, housing and medical care and necessary social services, and the right to security in the event of unemployment, sickness, disability, widowhood, old age or other lack of livelihood in circumstances beyond his control.
2. Motherhood and childhood are entitled to special care and assistance. All children, whether born in or out of wedlock, shall enjoy the same social protection.

Article 26

1. Everyone has the right to education. Education shall be free, at least in the elementary and fundamental stages. Elementary education shall be compulsory. Technical and professional education shall be made generally available and higher education shall be equally accessible to all on the basis of merit.
2. Education shall be directed to the full development of the human personality and to the strengthening of respect for human rights and fundamental freedoms. It shall promote understanding, tolerance and friendship among all nations, racial or religious groups, and shall further the activities of the United Nations for the maintenance of peace.
3. Parents have a prior right to choose the kind of education that shall be given to their children.

Article 27

1. Everyone has the right freely to participate in the cultural life of the community, to enjoy the arts and to share in scientific advancement and its benefits.
2. Everyone has the right to the protection of the moral and material interests resulting from any scientific, literary or artistic production of which he is the author.

Article 28

Everyone is entitled to a social and international order in which the rights and freedoms set forth in this Declaration can be fully realized.

Article 29

1. Everyone has duties to the community in which alone the free and full development of his personality is possible.
2. In the exercise of his rights and freedoms, everyone shall be subject only to such limitations as are determined by law solely for the purpose of securing due recognition and respect for the rights and freedoms of others and of meeting the just requirements of morality, public order and the general welfare in a democratic society.
3. These rights and freedoms may in no case be exercised contrary to the purposes and principles of the United Nations.

Article 30

Nothing in this Declaration may be interpreted as implying for any State, group or person any right to engage in any activity or to perform any act aimed at the destruction of any of the rights and freedoms set forth herein.

Additional Readings

1. Goodin, Robert E. 1995. *Utilitarianism as a Public Philosophy*. Cambridge; New York: Cambridge University press.

2. Letter from a Birmingham Jail—Martin Luther King, Jr. *http://www.stanford.edu/group/King/frequentdocs/birmingham.pdf*

3. Rawls, John. 2005; 1971. *A Theory of Justice*. Original ed. Cambridge, Mass.: Belknap Press.

4. Rawls, John, and Erin Kelly. 2001. *Justice as Fairness: a Restatement*. Cambridge, Mass.: Harvard University Press.

5. Young, Iris Marion. 2000. *Inclusion and Democracy*. Oxford; New York: Oxford University Press.

SECTION 2

Race—Deconstructing Myth and Power

11

Racial Formations

Michael Omi
Howard Winant

In 1982–83, Susie Guillory Phipps unsuccessfully sued the Louisiana Bureau of Vital Records to change her racial classification from black to white. The descendant of an eighteenth-century white planter and a black slave, Phipps was designated "black" in her birth certificate in accordance with a 1970 state law which declared anyone with at least one-thirty-second "Negro blood" to be black. The legal battle raised intriguing questions about the concept of race, its meaning in contemporary society, and its use (and abuse) in public policy. Assistant Attorney General Ron Davis defended the law by pointing out that some type of racial classification was necessary to comply with federal record-keeping requirements and to facilitate programs for the prevention of genetic diseases. Phipps's attorney, Brian Begue, argued that the assignment of racial categories on birth certificates was unconstitutional and that the one-thirty-second designation was inaccurate. He called on a retired Tulane University professor who cited research indicating that most whites have one-twentieth "Negro" ancestry. In the end, Phipps lost. The court upheld a state law which quantified racial identity, and in so doing affirmed the legality of assigning individuals to specific racial groupings.[1]

The Phipps case illustrates the continuing dilemma of defining race and establishing its meaning in institutional life. Today, to assert that variations in human physiognomy are racially based is to enter a constant and intense debate. *Scientific* interpretations of race have not been alone in sparking heated controversy; *religious* perspectives have done so as well.[2] Most centrally, of course, race has been a matter of *political* contention. This has been particularly true in the United States, where the concept of race varied enormously over time without ever leaving the center stage of US history.

What Is Race?

Race consciousness, and its articulation in theories of race, is largely a modern phenomenon. When European explorers in the New World "discovered" people who looked different than themselves, these "natives" challenged then existing conceptions of the origins of the human species, and raised disturbing questions as to whether *all* could be considered in the same "family of man."[3] Religious debates flared over the attempt to reconcile the Bible with the existence of "racially distinct" people. Arguments took place over creation itself, as theories of polygenesis questioned whether God had made only one species of humanity ("monogenesis"). Europeans wondered if the natives of the New World were indeed human beings with redeemable souls. At stake were not only the prospects for conversion, but the types of treatment to be accorded them. The expropriation of property, the denial of political rights, the introduction of slavery and other forms of coercive labor, as well as outright extermination, all presupposed a worldview which distinguished Europeans—children of God, human beings, etc.—from "others." Such a worldview was needed to explain why some should be "free" and others enslaved, why some had rights to land and property while others did not. Race, and the interpretation of racial differences, was a central factor in that worldview.

In the colonial epoch science was no less a field of controversy than religion in attempts to comprehend the concept of race and its meaning. Spurred on by the classificatory scheme of living organisms devised by Linnaeus in *Systema Naturae*, many scholars in the eighteenth and nineteenth centuries dedicated themselves to the identification and ranking of variations in humankind. Race was thought of as a *biological* concept, yet its precise definition was the subject of debates which, as we have noted, continue to rage today. Despite efforts ranging from Dr. Samuel Morton's studies of cranial capacity[4] to contemporary attempts to base racial classification on shared gene pools,[5] the concept of race has defied biological definition. . . .

Attempts to discern the *scientific meaning* of race continue to the present day. Although most physical anthropologists and biologists have abandoned the quest for a scientific basis to determine racial categories, controversies have recently flared in the area of genetics and educational psychology. For instance, an essay by Arthur Jensen which argued that hereditary factors shape intelligence not only revived the "nature or nurture" controversy, but raised highly volatile questions about racial equality itself.[6] Clearly the attempt to establish a *biological* basis of race has not been swept into the dust-bin of history, but is being resurrected in various scientific arenas. All such attempts seek to remove the concept of race from fundamental social, political, or economic determination. They suggest instead that the truth of race lies in the terrain of innate characteristics, of which skin color and other physical attributes provide only the most obvious, and in some respects most superficial, indicators.

Race As a Social Concept

The social sciences have come to reject biologistic notions of race in favor of an approach which regards race as a *social* concept. Beginning in the eighteenth century, this trend has been slow and uneven, but its direction clear. In the nineteenth century Max Weber discounted biological explanations for racial conflict and instead highlighted the social and political factors which engendered such conflict.[7] The work of pioneering cultural anthropologist Franz Boas was crucial in refuting the scientific racism of the early twentieth century by rejecting the connection between race and culture, and the assumption of a continuum of "higher" and "lower" cultural groups. Within the contemporary social science literature, race is assumed to be a variable which is shaped by broader societal forces.

Race is indeed a pre-eminently *sociohistorical* concept. Racial categories and the meaning of race are given concrete expression by the specific social relations and historical context in which they are embedded. Racial meanings have varied tremendously over time and between different societies.

In the United States, the black/white color line has historically been rigidly defined and enforced. White is seen as a "pure" category. Any racial intermixture makes one "nonwhite." In the movie *Raintree County*, Elizabeth Taylor describes the worst of fates to befall whites as "havin' a little Negra blood in ya'—just one little teeny drop and a person's all Negra."[8] This thinking flows from what Marvin Harris has characterized as the principle of *hypo-descent:*

> By what ingenious computation is the genetic tracery of a million years of evolution unraveled and each man [sic] assigned his proper social box? In the United States, the mechanism employed is the rule of hypo-descent. This descent rule requires Americans to believe that anyone who is known to have had a Negro ancestor is a Negro. We admit nothing in between. . . . "Hypo-descent" means affiliation with the subordinate rather than the superordinate group in order to avoid the ambiguity of intermediate identity. . . . The rule of hypo-descent is, therefore, an invention, which we in the United States have made in order to keep biological facts from intruding into our collective racist fantasies.[9]

The Susie Guillory Phipps case merely represents the contemporary expression of this racial logic.

By contrast, a striking feature of race relations in the lowland areas of Latin America since the abolition of slavery has been the relative absence of sharply defined racial groupings. No such rigid descent rule characterizes racial identity in many Latin American societies. Brazil, for example, has historically had less rigid conceptions of race, and thus a variety of "intermediate" racial categories exist. Indeed, as Harris notes, "One of the most striking consequences of the Brazilian system of racial identification is that parents and children and even brothers and sisters are frequently accepted as representatives of quite opposite racial types."[10] Such a possibility is incomprehensible within the logic of racial categories in the US.

To suggest another example: the notion of "passing" takes on new meaning if we compare various American cultures' means of assigning racial identity. In the United States, individuals who are actually "black" by the logic of hypo-descent have attempted to skirt the discriminatory barriers imposed by law and custom by attempting to "pass" for white.[11]

Ironically, these same individuals would not be able to pass for "black" in many Latin American societies.

Consideration of the term "black" illustrates the diversity of racial meanings which can be found among different societies and historically within a given society. In contemporary British politics the term "black" is used to refer to all nonwhites. Interestingly this designation has not arisen through the racist discourse of groups such as the National Front. Rather, in political and cultural movements, Asian as well as Afro-Caribbean youth are adopting the term as an expression of self-identity.[12] The wide-ranging meanings of "black" illustrate the manner in which racial categories are shaped politically.[13]

The meaning of race is defined and contested throughout society, in both collective action and personal practice. In the process, racial categories themselves are formed, transformed, destroyed, and re-formed. We use the term *racial formation* to refer to the process by which social, economic, and political forces determine the content and importance of racial categories, and by which they are in turn shaped by racial meanings. Crucial to this formulation is the treatment of race as a *central axis* of social relations which cannot be subsumed under or reduced to some broader category or conception.

Racial Ideology and Racial Identity

The seemingly obvious "natural" and "common sense" qualities which the existing racial order exhibits themselves testify to the effectiveness of the racial formation process in constructing racial meanings and racial identities.

One of the first things we notice about people when we meet them (along with their sex) is their race. We utilize race to provide clues about *who* a person is. This fact is made painfully obvious when we encounter someone whom we cannot conveniently racially categorize—someone who is, for example, racially "mixed" or of an ethnic/racial group with which we are not familiar. Such an encounter becomes a source of discomfort and momentarily a crisis of racial meaning. Without a racial identity, one is in danger of having no identity.

Our compass for navigating race relations depends on preconceived notions of what each specific racial group looks like. Comments such as, "Funny, you don't look black," betray an underlying image of what black should be. We also become disoriented when people do not act "black," "Latino," or indeed "white." The content of such stereotypes reveals a series of unsubstantiated beliefs about who these groups are and what "they" are like.[14]

In US society, then, a kind of "racial etiquette" exists, a set of interpretative codes and racial meanings which operate in the interactions of daily life. Rules shaped by our perception of race in a comprehensively racial society determine the "presentation of self,"[15] distinctions of status, and appropriate modes of conduct. "Etiquette" is not mere universal adherence to the dominant group's rules, but a more dynamic combination of these rules with the values and beliefs of subordinated groupings. This racial "subjection" is quintessentially ideological. Everybody learns some combination, some version, of the rules of racial classification, and of their own racial identity, often without obvious teaching or conscious inculcation. Race becomes "common sense"—a way of comprehending, explaining, and acting in the world.

Racial beliefs operate as an "amateur biology," a way of explaining the variations in "human nature."[16] Differences in skin color and other obvious physical characteristics supposedly provide visible clues to differences lurking underneath. Temperament, sexuality, intelligence, athletic ability, aesthetic preferences and so on are presumed to be fixed and discernible from the palpable mark of race. Such diverse questions as our confidence and trust in others (for example, clerks or salespeople, media figures, neighbors), our sexual preferences and romantic images, our tastes in music, films, dance, or sports, and our very ways of talking, walking, eating, and dreaming are ineluctably shaped by notions of race. Skin color "differences" are thought to explain perceived differences in intellectual, physical, and artistic temperaments, and to justify distinct treatment of racially identified individuals and groups.

The continuing persistence of racial ideology suggests that these racial myths and stereotypes cannot be exposed as such in the popular imagination. They are, we think, too essential, too integral, to the maintenance of the US social order. Of course, particular meanings, stereotypes, and myths can change, but the presence of a *system* of racial meanings and stereotypes, of racial ideology, seems to be a permanent feature of US culture.

Film and television, for example, have been notorious in disseminating images of racial minorities which establish for audiences what people from these groups look like, how they behave, and "who they are."[17] The power of the media lies not only in their ability to reflect the dominant racial ideology, but in their capacity to shape that ideology in the first place. D. W. Griffith's epic *Birth of a Nation*, a sympathetic treatment of the rise of the Ku Klux Klan during Reconstruction, helped to generate, consolidate, and "nationalize" images of blacks which had been more disparate (more regionally specific, for example) prior to the film's appearance.[18] In US television, the necessity to define characters in the briefest and most condensed manner has led to the perpetuation of racial caricatures, as racial stereotypes serve as shorthand for scriptwriters, directors and actors, in commercials, etc. Television's tendency to address the "lowest common denominator" in order to render programs "familiar" to an enormous and diverse audience leads it regularly to assign and reassign racial characteristics to particular groups, both minority and majority.

These and innumerable other examples show that we tend to view race as something fixed and immutable—something rooted in "nature." Thus we mask the historical construction of racial categories, the shifting meaning of race, and the crucial role of politics and ideology in shaping race relations. Races do not emerge full-blown. They are the results of diverse historical practices and are continually subject to challenge over their definition and meaning.

Racialization: The Historical Development of Race

In the United States, the racial category of "black" evolved with the consolidation of racial slavery. By the end of the seventeenth century, Africans whose specific identity was Ibo, Yoruba, Fulani, etc., were rendered "black" by an ideology of exploitation based on racial logic—the establishment and maintenance of a "color line." This of course did not occur overnight. A period of indentured servitude which was not rooted in racial logic preceded the consolidation of racial slavery. With slavery, however, a racially based understanding of society was set in motion which resulted in the shaping of a specific *racial* identity not only for the slaves but for the European settlers as well. Winthrop Jordan has observed: "From the initially common term *Christian*, at mid-century there was a marked shift toward the terms *English* and *free*. After about 1680, taking the colonies as a whole, a new term of self-identification appeared—*white*."[19]

We employ the term *racialization* to signify the extension of racial meaning to a previously racially unclassified relationship, social practice, or group. Racialization is an ideological process, a historically specific one. Racial ideology is constructed from pre-existing conceptual (or, if one prefers, "discursive") elements and emerges from the struggles of competing political projects and ideas seeking to articulate similar elements differently. An account of racialization processes that avoids the pitfalls of US ethnic history[20] remains to be written.

Particularly during the nineteenth century, the category of "white" was subject to challenges brought about by the influx of diverse groups who were not of the same Anglo-Saxon stock as the founding immigrants. In the nineteenth century, political and ideological struggles emerged over the classification of Southern Europeans, the Irish, and Jews, among other "non-white" categories.[21] Nativism was only effectively curbed by the institutionalization of a racial order that drew the color line *around*, rather than *within*, Europe.

By stopping short of racializing immigrants from Europe after the Civil War, and by subsequently allowing their assimilation, the American racial order was reconsolidated in the wake of the tremendous challenge placed before it by the abolition of racial slavery.[22] With the end of Reconstruction in 1877, an effective program for limiting the emergent class struggles of the later nineteenth century was forged: the definition of the working class *in racial terms*—as "white." This was not accomplished by any legislative decree or capitalist maneuvering to divide the working class, but rather by white workers themselves. Many of them were recent immigrants, who organized on racial lines as much as on traditionally defined class lines.[23] The Irish on the West Coast, for example, engaged in vicious anti-Chinese race-baiting and committed many pogrom-type assaults on Chinese in the course of consolidating the trade union movement in California.

Thus the very political organization of the working class was in important ways a racial project. The legacy of racial conflicts and arrangements shaped the definition of interests and in turn led to the consolidation of institutional patterns (e.g., segregated unions, dual labor markets, exclusionary legislation) which perpetuated the color line *within* the working class. Selig Perlman, whose study of the development of the labor movement is fairly sympathetic to this process, notes that:

> The political issue after 1877 was racial, not financial, and the weapon was not merely the ballot, but also "direct action"— violence. The anti-Chinese agitation in California, culminating as it did in the Exclusion Law passed by Congress in 1882, was doubtless the most important single factor in the history of American labor, for without it the entire country might have been overrun by Mongolian [sic] labor and *the labor movement might have become a conflict of races instead of one of classes.*[24]

More recent economic transformations in the US have also altered interpretations of racial identities and meanings. The automation of southern agriculture and the augmented labor demand of the postwar boom transformed Hacks from a largely rural, impoverished labor force to a largely urban, working-class group by 1970.[25] When boom became bust and liberal welfare statism moved rightwards, the majority of blacks came to be seen, increasingly, as part of the "underclass," as state "dependents." Thus the particularly deleterious effects on blacks of global and national economic shifts (generally rising unemployment rates, changes in the employment structure away from reliance on labor intensive work, etc.) were explained once again in the late 1970s and 1980s (as they had been in the 1940s and mid-1960s) as the result of defective black cultural norms, of familial disorganization, etc.[26] In this way new racial attributions, new racial myths, are affixed to "blacks."[27] Similar changes in racial identity are presently affecting Asians and Latinos, as such economic forces as increasing Third World impoverishment and indebtedness fuel immigration and high interest rates, Japanese competition spurs resentments, and US jobs seem to fly away to Korea and Singapore.[28] . . .

Once we understand that race overflows the boundaries of skin color, superexploitation, social stratification, discrimination and prejudice, cultural domination and cultural resistance, state policy (or of any other particular social relationship we list), once we recognize the racial dimension present to some degree in every identity, institution, and social practice in the United States—once we have done this, it becomes possible to speak of *racial formation*. This recognition is hard-won; there is a continuous temptation to think of race as an *essence*, as something fixed, concrete and objective, as (for example) one of the categories just enumerated. And there is also an opposite temptation: to see it as a mere illusion, which an ideal social order would eliminate.

In our view it is crucial to break with these habits of thought. The effort must be made to understand race as *an unstable and "decentered" complex of social meanings constantly being transformed by political struggle.* . . .

Endnotes

1. *San Francisco Chronicle*, 14 September 1982, 19 May 1983. Ironically, the 1970 Louisiana law was enacted to supersede an old Jim Crow statute which relied on the idea of "common report" in determining an infant's race. Following Phipps's unsuccessful attempt to change her classification and have the law declared unconstitutional, a legislative effort arose which culminated in the repeal of the law. See *San Francisco Chronicle*, 23 June 1983.

2. The Mormon church, for example, has been heavily criticized for its doctrine of black inferiority.

3. Thomas F. Gossett notes:

   > Race theory . . . had up until fairly modern times no firm hold on European thought. On the other hand, race theory and race prejudice were by no means unknown at the time when the English colonists came to North America. Undoubtedly, the age of exploration led many to speculate on race differences at a period when neither Europeans nor Englishmen were prepared to make allowances for vast cultural diversities. Even though race theories had not then secured wide acceptance or even sophisticated formulation, the first contacts of the Spanish with the Indians in the Americas can now be recognized as the beginning of a struggle between conceptions of the nature of primitive peoples which has not yet been wholly settled. (Thomas F. Gossett, *Race: The History of an Idea in America* (New York: Schocken Books, 1965), p. 16.)

   Winthrop Jordan provides a detailed account of early European colonialists' attitudes about color and race in *White Over Black: American Attitudes Toward the Negro, 1550–1812* (New York: Norton, 1977 [1968]), pp. 3–43.

4. Pro-slavery physician Samuel George Morton (1799–1851) compiled a collection of 800 crania from all parts of the world which formed the sample for his studies of race. Assuming that the larger the size of the cranium translated into greater intelligence, Morton established a relationship between race and skull capacity. Gossett reports that:

   > In 1849, one of his studies included the following results: The English skulls in his collection proved to be the largest, with an average cranial capacity of 96 cubic inches. The Americans and Germans were rather poor seconds, both with cranial capacities of 90 cubic inches. At the bottom of the list were the Negroes with 83 cubic inches, the Chinese with 82, and the Indians with 79. (Ibid., p. 74.)

   On Morton's methods, see Stephen J. Gould, "The Finagle Factor," *Human Nature* (July 1978).

5. Definitions of race founded upon a common pool of genes have not held up when confronted by scientific research which suggests that the differences *within* a given human population are greater than those *between* populations. See L. L. Cavalli-Sforza, "The Genetics of Human Populations," *Scientific American* (September 1974), pp. 81–89.

6. Arthur Jensen, "How Much Can We Boost IQ and Scholastic Achievement?" *Harvard Educational Review,* vol. 39 (1969), pp. 1–123.

7. Ernst Moritz Manasse, "Max Weber on Race," *Social Research,* vol. 14 (1947), pp. 191–221.

8. Quoted in Edward D. C. Campbell, Jr., *The Celluloid South: Hollywood and the Southern Myth* (Knoxville: University of Tennessee Press, 1981), pp. 168–70.

9. Marvin Harris, *Patterns of Race in the Americas* (New York: Norton, 1964), p. 56.

10. Ibid., p. 57.

11. After James Meredith had been admitted as the first black student at the University of Mississippi, Harry S. Murphy announced that he, and not Meredith, was the first black student to attend "Ole Miss." Murphy described himself as black but was able to pass for white and spent nine months at the institution without attracting any notice. (Ibid., p. 56.)

12. A. Sivanandan, "From Resistance to Rebellion: Asian and Afro-Caribbean Struggles in Britain," *Race and Class,* vol. 23, nos. 2–3 (Autumn-Winter 1981).

13. Consider the contradictions in racial status which abound in the country with the most rigidly defined racial categories—South Africa. There a race classification agency is employed to adjudicate claims for upgrading of official racial identity. This is particularly necessary for the "coloured" category. The apartheid system considers Chinese as "Asians" while the Japanese are accorded the status of "honorary whites." This logic nearly detaches race from any grounding in skin color and other physical attributes and nakedly exposes race as a juridical category subject to economic, social, and political influences. (We are indebted to Steve Talbot for clarification of some of these points.)

14. Gordon W. Allport, *The Nature of Prejudice* (Garden City, New York: Doubleday, 1958), pp. 184–200.

15. We wish to use this phrase loosely, without committing ourselves to a particular position on such social psychological approaches as symbolic interactionism, which are outside the scope of this study. An interesting study on this subject is S. M. Lyman and W. A. Douglass, "Ethnicity: Strategies of Individual and Collective Impression Management," *Social Research,* vol. 40, no. 2 (1973).

16. Michael Billig, "Patterns of Racism: Interviews with National Front Members," *Race and Class,* vol. 20, no. 2 (Autumn 1978), pp. 161–79.

17. "Miss San Antonio USA Lisa Fernandez and other Hispanics auditioning for a role in a television soap opera did not fit the Hollywood image of real Mexicans and had to darken their faces before filming." Model Aurora Garza said that their faces were

bronzed with powder because they looked too white. "I'm a real Mexican [Garza said] and very dark anyway. I'm even darker right now because I have a tan. But they kept wanting me to make my face darker and darker" (*San Francisco Chronicle*, 21 September 1984). A similar dilemma faces Asian American actors who feel that Asian character lead roles inevitably go to white actors who make themselves up to be Asian. Scores of Charlie Chan films, for example, have been made with white leads (the last one was the 1981 *Charlie Chan and the Curse of the Dragon Queen*). Roland Winters, who played in six Chan features, was asked by playwright Frank Chin to explain the logic of casting a white man in the role of Charlie Chan: "The only thing I can think of is, if you want to cast a homosexual in a show, and you get a homosexual, it'll be awful. It won't be funny . . . and maybe there's something there . . ." (Frank Chin, "Confessions of the Chinatown Cowboy," *Bulletin of Concerned Asian Scholars*, vol. 4, no. 3 (Fall 1972)).

18. Melanie Martindale-Sikes, "Nationalizing 'Nigger' Imagery Through 'Birth of a Nation'," paper prepared for the 73rd Annual Meeting of the American Sociological Association, 4–8 September 1978 in San Francisco.

19. Winthrop D. Jordan, op. cit., p. 95; emphasis added.

20. Historical focus has been placed either on particular racially defined groups or on immigration and the "incorporation" of ethnic groups. In the former case the characteristic ethnicity theory pitfalls and apologetics such as functionalism and cultural pluralism may be avoided, but only by sacrificing much of the focus on race. In the latter case, race is considered a manifestation of ethnicity.

21. The degree of antipathy for these groups should not be minimized. A northern commentator observed in the 1850s: "An Irish Catholic seldom attempts to rise to a higher condition than that in which he is placed, while the Negro often makes the attempt with success." Quoted in Gossett, op. cit., p. 288.

22. This analysis, as will perhaps be obvious, is essentially DuBoisian. Its main source will be found in the monumental (and still largely unappreciated) *Black Reconstruction in the United States 1860–1880* (New York: Atheneum, 1977 [1035]).

23. Alexander Saxton argues that:

> North Americans of European background have experienced three great racial confrontations: with the Indian, with the African, and with the Oriental. Central to each transaction has been a totally one-sided preponderance of power, exerted for the exploitation of nonwhites by the dominant white society. In each case (but especially in the two that began with systems of enforced labor), white workingmen have played a crucial, yet ambivalent role. They have been both exploited and exploiters. On the one hand, thrown into competition with nonwhites as enslaved or "cheap" labor, they suffered economically; on the other hand, being white, they benefited by that very exploitation which was compelling the nonwhites to work for low wages or for nothing. Ideologically they were drawn in opposite directions.

> *Racial identification cut at right angles to class consciousness.* (Alexander Saxton, *The Indispensable Enemy: Labor and the Anti-Chinese Movement in California* (Berkeley and Los Angeles: University of California Press, 1971), p. 1, emphasis added.)

24. Selig Perlman, *The History of Trade Unionism in the United States* (New York: Augustus Kelley, 1950), p. 52; emphasis added.

25. Whether Southern blacks were "peasants" or rural workers is unimportant in this context. Some time during the 1960s blacks attained a higher degree of urbanization than whites. Before World War II most blacks had been rural dwellers and nearly 80 percent lived in the South.

26. See George Gilder, *Wealth and Poverty* (New York: Basic Books, 1981); Charles Murray, *Losing Ground* (New York: Basic Books, 1984).

27. A brilliant study of the racialization process in Britain, focused on the rise of "mugging" as a popular fear in the 1970s, is Stuart Hall et al., *Policing the Crisis* (London: Macmillan, 1978).

28. The case of Vincent Chin, a Chinese American man beaten to death in 1982 by a laid-off Detroit auto worker and his stepson who mistook him for Japanese and blamed him for the loss of their jobs, has been widely publicized in Asian American communities. On immigration conflicts and pressures, see Michael Omi, "New Wave Dread: Immigration and Intra-Third World Conflict," *Socialist Review*, no. 60 (November–December 1981).

12

Constructing Race, Creating White Privilege

Pem Davidson Buck

Constructing Race

Improbable as it now seems, since Americans live in a society where racial characterization and self-definition appear to be parts of nature, in the early days of colonization before slavery was solidified and clearly distinguished from other forms of forced labor, Europeans and Africans seem not to have seen their physical differences in that way.[1] It took until the end of the 1700s for ideas about race to develop until they resembled those we live with today. Before Bacon's Rebellion, African and European indentured servants made love with each other, married each other, ran away with each other, lived as neighbors, liked or disliked each other according to individual personality. Sometimes they died or were punished together for resisting or revolting. And masters had to free both Europeans and Africans if they survived to the end of their indentures. Likewise, Europeans initially did not place all Native Americans in a single racial category. They saw cultural, not biological, differences among Native Americans as distinguishing one tribe from another and from themselves.

Given the tendency of slaves, servants, and landless free Europeans and Africans to cooperate in rebellion, the elite had to "teach Whites the value of whiteness" in order to divide and rule their labor force.[2] After Bacon's Rebellion they utilized their domination of colonial legislatures that made laws and of courts that administered them, gradually building a racial strategy based on the earlier tightening and lengthening of African indenture. Part of this process was tighter control of voting. Free property-owning blacks, mulattos, and Native Americans, all identified as not of European ancestry, were denied the vote in 1723.[3]

To keep the racial categories separate, a 1691 law increased the punishment of European women who married African or Indian men; toward the end of the 1600s a white woman could be whipped or enslaved for marrying a Black. Eventually enslavement for white women was abolished because it transgressed the definition of slavery as black. The problem of what to do with white women's "black" children was eventually partially solved by the control of white women's reproduction to prevent the existence of such children.

The potentially "white" children of black women were defined out of existence; they were "black" and shifted from serving a thirty-year indenture to being slaves. To facilitate these reproductive distinctions and to discourage the intimacy that can lead to solidarity and revolts, laws were passed requiring separate quarters for black and white laborers. Kathleen Brown points out that the control of women's bodies thus became critical to the maintenance of whiteness and to the production of slaves.[4] At the same time black men were denied the rights of colonial masculinity as property ownership, guns, and access to white women were forbidden. Children were made to inherit their mother's status, freeing European fathers from any vestiges of responsibility for their offspring born to indentured or enslaved African mothers. This legal shift has had a profound effect on the distribution of wealth in the United States ever since; slave-holding fathers were some of the richest men in the country, and their wealth, distributed among *all* their children, would have created a significant wealthy black segment of the population.

At the same time a changing panoply of specific laws molded European behavior into patterns that made slave revolt and cross-race unity more and more difficult.[5] These laws limited, for instance, the European right to teach slaves to read. Europeans couldn't use slaves in skilled jobs, which were reserved for Europeans. Europeans had to administer pre-scribed punishment for slave "misbehavior" and were expected to participate in patrolling at night. They did not have the legal right to befriend Blacks. A white servant who ran away with a Black was subject to additional punishment beyond that for simply running away. European rights to free their slaves were also curtailed.

Built into all this, rarely mentioned but nevertheless basic to the elite's ability to create and maintain whiteness, slavery, and exploitation, was the use of force against both Blacks and Whites. Fear kept many Whites from challenging, or even questioning, the system. It is worth quoting Lerone Bennett's analysis of how the differentiation between black and white was accomplished:

> The whole system of separation and subordination rested on official state terror. The exigencies of the situation required men to kill some white people to keep them white and to kill many blacks to keep them black. In the North and South, men and women were maimed, tortured, and murdered in a comprehensive campaign of mass conditioning. The severed heads of black and white rebels were impaled on poles along the road as warnings to black people and white people, and opponents of the status quo were starved to death in chains and roasted slowly over open fires. Some rebels were branded; others were castrated. This exemplary cruelty, which was carried out as a deliberate process of mass education, was an inherent part of the new system.[6]

Creating White Privilege

White privileges were established. The "daily exercise of white personal power over black individuals had become a cherished aspect of Southern culture," a critically important part of getting Whites to "settle for being white."[7] Privilege encouraged Whites to identify with the big slaveholding planters as members of the same "race." They were led to act on the belief that all Whites had an equal interest in the maintenance of whiteness and white privilege, and that it was the elite—those controlling the economic system, the political system, and the judicial system—who ultimately protected the benefits of being white.[8]

More pain could be inflicted on Blacks than on Whites.[9] Whites alone could bear arms; Whites alone had the right of self-defense. White servants could own livestock; Africans couldn't. It became illegal to whip naked Whites. Whites but not Africans had to be given their freedom dues at the end of their indenture. Whites were given the right to beat any Blacks, even those they didn't own, for failing to show proper respect. Only Whites could be hired to force black labor as overseers. White servants and laborers were given lighter tasks and a monopoly, for a time, on skilled jobs. White men were given the right to control "their" women without elite interference; Blacks as slaves were denied the right to family at all, since family would mean that slave husbands, not owners, controlled slave wives. In 1668, all free African women were defined as labor, for whom husbands or employers had to pay a tithe, while white women were defined as keepers of men's homes, not as labor; their husbands paid no tax on them. White women were indirectly given control of black slaves and the right to substitute slave labor for their own labor in the fields.

Despite these privileges, landless Whites, some of them living in "miserable huts," might have rejected white privilege if they saw that in fact it made little *positive* difference in their lives, and instead merely protected them from the worst *negative* effects of elite punishment and interference, such as were inflicted on those of African descent.[10] After all, the right to whip someone doesn't cure your own hunger or landlessness. By the end of the Revolutionary War unrest was in the air. Direct control by the elite was no longer politically or militarily feasible. Rebellions and attempted rebellions had been fairly frequent in the hundred years following Bacon's Rebellion.[11] They indicated the continuing depth of landless European discontent. Baptist ferment against the belief in the inherent superiority of the upper classes simply underscored the danger.[12]

So landless Europeans had to be given some *material* reason to reject those aspects of their lives that made them similar to landless Africans and Native Americans, and to focus instead on their similarity to the landed Europeans—to accept whiteness as their defining characteristic. Landless Europeans' only real similarity to the elite was their European ancestry itself, so that ancestry had to be given real significance: European ancestry was identified with upward mobility and the right to use the labor of the non-eligible in their upward climb. So, since land at that time was the source of upward mobility, land had to be made available, if only to a few.

Meanwhile, Thomas Jefferson advocated the establishment of a solid white Anglo-Saxon yeoman class of small farmers, who, as property owners, would acquire a vested interest in law and order and reject class conflict with the elite. These small farmers would, by upholding "law and order," support and sometimes administer the legal mechanisms—jails, workhouses and poorhouses, and vagrancy laws—that would control other Whites who would remain a landless labor force. They would support the legal and illegal mechanisms controlling Native Americans, Africans, and poor Whites, becoming a buffer class between the elite and those they most exploited, disguising the elite's continuing grip on power and wealth. . . .

The Psychological Wage

The initial construction of whiteness had been based on a material benefit for Whites: land, or the apparently realistic hope of land. By the 1830s and 1840s, most families identified by their European descent had had several generations of believing their whiteness was real. But its material benefit had faded. Many Whites were poor, selling their labor either as farm renters or as industrial workers, and they feared wage slavery, no longer certain they were much freer than slaves.[13] But this time, to control unrest, the elite had no material benefits they were willing to part with. Nor were employers willing to raise wages. Instead, politicians and elites emphasized whiteness as a benefit in itself.

The work of particular white intellectuals, who underscored the already existing belief in white superiority and the worries about white slavery, was funded by elites and published in elite-owned printing houses.[14] These intellectuals provided fodder for newspaper discussions, speeches, scientific analysis, novels, sermons, songs, and blackface minstrel shows in which white superiority was phrased as if whiteness in and of itself was naturally a benefit, despite its lack of material advantage. This sense of superiority allowed struggling northern Whites to look down their noses at free Blacks and at recent immigrants, particularly the Irish. This version of whiteness was supposed to make up for their otherwise difficult situation, providing them with a "psychological wage" instead of cash—a bit like being employee of the month and given a special parking place instead of a raise.

Many Whites bought into the psychological wage, expressing their superiority over non-Whites and defining them, rather than the capitalists, as the enemy. They focused, often with trade union help, on excluding Blacks and immigrants from skilled trades and better-paying jobs. Employers cooperated in confining Blacks and immigrants to manual labor and domestic work, making a clear definition of the work suitable for white men.[15] Native white men began shifting away from defining themselves by their landowning freedom and independence. Instead they accepted their dependence on capitalists and the control employers exercised over their lives, and began to define themselves by their class position as skilled "mechanics" working for better wages under better working conditions than other people. They became proud of their productivity, which grew with the growing efficiency of industrial technology, and began using it to define whiteness—and manhood. The ethnic of individual hard work gained far wider currency. Successful competition in the labor marketplace gradually became a mark of manhood, and "white man's work" became the defining characteristic of whiteness.[16] Freedom was equated with the right to own and sell your own labor, as opposed to slavery, which allowed neither right. Independence was now defined not only by property ownership but also by possession of skill and tools that allowed wage-earning men to acquire status as a head of household controlling dependents.[17]

This redefinition of whiteness was built as much on changing gender as on changing class relationships.[18] Many native white men and women, including workers, journalists, scientists, and politicians, began discouraging married women from working for wages, claiming that true women served only their own families. Despite this claim—the cult of domesticity, or of true womanhood—many wives of working class men actually did work outside the home. They were less likely to do so in those cases where native men were able, through strikes and the exclusion of women, immigrants, and free Blacks, to create an artificial labor shortage. Such shortages gave native working class men the leverage to force employers to pay them enough to afford a non-earning wife. Women in the families of such men frequently did "stay home" and frequently helped to promote the idea that people who couldn't do the same were genetically or racially or culturally inferior.

But native Whites whose wages actually weren't sufficient struggled on in poverty. If a native woman worked for wages, particularly in a factory, the family lost status. Many female factory workers were now immigrants rather than native Whites. Many had no husband or had husbands whose wages, when they could get work, came nowhere near supporting a family.[19] It is no wonder immigrant women weren't particularly "domestic." Such families didn't meet the cultural requirements for white privilege—male "productivity" in "white man's work" and dependent female "domesticity." These supposed white virtues became a bludgeon with which to defend white privilege and to deny it to not-quite-Whites and not-Whites, helping to construct a new working class hierarchy. This new hierarchy reserved managerial and skilled jobs for "productive" native Whites. So, for the price of reserving better jobs for some native Whites, the capitalist class gained native white consent to their own loss of independence and to keeping most of the working class on abysmally low wages.

In the South, where there was less industry, the psychological wage slowly developed an additional role. It was used not only to gain consent to oppressive industrial relations, but also to convince poor farming Whites to support Southern elites in their conflict with Northern elites. Du Bois points out that by the Civil War

> . . . it became the fashion to pat the disenfranchised poor white man on the back and tell him after all he was white and that he and the planters had a common object in keeping the white man superior. This virus increased bitterness and relentless hatred, and after the war it became a chief ingredient in the division of the working class in the Southern States.[20]

Endnotes

1. My discussion of the construction of race and racial slavery is deeply indebted to Lerone Bennett, *The Shaping of Black America* (New York: Penguin Books, 1993 [1975]), 1–109. See also Theodore Allen, *Invention of the White Race*, vol. II, *The Origin of Racial Oppression in Anglo-America* (New York: Verso, 1997), 75–109; Audrey Smedley, *Race in North America: Origin and Evolution of a Worldview* (Boulder: Westview Press, 1993), 100–1, 109, 142–3, 198; Kathleen Brown, *Good Wives, Nasty Wenches, and Anxious Patriarchs: Gender, Race, and Power in Colonial Virginia* (Chapel Hill: University of North Carolina Press, 1996), 107–244; bell hooks, *Ain't I a Woman: Black Women and Feminism* (Boston: South End Press, 1981), 15–51.

2. Bennett, *Shaping of Black America*, 74–5.

3. Allen, *Invention*, vol. II, 241.

4. Brown, *Good Wives*, pays particular attention to control of women's bodies and status in producing slavery and race (see especially 181, 129–33, 116); also see Allen, *Invention*, vol. II, 128–35, 146–7, 177–88; Bennett, *Shaping of Black America*, 75.

5. For this section see Bennett, *Shaping of Black America*, 72; Edmund Morgan, *American Slavery, American Freedom: The Ordeal of Colonial Virginia* (New York: W. W. Norton and Co, 1975), 311–3; Allen, *Invention*, vol. II, 249–53.

6. Bennett, *Shaping of Black America*, 73–4.

7. The first quote is from Smedley, *Race in North America*, 224; the second is from David Roediger, *The Wages of Whiteness: Race and the Making of the American Working Class* (New York: Verso, 1991), 6.

8. Allen, *Invention*, vol. II, 162, 248–53, emphasizes that elites invented white supremacy to protect their own interests, although working-class Whites did much of the "dirty work" of oppression.

9. Morgan, *American Slavery*, 312–3. On white privileges see Ronald Takaki, *A Different Mirror: A History of Multicultural America* (Boston: Little, Brown, 1993), 67–8; Allen, *Invention*, vol. II, 250–3; Brown, *Good Wives*, 180–3.

10. The quote is from Allen, *Invention*, vol. II, 256, citing a contemporary traveler.

11. Howard Zinn, *A People's History of the United States* (New York: HarperCollins, 1995, 2nd ed.), 58.

12. Smedley, *Race in North America*, 174–5.

13. Bennett, *Shaping of Black America*, 10, 44–5.

14. *Allen*, Invention, vol. I, 109.

15. On runaways see Morgan, *American Slavery, American Freedom*, 217; Smedley, *Race*, 103–5; Bennett, *Shaping of Black America*, 55.

16. On the tendency to make common cause, see Allen, *Invention*, vol. II, 148–58; Bennett, *Shaping of Black America*, 19–22, 74. On increasing anger and landlessness see Allen, *Invention*, vol. II, 208–9, 343 n. 33; Ronald Takaki, *A Different Mirror: A History of Multicultural America* (Boston: Little, Brown, 1993), 62.

17. Berkeley is quoted in Takaki, *Different Mirror*, 63.

18. On Bacon's Rebellion see Takaki, *Different Mirror*, 63–5; Morgan, *American Slavery, American Freedom*, 254–70; Allen, *Invention*, vol. II, 163–5, 208–17, 239; Brown, *Good Wives*, 137–86. Although interpretations of the rebellion vary widely, it does seem clear that the frightening aspect of the rebellion for those who controlled the drainage system was its dramatic demonstration of the power of a united opposition to those who monopolized land, labor, and trade with Native Americans.

19. Allan Kulikoff, *Tobacco and Slaves: The Development of Southern Cultures in the Chesapeake 1680–1800* (Chapel Hill: University of North Carolina Press, 1986), 77, 104–17.

20. Morgan, *American Slavery, American Freedom*, 271–9.

13

Defining Racism, "Can We Talk?"

Beverly Daniel Tatum

Early in my teaching career, a White student I knew asked me what I would be teaching the following semester. I mentioned that I would be teaching a course on racism. She replied, with some surprise in her voice, "Oh, is there still racism?" I assured her that indeed there was and suggested that she sign up for my course. Fifteen years later, after exhaustive media coverage of events such as the Rodney King beating, the Charles Stuart and Susan Smith cases, the O. J. Simpson trial, the appeal to racial prejudices in electoral politics, and the bitter debates about affirmative action and welfare reform, it seems hard to imagine that anyone would still be unaware of the reality of racism in our society. But in fact, in almost every audience I address, there is someone who will suggest that racism is a thing of the past. There is always someone who hasn't noticed the stereotypical images of people of color in the media, who hasn't observed the housing discrimination in their community, who hasn't read the newspaper articles about documented racial bias in lending practices among well-known banks, who isn't aware of the racial tracking pattern at the local school, who hasn't seen the reports of rising incidents of racially motivated hate crimes in America— in short, someone who hasn't been paying attention to issues of race. But if you are paying attention, the legacy of racism is not hard to see, and we are all affected by it.

The impact of racism begins early. Even in our preschool years, we are exposed to misinformation about people different from ourselves. Many of us grew up in neighborhoods where we had limited opportunities to interact with people different from our own families. When I ask my college students, "How many of you grew up in neighborhoods where most of the people were from the same racial group as your own?" almost every hand goes up. There is still a great deal of social segregation in our communities. Consequently, most of the early information we receive about "others"—people racially, religiously, or socioeconomically different from ourselves—does not come as the result of firsthand experience. The second-hand information we do receive has often been distorted, shaped by cultural stereotypes, and left incomplete.

Some examples will highlight this process. Several years ago one of my students con-ducted a research project investigating preschoolers' conceptions of Native Americans.[1] Using children at a local day care center as her participants, she asked these three- and four-year-olds to draw a picture of a native American. Most children were stumped by her request. They didn't know what a Native American was. But when she rephrased the ques-tion and asked them to draw a picture of an Indian, they readily complied. Almost every picture included one central feature: feathers. In fact, many of them also included a weapon—a knife or tomahawk—and depicted the person in violent or aggressive terms. Though this group of children, almost all of whom were White, did not live near a large Native American population and probably had had little if any personal interaction with American Indians, they all had internalized an image of what Indians were like. How did they know? Cartoon images, in particular the Disney movie *Peter Pan*, were cited by the children as their number-once source of information. At the age of three, these children already had a set of stereotypes in place. Though I would not describe three-year-olds as prej-udiced, the stereotypes to which they have been exposed become the foundation for the adult prejudices so many of us have.

Sometimes the assumptions we make about others come not from what have we been told or what we have seen on television or in books, but rather from what we have *not* been told. The distortion of historical information about people of color leads young people (and older people, too) to make assumptions that may go unchallenged for a long time. Consider this conversation between two White students following a discussion about the cultural transmission of racism:

"Yeah, I just found out that Cleopatra was actually a Black woman."

"What?"

The first student went on to explain her newly learned information. The second stu-dent exclaimed in disbelief, "That can't be true. Cleopatra was beautiful."

What had this young woman learned about who in our society is considered beautiful and who is not? Had she conjured up images of Elizabeth Taylor when she thought of Cleopatra? The new information her classmate had shared and her own deeply ingrained assumptions about who is beautiful and who is not were too incongruous to allow her to assimilate the information at that moment.

Omitted information can have similar effects. For example, another young woman, preparing to be a high school English teacher, expressed her dismay that she had never learned about any Black authors in any of her English courses. How was she to teach about them to her future students when she hadn't learned about them herself? A white male stu-dent in the class responded to this discussion with frustration in his response journal, writ-ing "It's not my fault that Blacks don't write books." Had one of his elementary, high school, or college teachers ever told him that there were not Black writers? Probably not. Yet because he had never been exposed to Black authors, he had drawn his own conclusion that there were none.

Stereotypes, omissions, and distortions all contribute to the development of prejudice. *Prejudice* is a preconceived judgment or opinion, usually based on limited information. I assume that we all have prejudices, not because we want them, but simply because we are so continually exposed to misinformation about others. Though I have often heard students or workshop participants describe someone as not having "a prejudiced bone in his body," I usually suggest that they look again. Prejudice is one of the inescapable consequences of living in a racist society. Cultural racism—the cultural images and messages that affirm the assumed superiority of Whites and the assumed inferiority of people of color—is like smog in the air. Sometimes it is so thick it is visible, other times it is less apparent, but always, day in and day out, we are breathing it in. None of us would introduce ourselves as "smog-breathers" (and most of us don't want to be described as prejudiced), but if we live in a smoggy place, how can we avoid breathing the air? If we live in an environment in which we are bombarded with stereotypical images in the media, are frequently exposed to the ethnic jokes of friends and family members, and are rarely informed of the accomplishments of oppressed groups, we will develop the negative categorizations of those groups that form the basis of prejudice.

People of color as well as Whites develop these categorizations. Even a member of the stereotyped group may internalize the stereotypical categories about his or her own group to some degree. In fact, this process happens so frequently that it has a name, *internalized oppression*. Some of the consequences of believing the distorted messages about one's own group will be discussed in subsequent chapters.

Certainly some people are more prejudiced than others, actively embracing and perpetuating negative and hateful images of those who are different from themselves. When we claim to be free of prejudice, perhaps what we are really saying is that we are not hatemongers. But none of us is completely innocent. Prejudice is an integral part of our socialization, and it is not our fault. Just as the preschoolers my student interviewed are not to blame for the negative messages they internalized, we are not at fault for the stereotypes, distortions, and omissions that shaped our thinking as we grew up.

To say that it is not our fault does not relieve us of responsibility, however. We may not have polluted the air, but we need to take responsibility, I along with others for cleaning it up. Each of us needs to look at our own behavior. Am I perpetuating and reinforcing the negative messages so pervasive in our culture, or am I seeking to challenge them? If I have not been exposed to positive images of marginalized groups, am I seeking them out, expanding my own knowledge base for myself and my children? Am I acknowledging and examining my own prejudices, my own rigid categorizations of others, thereby minimizing the adverse impact they might have on my interactions with those I have categorized? Unless we engage in these and other conscious acts of reflection and reeducation, we easily repeat the process with our children. We teach what we were taught. The unexamined prejudices of the parents are passed on to the children. It is not our fault, but it is our responsibility to interrupt this cycle.

Racism: A System of Advantage Based on Race

Many people use the terms *prejudice* and *racism* interchangeably. I do not, and I think it is important to make a distinction. In his book *Portraits of White Racism*, David Wellman argues convincingly that limiting our understanding of racism to prejudice does not offer a sufficient explanation for the persistence of racism. He defines racism as a "system of advantage based on race."[2] In illustrating this definition, he provides example after example of how Whites defend their racial advantage—access to better schools, housing, jobs—even when they do not embrace overtly prejudicial thinking. Racism cannot be fully explained as an expression of prejudice alone.

This definition of racism is useful because it allows us to see that racism, like other forms of oppression is not only a personal ideology based on racial prejudice, but a *system* involving cultural messages and institutional policies and practices as well as the beliefs and actions of individuals. In the context of the United States, this system clearly operates to the advantage of Whites and to the disadvantage of people of color. Another related definition of racism, commonly used by antiracist educators and consultants, is "prejudice plus power." Racial prejudice when combined with social power—access to social, cultural, and economic resources and decision-making—leads to the institutionalization of racist policies and practices. While I think this definition also captures the idea that racism is more than individual beliefs and attitudes, I prefer Wellman's definition because the idea of systematic advantage and disadvantage is critical to an understanding of how racism operates in American society.

In addition, I find that many of my white students and workshop participants do not feel powerful. Defining racism as prejudice plus power has little personal relevance. For some, their response to this definition is the following: "I'm not really prejudiced, and I have no power, so racism has nothing to do with me." However, most White people, if they are really being honest with themselves, can see that there are advantages to being White in the United States. Despite the current rhetoric about affirmative action and "reverse racism," every social indicator, from salary to life expectancy, reveals the advantages of being White.[3]

The systematic advantages of being White are often referred to as White privilege. In a now well-known article, "White Privilege: Unpacking the Invisible Knapsack," Peggy McIntosh, a White feminist scholar, identified a long list of societal privileges that she received simply because she was White.[4] She did not ask for them, and it is important to note that she hadn't always noticed that she was receiving them. They included major and minor advantages. Of course she enjoyed greater access to jobs and housing. But she was also able to shop in department stores without being followed by suspicious salespeople and could always find appropriate hair care products and makeup in any drugstore. She could send her child to school confident that the teacher would not discriminate against him on the basis of race. She could also be late for meetings, and talk with her mouth full, fairly confident that these behaviors would not be attributed to the fact that she was White. She could express an opinion in a meeting or in print and not have it labeled the "White" view-point. In other words, she was more often than not viewed as an individual, rather than as a member of a racial group.

This article rings true for most White readers, many of whom may have never considered the benefits of being White. It's one thing to have enough awareness of racism to describe the ways that people of color are disadvantaged by it. But this new understanding of racism is more elusive. In very concrete terms, it means that if a person of color is the victim of housing discrimination, the apartment that would otherwise have been rented to that person of color is still available for a White person. The White tenant is, knowingly or unknowingly, the beneficiary of racism, a system of advantage based on race. The unsuspecting tenant is not to blame for the prior discrimination, but she benefits from it anyway.

For many Whites, this new awareness of the benefits of a racist system elicits considerable pain, often accompanied by feelings of anger and guilt. These uncomfortable emotions can hinder further discussion. We all like to think that we deserve the good things we have received, and that others, too, get what they deserve. Social psychologists call this tendency a "belief in a just world."[5] Racism directly contradicts such notions of justice.

Understanding racism as a system of advantage based on race is antithetical to traditional notions of an American meritocracy. For those who have internalized this myth, this definition generates considerable discomfort. It is more comfortable simply to think of racism as a particular form of prejudice. Notions of power or privilege do not have to be addressed when our understanding of racism is constructed in that way.

The discomfort generated when a systemic definition of racism is introduced is usually quite visible in the workshops I lead. Someone in the group is usually quick to point out that this is not the definition you will find in most dictionaries. I reply "Who wrote the dictionary?" I am not being facetious with this response. Whose interests are served by a "prejudice only" definition of racism? It is important to understand that the system of advantage is perpetuated when we do not acknowledge its existence.

Racism: For Whites Only?

Frequently someone will say, "You keep talking about White people. People of color can be racist, too." I once asked a White teacher what it would mean to her if a student or parent of color accused her of being racist. She said she would feel as though she had been punched in the stomach or called a "low-life scum." She is not alone in this feeling. The word *racist* holds a lot of emotional power. For many White people, to be called racist is the ultimate insult. The idea that this term might only be applied to Whites becomes highly problematic for after all, can't people of color be "low-life scum" too?

Of course, people of any racial group can hold hateful attitudes and behave in racially discriminatory and bigoted ways. We can all cite examples of horrible hate crimes which have been perpetrated by people of color as well as Whites. Hateful behavior is hateful behavior no matter who does it. But when I am asked, "Can people of color be racist?" I reply, "The answer depends on your definition of racism." If one defines racism as racial prejudice, the answer is yes. People of color can and do have racial prejudices. However, if one defines racism as a system of advantage based on race, the answer is no. People of color are not racist because they do not systematically benefit from racism. And equally important, there is no systematic cultural and institutional support or sanction for the racial bigotry of people of color. In my view, reserving the term *racist* only for behaviors committed by Whites in the context of a White-dominated society is a way of acknowledging the ever-present power differentiated afforded Whites by the culture and institutions that make up the system of advantage and continue to reinforce notions of White superiority. (Using the same logic, I reserve the word *sexist* for men. Though women can and do have gender-based prejudices, only men systematically benefit from sexism.)

Despite my best efforts to explain my thinking on this point, there are some who will be troubled, perhaps even incensed, by my response. To call the racially motivated acts of a person of color acts of racial bigotry and to describe similar acts committed by Whites as racist will make no sense to some people, including some people of color. To those, I will respectfully say, "We can agree to disagree." At moments like these, it is not agreement that is essential, but clarity. Even if you don't like the definition of racism I am using, hopefully you are now clear about what it is. If I also understand how you are using the term, our conversation can continue—despite our disagreement.

Another provocative question I'm often asked is "Are you saying all Whites are racist?" When asked this question, I again remember that White teacher's response, and I am conscious that perhaps the question I am really being asked is, "Are you saying all Whites are bad people?" The answer to that question is of course not. However, all White people, intentionally or unintentionally, do benefit from racism. A more relevant question is what are White people as individuals doing to interrupt racism? For many White people, the image of a racist is a hood-wearing Klan member or a name-calling Archie Bunker figure. These images represent what might be called *active racism*, blatant, intentional acts of racial bigotry and discrimination. *Passive racism* is more subtle and can be seen in the collusion of laughing when a racist joke is told, of letting exclusionary hiring practices go unchallenged, of accepting as appropriate the omissions of people of color from the curriculum, and of avoiding difficult race-related issues. Because racism is so ingrained in the fabric of American institutions, it is easily self-perpetuating.[6] All that is required to maintain it is business as usual.

I sometimes visualize the ongoing cycle of racism as a moving walkway at the airport. Active racist behavior is equivalent to walking fast on the conveyor belt. This person engaged in active racist behavior has identified with the ideology of White supremacy and is moving with it. Passive racist behavior is equivalent to standing still on the walkway. No overt effort is being made, but the conveyor belt moves the bystanders along to the same destination as those who are actively walking. Some of the bystanders may feel the motion of the conveyor belt, see the active racists ahead of them, and choose to turn around, unwilling to go to the same destination as the White supremacists. But unless they are walking actively in the opposite direction at a speed faster than the conveyor belt—unless they are actively antiracist—they will find themselves carried along with the others.

So, not all Whites are actively racist. Many are passively racist. Some, though not enough, are actively antiracist. The relevant question is not whether all Whites are racist, but how we can move more White people from a position of active or passive racism to one of active antiracism. The task of interrupting racism is obviously not the task of Whites alone. But the fact of White privilege means that Whites have greater access to the societal institutions in need of transformation. To whom much is given, much is required.

It is important to acknowledge that while all Whites benefit from racism, they do not all benefit equally. Other factors, such as socioeconomic status, gender, age, religious affiliation, sexual orientation, mental and physical ability, also play a role in our access to social influence and power. A White woman on welfare is not privileged to the same extent as a wealthy White heterosexual man. In her case, the systematic disadvantages of sexism and classism intersect with her White privilege, but the privilege is still there. This point was brought home to me in a 1994 study conducted by a Mount Holyoke graduate student, Phyllis Wentworth.[7] Wentworth interviewed a group of female college students, who were both older than their peers and were the first members of their families to attend college, about the pathways that led them to college. All of the women interviewed were White, from working-class backgrounds, from families where women were expected to graduate from high school and get married or get a job. Several had experienced abusive relationships and other personal difficulties prior to coming to college. Yet their experiences were punctuated by "good luck" stories of apartments obtained without a deposit, good jobs offered without experience or extensive reference checks, and encouragement provided by willing mentors. While the women acknowledged their good fortune, none of them discussed their Whiteness. They had not considered the possibility that being White had worked in their favor and helped give them the benefit of the doubt at critical junctures. This study clearly showed that even under difficult circumstances, White privilege was still operating.

It is also true that not all people of color are equally targeted by racism. We all have multiple identities that shape our experience. I can describe myself as a light-skinned, well-educated, heterosexual, able-bodied, Christian African American woman raised in a middle-class suburb. As an African American woman, I am systematically disadvantaged by race and by gender, but I systematically receive benefits in the other categories, which then mediate my experience of racism and sexism. When one is targeted by multiple isms—racism, sexism, classism, heterosexism, albeism, anti-Semitism, ageism—in whatever combinations, the effect is intensified. The particular combination of racism and classism in many communities of color is life-threatening. Nonetheless, when I, the middle-class Black mother of two sons, read another story about a Black man's unlucky encounter with a White police officer's deadly force, I am reminded that racism by itself can kill.

Endnotes

1. C. O'Toole, "The effect of the media and multicultural education on children's perceptions of Native Americans" (senior thesis, Department of Psychology and Education, Mount Holyoke College, South Hadley, MA, May 1990).

2. For an extended discussion of this point, see David Wellman, *Portraits of White Racism* (Cambridge: Cambridge University Press, 1977), ch. 1

3. For specific statistical information, see R. Farley, "The common destiny of Blacks and Whites: observations about the social and economic status of the races," pp. 197–233 in H. Hill and J. E. Jones, Jr. (Eds.), *Race in America: The struggle for equality* (Madison: University of Wisconsin Press, 1993).

4. P. McIntosh, "White privilege: Unpacking the invisible knapsack," *Peace and Freedom* (July/August 1989): 10–12.

5. For further discussion of the concept of "belief in a just world," see M. J. Lerner, "Social psychology of justice and interpersonal attraction," in T. Huston (Ed.,), *Foundations of interpersonal attraction* (New York: Academic Press, 1974).

6. For a brief historical overview of the institutionalization of racism and sexism in our legal system, see "Part V: How it happened: Race and gender issues in U.S. law," in P. S. Rothenberg (Ed.), *Race, class, and gender in the United States: An integrated study,* 3d ed. (New York: St. Martin's Press, 1995).

7. P. A. Wentworth, "The identity development of non-traditionally aged first-generation women college students: An exploratory study" (master's thesis, Department of Psychology and Education, Mount Holyoke College, South Hadley, MA, 1994).

14

Differentiation and Hierarchy in Cultural Context: The Consequences of Constructed Identity for African-Americans

H. Mark Ellis

When identifying the mechanisms that create or contribute to the social construction of race based identity in a society, the sources and consequences are often blurred. While explaining how race is socially constructed it is often difficult to make careful distinctions between the consequences of race and the sources of its social construction. The devastating social consequences of race-based identity act to perpetuate our shared beliefs that the perceived biology of racial differences is a meaningful marker of innate behavioral differences and social outcomes when we know that it is not. The powerful myths of race-based biology and behavior have played and continue to play an interesting role in racism. These myths support a belief system that gets played out in real socio-economic and health disparities and disadvantages. These destructive ideas about biology and behavior are deeply embedded in American culture as tools for excluding and derogating African-Americans. These ideas about biological differentiation are embedded in the psyches of African-Americans who grow up in this culture. They are subjected to race- and class-based deprivation of opportunities and they often confront structural barriers that are kept in place by mythologies of racial difference. In this essay, I argue that this externally created biological mythology when implanted in the individual and collective psyche of a disenfranchised group (hence embraced by the group) becomes an oppressive and self-destructive way of identifying the self, "knowing" one's self and actualizing the self.

The role of power in constructing difference in systems of stratification has to be examined. Power is not easily shared nor is it quietly and easily taken. Power is not easily practiced and does not contribute to prosperous, efficient and egalitarian social organizations. The question becomes, do democratic systems that are organized around shared governance use language and practices of human difference while simultaneously promoting equality? Imagine a society where differentiations are thought of as variations and not stratifications.

Social Construction Theory and the "Meaning" of Racial Identity

What does a lazy ill prepared student look like? What does a welfare mother look like? To understand how difference is socially constructed and gets played out in daily life, we need to engage a theoretical framework that allows us to examine how micro behaviors of face-to-face encounters are socially derived, mediated and sanctioned. The roles that we are cast in and are foisted on us as identity markers are culturally created, socially performed, and engaged with audience interactions of responses to behavioral compliance or deviation. If we accept such a roles-based theoretical orientation to define and delineate social roles and interactions found in social life, this means all members of society are cast as having a role(s) based on race, ethnicity, beliefs, sex, gender, sexual orientation, age and social class.

What is the purpose of identifying differences within a population—hence engaging in differentiation? The following scenario adapted from Susan Crawford's, *Beyond Dolls and Guns: 101 Ways to Help Children Avoid Gender Bias* serves as an example of the purpose and power of differentiation in any setting or society at-large. Crawford describes the scene and morning ritual of a teacher in the typical kindergarten classroom as follows: "At the beginning of a typical school day, an older white female kindergarten teacher greets her 8:30 A.M. class with, "Good morning boys and girls." What does this statement convey? Why is this teacher's race used as a descriptor?

Ironically, the teacher's description is not the most noteworthy part of the initial statement. Why does the teacher focus on the students' sex? This ascription takes place because sex and gender along with age and race are used to shape identity. These labels of identity shape the roles we assume in life such as student, worker, athlete, sibling, son or daughter, contestant, and so on. Young children "learn" gender role expectations along with all of their other new and evolving roles. The acquisition of these predetermined cultural scripts is how social constructions of identities work. Why not greet the class with, "Good morning blonde, brown, brunette, and red-haired ones"? Or perhaps the teacher could use the variable height ([1] tall and [2] short ones) or weight ([1] thin and [2] plump ones) when greeting her students. Illuminating these differences is rooted in our acceptance of stratified systems that are based on both defining social differentiation and placing these differences into a culturally constructed status hierarchy.

Why focus on differences at all? Ultimately, why not focus on similarity stemming from a common and shared human experience or position? For example, the teacher could have greeted the class in the following manner: "Good morning students or children." However, the teacher's decision to focus on the differences across the individuals within the classroom is merely a snap shot of reductive orientation of the larger society and its broader stratified systems of power that promote positions of inequality and injustice.

In the social sciences, we observe and describe what people do and we attempt to understand why they do what they do. In order to reach this understanding about behavior, we use facts and categorical descriptions of people. If race and gender did not exist as categories in our society, how would we describe an accuser or a victim of a crime? Without these social categories we would find ourselves stuck, not knowing how to execute role expectations and interactions or understand statistical trends observed in a social context. However, we have to be mindful that our use of these socially constructed categories in our research does not reify differences we observe across groups at the expense of acknowledging their origins and propagation in the power structure of society. We also note how the creation of racial and gender slurs in our language contribute to maintaining these social distances, distinctions, and inequities of rewards while damaging the psyches of the "other." These and other mechanisms hold social constructions in place. The histories of race and gender in America are filled with examples of these categories being used to distribute and maintain power and privilege. However, they are also used as psychological tools that can contribute to poor self-concept and self-image among minority groups.

The Consequences of Racial Construction: The African-American Case

Carter G. Woodson wrote in his 1933 classic, "The Miseducation of the Negro,"

> "When you control a man's thinking, you do not have to worry about his actions. You do not have to tell him where to stand. He will find his proper place and he will stay in it. You do not have to send him to the back door. He will go there without being told. In fact, if there is no back door, he will cut one for his special benefit. His education makes it necessary." (Winbush, 1993).

What is this thing called race that socially constructs 'his' obedience to his own oppression? Theories of race posited by such theorists as Omi and Winant assert and acknowledge that the social construction of race is not embedded in biology or genetic evidence, rather race as a biological category was created to justify actions such as slavery, taking property and land, creating miscegenation laws, and denying full inclusion and participation in American life as outlined and stipulated in the constitution and in federal and local laws, policies and practices (Omi and Winant, 1986). Is it 'his' race that socially constructs his obedience to his own oppression? Will 'he' also provide the noose to 'his' own hanging? What has the system done to 'him' and for 'him'? What does 'he' do in response to this system of domination? What is 'he' doing for 'himself' to move toward self-defined liberation? It is time to look beyond civil rights and fight for basic human rights? Will 'his' shackles ever truly be severed? Or will 'he' be doomed to carry them forever? Is 'his' heart, mind, body and soul fed by fear and dependency and nourished by 'his' own enslaving diet of dissociation, apathy, atrophy, despondency, and self-loathing? To enslave can be defined as, to subjugate as in to subdue or bring under control. A slave is someone who is completely dominated by someone's influence, habit, or person. In Randall Jarrell's poem, *The Death of a Ball Turret Gunner*, he suggests that when we awake from our mothers' sleep we are born into and awake into the State (Abcarian and Klotz, 1986). The individual is born into society: a system that immediately processes individuals for social cataloguing. Some are packaged and shipped to the suburbs for idyllic existence and others are shipped to the slums and marked "inferior" with the mandate to spend money to approach maximum assimilation and climb to a narrow apogee. When the state is unable to achieve this through legitimate means that are economically supported and nourished by racism it pursues an alternate plan with the instructions, "go directly to jail."

From here on, I conflate the African-American racial and working class experiences when referring to African-Americans in general. Many of the mechanisms that I describe that contribute to the social construction and maintenance of inequality are also experienced by other marginalized social groups and all races in the working class. Also, this is not to suggest that people in other social classes do not experience the trappings, limitations and consequences of social constructions. A consequence of these external controls and categories is that they turn into internalized self-punishing behaviors. I do describe these "race"/constructs as they relate to African-Americans.

External mechanisms of social construction feed, nurture, and make inevitable persistent and stubborn internalizations of the social construction of race-based expected behaviors. There is little else to nurture identities on the starvation diet that endears people to their own self-loafing. The core task of breaking open the psychic shackles of race construction is education that heals and opens minds to independent thinking and enables people to seek out their own achievement and find their own mental health and positive self-concept.

The creation of race under American slavery created more than a prolific economic system that free white males controlled and benefited from. From slavery was born American Apartheid. When America declared independence, who was it free from and why? And who was independent and free to do what? Do independence and liberation give rise to freedom, individuality, individualism, individuation, and the immortality of capitalism? What does it mean for American racial and ethnic minorities to live liberated lives? Does making it out of the ghetto decrease minority group solidarity and does it give rise to a triple consciousness: us, them, and a within racial group variance identity?

Rodney King has become a modern icon to represent what we now call racial profiling in America. When the riots broke out following the acquittal of his police assailants, Mr. King pleaded and asked, "Can't we all just get along?" This statement summarizes the state of our racial dilemma and 9-11 has since even complicated the state of race relations both domestically and internationally even more. This is what the black scholar and leader WEB Du Bois called a century ago, "the problem with the color line."

Privilege, power, and difference are necessary tools required to build and maintain a slave culture. The organizational strategy used to facilitate maximum output in this hierarchical arrangement is predicated on the successful maintenance and management of the color line. Slavery had many tentacles and we note that slave status was not always based on color or race. Sociologist Allan Johnson reminds us that, "the trouble around diversity, then, isn't just that people differ from one another. The trouble is produced by a world organized in ways that encourage people to use difference to include or exclude, reward or punish, credit or discredit, elevate or oppress, value or devalue, leave alone or harass" (Johnson, 2001). Let's take for example the issue of racial difference/diversity. African American novelist James Baldwin once offered that there is no such thing as blackness, or whiteness, or more generally, race. To quote Baldwin, "No one was white before he/she came to America. It took generations, and a vast amount of coercion before this became a white country" (Johnson, 2001). What Baldwin is saying is that unless you live in a culture that recognizes those differences as significant, they are socially irrelevant and therefore do not exist. Also race and all its categories outside a system of privilege and oppression have no significance. It is the system that creates these categories. This is what sociologists call the social construction of reality. Once we give such things as skin color and sex a name, those things acquire significance they otherwise would not have (Johnson, 2001).

How do power, privilege, and difference work to oppress American minorities? One way that the dominant culture does this is to render people of color as minorities. Minorities are silenced, made invisible, problematized, defined and constructed as less than entire beings, and are made to believe that they must rely on the dominant culture for survival. Also, they come to know their value by how the popular culture depicts them. Hence, identity–dependency is paramount to the thriving and survival of enslaving processes.

Take for example the content analysis of sociologist Allen Johnson on Oscar-awarded best films over the last thirty years. His analysis examines privilege and prestige in American society. The Oscars are the most coveted award for achievement in acting. This raises two questions: (1) How many people of color have achieved this award? And (2) what film roles and narratives have been created for people of color—how are they being depicted? Whether people of color are playing pimps, prostitutes, mammies, thugs, and so on, the media feeds our collective psyches with an over abundance of negative images of people of color. As for Johnson's Oscar film analysis, he notes that in 2002 that the film to receive that Oscar was *Chicago*. In 2001 it was *A Beautiful Mind*. In 2000 it was *Gladiator*. Oscar award winning films from prior years also included: *American Beauty* (1999), *Shakespeare in Love* (1998), *Titanic* (1997), *The English Patient* (1996), *Braveheart* (1995), *Forrest Gump* (1994), and so on. Of these films judged better than all the rest in each year, none set in the United States place people of color at the center of the story without having to share it with white characters of equal importance—*Driving Miss Daisy* (1989) and *In the Heat of the Night* (1967). The one film that focuses on Native Americans—*Dances with Wolves* (1980)—is told from a white man's point of view with Native Americans clearly defined as the other. Only two focus on non-European cultures: *The Last Emperor* (1987) and *Gandhi* (1982). Although *Out of Africa* (1985) is set in Africa, the story focuses exclusively on whites and without any critical commentary on their exploitation of the African continent. For the most part these films address life experiences and the condition of the human spirit from the perspective of the white male (Johnson, 2001).

When Hollywood does award minority actors it is usually for violent or dependency roles that actors of color play. Take for example Denzel Washington's violent and corrupt role in the film, *Training Day* and Halle Berry's chronically dependent character in *Monster's Ball*. Both their performances in these films earned them Oscars. More generally, the lack of emotional range and complexity of minority characters or characters played by minorities send the message that minorities do not have the capacity to live the full human experience and the capacity to fully emote like whites, thus rendering minorities as not fully human. When a person views someone as less than him or herself and not fully human, it explains how they justify violence or indifference toward this thing that they call "other." Do minorities buy into these images and create their own enslavement? When they have the opportunity to make it in entertainment and they participate in the replication of these negative images, are they as culpable as the white man who airs and broadcasts these images? Are they to say no to these capitalistic opportunities? After all, it's just entertainment, right? Has this economic dogma bred so much discontent that they are willing participants in their own disenfranchisement and destruction?

Well, the goal of a minority group in its own liberation should not be to act like their oppressor, but to be better without exerting injurious intent or action. However, if the media tells African-Americans who they are and should be in the popular culture such as in song lyrics and music videos and in film and they learn and accept these messages and internalize these overwhelmingly negative images, what value will they put on their lives? Perhaps buying lots of things might satisfy a need for immediate gratification of self-value. Perhaps the appearance of pointers to external value embodied in things masks the pain or numbs the perception of a worthless inner self. Perhaps investing in a college education or buying a home might be too delayed in feeling some modicum of continuous and immediate self-worth.

The socially constructed commoditized (i.e., propertied) identity of African-Americans under slavery that was created and exploited by and for the benefit of racist white capitalism has been embraced by many African-Americans that seem to define the "self" via the constructs of contemporary commodities. The possible consequence of a socially constructed oppressive economic identity (particular in a capitalistic society) may be to unknowingly re-define one's self worth and value on similar terms and language used by the oppressor. Hence, one becomes his own oppressor by embracing inherently negative and debilitating constructions of identity. For example, what do the consumption patterns of minorities tell us about self-containment, self-enslavement, and the control of dominant white society over minorities? Why don't racial minorities and working class people save their money? Can they? Why do they overextend themselves with regard to gift giving as opposed to putting that money in the bank or an account that makes money? Why don't many minorities have savings accounts? Do they live on income alone, income and credit, mostly credit, on public assistance, or on some combination? Why? Why don't they invest their money in income-producing debt such as real estate or education? Why don't they take money from their parents for down payments on homes like their white counterparts? These are some of the interesting economic questions that Shapiro and Oliver ask in their book, *Black Wealth/White Wealth: A New Perspective on Racial Inequality.*

Conclusion

There are many external and internal social constructions of race. We can continue to examine slavery as a social, political and economic system that created wealth for white men and contributed economic disparity between wealthy white men and people of color and women. We can also look at how slavery contributed to self-enslaving and self-loathing while creating profound disadvantages and utter dependence. This color and class line separated the races and created whiteness and blackness by practices, policies and laws that lead to social inclusion and exclusion of various racial and ethnic groups. We also note that social and cultural systems create categories and meanings of difference that are arbitrary and not embedded in biology. Skin color as foundational to the definition of race created dependence on the inferior group. Cultural images of bodies and characteristics in the media have also contributed to this social construction. There have been many contributing factors to the social construction of race along with devastating consequences. We must now think about solutions to the racial destructiveness of the social construction of race. Can race be redeemed to be recreated as a positive category of identity or is that impossible within the American legacy of racial construction?

Thus, efforts to build new cultural understandings based on variations in human characteristics, shifting away from racist practices and interactions historically built on differentiation, must be based on deconstructing the invidious consequences of differentiation. History and legacies cannot be re-written and even revisionist historians cannot do this. Even if the teacher in the story discussed earlier were to greet the aggregated individuals in the physical and social space called a classroom by recognizing a shared status of "students or children (age as a master status)," once the door to the classroom closes, even in egalitarian learning environments, power dynamics still remain. Social scripts for the roles of teacher and student are short-lived and contextual. The participants do not always agree upon outcomes of decision-making processes between teachers and kindergarten students. Jointly negotiated power in this context is probably appropriately not shared.

To borrow from sociological phenomenology and the ideas of Alfred Schultz, one way to view aggregates such as classrooms, within a larger social system, is to examine the ways in which groups and individuals experience everyday life. We recognize that the rituals and experiences of everyday life are socially constructed and mediated by rules that are imposed and are at times at odds with an individual's ideas of how to live life. In addition, not all individuals are able to achieve these normative social expectations. An explanation for the inability of some people to fulfill this social contract could focus on ascribed and sociopolitical and historical differences that these individuals represent. We take the existence of others for granted as we assume that they share our own perspectives and assume that others can understand our own lived experiences (Outhwaite and Bottomore, 1994).

Social and physical inhabitance of constructed categories for existence become internalized psychological and daily-lived experiences and realities of inequality. Stereotypes, when they become embedded in social constructions of primary characteristics of people become invidious, pernicious and destructive mechanisms that enable people to be socially controlled.

References

Abcarian, Richard, and Marvin Klotz, eds. 1986. *Literature: The Human Experience*. New York: St. Martin's Press.

Crawford, Susan Hoy. 1996. *Beyond Dolls and Guns: 101 Ways to Help Children Avoid Gender Bias*. Portsmouth, NH: Heinemann Publishers.

The Criminal Justice Collective of Northern Arizona University. 2000. *Investigating Difference: Human and Cultural Relations in Criminal Justice*. Boston: Allyn and Bacon.

Diamond, Jared. 1999. *Guns, Germs, and Steel: The Fates of Human Societies*. New York: W.W. Norton & Company.

Glazer, Penina Migdal, and Miriam Slater. 1987. *Unequal Colleagues: The Entrance of Women into the Professions*. New Brunswick: Rutgers University Press.

Hochschild, Arlie, with Anne Machung. 1989. *The Second Shift*. New York: Avon Books.

Hurst, Charles E. 2007. *Social Inequality: Forms, Causes, and Consequences*. New York: Pearson Education, Inc.

Johnson, Allan G. 2001. *Privilege, Power, and Difference*. Mountain View, California: Mayfield Publishing Company.

Lorber, Judith. 2001. "The Social Construction of Gender." Pages 47–57 in *Race, Class and Gender in the United States*. New York: Worth Publishers.

Loewen, James W. 1995. *Lies My Teacher Told Me: Everything Your American History Textbook Got Wrong*. New York: Simon and Schuster.

McNamara, Robert, and Ronald Burns. 2009. *Multiculturalism in the Criminal Justice System*. New York: McGraw-Hill.

McIntosh, Peggy. 2002. "White Privilege: Unpacking the Invisible Knapsack." Pages 97–101 in *White Privilege: Essential Readings on the Other Side of Racism*. New York: Worth Publishers.

Ogawa, Brian K. 1999. *Color of Justice*. Boston: Allyn and Bacon.

Oliver, Melvin L., and Thomas M. Shapiro. *Black Wealth/White Wealth: A New Perspective on Racial Inequality*. 1997. New York: Routledge.

Omi, Michael, and Howard Winant. 2001. "Racial Formations." Pages 11–20 in *Race, Class and Gender in the United States*. New York: Worth Publishers.

Outhwaite, William, and Tom Bottomore. eds. 1994. *The Blackwell Dictionary of Twentieth-Century Social Thought*. Cambridge, Massachusetts: Blackwell Publishers.

Petchesky, Rosalind Pollack. 1990. *Abortion and Woman's Choice: The State, Sexuality and Reproductive Freedom*. Boston: Northeastern University Press.

Reagon, Bernice Johnson. 1995. *Greed*. Washington, DC: Songtalk Publishing Company.

Rosenblum, Karen E., and Toni-Michelle C. Travis. 2008. *The Meaning of Difference: American Constructions of Race, Sex and Gender, Social Class, Sexual Orientation, and Disability.* New York: McGraw-Hill.

Rothenberg, Paula. 2001. *Race, Class and Gender in the United States.* New York: Worth Publishers.

Rothenberg, Paula. ed. 2002. *White Privilege: Essential Readings on the Other Side of Racism.* New York: Worth Publishers.

Winbush, Raymond A. ed. 2003. *Should America Pay?: Slavery and the Raging Debate on Reparations.* New York: Amistad, an Imprint of HarperCollins Publishers.

15

Who and What is a Negro

Marcus Garvey

The New York World under date of January 15, 1923, published a statement of Drs. Clark Wissler and Franz Boaz (the latter a professor of anthropology at Columbia University), confirming the statement of the French that Moroccan and Algerian troops used in the invasion of Germany were not to be classified as Negroes, because they were not of that race. How the French and these gentlemen arrive at such a conclusion is marvelous to understand, but I feel it is the old-time method of depriving the Negro of anything that would tend to make him recognized in any useful occupation or activity.

The custom of these anthropologists is whenever a black man, whether he be Moroccan, Algerian, Senegalese or what not, accomplishes anything of importance, he is no longer a Negro. The question, therefore, suggests itself, "Who and what is a Negro?" The answer is, "A Negro is a person of dark complexion or race, who has not accomplished anything and to whom others are not obligated for any useful service." If the Moroccans and Algerians were not needed by France at this time to augment their occupation of Germany or to save the French nation from extinction, they would have been called Negroes as usual, but now that they have rendered themselves useful to the higher appreciation of France they are no longer members of the Negro race, but can be classified among a higher type as made out by the two professors above mentioned. Whether these professors or France desire to make the Moroccans other than Negroes we are satisfied that their propaganda before has made these people to understand that their destiny is linked up with all other men of color throughout the world, and now that the hundreds of millions of darker peoples are looking toward one common union and destiny through the effort of universal cooperation, we have no fear that the Moroccans and Algerians will take care of the situation in France and Germany peculiar to the interest of Negroes throughout the world.

Let us not be flattered by white anthropologists and statesmen who, from time to time, because of our success here, there or anywhere, try to make out that we are no longer members of the Negro race. If we were Negroes when we were down under the heel of oppression then we will be Negroes when we are up and liberated from such thraldom.

The Moroccans and Algerians have a splendid opportunity of proving the real worth of the Negro in Europe, and who to tell that one day Africa will colonize Europe, even as Europe has been endeavoring to colonize the world for hundreds of years.

Negroes Robbed of Their History

The white world has always tried to rob and discredit us of our history. They tell us that Tut-Ankh-Amen, a King of Egypt, who reigned about the year 1350 B.C. (before Christ), was not a Negro, that the ancient civilization of Egypt and the Pharaohs was not of our race, but that does not make the truth unreal. Every student of history, of impartial mind, knows that the Negro once ruled the world, when white men were savages and barbarians living in caves; that thousands of Negro professors at that time taught in the universities in Alexandria, then the seat of learning; that ancient Egypt gave to the world civilization and that Greece and Rome have robbed Egypt of her arts and letters, and taken all the credit to themselves. It is not surprising, however, that white men should resort to every means to keep Negroes in ignorance of their history, it would be a great shock to their pride to admit to the world today that 3,000 years ago black men excelled in government and were the founders and teachers of art, science and literature. The power and sway we once held passed away, but now in the twentieth century we are about to see a return of it in the rebuilding of Africa; yes, a new civilization, a new culture, shall spring up from among our people, and the Nile shall once more flow through the land of science, of art, and of literature, wherein will live black men of the highest learning and the highest accomplishments.

Professor George A. Kersnor, head of the Harvard–Boston expedition to the Egyptian Soudan, returned to America early in 1923 and, after describing the genius of the Ethiopians and their high culture during the period of 750 B.C. to 350 A.D. in middle Africa, he declared the Ethiopians were not African Negroes. He described them as dark colored races . . . showing a mixture of black blood. Imagine a dark colored man in middle Africa being anything else but a Negro. Some white men, whether they be professors or what not, certainly have a wide stretch of imagination. The above statements of the professors support my contention at all times that the prejudice against us as Negroes is not because of color, but because of our condition. If black men throughout the world as a race will render themselves so independent and useful as to be sought out by other race groups it will simply mean that all the problems of race will be smashed to pieces and the Negro would be regarded like anybody else—a man to be respected and admired.

16

"No Color Barrier": Italians, Race, and Power in the United States

Thomas A. Guglielmo

Looking back on their and their ancestors' early immigrant experiences in America, many Italian Americans, especially since the 1970s, have prided themselves on making it in America by working hard and shunning government assistance. Examining interviews of Chicago's Italian Americans conducted in the early 1980s, I came across these views over and over again. Leonard Giuliano stated: "With determination and perseverance . . . the Italian was able to . . . pull himself up by his own bootstraps. . . . His greatest desire, of course, was for his children and his family to have a better life than he had left in Italy, but he did not expect this for nothing. He had to work." Constance Muzzacavallo agreed: "I think we've updated ourselves. I'll give the Italian 100 percent credit for that. You didn't have the government helping you." Joseph Loguidice added: "The immigrants in those days didn't have . . . the things today . . . or the help that they have today. Today is a cake walk. Everybody gets help. They didn't have no aid . . . like you have today. . . . Those people were too proud."[1]

These views—coming to life most forcefully during the post-1960s "backlash" years—address far more than simply the value of hard work and the proper role of the federal government; they are also deeply about race. As one Al Riccardi told an interviewer in the early 1990s. "My people had a rough time, too. But nobody gave us something, so why do we owe them [African Americans] something? Let them pull their share like the rest of us had to do."[2]

This essay was written, in part, as a response to Giuliano, Muzzacavallo, Loguidice, Riccardi, and the countless others who share their views. Focusing on the early years of migration and settlement—approximately 1890–1918—I am interested in Italian immigrants' hardships, hard work, and perseverance, but also in something too often overlooked in romantic retrospectives on the European "immigrant experience"—white power and privilege. Most broadly, this essay examines where Italians were located within America's developing racial order and what consequences this had on their everyday lives and opportunities.

This essay is written as an invitation to other scholars to further explore Italians' (and other immigrants') encounters with race in the United States. If it demonstrates anything, it is that we still have much to learn about these critical issues.

Beginning in earnest with the onset of mass migration from Italy (particularly southern Italy) in the late nineteenth century and continuing well into the twentieth century, racial discrimination and prejudice aimed at Italians, southern Italians, Latins, Mediterraneans, and "new" immigrants were fierce, powerful, and pervasive. And some of this anti-Italian sentiment and behavior questioned Italians' whiteness on occasion. In the end, however, Italians' many perceived racial inadequacies aside, they were still largely accepted as whites by the widest variety of people and institutions—the U.S. census, race science, newspapers, unions, employers, neighbors, real estate agents, settlement houses, politicians, political parties, and countless federal and state laws regarding naturalization, segregation, voting rights, and "miscegenation." This widespread acceptance was reflected most concretely in Italians' ability to immigrate to the United States and become citizens, work certain jobs, live in certain neighborhoods, join certain unions, marry certain partners, patronize certain movie theaters, restaurants, saloons, hospitals, summer camps, parks, beaches, and settlement houses. In so many of these situations, one color line existed separating "whites" from the "colored races"— groups such as "Negroes," "Orientals," and "Mexicans." And from the moment they arrived in the United States—and forever after— Italians were consistently and unambiguously placed on the side of the former. If Italians were racially undesirable in the eyes of many Americans, they were white just the same.

They were so securely white, in fact, that Italians themselves rarely had to aggressively assert the point. Indeed, according to my work on Chicago, not until World War II did many Italians identify openly and mobilize politically as white. After the early years of migration and settlement, when Italy remained merely an abstraction to many newcomers, their strongest allegiance was to the Italian race, not the white one. In the end, however, how Italians chose to identify proved to be of little consequence when it came to the "wages of whiteness." As it turned out, Italians did not need to be openly and assertively white to benefit from the considerable rewards and resources of whiteness. For a good part of the late nineteenth and early twentieth centuries, then, Italians were white on arrival, not so much because of the way they viewed themselves but because of the way others viewed and treated them. For this reason, and because of space constraints, I will not focus on Italians' race/color self-identification here.

Two conceptual tools are critical to my analysis. First is the simple point that we take the structure of race seriously. Race is still too often talked about as simply an idea, an attitude, a consciousness, an identity, or an ideology. It is, to be sure, all of these things—but also much more. It is also rooted in various political, economic, social, and cultural institutions, and thus very much about power and resources (or lack thereof). Particularly helpful on this point is sociologist Eduardo Bonilla-Silva, who argues that we use "racialized social system" as an analytical tool. In all such systems, he argues,

The placement of people in racial categories involves some form of hierarchy that produces definite social relations between the races. The race placed in the superior position tends to receive greater economic remuneration and access to better occupations and/or prospects in the labor market, occupies a primary position in the political system, is granted higher social estimation . . . often has a license to draw physical (segregation) as well as social (racial etiquette) boundaries between itself and other races, and receives what Du Bois calls a "psychological wage." The totality of these racialized social relations and practices constitutes [a racialized social system).[3]

Such a system existed throughout the nineteenth- and twentieth-century United States. Whether one was white, black, red, yellow, or brown—and to some extent Anglo-Saxon, Alpine, South Italian, or North Italian—powerfully influenced (along with other systems of difference, such as class and gender) where one lived and worked, the kind of person one married, and the kinds of life chances one had. Thus, race was not (and is not) completely about ideas, ideologies, and identity. It is also about location in a social system and its consequences.

To fully understand these consequences, one more conceptual tool is critical: the distinction between race and color. Several years back, when I began research on Italians and race, I envisioned a "wop to white" story, an Italian version of Noel Ignatiev's *How the Irish Became White*. I quickly realized, however, that this approach had serious shortcomings. For one, Italians did not need to become white; they always were, in numerous, critical ways. For another, race was more than black and white. Though Italians' status as whites was relatively secure, they still suffered, as noted above, from extensive *racial* discrimination and prejudice as Italians, South Italians, Latins, and so on.

Nor was this simply "ethnic" discrimination. To be sure, few scholars agree on how best to conceptually differentiate between "race" and "ethnicity." Some have argued that whereas race is based primarily on physical characteristics subjectively chosen, ethnicity is based on cultural ones (e.g., language, religion, etc.). Others have maintained that "membership in an ethnic group is usually voluntary; membership in a racial group is not." Still others have argued that "while 'ethnic' social relations are not *necessarily* hierarchical, exploitative and conflictual, 'race relations'" almost always are.[4] None of these distinctions, though all are valid in certain ways, is very helpful for our purposes. None of them, that is, helps us to better understand Italians' social experiences and their particular social location in the United States. After all, a group like the "South Italian race" was purported to have particular "cultural" *and* "physical" characteristics; included both voluntary *and* involuntary members; and was created in Italy and used extensively in the United States to explicitly rank and exploit certain human beings.

How, then, to navigate between Italians' relatively secure whiteness *and* their highly problematical racial status, without resorting to unhelpful conceptual distinctions between race and ethnicity? The answer, I contend, is race and color. I argue that between the mid-nineteenth and mid-twentieth centuries there were primarily two ways of categorizing human beings based on supposedly inborn physical, mental, moral, emotional, and cultural traits. The first is color (or what might be called "color race," since this is what many Americans think of as race today): the black race, brown race, red race, white race, and yellow race. Color, as I use it, is a social category and not a physical description. "White" Italians, for instance, could be darker than "black" Americans. Second is race, which could mean many things: large groups like Nordics and Mediterraneans; medium-sized ones like the Celts and Hebrews; or smaller ones like the North and South Italians.

This race/color distinction was, of course, never absolute during this time period, and it certainly changed over time. But some people and institutions were very clear on the distinction. The federal government's naturalization applications throughout this time period, for instance, asked applicants to provide their race and color. For Italians, the only acceptable answers were North or South Italian for the former and white for the latter. Most important, for all of its discursive messiness, the race/color distinction was crystal clear throughout the United States when it came to resources and rewards. In other words, while Italians suffered for their supposed *racial* undesirability as Italians, South Italians, and so forth, they still benefited in countless ways from their privileged *color* status as whites.

Italians are a particularly good group on which to test this argument, because they faced such severe racial discrimination and prejudice in the United States, which all started prior to migration in Italy. In the late nineteenth century, an influential group of positivist anthropologists, including Cesare Lombroso, Giuseppe Sergi, and Alfredo Niceforo, emerged on the scene with scientific "proof" that southern Italians were racially distinct from and hopelessly inferior to their northern compatriots. Sergi, for instance, using skull measurements to trace the various origins and desirability of the Italian people, argued that while northern Italians descended from superior Aryan stock, southerners were primarily of inferior African blood. Similarly, Niceforo argued in his widely read study, *L'Italia barbara contemporanea*, that two Italies existed, whose fundamental racial differences made unification impossible. After all, "One of the two Italies, the northern one, shows a civilization greatly diffused, more fresh, and more modern. The Italy of the South [however] shows a moral and social structure reminiscent of primitive and even quasibarbarian times, a civilization quite inferior."[5]

Such ideas were by no means restricted to the academy; a great deal of Italian mass culture and many public officials absorbed and disseminated them as well. For instance, Italy's leading illustrated magazine of the time, *Illustrazione italiana*, repeatedly and "patronizingly celebrate[d] the South's anomalous position between Italy and the Orient, between the world of civilized progress and the spheres of either rusticity or barbarism." As one of the magazine's reporters noted after a trip through Sicily in 1893, "In the fields where I interviewed many peasants I found only types with the most unmistakable African origin. My how much strange intelligence is in those muddled brains." Similarly, Filippo Turati, a Socialist Party leader at the turn of the twentieth century, no doubt spoke for many of his compatriots when he referred to the "Southern Question" as a battle between "an incipient civilization and that putrid barbarity."[6]

Just at this moment—at the height of the scientific and popular racialist assault on the Mezzogiorno (southern Italy) and its people—the origins of Italian immigration to the United States shifted dramatically from the North to the South. As hundreds of thousands of these much-maligned *meridionali* (southern Italians) arrived in America each year, a wide variety of American institutions and individuals, alarmed by this massive influx, made great use of Italian positivist race arguments. In 1899, the U.S. Bureau of Immigration, for instance, began recording the racial backgrounds of immigrants and distinguishing between "Keltic" northern Italians and "Iberic" southern Italians. In 1911, the U.S. Immigration Commission, throughout its highly influential forty-two-volume report, made a similar distinction. Citing the works of Niceforo and Sergi, it argued that northern and southern Italians "differ from each other materially in language, physique, and character, as well as in geographical distribution." While the former was "cool, deliberate, patient, practical, as well as capable of great progress in the political and social organization of modern civilization," the latter was "excitable, impulsive, highly imaginative, impracticable," and had "little adaptability to highly organized society."[7]

Social scientists like Edward Ross, also citing the work of Italian positivists, made a similar set of arguments. In popular magazine articles and books, Ross warned that while northern Italians were well-fitted for citizenship, their southern counterparts certainly were not because of their horrifying "propensity for personal violence," "inaptness" for teamwork, strong dose of African blood, and "lack of mental ability." Deeply anxious about many of these characteristics, in 1914 the popular magazine *World's Work* urged the federal government to pass an exclusion law "aimed specifically at the southern Italians, similar to our immigration laws against Asiatics," since southern Italians "are a direct menace to our Government because they are not fit to take part in it."[8]

A wide range of local institutions shared these anti-*meridionali* racialist ideas. Newspapers from New York to Florida, and Chicago to Louisiana, regularly lambasted southern Italians as being "injurious," "undesirable," and of the "lowest order."[9] Typical for the time was the *Chicago Tribune*, which in 1910 sent anthropologist George A. Dorsey to the Mezzogiorno to study immigrants in their homeland. Traveling from one small hill town to the next and writing daily columns on his impressions, Dorsey offered, in the end, the most damning view of southern Italians. These people, he claimed, were unmanly and primitive barbarians who had clear "Negroid" ancestry, who shared much more in common with the East than the West, and who were "poor in health, stature, strength, initiative, education, and money." "They are," concluded Dorsey after five months, "of questionable value from a mental, moral, or physical standpoint."[10] And throughout the United States many local governments, local politicians, labor unions, and employers could not help but agree with Dorsey and the *Tribune*.[11]

These ideas had a popular appeal as well, which was reflected in Italians' rocky relations with their neighbors in a wide range of communities nationwide. In northern cities like

New York, Chicago, Milwaukee, Rochester, New Haven, Buffalo, and Philadelphia, various immigrant groups vigorously resisted the influx of Italians (particularly those from the South of Italy). In Rochester, one character in Jerre Mangione's *Monte Allegro* recalled that neighborhood animosity was so intense against Italians that "the storekeepers would not sell them food and the landlords would not rent them homes."[12] Likewise, on Chicago's Near North Side, bloody battles involving sticks, guns, knives, and blackjacks occurred regularly between Swedes and Sicilians. The former also held homeowner meetings to devise more genteel ways of ridding the neighborhood of the dreaded "dark people." The problem, in the words of one local Swedish pastor, was that Sicilians "do not keep their places clean; they tear up the cedar blocks of the sidewalk; and they also bring the district into disrepute in many other ways." Meanwhile, children engaged in similar battles on the playgrounds and streets of the neighborhood as Swedish girls kept Sicilians girls off the swings and out of the sandboxes at Seward Park by exclaiming: "Get out! Dagoes! Dagoes! You can't play here!" And Irish and Swedish boys regularly engaged in street battles with their Sicilian counterparts. On one occasion an Italian youngster led a charge of his compatriots against their neighborhood aggressors on horseback.[13]

Relations were often no friendlier in other parts of the country. Most dramatically, lynchings were none too rare an occurrence for Italians throughout the South, West, and Midwest at this time. Certainly the most infamous and shocking of these took place in New Orleans in 1891 when an angry mob, bent on avenging the murder of Police Chief David Hennessy, lynched eleven Sicilian suspects in one night. Other lynchings took place in locations as diverse as Denver, Tampa, Tallulah, Mississippi, and southern Illinois. Indeed, as late as 1915, an armed posse in Johnston, Illinois, a mining town some one hundred miles east of St. Louis, lynched Sicilian Joseph Strando for his alleged murder of a prominent town resident.[14]

Taken together, many Italians, particularly those from the Mezzogiorno, encountered powerful, pervasive, and often racialized discrimination and prejudice upon arrival in the United States. Thus, if *meridionali* emigrated from Italy in part to escape a racialized social system that relegated them to the bottom tier, they entered another social system in the United States fairly close to the bottom again. But the social systems of turn-of-the-century Italy and the United States were very different. Most important, in contrast to the Old World, southern Italians never occupied the lowest of social positions in the United States. This was because the United States had both racial *and* color hierarchies, and if Italians were denigrated and exploited in the former, they were greatly privileged in the latter. That is, for all of the racial prejudice and discrimination that Italians faced in these early years, they were still generally accepted as white and reaped the many rewards that came with this status.

To be sure, this statement needs serious qualification, for certainly at no other time in Italian American history was the color status of *meridionali* more hotly contested. We have already seen that prominent social scientists publicly ruminated on southern Italians' "Negroid" roots, and that lynching—a punishment often reserved for African Americans—

occurred with some frequency against Italians in these years. Color questions came in other forms. In 1911, the U.S. House Committee on Immigration openly debated and seriously questioned whether one should regard "the south Italian as a full-blooded Caucasian"; many representatives did not seem to think so. From the docks of New York to railroads in the West, some native-born American workers carefully drew distinctions between themselves—"white men"—and "new immigrant" foreigners like Italians.[15] Meanwhile, in the South, where color questioning may have been most severe, one Mississippi Delta town attempted to bar Italians from white schools, and Louisiana state legislators in 1898 fought to disenfranchise Italians, along with African Americans, at the state constitutional convention. As one local newspaper at the time wrote, "When we speak of white man's government, they [Italians] are as black as the blackest Negro in existence." In the sugarcane fields of Louisiana, one Sicilian American recalled, "The boss used to call us niggers" and "told us that we weren't white men."[16]

This important evidence notwithstanding, we should not exaggerate the precariousness of Italians' color status. Color questioning never led to any sustained or systematic positioning of Italians as nonwhite.[17] That is, if U.S. congressmen openly debated whether southern Italians were full-blooded Caucasians, they never went so far as to deny *meridionali* naturalization rights based on their doubts; if magazines like *World's Work* called for the exclusion of southern Italian immigration, Congress never enacted such measures; and if some Louisianans tried to disenfranchise Italians, their efforts, in direct contrast to those regarding African Americans, failed miserably.

Italians' whiteness, however, was most visible in communities all across the country. In Chicago, for example, when famous African American boxing champion Jack Johnson attempted to marry a "white" woman in 1912, a rowdy and menacing crowd of a thousand "whites" protested on the Near North Side by hanging Johnson in effigy. Italians, by contrast, could marry "white" women without anywhere near this level of resistance.[18] Regarding housing, battles took place to prevent Italian infiltration in places like the Near North Side and the Grand Avenue area. These efforts, however, were never as violent as those in areas just west of the Black Belt, where bombings, rioting, and gang attacks against African Americans occurred regularly as the Great Migration got under way during World War I. As a result, while the few wealthy Italians could move to any Chicago neighborhood that they could afford, African Americans (and many Asians) were forced to live in the most blighted of Chicago's neighborhoods, regardless of their wealth or education.[19]

In the workplace, Italians faced discrimination from both unions and employers. However, they always enjoyed far more employment options and opportunities than did the "colored races."[20] Finally, Italians were refused admission to a movie theater or restaurant on occasion. But such instances were rare indeed, and certainly paled in comparison to what many African Americans and some Asians had to endure: systematic exclusion from or segregation in countless Chicago restaurants, theaters, hotels, bars, prisons, hospitals, settlement houses, orphanages, schools, and cemeteries.[21] Thus, even in this early period when the "colored races" remained a small fraction of the city's population, a distinct and pervasive color line separated them from "whites." And for all their alleged racial inadequacies, Italians were placed firmly among the latter.[22]

A very similar story applies to Baltimore. Here, according to historian Gordon Shufelt, from the earliest days of Italian immigration, the "white citizens of Baltimore . . . invited Italian immigrants to join the white community." As in Chicago, this color position made all the difference in the world. In 1904, when a massive fire swept through the city, destroying almost everything in its path, the city distributed relief and relief jobs strictly according to color criteria—"whites" (Italians among them) got jobs and relief, "blacks" did not. Similarly, in the following decade, when local Democratic politicians repeatedly tried to pass anti-African American disfranchisement legislation and segregation housing ordinances, they never intentionally targeted Italians and instead welcomed them into the white fold as key constituents. By the early 1900s, one local politician for Italians campaigned openly as the "white man's ward leader," and began speeches with the boast: "There's no man in the state who hates the darky more than I do."[23]

Out West, Italians suffered from indignities on account of their race. They faced some workplace and neighborhood discrimination in cities like San Francisco, and severe violence throughout the West. Italians were lynched in Gunnison, Colorado, in 1890 and in Denver three years later. This mistreatment extended to explicit color questioning on occasion. One Italian from rural Washington recalled: "Many of the natives were kind and generous; but others spared no effort to let us know that we were intruders and undesirables." In fact, one classmate called him "a goddamn wop" and insisted that he did not "belong to the white race." Similarly, in Arizona, some copper companies categorized their workers into three main groups—whites, Mexicans, and Italians/Spaniards.[24]

As in other parts of the country, however, this color questioning seems to have been sporadic at best (probably more sporadic in the West, where far fewer Italian immigrants settled and where, of these, fewer came from the Mezzogiorno) and rarely institutionalized Indeed, as scholars like Tomás Almaguer and Yvette Huginnie have shown, whiteness mattered monumentally in the West, and all people of European descent belonged to this most privileged color category. In a region of "white man's towns"—where pervasive color lines prevented many African Americans, Asians, Latinos, and Native Americans from owning land, marrying anyone they chose, serving on juries, joining particular unions, claiming land to mine, swimming in the local pool, or attending the best schools—Italians were white and, as usual, benefited greatly from this arrangement.[25]

But what about the Deep South, where Italians' whiteness may have been most seriously challenged? Though far more research needs to be done, it appears that Italians' whiteness was more evident on a daily basis here than perhaps anywhere else. After all, the Deep South had, by the turn of the twentieth century, the most visible colorized social system in the form of disfranchisement, antimiscegenation laws, and Jim Crow segregation. And while evidence certainly exists that Southerners ("black" and "white") and some of their organizations occasionally categorized Italians as nonwhite. I have found no evidence that Italians were ever subjected in any systematic way to Jim Crow segregation or disfranchisement, or legally barred from marrying "white" men and women.[26]

Indeed, it was Italians' very whiteness that largely explains their arrival in the South in the first place. Many southern planters recruited Italians explicitly as "white" laborers who, in direct contrast to African Americans and Asians, could address their two major turn-of-the-century concerns: the "colored problem" and the declining pool of cheap labor. As historian J. Vincenza Scarpaci has pointed out, "The growing interest of the planters for Italians paralleled the post-war concern for an increased white population." As one southern newspaper joyfully announced in 1906. "The influx of the Italians between 1890–1900 made Louisiana a white state."[27]

To be sure, many Southerners, even planters among them, came to deeply regret recruiting Italians and other southern and eastern Europeans. Indeed, during the first few decades of the twentieth century growing anti-immigrant fervor swept through the region. Still, anti-Italian feelings and actions—while intense for a time—seldom lasted long. Having completed an extensive survey of southern towns in the early 1900s, the U.S. Immigration Commission found that in many locations Italians had "fought their way inch by inch through unreasoning hostility and prejudice to almost unqualified respect, or even admiration." Equally prevalent, reported the commission, was that if in some cases parents held fast to their anti-Italian prejudice, similar feelings were breaking down among the "American" children with whom Italians played and mingled freely in "white" schools.[28]

Furthermore, even at their height, anti-Italian feelings had their limits. Even the most virulent attacks on Italians often took their whiteness for granted. During Louisiana's debates about disfranchisement in 1898, for instance, New Orleans's main paper, the *Daily Picayune*, suggested under the headline "White Foreigners Should Not Have Privileges over White Natives"—that Italians might be too ignorant and illiterate to be trusted with the ballot. In 1906, the *Memphis Commercial Appeal* asked: "Does the South want white labor to piece out or to compete with its Negro labor? . . . What class of settlers are they bringing here? Are they of that character that they would help maintain a white man's Dixie; or are they so ignorant or careless as to become in effect allies of those *across* the color line? We want immigration to a certain extent, but we do not want 'just anybody'" (emphasis added). One journal article from 1903, titled "Italian Immigration into the South," put it best by asking: "Is the immigrant of today the kind of white man whom the South stands ready to welcome?" That Italians were white was assumed; that they were desirable was another question entirely.[29]

This point becomes even clearer, perhaps, when we compare Italians' experiences with those of another marginalized immigrant group in the South—the Chinese. As James Loewen has shown convincingly in his book *The Mississippi Chinese*, the Chinese were initially grouped along with African Americans and systematically excluded from white schools, organizations, and social institutions. By the 1930s and 1940s, when their reputations and status improved considerably, the Chinese were, generally speaking, still not accepted as white. Instead, many towns in the South developed triply segregated school systems. Nothing in Italians' experiences in the Deep South ever approached this sort of treatment.[30]

In sum, whether in the North, South, or West; whether by the government, newspapers, employers, social scientists, or neighbors; Italians faced their share of racial discrimination and prejudice. During these early years of migration and settlement, however, their whiteness was rarely challenged in any sustained or systematic way. Italians were white on arrival in America, then, regardless of where they happened to arrive.

Why was this the case? Given the widespread doubts about (chiefly) southern Italian *racial* fitness and desirability, why was their *color* status as whites not more seriously contested? First, scientists, for as long as they had attempted to construct racial/color taxonomies, placed Italians firmly within the white category. The weight of scientific opinion in the United States supported some variation of Johann Friedrich Blumenbach's classification scheme from the late eighteenth century, which divided humankind into "five principal varieties": the American ("red"), Caucasian ("white"), Ethiopian ("black"), Malay ("brown"), and Mongolian ("yellow"). As the U.S. Immigration Commission's *Dictionary of Races and Peoples* noted in 1911, "in preparing this dictionary . . . the author deemed it reasonable to follow the classification employed by Blumenbach. . . . The use of this classification as the basis for this present work is perhaps entirely justified by the general prevailing custom in the United States [to follow Blumenbach], but there is equal justification in the fact that recent writers, such as Keane and the American authority Brinton, have returned to practically the earlier [Blumenbach] classifications." Significantly, Blumenbach placed Italians (both southern and northern) within the Caucasian "variety." To question Italian whiteness, then, required one to challenge widely accepted theories in race science as well.[31]

Second, the history of the Italian peninsula—particularly that of the Roman Empire and the Renaissance—also supported the classification of Italians as white. As Eliot Lord argued in the early twentieth century, "The far-reaching ancestry of the natives of South and Central Italy runs back to the dawn of the earliest Greek civilization in the peninsula and to the Etruscan, driving bronze chariots and glittering in artful gold when the Angles, Saxons and Jutes, and all the wild men of Northern Europe were muffling their nakedness in the skins of wild beasts." As a result, asked Lord in conclusion: "Upon what examination worthy of the name has the Southern Latin stock, as exhibited in Italy, been stamped as 'undesirable'? Is it undesirable to perpetuate the blood, the memorials and traditions of the greatest empire of antiquity, which spread the light of its civilization from the Mediterranean to the North Sea and the Baltic?"[32] Given these points, anti-immigrant racialists had to exercise caution in their color-questioning of Italians, for if Italians were not white, a good deal of Western civilization might not have been either.

Finally, if various branches of the American state deeply institutionalized the *racial* differences between northern and southern Italians in their immigration statistics, studies, and applications, they just as surely secured the two groups' *color* commonalities. For one,

American naturalization laws during this time allowed only "free white male persons" or "aliens of African nativity or persons of African descent" to become U.S. citizens; and American courts repeatedly denied Asian and Middle Eastern immigrants access to American citizenship because of the color stipulation in the law. Italians never once encountered any problems.[33]

Just as important as naturalization laws was the U.S. census. The color/race category and the kinds of answers the census requested changed many times between 1880 and 1920; the census, for instance, alternated frequently between asking for people's "color," "race," and "color or race." At some points it also asked enumerators to distinguish between "whites" and "Mexicans," between "mulattos," "octoroons," "quadroons," and so forth. Throughout all of these variations, however, Italians were always listed as foreign-born or native-born "whites." Because the census represented the federal government's final word on color categories, this classification was no small thing. Indeed, census categorization schemes must have had an immense influence on everyday Americans and their color conceptions. With the largest collection of social data on Americans anywhere, the U.S. census offered invaluable information to countless people—from social scientists and politicians to government bureaucrats and journalists. When using this information, one often unwittingly reproduced the various ways the census organized it—and, in the process, reproduced Italian whiteness.[34]

In the end, Italians' firm hold on whiteness never loosened over time. They were, at different points, criminalized mercilessly, ostracized in various neighborhoods, denied jobs on occasion, and alternately ridiculed and demonized by American popular culture. Yet, through it all, their whiteness remained intact. The rise of immigration restriction in the early 1920s demonstrates this point well. Anti-immigrant racialists—front Madison Grant to Kenneth Roberts, from mass circulation magazines like *Collier's* to mass movements like the Klan—roundly condemned Italians (particularly, though not exclusively, those from the South) for mongrelizing and menacing the nation. Interestingly, however, they stopped well short of questioning Italians' whiteness. If all racialists agreed that Italians were a hopelessly inferior lot, they also agreed that they were "white" or "Caucasian" just the same. They were, in the fitting words of former Seattle Mayor Ole Hanson, "the White Peril of Europe."[35]

Lothrop Stoddard's popular book, *The Rising Tide of Color* (1920), typified this point. Stoddard, an ardent Nordic supremacist, sounded the alarm against the unrestricted immigration of the Alpine and Mediterranean races, who as "lower human types" "upset standards, sterilize better stocks, increase low types, and compromise national futures more than war, revolutions, or native deterioration." And yet for all this doom and gloom, Stoddard was much more concerned about "colored" immigrants from Asia, Africa, and Central/South America. "If the white immigrants can gravely disorder the national life," declared Stoddard passionately, "it is not too much to say that the colored immigrant would doom it to certain death." The Immigration Act of 1924 made eminently clear the practical implications of this distinction between "whites" and "coloreds": while "new" European immigrants, branded as racial inferiors, were severely reduced in numbers, the Japanese, branded as racial *and* color inferiors, were excluded altogether.[36]

Whiteness continued to deeply shape Italian Americans' lives and opportunities in the interwar and postwar years. The Federal Housing Administration redlined every major city in the country; local institutions distributed GI Bill benefits, ensuring that people of "color" would not receive their fair share: and Congress excluded farmers and domestic workers—the vast majority of whom were African Americans and Latinos—from receiving Social Security and labor union protections.[37] If whiteness, as historian Matthew Jacobson aptly put it, "opened the Golden Door" for so many European immigrants, it also kept it wide open for years to come.[38]

Many Italian Americans (among other people), as noted, have had a hard time appreciating this point. Often contrasting themselves explicitly with African Americans, they have spoken (and continue to speak) proudly of the ways in which they pulled themselves up by their bootstraps by working hard and shunning government assistance. And, of course, these narratives have sonic truth to them. Many Italian Americans did work hard and their success in the United States is, in part, a testament to this fact. However, the idea that they, unlike groups such as African Americans, did it all by themselves without government assistance could not be more inaccurate. Indeed, the opposite was often the case. Italian Americans' whiteness—conferred more powerfully by the federal government than by any other institution—was their single most powerful asset in the "New World"; it gave them countless advantages over "nonwhites" in housing, jobs, schools, politics, and virtually every other meaningful area of life. Without appreciating this fact, one has no hope of fully understanding Italian American history.

Endnotes

Those who wish to see a more extensive treatment and documentation of the subjects in this chapter should consult my book, *White on Arrival: Italians, Race, Color, and Power in Chicago, 1890–1945* (New York: Oxford University Press, 2003).

1. Leonard Giuliano, Jan. 2, 1980, Box 5, Folder 30, 90; Constance Muzzacavallo, June 12, 1980, Box 16, Folder 102, 54; Joseph Loguidice. July 21, 1980, Box 15, Folder 96, 18; all in the Italian-American Collection, University of Illinois at Chicago Special Collections (hereafter UIC). For evidence that these views extended beyond Chicago, see Richard Gambino, *Blood of My Blood* (Garden City, NY: Doubleday, 1974), 336–337; Robert Orsi, "The Religious Boundaries of an Inbetween People: Street *Feste* and the Problem of the Dark-Skinned 'Other' in Italian Harlem, 1920–1990," *American Quarterly* 44 (Sept. 1992): 319; Jonathan Rieder, *Canarsie: The Jews and Italians of Brooklyn Against Liberalism* (Cambridge, MA: Harvard University Press, 1985).
2. Lillian B. Rubin, *Families on the Fault Line: America's Working Class Speaks About the Family, the Economy, Race, and Ethnicity* (New York: HarperCollins, 1994), 187–188.

3. Eduardo Bonilla-Silva, "Rethinking Racism: Toward a Structural Interpretation," *American Sociological Review* 62 (June 1996): 469–470.

4. Richard Jenkins, *Rethinking Ethnicity: Arguments and Explorations* (London: Sage, 1997), 81, 74–75.

5. Leonard Covello, *The Social Background of the Italo-American School Child* (Leiden: E. J. Brill, 1967), 25.

6. John Dickie, "Stereotypes of the Italian South 1860–1900," 135; Gabriella Gribaudi, "Images of the South: The *Mezzogiorno* as Seen by Insiders and Outsiders," 96; both in Robert Lumley and Jonathan Morris, eds., *The New History of the Italian South: The Mezzogiorno Revisited* (Exeter, UK: Exeter Press, 1997).

7. Reports of the U.S. Immigration Commission, *Dictionary of Races and Peoples* (Washington, DC: U.S. Government Printing Office. 1911), 81, 82.

8. Edward A. Ross, *The Old World in the New: The Significance of Past and Present Immigration to the American People* (New York: Century, 1914), 95–119; "To Keep Out Southern Italians," *The World's Work* 28 (Aug. 1914); 378–379.

9. *Chicago Record Herald,* June 14, 1910, 2; *Chicago Record Herald,* Oct. 30, 1907, 1; Edward F. Haas, "Guns, Goats, and Italians: The Tallulah Lynching of 1899," *North Louisiana Historical Association Journal* 13 (1982): 50; George E. Pozzetta, "Foreigners in Florida: A Study of Immigration Promotion, 1865–1910," *Florida Historical Quarterly* 53 (Oct. 1974): 175; William B. Gatewood, Jr., "Strangers and the Southern Eden: The South and Immigration, 1900–1920," in Jerrel H. Shofner and Linda V. Ellsworth, eds., *Ethnic Minorities in Gulf Coast Society* (Pensacola, FL: Gulf Coast History and Humanities Conference, 1979), 8–10; Charles Shanabruch, "The Louisiana Immigration Movement, 1891–1907: An Analysis of Efforts, Attitudes, and Opportunities," *Louisiana History* 18 (Spring 1977): 217; Rowland T. Berthoff, "Southern Attitudes Toward Immigration, 1865–1914," *Journal of Southern History* 17 (Aug. 1951): 328–360; David D. Mays. "'Sivilizing Moustache Pete': Changing Attitudes Towards Italians in New Orleans. 1890–1918," in Jerrel H. Shofner and Linda V. Ellsworth, eds., *Ethnic Minorities* (Pensacola, FL: Gulf Coast History and Humanities Conference, 1979), 95, 103; Anthony V. Margavio, "The Reaction of the Press to the Italian-American in New Orleans, 1880 to 1920," *Italian Americana* 4 (Fall/Winter 1978): 72–83.

10. *Chicago Tribune,* Aug. 19, 1910, 9.

11. Jerre Mangione, *Monte Allegro: A Memoir of Italian American Life* (1942; New York: Columbia University Press, 1981), 65; Ray Stannard Baker, *Following the Color Line: American Negro Citizenship in the Progressive Era* (New York: Harper & Row, 1964), 268; Gatewood, "Strangers and the Southern Eden" 5–12; Pozzetta, "Foreigners in Florida," 175; Dino Cinel, *From Italy to San Francisco: The Immigrant Experience* (Stanford, CA: Stanford University Press, 1982), 115, 138, 282 nn. 63–64; Orsi, "The Religious Boundaries of an Inbetween People," 313–347; Rudolph J. Vecoli, "Prelates and Peasants: Italian Immigrants and the Catholic Church," *Journal of Social History* 2 (1969): 230, 233, 238, 250, 263 n. 160; Samuel L. Baily, *Immigrants in the Lands of*

Promise: Italians in Buenos Aires and New York City, 1870–1914 (Ithaca, NY: Cornell University Press, 1999), 83–89; Gary R. Mormino and George E. Pozzetta, *The Immigrant World of Ybor City: Italians and Their Latin Neighbors, 1885–1985* (Urbana: University of Illinois Press, 1987), 239–242.

12. Mangione, *Monte Allegro,* 65; Alexander DeConde, *Half Bitter, Half Sweet: An Excursion into Italian American History* (New York: Scribner's, 1971), 111: Jerre Mangione and Ben Morreale, *La Storia: Five Centuries of the Italian American Experience* (New York: HarperCollins, 1992), 153, 162–163; Robert Orsi, *The Madonna of 115th St.: Faith and Community in Italian Harlem, 1880–1950* (New Haven, CT: Yale University Press, 1985). 16; Virginia Yans-McGlaughlin, *Family and Community: Italian Immigrants in Buffalo, 1880–1930* (Ithaca, NY: Cornell University Press, 1971), 112–117.

13. For quotations, see *Skandinaven,* May 8, 1900, Chicago Foreign Language Press Survey (hereafter CFLPS), Reel 63, Immigration History Research Center (hereafter IHRC), University of Minnesota Minneapolis, MN; Harvey Warren Zorbaugh. *The Gold Coast and the Slum* (Chicago: University of Chicago Press, 1929), 160.

14. *L'Italia,* Oct. 15, 1904, 1; *Chicago Tribune,* June 11, 1915, 13. For further evidence of lynchings of Italians, see *L'Italia,* Dec. 21, 1907, 1; *L'Italia,* Sept. 24, 1910, 1; and the following secondary sources: John V. Baiamonte, Jr., "'Who Killa de Chief' Revisited: The Hennessey {sic} Assasination and Its Aftermath, 1890–1891," *Louisiana History* 33 (Spring 1992): 117–146; Barbara Botein, "The Hennessy Case: An Episode in Anti-Italian Nativism," *Louisiana History* 20 (Summer 1979): 261–279; Haas, "Guns, Goats, and Italians, "45–58; Robert P. Ingalls, "Lynching and Establishment Violence in Tampa, 1858–1935," *Journal of Southern History* 53 (Nov. 1987): 626–628; John S. Kendall, "Who Killa de Chief," *Lousiana Historical Quarterly* 22 (1939): 492–530; Marco Rumanelli and Sheryl L. Postman, eds., *The 1891 New Orleans Lynching and U.S.-Italian Relations: A Look Back* (New York: Peter Lang, 1992); Matthew Frye Jacobson, *Whiteness of a Different Color: European Immigrants and the Alchemy of Race* (Cambridge, MA: Harvard University Press, 1998), 56–62. On African Americans being the prime targets of lynching violence, see W. Fitzhugh Brundage, ed., *Under Sentence of Death: Lynching in the South* (Chapel Hill: University of North Carolina Press, 1997), 2; and *L'Italia,* Jan. 10, 1915, 7.

15. House Committee on Immigration and Naturalization, *Hearings Relative to the Further Restriction of Immigration,* 62d Cong., 2d Sess. (Washington, DC: U.S. Government Printing Office, 1912), 77–78; William M. Leiserson, *Adjusting Immigrant and Industry* (New York: Harpers and Brothers, 1924), 71–72; Charles B. Barnes, *The Longshoremen* (New York: Survey Associates, 1915), 8; John Higham, *Strangers in the Land: Patterns of American Nativism, 1860–1925,* 2nd ed. (New Brunswick, NJ: Rutgers University Press, 1988), 66. See also Rueben Gold Thwaites, *Afloat on the Ohio: An Historical Pilgrimage of a Thousand Miles in a Skiff, from Redstone to Cairo* (New York: Doubleday and McClure, 1900), 69: Rudolph J. Vecoli, "Chicago's Italians Prior

to World War I: A Study of Their Social and Economic Adjustment" (Ph.D. diss., University of Wisconsin, 1963), 320, 322, 330–331, 419; Gunther Peck, *Reinventing Free Labor: Padrone and Immigrant Workers in the North American West, 1880–1930* (Cambridge, Eng: Cambridge: Harvard University Press, 2000), 169.

16. George E. Cunningham, "The Italian, A Hindrance to White Solidarity, 1890–1898," *Journal of Negro History* 50 (July 1965): 34; Paul Campisi, "The Adjustment of the Italian Americans to the War Crisis" (M.A. thesis, University of Chicago, 1942), 83. See also John V. Baiamonte, Jr., *Spirit of Vengeance: Nativism and Louisiana Justice, 1921–1924* (Baton Rouge: Louisiana State University Press, 1986), 15; Jean Scarpaci, "A Tale of Selective Accommodation: Sicilians and Native Whites in Louisiana," *Journal of Ethnic Studies* 5 (Fall 1977): 38–39, 44: Hodding Carter, *Southern Legacy* (Baton Rouge: Louisiana State University Press, 1950), 105–112; Robert L. Brandfon, "The End of Immigration to the Cotton Fields," *Mississippi Valley Historical Review* 50(Mar. 1964): 610; Mormino and Pozzetta, *The Immigrant World of Ybor City,*241.

17. By "sustained" I mean color challenges that are not isolated incidents, but occur over a prolonged period of time. By "systematic" I mean color challenges that become entrenched in institutions such as the U.S. census, law, residential patters, restrictive covenants, hiring policies, union membership rules, dating and marriage customs, and so forth.

18. On the Near North Side riot, see *L'Italia*, Oct. 22, 1913, 3. Asians, like African Americans, also were quite restricted in their marriage options. See Ifu Chen, "Chinatown of Chicago," paper for Sociology 466, 1932. Ernest W. Burgess Papers, Box 128, Folder 8, University of Chicago Special Collections (hereafter UC), 14.

19. Thomas Lee Philpott, *The Slum and the Ghetto: Immigrants, Blacks, and Reformers in Chicago, 1880–1930,*2nd ed. (Belmont, CA: Wadsworth, 1991), 116–182; Allan Spear, *Black Chicago: The Making of a Negro Ghetto, 1890–1920* (Chicago: University of Chicago Press, 1967), 21–33; James R. Grossman, *Land of Hope: Chicago, Black Southerners, and the Great Migration* (Chicago: University of Chicago Press, 1989); Homer Hoyt, *One Hundred Years of Land Values in Chicago* (Chicago: University of Chicago Press, 1933), 315–319. William M. Tuttle, Jr., *Race Riot: Chicago in the Red Summer of 1919* (New York: Atheneum, 1970), 159–176; Edith Abbott, *The Tenements of Chicago, 1908–1935* (Chicago: University of Chicago Press, 1936), 117–126.

20. On discrimination against Italians by employers, unions, and fellow workers, see Vecoli, "Chicago's Italians Prior to World War I," 342–345, 350, 360, 419–424; *La Parola dei Socialisti*, Jan. 4, 1913, CFLPS, Chicago Historical Society (hereafter CHS). On the far more widespread discrimination against African Americans, see Philpott, *The Slum and the Ghetto,*, 119; Spear, *Black Chicago,* 30–41; Grossman, *Land of Hope,* chs. 7–8; Tuttle, *Race Riot,* 108–130; interview with Frank Mead, 1970, Box 25, Roosevelt University Labor Oral History Project, Roosevelt University, Chicago, 44–45.

21. Spear, *Black Chicago,* 42–49; Grossman, *Land of Hope,*127–128. See also *L'Italia*, Sept. 10, 1910, 2, on some Chicagoans' resistance to one Japanese and two Chinese students

attending a local high school. *L'Italia*, Apr. 10, 1909, CFLPS, CHS, talks about a theater owner, Louis Lang, who was on trial for refusing to admit several Italians into his "Nickel Show."

22. I have not discussed Mexicans here because they did not start arriving in Chicago in large numbers until World War I.

23. Gordon H. Shufelt, "Strangers in the Middle Land: Italian Immigrants and Race Relations in Baltimore, 1890–1920" (Ph.D. diss., American University, 1998), 208, 179. On the "Great Fire of 1904," see pp. 127–149; on the first disfranchisement campaign of 1905, see pp. 150–183; on the second disfranchisement campaign of 1910, see pp. 184-209; on the housing segregation ordinances of 1910–1913, see pp. 210–232. See also Shufelt's essay "Jim Crow Among Strangers: The Growth of Baltimore's Little Italy and Maryland's Disfranchisement Campaigns," *Journal of American Ethnic History* 19 (Summer 2000): 49–78.

24. On anti-Italian violence, see Andrew F. Rolle, *The Immigrant Upraised: Italian Adventures and Colonists in an Expanding America* (Norman: University of Oklahoma Press, 1968), 174–178: Alexander DeConde, *Half Bitter, Half Sweet*, 125; Luciano J. Iorizzo and Salvatore Mondello, *The Italian-Americans* (New York: Twayne, 1971), 67; and Patrick J. Gallo, *Old Bread New Wine: A Portrait of the Italian-Americans* (Chicago: Nelson Hall, 1981), 113. On discrimination in San Francisco, see Cinel *From Italy to San Francisco*, 115, 138, 282 nn. 63–64; on the "bully" quotation, see Mangione and Morreale, *La Storia*, 192; on the Arizona copper companies, see Linda Gordon, *The Great Arizona Orphan Abduction* (Cambridge, MA: Harvard University Press, 1999), 102.

25. For general histories of the West's particular color structure, see Tomas Almaguer, *Racial Fault Lines: The Historical Origins of White Supremacy in California* (Berkeley: University of California Press, 1994); A Yvette Hugginie, "'Mexican Labour' in a 'White Man's Town'; Racialism, Imperialism and Industrialization in the Making of Arizona, 1840–1905," in Peter Alexander and Rick Halpern, eds., *Racializing Class, Classifying Race: Labour and Difference in Britain, the USA, and Africa* (New York: St. Martin's Press, 2000), 32–56; Gordon, *The Great Arizona Orphan Abduction*, esp. 99–100, 175–195, 305; Richard White, "Race Relations in the American West," *American Quarterly* 38 (1986): 396–416; Peggy Pascoe, "Race, Gender, and the Privileges of Property: On the Significance of Miscegenation Law in the U.S. West," in Valerie J. Matsumoto and Blake Allmendinger, eds., *Over the Edge: Remapping the American West* (Berkeley: University of California Press, 1999), 215–230.

26. On the occasional categorizing of Italians as nonwhite, see note 15 above. On the South's color structure, there is, of course, a voluminous literature. For some general works, see C. Vann Woodward, *The Strange Career of Jim Crow*, 3rd rev. ed. (New York: Oxford University Press, 1974): Joel Williamson, *The Crucible of Race: Black/White Relations in the American South Since Emancipation* (New York: Oxford University Press, 1984); Howard N. Rabinowitz, *Race Relations in the Urban South,*

1865–1890 (New York: Oxford University Press, 1978); John Whitson Cell, *The Highest Stage of White Supremacy: The Origins of Segregation in South Africa and the American South* (Cambridge: Cambridge University Press, 1982); Grace Elizabeth Hale, *Making Whiteness: The Culture of Segregation in the South, 1890–1940* (New York: Pantheon, 1998); Leon F. Litwack, *Trouble in Mind : Black Southerners in the Age of Jim Crow* (New York: Knopf, 1998); Glenda Elizabeth Gilmore, *Gender and Jim Crow: Women and the Politics of White Supremacy in North Carolina, 1896–1920* (Chapel Hill: University of North Carolina Press, 1996). On miscegenation laws, see Peggy Pascoe, "Miscegenation Law, Court Cases, and Ideologies of 'Race' in Twentieth-Century America," *Journal of American History* 83 (June 1996): 44–69; Rachel F. Moran, *Interracial Intimacy: The Regulation of Race and Romance* (Chicago: University of Chicago Press, 2001); Randall Kennedy, *Interracial Intimacies: Sex, Marriages, Identity, and Adoption* (New York: Pantheon, 2003).

27. J. Vincenza Scarpaci, "Labor for Louisiana's Sugar Cane Fields: An Experiment in Immigrant Recruitment," *Italian Americana* 7 (Fall/Winter 1981): 27; Gatewood, "Strangers and the Southern Eden," p. 4. For more evidence on these points, see Berthoff, "Southern Attitudes Toward Immigration, 1865–1914," 334, 356–357; Botein, "The Hennessy Case," 262; Walter L. Fleming, "Immigration to the Southern States," *Political Science Quarterly* 20 (June 1905): 276–297; Emily Fogg Meade, "Italian Immigration into the South," *South Atlantic Quarterly* 4 (July 1905): 217–223; Alfred H. Stone, "The Italian Cotton Grower: The Negro's Problem," *South Atlantic Quarterly* 4 (January 1905): 42–47; Alfred Holt Stone, *Studies in the American Race Problem* (New York: Doubleday, Page, 1908); *Daily Picayune* (New Orleans), Mar. 13, 1898, 3.

28. U.S. Immigration Commission, *Reports of the U.S. Immigration Commission,* vol. 21, *Immigrants in Industries* (Washington, DC: U.S. Government Printing Office, 1911), pt. 24, 242, 295, 305, 353, 367–368. On the rise of anti-immigrant sentiment in the South, see Berthoff, "Southern Attitudes Toward Immigration," 343–360; Gatewood, "Strangers and the Southern Eden": Higham, *Strangers in the Land,* 164, 166–171, 191, 288.

29. *Daily Picayune* (New Orleans), Mar. 7, 1898, 7; the *Memphis Commercial Appeal* quotation is from Gatewood, "Strangers and the Southern Eden," 9; Meade, "Italian Immigration into the South," 217.

30. James W. Loewen, *The Mississippi Chinese: Between Black and White* (Cambridge, MA: Harvard University Press, 1971), see esp. 1–2, 58–83.

31. U.S. Immigration Commission, *Dictionary of Races and Peoples,* 3.

32. Eliot Lord, *The Italian in America* (New York: B. F. Buck, 1905), 20, 232.

33. For naturalization applications of Italians, see RG 21, National Archives Great Lakes Branch, Chicago, IL. See also Ian Haney Lopez, *White by Law: The Legal Construction of Race* (New York: New York University Press, 1996); Jacobson, *Whiteness of a Different Color,* 223–245.

34. For general information on changes in race/color census categories and related shifts in

how enumerators were instructed to fill in such categories, see *200 Years of United States Census Taking: Population and Housing Questions, 1790–1990,* prepared by Frederick G. Bohme and Walter C. Odom (Washington, DC: U.S. Government Printing Office, 1989), 26, 30, 36, 41, 50, 60, 69. On the power of censuses in general to construct social categories, see Benedict Anderson, *Imagined Communities: Reflections on the Origin and Spread of Nationalism,* rev. ed. (London: Verso, 1991), 163–170, 184–185.

35. *Chicago Daily News,* Feb. 9, 1921, 7.

36. Lothrop Stoddard, *The Rising Tide of Color against White World Supremacy* (New York: Scribner's, 1920), 267. On the Immigration Act of 1924, see Desmond S. King, *Making Americans: Immigration, Race, and the Origins of the Diverse Democracy* (Cambridge, MA: Harvard University Press, 2000); Mae Ngai, "The Architecture of Race in American Immigration Law: A Reexamination of the Immigration Act of 1924," *Journal of American History* 86 (June 1999): 67–92. The Japanese were singled out in 1924 only because the 1917 Immigration Act had already excluded virtually all other Asians from immigrating to the United States.

37. See especially George Lipsitz, *The Possessive Investment in Whiteness: How White People Profit from Identity Politics* (Philadelphia: Temple University Press, 1998), ch. 1.

38. Jacobson, *Whiteness of a Different Color,* 8.

17

Racialization of Language in the United States

J. T. Ghim

Introduction

When discussing an intricate set of concepts such as race and justice, it is necessary to develop clear definitions of the terms and to make particular distinctions of their usage. Social scientists generally agree that race is a socially constructed concept. That is, race is a sociopolitical category and the inclusion (or insertion) of individuals into a group is based on factors and rationales intends to create differences and divisions among human beings. These factors and rationales are more often than not driven by interests, usually political and economic, and in some instances religious and cultural. Thus, simply examining the history of the United States has shown that race as a concept, which operates to categorize individuals into groups based on differences, has constantly redefined what it means to be "White" and "Black," and, more recently, "Hispanic" and "Asian."

Justice is also a socially constructed concept insofar as each individual holds different views and beliefs about what is just and unjust. Depending on one's religious, philosophical, and cultural background, as well as one's political and social views, each of which are constantly being redefined by personal history (i.e., experience), each human being comes to realize and think of justice as one thing or another. However, because so much of our understanding of justice comes from, and is about, our experiences of other human beings in a societal environment, people have been able to agree that certain norms and rules are essential to justice. It is this agreement of norms and rules and their establishment that enables us to exist in a community. It is within a community of individuals that institutions are created in order to ensure that the norms and the rules of the community are followed by all of its members.

When we synthesize these two complex concepts, race and justice, and consider them in light of history and experience, the definition produced is contradictory. That is, if justice is about the coexistence of many, and different, individuals under the umbrella of a common community in which all members have come to agree on certain norms and rules, how do we explain the concept of race, which serves only differentiate groups and individuals? One way to answer this question is to discuss race and justice within a specific context.

The history of race and justice in the United States begins with race and injustice. As it exists in nearly all societies created by humans, the political community of the United States is based on hierarchy. The hierarchical relationships—differences created to establish a particular type of relationship between individuals and groups with unequal power—have largely been defined along categories of race, gender, and class. All three are often referred to as systems of oppression (Young, 1990). They are oppressive and unjust because society's resources are divided and justified along the hierarchical structure, which means that certain individuals and groups will have access to such resources, whereas other individuals and groups will not. Therefore, in this specific context, justice, or the lack of it, refers to those individuals and groups who have been unjustly denied access to those resources and consequently have been harmed by such societal arrangements. Thus, racial justice is what is achieved when the unequal distribution of society's resources has been modified or eradicated.

There are many examples of racial injustice throughout the history of the United States, and many exist today. It was the construction of race and its accompanying hierarchical system that justified African-American slavery and the genocide of Natives Americans. Today, these two "racial" groups, along with more recent immigrants from Asia and Latin America, are targets of racist political and economic policies and are subjected to racism in social and cultural settings. It is important to realize, however, that the social construction of race is not a simple process of declaring one group of people to be superior or inferior to another. The construction of race involves far more complex and subtle processes, which involve introducing race and its hierarchical system to various extant human and communal practices.

The process by which race is invoked and produced occurs when it and its hierarchical structure is extended to other realms and practices in society that were *not* defined along racial lines. Such process is referred to as *racialization* or racial formation (Omi & Winnant, 1986). All forms of racial injustice and its practices always begin with the process of racialization. A common example of racialization involves the waves of immigrants that arrived in the United States in the 19th and 20th centuries. Many of these immigrants—Irish, Italian, Greeks, and others from southern and eastern Europe—were not initially considered "White" because the racial hierarchy had placed them in categories below the Anglo-Saxons and other northern Europeans who made up the political and economic elites of the United States. However, as these immigrants grew in number and influence, the need to maintain the "White supremacist" racial hierarchy against the Blacks and the Native Americans, caused these often darker-skinned, Catholic and Jewish immigrants to be recategorized as "White" (Jacobson, 1998). Likewise, as the social positions of African Americans have changed, the classification of "Black" has gone through numerous transformations over the last two centuries (see below). Today, the U.S. Census Bureau uses five broad categories of race to define all those who live in the United States: "White," "Black," "Asian," "Hispanic," and "Native American." Although there exists hundreds (if not thousands) of people of different national, ethnic, cultural, and historic backgrounds within these five categories, the category of race dominates how all of us are defined, particularly by the dominant political and economic institutions of our society, e.g., national and state governments, corporations, and schools.

This structure, used by the most powerful institutions in society, is often called the *racial institutional order*. Its goal is "[to] seek and exercise governing power in ways that predictably shape people's statuses, resources, and opportunities by their placement in 'racial' categories" (King & Smith, 2005, p. 78). It is when the racial institutional is established through various processes of racialization that a race-based hierarchy becomes solidified and practices of racial injustice take place. This results in the formation of the racial structure: "the social relations between the races become institutionalized (forming a structure as well as a culture) and affect their social life whether individual members of the races want it or not" (Bonilla-Silva, p. 473). The racial structure of the United States today is different from its past. African Americans are no longer subjected to the dehumanizing practices of slavery and segregation. Native Americans have gained full citizenship rights and enjoy a certain level of autonomy and self-governance on their reservations. Yet, the new and current racial structure, although not as blatantly racist and unjust as older ones, nonetheless has held both groups in the lower strata of the political and economic hierarchy while new forms and practices of discrimination have emerged to continue the processes of racialization. The *de jure* segregation of the Jim Crow era has been replaced by a *de facto* economic isolation and impoverishment of African Americans in urban communities. Discriminatory law enforcement and criminal justice systems, targeting African Americans and other minority groups, have resulted in the disproportionate incarceration and the disfranchisement of millions of minority citizens (the sentencing project). The key point is that race, racism, racialization, racial institutional order, and racial structure have not disappeared; they have simply evolved in form and content.

What follows is an analysis of a topic not often discussed in conjunction with issues of race and justice: language. Some of the most pertinent discussions in race and justice involve issues dealing with political rights and liberties, specifically focusing on eliminating discriminatory practices and improving access to representation, the judicial system, education, housing, and other economic opportunities. However, considering the complexities of racism, the omnipotence of racialized domains and practices in society, and the continuing dominance of racial institutional orders, one cannot undermine the all-encompassing nature and presence of racial structure in the United States. Language is a powerful and essential tool needed to access nearly everything in society and life. Like all valuable resources, it is sought after by many individuals. Because language is a valuable commodity, it is not exempt from the purview of the racial structure. In fact, language itself as a concept shares many attributes and complexities with the concept of race: language, like race, is a phenomenon of modern history, and its categorization is socially constructed and externally assigned/imposed—like race—through social processes and institutions such as "universal education." Furthermore, it has become an issue of much contention in recent years, particularly involving various racial minorities in the United States and the rest of the world. The next part of this chapter addresses how language has been racialized at various times in the United States, followed by a discussion of contemporary debates surrounding language and race.

Racialization of Language in the 19th Century

When language is discussed, it is typically discussed in two contexts. The first context is the human *use* of language(s) as a mode of communication between individuals. The second context refers to the types of languages, i.e., this book is written in English rather than Portuguese. In the first context, humans typically communicate with one another by verbal means, i.e., spoken language. Just as we acquire the knowledge to speak and understand what others verbally communicate to us, we also gain literacy—a term used to indicate if someone has a certain level of proficiency to read and write in a language. When one is proficient in more than one language, she or he is commonly referred to as being "bilingual" or "multilingual." Not everyone speaks the same way nor are we all equally literate. It is common knowledge that such differences exist as the result of numerous factors, e.g., culture, the region one comes from, the level of education acquired, and the type of occupation. The emphasis is that language, like race, is socially constructed. Language is used in a variety of ways. There are established hierarchies associated with the variation.

Contemporary scholars and historians of modern nations have identified the role of language as a vital and defining component to the nation-building projects of those nations created and/or consolidated in the 18th and 19th centuries (Anderson, 1979; Hobsbawm, 1990). For example, European scholars of that time, e.g., Fichte (2001) and Herder (2001), sought to invent a national identity of the German people using a common language as the justification for why its various warring principalities should unite and fight against foreign enemies. Thus, in order to socially construct and produce a sense of common national identity (i.e., nationalism), the development of a national language was deemed essential to unify a diverse people. In the case of Germany, as well as many other European nations of that time, embarking on such a project required the establishment of a standard language, which necessitated 1) the elimination of variations of that language, i.e., dialects, and 2) the institutionalization of education to disseminate the new national language. Thus, the birth of standard language and education brought about classifications and categorizations of languages and dialects that were a product of social construction with specific political and economic interests, much like other socially constructed systems such as race, gender, and ethnicity (Joseph, 2004). Hence the traditional minority groups in Europe today are not racialized groups (although such groups do exist), but groups that were assimilated through such standardization/nationalization processes, with segments of them claiming the right to self-determination on the basis of linguistic differences—evidences of cultural uniqueness that were subsumed by their dominant "national" counterparts, e.g., Basque, Catalonia, and Galicia (in Spain); Corsica and the Bretons (in France); Scotland and Wales (in Britain); and the Walloons (in Belgium).

Although the historical development of the United States does not completely parallel that of Europe, nonetheless its European ancestors played a significant role in shaping its policies and practices. As in Europe, issues of language also became an essential piece of the national project in the United States, and the political and economic elite placed a particular focus on literacy and schooling. In 1828, Noah Webster produced the first American English dictionary, which included significant modifications from British English. It should be noted that Webster had hoped to establish a standard American English in order to minimize variations across the country for the sake of "political harmony" (quoted in Collins, 1999, p. 217). This new standard American English was then disseminated through public schools, as well as other agendas, such as "disciplinary potential of education, the utility of schooling and literacy [in] reshaping the character of the working class, inculcating virtues of punctuality, sobriety, thrift, and respect for authority, along with reading and writing" (p. 217).

Although the idea of standardizing language and adopting a multifunctional model of schooling were imported from Europe, the United States differed insofar as these language and education policies were immediately *racialized*. Literacy was a mark of civilization and social status for Whites, which was contrasted with the illiteracy and perceived ignorance of Black slaves (Collins, 1999; Schmidt, 2000). Political and economic elites were marked by not only their material possessions, but by having acquired an education that few could afford, either in terms of time or wealth. These "learned men"—the same men and their descendents whom Americans have been taught to refer to as the "founding fathers"— dominated the political and economic institutional orders of that time. Because they created the racialized political and economic institutional orders, i.e., slavery, they viewed language and literacy as something that belonged solely to them, much like property and slaves. To make such a socially valuable tool and commodity available to anyone else, particularly slaves, would have been not only contradictory but self-destructive.

Beneath such fear and insecurity lie the roots of how language became racialized in the antebellum South. The following is the title and preamble of legislation passed in North Carolina around the same time a standard American English was developed and illiteracy among working-class Whites began to decline:

> **An Act to Prevent All persons from Teaching Slaves to Read or Write, the Use of Figures Excepted,**
>
> Whereas the teaching of slaves to read and write, has a tendency to excite dissatisfaction in their minds, and to produce insurrection and rebellion, to the manifest injury of the citizens of this States. (From Acts Passed by the General Assembly of the State of North Carolina at the Session of 1830–31, cited in Rothenberg, p. 538)

Alabama, Georgia, Louisiana, South Carolina, and Virginia passed similar laws banning the teaching of slaves how to read and write (Cornelius, 1983, fn7; Du Bois, 1969), which punished both Whites and Blacks, although the punishments significantly varied (monetary for Whites, both monetary and corporeal for free Blacks, and purely corporeal for enslaved Blacks). The goal of this type of statute was to maintain the racial institutional order of slavery in these states, which preserved the power of the political and economic elites. Moreover, as indicated in the Preamble, above, slave owners were concerned that if the slaves learned how to read and write, they would be inclined to cooperate with free Blacks and abolitionists to "produce insurrection and rebellion." Slave owners knew of language's powerful "moral, technical and cultural dimensions" (Collins, 1999). A slave who knew how to read newspapers and write letters posed a grave threat to the racial structure in antebellum South, and thus, as W. E. B. Du Bois (1969) noted, "after the Nat Turner insurrection in Virginia, these laws [prohibiting the teaching of reading and writing to slaves] were strengthened and more carefully enforced" (p. 638).

The consequences of language having been racialized and incorporated into the racial structure produced appalling literacy rate among African Americans. According to Du Bois (1969), "illiteracy among the colored population was well over 95% in 1863, which meant that less than 150,000 of the four million slaves emancipated could read and write" (p. 638). Compare those statistics with the half-million *free* Blacks in 1860 with a literacy rate of over 80% (p. 638). These examples illustrate how two differing racial institutional orders existed in the United States prior to the Civil War. One racial institutional order was dominated by the interests of those individuals who regarded slavery as essential to their political and economic interests, hence every aspect of society was racialized, including language. The competing racial institutional order was an alliance of free slaves and abolitionists, who opposed the dominant racial institutional order in the South.

The result of the clash of these competing racial institutional orders was the American Civil War. After the Civil War, new constitutional, administrative, political, economic, educational, and social institutions to promote greater racial equality were built, but elements of the "White supremacist" racial order had not been eradicated.

For nearly 100 years, from the end of the Civil War until the passage of the Civil Rights Act (1964), African Americans were racially segregated and discriminated against in all aspects of life, including school. Although they were allowed to attend schools, which many of them could not do before the Civil War, these racially segregated schools were significantly underfunded and the level of illiteracy among African Americans remained high compared to Whites (Collins, 1999, p. 219). Thus, a new racial institutional order of Black segregation was accompanied by new modes and methods of racializing language and literacy. The logic behind language was no longer about the exclusivity/exclusion of the antebellum era, but one of economic, political, and social marginalization. This was because the dominant political and economic elite in the country had shifted from the agricultural economy of the South to industrial-capitalist economy of the North. As a result, education and literacy became even more valuable. Being illiterate almost always meant, as it does today, that a person would be denied access to social mobility and economic opportunities.

After adding segregation into the equation, one can imagine what the situation must have been like for African Americans.

Racializing Language Through Assimilation, Bilingualism, and Ebonics

With the new mode of economic production, the "way of life" in the United States changed tremendously, as did its racial structure. Another factor was the large influx of immigrants from various parts of the world, particularly in the latter half of the 20th century, which was different from the European immigration of the 19th century. The majority of these immigrants came from Asia and Latin America, whose "racial" backgrounds did not fit neatly into the Black/White categorization that had characterized the U.S. racial structure in the 19th century. Given the new racial composition of the United States, along with different economic and political interests, the dominant racial institutional orders went through significant transformations (King & Smith, 2005). Various institutional orders had competed and contested the racialization processes, which involved the development and implementation of policies for dealing with non-White "races." It is important to note the intricacies involved in this process, because such policies are hardly uniform. That is, the process of racialization involved and produced different experiences for different minority groups. The debate continued on through the 20th century through issues involving language, literacy, and education. The issues are defined and discussed below in the contexts of 1) the racialization of specific racial minorities (i.e., immigrants from Asia and Latin America) through bilingual education and 2) the perpetuation of de facto segregated schooling of African Americans and the ensuing racialization of linguistic behaviors.

As noted above, the birth of schooling and education is marked by, and runs parallel with, the standardization of a language in a society. It was also noted that the exclusion of African Americans from the social and economic capital of education and language was an essential component to the racial history of the United States. Although such exclusionary policies mark the racial structure, the same racial institutional order that upheld the structure sought to include new racial groups, and, as a result, various non-Anglo-Protestant Whites became "White" (Jacobson, 1998). At the same time, Native Americans—and the way they were treated—shifted from exclusion to assimilation: "The boarding schools tried to teach Indians skills and trades that would be useful in White society, utilizing stern disciplinary measures to force assimilation . . . [one of them being] the policy of deterring communication in native language" (U.S. Commission on Human Rights, 2007, pp. 530–531). The ideology that triggered this process depended on industrial capitalism and its need for laborers.

The demand for labor in the new racial institutional required increasing the literacy rate of the population, yet society continued to rely on schools and other educational practices to provide the disciplinary effects that had been initiated under the old racial structure. It is only with the shift in economic and political interests, complemented by the demand for greater equality and racial justice (i.e., the Civil Rights Movement), which ended de jure exclusionary practices in education (again, see the *Brown* decision). Institutionalizing the *Brown* decision came about through the enactment of the Civil Rights Act and other federal legislation.

The most pertinent judicial case involving language, and which made use of the Civil Rights Act, was *Lau v. Nichols* (1974). A group of Chinese students in San Francisco brought suit against their school district, claiming their civil rights had been violated as a result of not being able to be educated in their own language. The U.S. Supreme Court ruled unanimously in favor of the Chinese students, which led to significant changes and improvements in the development of access to bilingual education in the latter half of 1970s (Schmidt, 2000, pp. 11–13). These developments had significant consequences, intended and unintended, on the contemporary racialization(s) of language.

First, the *Lau* decision was followed by the Equal Education Opportunity Act (1975). It institutionalized bilingual education as it exists today in the United States. Although the objectives of these interrelated legislations appear to have been to eradicate discrimination of racial minorities in accessing education, by deliberately specifying funds for non-English speakers in school, it simultaneously revealed who the recipients of such resources were going to be: students who have recently immigrated to the United States, primarily speakers of Spanish and various Asian languages (Schmidt, 2000, p. 12). Even though much of the struggle for racial justice had been defined by and achieved under the leadership of African Americans, it was clear, at least in this instance, that they were not the racial minority that would benefit from these new policies. In fact, not having "established language" of their own meant that African Americans would be unable to claim any of the government resources for which they had fought so hard.

The significance of the racialization of language became more evident when one examines the debate surrounding the allocation of government resources for bilingual education. This is an issue that paired two historically unlikely bed fellows, Black and White Americans. What is important is that language had once again become the center of competition among different racial institutional orders. One order consisted of those who supported the funding of bilingual education; the other was composed of those who believed bilingualism in itself was a threat to "The American identity" (Collins, 1999; Huntington, 2004; Schmidt, 2000). These groups had once again racialized the issues and discussions of access to language and education. Those who opposed bilingual education schooling (and government funding for it) invoked policies seen previously in the United States, e.g., assimilation and discipline through schooling, eradication of diversity, national unity, controlling the medium of communication, and de facto exclusion of nonnataive/nonfluent speakers of the national language. The supporters of bilingual policies represent the other racialized institutional order. They may not be as ardent or blatant in their rhetoric as their opponents, yet the positions nonetheless created a racialized situation of language. The recent "Ebonics Controversy" illustrates this point.

In 1997, the Oakland school district passed a resolution that identified Ebonics as a separate language from Standard English. As a result, the school district sought state and federal government grants for bilingual programs. The students it served were primarily African Americans and the school district argued that these students used a form of "language" at home that was significantly different from Standard English, thus it had tremendous effect on their ability to perform adequately in school (Baugh, 2002; Collins, 1999). The "language" the school district referred to was Ebonics. Ebonics has been the subject of dozens of analyses of its social and systemic nature and usages; the "language" is socially constructed, and because "language or dialect" has been seen being used by African Americans, it contains racialized component. Consider the following statement from a professional association of linguists:

Linguistic Society of America: Resolution on the Oakland "Ebonics" Issue

a. The variety known as "Ebonics," "African American Vernacular English" (AAVE), and "Vernacular Black English" and by other names is systematic and rule-governed like all natural speech varieties. In fact, all human linguistic systems—spoken, signed, and written—are fundamentally regular. . . . Characterizations of Ebonics as "slang," "mutant," "lazy," "defective," "ungrammatical," or "broken English" are incorrect and demeaning.

b. The distinction between "languages" and "dialects" is usually made more on social and political grounds than on purely linguistic ones. . . . What is important from a linguistic and educational point of view is not whether AAVE is called a "language" or a "dialect" but rather that its systematicity be recognized.

3 January 1997: Approved by members attending the 71st Annual Business Meeting, Chicago, Illinois (Linguistics Society of America [LSA], 1997).

The point is not to define Ebonics and/or whether the Oakland school district's claim was valid on technical grounds. The district's goal was to gain additional economic resources to make their students perform better; if they did not, the students would effectively lose access to social mobility and economic opportunities. However, the discussion involving the issue of racial justice became a technical debate about the "language" of Ebonics (Baugh, 2002; Collins, 1999).

Although an earlier judicial case (*Martin Luther King, Jr. Elementary School* v. *Ann Arbor School District*) had already established the precedence that "Black English" was sufficiently different enough from Standard English to warrant appropriate remedies, the Oakland school district's action had ignited a series of reactions from all corners of U.S. society (Baugh, 2002). The reactions could be summarized to fit into two broad categories. The first group of reactions came from political commentators, institutional leaders, and media outlets, whose responses were almost unanimously critical. Some of these reactions came from prominent African-American political leaders, e.g., Jesse Jackson and the president of the NAACP (Baugh, 2002; Collins, 1999; Zernike, 1997). The second group of responses largely came from professional linguists, academics, and educators whose positions were more or less consistent with the LSA Resolution. Perhaps the strangest aspect of this controversy was that nearly everyone limited their discussion to the technical status of Ebonics as a language. It would be incorrect to claim that none of the comments explicitly (or even implicitly) addressed issues of race, yet the discussion took place within the confines of technical issues regarding language (Baugh, 2002).

The Oakland Ebonics case illustrates how little race is explicitly discussed in the current U.S. racial structure. Although newspapers in Montréal and Hong Kong immediately identified the issue of race and struggle for resources, comparing the issue to similar situations involving marginalized groups within their own societies (Gauthier, 1997), the debate in the United States was dominated by technical issues of language combined with an ahistorical and nonracial twist. These are common characteristic of the new racial structure of the post-Civil Rights era: "color-blind racism."

> [W]hites have developed a new, powerful ideology that justifies contemporary racial inequality and thus help maintain "systemic White privilege." I label this new ideology "color-blind racism" because this term fits quite well the language used by Whites to defend the racial status quo. This ideology emerged in the 1960s concurrently with what I have labeled "New Racism" [which consists of] practices [that] maintain White privilege, and, unlike those typical of Jim Crow, tend to be slippery, institutional, and apparently nonracial . . . Because the tactics for maintaining systemic White privilege changed in the 1960s, the rationalization for explaining racial inequality changed, too. Whereas Jim Crow racism explained Blacks' social standing as the product of their imputed biological and moral inferiorities, color-blind racism explains it as the product of market dynamics, naturally occurring phenomena, and presumed cultural deficiencies (Bonilla-Silva 132).

However, when analyzing the issues of language and education in the post-Civil Rights era, color-blind racism as an ideology and a strategy appears to have consumed not only Whites but racial minorities as well. As demonstrated in the case of Ebonics controversy, the debate regarding the condition of inequality and injustice of African-Americans students in Oakland was shifted into a discussion regarding language. Thus, the response by the racial institutional order(s) to this controversy was a nonracial one characteristic of the contemporary color-blind racial structure.

Conclusion: Is Racial Justice Possible?

As long as human beings continue to do or be incapable or unwilling to understand the omnipresence of race in human societies, inherited racialized parts of life will continue to be passed on to subsequent generations. What is particularly dangerous is that just as race's impact on language has greatly transformed the past 200 years, its face, capacity, and range of motion are constantly changing. Given the transformative character of race, it is not possible to realize its presence, never mind eradicating its injustices. One way to discover it is to acknowledge its embeddedness in nearly all aspects of society.

As for seeking racial justice, specifically in the realm of language, in light of the fact that the racialization of language has diverged into different paths for African Americans, compared to other racial minority groups, two different solutions seem to be in order. However, considering that non-African-American groups have had greater success in accessing government resources (e.g., the *Lau* decision), African Americans should continue to pursue the "bilingual" aspect of government provisions to gain greater resources. However, this objective cannot be accomplished by contesting the currently racialized understanding of language, i.e., discussing its technical details. The shift must be made by emphasizing the current economic conditions of African Americans, particularly in terms of resources and funds allocated for education, which are the lowest of all racial minority groups. In addition, the historical roots of African-American vernacular English, with its direct ties to American slavery (Baugh, 2002, p. 96), should be brought to light to further contest the very terrain on which language issues are discussed. Both of these factors (current economic conditions and historical roots) have gained academic and institutional recognition as "linguistic minority rights" (May, 2004). Understanding that history has shown how language is constructed, manipulated, then reconstructed, much like how race has been constantly redefined by the dominant racial institutional orders, it appears that racial contestation must begin with modifying the terms of the debate surrounding the relationship between race and language in order to at least contest the current racial structure and begin to minimize both the hidden and open racial injustices.

References

Anderson, B. (1979). *Imagined communities.* New York: Verso.

Baugh, J. (2002). *Beyond Ebonics: Linguistic pride and racial prejudice.* New York: Oxford University Press.

Bilingual Education Act (1967)

Bonilla-Silva, E. (1996). Rethinking racism: Toward a structural interpretation. *American Sociological Review, 62,* 465–480.

Bonilla-Silva, E. (2007). Color-blind racism. In P. Rothenberg (Ed.), *Race, class, and gender in the United States* (7th ed.). New York: Worth Publishers.

Collins, J. (1999). The Ebonics controversy in context: Literacies, subjectivities, and language ideologies in the United States. In J. Blommaert (Ed.), *Language ideology debates* (pp. 201–234). New York: Mouton de Gruyter.

Cornelius, J. (1983). "We slipped and learned to read": Slave accounts of the literacy process, 1830–1865. *Phylon, 44* (3), 171–186.

Du Bois, W. E. B. (1969). *Black Reconstruction in America: 1860–1880*. New York: Atheneum. (Originally published in 1935.)

Equal Education Opportunity Act (1975)

Fichte, J. G. (2001). Addresses to the German nation. In V. Pecora (Ed.). *Nations and identities*. London: Blackwell. (Original work published 1808.)

Gauthier, N. (1997). Ebonics argument parallels French vs. joual debate. *Gazette* (Montreal), February 9, D1.

Herder, J. G. von. (2001). Ideas for a philosophy of history of mankind. In V. Pecora (Ed.), *Nations and identities*. London: Blackwell. (Original work published in 1784.)

Hobsbawm, E. J. (1990). *Nations and nationalism since 1780: Programme, myth, reality*. Cambridge: Cambridge University Press.

Huntington, S. (2004). *Who are we? The challenge to America's national identity*. New York: Simon & Schuster.

Jacobson, M. F. (1998). *Whiteness of a different color: European immigrants and the alchemy of race*. Cambridge, MA: Harvard University Press.

Joseph, J. E. (2004). *Language and identity: National, ethnic, religious*. New York: Palgrave Macmillan.

Kashef, Z. (2003). This person doesn't sound White. *ColorLines*, 6 (3). Retrieved January 22, 2008, from www.colorlines.com/article.php?ID=63.

King, D., & Smith, R. (2005). Racial orders in American political development. *American Political Science Review*, 99 (1). 75–92.

Lau v. Nichols (1974)

Linguistic Society of America. (1997). Resolution on the Oakland "Ebonics" issue. Retrieved January 5, 2008, from www.lsadc.org/info/lsa-res-ebonics.cfm.

Martin Luther King, Jr. Elementary School v. Ann Arbor School District

Mauer, M. and King R. S. (2007). *Uneven Justice: State Rates of Incarceration by Race and Ethnicity*. Sentencing Project. Washington, DC.

May, S. (2004). Misconceiving minority language rights: Implications for liberal politial theory. In W. Kymlicka & A. Patten (Eds.), *Language rights and political theory*. New York: Oxford University Press.

Omi, M., & Winnant, H. (1986). *Racial formations in the United States: From the 1960s to the 1980s*. New York: Routledge.

Schmidt, R. (2000). *Language policy and identity politics in the United States*. Philadelphia: Temple University Press.

U.S. Commission on Human Rights. (2007). Indian tribes: A continuing quest for survival. In P. Rothenberg (Ed.), *Race, class, and gender in the United States* (7th ed.). New York: Worth Publishers.

Young, I. (1990). *Justice and the politics of difference*. Princeton, NJ: Princeton University Press.

Zernike, K. (1997). Goals go beyond language: Despite drop in test scores, LA embraces Ebonics. *Boston Globe*. January 16, p. A1.

18

The Souls of Black Folk

W.E.B. Du Bois

The Forethought

Herein lie buried many things which if read with patience may show the strange meaning of being black here in the dawning of the Twentieth Century. This meaning is not without interest to you, Gentle Reader; for the problem of the Twentieth Century is the problem of the color-line.

I pray you, then, receive my little book in all charity, studying my words with me, forgiving mistake and foible for sake of the faith and passion that is in me, and seeking the grain of truth hidden there.

I have sought here to sketch, in vague, uncertain outline, the spiritual world in which ten thousand thousand Americans live and strive. First, in two chapters I have tried to show what Emancipation meant to them, and what was its aftermath. In a third chapter I have pointed out the slow rise of personal leadership, and criticised candidly the leader who bears the chief burden of his race to-day. Then, in two other chapters I have sketched in swift outline the two worlds within and without the Veil, and thus have come to the central problem of training men for life. Venturing now into deeper detail, I have in two chapters studied the struggles of the massed millions of the black peasantry, and in another have sought to make clear the present relations of the sons of master and man.

Leaving, then, the world of the white man, I have stepped within the Veil, raising it that you may view faintly its deeper recesses,—the meaning of its religion, the passion of its human sorrow, and the struggle of its greater souls. All this I have ended with a tale twice told but seldom written.

Before each chapter, as now printed, stands a bar of the Sorrow Songs,—some echo of haunting melody from the only American music which welled up from black souls in the dark past. And, finally, need I add that I who speak here am bone of the bone and flesh of the flesh of them that live within the Veil?

W.E.B. Du B.

Chapter I.
Of Our Spiritual Strivings

O water, voice of my heart, crying in the sand,
    All night long crying with a mournful cry,
As I lie and listen, and cannot understand
    The voice of my heart in my side or the voice of the sea,
O water, crying for rest, is it I, is it I?
    All night long the water is crying to me.

Unresting water, there shall never be rest
    Till the last moon droop and the last tide fail,
And the fire of the end begin to burn in the west;
    And the heart shall be weary and wonder and cry like the sea,
All life long crying without avail,
    As the water all night long is crying to me.
    Arthur Symons.

Between me and the other world there is ever an unasked question: unasked by some through feelings of delicacy; by others through the difficulty of rightly framing it. All, nevertheless, flutter round it. They approach me in a half-hesitant sort of way, eye me curiously or compassionately, and then, instead of saying directly, How does it feel to be a problem? they say, I know an excellent colored man in my town; or, I fought at Mechanicsville; or, Do not these Southern outrages make your blood boil? At these I smile, or am interested, or reduce the boiling to a simmer, as the occasion may require. To the real question, How does it feel to be a problem? I answer seldom a word.

And yet, being a problem is a strange experience,—peculiar even for one who has never been anything else, save perhaps in babyhood and in Europe. It is in the early days of rollicking boyhood that the revelation first bursts upon one, all in a day, as it were. I remember well when the shadow swept across me. I was a little thing, away up in the hills of New England, where the dark Housatonic winds between Hoosac and Taghkanic to the sea. In a wee wooden schoolhouse, something put it into the boys' and girls' heads to buy gorgeous visiting-cards—ten cents a package—and exchange. The exchange was merry, till one girl, a tall newcomer, refused my card,—refused it peremptorily, with a glance. Then it dawned upon me with a certain suddenness that I was different from the others; or like, mayhap, in heart and life and longing, but shut out from their world by a vast veil. I had thereafter no desire to tear down that veil, to creep through; I held all beyond it in common contempt, and lived above it in a region of blue sky and great wandering shadows. That sky was bluest when I could beat my mates at examination-time, or beat them at a foot-race, or even beat their stringy heads. Alas, with the years all this fine contempt began to fade; for the worlds

I longed for, and all their dazzling opportunities, were theirs, not mine. But they should not keep these prizes, I said; some, all, I would wrest from them. Just how I would do it I could never decide: by reading law, by healing the sick, by telling the wonderful tales that swam in my head,—some way. With other black boys the strife was not so fiercely sunny: their youth shrunk into tasteless sycophancy, or into silent hatred of the pale world about them and mocking distrust of everything white; or wasted itself in a bitter cry, Why did God make me an outcast and a stranger in mine own house? The shades of the prison-house closed round about us all: walls strait and stubborn to the whitest, but relentlessly narrow, tall, and unscalable to sons of night who must plod darkly on in resignation, or beat unavailing palms against the stone, or steadily, half hopelessly, watch the streak of blue above.

After the Egyptian and Indian, the Greek and Roman, the Teuton and Mongolian, the Negro is a sort of seventh son, born with a veil, and gifted with second-sight in this American world,—a world which yields him no true self-consciousness, but only lets him see himself through the revelation of the other world. It is a peculiar sensation, this double-consciousness, this sense of always looking at one's self through the eyes of others, of measuring one's soul by the tape of a world that looks on in amused contempt and pity. One ever feels his two-ness,—an American, a Negro; two souls, two thoughts, two unreconciled strivings; two warring ideals in one dark body, whose dogged strength alone keeps it from being torn asunder.

The history of the American Negro is the history of this strife,—this longing to attain self-conscious manhood, to merge his double self into a better and truer self. In this merging he wishes neither of the older selves to be lost. He would not Africanize America, for America has too much to teach the world and Africa. He would not bleach his Negro soul in a flood of white Americanism, for he knows that Negro blood has a message for the world. He simply wishes to make it possible for a man to be both a Negro and an American, without being cursed and spit upon by his fellows, without having the doors of Opportunity closed roughly in his face.

This, then, is the end of his striving: to be a co-worker in the kingdom of culture, to escape both death and isolation, to husband and use his best powers and his latent genius. These powers of body and mind have in the past been strangely wasted, dispersed, or forgotten. The shadow of a mighty Negro past flits through the tale of Ethiopia the Shadowy and of Egypt the Sphinx. Throughout history, the powers of single black men flash here and there like falling stars, and die sometimes before the world has rightly gauged their brightness. Here in America, in the few days since Emancipation, the black man's turning hither and thither in hesitant and doubtful striving has often made his very strength to lose effectiveness, to seem like absence of power, like weakness. And yet it is not weakness,—it is the contradiction of double aims. The double-aimed struggle of the black artisan—on the one hand to escape white contempt for a nation of mere hewers of wood and drawers of water, and on the other hand to plough and nail and dig for a poverty-stricken horde—could only result in making him a poor craftsman, for he had but half a heart in either cause. By the poverty and ignorance of his people, the Negro minister or doctor was tempted toward quackery and demagogy; and by the criticism of the other world, toward ideals that made him ashamed of his lowly tasks. The would-be black *savant* was confronted by the paradox that the knowledge his people needed was a twice-told tale to his white neighbors, while the knowledge which would teach the white world was Greek to his own flesh and blood. The innate love of harmony and beauty that set the ruder souls of his people a-dancing and a-singing raised but confusion and doubt in the soul of the black artist; for the beauty revealed to him was the soul-beauty of a race which his larger audience despised, and he could not articulate the message of another people. This waste of double aims, this seeking to satisfy two unreconciled ideals, has wrought sad havoc with the courage and faith and deeds of ten thousand thousand people,—has sent them often wooing false gods and invoking false means of salvation, and at times has even seemed about to make them ashamed of themselves.

Away back in the days of bondage they thought to see in one divine event the end of all doubt and disappointment; few men ever worshipped Freedom with half such unquestioning faith as did the American Negro for two centuries. To him, so far as he thought and dreamed, slavery was indeed the sum of all villainies, the cause of all sorrow, the root of all prejudice; Emancipation was the key to a promised land of sweeter beauty than ever stretched before the eyes of wearied Israelites. In song and exhortation swelled one refrain—Liberty; in his tears and curses the God he implored had Freedom in his right hand. At last it came,—suddenly, fearfully, like a dream. With one wild carnival of blood and passion came the message in his own plaintive cadences:—

"Shout, O children!
Shout, you're free!
For God has bought your liberty!"

Years have passed away since then,—ten, twenty, forty; forty years of national life, forty years of renewal and development, and yet the swarthy spectre sits in its accustomed seat at the Nation's feast. In vain do we cry to this our vastest social problem:—

"Take any shape but that, and my firm nerves
Shall never tremble!"

The Nation has not yet found peace from its sins; the freedman has not yet found in freedom his promised land. Whatever of good may have come in these years of change, the shadow of a deep disappointment rests upon the Negro people,—a disappointment all the more bitter because the unattained ideal was unbounded save by the simple ignorance of a lowly people.

The first decade was merely a prolongation of the vain search for freedom, the boon that seemed ever barely to elude their grasp,—like a tantalizing will-o'-the-wisp, maddening and misleading the headless host. The holocaust of war, the terrors of the Ku-Klux Klan, the lies of carpet-baggers, the disorganization of industry, and the contradictory advice of friends and foes, left the bewildered serf with no new watchword beyond the old cry for freedom. As the time flew, however, he began to grasp a new idea. The ideal of liberty demanded for its attainment powerful means, and these the Fifteenth Amendment gave him. The ballot, which before he had looked upon as a visible sign of freedom, he now regarded as the chief means of gaining and perfecting the liberty with which war had partially endowed him. And why not? Had not votes made war and emancipated millions? Had not votes enfranchised the freedmen? Was anything impossible to a power that had done all this? A million black men started with renewed zeal to vote themselves into the kingdom. So the decade flew away, the revolution of 1876 came, and left the half-free serf weary, wondering, but still inspired. Slowly but steadily, in the following years, a new vision began gradually to replace the dream of political power,—a powerful movement, the rise of another ideal to guide the unguided, another pillar of fire by night after a clouded day. It was the ideal of "book-learning"; the curiosity, born of compulsory ignorance, to know and test the power of the cabalistic letters of the white man, the longing to know. Here at last seemed to have been discovered the mountain path to Canaan; longer than the highway of Emancipation and law, steep and rugged, but straight, leading to heights high enough to overlook life.

Up the new path the advance guard toiled, slowly, heavily, doggedly; only those who have watched and guided the faltering feet, the misty minds, the dull understandings, of the dark pupils of these schools know how faithfully, how piteously, this people strove to learn. It was weary work. The cold statistician wrote down the inches of progress here and there, noted also where here and there a foot had slipped or some one had fallen. To the tired climbers, the horizon was ever dark, the mists were often cold, the Canaan was always dim and far away. If, however, the vistas disclosed as yet no goal, no resting-place, little but flattery and criticism, the journey at least gave leisure for reflection and self-examination; it changed the child of Emancipation to the youth with dawning self-consciousness, self-realization, self-respect. In those sombre forests of his striving his own soul rose before him, and he saw himself,—darkly as through a veil; and yet he saw in himself some faint revelation of his power, of his mission. He began to have a dim feeling that, to attain his place in the world, he must be himself, and not another. For the first time he sought to analyze the burden he bore upon his back, that dead-weight of social degradation partially masked behind a half-named Negro problem. He felt his poverty; without a cent, without a home, without land, tools, or savings, he had entered into competition with rich, landed, skilled neighbors. To be a poor man is hard, but to be a poor race in a land of dollars is the very bottom of hardships. He felt the weight of his ignorance,—not simply of letters, but of life, of business, of the humanities; the accumulated sloth and shirking and awkwardness of decades and centuries shackled his hands and feet. Nor was his burden all poverty and ignorance. The red stain of bastardy, which two centuries of systematic legal defilement of Negro women had stamped upon his race, meant not only the loss of ancient African chastity, but also the hereditary weight of a mass of corruption from white adulterers, threatening almost the obliteration of the Negro home.

A people thus handicapped ought not to be asked to race with the world, but rather allowed to give all its time and thought to its own social problems. But alas! while sociologists gleefully count his bastards and his prostitutes, the very soul of the toiling, sweating black man is darkened by the shadow of a vast despair. Men call the shadow prejudice, and learnedly explain it as the natural defence of culture against barbarism, learning against ignorance, purity against crime, the "higher" against the "lower" races. To which the Negro cries Amen! and swears that to so much of this strange prejudice as is founded on just homage to civilization, culture, righteousness, and progress, he humbly bows and meekly does obeisance. But before that nameless prejudice that leaps beyond all this he stands helpless, dismayed, and well-nigh speechless; before that personal disrespect and mockery, the ridicule and systematic humiliation, the distortion of fact and wanton license of fancy, the cynical ignoring of the better and the boisterous welcoming of the worse, the all-pervading desire to inculcate disdain for everything black, from Toussaint to the devil,— before this there rises a sickening despair that would disarm and discourage any nation save that black host to whom "discouragement" is an unwritten word.

But the facing of so vast a prejudice could not but bring the inevitable self-questioning, self-disparagement, and lowering of ideals which ever accompany repression and breed in an atmosphere of contempt and hate. Whisperings and portents came borne upon the four winds: Lo! we are diseased and dying, cried the dark hosts; we cannot write, our voting is vain; what need of education, since we must always cook and serve? And the Nation echoed and enforced this self-criticism, saying: Be content to be servants, and nothing more; what need of higher culture for half-men? Away with the black man's ballot, by force or fraud,—and behold the suicide of a race! Nevertheless, out of the evil came something of good,—the more careful adjustment of education to real life, the clearer perception of the Negroes' social responsibilities, and the sobering realization of the meaning of progress.

So dawned the time of *Sturm and Drang*: storm and stress to-day rocks our little boat on the mad waters of the world-sea; there is within and without the sound of conflict, the burning of body and rending of soul; inspiration strives with doubt, and faith with vain questionings. The bright ideals of the past,—physical freedom, political power, the training of brains and the training of hands,—all these in turn have waxed and waned, until even the last grows dim and overcast. Are they all wrong,—all false? No, not that, but each alone was over-simple and incomplete,—the dreams of a credulous race-childhood, or the fond imaginings of the other world which does not know and does not want to know our power. To be really true, all these ideals must be melted and welded into one. The training of the schools we need to-day more than ever,—the training of deft hands, quick eyes and ears, and above all the broader, deeper, higher culture of gifted minds and pure hearts. The power of the ballot we need in sheer self-defence,—else what shall save us from a second slavery? Freedom, too, the long-sought, we still seek,—the freedom of life and limb, the freedom to work and think, the freedom to love and aspire. Work, culture, liberty, all these we need, not singly but together, not successively but together, each growing and aiding each, and all striving toward that vaster ideal that swims before the Negro people, the ideal of human brotherhood, gained through the unifying ideal of Race; the ideal of fostering and developing the traits and talents of the Negro, not in opposition to or contempt for other races, but rather in large conformity to the greater ideals of the American Republic, in order that some day on American soil two world-races may give each to each those characteristics both so sadly lack. We the darker ones come even now not altogether empty-handed: there are to-day no truer exponents of the pure human spirit of the Declaration of Independence than the American Negroes; there is no true American music but the wild sweet melodies of the Negro slave; the American fairy tales and folk-lore are Indian and African; and, all in all, we black men seem the sole oasis of simple faith and reverence in a dusty desert of dollars and smartness. Will America be poorer if she replace her brutal dyspeptic blundering with light-hearted but determined Negro humility? or her coarse and cruel wit with loving jovial good-humor? or her vulgar music with the soul of the Sorrow Songs?

Merely a concrete test of the underlying principles of the great republic is the Negro Problem, and the spiritual striving of the freedmen's sons is the travail of souls whose burden is almost beyond the measure of their strength, but who bear it in the name of an historic race, in the name of this the land of their fathers' fathers, and in the name of human opportunity.

19

When Are WE Going to Get Over It?

Andrew Manis

For much of the last forty years, ever since America "fixed" its race problem in the Civil Rights and Voting Rights Acts, we white people have been impatient with African Americans who continued to blame race for their difficulties. Often we have heard whites ask, "When are African Americans finally going to get over it? Now I want to ask "When are we White Americans going to get over our ridiculous obsession with skin color?"

Recent reports that "Election Spurs 'Hundreds' of Race Threats, Crimes" should frighten and infuriate every one of us. Having grown up in "Bombingham," Alabama, in the 1960s, I remember overhearing an avalanche of comments about what many white classmates and their parents wanted to do to John and Bobby Kennedy and Martin Luther King. Eventually, as you may recall, in all three cases, someone decided to do more than "talk the talk." Since our recent presidential election, to our eternal shame we are once again hearing the same reprehensible talk I remember from my boyhood.

We white people have controlled political life in the disunited colonies and United States for some 400 years on this continent. Conservative whites have been in power 28 of the last 40 years. Even during the eight Clinton years, conservatives in Congress blocked most of his agenda and pulled him to the right. Yet never in that period did I read any headlines suggesting that anyone was calling for the assassinations of presidents Nixon, Ford, Reagan, or either of the Bushes. Criticize them, yes. Call for their impeachment, perhaps. But there were no bounties on their heads. And even when someone did try to kill Ronald Reagan, the perpetrator was a non-political mental case who wanted merely to impress Jody Foster.

But elect a liberal who happens to be black and we're back in the sixties again. At this point in our history, we should be proud that we've proven what conservatives are always saying—that in America anything is possible, EVEN electing a black man as president. But instead we now hear that schoolchildren from Maine to California are talking about wanting to "assassinate Obama."

Fighting the urge to throw up, I can only ask, "How long?" How long before we white people realize we can't make our nation, much less the whole world, look like us? How long until we white people can—once and for all—get over this hell-conceived preoccupation with skin color? How long until we white people get over the demonic conviction that white skin makes us superior? How long before we white people get over our bitter resentments about being demoted to the status of equality with non-whites? How long before we get over our expectations that we should be at the head of the line merely because of our white skin? How long until we white people end our silence and call out our peers when they share the latest racist jokes in the privacy of our white-only conversations? I believe in free speech, but how long until we white people start making racist loudmouths as socially uncomfortable as we do flag burners? How long until we white people will stop insisting that blacks exercise personal responsibility, build strong families, educate themselves enough to edit the *Harvard Law Review,* and work hard enough to become President of the United States, only to threaten to assassinate them when they do? How long before we start "living out the true meaning" of our creeds, both civil and religious, that all men and women are created equal and that "red and yellow, black and white" all are precious in God's sight?

Until this past November 4, I didn't believe this country would ever elect an African American to the presidency. I still don't believe I'll live long enough to see us white people get over our racism problem. But here's my three-point plan during the Obama administration: First, every day that Barack Obama lives in the White House that Black Slaves Built I'm going to pray that God (and the Secret Service) will protect him and his family from harm. Second, I'm going to report to the FBI anyone I overhear saying, in seriousness or in jest, anything of a threatening nature about President Obama. Third, I'm going to pray to live long enough to see America surprise the world once again, when white people can sing of our damnable color prejudice, "We HAVE overcome."

Additional Readings

1. Chen, Michelle. "Doublespeak on Racism".
   http://www.racewire.org/archives/2009/04/doublespeak_on_race_relations_1.html

2. Holder, Eric. "We Should Have an Open Dialogue on Race".
   http://www.clipsandcomment.com/2009/02/18/full-text-us-attorney-general-eric-holder-remarks-on-black-history-month-nation-of-cowards/

3. Garcia, Michelle and Julissa Reynoso. "As Long as 'Latino' Is Synonymous With 'Immigrant,' We Will Remain a Class Apart".
   http://www.racewire.org/archives/2009/04/as_long_as_latino_is_synonymou.html

4. Lehrman, Sally. "Colorblind Racism".
   http://www.alternet.org/story/16792.

5. Moore, Robert B. "Racism in the English Language," from Racism in the English Language. New York: Council on Interracial Books for Children, 1976.

6. Obama, Barack. "A More Perfect Union".
   http://www.npr.org/templates/story/story.php?storyId=88478467

SECTION 3

Confronting the Myth and Power of Race in America Law

20

A Brief History of Blacks in America before the Civil War

R. L. Raines

The Beginning: Africans In Colonial America

The first Africans to arrive and permanently settle in North America were brought to Jamestown, Virginia in April 1619. The arrival of these 20 Africans to Jamestown in this particular year, the way in which they came to be brought here, and their initial legal status are significant in many aspects. This is a full 15 months before the Puritans aboard the Mayflower landed at Plymouth Rock, MA. Why is this significant? To most Americans the founding of this nation began with the arrival of the Mayflower in November of 1620. We point to the Mayflower Compact as a precursor of the democratic form of government that was to define America, government by the consent of the governed. We have indelibly imprinted in our minds from the earliest years of schooling the travails and hardships of these settlers during their first winter in America and how, after somehow surviving against overwhelming odds, they planted crops and then gathered their first harvest, which we celebrate today as Thanksgiving Day.

The failed settlement of Jamestown, VA, founded in 1607, seems more imaginary than real. It is the stuff of Hollywood, especially Walt Disney, a romantic tale of Pocahontas and Captain John Smith (she may have saved Smith from being killed by her people, but she married a man named John Rolfe). With this said, it is ironic that the Africans were here before the Mayflower. If it is a profound point of pride for some to be able to trace their ancestry back to the founding of America, then what of the fact that Africans in America pre-date this prideful fortuity? If it had been possible to keep accurate records of the descendants of those 20 Africans who were brought here in 1619, albeit under very different circumstances than the Puritans, there would be African-Americans today who could proudly name specific ancestors who were here before the "founding of America." It would not be the same kind of pride as white descendants of the Mayflower, since Africans came here by force, but it would be the kind of pride that would quiet the boastful but uninformed Mayflower descendant, who may believe that they have a special claim to all things American solely because his ancestors were here first.

How the Africans Came to America

Secondly, what significance can we make of the manner in which the 20 Africans happened to arrive in Jamestown? It is important to note that those Africans did not come here via a direct route from Africa. They were not intended for North America at all. They were slaves aboard a Spanish ship and presumably on their way to a New World Spanish port in the Caribbean, when their ship was attacked by a Dutch ship. When the Dutch plundered the Spanish ship, it took the 20 Africans as they would take any other cargo of value. The Dutch ship arrived at the recently established English settlement of Jamestown badly in need of supplies. The Dutch captain offered as barter these 20 "Negers" to the Jamestown settlers in exchange for the sorely needed supplies (Higginbotham, 41). At least two of the English settlers provided what the Dutch ship required and claimed the Africans. Thus the first Africans to arrive and permanently settle in North America did not come here as a direct result of the transatlantic African slave trade, nor in response to a direct effort by Virginia colonist, at this time, to import slave labor, as would be the case after 1650.

Legal Status upon Arrival in Virginia

What was the legal status of the first Africans to arrive in North America? They were likely christened, as was the Spanish Jesuit practice, either aboard ship or in the Spanish colony, and prepped for sale. It is presumed that they were on their way to their final destination when the Dutch ship attacked. The point here is that these 20 Africans were considered Christians. This fact would have had significance to the Jamestown settlers. Christians did not enslave Christians, so the English and all of Europe came to believe sometime after the 1066 conquest of England (Higginbotham, 323). Prior to this, in keeping with traditional slave societies, it was common to enslave the conquered. Thus, the very fact that these "heathens" had been christened gave pause to the English settlers and it would not resolve the professed incongruity between slavery and Christianity for nearly 50 years after the arrival of the Africans. "[A] Spanish subject who had been christened or baptized was by that act enfranchised or set free under English law and admitted to the privileges of a free person" (Higginbotham, 21). Therefore, upon their arrival and for a brief period thereafter, their Christianity would prevent permanent enslavement.

English settlers would know little of slavery from personal experience. While there is evidence of African slaves being brought to England as early as 1562, England would not become a major participant in the slave trade until 1660, some 40 years after the first Africans were brought to English North America. The vast majority of English slaves went to its colonies in the New World. These English settlers in Jamestown knew only one form of legal bondage: indentured servitude, a bonded servant for a specific term of years, not lifetime servitude, which is slavery. In fact, all the original settlers of Jamestown were indentured servants themselves, as were the 1620 Puritans of Massachusetts.[i]

The Colonial Experience: Virginia

A. Leon Higginbotham, Jr., in his book *In the Matter of Color, Race, and the American Legal Process: The Colonial Period*, states that "from 1619 to approximately 1660 there appears to have been no systematic effort in Virginia to define broadly the rights or non-rights of blacks" (Higginbotham, 19). In fact, blacks were not denied the right to vote in Virginia until 1723 (Bennett, 38). Instead the racial discrimination that was to characterize Virginia happened case by case, statute by statute, over the 41 years between 1619 and 1660. It is the story of *de facto* racism (what people, in fact, do by custom) becoming *de jure* racism (what is required by law), namely the institutionalization of racism. While the deprivation of legal rights such as the right to vote, testify in court, hold elective office, etc., happened over time, socially, these blacks, from the very beginning, were never treated equally by whites.

> Although the American colonists seemed to have practiced from the beginning the same discrimination which white men had practiced against the negro all along and before any statutes decreed it, these first blacks were not exposed to the systematic degradation to which later blacks would be subjected to. (Higginbotham, 20)

It shall come as no surprise that our legislative and judicial systems generally followed the majority public racist sentiment over the last 200 plus years of the African-American experience. If, *de facto*, the majority of whites did not want to eat with, ride with, intermarry with blacks or live in the same neighborhoods or go to the same schools as blacks, laws were passed (*de jure*) to accommodate these racist proclivities.

We see in Virginia the earliest example of this institutionalization of racism. Again, case by case, statute by statute, Virginia groped its way toward systematic degradation of blacks—slave or free—and development of a slave code that was to emulated throughout the slaveholding colonies, later states. By 1705 Virginia presumed that all blacks were slaves, unless proven otherwise. "Just how then did the legal process, haltingly at first and later without hesitation, help fix those social prejudices by which an individual's status was determined solely on the basis of race?" (Higginbotham, 20)

Fear, Greed & Prejudice

To understand the motivations of the Virginia colonists that pertain to their judicial and legislative treatment of blacks, one only has to look to their greed, fear, and prejudice. As early as 1639, just 19 years after the arrival of the first Africans to Jamestown, the Virginia legislature enacted the following statute: "All persons except Negroes are to be provided with arms and ammunition . . ."(Henning, 226).

We can assume that the need to issue guns and ammunition was to repel an attack by Native Americans. After all, who else was there to fear in 1639? Why are blacks excluded from a fight that may determine the very survival of the now young settlements in and around Jamestown? The entire Jamestown settlement was almost wiped out by an Indian attack of 1622, called a massacre, just two years after the first blacks arrived and only 17 years earlier than this 1639 edict. Why did the law make no distinction between indentured, slave or free blacks?

To both questions, we must conclude that fear motivated this legislation. Fear that the blacks in the colonies—free, slave, or indentured—if given weapons might point them at the white colonists instead of the Indians. This begs another question: what happened between 1619 and 1639 to even make such a possibility likely? Had race relations sunk to the point of outward hatred and hostility? Sadly, we do not have enough information to answer these questions.

The next two cases, both in 1640, further illustrate the state of deteriorating race relations in Virginia and the kind of disparate justice blacks could expect. In the first case, a black named Emmanuel escaped along with six white indentured servants. Upon their capture the six white men were given various forms of punishment ranging from being whipped, branded, chained, and years added to their terms of indenture. Emmanuel, however, received all of the above, except added time (Higginbotham, 27). It is believed that this meant Emmanuel could receive no additional time of servitude because he had none to give—he was already a slave for life.

Next is the curious case of a black indentured servant named John Punch. Punch and two white indentured servants ran away. After capture the two whites received punishments of additional terms of indenture, an extra year to their respective masters and then three additional years to the colony. But John Punch, "being a Negro . . . shall serve his master . . . for the time of his natural life here or elsewhere" (Higginbotham, 28–29).

Just 21 years after the arrival of the first Africans to Jamestown, initially given the legal status of indentured servants could now be reduced to slavery as a form of penal punishment. There is greed here: free labor for life. One can imagine the aggrieved master whispering into the judge's ear, "why not set an example and make him a slave for life. It will deter future attempted escapes by black indentured servants." Ostensibly, the motive is to curb running away, allay the fear of such happening in the future, but the real motivation is economic, and of course prejudice. We will see that the need for labor will trump all else, notwithstanding moral, religious, and legal contradictions. When exactly did it occur to Virginians that blacks were so beneath them that justice no longer applied in their cases? Color instead of justice came to determine judicial outcomes.

One of the justifications for enslavement of blacks is that they were heathens—non Christians. But as more and more American slaves accepted Christianity, the problem became obvious. "How can I give my slave the benefit of salvation and still have his or her (free) labor?" the slave master asked himself. After all, at that time slavery and Christianity were incompatible. As you might imagine, the Virginia colonists solved this dilemma by deciding to have their cake and eat it too. It was decreed that conversion to Christianity did not alter the slaves' legal status as a bonded servant for life:

1667: *Virginia Statute*

Whereas some doubts have arisen whether children that are slaves By birth, and charity and pity of their owners made partakers of the blessed sacrament of baptism, should by virtue of their baptism be made free, it is enacted that *baptism does not alter the condition of the person as to his bondage . . . , masters freed from this doubt may more carefully propagate Christianity by permitting slaves to be admitted to the sacrament.* (Hening, 260)

The motivation was fear of losing free labor, greed. If it had come down to choosing between giving slaves Christianity or having their labor, there is little doubt of the Virginian's decision. The legislature solved their dilemma by giving them their precious free slave labor and assuaged their conscience at the same time, to say nothing of helping them gain points in heaven for proselytizing and converting the heathens.

Miscegenation

Interracial sexual relations and marriage—miscegenation—seemed at first to catch the Virginia colonists by surprise. The first known case was reported in 1630, just 11 years after the arrival of Africans in Jamestown:

Hugh Davis to be soundly whipt before an assembly of Negroes and others for abusing himself to the dishonor of God and shame of Christianity by defiling his body in lying with a Negro which fault his to acknowledge next Sabbath day. (Higginbotham, 23)

The language of this case bears close examination and raises many questions. First, why is it important that blacks be witnesses to Davis' punishment? How does sex with a black woman cause Davis to abuse himself, defile his body, dishonor God, and bring shame on Christianity? And finally, assuming it was consensual, why the seeming surprise and shock that such an assignation took place?

In the social pecking order of the early 17th century Virginia, the white indentured servants was above black indentured and enslaved persons. To have Davis bare his chest and be whipped in front of his inferiors was meant to shame and humiliate him. How was he to ever again walk among blacks with the usual air of social superiority that his color previously afforded him when he had been so debased in front of those at the bottom of the social ladder? This form of punishment meant ridicule not only from his white peers, but also from those much lower in status.

Davis' act caused him to "defile" and "abuse" himself, dishonored God and shamed Christianity. These are very strong words for one white male braving intercourse with a heathen female, even in the year 1630. The tenor of the language shows surprise that a white man would even think of the black women in a sexual way. It must also be noted that there is no record of the black woman being punished, just Davis (Higginbotham, 23).

The shock and surprise that white men would have sex with black women seems to have abated considerably within 10 years after the *Davis* case. In a 1640 case, the court's tone, language, and punishment took quite a different turn:

> Robert Sweat has begotten with child a Negro woman . . . the said Negro women shall be whipt at the whipping post and the said Sweat shall tomorrow in the forenoon do public pennance for his offense at James City Church in the time of devine service according to the laws of England in the case provided. (Higginbotham, 23–24)

Except for the fact that the black woman was impregnated—which one might consider worse than that crime of 10 years earlier—is this not the same offense for which Davis was found guilty? Where is the moral and religious outrage of 10 years earlier? Why is the white man, unlike Davis, not punished, but the black woman is? The simple answer to these questions is the realization within a short span of 10 years that white men like Davis, Sweat and many others did and would continue to engage in such conduct. In essence, it is a decision by the white men of the colony to no longer punish themselves for sexual intercourse with black women. And from this year forward and for the next 125 years of slavery in America this would be the case. Except for intermarrying with blacks, white men would no longer receive punishment or official condemnation for either consensual sex with or the rape of the black female. Going forward only black men and women, black and white, are severely punished for interracial sex. Given the male to female ratio early in the history of Virginia, it should have been a foregone conclusion that such interracial sexual activity would take place. During the earliest years, there were three men to every woman in the entire Virginia colony, while in Jamestown itself the ratio was close to 15 to 1 (Bridenbaugh, 126–127).

The resolve to allow white men almost complete immunity from punishment in their sexual transgressions with either black females or white female indentured servants had adverse effects on the women and the offspring of those relationships. What happens when the master impregnates the white indentured servant? What happens when he impregnates the black female slave?

1662: Virginia Statute

> In the preamble the legislature noted that 'some dissolute masters' had 'gotten their maids with child' in order to 'claim the benefit of their service,' and that some loose women, hoping to gain their freedom, had laid 'all their bastards to their masters.' And accordingly, the following provision was enacted: 'each women servant got with child by her master shall after her indenture is expired be sold for two years by the church wardens.'" . . . "Children got by an Englishman upon a Negro woman shall be bond or free according to the condition of the mother, and if any Christian shall commit fornication with a Negro man or woman, he [she] shall pay double fines of the former act. (Hening, 127)

This legislative act attempted to address what it considered to be two distinct concerns. The first problem appears to have been one of immoral ("dissolute") masters getting their indentured servants pregnant for the purpose of benefitting from more years of their ser-vice (extending her term of indenture), while the second concern is that of these same masters being taken advantage of by their black female slaves who entice them into sex with the expectation of gaining freedom for themselves and their offspring.

It is curious that the same master can be both victimizer and victim while engaged in the same sexual conduct. The distinction is in the two different classes of women involved. In the first instance, the female indentured servant is probably white and is seen as being preyed upon by the master for his own selfish ends. She is the victim. In the latter case, the black woman is obviously seen as the predator, and the master the victim. Since the white master (slave owner or holder of the contract of indenture) was usually the aggressor, the distinction made in this case about victimizer and victim is purely self-serving for the white male.

What of the remedies? In the case of the white female indentured servant, the only punishment for the master is the denial of her services after the expiration of her term of indenture. Real justice would have called for the immediate end of the contract. What did she do to justify two additional years of indenture? Why punish the victim? Was this for her and her child's benefit or for that of a colony that sorely needed labor?

As to the black slave woman, the legislature decrees, in departure from centuries-old English law, the status of the child from the sexual liaison between the white ("Christian") male and the black woman follows, not that of the father, but that of the mother. Know-ing, in this case, that the woman is a slave, the law effectively perpetuates slavery by extend-ing it to the slave progeny of the slave master. Thus, the "temptress" black slave woman hoping to gain her freedom through producing offspring of the master discovered, not only would she remain a slave, her child by the master would also be a slave . The prejudice is obvious. The white indentured woman is good and a victim while the black slave woman is bad and the white man, the master, her victim. Note that the only punishment for the white male is the payment of a monetary fine.

A Virginia statute of 1691 called for banishment from the colony of any white man or woman who intermarried with blacks, mulattos, or Indians. This law was also meant to deal with "that abominable mixture and spurious issue (offspring)" by such interracial marriages or offspring from interracial coupling of any kind. The act provides:

> . . . Whatsoever English or other white man or woman, bond or free shall inter-marry with a Negro, mulatto, or Indian man or woman, bond or free, he shall within three months be banished from this dominion forever.
>
> And it is further enacted, that if any English woman being free shall have a bas-tard child by a Negro she shall pay fifteen pounds to the church wardens, and in default of such payment, she shall be taken into possession by the church wardens and disposed of for five years and the amount she brings shall be paid one-third to their majesties for the support of the government, one-third to the parish where

the offense is committed and the other third to the informer. The child shall be bound out to the church wardens until he is thirty years of age. In case the English woman that shall have a bastard is a servant she shall be sold by the church wardens (after her time is expired) for five years, and the child serve as aforesaid. (Higginbotham 44–45)

The white woman, unlike the white male, is dealt with severely for her interracial indiscretion. If she is a free woman and has a child by a black man, she is to pay a significant fine, one which she probably cannot pay, and in default, she is to be reduced to an indentured servant for five years. Her bastard/mulatto child is to be indentured for a period of 30 years, a life sentence in many instances. The child's only offense is to be born part black and part white and be that "spurious issue" which the statute was aimed at preventing. In 1705, Virginia provided that all mulatto children would be indentured servants until age 31. If the white woman is already an indentured servant, she is to serve an additional five years after her original term of indenture and her mulatto offspring will also serve the colony for 30 years.

1705: Virginia Statute

Whatsoever white man or woman being free shall intermarry with a Negro shall be committed to prison for six months without bail, and pay 10 pounds to the use of the parish. Ministers marrying such persons shall pay a fine of 10,000 pounds of tobacco. (Higginbotham, 46)

There is no imprisonment for the black mulatto partner (presumably a slave) person, probably because the colony needed the labor. In 1848 the prison term was increased to one year. In 1932, imprisonment was imposed on both blacks and whites for a term of one to five years. With the end of slavery, blacks would now be sentenced to prison as well as whites.

The white husband could easily obtain a divorce or annulment of a marriage in the event of his wife's infidelity with a black man. It was rare for the white wife to exercise such an option.

Virginia Acts (1705)

The marriage between Benjamin Butt, Jr., and a certain Lydia Bright, who is of respectable family, and was at the time of the marriage supposed to be unsullied in her reputation, is dissolved because Lydia has been delivered of a mulatto child and has publicly acknowledged that the father of the child is a slave.

A marriage solemnized between Richard Jones . . . and his wife Peggy, is dissolved and Richard is forever divorced from Peggy provided that a jury find that the child of Peggy is not the child of Richard, but is the offspring of a man of color. (Guild, 31)

Ironically, it was a Virginia case, *Loving vs. Virginia*, that reached the Supreme Court in 1967 that successfully challenged the legality of a state denying the right of interracial couples to marry, and the imposition of prison terms for such marriages. The Court's decision finally ended this ban which was still in effect in at least 16 states (Higginbotham, 42).

Legalization of Slavery in Virginia (Prejudice, Greed)

By 1705, the Virginia legislature erased all doubt as to the status of black servants arriving in the colony.

> [A]ll servants imported and brought in this country [Virginia] by sea or land, who were not Christians in their native country . . . shall be accounted and be slaves, and as such be here brought and sold notwithstanding a conversion to Christianity afterwards." (Higginbotham, 53)

Absolute Power over Life and Death (Fear, Prejudice)

Normally one would be liable for causing the death of another person, absent self defense or some other mitigating factor. Just as the slave owners of Virginia had once been concerned about the seeming contradiction between converting their slaves to Christianity and its effects on the slave status of those converted, questions (fear) must have arisen about criminal liability for causing the death of a slave due to overly harsh or over zealous corporal punishment. Just as the Virginia legislature allayed the concern of slave owners in 1667 about slavery not being incompatible with Christianity, in 1669 it assured the slave owners that they would not face criminal charges for the accidental or "casuall" killing of slaves.

> *An Act about the casuall killing of slaves.* Whereas the only law in force for the punishment of refractory servants resisting their master, mistress or overseer, cannot be inflicted on negroes [because the punishment was extension of time], Nor the obstinacy of many of them by other than violent means supprest. *Be it enacted and declared by this grand assembly,* if any slave resist his master . . . and by the extremity of the correction should chance to die that this death shall not be accompted Felony, but the master (or that other person appointed by the master to punish him) be acquit from molestation, since it cannot be presumed that propensed malice (which alone makes murther Felony) should induce any man to destroy his own estate (Hening, 270).

Lack of premeditation by the slave owner is part of the logic of this law, and the presumption that one would not willingly destroy his own property. Slaves could not be given additional time of service, as in the case of an indentured servant, for acts of disobedience, stubbornness, running away, etc. Therefore, the slave owner, the legislature reasoned, must be given immunity when it came to excessive punitive, corporal punishment. If the slave died as a result of the whipping, for example, the slave owner need not fear any criminal repercussions from the authorities. As a result, in Virginia from 1669 to the end of slavery in 1865, white slave owners and their white overseers exercised the absolute power of life or death over their slaves without any fear of criminal liability.

No Blacks in Positions of Authority (Fear, Prejudice)

"Hannah Warwick's case extenuated because she was overseen by a negro overseer." (Higginbotham, 29)

This one line judgment by a Virginia court in 1669 is powerfully revealing as to white prejudice and fear of having blacks in any position of authority. The defendant is legally excused from her act or crime simply because her boss was black. It is the very fact of a black person being put in charge that is determinative in this case. As noted by one historian,

> The clear inference to be drawn from the decision is that the society was more interested in making sure that blacks did not exercise authority over whites, and that white servants knew this, than in prosecuting the infraction of Hanna Warwick. Thus, the court intimated, by extension, that whites, although wrong, could refuse to submit to the authority of blacks even when blacks were performing as agents of the common master (Higginbotham, 30).

The fact that a black was an overseer means that up to this point racial hierarchies were not as rigid. The verdict in the case sent a strong message that blacks are inferior and should not be placed in positions of authority, blacks are to be directed not give direction.

Black Assembly: Conspiracies and Revolt (Fear)

Virginia Statute (1680)

> Whereas the frequent meetings of considerable number of Negro slaves under the pretense of feast and burials is judged of dangerous consequence [it is]enacted that no Negro or slave may carry arms, such as any club, staff, gun, sword, or other weapon, nor go from his owner's plantation without a certificate and then only on necessary occasions; the punishment of twenty lashes on the bare back, well laid on. And further, if any Negro lift up his hand against any Christian he shall receive thirty lashes, and if he absent himself or lie out from his master's service and resist lawful apprehension, he may be killed and this *law* shall be published every six months. (Higginbotham, 63)

By 1680, the large slave population caused concern and fear of slave conspiracies to revolt. This law assumes that slaves, while attending rites of passage such as funerals, births, and feasts, are really getting together to plan rebellion. Note the solution. While the stated problem is slaves assembling for the purpose of plotting, all blacks, slave or free, are now restricted in assembly and movement. No black person, slave or free, can carry anything that might be construed by whites to be a weapon. And if any black person, slave or free, raises his hand against a white person (even in 1680 "Christian" meant a white person, further proof of the limited number of Christian blacks), he was to receive 30 lashes.

Restrictions on Manumission (Greed)

Virginia Statute (1691)

> A great inconvenience may happen to this country by the setting of Negroes and mulattoes free, by their entertaining Negroes from their masters' service, or receiving stolen goods, or being grown old bringing a charge upon the country, it is enacted that no Negroes, or mulattoes be set free by any person whatsoever, unless such person pay for the transportation of such Negro out of the country within six months after such setting free, upon penalty of ten pounds sterling to the church wardens, with which the church wardens are to cause the Negro to be transported out of the country and the remainder given to the use of the poor in the parish. (Higginbotham, 48)

Apparently, just some 70 years after arrival of the first blacks in Virginia and 40 years after the mass importation of slaves, the colony has to address the problem of slave owners releasing their slaves onto the community at large. Why were masters manumitting their slaves in significant numbers, enough to cause the legislature to act? The simple fact is that these slaves, having grown too old to be productive, are now overhead, a cost without any monetary value to the owner because they are no longer contributing to the profit margin. The law implies that these elderly former slaves are a public nuisance (distracting and keeping other slaves from doing their work, stealing, etc.) and a cost "charge" to the public. Many, with nowhere to go, would be a burden on the colony itself. The solution is to have the slave owner either live up to his contract for life or pay for the removal of the former slave out of the colony.

The Colonial Experience: Massachusetts

Like Virginia, the story of enslaving only blacks in Massachusetts seems to have been an evolutionary process. The first recorded arrival of blacks in Massachusetts was in 1638. This was when ". . . Captain W. Pierce returned to Salem on the ship *Desire* from the Tortugas, where he had exchanged a group of Pequod Indian warriors for 'salt, cotton, tobacco, and Negroes." Unlike Virginia, however, where *de facto* slavery developed gradually in "response to societal custom" (Higginbotham, 61), and the acute need for labor, slavery in Massachusetts was legalized by statute as early as 1641, just 20 years after the first Puritans arrived at Plymouth Rock and, as such, it was the first English colony in North America to enact such a statute. One would think that colonies such as Virginia, South Carolina, or Georgia would be the first, not Massachusetts. Why would Massachusetts need to do so?

It was the practice of the colony to reduce Native Americans found guilty of crimes or warfare against the colony to either specific terms of slavery or for life. Those thought to be a serious threat or incorrigible were sold into slavery and deported to the Caribbean, as seen in the 1638 case of the Pequod Indians above. Blacks were never essential to the economy of the colony. In 1700 they numbered less than 1,000 in all of New England and were never more than 3% of the total population in the 18th century. (Higginbotham, 71) From 1680 to 1783 when slavery ended in Massachusetts, black slaves worked primarily as domestics, farm hands on family farms, dockworkers, and skilled laborers. Unlike the South, Massachusetts and other northern colonies had no staple crops, therefore no large plantations, no great reliance on agriculture as a means of colonial wealth.

The 1641 statute (ironically named the "Body of Liberties") allowed enslavement under the following conditions:

1. "lawful captives taken in juste warres . . .";
2. such strangers as willfully sell themselves or are sold to us" ;
3. those sentenced to servitude as a means of penal punishment. (Higginbotham, 62)

> This statute was tested in a very early 1646 case of *Smith v Keyser*.

In 1645, Smith and Keyser of Massachusetts joined a party of English slavers in a raid of an African village, killing 100 and wounding others. Smith, the ship's captain, sued his first mate Keyser for failing to deliver the remainder of the slave cargo.

The civil case resulted in the captain receiving monetary damages. This illustrates that as early as 1646 black slaves were viewed as personal property, like livestock, or a commercial commodity that one could legally recover recompense if wrongfully converted, loss or otherwise damaged by another. It was as though Keyser had sold, to his own advantage, bales of wheat belonging to the ship or through negligence left them on the dock. The Massachusetts court does not say if this kind of case (financial damages for loss of human cargo) was its first.

> A similar case came some 30 years later, before an English court in 1677. In that case the court was tackling this concept for the first time. After considering the novelty of the facts, the court concluded that a civil action to recover the value of the lost human merchandise was allowable because blacks were "usually bought and sold among merchants, as merchandise, and also being infidels, there might be a property in them sufficient to maintain trover [wrongful taking or use of another's property]. . . ." (Higginbotham, 321).

In the case of *Smith v. Keyser*, there is no evidence that the court grappled with the legal issue of the right to damages in a case involving human property as the English court did. It does not seem to have even been a question. Slaves *were* clearly property. The captain had been deprived of this property and damages were awarded.

Walker v. Jennison, et.al.*ii*

We now examine a case that represents the end of slavery in Massachusetts, some 142 years after the statutory recognition of slavery. Quock Walker was a slave farm hand owned by a man named Caldwell who promised Walker his freedom upon his 25th birthday. Caldwell died prior to Walker reaching this age. Caldwell's widow remarried a man named Jennison. Upon his 25th birthday, Walker reminded Jennison of the promise made to him by his deceased prior owner, Caldwell. Jennison refused to acknowledge this oral agreement. The Caldwell widow, now Mrs. Jennison, appears to have remained silent. It would have been rare for her to go against the will of her new husband, who was now in control of her property, both land and workers. Walker refused to work for Jennison and fled to the nearby farm of the brothers of his deceased owner. Hearing of this, Jennison, with the aid of other men, pursued Walker and forcibly brought him back to his farm, delivering a beating in the process. Walker sues Jennison, asserting his freedom, and monetary damages resulting from the assault and battery. Walker stated that Jennison knew of the deceased Caldwell's promise when he married the widow Caldwell. In the meantime Jennison sues the Caldwell brothers for the loss of Walker's services and finally the state of Massachusetts sues Jennison for unlawful assault and battery on a "free man, citizen, not a chattel slave."

Jennison argued that since Walker was his slave he had a right to discipline him. In June of 1781 *Quock Walker v. Jennison* was decided in favor of Walker and he was awarded damages for Jennison's assault and battery.

In Walker's suit against Jennison, the jury concluded that Walker was not a slave. However, a different jury seems to have come to a different conclusion in Jennison's suit against the Caldwells. It awards Jennison damages for the Caldwells' wrongful interference with Jennison's property (Walker). If Walker was free, then he could work for whoever he pleased. Higginbotham says that these inconsistent rulings are: ". . . due to the proclivity of Massachusetts juries to rule in favor of slaves who challenged the legality of their enslavement" (Higginbotham, 92). This just begs the question, if Massachusetts juries favored freedom over enslavement, the second jury should have also found for Walker and denied Jennison damages for loss of services of a man he did not own.

The state in April, 1783, in a criminal action, indicted Jennison for assault and battery upon a "free citizen." The case, *Massachusetts v. Jennison*, was heard by the state's highest court. The prosecutor produced proof that the deceased Caldwell had promised to free Walker upon his 25th birthday and that Jennison knew of this promise when he married Caldwell's widow.

The defense argued that Walker was indeed Jennison's slave and as such he had the right to take the actions necessary to retrieve and discipline his servant. It also argued that Massachusetts had since 1641 recognized one's right to "hold property in slaves," and that without any intervening "specific prohibition" by the state, this right still existed.

Judge Cushing decided to instruct the jury in such a manner that ignored both parties' contentions. Instead, he looked to the words of the Massachusetts Constitution of 1780 and instructed the jury to rely on the following wording of the Declaration of Rights in that Constitution, "All men are born free and equal . . ." (Higginbotham, 95).

Cushing asserted that while probably not intending to, the legislature with these words effectively ended slavery in Massachusetts as of 1781. He reasoned: Are blacks not men? Does the document exclude any specific kind of man? The jury, so instructed, returned a verdict that found Jennison guilty and officially emancipated Quock Walker.

There was no great public outcry, no riots, no legislative effort to amend the constitution to reinstate slavery. The court ruled and the public simply complied. Imagine if a court in a southern slave holding state dared rule slavery unconstitutional? Massachusetts is unique among Northern states in that it ended slavery through judicial action while the other states did so through legislative action.

Access to the judicial process, parity of justice in court rulings, 30 years of growing public sentiment against slavery (was the abolitionist movement stronger anywhere than Massachusetts?), economics, and finally the Massachusetts Constitution of 1780 led up to the dramatic decision in the *Quock Walker* case, which effectively ended slavery in Massachusetts.

These cases offer a fascinating look at how the Massachusetts judicial and public sentiment developed since 1641 regarding the treatment of blacks in general and the issue of slavery in particular. The first observation has to be access to the courts by blacks in Massachusetts and secondly the apparent parity of justice once getting to court, unheard of in Virginia or other southern states. Quock Walker benefitted from years of judicial fairness toward blacks and the changing public attitude toward slavery. In Virginia, the kind of justice one received depended on the color of one's skin, while in Massachusetts the courts had developed to the point that justice was not dependent on skin color but on the actual facts of the case. What a rarity!

Higginbotham concluded that ". . . one will discover that the New England institution of slavery was probably the most 'benign' system in the original English Colonies—black servants and slaves were apparently accorded the same legal rights as white servants in terms of their ability to petition the court for protection against masters, and in their ability to obtain the same panoply of legal protections available to white men when they were criminal defendants" (Higginbotham, 72).

Massachusetts could end the institution of slavery so easily because its economy did not rely on slave labor, it had no staple crop, it had small family farms instead of large plantations, it focused on manufactured goods and shipping instead of agriculture (it was the largest slave trader in the New World during the colonial period after 1715), it had a large white labor force (both indentured and free), and anti-slavery public sentiment had grown over a 30 year period prior to the Walker case.

"The Peculiar Institution"

American historian Kenneth M. Stampp is credited with coining this phrase in his 1956 study of slavery, *The Peculiar Institution: Slavery in the Ante-Bellum South.* American slavery was "peculiar in many ways. First, it was radically different from traditional forms of slavery. From time immemorial one could become enslaved primarily through conquest, debt, or penal punishment. Although early in the colonial period at least one American colony, Massachusetts, enacted a statute providing for slavery in these instances, all the colonies at some point resorted exclusively to non-white (blacks, Indians, and those of mixed race) slavery. And finally, after the failure of attempts to enslave Native Americans, due primarily to their mass extermination resulting from war and lack of immunity to European diseases, the colonists turned solely to enslavement of Africans. Thus, at some early point in the American colonial period and continuing into the 19th century up until the end of the Civil War, American slavery was based solely on race.

Secondly, the American system of slavery was peculiar because, by the early 19th century, it was geographic. As Abraham Lincoln noted, America was a house divided. The malignancy that was slavery existed primarily in the South. The North, having abolished slavery, agitated for its abolition and/or stemming its spread. The South, utterly dependent on slavery for its economic wealth, vigorously resisted.

Thirdly, American slaves were legally classified as chattel, a designation which essentially reduced a human being to personal property akin to livestock. And when this legal definition became too narrow to fit the needs of the slave-owning South, they (slaves) could at the same time, be assigned the status of real estate.

For example, consider the Virginia Statute of 1715:

> All Negro, mulatto, and Indian slaves within this dominion shall be held to be real estate and not chattels and shall descend unto heirs and widows according to the custom of land inheritance . . . Provided that any merchant bringing slaves into this dominion shall hold such slaves whilst they remain unsold as personal estate. All such slaves may be taken on execution as other chattels; . . . No person selling any slave shall be obliged to have the sale recorded . . . Nothing in this act shall be construed to give the owner of a slave not seized of other real estate the right to vote as a freeholder (Higginbotham, 52).

The objective here was to preserve estates for the benefit of heirs and creditors. If, upon the death of the slave owner, the slaves were treated as chattel (personal property) instead of real estate, they could be passed outside the then laws governing real property. Under the English law of primogeniture, all real property must pass to the eldest son, while personal property could be disposed of as the deceased saw fit. Therefore, if the slaves were not treated as real (estate) property, the heir could inherit house and land without slave labor to work that land. Also, creditors' secured interest is usually in the land and structures built thereon: real estate. If the slaves, upon the death of the debtor were not designated as real property then the creditors could lose out.

Observe the competing interests in the above statute which cause the law to swing back and forth between assigning slaves as chattel and as real estate. First, there is the need to have slaves treated as real estate upon the death of the slave owner as discussed above.

But then, while the slave owner is alive the slaves, by law, are his personal property and may be disposed of as he wishes. To accommodate the easy flow of commerce, the slave merchant must be allowed to hold slaves as personal property. To do otherwise would require a trip to the county courthouse or clerk to record every single sale of a slave as you would for the sale of land. And lastly, since ownership of real estate entitled one to the right to vote, the law had to make certain that ownership of a slave without ownership of *actual* real estate did not entitle one to the franchise.

The last aspect of American slavery that makes it peculiar is that it is so contrary to the basic ideals upon which this country was founded. The Declaration of Independence states,

> We hold these truths to be self-evident, that all men are created equal, that they are endowed by their Creator with certain unalienable rights, that among these are life, liberty, and the pursuit of happiness.

Of course, Thomas Jefferson and the other founding fathers (most of whom were slave owners) would tell us that African-Americans, Native Americans and women were not considered in this Declaration of Independence. They were talking primarily about men like themselves: white, landowning Anglo-Saxon Protestant (WASP) males.

It should also be noted that the slave owning South at various times felt beleaguered by the growing opposition to slavery in America. At times simply asserting that this form of labor was the most cost effective way to grow and harvest their crops, and that it was essential to its livelihood was not enough. Moral opposition to slavery needed to be blunted with arguments other than those economic. Therefore, proslavery forces found justification for their cherished "peculiar" institution elsewhere: religion and pseudo-science.

As to religious justification, three examples will suffice, one from the Old Testament and two from the New Testament. In Genesis, the first chapter of the Old Testament, Noah lay in his tent nude after passing out from too much wine. His son Ham happens upon him and then proceeds to tell others of his father's condition. Upon hearing this, two of his brothers enter the tent with eyes averted, and walking backward they place a garment over Noah. Upon hearing of Ham's ridicule, Noah curses him: "And he said, cursed be Canaan [Ham], a servant of servants shall he be unto his brethren" (Genesis 9:25). Slave owners identified Africans as the descendants of Ham and reasoned that as a result of this biblical curse they were destined to be slaves of whites, making American whites, by extension of this logic, the descendants of Shem and Japheth, the brothers who Noah blessed while cursing Ham.

This is a fascinating justification for American slavery. Apparently, Africans were meant to be slaves because Europeans, and later New World colonists, went to Africa and enslaved them. What were they and what were they meant to be *before* the Europeans and New World colonists discovered this cheap form of labor? Additionally, at various times, many slave owning whites denied the very humanity of Africans, arguing that they descended from apes while whites descended from Adam and Eve. These apparent contradictions did not inhibit their belief that Africans were ordained by the bible to be in a state of enslavement.

From the New Testament, we read in 1 Peter 2:18: "Servants, be subject to your masters with all fear, not only to the good and gentle but also to the [perverse]." In the first part of Hebrews 13:17, it states "Obey them that have the rule over you, and submit yourselves . . ."

When reading the passage from 1 Peter in context, it exhorts the Christian to suffer as Job did, for the glory of God, not submit to a cruel master for pecuniary ends, for personal greed and profit. How would this glorify Christ? And the passage from Hebrews taken in context refers to Christians obeying those who are their elders in Christ. The section of scripture immediately following the above quote states, "for they watch for your souls" (Hebrews 13:17). Thus, according to the religious slave owner, slavery was justified in the bible and a Christian slave's duty was to love and obey their slave masters if they hoped to reach heaven.

In both instances the slave owner, for his own benefit, takes these quotes out of context, but to the illiterate slave, not being able to read and interpret for himself, the message was simple and powerful. Having converted to Christianity the slave was expected to live according to the tenets as told him by his master. In addition to justifications for slavery, these scriptures were also used to keep the slave docile. These passages served the American system of slavery well.

Then there is the use of pseudo-science to justify slavery, the most popular being the theory of social Darwinism. In essence, whites were the dominant race, the theory goes, because they were the fittest. Just as nature favored specific species to survive at the expense of others, so too in the realm of mankind, the white race was destined through "natural selection" to be master over the black race. The evidence of this claim is entirely speculative, with no basis in fact. As in the case of the biblical justification involving Ham, white slave owners used past and existing condition of blacks as slaves—one whites were responsible for—to theorize why they were meant to be slaves.

Events Leading to the Civil War

The Constitution

The seeds for the American Civil War were sown in the document that created this nation, the Constitution. There were many issues that had to be addressed and solutions hammered out before a constitution could be approved by the 13 separate states. None, however, was more important than the question of slavery.

There are three instances in the Constitution where concessions are made to the southern slave holding states. The first and most significant concession is known as the Three-Fifths Compromise. The importance of this concession by the northern states can be readily seen by its very placement in the Constitution. It is found in the fourth paragraph, specifically Article I, Section 2, Paragraph 3 of the Constitution. The issue: how to count each states population to determine how many representatives each state would have in the House of Representatives.

In most Southern states the overwhelmingly slave population ranged from 21.6% to 43.7%, according to the first national census taken in 1790. In the North the black population, slave and free, ranged from .6% to 7.7% (Higginbotham, 52). It was obvious that if its slaves were not counted in population totals, the South would be at a numerical disadvantage, compared to the north in the House of Representatives. The North, of course, argued that the south could not count "chattel," beings with no rights whatsoever, and mere livestock by southern slave codes. Without a compromise, however, there would be no union, no United States. And while slavery in 1789 existed, in most states except Massachusetts and the settlement of Vermont, its gradual abolishment in the North was clearly written on the wall. Knowing this, the South insisted that its slaves be counted for purposes of determining the number of representatives it could send to Congress. It was agreed that every five "other persons" would count as three persons. While slavery is not specifically mentioned, it is clear that these "other persons" were slaves. Article I, Section 2, Paragraph 3 states:

> Representatives and direct Taxes shall be apportioned among the several States which may be included within this Union, according to their respective Numbers, [which shall be determined by adding to the whole number of free Persons, including those bound to Service for a Term of Years, And excluding Indians not taxed, *three fifths of all other Persons.* (emphasis added)

From this Compromise, the slave holding states, from Delaware on down, sent a total of 20 representatives to the first Congress, compared to 36 from the North. What would these numbers have been if just the white populations from the Southern states had been counted? The irony is that millions of disenfranchised people (the slave population was approximately 4,000,000 prior to the Civil War) were used by the enfranchised to ensure higher levels of representation in Congress for those who desired to protect their continued right of ownership of slaves. And while this difference of 16 representatives may seem large, at the signing of the Constitution, New York and New Jersey had yet to abolish slavery. New York would not do so until 1799, New Jersey not until 1846. And so for a period of time the South could rely on another 10 votes, narrowing the gap to only six.

The second reference to slavery in the Constitution states that Congress can pass no legislation, prior to 1808, that would end the flow of slaves from outside the U. S. (e.g., from Africa or the Caribbean). Article I, Section 9 states:

> The Migration or Importation of such Persons as any of the States now existing shall think proper to admit, shall not be prohibited by the Congress prior to the year one thousand eight hundred and eight. . .

Since people migrate and goods are imported, this provision refers to that commodity known as the African slave. This constitutional clause exacted a promise from the soon to-be-formed federal government that it would not interfere with access to slaves from outside the U.S. for at least 21 years. On March 2, 1807 Congress passed legislation, to become effective January 1, 1808—the first opportunity provided by the Constitution—that ended this nation's participation in the international slave trade. From 1808 on all slaves bought and sold in this country had to already exist here or be born here, It is ironic that this legislation was passed largely due to the urging of a southern (often ambivalent) slave-owning President. This president was Thomas Jefferson. He asked Congress to act at the earliest time allowed by the Constitution to end "all further participation in those violations of human rights which have been so long continued on the unoffending inhabitants of Africa." (Quarles, 78). Notwithstanding this provision, slaves continued to be smuggled into the United States well into the mid 1800's.

Lastly, Article IV, Section 3 provides that runaway slaves must be returned to their lawful owners and states from which they escaped. This constitutional provision is referred to as the fugitive slave law. It reads,

> No person held to service or labor in one State under the laws thereof, escaping into another, shall, in consequence of any law or regulation therein, be discharged from such service or labor, but shall be delivered up on claim of the party to whom such service or labor may be due.

The Missouri Compromise of 1820

The next significant event leading up to the Civil War occurred 32 years after the ratification of the Constitution. Within that period the nation had grown rapidly from the original 13 states to 22. In 1803, with the Louisiana Purchase, the United States had more than doubled in size with a then unknown number of states to emerge from this vast territory. The immediate concern in 1820 was the balance of power in Congress between the now almost completely slave free North (New Jersey and Delaware being the exceptions) and the slave owning South. From 1790 to 1817 Vermont, Ohio, Indiana, and Illinois joined the Union as free states and Kentucky, Tennessee, Louisiana, Mississippi, and Alabama entered as slave states, keeping the free-slave state balance evenly at 11 each.

Maine applied for admission. Knowing that Maine will enter as a free state, the South holds up admission over its concern of being outnumbered. This is not folly. A growing number of free states would disadvantage the South, whose primary concern is preserving and expanding slavery. A Northern majority in Congress could result in Northern control, and its setting the national agenda. This Northern agenda included abolition of slavery and failing that, stemming its spread. Southern legislators held up the admission of Maine as hostage until exacting a promise (compromise) that the Northern members of Congress agree to admit Missouri (the first state to be admitted above the 36° 30' line, the southernmost border of the Louisiana Purchase Territory) as a slave state. The North countered by exacting a commitment that Missouri would be the only slave state to exist above the 36° 30' line. This compromise kept the free-slave balance at 12 each, with the admission of Maine in March of 1820 and the admission of Missouri in August of 1821. Again, the issue of slavery played a vital part in whether this nation would remain one. Compromise in the Constitution enabled the founding of this country. This Compromise of 1820, as well numerous others to follow would avert for a while the inevitable split between free America and slave America.

The Kansas-Nebraska Act, 1854

By 1848, the United States had grown to 30 states, 15 free and 15 slave-owning. The desired balance, at least in the mind of the South, had held. In September, 1850, California is admitted as a free state. This large state with its sizable population could upset this delicate free-slave state balance. Foreseeing more and more states being formed out of the vast Louisiana Purchase Territory, the South sought recession of the Missouri Compromise of 30 years earlier. The compromise that emerged was to allow people in the territories to decide for themselves if they would enter the Union as a free or slave state. No longer was slavery forbidden by the federal government in that area north of the 36° 30' line. Hoping that more territories entering the Union would choose slavery did not happen. After California's admission in 1850 and just prior to the Civil War, Minnesota (1858) and Oregon (1859) and then Kansas (January, 1861) entered as free states. The fight for Kansas between abolitionists and pro-slavery forces was so violent that the struggle was know as "Bloody Kansas." Failure to persuade Kansas voters, along with Lincoln's election was the last straw for the South. The Union was now comprised of 15 slave states and 19 free states, with plenty of space in the western states to accommodate expanding, likely, free states.

The Dred Scott Decision (1857)

While losing in the free versus slave statehood battle, the South would in 1857 receive the validation from our highest court. Among other things the court found explicitly for the first time a constitutional right for one man to own another, and that the federal government lacked the authority to prevent the spread of slavery.

Dred Scott was a slave whose first master moved him from Virginia to Missouri. While in Missouri, Scott was sold to an army surgeon, Emerson. This army doctor moved from military post to military post between 1832 and 1843, first Illinois, then what is current-day St. Paul, Minnesota, then to Louisiana, and finally back to Missouri in 1843. Scott and his wife Harriet were with Emerson in each of these moves. The Scotts were back in Missouri for three years before suing for their freedom in 1846. They had learned that they had once lived in a free state (Illinois) and then territory where slavery was prohibited by the federal government in the Missouri Compromise of 1820. Scott's claims were that since he had once lived in a free state and free territory, he was therefore free.

The U.S. Supreme Court Chief Justice Roger B. Taney, a former Southern slave owner, wrote the majority opinion, and framed the question before the Court in such a way that the answer was inevitable:

Can a negro, whose ancestors were imported into this country, and sold, as slaves, become a member of the political community formed and brought into existence by the Constitution of the United States, and as such become entitled to all the rights, and privileges, and immunities, guaranteed by that instrument to the citizen? One of which rights is the privilege of suing in a court of the United States in the cases specified in the Constitution.

The Court answered, "no." Taney asserts blacks, slave or free, were never intended to be included in the "community" formed by the Constitution. And since they were never meant to be included as citizens, they had no rights ("privileges and immunities") of citizenship. One of these rights is that of bringing suit in federal court. Thus, Scott doesn't even have the right to petition the Supreme Court. The practical result is that the Court lacked jurisdiction to hear the case. In such cases, the ruling of the lower court would stand as the final decision. The Missouri Supreme Court had ruled against Scott. But a most curious thing happens, something completely outside the usual rules of jurisdiction. *Having said that it lacks jurisdiction to hear the case, the U.S. Supreme Court goes on to do just that*, in the process it not only ruled on Scott's fate but on past congressional legislation regarding slavery and one's property rights to slave ownership.

But again, why does the Court decide to hear a case it says it has no authority to hear? This Court, specifically Taney, took a similar approach six years earlier when it commented on the *Strader* case of 1851.[iii] In that case, a Kentucky slave owner allowed three of his slaves who were musicians to regularly cross over into Ohio to perform. With the help of a man named Strader, they escaped into Canada. The slave owner sued Strader and his case reached the U.S. Supreme Court. While noting that it lacked jurisdiction, the Court went on to say that if the runaways returned to Kentucky, they would once again have the legal status of slaves. The theory was that if a runaway slave escaped into a free state or territory and returned to a slave state, he "reverted" to his former slave status.

The *Strader* case (1851) and now the *Dred Scott* case were attempts by the U.S. Supreme Court to advance the aggrieved rights and interests of slave owners. The objective was no grander than that of settling once and for all the legal questions regarding slavery that had plagued this nation since its inception: is slavery legal? Where can slavery exist and where can it be banned? The Court would, in one fell swoop, end the national debate (so it thought) over slavery. No more Missouri Compromises, Kansas-Nebraska Acts, or other congressional attempts to accommodate competing interests. The issues in *Strader* did not afford them the opportunity to accomplish their purpose, but the *Scott* case did.

The Court first says it lacks jurisdiction to hear Scott's case and in the same paragraph denies citizenship to all blacks, slave or free. Having accomplished this the Court now decides that an act of Congress, the Missouri Compromise passed some 37 years ago, and nullified by the Kansas-Nebraska Act of 1854, was unconstitutional. It also held that the Fifth Amendment denied Congress this authority. The Court relied on that clause of the Fifth Amendment which says that no person could be "deprived of . . . property, without due process of law."

Since the Court recognized the rights of whites to hold property in another person (slaves), Congress by prohibiting ownership of slave property in the lands north of the 36°30' latitude was depriving the slave owner of his lawful property without due process. The Court said that ownership of slave property was like ownership of any other kind of property. The federal government could not grant ownership of this property in one place and deny it in another.

In examining the Court's rationale for its rulings, it is easy to dismiss it as pure racism (five of the nine justices were from the South). However, there are other crucial objectives, such as the protection of states' rights and individual rights to property and limiting the interference of the federal government in the expansion of the nation. The *Dred Scott* case was like the perfect storm. All of the elements were so aligned as to give the Court sway to settle slavery matters that it was probably itching to do for years. It just needed the right case.

The Court's primary justification for the exclusion of blacks, slave or free, from all aspects of American-hood was based on the history of the African in America. As with the troublesome justifications discussed earlier, blacks' condition, as brought upon by the white man, was used as a rationale for this very condition. This needs analysis.

The narrow issue before the Court was whether the slave Dred Scott could claim his freedom based on the facts presented. But Taney uses this case to inform free blacks that they too were excluded from citizenship. While it would be illogical to think that a slave in any society, now or thousands of years ago, would have the rights of citizenship, those free blacks, overwhelmingly in the North, had enjoyed the benefits of citizenship afforded by these states (some as early as 1787) and exercised such rights as that of the right to vote, own property, sue in court, or hold elective office. The highest Court now tells these blacks that not only were they not citizens of the United States but were not even citizens of the state wherein they resided. The circumstances under which Africans came to America and subsequent social and legal treatment justified their exclusion from the privileges and immunities of citizenship:

> No one of that race had ever migrated to the United States voluntarily; all of them had been brought here as articles of merchandise . . . It is obvious that they were not even in the minds of the framers of the Constitution when they were conferring special rights and privileges upon the citizens of a State in every other part of the union.

Thus, because they did not come here voluntarily, but were imported as a commodity, they and their descendants, including free blacks, were not fit to "associate with the white race."

Taney even uses the Constitution and the Declaration of Independence to make his case. He cites two of the references discussed (Article I, Section 9 and Article IV, Section 3) as proof of slavery's acceptance by the founding fathers.

As to the Declaration of Independence, the Court concludes, again from past treatment of blacks that they were not part of those addressed by that document:

... In the opinion of the court, the legislation and histories of the times, and the language used in the Declaration of Independence, show, that neither the class of persons who had been imported as slaves, nor their descendants, whether they had become free or not, were then acknowledged as part of the people, nor intended to be included in the general words used in that memorable instrument.

The U.S. Supreme Court confirms the basest of American prejudices. This is not the Court's finest hour. Instead of quelling the brewing separatists' storm, it fueled it. While the South was elated, the North was infuriated. The Supreme Court, whose decisions are the law of the land, had just determined that slavery and the inferiority of the black race were written in and thus guaranteed by the Constitution, that ownership in a person of the black race was also guaranteed by that founding document, which all states were obligated to obey. This meant that a slave owner from Virginia, for example, could bring his slaves to Massachusetts and under his guaranteed constitutional rights, and Massachusetts was powerless to do anything about it. It meant that the effort to stem the spread of slavery could no longer by affected by the federal government.

Assuming that Taney is right in all his assumptions about the intent of the Founding Fathers' to exclude all blacks from this American Democracy, and aside from it being morally repugnant, why is this still a very bad decision? In answer, the Supreme Court could have simply looked to the *actual words* of the two founding documents. Why rely on suspect history and self-serving assumptions? Neither document, technically, excludes anyone from participation in the freedoms, rights, privileges *and citizenship* in the nation formed by these documents. Indeed, why not just look to ". . . all men are created equal."

Lincoln's Views and His Election

The newly formed Republican Party's 1860 presidential platform included the overturn of the Dred Scott decision and a halt to any further spread of slavery beyond existing states and a return to prohibiting slavery in the territories, from which some 14 states would eventually come. Abraham Lincoln's overwhelming victory sealed the fate of a soon-to-be divided nation and a civil war. John C. Breckinridge of the Southern Democratic Party carried the nine southern states that would later become the Confederate States of America with 72 electoral votes. Stephen A. Douglas of the Northern Democratic Party received 12 electoral votes to Lincoln's 180.

Following the election, in December 1860 South Carolina seceded from the Union. On January 29, 1861, Kansas enters the Union as a free state. In February, one month before Lincoln's inauguration, the states of Mississippi, Alabama, Louisiana, and Georgia also secede. In April, after the Confederate army attempts to capture Fort Sumter, Virginia, North Carolina, Tennessee, and Arkansas completed the process of nine states seceding. A separate nation, called the Confederate States of America, was created. Lincoln, determined to keep one nation intact, stated in his inaugural address that "plainly, the central idea of secession is the essence of anarchy" (Hines et. al, 256).

It is ironic that the issue of slavery, which the nation grappled with since its inception, brought on the war, but the war was not fought to end slavery. Rather it was to preserve that Union formed some 72 years earlier. While Lincoln opposed slavery, his speeches during the 1860 presidential campaign focused not on his personal belief but rather on his party's platform of halting the spread of slavery. He also stated in that inaugural speech, in the hope of appeasing the seceding states:

> I have no purpose, directly or indirectly, to interfere with the institution of slavery in the States where it exists. I believe I have no lawful right to do so, and I have no inclination to do so. (Hines et. al., 255)

Since this was Lincoln's position from the day he was nominated and throughout the campaign, why did his election spark rebellion? Why couldn't the south accept any further expansion of slavery?

The Supreme Court's decision in the *Dred Scott* case was a tremendous victory for pro-slavery states. It validated their cherished institution. The presidency going to a party and person dedicated to its refusal was unacceptable. With the 1860 election of Lincoln and losing the cherished balance of power in both houses of Congress, the South thought it inevitable that *Scott* would indeed be overturned through either legislation or constitutional amendment, efforts it would be powerless to stop. Further, if *Scott* was overturned there would be no possibility of further extension of slavery in the yet to be settled vast western territory which would one day carve out a then unknown number of states. This would put anti-slavery proponents in an even stronger position to control the national agenda. To the South, the death of expansion of slavery meant the inevitable death of slavery in America to the South. And further, the fine distinction made by Lincoln in opposing slavery on moral grounds but accepting it where it currently existed was probably lost on the average Southerner.

Lincoln's Views on Race

To the popular mind Abraham Lincoln was a stalwart opponent of slavery and a great friend of the black race. While the former is true, the latter was not always the case. In fact, using language much like that in the *Dred Scott* case, a case which he and his party were bent on overturning, Lincoln says that blacks are neither socially nor politically equal to whites, therefore not worthy of association. Lincoln's solution for the two races was for all blacks to leave this country and resettle elsewhere.

During his presidential debates with Stephen Douglas, Lincoln repeatedly corrected the portrayal of him and his party as promoters of racial equality. Opposing slavery, he said, did not mean a belief in equality of the races:

> I do not understand that because I do not want a negro woman for a slave I must necessarily have her for a wife . . . I am not, nor ever have been in favor of bring-

ing about in any way the social and political equality with black races—that I am not nor ever have been in favor of making voters or jurors of negroes, nor of qualifying them to hold office, nor intermarry with white people; and I will say in addition to this that there is a physical difference between the races which I believe will forever forbid the two races living together on terms of social and political equity (Hines et. al, 250).

On August 14, 1862, Lincoln told a group of black leaders he had invited to the White House:

> You and we are different races. We have between us a broader difference than exists between almost any other two races. Whether it is right or wrong I need not discuss, but this physical difference is a great disadvantage to us both, as I think your race suffers greatly, many of them by living among us, while ours suffers from your presence (Bennett, 192).

The solution? Blacks would have to leave America. Lincoln supported the resettlement of free blacks in Liberia, Haiti, or Central America (present day Panama). Lincoln's social views soften before the end of the war. Many attribute this to his recognition of the invaluable assistance of black soldiers in the war and the life and intellect of Frederick Douglass.

This brief history of blacks in America prior to the Civil War explores the genesis of race relations in the United States. The reader should take away from this history three important points. First, that racial policy in the United States was motivated by prejudice, greed and fear. Second, Federal and State Courts have played an important role in hindering and aiding the struggle for racial equality. And lastly, there was no common experience for blacks, free and slave. Opportunities and obstacles varied by geographical arena.

Supreme Court Cases Cited

Dred Scott v. Sandford, 60 U.S. (19How.) 393 (1857)
Loving v. Virginia, 338 U.S. 1 (1967)
Strader v. Graham 51 U.S. (10How.) 82 (1851)

Sources

Lerone Bennett, Jr., *Before The Mayflower: A History of Black America* (New York: Penguin Books, 6th revised, 1993).

Carl Bridenbaugh, *Jamestown: 1544–1699* (Bridgewater, NJ: Replica Books, 2000).

Helen Catterall, ed., *Judicial Cases Concerning American Slavery and the Negro*, vol. 1 (Washington , D.C., : Negro University. 1926).

Abraham L. Davis and Barbara Luck Graham, *The Supreme Court, Race and Civil Rights*, Thousand Oaks, California: 1995).

Fred W. Friendly and Martha J. H. Elliott, *The Constitution, That Delicate Balance; Landmark Cases that Shaped the Constitution,* (New York: Random House, 1984).

Don E. Fehrenbacher, *The Dred Scott Case, Its Significance in American Law and Politics,* (New York: Oxford University Press, 1978).

John Hope Franklin and Alfred A. Moss, Jr., *From Slavery To Freedom, A History of African Americans,* 7th ed. (New York: McGraw-Hill, 1994).

John Gunther, *Inside Africa* (New York: Harper & Brothers, 1955).

Willliam W. Hening, *Statutes at Large of Virginia,* vol. 1 (Richmond, Va.; Franklin Press, 1819–1820).

Leon Higginbotham, Jr., *In The Matter of Color, Race & The Legal Process: The Colonial Period* (New York: Oxford Univ. Press, 1980).

Darlene Clark Hine, William C. Hine and Stanley Harrold, *The African-American Odyssey,* 4th ed., combined vol. (Upper Saddle River, New Jersey: Pearson/Prentice Hall, 2008).

Kenneth Morgan, *Slavery and Servitude in Colonial North America,* (New York: New York Univ. Press, 2000).

Allan Nevins, *War For The Union, 1864–1865, The Organized War To Victory,* 4 vol. set (New York: Koneck & Konecky, 1971.)

Nathaniel Philbrick, *Mayflower: A Story of Courage, Community, and War* (New York: Viking. Penguin Group, 2006).

David A. Price, *Love And Hate In Jamestown: John Smith, Pocahontas, And The Heart Of A New Nation* (New York: Alfred A. Knopf, 2003).

Benjamin Quarles, *The Negro in the Making of America,* 3rd ed., (New York: MacMillan Publishing, 1964).

Paula S. Rothenberg, ed. *Race, Class, and Gender in the United States,* 5th ed. (New York: Worth Publishers, 2001).

Kenneth M. Stampp, *The Peculiar Institution, Slavery in the Ante-Bellum South,* New York: Vintage Books, 1056).

John C. Waugh, *Reelecting Lincoln, The Battle for the 1864 Presidency* (New York: Crown Publishers, 1997).

Betty Wood, *Slavery in Colonial American: 1619–1776,* (New York: Rowan & Littlefield, 2005).

Endnotes

i. See, generally, Nathaniel Philbrick *Mayflower: A Story of Courage, Community, and War* (New York: Viking. Penguin Group, 2006); and David A. Price *Love And Hate In Jamestown: John Smith, Pocahontas, And The Heart Of A New Nation* (New York: Alfred A. Knopf, 2003).

ii.. Quock Walker v. Jennison; Jennison v. Caldwell, Proc. Mass. Hist. Soc. 1873–1875, 296 (September. 1781)

iii. In his exhaustive study (595 pages), *The Dred Scott Case, Its Significance in American Law and Politics*, (New York: Oxford University Press, 1978), Don E. Fehrenbacher, casts real doubt as to whether Chief Justice Roger Taney had a majority vote of the court when he rushed *his* opinion to the printers, especially on the issues of citizenship for free blacks and the constitutionality of the Missouri Compromise. The publication of the decision actually caught the other justices off guard, in particular the four from the North.

21

The Black Codes

W. E. B. Du Bois

The whole proof of what the South proposed to do to the emancipated Negro, unless restrained by the nation, was shown in the Black Codes passed after [President Andrew] Johnson's accession, but representing the logical result of attitudes of mind existing when Lincoln still lived. Some of these were passed and enforced. Some were passed and afterward repealed or modified when the reaction of the North was realized. In other cases, as for instance, in Louisiana, it is not clear just which laws were retained and which were repealed. In Alabama, the Governor induced the legislature not to enact some parts of the proposed code which they overwhelmingly favored.

The original codes favored by the Southern legislatures were an astonishing affront to emancipation and dealt with vagrancy, apprenticeship, labor contracts, migration, civil and legal rights. In all cases, there was plain and indisputable attempt on the part of the Southern states to make Negroes slaves in everything but name. They were given certain civil rights: the right to hold property, to sue and be sued. The family relations for the first time were legally recognized. Negroes were no longer real estate.

Yet, in the face of this, the Black Codes were deliberately designed to take advantage of every misfortune of the Negro. Negroes were liable to a slave trade under the guise of vagrancy and apprenticeship laws; to make the best labor contracts, Negroes must leave the old plantations and seek better terms; but if caught wandering in search of work, and thus unemployed and without a home, this was vagrancy, and the victim could be whipped and sold into slavery. In the turmoil of war, children were separated from parents, or parents unable to support them properly. These children could be sold into slavery, and "the former owner of said minors shall have the preference." Negroes could come into court as witnesses only in cases in which Negroes were involved. And even then, they must make their appeal to a jury and judge who would believe the word of any white man in preference to that of any Negro on pain of losing office and caste.

The Negro's access to the land was hindered and limited; his right to work was curtailed; his right of self-defense was taken away, when his right to bear arms was stopped; and his employment was virtually reduced to contract labor with penal servitude as a punishment for leaving his job. And in all cases, the judges of the Negro's guilt or innocence, rights and obligations were men who believed firmly, for the most part, that he had "no rights which a white man was bound to respect."

Making every allowance for the excitement and turmoil of war, and the mentality of a defeated people, the Black Codes were infamous pieces of legislation.

Let us examine these codes in detail.[1] They covered, naturally, a wide range of subjects. First, there was the question of allowing Negroes to come into the state. In South Carolina the constitution of 1865 permitted the Legislature to regulate immigration, and the consequent law declared "that no person of color shall migrate into and reside in this State, unless, within twenty days after his arrival within the same, he shall enter into a bond, with two freeholders as sureties . . . in a penalty of one thousand dollars, conditioned for his good behavior, and for his support."

Especially in the matter of work was the Negro narrowly restricted. In South Carolina, he must be especially licensed if he was to follow on his own account any employment, except that of farmer or servant. Those licensed must not only prove their fitness, but pay an annual tax ranging front $10–$100. Under no circumstances could they manufacture or sell liquor. Licenses for work were to be granted by a judge and were revokable on complaint. The penalty was a fine double the amount of the license, one-half of which went to the informer.

Mississippi provided that "every freedman, free Negro, and mulatto shall on the second Monday of January, one thousand eight hundred and sixty-six, and annually thereafter, have a lawful home or employment, and shall have written evidence thereof . . . from the Mayor . . . or from a member of the board of police . . . which licenses may be revoked for cause at any time by the authority granting the same."

Detailed regulation of labor was provided for in nearly all these states.

Louisiana passed an elaborate law in 1865, to "regulate labor contracts for agricultural pursuits." Later, it was denied that this legislation was actually enacted but the law was published at the time and the constitutional convention of 1868 certainly regarded this statute as law, for they formally repealed it. The law required all agricultural laborers to make labor contracts for the next year within the first ten days of January, the contracts to be in writing, to be with heads of families, to embrace the labor of all the members, and to be "binding on all minors thereof." Each laborer, after choosing his employer, "shall not be allowed to leave his place of employment, until the fulfillment of his contract, unless by consent of his employer, or on account of harsh treatment, or breach of contract on the part of the employer; and if they do so leave, without cause or permission, they shall forfeit all wages earned to the time of abandonment. . . .

"In case of sickness of the laborer, wages for the time lost shall be deducted, and where the sickness is feigned for purposes of idleness, . . . and also should refusal to work be continued beyond three days, the offender shall be reported to a justice of the peace, and shall be forced to labor on roads, levees, and other public works, without pay, until the offender consents to return to his labor. . . .

"When in health, the laborer shall work ten hours during the day in summer, and nine hours during the day in winter, unless otherwise stipulated in the labor contract; he shall obey all proper orders of his employer or his agent; take proper care of his work mules, horses, oxen, stock; also of all agricultural implements; and employers shall have the right to make a reasonable deduction from the laborer's wages for injuries done to animals or agricultural implements committed to his care, or for bad or negligent work. Bad work shall not be allowed. Failing to obey reasonable orders, neglect of duty and leaving home without permission, will be deemed disobedience. . . . For any disobedience a fine of one dollar shall be imposed on the offender. For all lost time from work hours, unless in case of sickness, the laborer shall be fined twenty-five cents per hour. For all absence from home without leave, the laborer will be fined at the rate of two dollars per day. Laborers will not be required to labor on the Sabbath except to take the necessary care of stock and other property on plantations and do the necessary cooking and household duties, unless by special contract. For all thefts of the laborers from the employer of agricultural products, hogs, sheep, poultry or any other property of the employer, or willful destruction of property or injure, the laborer shall pay the employer double the amount of the value of the property stolen, destroyed or injured, one half to be paid to the employer, and the other half to be placed in the general fund provided for in this section. No live stock shall be allowed to laborers without the permission of the employer. Laborers shall not receive visitors during work hours. All difficulties arising between the employers and laborers, under this section, shall be settled, and all fines be imposed, by the former; if not satisfactory to the laborers, an appeal may be had to the nearest justice of the peace and two freeholders, citizens, one of said citizens to be selected by the employer and the other by the laborer; and all fines imposed and collected under this section shall be deducted from the wages due, and shall be placed in a common fund, to be divided among the other laborers employed on the plantation at the time when their full wages fall due, except as provided for above."

Similar detailed regulations of work were in the South Carolina law. Elaborate provision was made for contracting colored "servants" to white "masters." Their masters were given the right to whip "moderately" servants under eighteen. Others were to be whipped on authority of judicial officers. These officers were given authority to return runaway servants to their masters. The servants, on the other hand, were given certain rights. Their wages and period of service must be specified in writing, and they were protected against "unreasonable" tasks, Sunday and night work, unauthorized attacks on their persons, and inadequate food.

Contracting Negroes were to be known as "servants" and contractors as "masters." Wages were to be fixed by the judge, unless stipulated. Negroes of ten years of age or more without a parent living in the district might make a valid contract for a year or less. Failure to make written contracts was a misdemeanor, punishable by a fine of $5 to $50; farm labor to be from sunrise to sunset, with intervals for meals; servants to rise at dawn, to be careful of master's property and answerable for property lost or injured. Lost time was to be deducted from wages. Food and clothes might be deducted. Servants were to be quiet and orderly and to go to bed at reasonable hours. No night work or outdoor work in bad weather was to be asked, except in cases of necessity, visitors not allowed without the master's consent. Servants leaving employment without good reason must forfeit wages. Masters might discharge servants for disobedience, drunkenness, disease, absence, etc. Enticing away the services of a servant was punishable by a fine of $20 to $100. A master could command a servant to aid him in defense of his own person, family or property. House servants at all hours of the day and night, and at all days of the weeks, "must answer promptly all calls and execute all lawful orders. . . ."

Mississippi provided "that every civil officer shall, and every person may, arrest and carry back to his or her legal employer any freedman, free Negro, or mulatto who shall have quit the service of his or her employer before the expiration of his or her term of service without good cause; and said officer and person shall be entitled to receive for arresting and carrying back every deserting employee aforesaid the sum of five dollars, and ten cents per mile from the place of arrest to the place of delivery, and the same shall be paid by the employer and held as a set-off for so much against the wages of said deserting employee."

It was provided in some states, like South Carolina, that any white man, whether an officer or not, could arrest a Negro. "Upon view of a misdemeanor committed by a person of color, any person present may arrest the offender and take him before a magistrate, to be dealt with as the case may require. In case of a misdemeanor committed by a white person toward a person of color, any person may complain to a magistrate, who shall cause the offender to be arrested, and according to the nature of the case, to be brought before himself, or be taken for trial in the district court."

On the other hand, in Mississippi, it was dangerous for a Negro to try to bring a white person to court on any charge. "In every case where any white person has been arrested and brought to trial, by virtue of the provisions of the tenth section of the above recited act, in any court in this State, upon sufficient proof being made to the court or jury, upon the trial before said court, that any freedman, free Negro or mulatto has falsely and maliciously caused the arrest and trial of said white person or persons, the court shall render up a judgment against said freedman, free Negro or mulatto for all costs of the case, and impose a fine not to exceed fifty dollars, and imprisonment in the county jail not to exceed twenty days; and for a failure of said freedman, free Negro or mulatto to pay, or cause to be paid, all costs, fines and jail fees, the sheriff of the county is hereby authorized and required, after giving ten days' public notice, to proceed to hire out at public outcry, at the courthouse of the county, said freedman, free Negro or mulatto, for the shortest time to raise the amount necessary to discharge said freedman, free Negro or mulatto from all costs, fines, and jail fees aforesaid."

Mississippi declared that: "Any freedman, free Negro, or mulatto, committing riots, routs, affrays, trespasses, malicious mischief and cruel treatment to animals, seditious speeches, instilling gestures, language or acts, or assaults on any person, disturbance of the peace, exercising the functions of a minister of the gospel without a license from some regularly organized church, vending spirituous or intoxicating liquors, or committing any other misdemeanor, the punishment of which is not specifically provided for by law, shall, upon conviction thereof, in the county court, be fined not less than ten dollars, and not more than one hundred dollars, and may be imprisoned, at the discretion of the court, not exceeding thirty days. . . ."

The most important and oppressive laws were those with regard to vagrancy and apprenticeship. Sometimes they especially applied to Negroes; in other cases, they were drawn in general terms but evidently designed to fit the Negro's condition and to be enforced particularly with regard to Negroes.

The Virginia Vagrant Act enacted that "any justice of the peace, upon the complaint of any one of certain officers therein named, may issue his warrant for the apprehension of any person alleged to be a vagrant and cause such person to be apprehended and brought before hint; and that if upon due examination said justice of the peace shall find that such person is a vagrant within the definition of vagrancy contained in said statute, he shall issue his warrant, directing such person to be employed for a term not exceeding three months, and by any constable of the county wherein the proceedings are had, be hired out for the best wages which can be procured, his wages to be applied to the support of himself and his family. The said statute further provides, that in case any vagrant so hired shall, during his term of service, run away from his employer without sufficient cause, he shall be apprehended on the warrant of a justice of the peace and returned to the custody of his employer, who shall then have free from any other hire, the services of such vagrant for one month in addition to the original term of hiring, and that the employer shall then have power, if authorized by a justice of the peace, to work such vagrant with ball and chain. The said statute specified the persons who shall be considered vagrants and liable to the penalties imposed by it. Among those declared to be vagrants are all persons who, not having the wherewith to support their families, live idly and without employment, and refuse to work for the usual and common wages given to other laborers in the like work in the place where they are."

In Florida, January 12, 1866: "It is provided that when any person of color shall enter into a contract as aforesaid, to serve as a laborer for a year, or any other specified term, on any farm or plantation in this State, if he shall refuse or neglect to perform the stipulations of his contract by willful disobedience of orders, wanton impudence or disrespect to his employer, or his authorized agent, failure or refusal to perform the work assigned to him, idleness, or abandonment of the premises or the employment of the party with whom the contract was made, he or she shall be liable, upon the complaint of his employer or his agent, made under oath before any justice of the peace of the county, to be arrested and tried before the criminal court of the county, and upon conviction shall be subject to all the pains and penalties prescribed for the punishment of vagrancy."

In Georgia, it was ruled that "All persons wandering or strolling about in idleness, who are able in work, and who have no property to support them; all persons leading an idle, immoral, or profligate life, who have no property to support them and are able to work and do not work; all persons able to work having no visible and known means of a fair, honest, and respectable livelihood; all persons having a fixed abode, who have no visible property to support them, and who live by stealing or by trading in, bartering for, or buying stolen property; and all professional gamblers living in idleness, shall be deemed and considered vagrants, and shall be indicated as such, and it shall be lawful for any person to arrest said vagrants and have them bound over for trial to the next term of the county court, and upon conviction, they shall be fined and imprisoned or sentenced to work on the public works, for not longer than a year, or shall, in the discretion of the court, be bound over for trial to the next term of the county court, and upon conviction, they shall be fined and imprisoned or sentenced to work on the public works, for not longer than a year, or shall, in the discretion of the court, be bound out to some person for a time not longer than one year, upon such valuable consideration as the court may prescribe."

Mississippi provided "That all freedmen, free Negroes, and mulattoes in this state over the age of eighteen years, found on the second Monday in January, 1866, or thereafter, with no lawful employment or business, or found unlawfully assembling themselves together, either in the day or night time, and all white persons so assembling with freedmen, free Negroes or mulattoes, or usually associating with freedmen, free Negroes or mulattoes on terms of equality, or living in adultery or fornication with a freedwoman, free Negro or mulatto, shall be deemed vagrants, and on conviction thereof shall be fined in the sum of not exceeding, in the case of a freedman, free Negro or mulatto, fifty dollars, and a white man two hundred dollars and imprisoned, at the discretion of the court, the free Negro not exceeding ten days, and the white men not exceeding six months."

Sec. 5 provides that all fines and forfeitures collected under the provisions of this act shall be paid into the county treasury for general county purposes, and in case any freedman, free Negro or mulatto, shall fail for five days after the imposition of any fine or forfeiture upon him or her, for violation of any of the provisions of this act to pay the same, that it shall be, and is hereby made, the duty of the Sheriff of the proper county to hire out said freedman, free Negro or mulatto, to any person who will, for the shortest period of service, pay said fine or forfeiture and all costs; *Provided*, a preference shall be given to the employer, if there be one, in which case the employer shall be entitled to deduct and retain the amount so paid from the wages of such freedman, free Negro or mulatto, then due or to become due; and in case such freedman, free Negro or mulatto cannot be hired out, he or she may be dealt with as a pauper. . . ."

In Alabama, the "former owner" was to have preference in the apprenticing of a child. This was true in Kentucky and Mississippi.

Mississippi "provides that it shall be the duty of all sheriffs, justices of the peace, and other civil officers of the several counties in this state to report to the probate courts of their respective counties semi-annually, at the January and July terms of said courts, all freedmen, free Negroes and mulattoes, under the age of eighteen, within their respective counties, beats, or districts, who are orphans, or whose parent or parents have not the means, or who refuse to provide for and support said minors, and thereupon it shall be the duty of said probate court to order the clerk of said court to apprentice said minors to some competent and suitable person, on such terms as the court may direct, having a particular care to the interest of said minors; *Provided*, that the former owner of said minors shall have the preference when, in the opinion of the court, he or she shall be a suitable person for that purpose. . . ."

"Capital punishment was provided for colored persons guilty of willful homicide, assault upon a white woman, impersonating her husband for carnal purposes, raising an insurrection, stealing a horse, a mule, or baled cotton, and housebreaking. For crimes not demanding death Negroes might be confined at hard labor, whipped, or transported; 'but punishments more degrading than imprisonment shall not be imposed upon a white person for a crime not infamous.'"[2]

In most states Negroes were allowed to testify in courts but the testimony was usually confined to cases where colored persons were involved, although in some states, by consent of the parties, they could testify in cases where only white people were involved. . . .

Mississippi simply reenacted her slave code and made it operative so far as punishments were concerned. "That all the penal and criminal laws now in force in this State, defining offenses, and prescribing the mode of punishment for crimes and misdemeanors committed by slaves, free Negroes or mulattoes, be and the same are hereby reenacted, and declared to be in full force and effect, against freedmen, free Negroes, and mulattoes, except so far as the mode and manner of trial and punishment have been changed or altered by law."

North Carolina, on the other hand, abolished her slave code, making difference of punishment only in the case of Negroes convicted of rape. Georgia placed the fines and costs of a servant upon the master. "Where such cases shall go against the servant, the judgment for costs upon written notice to the master shall operate as a garnishment against him, and he shall retain a sufficient amount for the payment thereof, out of any wages due to said servant, or to become due during the period of service, and may be cited at any time by the collecting officer to make answer thereto."

The celebrated ordinance of Opelousas, Louisiana, shows the local ordinances regulating Negroes. "No Negro or freedman shall be allowed to come within the limits of the town of Opelousas without special permission from his employer, specifying the object of his visit and the time necessary for the accomplishment of the same.

"Every Negro freedman who shall be found on the streets of Opelousas after ten o'clock at night without a written pass or permit from his employer, shall be imprisoned and compelled to work five days on the public streets, or pay a fine of five dollars.

"No Negro or freedman shall be permitted to rent or keep a house within the limits of the town under any circumstances, and anyone thus offending shall be ejected, and compelled to find an employer or leave the town within twenty-four hours.

"No Negro or freedman shall reside within the limits of the town of Opelousas who is not in the regular service of some white person or former owner, who shall be held responsible for the conduct of said freedman.

"No Negro or freedman shall be permitted to preach, exhort, or otherwise declaim to congregations of colored people without a special permission from the Mayor or President of the Board of Police, under the penalty of a fine of ten dollars or twenty days' work on the public streets.

"No freedman who is not in the military service shall be allowed to carry firearms, or any kind of weapons within the limits of the town of Opelousas without the special permission of his employer, in writing, and approved by the Mayor or President of the Board.

"Any freedman not residing in Opelousas, who shall be found within its corporate limits after the hour of 3 o'clock, on Sunday, without a special permission from his employer or the Mayor, shall be arrested and imprisoned and made to work two days on the public streets, or pay two dollars in lieu of said work."[3]

Of Louisiana, Thomas Conway testified February 22, 1866: "Some of the leading officers of the state down there—men who do much to form and control the opinions of the masses—instead of doing as they promised, and quietly submitting to the authority of the government, engaged in issuing slave codes and in promulgating them to their subordinates, ordering them to carry them into execution, and this to the knowledge of state officials of a higher character, the governor and others. And the men who issued them were not punished except as the military authorities punished them. The governor inflicted no punishment on them while I was there, and I don't know that, up to this day, he has ever punished one of them. These codes were simply the old black code of the state, with the word 'slave' expunged, and 'Negro' substituted. The most odious features of slavery were preserved in them. . . ."[4]

Endnotes

1. Quotations from McPherson, *History of United States during Reconstruction*, pp. 29–44.
2. Simkins and Woody, *South Carolina during Reconstruction*, pp. 49, 50.
3. Warmoth, *War, Politics and Reconstruction*, p. 274.
4. *Report on the Joint Committee on Reconstruction*, 1866, Part IV, pp. 78–79.

22

Narrative of the Life of Frederick Douglass, An American Slave

Chapter I

I was born in Tuckahoe, near Hillsborough, and about twelve miles from Easton, in Talbot county, Maryland. I have no accurate knowledge of my age, never having seen any authentic record containing it. By far the larger part of the slaves know as little of their ages as horses know of theirs, and it is the wish of most masters within my knowledge to keep their slaves thus ignorant. I do not remember to have ever met a slave who could tell of his birthday. They seldom come nearer to it than planting-time, harvest-time, cherry-time, spring-time, or fall-time. A want of information concerning my own was a source of unhappiness to me even during childhood. The white children could tell their ages. I could not tell why I ought to be deprived of the same privilege. I was not allowed to make any inquiries of my master concerning it. He deemed all such inquiries on the part of a slave improper and impertinent, and evidence of a restless spirit. The nearest estimate I can give makes me now between twenty-seven and twenty-eight years of age. I come to this, from hearing my master say, some time during 1835, I was about seventeen years old.

My mother was named Harriet Bailey. She was the daughter of Isaac and Betsey Bailey, both colored, and quite dark. My mother was of a darker complexion than either my grandmother or grandfather.

My father was a white man. He was admitted to be such by all I ever heard speak of my parentage. The opinion was also whispered that my master was my father; but of the correctness of this opinion, I know nothing; the means of knowing was withheld from me. My mother and I were separated when I was but an infant—before I knew her as my mother. It is a common custom, in the part of Maryland from which I ran away, to part children from their mothers at a very early age. Frequently, before the child has reached its twelfth month, its mother is taken from it, and hired out on some farm a considerable distance off, and the child is placed under the care of an old woman, too old for field labor. For what this separation is done, I do not know, unless it be to hinder the development of the child's affection toward its mother, and to blunt and destroy the natural affection of the mother for the child. This is the inevitable result.

I never saw my mother, to know her as such, more than four or five times in my life; and each of those times was very short in duration, and at night. She was hired by a Mr. Stewart, who lived about twelve miles from my home. She made her journeys to see me in the night, travelling the whole distance on foot, after the performance of her day's work. She was a field hand, and a whipping is the penalty of not being in the field at sunrise, unless a slave has special permission from his or her master to the contrary—a permission which they seldom get, and one that gives to him that gives it the proud name of being a kind master. I do not recollect of ever seeing my mother by the light of day. She was with me in the night. She would lie down with me, and get me to sleep, but long before I waked she was gone. Very little communication ever took place between us. Death soon ended what little we could have while she lived, and with it her hardships and suffering. She died when I was about seven years old, on one of my master's farms, near Lee's Mill. I was not allowed to be present during her illness, at her death, or burial. She was gone long before I knew any thing about it. Never having enjoyed, to any considerable extent, her soothing presence, her tender and watchful care, I received the tidings of her death with much the same emotions I should have probably felt at the death of a stranger.

Called thus suddenly away, she left me without the slightest intimation of who my father was. The whisper that my master was my father, may or may not be true; and, true or false, it is of but little consequence to my purpose whilst the fact remains, in all its glaring odiousness, that slaveholders have ordained, and by law established, that the children of slave women shall in all cases follow the condition of their mothers; and this is done too obviously to administer to their own lusts, and make a gratification of their wicked desires profitable as well as pleasurable; for by this cunning arrangement, the slaveholder, in cases not a few, sustains to his slaves the double relation of master and father.

I know of such cases; and it is worthy of remark that such slaves invariably suffer greater hardships, and have more to contend with, than others. They are, in the first place, a constant offence to their mistress. She is ever disposed to find fault with them; they can seldom do any thing to please her; she is never better pleased than when she sees them under the lash, especially when she suspects her husband of showing to his mulatto children favors which he withholds from his black slaves. The master is frequently compelled to sell this class of his slaves, out of deference to the feelings of his white wife; and, cruel as the deed may strike any one to be, for a man to sell his own children to human flesh-mongers, it is often the dictate of humanity for him to do so; for, unless he does this, he must not only whip them himself, but must stand by and see one white son tie up his brother, of but few shades darker complexion than himself, and ply the gory lash to his naked back; and if he lisp one word of disapproval, it is set down to his parental partiality, and only makes a bad matter worse, both for himself and the slave whom he would protect and defend.

Every year brings with it multitudes of this class of slaves. It was doubtless in consequence of a knowledge of this fact, that one great statesman of the south predicted the downfall of slavery by the inevitable laws of population. Whether this prophecy is ever fulfilled or not, it is nevertheless plain that a very different-looking class of people are springing up at the south, and are now held in slavery, from those originally brought to this country from Africa; and if their increase will do no other good, it will do away the force of the argument, that God cursed Ham, and therefore American slavery is right. If the lineal descendants of Ham are alone to be scripturally enslaved, it is certain that slavery at the south must soon become unscriptural; for thousands are ushered into the world, annually, who, like myself, owe their existence to white fathers, and those fathers most frequently their own masters.

I have had two masters. My first master's name was Anthony. I do not remember his first name. He was generally called Captain Anthony—a title which, I presume, he acquired by sailing a craft on the Chesapeake Bay. He was not considered a rich slaveholder. He owned two or three farms, and about thirty slaves. His farms and slaves were under the care of an overseer. The overseer's name was Plummer. Mr. Plummer was a miserable drunkard, a profane swearer, and a savage monster. He always went armed with a cowskin and a heavy cudgel. I have known him to cut and slash the women's heads so horribly, that even master would be enraged at his cruelty, and would threaten to whip him if he did not mind himself. Master, however, was not a humane slaveholder. It required extraordinary barbarity on the part of an overseer to affect him. He was a cruel man, hardened by a long life of slaveholding. He would at times seem to take great pleasure in whipping a slave. I have often been awakened at the dawn of day by the most heart-rending shrieks of an own aunt of mine, whom he used to tie up to a joist, and whip upon her naked back till she was literally covered with blood. No words, no tears, no prayers, from his gory victim, seemed to move his iron heart from its bloody purpose. The louder she screamed, the harder he whipped; and where the blood ran fastest, there he whipped longest. He would whip her to make her scream, and whip her to make her hush; and not until overcome by fatigue, would he cease to swing the blood-clotted cowskin. I remember the first time I ever witnessed this horrible exhibition. I was quite a child, but I well remember it. I never shall forget it whilst I remember any thing. It was the first of a long series of such outrages, of which I was doomed to be a witness and a participant. It struck me with awful force. It was the blood-stained gate, the entrance to the hell of slavery, through which I was about to pass. It was a most terrible spectacle. I wish I could commit to paper the feelings with which I beheld it.

This occurrence took place very soon after I went to live with my old master, and under the following circumstances. Aunt Hester went out one night,—where or for what I do not know,—and happened to be absent when my master desired her presence. He had ordered her not to go out evenings, and warned her that she must never let him catch her in company with a young man, who was paying attention to her belonging to Colonel Lloyd. The young man's name was Ned Roberts, generally called Lloyd's Ned. Why master was so careful of her, may be safely left to conjecture. She was a woman of noble form, and of graceful proportions, having very few equals, and fewer superiors, in personal appearance, among the colored or white women of our neighborhood.

Aunt Hester had not only disobeyed his orders in going out, but had been found in company with Lloyd's Ned; which circumstance, I found, from what he said while whipping her, was the chief offence. Had he been a man of pure morals himself, he might have been thought interested in protecting the innocence of my aunt; but those who knew him will not suspect him of any such virtue. Before he commenced whipping Aunt Hester, he took her into the kitchen, and stripped her from neck to waist, leaving her neck, shoulders, and back, entirely naked. He then told her to cross her hands, calling her at the same time a d——b b——h. After crossing her hands, he tied them with a strong rope, and led her to a stool under a large hook in the joist, put in for the purpose. He made her get upon the stool, and tied her hands to the hook. She now stood fair for his infernal purpose. Her arms were stretched up at their full length, so that she stood upon the ends of her toes. He then said to her, "Now, you d——b b——h, I'll learn you how to disobey my orders!" and after rolling up his sleeves, he commenced to lay on the heavy cowskin, and soon the warm, red blood (amid heartrending shrieks from her, and horrid oaths from him) came dripping to the floor. I was so terrified and horror-stricken at the sight, that I hid myself in a closet, and dared not venture out till long after the bloody transaction was over. I expected it would be my turn next. It was all new to me. I had never seen any thing like it before. I had always lived with my grandmother on the outskirts of the plantation, where she was put to raise the children of the younger women. I had therefore been, until now, out of the way of the bloody scenes that often occurred on the plantation.

Chapter VII

I lived in Master Hugh's family about seven years. During this time, I succeeded in learning to read and write. In accomplishing this, I was compelled to resort to various stratagems. I had no regular teacher. My mistress, who had kindly commenced to instruct me, had, in compliance with the advice and direction of her husband, not only ceased to instruct, but had set her face against my being instructed by any one else. It is due, however, to my mistress to say of her, that she did not adopt this course of treatment immediately. She at first lacked the depravity indispensable to shutting me up in mental darkness. It was at least necessary for her to have some training in the exercise of irresponsible power, to make her equal to the task of treating me as though I were a brute.

My mistress was, as I have said, a kind and tenderhearted woman; and in the simplicity of her soul she commenced, when I first went to live with her, to treat me as she supposed one human being ought to treat another. In entering upon the duties of a slaveholder, she did not seem to perceive that I sustained to her the relation of a mere chattel, and that for her to treat me as a human being was not only wrong, but dangerously so. Slavery proved as injurious to her as it did to me. When I went there, she was a pious, warm, and tenderhearted woman. There was no sorrow or suffering for which she had not a tear. She had bread for the hungry, clothes for the naked, and comfort for every mourner that came within her reach. Slavery soon proved its ability to divest her of these heavenly qualities. Under its influence, the tender heart became stone, and the lamblike disposition gave way to one of tiger-like fierceness. The first step in her downward course was in her ceasing to instruct me. She now commenced to practise her husband's precepts. She finally became even more violent in her opposition than her husband himself. She was not satisfied with simply doing as well as he had commanded; she seemed anxious to do better. Nothing seemed to make her more angry than to see me with a newspaper. She seemed to think that here lay the danger. I have had her rush at me with a face made all up of fury, and snatch from me a newspaper, in a manner that fully revealed her apprehension. She was an apt woman; and a little experience soon demonstrated, to her satisfaction, that education and slavery were incompatible with each other.

From this time I was most narrowly watched. If I was in a separate room any considerable length of time, I was sure to be suspected of having a book, and was at once called to give an account of myself. All this, however, was too late. The first step had been taken. Mistress, in teaching me the alphabet, had given me the *inch*, and no precaution could prevent me from taking the *ell*.

The plan which I adopted, and the one by which I was most successful, was that of making friends of all the little white boys whom I met in the street. As many of these as I could, I converted into teachers. With their kindly aid, obtained at different times and in different places, I finally succeeded in learning to read. When I was sent of errands, I always took my book with me, and by going one part of my errand quickly, I found time to get a lesson before my return. I used also to carry bread with me, enough of which was always in the house, and to which I was always welcome; for I was much better off in this regard than many of the poor white children in our neighborhood. This bread I used to bestow upon the hungry little urchins, who, in return, would give me that more valuable bread of knowledge. I am strongly tempted to give the names of two or three of those little boys, as a testimonial of the gratitude and affection I bear them; but prudence forbids;—not that it would injure me, but it might embarrass them; for it is almost an unpardonable offence to teach slaves to read in this Christian country. It is enough to say of the dear little fellows, that they lived on Philpot Street, very near Durgin and Bailey's ship-yard. I used to talk this matter of slavery over with them. I would sometimes say to them, I wished I could be as free as they would be when they got to be men. "You will be free as soon as you are twenty-one, *but I am a slave for life!* Have not I as good a right to be free as you have?" These words used to trouble them; they would express for me the liveliest sympathy, and console me with the hope that something would occur by which I might be free.

I was now about twelve years old, and the thought of being *a slave for life* began to bear heavily upon my heart. Just about this time, I got hold of a book entitled "The Columbian Orator." Every opportunity I got, I used to read this book. Among much of other interesting matter, I found in it a dialogue between a master and his slave. The slave was represented as having run away from his master three times. The dialogue represented the conversation which took place between them, when the slave was retaken the third time. In this dialogue, the whole argument in behalf of slavery was brought forward by the master, all of which was disposed of by the slave. The slave was made to say some very smart as well as impressive things in reply to his master—things which had the desired though unexpected effect; for the conversation resulted in the voluntary emancipation of the slave on the part of the master.

In the same book, I met with one of Sheridan's mighty speeches on and in behalf of Catholic emancipation. These were choice documents to me. I read them over and over again with unabated interest. They gave tongue to interesting thoughts of my own soul, which had frequently flashed through my mind, and died away for want of utterance. The moral which I gained from the dialogue was the power of truth over the conscience of even a slaveholder. What I got from Sheridan was a bold denunciation of slavery, and a powerful vindication of human rights. The reading of these documents enabled me to utter my thoughts, and to meet the arguments brought forward to sustain slavery; but while they relieved me of one difficulty, they brought on another even more painful than the one of which I was relieved. The more I read, the more I was led to abhor and detest my enslavers. I could regard them in no other light than a band of successful robbers, who had left their homes, and gone to Africa, and stolen us from our homes, and in a strange land reduced us to slavery. I loathed them as being the meanest as well as the most wicked of men. As I read and contemplated the subject, behold! that very discontentment which Master Hugh had predicted would follow my learning to read had already come, to torment and sting my soul to unutterable anguish. As I writhed under it, I would at times feel that learning to read had been a curse rather than a blessing. It had given me a view of my wretched condition, without the remedy. It opened my eyes to the horrible pit, but to no ladder upon which to get out. In moments of agony, I envied my fellow-slaves for their stupidity. I have often wished myself a beast. I preferred the condition of the meanest reptile to my own. Any thing, no matter what, to get rid of thinking! It was this everlasting thinking of my condition that tormented me. There was no getting rid of it. It was pressed upon me by every object within sight or hearing, animate or inanimate. The silver trump of freedom had roused my soul to eternal wakefulness. Freedom now appeared, to disappear no more forever. It was heard in every sound, and seen in every thing. It was ever present to torment me with a sense of my wretched condition. I saw nothing without seeing it, I heard nothing without hearing it, and felt nothing without feeling it. It looked from every star, it smiled in every calm, breathed in every wind, and moved in every storm.

I often found myself regretting my own existence, and wishing myself dead; and but for the hope of being free, I have no doubt but that I should have killed myself, or done something for which I should have been killed. While in this state of mind, I was eager to hear any one speak of slavery. I was a ready listener. Every little while, I could hear something about the abolitionists. It was some time before I found what the word meant. It was always used in such connections as to make it an interesting word to me. If a slave ran away and succeeded in getting clear, or if a slave killed his master, set fire to a barn, or did any thing very wrong in the mind of a slaveholder, it was spoken of as the fruit of *abolition*. Hearing the word in this connection very often, I set about learning what it meant. The dictionary afforded me little or no help. I found it was "the act of abolishing;" but then I did not know what was to be abolished. Here I was perplexed. I did not dare to ask any one about its meaning, for I was satisfied that it was something they wanted me to know very little about. After a patient waiting, I got one of our city papers, containing an account of the number of petitions from the north, praying for the abolition of slavery in the District of Columbia, and of the slave trade between the States. From this time I understood the words *abolition* and *abolitionist,* and always drew near when that word was spoken, expecting to hear something of importance to myself and fellow-slaves. The light broke in upon me by degrees. I went one day down on the wharf of Mr. Waters; and seeing two Irishmen unloading a scow of stone, I went, unasked, and helped them. When we had finished, one of them came to me and asked me if I were a slave. I told him I was. He asked, "Are ye a slave for life?" I told him that I was. The good Irishman seemed to be deeply affected by the statement. He said to the other that it was a pity so fine a little fellow as myself should be a slave for life. He said it was a shame to hold me. They both advised me to run away to the north; that I should find friends there, and that I should be free. I pretended not to be interested in what they said, and treated them as if I did not understand them; for I feared they might be treacherous. White men have been known to encourage slaves to escape, and then, to get the reward, catch them and return them to their masters. I was afraid that these seemingly, good men might use me so; but I nevertheless remembered their advice, and from that time I resolved to run away. I looked forward to a time at which it would be safe for me to escape. I was too young to think of doing so immediately; besides, I wished to learn how to write, as I might have occasion to write my own pass. I consoled myself with the hope that I should one day find a good chance. Meanwhile, I would learn to write.

The idea as to how I might learn to write was suggested to me by being in Durgin and Bailey's ship-yard, and frequently seeing the ship carpenters, after hewing, and getting a piece of timber ready for use, write on the timber the name of that part of the ship for which it was intended. When a piece of timber was intended for the larboard side, it would be marked thus—"L." When a piece was for the starboard side, it would be marked thus—"S." A piece for the larboard side forward, would be marked thus—"L.F." When a piece was for starboard side forward, it would be marked thus—"S.F." For larboard aft, it would be marked thus—"L.A." For starboard aft, it would be marked thus-"S.A." I soon learned the names of these letters, and for what they were intended when placed upon a piece of timber in the ship-yard. I immediately commenced copying them, and in a short time was able to make the four letters named. After that, when I met with any boy who I knew could write, I would tell him I could write as well as he. The next word would be, "I don't believe you. Let me see you try it." I would then make the letters which I had been so fortunate as to learn, and ask him to beat that. In this way I got a good many lessons in writing, which it is quite possible I should never have gotten in any other way. During this time, my copy-book was the board fence, brick wall, and pavement; my pen and ink was a lump of chalk. With these, I learned mainly how to write. I then commenced and continued copying the Italics in Webster's Spelling Book, until I could make them all without looking on the book.

By this time, my little Master Thomas had gone to school, and learned how to write, and had written over a number of copybooks. These had been brought home, and shown to some of our near neighbors, and then laid aside. My mistress used to go to class meeting at the Wilk Street meetinghouse every Monday afternoon, and leave me to take care of the house. When left thus, I used to spend the time in writing in the spaces left in Master Thomas's copy-book, copying what he had written. I continued to do this until I could write a hand very similar to that of Master Thomas. Thus, after a long, tedious effort for years, I finally succeeded in learning how to write.

Chapter XI

I now come to that part of my life during which I planned, and finally succeeded in making, my escape from slavery. But before narrating any of the peculiar circumstances, I deem it proper to make known my intention not to state all the facts connected with the transaction. My reasons for pursuing this course may be understood from the following: First, were I to give a minute statement of all the facts, it is not only possible, but quite probable, that others would thereby be involved in the most embarrassing difficulties. Secondly, such a statement would most undoubtedly induce greater vigilance on the part of slaveholders than has existed heretofore among them; which would, of course, be the means of guarding a door whereby some dear brother bondman might escape his galling chains. I deeply regret the necessity that impels me to suppress any thing of importance connected with my experience in slavery. It would afford me great pleasure indeed, as well as materially add to the interest of my narrative, were I at liberty to gratify a curiosity, which I know exists in the minds of many, by an accurate statement of all the facts pertaining to my most fortunate escape. But I must deprive myself of this pleasure, and the curious of the gratification which such a statement would afford. I would allow myself to suffer under the greatest imputations which evil-minded men might suggest, rather than exculpate myself, and thereby run the hazard of closing the slightest avenue by which a brother slave might clear himself of the chains and fetters of slavery.

I have never approved of the very public manner in which some of our western friends have conducted what they call the *underground railroad*, but which, I think, by their open declarations, has been made most emphatically the *upperground railroad*. I honor those good men and women for their noble daring, and applaud them for willingly subjecting themselves to bloody persecution, by openly avowing their participation in the escape of slaves. I, however, can see very little good resulting from such a course, either to themselves or the slaves escaping; while, upon the other hand, I see and feel assured that those open declarations are a positive evil to the slaves remaining, who are seeking to escape. They do nothing towards enlightening the slave, whilst they do much towards enlightening the master. They stimulate him to greater watchfulness, and enhance his power to capture his slave. We owe something to the slaves south of the line as well as to those north of it; and in aiding the latter on their way to freedom, we should be careful to do nothing which would be likely to hinder the former from escaping from slavery. I would keep the merciless slave-holder profoundly ignorant of the means of flight adopted by the slave. I would leave him to imagine himself surrounded by myriads of invisible tormentors, ever ready to snatch from his infernal grasp his trembling prey. Let him be left to feel his way in the dark; let darkness commensurate with his crime hover over him; and let him feel that at every step he takes, in pursuit of the flying bondman, he is running the frightful risk of having his hot brains dashed out by an invisible agency. Let us render the tyrant no aid; let us not hold the light by which he can trace the footprints of our flying brother. But enough of this. I will now proceed to the statement of those facts, connected with my escape, for which I am alone responsible, and for which no one can be made to suffer but myself.

In the early part of the year 1838, I became quite restless. I could see no reason why I should, at the end of each week, pour the reward of my toil into the purse of my master. When I carried to him my weekly wages, he would, after counting the money, look me in the face with a robber-like fierceness, and ask, "Is this all?" He was satisfied with nothing less than the last cent. He would, however, when I made him six dollars, sometimes give me six cents, to encourage me. It had the opposite effect. I regarded it as a sort of admission of my right to the whole. The fact that he gave me any part of my wages was proof, to my mind, that he believed me entitled to the whole of them. I always felt worse for having received any thing; for I feared that the giving me a few cents would ease his conscience, and make him feel himself to be a pretty honorable sort of robber. My discontent grew upon me. I was ever on the look-out for means of escape; and, finding no direct means, I determined to try to hire my time, with a view of getting money with which to make my escape. In the spring of 1838, when Master Thomas came to Baltimore to purchase his spring goods, I got an opportunity, and applied to him to allow me to hire my time. He unhesitatingly refused my request, and told me this was another stratagem by which to escape. He told me I could go nowhere but that he could get me; and that, in the event of my running away, he should spare no pains in his efforts to catch me. He exhorted me to content myself, and be obedient. He told me, if I would be happy, I must lay out no plans for the future. He said, if I behaved myself properly, he would take care of me. Indeed, he advised me to complete thoughtlessness of the future, and taught me to depend solely upon him for happiness. He seemed to see fully the pressing necessity of setting aside my intellectual nature, in order to contentment in slavery. But in spite of him, and even in spite of myself, I continued to think, and to think about the injustice of my enslavement, and the means of escape.

About two months after this, I applied to Master Hugh for the privilege of hiring my time. He was not acquainted with the fact that I had applied to Master Thomas, and had been refused. He too, at first, seemed disposed to refuse; but, after some reflection, he granted me the privilege, and proposed the following terms: I was to be allowed all my time, make all contracts with those for whom I worked, and find my own employment; and, in return for this liberty, I was to pay him three dollars at the end of each week; find myself in calking tools, and in board and clothing. My board was two dollars and a half per week.

This, with the wear and tear of clothing and calking tools, made my regular expenses about six dollars per week. This amount I was compelled to make up, or relinquish the privilege of hiring my time. Rain or shine, work or no work, at the end of each week the money must be forthcoming, or I must give up my privilege. This arrangement, it will be perceived, was decidedly in my master's favor. It relieved him of all need of looking after me. His money was sure. He received all the benefits of slaveholding without its evils; while I endured all the evils of a slave, and suffered all the care and anxiety of a freeman. I found it a hard bargain. But, hard as it was, I thought it better than the old mode of getting along. It was a step towards freedom to be allowed to bear the responsibilities of a freeman, and I was determined to hold on upon it. I bent myself to the work of making money. I was ready to work at night as well as day, and by the most untiring perseverance and industry, I made enough to meet my expenses, and lay up a little money every week. I went on thus from May till August. Master Hugh then refused to allow me to hire my time longer. The ground for his refusal was a failure on my part, one Saturday night, to pay him for my week's time. This failure was occasioned by my attending a camp meeting about ten miles from Baltimore. During the week, I had entered into an engagement with a number of young friends to start from Baltimore to the camp ground early Saturday evening; and being detained by my employer, I was unable to get down to Master Hugh's without disappointing the company. I knew that Master Hugh was in no special need of the money that night. I therefore decided to go to camp meeting, and upon my return pay him the three dollars. I staid [sic] at the camp meeting one day longer than I intended when I left. But as soon as I returned, I called upon him to pay him what he considered his due. I found him very angry; he could scarce restrain his wrath. He said he had a great mind to give me a severe whipping. He wished to know how I dared go out of the city without asking his permission. I told him I hired my time, and while I paid him the price which he asked for it, I did not know that I was bound to ask him when and where I should go. This reply troubled him; and, after reflecting a few moments, he turned to me, and said I should hire my time no longer; that the next thing he should know of, I would be running away. Upon the same plea, he told me to bring my tools and clothing home forthwith. I did so; but instead of seeking work, as I had been accustomed to do previously to hiring my time, I spent the whole week without the performance of a single stroke of work. I did this in retaliation. Saturday night, he called upon me as usual for my week's wages. I told him I had no wages; I had done no work that week. Here we were upon the point of coming to blows. He raved, and swore his determination to get hold of me. I did not allow myself a single word; but was resolved, if he laid the weight of his hand upon me, it should be blow for blow. He did not strike me, but told me that he would find me in constant employment in future. I thought the matter over during the next day, Sunday, and finally resolved upon the third day of September, as the day upon which I would make a second attempt to secure my freedom. I now had three weeks during which to prepare for my journey. Early on Monday morning, before Master Hugh had time to make any engagement for me, I went out and got employment of Mr. Butler, at his ship-yard near the drawbridge, upon what is called the City Block, thus making it unnecessary for him to seek employment for me. At the end of the week, I brought him between eight and nine dollars. He seemed very well pleased, and asked me why I did not do the same the week before. He little knew what my plans were. My object in working steadily was to remove any suspicion he might entertain of my intent to run away; and in this I succeeded admirably. I suppose he thought I was never better satisfied with my condition than at the very time during which I was planning my escape. The second week passed, and again I carried him my full wages; and so well pleased was he, that he gave me twenty-five cents, (quite a large sum for a slaveholder to give a slave,) and bade me to make a good use of it. I told him I would.

Things went on without very smoothly indeed, but within there was trouble. It is impossible for me to describe my feelings as the time of my contemplated start drew near. I had a number of warm-hearted friends in Baltimore,—friends that I loved almost as I did my life,—and the thought of being separated from them forever was painful beyond expression. It is my opinion that thousands would escape from slavery, who now remain, but for the strong cords of affection that bind them to their friends. The thought of leaving my friends was decidedly the most painful thought with which I had to contend. The love of them was my tender point, and shook my decision more than all things else. Besides the pain of separation, the dread and apprehension of a failure exceeded what I had experienced at my first attempt. The appalling defeat I then sustained returned to torment me. I felt assured that, if I failed in this attempt, my case would be a hopeless one—it would seal my fate as a slave forever. I could not hope to get off with any thing less than the severest punishment, and being placed beyond the means of escape. It required no very vivid imagination to depict the most frightful scenes through which I should have to pass, in case I failed. The wretchedness of slavery, and the blessedness of freedom, were perpetually before me. It was life and death with me. But I remained firm, and, according to my resolution, on the third day of September, 1838, I left my chains, and succeeded in reaching New York without the slightest interruption of any kind. How I did so,—what means I adopted,—what direction I travelled, and by what mode of conveyance,—I must leave unexplained, for the reasons before mentioned.

I have been frequently asked how I felt when I found myself in a free State. I have never been able to answer the question with any satisfaction to myself. It was a moment of the highest excitement I ever experienced. I suppose I felt as one may imagine the unarmed mariner to feel when he is rescued by a friendly man-of-war from the pursuit of a pirate. In writing to a dear friend, immediately after my arrival at New York, I said I felt like one who had escaped a den of hungry lions. This state of mind, however, very soon subsided; and I was again seized with a feeling of great insecurity and loneliness. I was yet liable to be taken back, and subjected to all the tortures of slavery. This in itself was enough to damp the ardor of my enthusiasm. But the loneliness overcame me. There I was in the midst of thousands, and yet a perfect stranger; without home and without friends, in the midst of thousands of my own brethren—children of a common Father, and yet I dared not to unfold to any one of them my sad condition. I was afraid to speak to any one for fear of speaking to the wrong one, and thereby falling into the hands of money-loving kidnappers, whose business it was to lie in wait for the panting fugitive, as the ferocious beasts of the forest lie in wait for their prey. The motto which I adopted when I started from slavery was this—"Trust no man!" I saw in every white man an enemy, and in almost every colored man cause for distrust. It was a most painful situation; and, to understand it, one must needs experience it, or imagine himself in similar circumstances. Let him be a fugitive slave in a strange land—a land given up to be the hunting-ground for slaveholders—whose inhabitants are legalized kidnappers—where he is every moment subjected to the terrible liability of being seized upon by his fellow-men, as the hideous crocodile seizes upon his prey!—I say, let him place himself in my situation— without home or friends—without money or credit—wanting shelter, and no one to give it—wanting bread, and no money to buy it,—and at the same time let him feel that he is pursued by merciless men-hunters, and in total darkness as to what to do, where to go, or where to stay,—perfectly helpless both as to the means of defence and means of escape,—in the midst of plenty, yet suffering the terrible gnawings of hunger,—in the midst of houses, yet having no home,—among fellow-men, yet feeling as if in the midst of wild beasts, whose greediness to swallow up the trembling and half-famished fugitive is only equalled by that with which the monsters of the deep swallow up the helpless fish upon which they subsist,—I say, let him be placed in this most trying situation,—the situation in which I was placed,—then, and not till then, will he fully appreciate the hardships of, and know how to sympathize with, the toil-worn and whip-scarred fugitive slave.

Thank Heaven, I remained but a short time in this distressed situation. I was relieved from it by the humane hand of Mr. DAVID RUGGLES, whose vigilance, kindness, and perseverance, I shall never forget. I am glad of an opportunity to express, as far as words can, the love and gratitude I bear him. Mr. Ruggles is now afflicted with blindness, and is himself in need of the same kind offices which he was once so forward in the performance of toward others. I had been in New York but a few days, when Mr. Ruggles sought me out, and very kindly took me to his boarding-house at the corner of Church and Lespenard Streets. Mr. Ruggles was then very deeply engaged in the memorable *Darg* case, as well as attending to a number of other fugitive slaves, devising ways and means for their successful escape; and, though watched and hemmed in on almost every side, he seemed to be more than a match for his enemies.

Very soon after I went to Mr. Ruggles, he wished to know of me where I wanted to go; as he deemed it unsafe for me to remain in New York. I told him I was a calker, and should like to go where I could get work. I thought of going to Canada; but he decided against it, and in favor of my going to New Bedford, thinking I should be able to get work there at my trade. At this time, Anna,* my intended wife, came on; for I wrote to her immediately after my arrival at New York, (notwithstanding my homeless, houseless, and helpless condition,) informing her of my successful flight, and wishing her to come on forthwith. In a few days

---

*She was free.

after her arrival, Mr. Ruggles called in the Rev. J. W. C. Pennington, who, in the presence of Mr. Ruggles, Mrs. Michaels, and two or three others, performed the marriage ceremony, and gave us a certificate, of which the following is an exact copy:—

> "This may certify, that I joined together in holy matrimony Frederick Johnson† and Anna Murray, as man and wife, in the presence of Mr. David Ruggles and Mrs. Michaels.
>
> "James W. C. Pennington.
> "*New York, Sept.* 15, 1838."

Upon receiving this certificate, and a five-dollar bill from Mr. Ruggles, I shouldered one part of our baggage, and Anna took up the other, and we set out forthwith to take passage on board of the steamboat John W. Richmond for Newport, on our way to New Bedford. Mr. Ruggles gave me a letter to a Mr. Shaw in Newport, and told me, in case my money did not serve me to New Bedford, to stop in Newport and obtain further assistance; but upon our arrival at Newport, we were so anxious to get to a place of safety, that, notwithstanding we lacked the necessary money to pay our fare, we decided to take seats in the stage, and promise to pay when we got to New Bedford. We were encouraged to do this by two excellent gentlemen, residents of New Bedford, whose names I afterward ascertained to be Joseph Ricketson and William C. Taber. They seemed at once to understand our circumstances, and gave us such assurance of their friendliness as put us fully at ease in their presence. It was good indeed to meet with such friends, at such a time. Upon reaching New Bedford, we were directed to the house of Mr. Nathan Johnson, by whom we were kindly received, and hospitably provided for. Both Mr. and Mrs. Johnson took a deep and lively interest in our welfare. They proved themselves quite worthy of the name of abolitionists. When the stage-driver found us unable to pay our fare, he held on upon our baggage as security for the debt. I had but to mention the fact to Mr. Johnson, and he forthwith advanced the money.

We now began to feel a degree of safety, and to prepare ourselves for the duties and responsibilities of a life of freedom. On the morning after our arrival at New Bedford, while at the breakfast-table, the question arose as to what name I should be called by. The name given me by my mother was, "Frederick Augustus Washington Bailey." I, however, had dispensed with the two middle names long before I left Maryland so that I was generally known by the name of "Frederick Bailey." I started from Baltimore bearing the name of "Stanley." When I got to New York, I again changed my name to "Frederick Johnson," and thought that would be the last change. But when I got to New Bedford, I found it necessary again to change my name. The reason of this necessity was, that there were so many Johnsons in New Bedford, it was already quite difficult to distinguish between them. I gave Mr. Johnson the privilege of choosing me a name, but told him he must not take from me the name

---

†I had changed my name from Frederick *Bailey* to that of *Johnson*.

of "Frederick." I must hold on to that, to preserve a sense of my identity. Mr. Johnson had just been reading the "Lady of the Lake," and at once suggested that my name be "Douglass." From that time until now I have been called "Frederick Douglass;" and as I am more widely known by that name than by either of the others, I shall continue to use it as my own.

I was quite disappointed at the general appearance of things in New Bedford. The impression which I had received respecting the character and condition of the people of the north, I found to be singularly erroneous. I had very strangely supposed, while in slavery, that few of the comforts, and scarcely any of the luxuries, of life were enjoyed at the north, compared with what were enjoyed by the slaveholders of the south. I probably came to this conclusion from the fact that northern people owned no slaves. I supposed that they were about upon a level with the non-slaveholding population of the south. I knew *they* were exceedingly poor, and I had been accustomed to regard their poverty as the necessary consequence of their being non-slaveholders. I had somehow imbibed the opinion that, in the absence of slaves, there could be no wealth, and very little refinement. And upon coming to the north, I expected to meet with a rough, hard-handed, and uncultivated population, living in the most Spartan-like simplicity, knowing nothing of the ease, luxury, pomp, and grandeur of southern slaveholders. Such being my conjectures, any one acquainted with the appearance of New Bedford may very readily infer how palpably I must have seen my mistake.

In the afternoon of the day when I reached New Bedford, I visited the wharves, to take a view of the shipping. Here I found myself surrounded with the strongest proofs of wealth. Lying at the wharves, and riding in the stream, I saw many ships of the finest model, in the best order, and of the largest size. Upon the right and left, I was walled in by granite warehouses of the widest dimensions, stowed to their utmost capacity with the necessaries and comforts of life. Added to this, almost every body seemed to be at work, but noiselessly so, compared with what I had been accustomed to in Baltimore. There were no loud songs heard from those engaged in loading and unloading ships. I heard no deep oaths or horrid curses on the laborer. I saw no whipping of men; but all seemed to go smoothly on. Every man appeared to understand his work, and went at it with a sober, yet cheerful earnestness, which betokened the deep interest which he felt in what he was doing, as well as a sense of his own dignity as a man. To me this looked exceedingly strange. From the wharves I strolled around and over the town, gazing with wonder and admiration at the splendid churches, beautiful dwellings, and finely-cultivated gardens; evincing an amount of wealth, comfort, taste, and refinement, such as I had never seen in any part of slaveholding Maryland.

Every thing looked clean, new, and beautiful. I saw few or no dilapidated houses, with poverty-stricken inmates; no half-naked children and barefooted women, such as I had been accustomed to see in Hillsborough, Easton, St. Michael's, and Baltimore. The people looked more able, stronger, healthier, and happier, than those of Maryland. I was for once made glad by a view of extreme wealth, without being saddened by seeing extreme poverty. But the most astonishing as well as the most interesting thing to me was the condition of the colored people, a great many of whom, like myself, had escaped thither as a refuge from the hunters of men. I found many, who had not been seven years out of their chains, living in finer houses, and evidently enjoying more of the comforts of life, than the average of slave-holders in Maryland. I will venture to assert that my friend Mr. Nathan Johnson (of whom I can say with a grateful heart, "I was hungry, and he gave me meat; I was thirsty, and he gave me drink; I was a stranger, and he took me in") lived in a neater house; dined at a better table; took, paid for, and read, more newspapers; better understood the moral, religious, and political character of the nation,—than nine tenths of the slaveholders in Talbot county Maryland. Yet Mr. Johnson was a working man. His hands were hardened by toil, and not his alone, but those also of Mrs. Johnson. I found the colored people much more spirited than I had supposed they would be. I found among them a determination to protect each other from the blood-thirsty kidnapper, at all hazards. Soon after my arrival, I was told of a circumstance which illustrated their spirit. A colored man and a fugitive slave were on unfriendly terms. The former was heard to threaten the latter with informing his master of his whereabouts. Straightway a meeting was called among the colored people, under the stereotyped notice, "Business of importance!" The betrayer was invited to attend. The people came at the appointed hour, and organized the meeting by appointing a very religious old gentleman as president, who, I believe, made a prayer, after which he addressed the meeting as follows: *"Friends, we have got him here, and I would recommend that you young men just take him outside the door, and kill him!"* With this, a number of them bolted at him; but they were intercepted by some more timid than themselves, and the betrayer escaped their vengeance, and has not been seen in New Bedford since. I believe there have been no more such threats, and should there be hereafter, I doubt not that death would be the consequence.

I found employment, the third day after my arrival, in stowing a sloop with a load of oil. It was new, dirty, and hard work for me; but I went at it with a glad heart and a willing hand. I was now my own master. It was a happy moment, the rapture of which can be understood only by those who have been slaves. It was the first work, the reward of which was to be entirely my own. There was no Master Hugh standing ready, the moment I earned the money, to rob me of it. I worked that day with a pleasure I had never before experienced. I was at work for myself and newly-married wife. It was to me the starting-point of a new existence. When I got through with that job, I went in pursuit of a job of calking; but such was the strength of prejudice against color, among the white calkers, that they refused to work with me, and of course I could get no employment.* Finding my trade of no immediate benefit, I threw off my calking habiliments, and prepared myself to do any kind of work I could get to do. Mr. Johnson kindly let me have his wood-horse and saw, and I very soon found myself a plenty of work. There was no work too hard—none too dirty. I was ready to

---

*I am told that colored persons can now get employment at calking in New Bedford—a result of anti-slavery effort.

saw wood, shovel coal, carry the hod, sweep the chimney, or roll oil casks,—all of which I did for nearly three years in New Bedford, before I became known to the anti-slavery world.

In about four months after I went to New Bedford, there came a young man to me, and inquired if I did not wish to take the "Liberator." I told him I did; but, just having made my escape from slavery, I remarked that I was unable to pay for it then. I, however, finally became a subscriber to it. The paper came, and I read it from week to week with such feelings as it would be quite idle for me to attempt to describe. The paper became my meat and my drink. My soul was set all on fire. Its sympathy for my brethren in bonds—its scathing denunciations of slaveholders—its faithful exposures of slavery—and its powerful attacks upon the upholders of the institution—sent a thrill of joy through my soul, such as I had never felt before!

I had not long been a reader of the "Liberator," before I got a pretty correct idea of the principles, measures and spirit of the anti-slavery reform. I took right hold of the cause. I could do but little; but what I could, I did with a joyful heart, and never felt happier than when in an anti-slavery meeting. I seldom had much to say at the meetings, because what I wanted to say was said so much better by others. But, while attending an anti-slavery convention at Nantucket, on the 11th of August, 1841, I felt strongly moved to speak, and was at the same time much urged to do so by Mr. William C. Coffin, a gentleman who had heard me speak in the colored people's meeting at New Bedford. It was a severe cross, and I took it up reluctantly. The truth was, I felt myself a slave, and the idea of speaking to white people weighed me down. I spoke but a few moments, when I felt a degree of freedom, and said what I desired with considerable ease. From that time until now, I have been engaged in pleading the cause of my brethren—with what success, and with what devotion, I leave those acquainted with my labors to decide.

23

The Emancipation Proclamation

Abraham Lincoln

A Proclamation

Whereas, on the twenty-second day of September, in the year of our Lord one thousand eight hundred and sixty-two, a proclamation was issued by the President of the United States, containing, among other things, the following, to wit:

"That on the first day of January, in the year of our Lord one thousand eight hundred and sixty-three, all persons held as slaves within any State or designated part of a State, the people whereof shall then be in rebellion against the United States, shall be then, thenceforward, and forever free; and the Executive Government of the United States, including the military and naval authority thereof, will recognize and maintain the freedom of such persons, and will do no act or acts to repress such persons, or any of them, in any efforts they may make for their actual freedom.

"That the Executive will, on the first day of January aforesaid, by proclamation, designate the States and parts of States, if any, in which the people thereof, respectively, shall then be in rebellion against the United States; and the fact that any State, or the people thereof, shall on that day be, in good faith, represented in the Congress of the United States by members chosen thereto at elections wherein a majority of the qualified voters of such State shall have participated, shall, in the absence of strong countervailing testimony, be deemed conclusive evidence that such State, and the people thereof, are not then in rebellion against the United States."

Now, therefore I, Abraham Lincoln, President of the United States, by virtue of the power in me vested as Commander-in-Chief, of the Army and Navy of the United States in time of actual armed rebellion against the authority and government of the United States, and as a fit and necessary war measure for suppressing said rebellion, do, on this first day of January, in the year of our Lord one thousand eight hundred and sixty-three, and in accordance with my purpose so to do publicly proclaimed for the full period of one hundred days, from the day first above mentioned, order and designate as the States and parts of

States wherein the people thereof respectively, are this day in rebellion against the United States, the following, to wit:

Arkansas, Texas, Louisiana, (except the Parishes of St. Bernard, Plaquemines, Jefferson, St. John, St. Charles, St. James Ascension, Assumption, Terrebonne, Lafourche, St. Mary, St. Martin, and Orleans, including the City of New Orleans) Mississippi, Alabama, Florida, Georgia, South Carolina, North Carolina, and Virginia, (except the forty-eight counties designated as West Virginia, and also the counties of Berkley, Accomac, Northampton, Elizabeth City, York, Princess Ann, and Norfolk, including the cities of Norfolk and Portsmouth[)], and which excepted parts, are for the present, left precisely as if this proclamation were not issued.

And by virtue of the power, and for the purpose aforesaid, I do order and declare that all persons held as slaves within said designated States, and parts of States, are, and henceforward shall be free; and that the Executive government of the United States, including the military and naval authorities thereof, will recognize and maintain the freedom of said persons.

And I hereby enjoin upon the people so declared to be free to abstain from all violence, unless in necessary self-defence; and I recommend to them that, in all cases when allowed, they labor faithfully for reasonable wages.

And I further declare and make known, that such persons of suitable condition, will be received into the armed service of the United States to garrison forts, positions, stations, and other places, and to man vessels of all sorts in said service.

And upon this act, sincerely believed to be an act of justice, warranted by the Constitution, upon military necessity, I invoke the considerate judgment of mankind, and the gracious favor of Almighty God.

In witness whereof, I have hereunto set my hand and caused the seal of the United States to be affixed.

Done at the City of Washington, this first day of January, in the year of our Lord one thousand eight hundred and sixty three, and of the Independence of the United States of America the eighty-seventh.

By the President: ABRAHAM LINCOLN
WILLIAM H. SEWARD, Secretary of State.

24

The First Thirteenth Amendment[a]

Hanes Walton, Jr. and Robert C. Smith

As the prospects of secession and civil war increased, the House and Senate appointed special committees to investigate the situation and make recommendations that might avoid war. Among the recommendations proposed by the House committee was an amendment to the Constitution that would have prohibited any amendment to the Constitution granting the Congress the power to interfere in any way with slavery in any state. The text of the amendment read:

> No amendment shall be made to the Constitution which will authorize or give to Congress the Power to abolish or interfere, within any state, with the domestic institutions thereof, including that of persons held to labor or service by the laws of said state.

This extraordinary amendment, intended to freeze slavery into the Constitution forever, was adopted on March 2, 1861, by a Congress that was overwhelmingly northern, since by that time the senators and representatives from seven southern states that had already seceded were not present. President Lincoln took the extraordinary and completely unnecessary step of personally signing the amendment, the first time a president has signed a constitutional amendment. Three states—Ohio, Illinois, and Maryland—quickly ratified the amendment. However; the attack one month later on Fort Sumter that brought on the Civil War ended any prospect of preserving the Union by preserving slavery, and no other state ratified this first Thirteenth Amendment. Ironically, the second Thirteenth Amendment, adopted four years later; abolished slavery throughout the United States. (Lincoln also signed this amendment.)

---

[a]For a history of the first Thirteenth Amendment and an analysis of whether it would have been constitutional if it had been ratified, see Mark Brandon. "The 'Original' Thirteenth Amendment and the Limits to Formal Constitutional Change," in Sanford Levinson, ed., *Responding to Imperfection: The Theory and Practice of Constitutional Amendment* (Princeton, NJ: Princeton University Press, 1995).

25

Scott v. Sandford (1857)

. . . it becomes, therefore, our duty to decide whether the facts stated in the plea are or are not sufficient to show that the plaintiff is not entitled to sue as a citizen in a court of the United States.

This is certainly a very serious question, and one that now for the first time has been brought for decision before this court. But it is brought here by those who have a right to bring it, and it is our duty to meet it and decide it.

The question is simply this: can a negro whose ancestors were imported into this country and sold as slaves become a member of the political community formed and brought into existence by the Constitution of the United States, and as such become entitled to all the rights, and privileges, and immunities, guarantied by that instrument to the citizen, one of which rights is the privilege of suing in a court of the United States in the cases specified in the Constitution?

It will be observed that the plea applies to that class of persons only whose ancestors were negroes of the African race, and imported into this country and sold and held as slaves. The only matter in issue before the court, therefore, is, whether the descendants of such slaves, when they shall be emancipated, or who are born of parents who had become free before their birth, are citizens of a State in the sense in which the word "citizen" is used in the Constitution of the United States. And this being the only matter in dispute on the pleadings, the court must be understood as speaking in this opinion of that class only, that is, of those persons who are the descendants of Africans who were imported into this country and sold as slaves.

The situation of this population was altogether unlike that of the Indian race. The latter, it is true, formed no part of the colonial communities, and never amalgamated with them in social connections or in government. But although they were uncivilized, they were yet a free and independent people, associated together in nations or tribes and governed by their own laws. Many of these political communities were situated in territories to which the white race claimed the ultimate right of dominion. But that claim was acknowledged to be subject to the right of the Indians to occupy it as long as they thought proper, and neither the English nor colonial Governments claimed or exercised any dominion over the tribe or nation by whom it was occupied, nor claimed the right to the possession of the territory, until the tribe or nation consented to cede it. These Indian Governments were regarded and treated as foreign Governments as much so as if an ocean had separated the red man from the white, and their freedom has constantly been acknowledged, from the time of the first emigration to the English colonies to the present day, by the different Governments which succeeded each other. Treaties have been negotiated with them, and their alliance sought for in war, and the people who compose these Indian political communities have always been treated as foreigners not living under our Government. It is true that the course of events has brought the Indian tribes within the limits of the United States under subjection to the white race, and it has been found necessary, for their sake as well as our own, to regard them as in a state of pupilage, and to legislate to a certain extent over them and the territory they occupy. But they may, without doubt, like the subjects of any other foreign Government, be naturalized by the authority of Congress, and become citizens of a State, and of the United States, and if an individual should leave his nation or tribe and take up his abode among the white population, he would be entitled to all the rights and privileges which would belong to an emigrant from any other foreign people.

We proceed to examine the case as presented by the pleadings.

The words "people of the United States" and "citizens" are synonymous terms, and mean the same thing. They both describe the political body who, according to our republican institutions, form the sovereignty and who hold the power and conduct the Government through their representatives. They are what we familiarly call the "sovereign people," and every citizen is one of this people, and a constituent member of this sovereignty. The question before us is whether the class of persons described in the plea in abatement compose a portion of this people, and are constituent members of this sovereignty? We think they are not, and that they are not included, and were not intended to be included, under the word "citizens" in the Constitution, and can therefore claim none of the rights and privileges which that instrument provides for and secures to citizens of the United States. On the contrary, they were at that time considered as a subordinate and inferior class of beings who had been subjugated by the dominant race, and, whether emancipated or not, yet remained subject to their authority, and had no rights or privileges but such as those who held the power and the Government might choose to grant them.

It is not the province of the court to decide upon the justice or injustice, the policy or impolicy, of these laws. The decision of that question belonged to the political or lawmaking power, to those who formed the sovereignty and framed the Constitution. The duty of the court is to interpret the instrument they have framed with the best lights we can obtain on the subject, and to administer it as we find it, according to its true intent and meaning when it was adopted.

In discussing this question, we must not confound the rights of citizenship which a State may confer within its own limits and the rights of citizenship as a member of the Union. It does not by any means follow, because he has all the rights and privileges of a citizen of a State, that he must be a citizen of the United States. He may have all of the rights and privileges of the citizen of a State and yet not be entitled to the rights and privileges of a citizen in any other State. For, previous to the adoption of the Constitution of the United States, every State had the undoubted right to confer on whomsoever it pleased the character of citizen, and to endow him with all its rights. But this character, of course, was confined to the boundaries of the State, and gave him no rights or privileges in other States beyond those secured to him by the laws of nations and the comity of States. Nor have the several States surrendered the power of conferring these rights and privileges by adopting the Constitution of the United States. Each State may still confer them upon an alien, or anyone it thinks proper, or upon any class or description of persons, yet he would not be a citizen in the sense in which that word is used in the Constitution of the United States, nor entitled to sue as such in one of its courts, nor to the privileges and immunities of a citizen in the other States. The rights which he would acquire would be restricted to the State which gave them. The Constitution has conferred on Congress the right to establish an uniform rule of naturalization, and this right is evidently exclusive, and has always been held by this court to be so. Consequently, no State, since the adoption of the Constitution, can, by naturalizing an alien, invest him with the rights and privileges secured to a citizen of a State under the Federal Government, although, so far as the State alone was concerned, he would undoubtedly be entitled to the rights of a citizen and clothed with all the rights and immunities which the Constitution and laws of the State attached to that character.

It is very clear, therefore, that no State can, by any act or law of its own, passed since the adoption of the Constitution, introduce a new member into the political community created by the Constitution of the United States. It cannot make him a member of this community by making him a member of its own. And, for the same reason, it cannot introduce any person or description of persons who were not intended to be embraced in this new political family which the Constitution brought into existence, but were intended to be excluded from it.

The question then arises, whether the provisions of the Constitution, in relation to the personal rights and privileges to which the citizen of a State should be entitled, embraced the negro African race, at that time in this country or who might afterwards be imported, who had then or should afterwards be made free in any State, and to put it in the power of a single State to make him a citizen of the United States and endue him with the full rights of citizenship in every other State without their consent? Does the Constitution of the United States act upon him whenever he shall be made free under the laws of a State, and raised there to the rank of a citizen, and immediately clothe him with all the privileges of a citizen in every other State, and in its own courts?

The court think the affirmative of these propositions cannot be maintained. And if it cannot, the plaintiff in error could not be a citizen of the State of Missouri within the meaning of the Constitution of the United States, and, consequently, was not entitled to sue in its courts.

It is true, every person, and every class and description of persons who were, at the time of the adoption of the Constitution, recognised as citizens in the several States became also citizens of this new political body, but none other; it was formed by them, and for them and their posterity, but for no one else. And the personal rights and privileges guarantied to citizens of this new sovereignty were intended to embrace those only who were then members of the several State communities, or who should afterwards by birthright or otherwise become members according to the provisions of the Constitution and the principles on which it was founded. It was the union of those who were at that time members of distinct and separate political communities into one political family, whose power, for certain specified purposes, was to extend over the whole territory of the United States. And it gave to each citizen rights and privileges outside of his State which he did not before possess, and placed him in every other State upon a perfect equality with its own citizens as to rights of person and rights of property; it made him a citizen of the United States.

It becomes necessary, therefore, to determine who were citizens of the several States when the Constitution was adopted. And in order to do this, we must recur to the Governments and institutions of the thirteen colonies when they separated from Great Britain and formed new sovereignties, and took their places in the family of independent nations. We must inquire who, at that time, were recognised as the people or citizens of a State whose rights and liberties had been outraged by the English Government, and who declared their independence and assumed the powers of Government to defend their rights by force of arms.

In the opinion of the court, the legislation and histories of the times, and the language used in the Declaration of Independence, show that neither the class of persons who had been imported as slaves nor their descendants, whether they had become free or not, were then acknowledged as a part of the people, nor intended to be included in the general words used in that memorable instrument.

It is difficult at this day to realize the state of public opinion in relation to that unfortunate race which prevailed in the civilized and enlightened portions of the world at the time of the Declaration of Independence and when the Constitution of the United States was framed and adopted. But the public history of every European nation displays it in a manner too plain to be mistaken.

They had for more than a century before been regarded as beings of an inferior order, and altogether unfit to associate with the white race either in social or political relations, and so far inferior that they had no rights which the white man was bound to respect, and that the negro might justly and lawfully be reduced to slavery for his benefit. He was bought and sold, and treated as an ordinary article of merchandise and traffic whenever a profit could be made by it. This opinion was at that time fixed and universal in the civilized portion of the white race. It was regarded as an axiom in morals as well as in politics which no one thought of disputing or supposed to be open to dispute, and men in every grade and position in society daily and habitually acted upon it in their private pursuits, as well as in matters of public concern, without doubting for a moment the correctness of this opinion.

And in no nation was this opinion more firmly fixed or more uniformly acted upon than by the English Government and English people. They not only seized them on the coast of Africa and sold them or held them in slavery for their own use, but they took them as ordinary articles of merchandise to every country where they could make a profit on them, and were far more extensively engaged in this commerce than any other nation in the world.

The opinion thus entertained and acted upon in England was naturally impressed upon the colonies they founded on this side of the Atlantic. And, accordingly, a negro of the African race was regarded by them as an article of property, and held, and bought and sold as such, in every one of the thirteen colonies which united in the Declaration of Independence and afterwards formed the Constitution of the United States. The slaves were more or less numerous in the different colonies as slave labor was found more or less profitable. But no one seems to have doubted the correctness of the prevailing opinion of the time.

The legislation of the different colonies furnishes positive and indisputable proof of this fact.

It would be tedious, in this opinion, to enumerate the various laws they passed upon this subject. It will be sufficient, as a sample of the legislation which then generally prevailed throughout the British colonies, to give the laws of two of them, one being still a large slaveholding State and the other the first State in which slavery ceased to exist.

The province of Maryland, in 1717, ch. 13, s. 5, passed a law declaring

> that if any free negro or mulatto intermarry with any white woman, or if any white man shall intermarry with any negro or mulatto woman, such negro or mulatto shall become a slave during life, excepting mulattoes born of white women, who, for such intermarriage, shall only become servants for seven years, to be disposed of as the justices of the county court where such marriage so happens shall think fit, to be applied by them towards the support of a public school within the said county. And any white man or white woman who shall intermarry as aforesaid with any negro or mulatto, such white man or white woman shall become servants during the term of seven years, and shall be disposed of by the justices as aforesaid, and be applied to the uses aforesaid.

The other colonial law to which we refer was passed by Massachusetts in 1705 (chap. 6). It is entitled "An act for the better preventing of a spurious and mixed issue," &c., and it provides, that

> if any negro or mulatto shall presume to smite or strike any person of the English or other Christian nation, such negro or mulatto shall be severely whipped, at the discretion of the justices before whom the offender shall be convicted.

And

> that none of her Majesty's English or Scottish subjects, nor of any other Christian nation, within this province, shall contract matrimony with any negro or mulatto; nor shall any person, duly authorized to solemnize marriage, presume to join any such in marriage, on pain of forfeiting the sum of fifty pounds; one moiety thereof to her Majesty, for and towards the support of the Government within this province, and the other moiety to him or them that shall inform and sue for the same, in any of her Majesty's courts of record within the province, by bill, plaint, or information.

We give both of these laws in the words used by the respective legislative bodies because the language in which they are framed, as well as the provisions contained in them, show, too plainly to be misunderstood the degraded condition of this unhappy race. They were still in force when the Revolution began, and are a faithful index to the state of feeling towards the class of persons of whom they speak, and of the position they occupied throughout the thirteen colonies, in the eyes and thoughts of the men who framed the Declaration of Independence and established the State Constitutions and Governments. They show that a perpetual and impassable barrier was intended to be erected between the white race and the one which they had reduced to slavery, and governed as subjects with absolute and despotic power, and which they then looked upon as so far below them in the scale of created beings, that intermarriages between white persons and negroes or mulattoes were regarded as unnatural and immoral, and punished as crimes, not only in the parties, but in the person who joined them in marriage. And no distinction in this respect was made between the free negro or mulatto and the slave, but this stigma of the deepest degradation was fixed upon the whole race.

We refer to these historical facts for the purpose of showing the fixed opinions concerning that race upon which the statesmen of that day spoke and acted. It is necessary to do this in order to determine whether the general terms used in the Constitution of the United States as to the rights of man and the rights of the people was intended to include them, or to give to them or their posterity the benefit of any of its provisions.

The language of the Declaration of Independence is equally conclusive:

It begins by declaring that,

> [w]hen in the course of human events it becomes necessary for one people to dissolve the political bands which have connected them with another, and to assume among the powers of the earth the separate and equal station to which the laws of nature and nature's God entitle them, a decent respect for the opinions of mankind requires that they should declare the causes which impel them to the separation.

It then proceeds to say:

> We hold these truths to be self-evident: that all men are created equal; that they are endowed by their Creator with certain unalienable rights; that among them is life, liberty, and the pursuit of happiness; that to secure these rights, Governments are instituted, deriving their just powers from the consent of the governed.

The general words above quoted would seem to embrace the whole human family, and if they were used in a similar instrument at this day would be so understood. But it is too clear for dispute that the enslaved African race were not intended to be included, and formed no part of the people who framed and adopted this declaration, for if the language, as understood in that day, would embrace them, the conduct of the distinguished men who framed the Declaration of Independence would have been utterly and flagrantly inconsistent with the principles they asserted, and instead of the sympathy of mankind to which they so confidently appealed, they would have deserved and received universal rebuke and reprobation.

Yet the men who framed this declaration were great men—high in literary acquirements, high in their sense of honor, and incapable of asserting principles inconsistent with those on which they were acting. They perfectly understood the meaning of the language they used, and how it would be understood by others, and they knew that it would not in any part of the civilized world be supposed to embrace the negro race, which, by common consent, had been excluded from civilized Governments and the family of nations, and doomed to slavery. They spoke and acted according to the then established doctrines and principles, and in the ordinary language of the day, and no one misunderstood them. The unhappy black race were separated from the white by indelible marks, and laws long before established, and were never thought of or spoken of except as property, and when the claims of the owner or the profit of the trader were supposed to need protection.

This state of public opinion had undergone no change when the Constitution was adopted, as is equally evident from its provisions and language.

The brief preamble sets forth by whom it was formed, for what purposes, and for whose benefit and protection. It declares that it is formed by the people of the United States—that is to say, by those who were members of the different political communities in the several States—and its great object is declared to be to secure the blessings of liberty to themselves and their posterity. It speaks in general terms of the people of the United States, and of citizens of the several States, when it is providing for the exercise of the powers granted or the privileges secured to the citizen. It does not define what description of persons are intended to be included under these terms, or who shall be regarded as a citizen and one of the people. It uses them as terms so well understood that no further description or definition was necessary.

But there are two clauses in the Constitution which point directly and specifically to the negro race as a separate class of persons, and show clearly that they were not regarded as a portion of the people or citizens of the Government then formed.

One of these clauses reserves to each of the thirteen States the right to import slaves until the year 1808 if it thinks proper. And the importation which it thus sanctions was unquestionably of persons of the race of which we are speaking, as the traffic in slaves in the United States had always been confined to them. And by the other provision the States pledge themselves to each other to maintain the right of property of the master by delivering up to him any slave who may have escaped from his service, and be found within their respective territories. By the first above-mentioned clause, therefore, the right to purchase and hold this property is directly sanctioned and authorized for twenty years by the people who framed the Constitution. And by the second, they pledge themselves to maintain and uphold the right of the master in the manner specified, as long as the Government they then formed should endure. And these two provisions show conclusively that neither the description of persons therein referred to nor their descendants were embraced in any of the other provisions of the Constitution, for certainly these two clauses were not intended to confer on them or their posterity the blessings of liberty, or any of the personal rights so carefully provided for the citizen.

No one of that race had ever migrated to the United States voluntarily; all of them had been brought here as articles of merchandise. The number that had been emancipated at that time were but few in comparison with those held in slavery, and they were identified in the public mind with the race to which they belonged, and regarded as a part of the slave population rather than the free. It is obvious that they were not even in the minds of the framers of the Constitution when they were conferring special rights and privileges upon the citizens of a State in every other part of the Union.

Indeed, when we look to the condition of this race in the several States at the time, it is impossible to believe that these rights and privileges were intended to be extended to them.

It is very true that, in that portion of the Union where the labor of the negro race was found to be unsuited to the climate and unprofitable to the master, but few slaves were held at the time of the Declaration of Independence, and when the Constitution was adopted, it had entirely worn out in one of them, and measures had been taken for its gradual abolition in several others. But this change had not been produced by any change of opinion in relation to this race, but because it was discovered from experience that slave labor was unsuited to the climate and productions of these States, for some of the States where it had ceased or nearly ceased to exist were actively engaged in the slave trade, procuring cargoes on the coast of Africa and transporting them for sale to those parts of the Union where their labor was found to be profitable and suited to the climate and productions. And this traffic was openly carried on, and fortunes accumulated by it, without reproach from the people of the States where they resided. And it can hardly be supposed that, in the States where it was then countenanced in its worst form—that is, in the seizure and transportation—the people could have regarded those who were emancipated as entitled to equal rights with themselves.

And we may here again refer in support of this proposition to the plain and unequivocal language of the laws of the several States, some passed after the Declaration of

Independence and before the Constitution was adopted and some since the Government went into operation.

We need not refer on this point particularly to the laws of the present slaveholding States. Their statute books are full of provisions in relation to this class in the same spirit with the Maryland law which we have before quoted. They have continued to treat them as an inferior class, and to subject them to strict police regulations, drawing a broad line of distinction between the citizen and the slave races, and legislating in relation to them upon the same principle which prevailed at the time of the Declaration of Independence. As relates to these States, it is too plain for argument that they have never been regarded as a part of the people or citizens of the State, nor supposed to possess any political rights which the dominant race might not withhold or grant at their pleasure. And as long ago as 1822, the Court of Appeals of Kentucky decided that free negroes and mulattoes were not citizens within the meaning of the Constitution of the United States, and the correctness of this decision is recognized, and the same doctrine affirmed, in 1 Meigs's Tenn. Reports, 331.

And if we turn to the legislation of the States where slavery had worn out, or measures taken for its speedy abolition, we shall find the same opinions and principles equally fixed and equally acted upon.

Thus, Massachusetts, in 1786, passed a law similar to the colonial one of which we have spoken. The law of 1786, like the law of 1705, forbids the marriage of any white person with any negro, Indian, or mulatto, and inflicts a penalty of fifty pounds upon anyone who shall join them in marriage, and declares all such marriage absolutely null and void, and degrades thus the unhappy issue of the marriage by fixing upon it the stain of bastardy. And this mark of degradation was renewed, and again impressed upon the race, in the careful and deliberate preparation of their revised code published in 1836. This code forbids any person from joining in marriage any white person with any Indian, negro, or mulatto, and subjects the party who shall offend in this respect to imprisonment not exceeding six months in the common jail or to hard labor, and to a fine of not less than fifty nor more than two hundred dollars, and, like the law of 1786, it declares the marriage to be absolutely null and void. It will be seen that the punishment is increased by the code upon the person who shall marry them, by adding imprisonment to a pecuniary penalty.

So, too, in Connecticut. We refer more particularly to the legislation of this State, because it was not only among the first to put an end to slavery within its own territory, but was the first to fix a mark of reprobation upon the African slave trade. The law last mentioned was passed in October, 1788, about nine months after the State had ratified and adopted the present Constitution of the United States, and, by that law, it prohibited its own citizens, under severe penalties, from engaging in the trade, and declared all policies of insurance on the vessel or cargo made in the State to be null and void. But up to the time of the adoption of the Constitution, there is nothing in the legislation of the State indicating any change of opinion as to the relative rights and position of the white and black races in this country, or indicating that it meant to place the latter, when free, upon a level with its citizens. And certainly nothing which would have led the slaveholding States to suppose that Connecticut designed to claim for them, under the new Constitution, the equal rights and privileges and rank of citizens in every other State.

The first step taken by Connecticut upon this subject was as early as 1774, when it passed an act forbidding the further importation of slaves into the State. But the section containing the prohibition is introduced by the following preamble:

> And whereas the increase of slaves in this State is injurious to the poor, and inconvenient.

This recital would appear to have been carefully introduced in order to prevent any misunderstanding of the motive which induced the Legislature to pass the law, and places it distinctly upon the interest and convenience of the white population—excluding the inference that it might have been intended in any degree for the benefit of the other.

And in the act of 1784, by which the issue of slaves born after the time therein mentioned were to be free at a certain age, the section is again introduced by a preamble assigning a similar motive for the act. It is in these words:

> Whereas sound policy requires that the abolition of slavery should be effected as soon as may be consistent with the rights of individuals, and the public safety and welfare—showing that the right of property in the master was to be protected, and that the measure was one of policy, and to prevent the injury and inconvenience to the whites of a slave population in the State.

And still further pursuing its legislation, we find that, in the same statute passed in 1774, which prohibited the further importation of slaves into the State, there is also a provision by which any negro, Indian, or mulatto servant who was found wandering out of the town or place to which he belonged without a written pass such as is therein described was made liable to be seized by anyone, and taken before the next authority to be examined and delivered up to his master—who was required to pay the charge which had accrued thereby. And a subsequent section of the same law provides that if any free negro shall travel without such pass, and shall be stopped, seized, or taken up, he shall pay all charges arising thereby. And this law was in full operation when the Constitution of the United States was adopted, and was not repealed till 1797. So that, up to that time, free negroes and mulattoes were associated with servants and slaves in the police regulations established by the laws of the State.

And again, in 1833, Connecticut passed another law which made it penal to set up or establish any school in that State for the instruction of persons of the African race not inhabitants of the State, or to instruct or teach in any such school or institution, or board or harbor for that purpose, any such person without the previous consent in writing of the civil authority of the town in which such school or institution might be.

And it appears by the case of *Crandall v. The State*, reported in 10 Conn. Rep. 340, that upon an information filed against Prudence Crandall for a violation of this law, one of the points raised in the defence was that the law was a violation of the Constitution of the United States, and that the persons instructed, although of the African race, were citizens of other States, and therefore entitled to the rights and privileges of citizens in the State of Connecticut. But Chief Justice Dagget, before whom the case was tried, held that persons of that description were not citizens of a State, within the meaning of the word citizen in the Constitution of the United States, and were not therefore entitled to the privileges and immunities of citizens in other States.

The case was carried up to the Supreme Court of Errors of the State, and the question fully argued there. But the case went off upon another point, and no opinion was expressed on this question.

We have made this particular examination into the legislative and judicial action of Connecticut because, from the early hostility it displayed to the slave trade on the coast of Africa, we may expect to find the laws of that State as lenient and favorable to the subject race as those of any other State in the Union, and if we find that, at the time the Constitution was adopted, they were not even there raised to the rank of citizens, but were still held and treated as property, and the laws relating to them passed with reference altogether to the interest and convenience of the white race, we shall hardly find them elevated to a higher rank anywhere else.

A brief notice of the laws of two other States, and we shall pass on to other considerations.

By the laws of New Hampshire, collected and finally passed in 1815, no one was permitted to be enrolled in the militia of the State but free white citizens, and the same provision is found in a subsequent collection of the laws made in 1855. Nothing could more strongly mark the entire repudiation of the African race. The alien is excluded because, being born in a foreign country, he cannot be a member of the community until he is naturalized. But why are the African race, born in the State, not permitted to share in one of the highest duties of the citizen? The answer is obvious; he is not, by the institutions and laws of the State, numbered among its people. He forms no part of the sovereignty of the State, and is not therefore called on to uphold and defend it.

Again, in 1822, Rhode Island, in its revised code, passed a law forbidding persons who were authorized to join persons in marriage from joining in marriage any white person with any negro, Indian, or mulatto, under the penalty of two hundred dollars, and declaring all such marriages absolutely null and void, and the same law was again reenacted in its revised code of 1844. So that, down to the last-mentioned period, the strongest mark of inferiority and degradation was fastened upon the African race in that State.

It would be impossible to enumerate and compress in the space usually allotted to an opinion of a court the various laws, marking the condition of this race which were passed from time to time after the Revolution and before and since the adoption of the Constitution of the United States. In addition to those already referred to, it is sufficient to say that Chancellor Kent, whose accuracy and research no one will question, states in the sixth edition of his Commentaries (published in 1848, 2 vol., 258, note b) that in no part of the country except Maine did the African race, in point of fact, participate equally with the whites in the exercise of civil and political rights.

The legislation of the States therefore shows in a manner not to be mistaken the inferior and subject condition of that race at the time the Constitution was adopted and long afterwards, throughout the thirteen States by which that instrument was framed, and it is hardly consistent with the respect due to these States to suppose that they regarded at that time as fellow citizens and members of the sovereignty, a class of beings whom they had thus stigmatized, whom, as we are bound out of respect to the State sovereignties to assume they had deemed it just and necessary thus to stigmatize, and upon whom they had impressed such deep and enduring marks of inferiority and degradation, or, that, when they met in convention to form the Constitution, they looked upon them as a portion of their constituents or designed to include them in the provisions so carefully inserted for the security and protection of the liberties and rights of their citizens. It cannot be supposed that they intended to secure to them rights and privileges and rank, in the new political body throughout the Union which every one of them denied within the limits of its own dominion. More especially, it cannot be believed that the large slaveholding States regarded them as included in the word citizens, or would have consented to a Constitution which might compel them to receive them in that character from another State. For if they were so received, and entitled to the privileges and immunities of citizens, it would exempt them from the operation of the special laws and from the police regulations which they considered to be necessary for their own safety. It would give to persons of the negro race, who were recognised as citizens in any one State of the Union, the right to enter every other State whenever they pleased, singly or in companies, without pass or passport, and without obstruction, to sojourn there as long as they pleased, to go where they pleased at every hour of the day or night without molestation, unless they committed some violation of law for which a white man would be punished; and it would give them the full liberty of speech in public and in private upon all subjects upon which its own citizens might speak; to hold public meetings upon political affairs, and to keep and carry arms wherever they went. And all of this would be done in the face of the subject race of the same color, both free and slaves, and inevitably producing discontent and insubordination among them, and endangering the peace and safety of the State.

It is impossible, it would seem, to believe that the great men of the slaveholding States, who took so large a share in framing the Constitution of the United States and exercised so much influence in procuring its adoption, could have been so forgetful or regardless of their own safety and the safety of those who trusted and confided in them.

Besides, this want of foresight and care would have been utterly inconsistent with the caution displayed in providing for the admission of new members into this political family. For, when they gave to the citizens of each State the privileges and immunities of citizens in the several States, they at the same time took from the several States the power of naturalization, and confined that power exclusively to the Federal Government. No State was willing to permit another State to determine who should or should not be admitted as one of its citizens, and entitled to demand equal rights and privileges with their own people, within their own territories. The right of naturalization was therefore, with one accord, surrendered by the States, and confided to the Federal Government. And this power granted to Congress to establish an uniform rule of naturalization is, by the well understood meaning of the word, confined to persons born in a foreign country, under a foreign Government. It is not a power to raise to the rank of a citizen anyone born in the United States who, from birth or parentage, by the laws of the country, belongs to an inferior and subordinate class. And when we find the States guarding themselves from the indiscreet or improper admission by other States of emigrants from other countries by giving the power exclusively to Congress, we cannot fail to see that they could never have left with the States a much more important power—that is, the power of transforming into citizens a numerous class of persons who, in that character, would be much more dangerous to the peace and safety of a large portion of the Union than the few foreigners one of the States might improperly naturalize. The Constitution upon its adoption obviously took from the States all power by any subsequent legislation to introduce as a citizen into the political family of the United States anyone, no matter where he was born or what might be his character or condition, and it gave to Congress the power to confer this character upon those only who were born outside of the dominions of the United States. And no law of a State, therefore, passed since the Constitution was adopted, can give any right of citizenship outside of its own territory.

. . . the Constitution does not limit the power of Congress in this respect to white persons. And they may, if they think proper, authorize the naturalization of anyone, of any color, who was born under allegiance to another Government. But the language of the law above quoted shows that citizenship at that time was perfectly understood to be confined to the white race; and that they alone constituted the sovereignty in the Government.

Congress might, as we before said, have authorized the naturalization of Indians because they were aliens and foreigners. But, in their then untutored and savage state, no one would have thought of admitting them as citizens in a civilized community. And, moreover, the atrocities they had but recently committed, when they were the allies of Great Britain in the Revolutionary war, were yet fresh in the recollection of the people of the United States, and they were even then guarding themselves against the threatened renewal of Indian hostilities. No one supposed then that any Indian would ask for, or was capable of enjoying, the privileges of an American citizen, and the word white was not used with any particular reference to them.

Neither was it used with any reference to the African race imported into or born in this country; because Congress had no power to naturalize them, and therefore there was no necessity for using particular words to exclude them.

It would seem to have been used merely because it followed out the line of division which the Constitution has drawn between the citizen race, who formed and held the Government, and the African race, which they held in subjection and slavery and governed at their own pleasure.

. . . .

Upon the whole, therefore, it is the judgment of this court that it appears by the record before us that the plaintiff in error is not a citizen of Missouri in the sense in which that word is used in the Constitution, and that the Circuit Court of the United States, for that reason, had no jurisdiction in the case, and could give no judgment in it. Its judgment for the defendant must, consequently, be reversed, and a mandate issued directing the suit to be dismissed for want of jurisdiction.

26

Speech on the Dred Scott Decision

Abraham Lincoln
June 26, 1857
Speech at Springfield, Illinois

FELLOW CITIZENS:—I am here to-night, partly by the invitation of some of you, and partly by my own inclination. Two weeks ago Judge Douglas spoke here on the several subjects of Kansas, the Dred Scott decision, and Utah. I listened to the speech at the time, and have read the report of it since. It was intended to controvert opinions which I think just, and to assail (politically, not personally,) those men who, in common with me, entertain those opinions. For this reason I wished then, and still wish, to make some answer to it, which I now take the opportunity of doing.

I begin with Utah. If it prove to be true, as is probable, that the people of Utah are in open rebellion to the United States, then Judge Douglas is in favor of repealing their territorial organization, and attaching them to the adjoining States for judicial purposes. I say, too, if they are in rebellion, they ought to be somehow coerced to obedience; and I am not now prepared to admit or deny that the Judge's mode of coercing them is not as good as any. The Republicans can fall in with it without taking back anything they have ever said. To be sure, it would be a considerable backing down by Judge Douglas from his much vaunted doctrine of self-government for the territories; but this is only additional proof of what was very plain from the beginning, that that doctrine was a mere deceitful pretense for the benefit of slavery. Those who could not see that much in the Nebraska act itself, which forced Governors, and Secretaries, and Judges on the people of the territories, without their choice or consent, could not be made to see, though one should rise from the dead to testify.

But in all this, it is very plain the Judge evades the only question the Republicans have ever pressed upon the Democracy in regard to Utah. That question the Judge well knows to be this: "If the people of Utah shall peacefully form a State Constitution tolerating polygamy, will the Democracy admit them into the Union?" There is nothing in the United States Constitution or law against polygamy; and why is it not a part of the Judge's "sacred right of self-government" for that people to have it, or rather to keep it, if they choose? These questions, so far as I know, the Judge never answers. It might involve the Democracy to answer them either way, and they go unanswered.

As to Kansas. The substance of the Judge's speech on Kansas is an effort to put the free State men in the wrong for not voting at the election of delegates to the Constitutional Convention. He says: "There is every reason to hope and believe that the law will be fairly interpreted and impartially executed, so as to insure to every bona fide inhabitant the free and quiet exercise of the elective franchise."

It appears extraordinary that Judge Douglas should make such a statement. He knows that, by the law, no one can vote who has not been registered; and he knows that the free State men place their refusal to vote on the ground that but few of them have been registered. It is possible this is not true, but Judge Douglas knows it is asserted to be true in letters, newspapers and public speeches, and borne by every mail, and blown by every breeze to the eyes and ears of the world. He knows it is boldly declared that the people of many whole counties, and many whole neighborhoods in others, are left unregistered; yet, he does not venture to contradict the declaration, nor to point out how they can vote without being registered; but he just slips along, not seeming to know there is any such question of fact, and complacently declares: "There is every reason to hope and believe that the law will be fairly and impartially executed, so as to insure to every bona fide inhabitant the free and quiet exercise of the elective franchise."

I readily agree that if all had a chance to vote, they ought to have voted. If, on the contrary, as they allege, and Judge Douglas ventures not to particularly contradict, few only of the free State men had a chance to vote, they were perfectly right in staying from the polls in a body.

By the way since the Judge spoke, the Kansas election has come off. The Judge expressed his confidence that all the Democrats in Kansas would do their duty—including "free state Democrats" of course. The returns received here as yet are very incomplete; but so far as they go, they indicate that only about one sixth of the registered voters, have really voted; and this too, when not more, perhaps, than one half of the rightful voters have been registered, thus showing the thing to have been altogether the most exquisite farce ever enacted. I am watching with considerable interest, to ascertain what figure "the free state Democrats" cut in the concern. Of course they voted—all democrats do their duty—and of course they did not vote for slave-state candidates. We soon shall know how many delegates they elected, how many candidates they had, pledged for a free state; and how many votes were cast for them.

Allow me to barely whisper my suspicion that there were no such things in Kansas "as free state Democrats"—that they were altogether mythical, good only to figure in newspapers and speeches in the free states. If there should prove to be one real living free state Democrat in Kansas, I suggest that it might be well to catch him, and stuff and preserve his skin, as an interesting specimen of that soon to be extinct variety of the genus, Democrat.

And now as to the Dred Scott decision. That decision declares two propositions—first, that a negro cannot sue in the U.S. Courts; and secondly, that Congress cannot prohibit slavery in the Territories. It was made by a divided court—dividing differently on the different points. Judge Douglas does not discuss the merits of the decision; and, in that respect,

I shall follow his example, believing I could no more improve on McLean and Curtis, than he could on Taney.

He denounces all who question the correctness of that decision, as offering violent resistance to it. But who resists it? Who has, in spite of the decision, declared Dred Scott free, and resisted the authority of his master over him?

Judicial decisions have two uses—first, to absolutely determine the case decided, and secondly, to indicate to the public how other similar cases will be decided when they arise. For the latter use, they are called "precedents" and "authorities."

We believe, as much as Judge Douglas, (perhaps more) in obedience to, and respect for the judicial department of government. We think its decisions on Constitutional questions, when fully settled, should control, not only the particular cases decided, but the general policy of the country, subject to be disturbed only by amendments of the Constitution as provided in that instrument itself. More than this would be revolution. But we think the Dred Scott decision is erroneous. We know the court that made it, has often over-ruled its own decisions, and we shall do what we can to have it to over-rule this. We offer no resistance to it.

Judicial decisions are of greater or less authority as precedents, according to circumstances. That this should be so, accords both with common sense, and the customary understanding of the legal profession.

If this important decision had been made by the unanimous concurrence of the judges, and without any apparent partisan bias, and in accordance with legal public expectation, and with the steady practice of the departments throughout our history, and had been in no part, based on assumed historical facts which are not really true; or, if wanting in some of these, it had been before the court more than once, and had there been affirmed and re-affirmed through a course of years, it then might be, perhaps would be, factious, nay, even revolutionary, to not acquiesce in it as a precedent.

But when, as it is true we find it wanting in all these claims to the public confidence, it is not resistance, it is not factious, it is not even disrespectful, to treat it as not having yet quite established a settled doctrine for the country—But Judge Douglas considers this view awful. Hear him:

"The courts are the tribunals prescribed by the Constitution and created by the authority of the people to determine, expound and enforce the law. Hence, whoever resists the final decision of the highest judicial tribunal, aims a deadly blow to our whole Republican system of government—a blow, which if successful would place all our rights and liberties at the mercy of passion, anarchy and violence. I repeat, therefore, that if resistance to the decisions of the Supreme Court of the United States, in a matter like the points decided in the Dred Scott case, clearly within their jurisdiction as defined by the Constitution, shall be forced upon the country as a political issue, it will become a distinct and naked issue between the friends and the enemies of the Constitution—the friends and the enemies of the supremacy of the laws."

Why this same Supreme court once decided a national bank to be constitutional; but Gen. Jackson, as President of the United States, disregarded the decision, and vetoed a bill for a re-charter, partly on constitutional ground, declaring that each public functionary must support the Constitution, "as he understands it." But hear the General's own words. Here they are, taken from his veto message:

"It is maintained by the advocates of the bank, that its constitutionality, in all its features, ought to be considered as settled by precedent, and by the decision of the Supreme Court. To this conclusion I cannot assent. Mere precedent is a dangerous source of authority, and should not be regarded as deciding questions of constitutional power, except where the acquiescence of the people and the States can be considered as well settled. So far from this being the case on this subject, an argument against the bank might be based on precedent. One Congress in 1791, decided in favor of a bank; another in 1811, decided against it. One Congress in 1815 decided against a bank; another in 1816 decided in its favor. Prior to the present Congress, therefore the precedents drawn from that source were equal. If we resort to the States, the expressions of legislative, judicial and executive opinions against the bank have been probably to those in its favor as four to one. There is nothing in precedent, therefore, which if its authority were admitted, ought to weigh in favor of the act before me."

I drop the quotations merely to remark that all there ever was, in the way of precedent up to the Dred Scott decision, on the points therein decided, had been against that decision. But hear Gen. Jackson further—

"If the opinion of the Supreme court covered the whole ground of this act, it ought not to control the co-ordinate authorities of this Government. The Congress, the executive and the court, must each for itself be guided by its own opinion of the Constitution. Each public officer, who takes an oath to support the Constitution, swears that he will support it as he understands it, and not as it is understood by others."

Again and again have I heard Judge Douglas denounce that bank decision, and applaud Gen. Jackson for disregarding it. It would be interesting for him to look over his recent speech, and see how exactly his fierce philippics against us for resisting Supreme Court decisions, fall upon his own head. It will call to his mind a long and fierce political war in this country, upon an issue which, in his own language, and, of course, in his own changeless estimation, was "a distinct and naked issue between the friends and the enemies of the Constitution," and in which war he fought in the ranks of the enemies of the Constitution.

I have said, in substance, that the Dred Scott decision was, in part, based on assumed historical facts which were not really true; and I ought not to leave the subject without giving some reasons for saying this; I therefore give an instance or two, which I think fully sustain me. Chief Justice Taney, in delivering the opinion of the majority of the Court, insists at great length that negroes were no part of the people who made, or for whom was made, the Declaration of Independence, or the Constitution of the United States.

On the contrary, Judge Curtis, in his dissenting opinion, shows that in five of the then thirteen states, to wit, New Hampshire, Massachusetts, New York, New Jersey and North Carolina, free negroes were voters, and, in proportion to their numbers, had the same part in making the Constitution that the white people had. He shows this with so much particularity as to leave no doubt of its truth; and, as a sort of conclusion on that point, holds the following language:

"The Constitution was ordained and established by the people of the United States, through the action, in each State, of those persons who were qualified by its laws to act thereon in behalf of themselves and all other citizens of the State. In some of the States, as we have seen, colored persons were among those qualified by law to act on the subject. These colored persons were not only included in the body of 'the people of the United States,' by whom the Constitution was ordained and established; but in at least five of the States they had the power to act, and, doubtless, did act, by their suffrages, upon the question of its adoption."

Again, Chief Justice Taney says: "It is difficult, at this day to realize the state of public opinion in relation to that unfortunate race, which prevailed in the civilized and enlightened portions of the world at the time of the Declaration of Independence, and when the Constitution of the United States was framed and adopted." And again, after quoting from the Declaration, he says: "The general words above quoted would seem to include the whole human family, and if they were used in a similar instrument at this day, would be so understood."

In these the Chief Justice does not directly assert, but plainly assumes, as a fact, that the public estimate of the black man is more favorable now than it was in the days of the Revolution. This assumption is a mistake. In some trifling particulars, the condition of that race has been ameliorated; but, as a whole, in this country, the change between then and now is decidedly the other way; and their ultimate destiny has never appeared so hopeless as in the last three or four years. In two of the five States—New Jersey and North Carolina—that then gave the free negro the right of voting, the right has since been taken away; and in a third—New York—it has been greatly abridged; while it has not been extended, so far as I know, to a single additional State, though the number of the States has more than doubled. In those days, as I understand, masters could, at their own pleasure, emancipate their slaves; but since then, such legal restraints have been made upon emancipation, as to amount almost to prohibition. In those days, Legislatures held the unquestioned power to abolish slavery in their respective States; but now it is becoming quite fashionable for State Constitutions to withhold that power from the Legislatures. In those days, by common consent, the spread of the black man's bondage to new countries was prohibited; but now, Congress decides that it will not continue the prohibition, and the Supreme Court decides that it could not if it would. In those days, our Declaration of Independence was held sacred by all, and thought to include all; but now, to aid in making the bondage of the negro universal and eternal, it is assailed, and sneered at, and construed, and hawked at, and torn, till, if its framers could rise from their graves, they could not at all recognize it. All the powers of earth seem rapidly combining against him. Mammon is after him; ambition follows, and philosophy follows, and the Theology of the day is fast joining the cry. They have him in his prison house; they have searched his person, and left no prying instrument with him. One after another they have closed the heavy iron doors upon him, and now they have him, as it were, bolted in with a lock of a hundred keys, which can never be unlocked without the concurrence of every key; the keys in the hands of a hundred different men, and they scattered to a hundred different and distant places; and they stand musing as to what invention, in all the dominions of mind and matter, can be produced to make the impossibility of his escape more complete than it is.

It is grossly incorrect to say or assume, that the public estimate of the negro is more favorable now than it was at the origin of the government.

Three years and a half ago, Judge Douglas brought forward his famous Nebraska bill. The country was at once in a blaze. He scorned all opposition, and carried it through Congress. Since then he has seen himself superseded in a Presidential nomination, by one indorsing the general doctrine of his measure, but at the same time standing clear of the odium of its untimely agitation, and its gross breach of national faith; and he has seen that successful rival Constitutionally elected, not by the strength of friends, but by the division of adversaries, being in a popular minority of nearly four hundred thousand votes. He has seen his chief aids in his own State, Shields and Richardson, politically speaking, successively tried, convicted, and executed, for an offense not their own, but his. And now he sees his own case, standing next on the docket for trial.

There is a natural disgust in the minds of nearly all white people, to the idea of an indiscriminate amalgamation of the white and black races; and Judge Douglas evidently is basing his chief hope, upon the chances of being able to appropriate the benefit of this disgust to himself. If he can, by much drumming and repeating, fasten the odium of that idea upon his adversaries, he thinks he can struggle through the storm. He therefore clings to this hope, as a drowning man to the last plank. He makes an occasion for lugging it in from the opposition to the Dred Scott decision. He finds the Republicans insisting that the Declaration of Independence includes ALL men, black as well as white; and forth-with he boldly denies that it includes negroes at all, and proceeds to argue gravely that all who contend it does, do so only because they want to vote, and eat, and sleep, and marry with negroes! He will have it that they cannot be consistent else. Now I protest against that counterfeit logic which concludes that, because I do not want a black woman for a slave I must necessarily want her for a wife. I need not have her for either, I can just leave her alone. In some respects she certainly is not my equal; but in her natural right to eat the bread she earns with her own hands without asking leave of any one else, she is my equal, and the equal of all others.

Chief Justice Taney, in his opinion in the Dred Scott case, admits that the language of the Declaration is broad enough to include the whole human family, but he and Judge Douglas argue that the authors of that instrument did not intend to include negroes, by the fact that they did not at once, actually place them on an equality with the whites. Now this grave argument comes to just nothing at all, by the other fact, that they did not at once, or ever afterwards, actually place all white people on an equality with one or another. And this is the staple argument of both the Chief Justice and the Senator, for doing this obvious violence to the plain unmistakable language of the Declaration. I think the authors of that notable instrument intended to include all men, but they did not intend to declare all men equal in all respects. They did not mean to say all were equal in color, size, intellect, moral developments, or social capacity. They defined with tolerable distinctness, in what respects they did consider all men created equal—equal in "certain inalienable rights, among which are life, liberty, and the pursuit of happiness." This they said, and this meant. They did not mean to assert the obvious untruth, that all were then actually enjoying that equality, nor yet, that they were about to confer it immediately upon them. In fact they had no power to confer such a boon. They meant simply to declare the right, so that the enforcement of it might follow as fast as circumstances should permit. They meant to set up a standard maxim for free society, which should be familiar to all, and revered by all; constantly looked to, constantly labored for, and even though never perfectly attained, constantly approximated, and thereby constantly spreading and deepening its influence, and augmenting the happiness and value of life to all people of all colors everywhere. The assertion that "all men are created equal" was of no practical use in effecting our separation from Great Britain; and it was placed in the Declaration, nor for that, but for future use. Its authors meant it to be, thank God, it is now proving itself, a stumbling block to those who in after times might seek to turn a free people back into the hateful paths of despotism. They knew the proneness of prosperity to breed tyrants, and they meant when such should re-appear in this fair land and commence their vocation they should find left for them at least one hard nut to crack.

I have now briefly expressed my view of the meaning and objects of that part of the Declaration of Independence which declares that "all men are created equal."

Now let us hear Judge Douglas' view of the same subject, as I find it in the printed report of his late speech. Here it is:

> "No man can vindicate the character, motives and conduct of the signers of the Declaration of Independence except upon the hypothesis that they referred to the white race alone, and not to the African, when they declared all men to have been created equal—that they were speaking of British subjects on this continent being equal to British subjects born and residing in Great Britain—that they were entitled to the same inalienable rights, and among them were enumerated life, liberty and the pursuit of happiness. The Declaration was adopted for the purpose of justifying the colonists in the eyes of the civilized world in withdrawing their allegiance from the British crown, and dissolving their connection with the mother country."

My good friends, read that carefully over some leisure hour, and ponder well upon it—see what a mere wreck—mangled ruin—it makes of our once glorious Declaration.

"They were speaking of British subjects on this continent being equal to British subjects born and residing in Great Britain!" Why, according to this, not only negroes but white people outside of Great Britain and America are not spoken of in that instrument. The English, Irish and Scotch, along with white Americans, were included to be sure, but the French, Germans and other white people of the world are all gone to pot along with the

Judge's inferior races. I had thought the Declaration promised something better than the condition of British subjects; but no, it only meant that we should be equal to them in their own oppressed and unequal condition. According to that, it gave no promise that having kicked off the King and Lords of Great Britain, we should not at once be saddled with a King and Lords of our own.

I had thought the Declaration contemplated the progressive improvement in the condition of all men everywhere; but no, it merely "was adopted for the purpose of justifying the colonists in the eyes of the civilized world in withdrawing their allegiance from the British crown, and dissolving their connection with the mother country." Why, that object having been effected some eighty years ago, the Declaration is of no practical use now—mere rubbish—old wadding left to rot on the battle-field after the victory is won.

I understand you are preparing to celebrate the "Fourth," tomorrow week. What for? The doings of that day had no reference to the present; and quite half of you are not even descendants of those who were referred to at that day. But I suppose you will celebrate; and will even go so far as to read the Declaration. Suppose after you read it once in the old fashioned way, you read it once more with Judge Douglas' version. It will then run thus: "We hold these truths to be self-evident that all British subjects who were on this continent eighty-one years ago, were created equal to all British subjects born and then residing in Great Britain."

And now I appeal to all—to Democrats as well as others,—are you really willing that the Declaration shall be thus frittered away?—thus left no more at most, than an interesting memorial of the dead past? thus shorn of its vitality, and practical value; and left without the germ or even the suggestion of the individual rights of man in it?

But Judge Douglas is especially horrified at the thought of the mixing blood by the white and black races: agreed for once—a thousand times agreed. There are white men enough to marry all the white women, and black men enough to marry all the black women; and so let them be married. On this point we fully agree with the Judge; and when he shall show that his policy is better adapted to prevent amalgamation than ours we shall drop ours, and adopt his. Let us see. In 1850 there were in the United States, 405,751, mulattoes. Very few of these are the offspring of whites and free blacks; nearly all have sprung from black slaves and white masters. A separation of the races is the only perfect preventive of amalgamation but as an immediate separation is impossible the next best thing is to keep them apart where they are not already together. If white and black people never get together in Kansas, they will never mix blood in Kansas. That is at least one self-evident truth. A few free colored persons may get into the free States, in any event; but their number is too insignificant to amount to much in the way of mixing blood. In 1850 there were in the free states, 56,649 mulattoes; but for the most part they were not born there—they came from the slave States, ready made up. In the same year the slave States had 348,874 mulattoes all of home production. The proportion of free mulattoes to free blacks—the only colored classes in the free states—is much greater in the slave than in the free states. It is worthy of note too, that among the free states those which make the colored man the nearest to equal the white, have, proportionably the fewest mulattoes the least of amalgamation. In New Hampshire, the State which goes farthest towards equality between the races, there are just 184 Mulattoes while there are in Virginia—how many do you think? 79,775, being 23,126 more than in all the free States together. These statistics show that slavery is the greatest source of amalgamation; and next to it, not the elevation, but the degeneration of the free blacks. Yet Judge Douglas dreads the slightest restraints on the spread of slavery, and the slightest human recognition of the negro, as tending horribly to amalgamation.

This very Dred Scott case affords a strong test as to which party most favors amalgamation, the Republicans or the dear Union-saving Democracy. Dred Scott, his wife and two daughters were all involved in the suit. We desired the court to have held that they were citizens so far at least as to entitle them to a hearing as to whether they were free or not; and then, also, that they were in fact and in law really free. Could we have had our way, the chances of these black girls, ever mixing their blood with that of white people, would have been diminished at least to the extent that it could not have been without their consent. But Judge Douglas is delighted to have them decided to be slaves, and not human enough to have a hearing, even if they were free, and thus left subject to the forced concubinage of their masters, and liable to become the mothers of mulattoes in spite of themselves—the very state of case that produces nine tenths of all the mulattoes—all the mixing of blood in the nation.

Of course, I state this case as an illustration only, not meaning to say or intimate that the master of Dred Scott and his family, or any more than a percentage of masters generally, are inclined to exercise this particular power which they hold over their female slaves.

I have said that the separation of the races is the only perfect preventive of amalgamation. I have no right to say all the members of the Republican party are in favor of this, nor to say that as a party they are in favor of it. There is nothing in their platform directly on the subject. But I can say a very large proportion of its members are for it, and that the chief plank in their platform—opposition to the spread of slavery—is most favorable to that separation.

Such separation, if ever effected at all, must be effected by colonization; and no political party, as such, is now doing anything directly for colonization. Party operations at present only favor or retard colonization incidentally. The enterprise is a difficult one; but "when there is a will there is a way;" and what colonization needs most is a hearty will. Will springs from the two elements of moral sense and self-interest. Let us be brought to believe it is morally right, and, at the same time, favorable to, or, at least, not against, our interest, to transfer the African to his native clime, and we shall find a way to do it, however great the task may be. The children of Israel, to such numbers as to include four hundred thousand fighting men, went out of Egyptian bondage in a body.

How differently the respective courses of the Democratic and Republican parties incidentally bear on the question of forming a will—a public sentiment—for colonization, is easy to see. The Republicans inculcate, with whatever of ability they can, that the negro is a man; that his bondage is cruelly wrong, and that the field of his oppression ought not to be enlarged. The Democrats deny his manhood; deny, or dwarf to insignificance, the wrong of his bondage; so far as possible, crush all sympathy for him, and cultivate and excite hatred and disgust against him; compliment themselves as Union-savers for doing so; and call the indefinite outspreading of his bondage "a sacred right of self-government."

The plainest print cannot be read through a gold eagle; and it will be ever hard to find many men who will send a slave to Liberia, and pay his passage while they can send him to a new country, Kansas for instance, and sell him for fifteen hundred dollars, and the rise.

27

The Civil Rights Act of 1866

CHAP. XXXI.

An Act to protect all Persons in the United States in their Civil Rights, and furnish the Means of their Vindication.

Be it enacted by the Senate and House of Representatives of the United States of America in Congress assembled, That all persons born in the United States and not subject to any foreign power, excluding Indians not taxed, are hereby declared to be citizens of the United States; and such citizens, of every race and color, without regard to any previous condition of slavery or involuntary servitude, except as a punishment for crime whereof the party shall have been duly convicted, shall have the same right, in every State and Territory in the United States, to make and enforce contracts, to sue, be parties, and give evidence, to inherit, purchase, lease, sell, hold, and convey real and personal property, and to full and equal benefit of all laws and proceedings for the security of person and property, as is enjoyed by white citizens, and shall be subject to like punishment, pains, and penalties, and to none other, any law, statute, ordinance, regulation, or custom, to the contrary notwithstanding.

Sec. 2. *And be it further enacted,* That any person who, under color of any law, statute, ordinance, regulation, or custom, shall subject, or cause to be subjected, any inhabitant of any State or Territory to the deprivation of any right secured or protected by this act, or to different punishment, pains, or penalties on account of such person having at any time been held in a condition of slavery or involuntary servitude, except as a punishment for crime whereof the party shall have been duly convicted, or by reason of his color or race, than is prescribed for the punishment of white persons, shall be deemed guilty of a misdemeanor, and, on conviction, shall be punished by fine not exceeding one thousand dollars, or imprisonment not exceeding one year, or both, in the discretion of the court.

Sec. 3. *And be it further enacted,* That the district courts of the United States, within their respective districts, shall have, exclusively of the courts of the several States, cognizance of all crimes and offences committed against the provisions of this act, and also, concurrently with the circuit courts of the United States, of all causes, civil and criminal, affecting persons who are denied or cannot enforce in the courts or judicial tribunals of the State or locality where they may be any of the rights secured to them by the first section of this act;

and if any suit or prosecution, civil or criminal, has been or shall be commenced in any State court, against any such person, for any cause whatsoever, or against any officer, civil or military, or other person, for any arrest or imprisonment, trespasses, or wrongs done or committed by virtue or under color of authority derived from this act or the act establishing a Bureau for the relief of Freedmen and Refugees, and all acts amendatory thereof, or for refusing to do any act upon the ground that it would be inconsistent with this act, such defendant shall have the right to remove such cause for trial to the proper district or circuit court in the manner prescribed by the "Act relating to habeas corpus and regulating judicial proceedings in certain cases," approved March three, eighteen hundred and sixty-three, and all acts amendatory thereof. The jurisdiction in civil and criminal matters hereby conferred on the district and circuit courts of the United States shall be exercised and enforced in conformity with the laws of the United States, so far as such laws are suitable to carry the same into effect; but in all cases where such laws are not adapted to the object, or are deficient in the provisions necessary to furnish suitable remedies and punish offences against law, the common law, as modified and changed by the constitution and statutes of the State wherein the court having jurisdiction of the cause, civil or criminal, is held, so far as the same is not inconsistent with the Constitution and laws of the United States, shall be extended to and govern said courts in the trial and disposition of such cause, and, if of a criminal nature, in the infliction of punishment on the party found guilty.

Sec. 4. *And be it further enacted,* That the district attorneys, marshals, and deputy marshals of the United States, the commissioners appointed by the circuit and territorial courts of the United States, with powers of arresting, imprisoning, or bailing offenders against the laws of the United States, the officers and agents of the Freedmen's Bureau, and every other officer who may be specially empowered by the President of the United States, shall be, and they are hereby, specially authorized and required, at the expense of the United States, to institute proceedings against all and every person who shall violate the provisions of this act, and cause him or them to be arrested and imprisoned, or bailed, as the case may be, for trial before such court of the United States or territorial court as by this act has cognizance of the offence. And with a view to affording reasonable protection to all persons in their constitutional rights of equality before the law, without distinction of race or color, or previous condition of slavery or involuntary servitude, except as a punishment for crime, whereof the party shall have been duly convicted, and to the prompt discharge of the duties of this act, it shall be the duty of the circuit courts of the United States and the superior courts of the Territories of the United States, from time to time, to increase the number of commissioners, so as to afford a speedy and convenient means for the arrest and examination of persons charged with a violation of this act; and such commissioners are hereby authorized and required to exercise and discharge all the powers and duties conferred on them by this act, and the same duties with regard to offences created by this act, as they are authorized by law to exercise with regard to other offences against the laws of the United States.

Sec. 5. *And be it further enacted,* That it shall be the duty of all marshals and deputy marshals to obey and execute all warrants and precepts issued under the provisions of this act, when to them directed; and should any marshal or deputy marshal refuse to receive such warrant or other process when tendered, or to use all proper means diligently to execute the same, he shall, on conviction thereof, be fined in the sum of one thousand dollars, to the use of the person upon whom the accused is alleged to have committed the offense. And the better to enable the said commissioners to execute their duties faithfully and efficiently, in conformity with the Constitution of the United States and the requirements of this act, they are hereby authorized and empowered, within their counties respectively, to appoint, in writing, under their hands, any one or more suitable persons, from time to time, to execute all such warrants and other process as may be issued by them in the lawful performance of their respective duties; and the persons so appointed to execute any warrant or process as aforesaid shall have authority to summon and call to their aid the bystanders or posse comitatus of the proper county, or such portion of the land or naval forces of the United States, or of the militia, as may be necessary to the performance of the duty with which they are charged, and to insure a faithful observance of the clause of the Constitution which prohibits slavery, in conformity with the provisions of this act; and said warrants shall run and be executed by said officers anywhere in the State or Territory within which they are issued.

Sec. 6. *And be it further enacted,* That any person who shall knowingly and willfully obstruct, hinder, or prevent any officer, or other person charged with the execution of any warrant or process issued under the provisions of this act, or any person or persons lawfully assisting him or them, from arresting any person for whose apprehension such warrant or process may have been issued, or shall rescue or attempt to rescue such person from the custody of the officer, other person or persons, or those lawfully assisting as aforesaid, when so arrested pursuant to the authority herein given and declared, or shall aid, abet, or assist any person so arrested as aforesaid, directly or indirectly, to escape from the custody of the officer or other person legally authorized as aforesaid, or shall harbor or conceal any person for whose arrest a warrant or process shall have been issued as aforesaid, so as to prevent his discovery and arrest after notice or knowledge of the fact that a warrant has been issued for the apprehension of such person, shall, for either of said offences, be subject to a fine not exceeding one thousand dollars, and imprisonment not exceeding six months, by indictment and conviction before the district court of the United States for the district in which said offense may have been committed, or before the proper court of criminal jurisdiction, if committed within any one of the organized Territories of the United States.

Sec. 7. *And be it further enacted,* That the district attorneys, the marshals, their deputies, and the clerks of the said district and territorial courts shall be paid for their services the like fees as may be allowed to them for similar services in other cases; and in all cases where the proceedings are before a commissioner, he shall be entitled to a fee of ten dollars in full for his services in each case, inclusive of all services incident to such arrest and examination. The person or persons authorized to execute the process to be issued by such commissioners for the arrest of offenders against the provisions of this act shall be entitled to a fee of five dollars for each person he or they may arrest and take before any such commissioner as aforesaid, with such other fees as may be deemed reasonable by such commissioner for such other additional services as may be necessarily performed by him or them, such as attending at the examination, keeping the prisoner in custody, and providing him with food and lodging during his detention, and until the final determination of such commissioner, and in general for performing such other duties as may be required in the premises; such fees to be made up in conformity with the fees usually charged by the officers of the courts of justice within the proper district or county, as near as may be practicable, and paid out of the Treasury of the United States on the certificate of the judge of the district within which the arrest is made, and to be recoverable from the defendant as part of the judgment in case of conviction.

Sec. 8. *And be it further enacted*, that whenever the President of the United States shall have reason to believe that offences have been or are likely to be committed against the provisions of this act within any judicial district, it shall be lawful for him, in his discretion, to direct the judge, marshal, and district attorney of such district to attend at such place within the district, and for such time as he may designate, for the purpose of the more speedy arrest and trial of persons charged with a violation of this act; and it shall be the duty of every judge or other officer, when any such requisition shall be received by him, to attend at the place and for the time therein designated.

Sec. 9. *And be it further enacted*, that it shall be lawful for the President of the United States, or such person as he may empower for that purpose, to employ such part of the land or naval forces of the United States, or of the militia, as shall be necessary to prevent the violation and enforce the due execution of this act.

Sec. 10. *And be it further enacted*, That upon all questions of law arising in any cause under the provisions of this act a final appeal may be taken to the Supreme Court of the United States.

28

Plessy v. Ferguson (1896)

MR. JUSTICE BROWN, after stating the case, delivered the opinion of the court.

This case turns upon the constitutionality of an act of the General Assembly of the State of Louisiana, passed in 1890, providing for separate railway carriages for the white and colored races. Acts 1890, No. 111, p. 152.

The first section of the statute enacts

> that all railway companies carrying passengers in their coaches in this State shall provide equal but separate accommodations for the white and colored races by providing two or more passenger coaches for each passenger train, or by dividing the passenger coaches by a partition so as to secure separate accommodations: *Provided,* That this section shall not be construed to apply to street railroads. No person or persons, shall be admitted to occupy seats in coaches other than the ones assigned to them on account of the race they belong to.

By the second section, it was enacted

> that the officers of such passenger trains shall have power and are hereby required to assign each passenger to the coach or compartment used for the race to which such passenger belongs; any passenger insisting on going into a coach or compartment to which by race he does not belong shall be liable to a fine of twenty-five dollars, or in lieu thereof to imprisonment for a period of not more than twenty days in the parish prison, and any officer of any railroad insisting on assigning a passenger to a coach or compartment other than the one set aside for the race to which said passenger belongs shall be liable to a fine of twenty-five dollars, or in lieu thereof to imprisonment for a period of not more than twenty days in the parish prison; and should any passenger refuse to occupy the coach or compartment to which he or she is assigned by the officer of such railway, said officer shall have power to refuse to carry such passenger on his train, and for such refusal neither he nor the railway company which he represents shall be liable for damages in any of the courts of this State.

The third section provides penalties for the refusal or neglect of the officers, directors, conductors, and employees of railway companies to comply with the act, with a proviso that "nothing in this act shall be construed as applying to nurses attending children of the other race." The fourth section is immaterial.

The information filed in the criminal District Court charged in substance that Plessy, being a passenger between two stations within the State of Louisiana, was assigned by officers of the company to the coach used for the race to which he belonged, but he insisted upon going into a coach used by the race to which he did not belong. Neither in the information nor plea was his particular race or color averred. The petition for the writ of prohibition averred that petitioner was seven-eighths Caucasian and one eighth African blood; that the mixture of colored blood was not discernible in him, and that he was entitled to every right, privilege and immunity secured to citizens of the United States of the white race; and that, upon such theory, he took possession of a vacant seat in a coach where passengers of the white race were accommodated, and was ordered by the conductor to vacate said coach and take a seat in another assigned to persons of the colored race, and, having refused to comply with such demand, he was forcibly ejected with the aid of a police officer, and imprisoned in the parish jail to answer a charge of having violated the above act.

The constitutionality of this act is attacked upon the ground that it conflicts both with the Thirteenth Amendment of the Constitution, abolishing slavery, and the Fourteenth Amendment, which prohibits certain restrictive legislation on the part of the States.

1. That it does not conflict with the Thirteenth Amendment, which abolished slavery and involuntary servitude, except as a punishment for crime, is too clear for argument. Slavery implies involuntary servitude—a state of bondage; the ownership of mankind as a chattel, or at least the control of the labor and services of one man for the benefit of another, and the absence of a legal right to the disposal of his own person, property and services.

So, too, in the *Civil Rights Cases*, 109 U.S. 3, 24, it was said that the act of a mere individual, the owner of an inn, a public conveyance or place of amusement, refusing accommodations to colored people cannot be justly regarded as imposing any badge of slavery or servitude upon the applicant, but [p543] only as involving an ordinary civil injury, properly cognizable by the laws of the State and presumably subject to redress by those laws until the contrary appears. "It would be running the slavery argument into the ground," said Mr. Justice Bradley,

> to make it apply to every act of discrimination which a person may see fit to make as to the guests he will entertain, or as to the people he will take into his coach or cab or car, or admit to his concert or theatre, or deal with in other matters of intercourse or business.

A statute which implies merely a legal distinction between the white and colored races—a distinction which is founded in the color of the two races and which must always exist so long as white men are distinguished from the other race by color—has no tendency to destroy the legal equality of the two races, or reestablish a state of involuntary servitude.

Indeed, we do not understand that the Thirteenth Amendment is strenuously relied upon by the plaintiff in error in this connection.

2. By the Fourteenth Amendment, all persons born or naturalized in the United States and subject to the jurisdiction thereof are made citizens of the United States and of the State wherein they reside, and the States are forbidden from making or enforcing any law which shall abridge the privileges or immunities of citizens of the United States, or shall deprive any person of life, liberty, or property without due process of law, or deny to any person within their jurisdiction the equal protection of the laws.

The object of the amendment was undoubtedly to enforce the absolute equality of the two races before the law, but, in the nature of things, it could not have been intended to abolish distinctions based upon color, or to enforce social, as distinguished from political, equality, or a commingling of the two races upon terms unsatisfactory to either. Laws permitting, and even requiring, their separation in places where they are liable to be brought into contact do not necessarily imply the inferiority of either race to the other, and have been generally, if not universally, recognized as within the competency of the state legislatures in the exercise of their police power. The most common instance of this is connected with the establishment of separate schools for white and colored children, which has been held to be a valid exercise of the legislative power even by courts of States where the political rights of the colored race have been longest and most earnestly enforced.

Laws forbidding the intermarriage of the two races may be said in a technical sense to interfere with the freedom of contract, and yet have been universally recognized as within the police power of the State. *State v. Gibson*, 36 Indiana 389.

The distinction between laws interfering with the political equality of the negro and those requiring the separation of the two races in schools, theatres and railway carriages has been frequently drawn by this court. Thus, in *Strauder v. West Virginia*, 100 U.S. 303, it was held that a law of West Virginia limiting to white male persons, 21 years of age and citizens of the State, the right to sit upon juries was a discrimination which implied a legal inferiority in civil society, which lessened the security of the right of the colored race, and was a step toward reducing them to a condition of servility. Indeed, the right of a colored man that, in the selection of jurors to pass upon his life, liberty and property, there shall be no exclusion of his race and no discrimination against them because of color has been asserted in a number of cases. *Virginia v. Rives*, 100 U.S. 313; *Neal v. Delaware*, 103 U.S. 370; *Bush v. Kentucky*, 107 U.S. 110; *Gibson v. Mississippi*, 162 U.S. 565. So, where the laws of a particular locality or the charter of a particular railway corporation has provided that no person shall be excluded from the cars on account of color, we have held that this meant that persons of color should travel in the same car as white ones, and that the enactment was not satisfied by the company's providing cars assigned exclusively to people of color, though they were as good as those which they assigned exclusively to white persons. *Railroad Company v. Brown*, 17 Wall. 445.

Upon the other hand, where a statute of Louisiana required those engaged in the transportation of passengers among the States to give to all persons traveling within that State, upon vessels employed in that business, equal rights and privileges in all parts of the vessel, without distinction on account of race or color, and subjected to an action for damages the owner of such a vessel, who excluded colored passengers on account of their color from the cabin set aside by him for the use of whites, it was held to be, so far as it applied to interstate commerce, unconstitutional and void. *Hall v. De Cuir*, 95 U.S. 48. The court in this case, however, expressly disclaimed that it had anything whatever to do with the statute as a regulation of internal commerce, or affecting anything else than commerce among the States.

While we think the enforced separation of the races, as applied to the internal commerce of the State, neither abridges the privileges or immunities of the colored man, deprives him of his property without due process of law, nor denies him the equal protection of the laws within the meaning of the Fourteenth Amendment, we are not prepared to say that the conductor, in assigning passengers to the coaches according to their race, does not act at his peril, or that the provision of the second section of the act that denies to the passenger compensation in damages for a refusal to receive him into the coach in which he properly belongs is a valid exercise of the legislative power. Indeed, we understand it to be conceded by the State's Attorney that such part of the act as exempts from liability the railway company and its officers is unconstitutional. The power to assign to a particular coach obviously implies the power to determine to which race the passenger belongs, as well as the power to determine who, under the laws of the particular State, is to be deemed a white and who a colored person. This question, though indicated in the brief of the plaintiff in error, does not properly arise upon the record in this case, since the only issue made is as to the unconstitutionality of the act so far as it requires the railway to provide separate accommodations and the conductor to assign passengers according to their race.

It is claimed by the plaintiff in error that, in any mixed community, the reputation of belonging to the dominant race, in this instance the white race, is property in the same sense that a right of action or of inheritance is property. Conceding this to be so for the purposes of this case, we are unable to see how this statute deprives him of, or in any way affects his right to, such property. If he be a white man and assigned to a colored coach, he may have his action for damages against the company for being deprived of his so-called property. Upon the other hand, if he be a colored man and be so assigned, he has been deprived of no property, since he is not lawfully entitled to the reputation of being a white man.

So far, then, as a conflict with the Fourteenth Amendment is concerned, the case reduces itself to the question whether the statute of Louisiana is a reasonable regulation, and, with respect to this, there must necessarily be a large discretion on the part of the legislature. In determining the question of reasonableness, it is at liberty to act with reference to the established usages, customs, and traditions of the people, and with a view to the promotion of their comfort and the preservation of the public peace and good order. Gauged by this standard, we cannot say that a law which authorizes or even requires the separation of the two races in public conveyances is unreasonable, or more obnoxious to the Fourteenth Amendment than the acts of Congress requiring separate schools for colored children in the District of Columbia, the constitutionality of which does not seem to have been questioned, or the corresponding acts of state legislatures.

We consider the underlying fallacy of the plaintiff's argument to consist in the assumption that the enforced separation of the two races stamps the colored race with a badge of inferiority. If this be so, it is not by reason of anything found in the act, but solely because the colored race chooses to put that construction upon it. The argument necessarily assumes that if, as has been more than once the case and is not unlikely to be so again, the colored race should become the dominant power in the state legislature, and should enact a law in precisely similar terms, it would thereby relegate the white race to an inferior position. We imagine that the white race, at least, would not acquiesce in this assumption. The argument also assumes that social prejudices may be overcome by legislation, and that equal rights cannot be secured to the negro except by an enforced commingling of the two races. We cannot accept this proposition. If the two races are to meet upon terms of social equality, it must be the result of natural affinities, a mutual appreciation of each other's merits, and a voluntary consent of individuals. As was said by the Court of Appeals of New York in *People v. Gallagher*, 93 N. Y. 438, 448,

> this end can neither be accomplished nor promoted by laws which conflict with the general sentiment of the community upon whom they are designed to operate. When the government, therefore, has secured to each of its citizens equal rights before the law and equal opportunities for improvement and progress, it has accomplished the end for which it was organized, and performed all of the functions respecting social advantages with which it is endowed.

Legislation is powerless to eradicate racial instincts or to abolish distinctions based upon physical differences, and the attempt to do so can only result in accentuating the difficulties of the present situation. If the civil and political rights of both races be equal, one cannot be inferior to the other civilly or politically. If one race be inferior to the other socially, the Constitution of the United States cannot put them upon the same plane.

It is true that the question of the proportion of colored blood necessary to constitute a colored person, as distinguished from a white person, is one upon which there is a difference of opinion in the different States, some holding that any visible admixture of black blood stamps the person as belonging to the colored race (*State v. Chaver*, 5 Jones [N.C.] 1, p. 11); others that it depends upon the preponderance of blood (*Gray v. State*, 4 Ohio 354; *Monroe v. Collins*, 17 Ohio St. 665); and still others that the predominance of white blood must only be in the proportion of three-fourths. (*People v. Dean*, 4 Michigan 406; *Jones v. Commonwealth*, 80 Virginia 538). But these are questions to be determined under the laws of each State, and are not properly put in issue in this case. Under the allegations of his petition, it may undoubtedly become a question of importance whether, under the laws of Louisiana, the petitioner belongs to the white or colored race.

The judgment of the court below is, therefore,

Affirmed.

29

A Survey of Important Cases in the History of Racial Equality

R. L. Raines

Plessy v. Ferguson (1896)

Introduction

With the end of the Civil War and passage of constitutional amendments ending slavery (13th Amend., 1865), giving blacks citizenship and equal protection under the law (14th Amend., 1868), and the right to vote (15th Amend., 1870), the nation's highest court was called upon in 1896 to once again decide a case of historic proportions as it pertained to the social status of post-slavery African Americans. And, as had prior courts for the preceding 100 years, this court in *Plessy v. Ferguson*, ratified and legitimized the de facto racist preferences of whites to the detriment of blacks. The separate-but-equal doctrine of Plessy meant racial apartheid for blacks in the south and Jim Crow practices through most of this country. It would take the Civil Rights Movement of the 1950's-1960's to topple this seminal court decision.

In 1890, Louisiana passed a law like so many others that mandated the segregation of the races on intrastate rail travel. Not all rail companies welcomed the law because it meant increased costs. Various civil organizations opposed it as well. These unlikely parties combined to challenge the law. Plessy, an octoroon (1/8 black), was chosen to test the legality of the statute. Since he was apparently white, in 1892 he succeeded in purchasing a first class ticket to travel from Covington, LA, to New Orleans. He or someone else must have alerted the conductor to his racial status. Plessy was told to remove himself to the black only coach. Upon his refusal, he was arrested, jailed, and fined. The Louisiana Supreme Court found him guilty. Plessy appealed to the US Supreme Court, naming the Louisiana District Court judge, Ferguson, as the defendant. The US Supreme Court relied more on the social and economic history of blacks in America rather than jurisprudence, as it had in *Dred Scott* some 40 years earlier.

Plessy claimed that the Louisiana statute violated both his 13th and 14th Amendment rights. The Court's majority opinion reaffirmed white supremacy in America. It ruled that it was not a violation of his rights under the 13th Amendment because the segregation requirement did not reduce Plessy to a slave-like condition. The Court also denied that the Louisiana statute violated Plessy's 14th Amendment rights. Neither Plessy's rights as a citizen or the mandate that the state treat all its citizens equally were violated.

The state would argue that Plessy's ostensible objective was to travel from one city in Louisiana to another. The railroad could accommodate this objective. It simply required that he do so with members of his own race. The state's claim was that the requirement did not violate the equal treatment of citizens' requirement of the 14th Amendment because the treatment was "equal," it just happened to be "separate."

In yet another historic case where racism, instead of judicial parity, held sway, the nation's highest court once again pandered to the *de facto* racist attitudes and preferences of whites. Whites did not wish to sit with blacks so it became *de jure* (required by law). Is this not what this country had done since its inception? Even in its colonial period, the racist social practices were enacted into law. Didn't the 14th Amendment intend to end such state sanctioned discriminatory laws? The ruling in this case showed that the stigma of slavery had not yet been removed. Blacks were still inherently inferior and as such could be prohibited from association with whites in public places.

The Court rejected Plessy's 13th Amendment argument stating that a law can make a legal distinction between the races without destroying legal equality, therefore no imposition of involuntary servitude.

While making short shrift of Plessy's 13th Amendment argument, the Court expends considerable effort rebutting his 14th Amendment violation claim. The Court says:

> The object of the [14th] amendment was undoubtedly to enforce the *absolute equality of the two races before the law,* but in the nature of things it could not have been intended to abolish distinctions based upon color, or to enforce social, as distinguished from political equality, or a commingling of the two races upon terms unsatisfactory to either. [emphasis added]

This means that blacks are assured political rights, e.g., they can vote, hold elective office, enjoy all the protections of the Bill of Rights, etc. But, as it pertains to social equality, the 14th Amendment was not meant to force whites and blacks to exist on an equal footing "upon terms unsatisfactory to either." This latter observation is disingenuous since as Justice Harlan points out in his dissent, the real intent of the statute was to keep blacks away from whites, not the reverse.

The Court goes on to conclude that laws requiring separation of the races do not imply inferiority of either race to the other. If separation is a "badge of inferiority," well then, it is because blacks choose to feel that way. Further, the Court states that social preference cannot be legislated. Perhaps the Court's most controversial conclusion was that being white had value, while being black did not. It warned Louisiana that if it were to mistakenly assign a white person to a blacks only coach, believing the person to be black, then it could be sued for damages since the white person's "property value" of being known as white would have been damaged, his reputation impugned, defamed. The Court admonished Plessy. While he looked white, he was in fact black and as such he was properly assigned to the blacks only coach.

Separating social equality from political equality is tricky. This distinction assumes that one can enjoy one type of equality as opposed to the other, in a vacuum. But more importantly, by upholding the social preferences of whites the Court is doing exactly what it purports not to do: upholding one race's desires over another's. The Court denies that the Louisiana statutes place a "badge of inferiority" on blacks. Why else would blacks be denied access to areas where whites sit? The very act of segregation, in and of itself, suggests an ulterior motive.

Justice Harlan, in dissent, gets to the crux of the matter:

> Such legislation, as that here in question, is inconsistent not only with that equality of rights which pertains to citizenship, National or State, but with the personal liberty enjoyed by everyone within the United States.

Harlan argues that Plessy's 13th and 14th Amendment rights were violated, but his 14th Amendment argument is far more convincing. He states:

> Everyone knows that the statute in question had its origin in the purpose, not so much to exclude white persons from railroad cars occupied by blacks, as to exclude colored people from coaches occupied by or assigned to white persons . . . The thing to accomplish was, under the guise of giving equal accommodation for whites and blacks, to compel the latter to keep to themselves while traveling in railroad passenger coaches. . . .

He further reminds the other justices that there is no superior, dominant, ruling class of citizens in America. The Constitution is "color blind" and that all citizens are equal before the law. Harlan is prescient. He foresees that "the judgment this day rendered will, in time, prove to be quite as pernicious as that decision made by this tribunal in the *Dred Scott* case."

The *Plessy v. Ferguson* decision validated white social preferences (*de facto* segregation) and American Southern apartheid was legitimized, indeed segregation anywhere. This decision paved the way for separate bathrooms, water fountains, seating arrangement in public buildings, park benches, etc. "Colored only" and "White Only" signs proliferated throughout the South.

The Court Begins to Get it Right

Shelley v. Kraemer (1948)

Six years before the case that was to provide the first crack in the wall that was the *Plessy* doctrine of separate but equal, the US Supreme Court decided a case involving blatant racism in home ownership.

The practice of restrictive covenants provided that the seller of a home in a particular neighborhood could only sell to certain persons. If one wanted to exclude non-whites or Jews, they and their neighbors would insert in their deeds a promise not to sell their properties to such persons. Since these restrictions ran with the property in perpetuity, it was successful in keeping entire neighborhoods "ethnically pure." Even if a successor homeowner wanted to sell to another ethnicity, he was restrained by the covenant in his deed from doing so.

The *Shelley* case involved cases brought from Missouri and Michigan. In the Michigan case, 30 of 39 homeowners had in 1911 agreed to restrict, for a period of 50 years, ownership in the area to the "Caucasian race" and excluded people of the "Negro or Mongolian races." One of the property owners, subject to these covenant restrictions, sold his home to blacks. The other homeowners sued to stop the black family from taking possession of the property.

The Court recognizes the seminal nature of the case:

> Whether the equal protection clause [inhibits] judicial enforcement of restrictive covenants based on race or color is a question which this Court has not heretofore been called upon to consider.

This time the court interprets the 14th Amendment provision of "equal protection under the laws" correctly. It's answer:

> [It] cannot be doubted that among the civil rights intended to be protected from discriminatory state action by the 14th Amendment are the rights to acquire, enjoy, own and dispose of property.

The Court understands that the intent of the covenants is to discriminate against specific races, and that the state courts were complicit in these efforts. The Court observes:

> The undisputed facts disclose that petitioners (blacks) were willing purchasers of property upon which they wished to establish homes. The owners of the properties were willing sellers, and contracts for sale were accordingly consummated. It is clear that but for the active intervention of the state courts, supported by the full panoply of state power, petitioners would have been free to occupy the properties in question without restraint.

Therefore, beginning in 1948, some 80 years after its enactment, the equal protection of the laws clause of the 14th Amendment begins to fulfill its original intent.

Brown v. Board of Education (1954)

The school districts in the various states included in this landmark case required by law, pursuant to the *Plessy* doctrine of "separate-but-equal," that its public schools segregate its students based on race; i.e., black students had to attend all black schools and white students all white schools. The NAACP Legal Defense Fund, Thurgood Marshall leading, brought a lawsuit to end this practice, claiming that it violated the equal protection clause of the 14th Amendment. This argument asserts that the school districts and states requiring this segregation were not treating its black citizens equally or the same under the law; a direct challenge to *Plessy* doctrine. How could Marshall and the NAACP hope to win this case in light of the fact that *Plessy* had withstood almost 60 years of legal challenges? Each time a challenge was made, the courts invariably looked to see if the separate facilities provided by the state or local government for blacks and whites were equal. If a court found them unequal for blacks it would order that they be made equal. For example, if whites had, say, a dental school and blacks did not, the (federal) court would order the state to provide one. If the white school had a swimming pool and the black school did not, the (federal) court would order the building of a pool. As you can plainly see, all this did was to perpetuate the *Plessy* doctrine of "separate but equal" public facilities for the races.

So, what do you do if you want to end the *Plessy* doctrine as it pertains to public education? You can not go into court asserting that the black schools are physically unequal (antiquated plumbing, leaky ceilings, the building is falling apart because of age, no swimming pool, etc.); or that the black teachers are poorly trained and poorly paid. If you argue this, what do you get? An order from the court directing better and equal facilities, better trained and better paid teachers, etc. Again, this does not put an end to the practice of segregation in the schools, and this is your objective.

Given the above, Marshall's strategy had to be different from anything yet attempted. At first, he disarmed the other side (school districts) by asserting for the record that the segregated public schools were "equal" when it came to facilities, teachers, textbooks, etc. (although this was really not the case). Again, his goal was not a court order addressing those things, but to end the practice of racial segregation in public schools. The Court took note of this in its ruling, stating that the petitioners agree that the "physical facilities" for black and white students were equal. The defendants (school districts), at first blush, had to be wondering why they were in court at all. If blacks had the same quality schools and education as whites and *Plessy* was well established law, what were they doing in court? But they soon realized that this case was not about making the schools equal but rather about integrating them, carving out a niche, an exception, to the *Plessy* doctrine.

So, what was the Marshall strategy? *He would have to prove that the separate public education of blacks and whites was* **"inherently unequal."** If it is, in and of itself (innately), unequal, then school segregation did not meet the requirement of the 14th Amendment that states must provide *all* its citizens the "equal protection of the laws." How do you prove this? Part of the proof was results of psychological tests and social impact studies showing the adverse and lasting effects on blacks who are required to attend segregated schools.

The legal question (issue) before the court was: Do separate but equal public school facilities violate the Equal Protection Clause of the 14th Amendment?

The court ruled yes, they do.

> We come to the question presented: Does segregation of children in public schools solely on the basis of race, even though the physical facilities and other 'tangible' factors may be equal, deprive children of the minority group of equal education opportunities? We believe it does . . . To separate them from others of similar age and qualifications solely based on race generate feeling of inferiority as to the status in the community that may affect their hearts and minds in a way unlikely ever to be undone . . . We conclude that in the field of public education the doctrine of "separate but equal" has no place. Separate educational facilities are inherently unequal.

The Court accepted Marshall's psychological and social impact data that showed, among other things, the following: 1) *Forced segregation of black children promoted life-long feelings of inferiority and "[a] sense of inferiority affects the motivation of a child to learn."* Black children surmised that they could not be with whites because they (blacks) were not good enough. The segregated schools fit right into the daily and life-long pattern of Jim Crow segregation, which was meant to suppress and demean them. And, at the time, all the positive cultural images of beauty, happiness and success were white. There was no Michael Jordan, Halle Berry, Denzel Washington, or Barack Obama being splashed all over the dominant magazines, movies and television. One of the psychological studies conducted was with preschool aged black girls. When given the choice of a white doll or black doll, the black child invariably chose the white one. In short, blacks felt that they were required to go to school only with members of their own race because they, individually, and the African-American race collectively, were not good enough to associate with whites; and these feelings of inferiority lasted a lifetime.

Forced segregation of black children limited their opportunities in life. The Court notes the crucial role that education plays in the economic and social opportunities that one has in life. In the white world, the kind of school and the friends one makes during this period can have a decisive impact on one's future success. For example, even poor white child still got to go to the same public school as the town's richest white kid. Befriending one or more of these people can change forever the economic and social prospects for this very poor white person. On the other hand, who are the black kids going to school with? Overwhelmingly they are going to school with kids whose parents share the same socio-economic status as theirs, menial laborers: maids, cooks, chauffeurs, bootblacks, skycaps, railroad porters, ditch diggers, etc. There is little or no chance that one's school associations will help lift one to a better socio-economic level.

Given the above, the Court agreed with the NAACP Legal Defense Fund: ***"We conclude," said the Court, "that in the field of public education the doctrine of 'separate but equal' has no place. Separate educational facilities are** inherently **unequal."***

Thus, *Brown v. Bd. of Education* becomes the first successful assault on the *Plessy* doctrine in 57 years. Notice I say assault, not the end of *Plessy*. If it had been the complete end there would have been no need to the Civil Rights Movement of the 1950s–1960s, and additional court rulings and federal civil rights legislation.

Court Cases Cited

Brown v. Board of Education, 347 U.S. 483 (1954)
Plessy v. Ferguson, 163 U.S. 537 (1896)
Shelley v. Kraemer, 334 U.S. 1 (1948)

30

The Constitution, the Supreme Court, and Racial Justice

Michael Luis Principe

A review of U.S. constitutional history shows three things pertinent to this essay. First, there is a tradition of principles of civil rights in the United States that has expanded over the past two centuries. Second, rather than developing in a consistent and gradual basis, the major expansions of civil and political rights have generally come in large eruptions, during periods of civil unrest, and as a result of the leadership of progressive leaders. Third, although the U.S. Supreme Court has at times been the leader in the development of rights protections, it has far more often turned its back on those people who are the weakest politically and have the greatest need of protection. This essay examines U.S. constitutional and judicial history, with the goal of demonstrating how these precious constitutional principles have often been ignored, especially when the concept of racial justice was at issue.

Beginning with these words, "Let me add that a bill of rights is what the people are entitled to against every government on earth, general or particular, and what no just government should refuse, or rest on inference,"[1] Thomas Jefferson attempted to convince James Madison of the need for a bill of rights (letter from Thomas Jefferson to James Madison, December 20, 1787, quoted in Mason & Baker, 1985, p. 285). Having never believed the omission of such a document was a material defect (p. 286), Madison was somewhat in agreement with Alexander Hamilton, who expressed his view in *Federalist* No. 84, specifically, that to list certain rights against the government would be in effect to limit an individual to those specific rights. Yet, within 18 months of Jefferson's first letter on the subject, Madison placed the proposed bill of rights before the House of Representatives (p. 290). In proposing the amendments to Congress, Madison stated,

> If they are incorporated into the Constitution, independent tribunals of justice will consider themselves in a peculiar manner the guardians of those rights, they will be an impenetrable bulwark against every assumption of power in the legislative or executive; they will be naturally led to resist every encroachment upon rights expressly stipulated for in the constitution by the declaration of rights (quoted in Mason & Baker, 1985, p. 293).

The resulting ratification of the first 10 amendments to the U.S. Constitution was the beginning of a constitutional legacy found nowhere else in history. Building upon some of the principles heralded by John Locke (in his *Second Treatise on Civil Government*) and Thomas Jefferson (in the *Declaration of Independence*), the framers reversed centuries of political thought by recognizing the value of the individual to civil society. Rather than subjecting an individual's interests to the needs of the state (such as with Plato's attempt to achieve the just state) or prohibiting the individual from defying the sovereign except in the event they are subjected to a state of nature (such as with Thomas Hobbes's notion of the social contract), the framers of the constitution, influenced by the Enlightenment thinkers, recognized the importance of the individual in society by granting them constitutional protections against intrusion from the federal government.

Yet despite this monumental recognition of the principle of constitutionally protected civil and political rights, the reality was that most people were not initially included within its protections. The most egregious example of this contradiction between principle and practice was with slavery. Although the word "slavery" is not used in the Constitution, the document did include three separate provisions from which it could be inferred. Article I, section 2, clause 3 apportioned representatives and direct taxes among the states according to their populations, "which shall be determined by adding to the whole Number of Free Persons, including those bound to Service for a Term of Years, and excluding Indians not taxed, *three fifths of all other persons*" (emphasis added). Article I, section 9, clause 1 prohibited Congress from banning the "Migration or Importation of such Persons as any of the States now existing shall think proper to admit" before 1808. Article IV, section 2, clause 3 prohibited any state's laws from discharging the obligation of service for a person escaping from another state, who is under a legal duty of service in that prior state.

> Another example was in the area of voting rights, where the Constitution of 1787 left voting qualifications entirely in the hands of the states, with the result that most Americans—women, blacks, and some white adult males—were initially kept from the ballot box. By the 1820s the national trend was to chip away at those restrictions, first with removal of property qualifications for voting, followed by the Fifteenth, Nineteenth, and Twenty-sixth Amendments in 1870, 1920, and 1971 that dealt with race, gender, and age, respectively. With race, however, many years would pass before the promise of the Fifteenth Amendment was realized (Mason & Stephenson, 2009, p. 187).

As a result, after Madison's initial shepherding of the Bill of Rights through Congress, there was little expansion of civil liberties until the Civil War. As stated by C. Herman Pritchett (1984), "The Supreme Court's involvement in civil liberties issues during the first half of the nineteenth century was infrequent" (p. 4). In fact, with the acceptance of slavery, the recognition of women as little more than chattel, the Sedition Act of 1798 (which made virtually any criticism of the government a crime) (p. 4),[2] the Supreme Court's unanimous decision that the first eight amendments were inapplicable to the states (see *Barron v. Baltimore*, 7 Pet. 243 [1833]), and the fact that approximately half of the state constitutions did not initially include bills of rights (Pritchett, 1984, p. 4), it could be argued that the focus of the government during this period was actually on limiting rights.

After the Civil War, there was an explosion of civil liberties protections by the government. The 13th, 14th, and 15th Amendments, as well as the Civil Rights Acts of 1866, 1870, 1871, and 1875, guaranteed political and civil rights for the former slaves. Of these, the 14th Amendment was the most important addition. One of the main purposes of the Amendment was to constitutionalize the provisions of the Civil Rights Act of 1866, which protected the rights of former slaves to make and enforce contracts; sue and give testimony in court; inherit, sell, or lease property; and enjoy the full and equal benefit of all laws.

Section 1 of the 14th Amendment redefined citizenship and rights, formed the basis for limitations on state power, and included the privileges on immunities, due process, and equal protection clauses. Section 5 authorized Congress to enforce the provisions of the Amendment "by appropriate legislation." Intending this section to be similar to the necessary and proper clause of Article I, Congress assumed they could redress discrimination by private individuals as well as by affirmative state action. Evidence of their intention to assume broad authority to correct abuses of the Amendment came when Congress passed the 1875 Civil Rights Act. The Act prohibited racial discrimination or separation in hotels, theatres, or public conveyances, and required equality in jury service.

Despite these monumental efforts by Congress to correct injustices to former slaves, it only took the Supreme Court a few years to drastically water down or eliminate many of these important protections. For example, in the Civil Rights Cases of 1883 (109 U.S. 3 [1883]), the Court stated that although Congress had drafted the 14th Amendment, they had in fact misunderstood its meaning and the powers pursuant to it. The Court ruled that Congress only had the power to redress affirmative state discrimination, such as by hotel and theatre owners, not discrimination by private individuals. Thus, although Congress could prohibit states from discriminating on the basis of race, private parties were free to discriminate without fear of Congressional action. In describing the Supreme Court's decision, Pritchett (1984) stated, "There is scarcely a more striking instance in American constitutional history of outright judicial disregard of congressional intent" (p. 252).

In the case of *Santa Clara County v. Southern Pacific Railroad* (118 U.S. 394 [1886]), the Court opened the door for the judiciary to protect corporations by unanimously ruling that the 14th Amendment protects corporate interests as well as individuals. As a result of this decision, of the 554 Supreme Courts between 1886 and 1960 decisions that involved equal protection, 426 (77%) dealt with economic legislation, whereas only 78 (14%) dealt with racial discrimination (Pritchett, 1984, p. 315). Thus, the Court established itself as a branch of government with an economic perspective.

The final decision that severely limited the effect of the 14th Amendment was *Plessy v. Ferguson* (163 U.S. 537 [1896]). Here, the Court ruled that the Equal Protection Clause would not be violated by the "separate but equal" doctrine. This decision provided states with a legal principle that justified discriminatory policies in public services (e.g., education) and the political process (e.g., voting). As a result, Southern states almost immediately passed laws segregating virtually every aspect of life; Blacks were systematically excluded from the political process and denied their share of public services. This discrimination continued well into the 20th century.

Although, over the course of the next few decades, there were some instances where specific rights were expanded,[3] the next major explosion of rights did not occur until the era of the Warren Court. Like the Civil War period, the Warren Court existed amidst a nation coming apart at the seams, due in part to reactions against the civil rights movement and the anti-Viet Nam War effort. Yet, it was this Court's efforts to assume the responsibilities addressed by Madison (in his statement to Congress upon his delivery of the proposed Bill of Rights Amendments) (Mason & Baker, 1985, p. 293) that greatly expanded civil liberties protections for individuals. Perhaps nowhere was this more evident than in the series of cases decided in *Brown v. Board of Education* (347 U.S. 483 [1954]). These cases addressed the issue of racial segregation in public education and the Court's decision would affect school systems within 21 states and the District of Columbia, involving some 8 million White children and 2½ million Black children. Because of the importance of their decision, the Court was cautious in its approach. In fact, the Court had been unable to reach a decision when the case was first presented to it during the 1952 term. In scheduling the cases for re-argument during the 1953 term, the Court submitted a lengthy list of questions to the attorneys concerning the intentions of the framers of the 14th Amendment as well as requesting advice on the type of orders the Court should issue. One concept that had to be addressed by the Court in *Brown* was the "separate but equal" doctrine.

On May 17, 1954, Chief Justice Warren delivered the unanimous opinion of the Court. In ruling that segregation of the races was not permissible under the equal protection clause of the 14th Amendment, Warren stated, "We conclude that in the field of public education the doctrine of 'separate but equal' has no place. Separate educational facilities are inherently unequal." Although the process of desegregating public schools took many years, this decision was monumental in its influence on how the country viewed the government's obligation to provide public services and protect the civil rights of all its citizens.

Unfortunately, this progress towards greater civil liberties recognition was, as in the Civil War legislation era, short lived. The subsequent Burger and Rehnquist Courts, despite a few notable exceptions (e.g., *Furman v. Georgia*, 408 U.S. 238 [1972]; *Roe v. Wade*, 410 U.S. 113 [1973]; *Frontiero v. Richardson*, 411 U.S. 677 [1973]), adopted the same agenda maintained by a majority of Supreme Court justices, which resulted in narrowing or extinguishing a variety of civil and political rights (e.g., *Gregg v. Georgia*, 428 U.S. 153 [1976]; *United States v. Leon*, 468 U.S. 897 [1984]; *Adarand Constructors Co. v. Pena*, 515 U.S. 200 [1995]; *Planned Parenthood of Southeastern Pennsylvania v. Casey*, 505 U.S. 833 [1992]; *Wyoming v. Houghton*, 526 U.S. 295 [1999]; *Illinois v. Wardlow*, 528 U.S. 119 [2000]). As stated by David O'Brien (1985), this agenda was reflected in the Court's promotion and protection of corporate interests, while "pushing the New Right's social agenda on abortion and affirmative action" (p. 1).

During the tenure of the Burger Court, the standard of review for equal protection cases was expanded by adding a middle-tier level of analysis. Because virtually all legislation involves classification, when reviewing a challenged classification within a statute, regulation, or policy, the Court generally applies the "rational basis test." This test requires that any classification must be "rationally related to a permissible government interest" and provides states with a wide measure of discretion when developing classifications for legislation. Because the burden of proof (showing that the challenged classification is arbitrary) is placed upon the challenger, the initial presumption is that the regulation is proper and the state usually wins under this level of scrutiny.

But if a law, regulation, or policy employs a suspect classification (e.g., race, national origin, religion) or significantly burdens a fundamental right (e.g., 1st Amendment rights, privacy, right to travel), then the Court examines that classification more closely by applying the "strict scrutiny test." This test requires the classification to be "necessarily related to a compelling government interest" and the burden of proof is on the government to show that the legislation meets the test. Because the initial presumption under this level of scrutiny is that the regulation is improper, it is difficult for a classification to pass this test (especially if the government can demonstrate the classification serves a compelling state interest, there also must not be a less burdensome alternative available for achieving the government's objective).

Finally, a third, intermediate standard of review—"quasi-suspect scrutiny"—was developed by the Burger Court to deal with gender and illegitimacy cases. The test requires the classification to be "substantially related to an important government interest" and it places the presumption of regulatory constitutionality on equal footing. The result of these three tests has been that the Court requires greater legislative justifications for those classifications that are based on race, religion, gender, illegitimacy, or that significantly burden fundamental rights.

In the case of *Adarand Constructors Inc. v. Pena* (515 U.S. 200 [1995]), however, the Rehnquist Court was able to reverse the intentions of the framers of the 14th Amendment by placing all legislation classifying race (including legislation favoring the historically disadvantaged) under strict scrutiny analysis. The Court reviewed a prime contractor's contract with the Department of Transportation that rewarded prime contractors with an additional payment for subcontracting with small businesses controlled by "socially and economically disadvantaged individuals." A subcontractor with a lower bid challenged the regulation, claiming that it discriminated on the basis of race and therefore violated the 5th Amendment's equal protection component. Ignoring the intentions of the framers of the 14th Amendment and 1866 Civil Rights Act (as well as the justices who developed the strict scrutiny analysis), the Rehnquist Court ruled "all racial classifications, imposed by whatever federal, state, or local governmental actor, must be analyzed by a reviewing court under strict scrutiny. In other words, such classifications are constitutional only if they are narrowly tailored measures that further compelling governmental interests." Prior to this line of cases only legislation that classified people the basis of race and that disadvantaged people belonging to that suspect class would be analyzed under strict scrutiny; after *Adarand*, all legislation classifying on the basis of race (whether in support of the historically disadvantaged or not) would now have to satisfy strict scrutiny analysis, which was a difficult challenge.

Two of the more recent Supreme Court decisions involving issues of race were *Grutter v. Bollinger* (539 U.S. 306 [2003]) and *Gratz v. Bollinger* (539 U.S. 244 [2003]). *Grutter* involved the graduate admissions policy at the University of Michigan's law school; *Gratz* focused on Michigan's undergraduate admissions policy in the College of Literature, Science, and the Arts. Although both policies were designed to promote racial diversity, the law school used race in order to obtain a critical mass of minority students, whereas the undergraduate policy was based upon a point system (that awarded minority applicants with additional points). Challenged as violations of the 14th Amendment's equal protection clause and Title VI of the Civil Rights Act of 1964 (prohibiting racial discrimination in programs receiving federal financial assistance), the Court agreed race may be considered as a factor in achieving a diverse student body (upholding the law school policy), but found that separate admission tracks for specific racial groups is unconstitutional (striking down the undergraduate policy). Instead, the Court stated that Constitution allows a "truly individualized consideration" in which race is merely one of the factors used.

Despite the fact it is clear Congress drafted the 14th Amendment (as well as many other civil rights enactments) in order to protect and provide opportunities for newly freed Blacks, two issues must be remembered when considering constitutional protections in the area of racial justice. First, there has always been disagreement about how far these protections go in terms of civil and political rights. Second, although there may be debate over the level of these protections, the 14th Amendment and its progeny were intended to elevate the status of the historically disadvantaged to that of the majority, not protect the majority from the politically weak. Thus, although every U.S. citizen (regardless of race or gender) has equal protection rights and, in the event a classification burdens a suspect classification (e.g., national origin or religion) or a fundamental right (e.g., privacy, free speech, voting), can seek a court's review of that classification under the strict scrutiny analysis, it is specifically in the area of race that the framers intended historically disadvantaged people should have certain protections that the majority would not. Yet, over the course of Supreme Court history, through cases such as the *Civil Rights Cases*, *Santa Clara County*, *Plessy*, *Adarand*, and *Gratz*, the Court has often forgotten its role and instead focused on what benefitted the majority or the powerful.

This type of decision making should no longer be acceptable by the public. Rather than ignoring the will of the post-Civil War Congress (in drafting the 14th Amendment) and those Supreme Court justices who developed the strict scrutiny analysis, the Supreme Court should be required to abide by its constitutional responsibilities and protect those people who have historically been disadvantaged in their access to civil and political rights. This could be achieved in two ways: First, by properly educating the public on the Court's proper role; second, by insisting that the press do a better job of reporting biased and prejudiced Court decisions. The public will therefore be better armed to demand the Court abide by its constitutional duties so that racial justice can finally be achieved.

References

Locke, J. *Second treatise on civil government.*

Madison, J., Hamilton, A., & Jay, J. *The Federalist papers.*

Mason, A., & Baker, G. E. (1985). *Free government in the making: Readings in American political thought* (4th ed.). New York: Oxford University Press.

Mason, A., & Stephenson, D. G., Jr. (2009). *American constitutional law: Introductory essays and selected cases* (15th ed.). Upper Saddle River, NJ: Pearson/Prentice Hall.

O'Brien, D. (1987). Ginsburg and the Chicago school of thought. *Los Angeles Times,* November 8, Part V, p. 1.

Pritchett, C. H. (1984). *Constitutional civil liberties.* Englewood Cliffs, NJ: Prentice Hall.

Endnotes

1. During the course of a series of letters, Jefferson wrote: "There is a remarkable difference between the characters of the inconveniences which attend a Declaration of rights, and those which attend the want of it. The inconveniences of the Declaration are that it may cramp government in its useful exertions. But the evil of this is short lived, moderate, and reparable. The inconveniences of the want of a Declaration are permanent, afflicting, and irreparable; they are in constant progression from bad to worse" (p. 290).

2. Believing the legislation was not barred by the 1st Amendment, the Federalist members of Congress who passed the Act were trying to punish their Jeffersonian critics. Although many convictions were secured under it, the Act expired under its own terms in 1801, a subsequent Act of Congress repaid the fines, and President Jefferson later pardoned all who had been found guilty under the Act.

3. The 19th Amendment, guaranteeing women the right to vote, was ratified in 1920. Likewise, the decisions to extend the freedoms of speech and press, free exercise of religion, and prohibition against the establishment of religion to the states were decided in this period. Yet, despite these rights expansions, discrimination against women continued; free speech was severely limited by the Espionage Act of 1917, Sedition Act of 1918, various state statutes, and the Alien Registration Act of 1940 (also known as the Smith Act); and state action promoting religious preferences continued.

31

Indian Citizenship Act of 1924

The 1924 Indian Citizenship Act (43 U.S. Stats. At Large, Ch. 233, p. 253 (1924):

BE IT ENACTED by the Senate and house of Representatives of the the United States of America in Congress assembled, That all non citizen Indians born within the territorial limits of the United States be, and they are hereby, declared to be citizens of the United States: Provided That the granting of such citizenship shall not in any manner impair or otherwise affect the right of any Indian to tribal or other property." Approved, June 2, 1924, June 2, 1924. [H. R. 6355.] [Public, No. 175.] SIXTY-EIGHTH CONGRESS. Sess. I. CHS. 233. 1924. See House Report No. 222, Certificates of Citizenship to Indians, 68th Congress, 1st Session, Feb. 22, 1924. Note: This statute has been codified in the United States Code at Title 8, Sec. 1401(a)(2).

32

Korematsu v. United States
Supreme Court of the United States (1944)

323 U.S. 214
December 18, 1944, Decided

MR. JUSTICE BLACK delivered the opinion of the Court.

The petitioner, an American citizen of Japanese descent, was convicted in a federal district court for remaining in San Leandro, California, a "Military Area," contrary to Civilian Exclusion Order No. 34 of the Commanding General of the Western Command, U.S. Army, which directed that after May 9, 1942, all persons of Japanese ancestry should be excluded from that area. No question was raised as to petitioner's loyalty to the United States. The Circuit Court of Appeals affirmed, and the importance of the constitutional question involved caused us to grant certiorari.

It should be noted, to begin with, that all legal restrictions which curtail the civil rights of a single racial group are immediately suspect. That is not to say that all such restrictions are unconstitutional. It is to say that courts must subject them to the most rigid scrutiny. Pressing public necessity may sometimes justify the existence of such restrictions; racial antagonism never can.

In the instant case prosecution of the petitioner was begun by information charging violation of an Act of Congress, of March 21, 1942, 56 Stat. 173, which provides that

> ". . . whoever shall enter, remain in, leave, or commit any act in any military area or military zone prescribed, under the authority of an Executive order of the President, by the Secretary of War, or by any military commander designated by the Secretary of War, contrary to the restrictions applicable to any such area or zone or contrary to the order of the Secretary of War or any such military commander, shall, if it appears that he knew or should have known of the existence and extent of the restrictions or order and that his act was in violation thereof, be guilty of a misdemeanor and upon conviction shall be liable to a fine of not to exceed $5,000 or to imprisonment for not more than one year, or both, for each offense."

Exclusion Order No. 34, which the petitioner knowingly and admittedly violated, was one of a number of military orders and proclamations, all of which were substantially based upon Executive Order No. 9066, 7 Fed. Reg. 1407. That order, issued after we were at war with Japan, declared that "the successful prosecution of the war requires every possible protection against espionage and against sabotage to national-defense material, national-defense premises, and national-defense utilities. . . ."

One of the series of orders and proclamations, a curfew order, which like the exclusion order here was promulgated pursuant to Executive Order 9066, subjected all persons of Japanese ancestry in prescribed West Coast military areas to remain in their residences from 8 P.M. to 6 A.M. As is the case with the exclusion order here, that prior curfew order was designed as a "protection against espionage and against sabotage." In *Hirabayashi v. United States*, 320 U.S. 81, we sustained a conviction obtained for violation of the curfew order. The Hirabayashi conviction and this one thus rest on the same 1942 Congressional Act and the same basic executive and military orders, all of which orders were aimed at the twin dangers of espionage and sabotage.

The 1942 Act was attacked in the *Hirabayashi* case as an unconstitutional delegation of power; it was contended that the curfew order and other orders on which it rested were beyond the war powers of the Congress, the military authorities and of the President, as Commander in Chief of the Army; and finally that to apply the curfew order against none but citizens of Japanese ancestry amounted to a constitutionally prohibited discrimination solely on account of race. To these questions, we gave the serious consideration which their importance justified. We upheld the curfew order as an exercise of the power of the government to take steps necessary to prevent espionage and sabotage in an area threatened by Japanese attack.

In the light of the principles we announced in the *Hirabayashi* case, we are unable to conclude that it was beyond the war power of Congress and the Executive to exclude those of Japanese ancestry from the West Coast war area at the time they did. True, exclusion from the area in which one's home is located is a far greater deprivation than constant confinement to the home from 8 P.M. to 6 A.M. Nothing short of apprehension by the proper military authorities of the gravest imminent danger to the public safety can constitutionally justify either. But exclusion from a threatened area, no less than curfew, has a definite and close relationship to the prevention of espionage and sabotage. The military authorities, charged with the primary responsibility of defending our shores, concluded that curfew provided inadequate protection and ordered exclusion. They did so, as pointed out in our *Hirabayashi* opinion, in accordance with Congressional authority to the military to say who should, and who should not, remain in the threatened areas.

In this case the petitioner challenges the assumptions upon which we rested our conclusions in the *Hirabayashi* case. He also urges that by May 1942, when Order No. 34 was promulgated, all danger of Japanese invasion of the West Coast had disappeared. After careful consideration of these contentions we are compelled to reject them.

Here, as in the *Hirabayashi* case, ". . . we cannot reject as unfounded the judgment of the military authorities and of Congress that there were disloyal members of that population, whose number and strength could not be precisely and quickly ascertained. We cannot say that the war-making branches of the Government did not have ground for believing that in a critical hour such persons could not readily be isolated and separately dealt with, and constituted a menace to the national defense and safety, which demanded that prompt and adequate measures be taken to guard against it."

Like curfew, exclusion of those of Japanese origin was deemed necessary because of the presence of an unascertained number of disloyal members of the group, most of whom we have no doubt were loyal to this country. It was because we could not reject the finding of the military authorities that it was impossible to bring about an immediate segregation of the disloyal from the loyal that we sustained the validity of the curfew order as applying to the whole group. In the instant case, temporary exclusion of the entire group was rested by the military on the same ground. The judgment that exclusion of the whole group was for the same reason a military imperative answers the contention that the exclusion was in the nature of group punishment based on antagonism to those of Japanese origin. . . .

We uphold the exclusion order as of the time it was made and when the petitioner violated it. In doing so, we are not unmindful of the hardships imposed by it upon a large group of American citizens. But hardships are part of war, and war is an aggregation of hardships. All citizens alike, both in and out of uniform, feel the impact of war in greater or lesser measure. Citizenship has its responsibilities as well as its privileges, and in time of war the burden is always heavier. Compulsory exclusion of large groups of citizens from their homes, except under circumstances of direst emergency and peril, is inconsistent with our basic governmental institutions. But when under conditions of modern warfare our shores are threatened by hostile forces, the power to protect must be commensurate with the threatened danger. . . .

Since the petitioner has not been convicted of failing to report or to remain in an assembly or relocation center, we cannot in this case determine the validity of those separate provisions of the order. It is sufficient here for us to pass upon the order which petitioner violated. To do more would be to go beyond the issues raised, and to decide momentous questions not contained within the framework of the pleadings or the evidence in this case. It will be time enough to decide the serious constitutional issues which petitioner seeks to raise when an assembly or relocation order is applied or is certain to be applied to him, and we have its terms before us.

Some of the members of the Court are of the view that evacuation and detention in an Assembly Center were inseparable. After May 3, 1942, the date of Exclusion Order No. 34, Korematsu was under compulsion to leave the area not as he would choose but via an Assembly Center. The Assembly Center was conceived as a part of the machinery for group evacuation. The power to exclude includes the power to do it by force if necessary. And any forcible measure must necessarily entail some degree of detention or restraint whatever method of removal is selected. But whichever view is taken, it results in holding that the order under which petitioner was convicted was valid.

It is said that we are dealing here with the case of imprisonment of a citizen in a concentration camp solely because of his ancestry, without evidence or inquiry concerning his loyalty and good disposition towards the United States. Our task would be simple, our duty clear, were this a case involving the imprisonment of a loyal citizen in a concentration camp because of racial prejudice. Regardless of the true nature of the assembly and relocation centers—and we deem it unjustifiable to call them concentration camps with all the ugly connotations that term implies—we are dealing specifically with nothing but an exclusion order. To cast this case into outlines of racial prejudice, without reference to the real military dangers which were presented, merely confuses the issue. Korematsu was not excluded from the Military Area because of hostility to him or his race. He was excluded because we are at war with the Japanese Empire, because the properly constituted military authorities feared an invasion of our West Coast and felt constrained to take proper security measures, because they decided that the military urgency of the situation demanded that all citizens of Japanese ancestry be segregated from the West Coast temporarily, and finally, because Congress, reposing its confidence in this time of war in our military leaders—as inevitably it must—determined that they should have the power to do just this. There was evidence of disloyalty on the part of some, the military authorities considered that the need for action was great, and time was short. We cannot—by availing ourselves of the calm perspective of hindsight—now say that at that time these actions were unjustified.

33

Executive Order 9981

Harry S. Truman
July 26, 1948

Establishing the President's Committee on Equality of Treatment and Opportunity In the Armed Forces.

WHEREAS it is essential that there be maintained in the armed services of the United States the highest standards of democracy, with equality of treatment and opportunity for all those who serve in our country's defense:

NOW THEREFORE, by virtue of the authority vested in me as President of the United States, by the Constitution and the statutes of the United States, and as Commander in Chief of the armed services, it is hereby ordered as follows:

1. It is hereby declared to be the policy of the President that there shall be equality of treatment and opportunity for all persons in the armed services without regard to race, color, religion or national origin. This policy shall be put into effect as rapidly as possible, having due regard to the time required to effectuate any necessary changes without impairing efficiency or morale.

2. There shall be created in the National Military Establishment an advisory committee to be known as the President's Committee on Equality of Treatment and Opportunity in the Armed Services, which shall be composed of seven members to be designated by the President.

3. The Committee is authorized on behalf of the President to examine into the rules, procedures and practices of the Armed Services in order to determine in what respect such rules, procedures and practices may be altered or improved with a view to carrying out the policy of this order. The Committee shall confer and advise the Secretary of Defense, the Secretary of the Army, the Secretary of the Navy, and the Secretary of the Air Force, and shall make such recommendations to the President and to said Secretaries as in the judgment of the Committee will effectuate the policy hereof.

4. All executive departments and agencies of the Federal Government are authorized and directed to cooperate with the Committee in its work, and to furnish the Committee such information or the services of such persons as the Committee may require in the performance of its duties.

5. When requested by the Committee to do so, persons in the armed services or in any of the executive departments and agencies of the Federal Government shall testify before the Committee and shall make available for use of the Committee such documents and other information as the Committee may require.
6. The Committee shall continue to exist until such time as the President shall terminate its existence by Executive order.

Harry Truman
The White House
July 26, 1948

34

Brown v. Board of Education I, 1954

Supreme Court of the United States
347 U.S. 483
Brown v. Board of Education of Topeka
APPEAL FROM THE UNITED STATES DISTRICT COURT
FOR THE DISTRICT OF KANSAS
Argued December 9, 1952
Reargued December 8, 1953
Decided May 17, 1954

MR. CHIEF JUSTICE WARREN delivered the opinion of the Court.

These cases come to us from the States of Kansas, South Carolina, Virginia, and Delaware. They are premised on different facts and different local conditions, but a common legal question justifies their consideration together in this consolidated opinion.[1]

In each of the cases, minors of the Negro race, through their legal representatives, seek the aid of the courts in obtaining admission to the public schools of their community on a nonsegregated basis. In each instance, they had been denied admission to schools attended by white children under laws requiring or permitting segregation according to race. This segregation was alleged to deprive the plaintiffs of the equal protection of the laws under the Fourteenth Amendment. In each of the cases other than the Delaware case, a three-judge federal district court denied relief to the plaintiffs on the so-called "separate but equal" doctrine announced by this Court in *Plessy v. Fergson*, 163 U.S. 537. Under that doctrine, equality of treatment is accorded when the races are provided substantially equal facilities, even though these facilities be separate. In the Delaware case, the Supreme Court of Delaware adhered to that doctrine, but ordered that the plaintiffs be admitted to the white schools because of their superiority to the Negro schools.

The plaintiffs contend that segregated public schools are not "equal" and cannot be made "equal," and that hence they are deprived of the equal protection of the laws. Because of the obvious importance of the question presented, the Court took jurisdiction.[2] Argument was heard in the 1952 Term, and reargument was heard this Term on certain questions propounded by the Court.[3]

Reargument was largely devoted to the circumstances surrounding the adoption of the Fourteenth Amendment in 1868. It covered exhaustively consideration of the Amendment in Congress, ratification by the states, then—existing practices in racial segregation, and the views of proponents and opponents of the Amendment. This discussion and our own investigation convince us that, although these sources cast some light, it is not enough to resolve the problem with which we are faced. At best, they are inconclusive. The most avid proponents of the post-War Amendments undoubtedly intended them to remove all legal distinctions among "all persons born or naturalized in the United States." Their opponents, just as certainly, were antagonistic to both the letter and the spirit of the Amendments and wished them to have the most limited effect. What others in Congress and the state legislatures had in mind cannot be determined with any degree of certainty.

An additional reason for the inconclusive nature of the Amendment's history with respect to segregated schools is the status of public education at that time.[4] In the South, the movement toward free common schools, supported by general taxation, had not yet taken hold. Education of white children was largely in the hands of private groups. Education of Negroes was almost nonexistent, and practically all of the race were illiterate. In fact, any education of Negroes was forbidden by law in some states. Today, in contrast, many Negroes have achieved outstanding success in the arts and sciences, as well as in the business and professional world. It is true that public school education at the time of the Amendment had advanced further in the North, but the effect of the Amendment on Northern States was generally ignored in the congressional debates. Even in the North, the conditions of public education did not approximate those existing today. The curriculum was usually rudimentary; ungraded schools were common in rural areas; the school term was but three months a year in many states, and compulsory school attendance was virtually unknown. As a consequence, it is not surprising that there should be so little in the history of the Fourteenth Amendment relating to its intended effect on public education.

In the first cases in this Court construing the Fourteenth Amendment, decided shortly after its adoption, the Court interpreted it as proscribing all state-imposed discriminations against the Negro race.[5] The doctrine of "separate but equal" did not make its appearance in this Court until 1896 in the case of *Plessy v. Ferguson*, supra, involving not education but transportation.[6] American courts have since labored with the doctrine for over half a century. In this Court, there have been six cases involving the "separate but equal" doctrine in the field of public education.[7] In *Cumming v. County Board of Education*, 175 U.S. 528, and *Gong Lum v. Rice*, 275 U.S. 78, the validity of the doctrine itself was not challenged.[8] In more recent cases, all on the graduate school level, inequality was found in that specific benefits enjoyed by white students were denied to Negro students of the same educational qualifications. *Missouri ex rel. Gaines v. Canada*, 305 U.S. 337; *Sipuel v. Oklahoma*, 332 U.S. 631; *Sweatt v. Painter*, 339 U.S. 629; *McLaurin v. Oklahoma State Regents*, 339 U.S. 637. In none of these cases was it necessary to reexamine the doctrine to grant relief to the Negro plaintiff. And in *Sweatt v. Painter, supra,* the Court expressly reserved decision on the question whether *Plessy v. Ferguson* should be held inapplicable to public education.

In the instant cases, that question is directly presented. Here, unlike *Sweatt v. Painter,* there are findings below that the Negro and white schools involved have been equalized, or are being equalized, with respect to buildings, curricula, qualifications and salaries of teachers, and other "tangible" factors.[9] Our decision, therefore, cannot turn on merely a comparison of these tangible factors in the Negro and white schools involved in each of the cases. We must look instead to the effect of segregation itself on public education.

In approaching this problem, we cannot turn the clock back to 1868, when the Amendment was adopted, or even to 1896, when *Plessy v. Ferguson* was written. We must consider public education in the light of its full development and its present place in American life throughout the Nation. Only in this way can it be determined if segregation in public schools deprives these plaintiffs of the equal protection of the laws.

Today, education is perhaps the most important function of state and local governments. Compulsory school attendance laws and the great expenditures for education both demonstrate our recognition of the importance of education to our democratic society. It is required in the performance of our most basic public responsibilities, even service in the armed forces. It is the very foundation of good citizenship. Today it is a principal instrument in awakening the child to cultural values, in preparing him for later professional training, and in helping him to adjust normally to his environment. In these days, it is doubtful that any child may reasonably be expected to succeed in life if he is denied the opportunity of an education. Such an opportunity, where the state has undertaken to provide it, is a right which must be made available to all on equal terms.

We come then to the question presented: Does segregation of children in public schools solely on the basis of race, even though the physical facilities and other "tangible" factors may be equal, deprive the children of the minority group of equal educational opportunities? We believe that it does.

In *Sweatt v. Painter, supra,* in finding that a segregated law school for Negroes could not provide them equal educational opportunities, this Court relied in large part on "those qualities which are incapable of objective measurement but which make for greatness in a law school." In *McLaurin v. Oklahoma State Regents, supra,* the Court, in requiring that a Negro admitted to a white graduate school be treated like all other students, again resorted to intangible considerations: ". . . his ability to study, to engage in discussions and exchange views with other students, and, in general, to learn his profession." Such considerations apply with added force to children in grade and high schools. To separate them from others of similar age and qualifications solely because of their race generates a feeling of inferiority as to their status in the community that may affect their hearts and minds in a way unlikely ever to be undone. The effect of this separation on their educational opportunities was well stated by a finding in the Kansas case by a court which nevertheless felt compelled to rule against the Negro plaintiffs: Segregation of white and colored children in public schools has a detrimental effect upon the colored children. The impact is greater when it has the sanction of the law, for the policy of separating the races is usually interpreted as denoting the inferiority of the negro group. A sense of inferiority affects the motivation of a child to learn. Segregation with the sanction of law, therefore, has a tendency to [retard] the educational and mental development of negro children and to deprive them of some of the benefits they would receive in a racial[ly] integrated school system.[10] Whatever may have been the extent of psychological knowledge at the time of *Plessy v. Ferguson*, this finding is amply supported by modern authority.[11] Any language in *Plessy v. Ferguson* contrary to this finding is rejected.

We conclude that, in the field of public education, the doctrine of "separate but equal" has no place. Separate educational facilities are inherently unequal. Therefore, we hold that the plaintiffs and others similarly situated for whom the actions have been brought are, by reason of the segregation complained of, deprived of the equal protection of the laws guaranteed by the Fourteenth Amendment. This disposition makes unnecessary any discussion whether such segregation also violates the Due Process Clause of the Fourteenth Amendment.[12]

Because these are class actions, because of the wide applicability of this decision, and because of the great variety of local conditions, the formulation of decrees in these cases presents problems of considerable complexity. On reargument, the consideration of appropriate relief was necessarily subordinated to the primary question—the constitutionality of segregation in public education. We have now announced that such segregation is a denial of the equal protection of the laws. In order that we may have the full assistance of the parties in formulating decrees, the cases will be restored to the docket, and the parties are requested to present further argument on Questions 4 and 5 previously propounded by the Court for the reargument this Term.[13] The Attorney General of the United States is again invited to participate. The Attorneys General of the states requiring or permitting segregation in public education will also be permitted to appear as *amici curiae* upon request to do so by September 15, 1954, and submission of briefs by October 1, 1954.[14]

It is so ordered.

Endnotes

*Together with No. 2, Briggs et al. v. Elliott et al., on appeal from the United States District Court for the Eastern District of South Carolina, argued December 9–10, 1952, reargued December 7–8, 1953; No. 4, Davis et al. v. County School Board of Prince Edward County, Virginia, et al., on appeal from the United States District Court for the Eastern District of Virginia, argued December 10, 1952, reargued December 7–8, 1953, and No. 10, Gebhart et al. v. Belton et al., on certiorari to the Supreme Court of Delaware, argued December 11, 1952, reargued December 9, 1953.

1. In the Kansas case, Brown v. Board of Education, the plaintiffs are Negro children of elementary school age residing in Topeka. They brought this action in the United States District Court for the District of Kansas to enjoin enforcement of a Kansas statute which permits, but does not require, cities of more than 15,000 population to maintain separate school facilities for Negro and white students. Kan.Gen.Stat. § 72–1724 (1949). Pursuant to that authority, the Topeka Board of Education elected to establish segregated elementary schools. Other public schools in the community, however, are operated on a nonsegregated basis. The three-judge District Court, convened under 28 U.S.C. §§ 2281 and 2284, found that segregation in public education has a detrimental effect upon Negro children, but denied relief on the ground that the Negro and white schools were substantially equal with respect to buildings, transportation, curricula, and educational qualifications of teachers. 98 F.Supp. 797. The case is here on direct appeal under 28 U.S.C. § 1253.

   In the South Carolina case, *Briggs v. Elliott,* the plaintiffs are Negro children of both elementary and high school age residing in Clarendon County. They brought this action in the United States District Court for the Eastern District of South Carolina to enjoin enforcement of provisions in the state constitution and statutory code which require the segregation of Negroes and whites in public schools. S.C.Const., Art. XI, § 7; S.C.Code § 5377 (1942). The three-judge District Court, convened under 28 U.S.C. §§ 2281 and 2284, denied the requested relief. The court found that the Negro schools were inferior to the white schools, and ordered the defendants to begin immediately to equalize the facilities. But the court sustained the validity of the contested provisions and denied the plaintiffs admission to the white schools during the equalization program. 98 F.Supp. 529. This Court vacated the District Court's judgment and remanded the case for the purpose of obtaining the court's views on a report filed by the defendants concerning the progress made in the equalization program. 342 U.S. 350. On remand, the District Court found that substantial equality had been achieved except for buildings and that the defendants were proceeding to rectify this inequality as well. 103 F.Supp. 920. The case is again here on direct appeal under 28 U.S.C. § 1253.

   In the Virginia case, *Davis v. County School Board,* the plaintiffs are Negro children of high school age residing in Prince Edward County. They brought this action in the United States District Court for the Eastern District of Virginia to enjoin enforcement of provisions in the state constitution and statutory code which require the segregation of Negroes and whites in public schools. Va.Const., § 140; Va.Code § 22–221 (1950). The three-judge District Court, convened under 28 U.S.C. §§ 2281 and 2284, denied the requested relief. The court found the Negro school inferior in physical plant, curricula, and transportation, and ordered the defendants forthwith to provide substantially equal curricula and transportation and to "proceed with all reasonable diligence and dispatch to remove" the inequality in physical plant. But, as in the South

Carolina case, the court sustained the validity of the contested provisions and denied the plaintiffs admission to the white schools during the equalization program. 103 F.Supp. 337. The case is here on direct appeal under 28 U.S.C. § 1253.

In the Delaware case, *Gebhart v. Belton,* the plaintiffs are Negro children of both elementary and high school age residing in New Castle County. They brought this action in the Delaware Court of Chancery to enjoin enforcement of provisions in the state constitution and statutory code which require the segregation of Negroes and whites in public schools. Del.Const., Art. X, § 2; Del.Rev.Code § 2631 (1935). The Chancellor gave judgment for the plaintiffs and ordered their immediate admission to schools previously attended only by white children, on the ground that the Negro schools were inferior with respect to teacher training, pupil-teacher ratio, extracurricular activities, physical plant, and time and distance involved in travel. 87 A.2d 862. The Chancellor also found that segregation itself results in an inferior education for Negro children (see note 10, *infra*), but did not rest his decision on that ground. *Id.* at 865. The Chancellor's decree was affirmed by the Supreme Court of Delaware, which intimated, however, that the defendants might be able to obtain a modification of the decree after equalization of the Negro and white schools had been accomplished. 91 A.2d 137, 152. The defendants, contending only that the Delaware courts had erred in ordering the immediate admission of the Negro plaintiffs to the white schools, applied to this Court for certiorari. The writ was granted, 344 U.S. 891. The plaintiffs, who were successful below, did not submit a cross-petition.

2. 344 U.S. 1, 141, 891.

3. 345 U.S. 972. The Attorney General of the United States participated both Terms as amicus curiae.

4. For a general study of the development of public education prior to the Amendment, see Butts and Cremin, A History of Education in American Culture (1953), Pts. I, II; Cubberley, Public Education in the United States (1934 ed.), cc. II–XII. School practices current at the time of the adoption of the Fourteenth Amendment are described in Butts and Cremin, supra, at 269–275; Cubberley, supra, at 288–339, 408–431; Knight, Public Education in the South (1922), cc. VIII, IX. See also H. Ex.Doc. No. 315, 41st Cong., 2d Sess. (1871). Although the demand for free public schools followed substantially the same pattern in both the North and the South, the development in the South did not begin to gain momentum until about 1850, some twenty years after that in the North. The reasons for the somewhat slower development in the South (e.g., the rural character of the South and the different regional attitudes toward state assistance) are well explained in Cubberley, supra, at 408–423. In the country as a whole, but particularly in the South, the War virtually stopped all progress in public education. Id. at 427–428. The low status of Negro education in all sections of the country, both before and immediately after the War, is described in Beale, A History of Freedom of Teaching in American Schools (1941), 112–132, 175–195. Compulsory school attendance laws were not generally adopted until after the ratification of the

Fourteenth Amendment, and it was not until 1918 that such laws were in force in all the states. Cubberley, supra, at 563–565.

5. Slaughter-House Cases, 16 Wall. 36, 67–72 (1873); Strauder v. West Virginia, 100 U.S. 303, 307–308 (1880): It ordains that no State shall deprive any person of life, liberty, or property, without due process of law, or deny to any person within its jurisdiction the equal protection of the laws. What is this but declaring that the law in the States shall be the same for the black as for the white; that all persons, whether colored or white, shall stand equal before the laws of the States, and, in regard to the colored race, for whose protection the amendment was primarily designed, that no discrimination shall be made against them by law because of their color? The words of the amendment, it is true, are prohibitory, but they contain a necessary implication of a positive immunity, or right, most valuable to the colored race—the right to exemption from unfriendly legislation against them distinctively as colored—exemption from legal discriminations, implying inferiority in civil society, lessening the security of their enjoyment of the rights which others enjoy, and discriminations which are steps towards reducing them to the condition of a subject race. See also Virginia v. Rives, 100 U.S. 313, 318 (1880); Ex parte Virginia, 100 U.S. 339, 344–345 (1880).

6. The doctrine apparently originated in Roberts v. City of Boston, 59 Mass.198, 206 (1850), upholding school segregation against attack as being violative of a state constitutional guarantee of equality. Segregation in Boston public schools was eliminated in 1855. Mass.Acts 1855, c. 256. But elsewhere in the North, segregation in public education has persisted in some communities until recent years. It is apparent that such segregation has long been a nationwide problem, not merely one of sectional concern.

7. See also Berea College v. Kentucky, 211 U.S. 45 (1908).

8. In the Cummin case, Negro taxpayers sought an injunction requiring the defendant school board to discontinue the operation of a high school for white children until the board resumed operation of a high school for Negro children. Similarly, in the Gong Lum case, the plaintiff, a child of Chinese descent, contended only that state authorities had misapplied the doctrine by classifying him with Negro children and requiring him to attend a Negro school.

9. In the Kansas case, the court below found substantial equality as to all such factors. 98 F.Supp. 797, 798. In the South Carolina case, the court below found that the defendants were proceeding "promptly and in good faith to comply with the court's decree." 103 F.Supp. 920, 921. In the Virginia case, the court below noted that the equalization program was already "afoot and progressing" (103 F.Supp. 337, 341); since then, we have been advised, in the Virginia Attorney General's brief on reargument, that the program has now been completed. In the Delaware case, the court below similarly noted that the state's equalization program was well under way. 91 A.2d 137, 149.

10. A similar finding was made in the Delaware case: I conclude from the testimony that, in our Delaware society, State-imposed segregation in education itself results in the Negro children, as a class, receiving educational opportunities which are substantially

inferior to those available to white children otherwise similarly situated. 87 A.2d 862, 865.

11. K.B. Clark, Effect of Prejudice and Discrimination on Personality Development (Mid-century White House Conference on Children and Youth, 1950); Witmer and Kotin-sky, Personality in the Making (1952), c. VI; Deutscher and Chein, The Psychological Effects of Enforced Segregation A Survey of Social Science Opinion, 26 J. Psychol. 259 (1948); Chein, What are the Psychological Effects of Segregation Under Conditions of Equal Facilities?, 3 Int. J.Opinion and Attitude Res. 229 (1949); Brameld, Educational Costs, in Discrimination and National Welfare (MacIver, ed., 1949), 44–48; Frazier, The Negro in the United States (1949), 674–681. And see generally Myrdal, An American Dilemma (1944).

12. See Bolling v. Sharpe, post, p. 497, concerning the Due Process Clause of the Fifth Amendment.

13. 4. Assuming it is decided that segregation in public schools violates the Fourteenth Amendment (a) would a decree necessarily follow providing that, within the limits set by normal geographic school districting, Negro children should forthwith be admitted to schools of their choice, or (b) may this Court, in the exercise of its equity powers, permit an effective gradual adjustment to be brought about from existing segregated systems to a system not based on color distinctions? 5. On the assumption on which questions 4(a) and (b) are based, and assuming further that this Court will exercise its equity powers to the end described in question 4(b),(a) should this Court formulate detailed decrees in these cases; (b) if so, what specific issues should the decrees reach;(c) should this Court appoint a special master to hear evidence with a view to recommending specific terms for such decrees; (d) should this Court remand to the courts of first instance with directions to frame decrees in these cases and, if so, what general directions should the decrees of this Court include and what procedures should the courts of first instance follow in arriving at the specific terms of more detailed decrees?

14. See Rule 42, Revised Rules of this Court (effective July 1, 1954).

35

Brown v. Board of Education II, 1955

MR. CHIEF JUSTICE WARREN delivered the opinion of the Court.

These cases were decided on May 17, 1954. The opinions of that date, declaring the fundamental principle that racial discrimination in public education is unconstitutional, are incorporated herein by reference. All provisions of federal, state, or local law requiring or permitting such discrimination must yield to this principle. There remains for consideration the manner in which relief is to be accorded.

Because these cases arose under different local conditions and their disposition will involve a variety of local problems, we requested further argument on the question of relief. In view of the nationwide importance of the decision, we invited the Attorney General of the United States and the Attorneys General of all states requiring or permitting racial discrimination in public education to present their views on that question. The parties, the United States, and the States of Florida, North Carolina, Arkansas, Oklahoma, Maryland, and Texas filed briefs and participated in the oral argument.

These presentations were informative and helpful to the Court in its consideration of the complexities arising from the transition to a system of public education freed of racial discrimination. The presentations also demonstrated that substantial steps to eliminate racial discrimination in public schools have already been taken, not only in some of the communities in which these cases arose, but in some of the states appearing as *amici curiae*, and in other states as well. Substantial progress has been made in the District of Columbia and in the communities in Kansas and Delaware involved in this litigation. The defendants in the cases coming to us from South Carolina and Virginia are awaiting the decision of this Court concerning relief.

Full implementation of these constitutional principles may require solution of varied local school problems. School authorities have the primary responsibility for elucidating, assessing, and solving these problems; courts will have to consider whether the action of school authorities constitutes good faith implementation of the governing constitutional principles. Because of their proximity to local conditions and the possible need for further hearings, the courts which originally heard these cases can best perform this judicial appraisal. Accordingly, we believe it appropriate to remand the cases to those courts.

In fashioning and effectuating the decrees, the courts will be guided by equitable principles. Traditionally, equity has been characterized by a practical flexibility in shaping its remedies and by a facility for adjusting and reconciling public and private needs. These cases call for the exercise of these traditional attributes of equity power. At stake is the personal interest of the plaintiffs in admission to public schools as soon as practicable on a nondiscriminatory basis. To effectuate this interest may call for elimination of a variety of obstacles in making the transition to school systems operated in accordance with the constitutional principles set forth in our May 17, 1954, decision. Courts of equity may properly take into account the public interest in the elimination of such obstacles in a systematic and effective manner. But it should go without saying that the vitality of these constitutional principles cannot be allowed to yield simply because of disagreement with them.

While giving weight to these public and private considerations, the courts will require that the defendants make a prompt and reasonable start toward full compliance with our May 17, 1954, ruling. Once such a start has been made, the courts may find that additional time is necessary to carry out the ruling in an effective manner. The burden rests upon the defendants to establish that such time is necessary in the public interest and is consistent with good faith compliance at the earliest practicable date. To that end, the courts may consider problems related to administration, arising from the physical condition of the school plant, the school transportation system, personnel, revision of school districts and attendance areas into compact units to achieve a system of determining admission to the public schools on a nonracial basis, and revision of local laws and regulations which may be necessary in solving the foregoing problems. They will also consider the adequacy of any plans the defendants may propose to meet these problems and to effectuate a transition to a racially nondiscriminatory school system. During this period of transition, the courts will retain jurisdiction of these cases.

The judgments below, except that, in the Delaware case, are accordingly reversed, and the cases are remanded to the District Courts to take such proceedings and enter such orders and decrees consistent with this opinion as are necessary and proper to admit to public schools on a racially nondiscriminatory basis with all deliberate speed the parties to these cases. The judgment in the Delaware case—ordering the immediate admission of the plaintiffs to schools previously attended only by white children—is affirmed on the basis of the principles stated in our May 17, 1954, opinion, but the case is remanded to the Supreme Court of Delaware for such further proceedings as that Court may deem necessary in light of this opinion.

It is so ordered.

36

The Civil Rights Act of 1964

An Act

To enforce the constitutional right to vote, to confer jurisdiction upon the district courts of the United States to provide injunctive relief against discrimination in public accommodations, to authorize the Attorney General to institute suits to protect constitutional rights in public facilities and public education, to extend the Commission on Civil Rights, to prevent discrimination in federally assisted programs, to establish a Commission on Equal Employment Opportunity, and for other purposes.

Be it enacted by the Senate and House of Representatives of the United States of America in Congress assembled, That this Act may be cited as the "Civil Rights Act of 1964".

Title I—Voting Rights

SEC. 101. Section 2004 of the Revised Statutes (42 U.S.C. 1971), as amended by section 131 of the Civil Rights Act of 1957 (71 Stat. 637), and as further amended by section 601 of the Civil Rights Act of 1960 (74 Stat. 90), is further amended as follows:

(a) Insert "1" after "(a)" in subsection (a) and add at the end of subsection (a) the following new paragraphs:

"(2) No person acting under color of law shall—

"(A) in determining whether any individual is qualified under State law or laws to vote in any Federal election, apply any standard, practice, or procedure different from the standards, practices, or procedures applied under such law or laws to other individuals within the same county, parish, or similar political subdivision who have been found by State officials to be qualified to vote;

"(B) deny the right of any individual to vote in any Federal election because of an error or omission on any record or paper relating to any application, registration, or other act requisite to voting, if such error or omission is not material in determining whether such individual is qualified under State law to vote in such election; or

"(C) employ any literacy test as a qualification for voting in any Federal election unless (i) such test is administered to each individual and is conducted wholly in writing, and (ii) a certified copy of the test and of the answers given by the individual is furnished to him within twenty-five days of the submission of his request made within the period of time during which records and papers are required to be retained and preserved pursuant to title III of the Civil Rights Act of 1960 (42 U.S.C. 1974—74e; 74 Stat. 88): Provided, however, That the Attorney General may enter into agreements with appropriate State or local authorities that preparation, conduct, and maintenance of such tests in accordance with the provisions of applicable State or local law, including such special provisions as are necessary in the preparation, conduct, and maintenance of such tests for persons who are blind or otherwise physically handicapped, meet the purposes of this subparagraph and constitute compliance therewith.

"(3) For purposes of this subsection—

"(A) the term 'vote' shall have the same meaning as in subsection (e) of this section;

"(B) the phrase 'literacy test' includes any test of the ability to read, write, understand, or interpret any matter."

(b) Insert immediately following the period at the end of the first sentence of subsection (c) the following new sentence: "If in any such proceeding literacy is a relevant fact there shall be a rebuttable presumption that any person who has not been adjudged an incompetent and who has completed the sixth grade in a public school in, or a private school accredited by, any State or territory, the District of Columbia, or the Commonwealth of Puerto Rico where instruction is carried on predominantly in the English language, possesses sufficient literacy, comprehension, and intelligence to vote in any Federal election."

(c) Add the following subsection "(f)" and designate the present subsection "(f)" as subsection "(g)": "(f) When used in subsection (a) or (c) of this section, the words 'Federal election' shall mean any general, special, or primary election held solely or in part for the purpose of electing or selecting any candidate for the office of President, Vice President, presidential elector, Member of the Senate, or Member of the House of Representatives."

(d) Add the following subsection "(h)":

"(h) In any proceeding instituted by the United States in any district court of the United States under this section in which the Attorney General requests a finding of a pattern or practice of discrimination pursuant to subsection (e) of this section the Attorney General, at the time he files the complaint, or any defendant in the proceeding, within twenty days after service upon him of the complaint, may file with the clerk of such court a request that a court of three judges be convened to hear and determine the entire case. A copy of the request for a three-judge court shall be immediately furnished by such clerk to the chief judge of the circuit (or in his absence, the presiding circuit judge of the circuit) in which the case is pending. Upon receipt of the copy of such request it shall be the duty of the chief justice of the circuit or the presiding circuit judge, as the case may be, to designate immediately three judges in such circuit, of whom at least one shall be a circuit judge and another of whom shall be a district judge of the court in which the proceeding was instituted, to hear and determine such case, and it shall be the duty of the judges so designated to assign the case for hearing at the earliest practicable date, to participate in the hearing and determination thereof, and to cause the case to be in every way expedited.

An appeal from the final judgment of such court will lie to the Supreme Court.

"In any proceeding brought under subsection (c) of this section to enforce subsection (b) of this section, or in the event neither the Attorney General nor any defendant files a request for a three-judge court in any proceeding authorized by this subsection, it shall be the duty of the chief judge of the district (or in his absence, the acting chief judge) in which the case is pending immediately to designate a judge in such district to hear and determine the case. In the event that no judge in the district is available to hear and determine the case, the chief judge of the district, or the acting chief judge, as the case may be, shall certify this fact to the chief judge of the circuit (or, in his absence, the acting chief judge) who shall then designate a district or circuit judge of the circuit to hear and determine the case.

"It shall be the duty of the judge designated pursuant to this section to assign the case for hearing at the earliest practicable date and to cause the case to be in every way expedited."

Title II—Injunctive Relief Against Discrimination In Places of Public Accommodation

SEC. 201. (a) All persons shall be entitled to the full and equal enjoyment of the goods, services, facilities, and privileges, advantages, and accommodations of any place of public accommodation, as defined in this section, without discrimination or segregation on the ground of race, color, religion, or national origin.

(b) Each of the following establishments which serves the public is a place of public accommodation within the meaning of this title if its operations affect commerce, or if discrimination or segregation by it is supported by State action:

(1) any inn, hotel, motel, or other establishment which provides lodging to transient guests, other than an establishment located within a building which contains not more than five rooms for rent or hire and which is actually occupied by the proprietor of such establishment as his residence;

(2) any restaurant, cafeteria, lunchroom, lunch counter, soda fountain, or other facility principally engaged in selling food for consumption on the premises, including, but not limited to, any such facility located on the premises of any retail establishment; or any gasoline station;

(3) any motion picture house, theater, concert hall, sports arena, stadium or other place of exhibition or entertainment; and

(4) any establishment (A)(i) which is physically located within the premises of any establishment otherwise covered by this subsection, or (ii) within the premises of which is

physically located any such covered establishment, and (B) which holds itself out as serving patrons of such covered establishment.

(c) The operations of an establishment affect commerce within the meaning of this title if (1) it is one of the establishments described in paragraph (1) of subsection (b); (2) in the case of an establishment described in paragraph (2) of subsection (b), it serves or offers to serve interstate travelers or a substantial portion of the food which it serves, or gasoline or other products which it sells, has moved in commerce; (3) in the case of an establishment described in paragraph (3) of subsection (b), it customarily presents films, performances, athletic teams, exhibitions, or other sources of entertainment which move in commerce; and (4) in the case of an establishment described in paragraph (4) of subsection (b), it is physically located within the premises of, or there is physically located within its premises, an establishment the operations of which affect commerce within the meaning of this subsection. For purposes of this section, "commerce" means travel, trade, traffic, commerce, transportation, or communication among the several States, or between the District of Columbia and any State, or between any foreign country or any territory or possession and any State or the District of Columbia, or between points in the same State but through any other State or the District of Columbia or a foreign country.

(d) Discrimination or segregation by an establishment is supported by State action within the meaning of this title if such discrimination or segregation (1) is carried on under color of any law, statute, ordinance, or regulation; or (2) is carried on under color of any custom or usage required or enforced by officials of the State or political subdivision thereof; or (3) is required by action of the State or political subdivision thereof.

(e) The provisions of this title shall not apply to a private club or other establishment not in fact open to the public, except to the extent that the facilities of such establishment are made available to the customers or patrons of an establishment within the scope of subsection (b).

SEC. 202. All persons shall be entitled to be free, at any establishment or place, from discrimination or segregation of any kind on the ground of race, color, religion, or national origin, if such discrimination or segregation is or purports to be required by any law, statute, ordinance, regulation, rule, or order of a State or any agency or political subdivision thereof.

SEC. 203. No person shall (a) withhold, deny, or attempt to withhold or deny, or deprive or attempt to deprive, any person of any right or privilege secured by section 201 or 202, or (b) intimidate, threaten, or coerce, or attempt to intimidate, threaten, or coerce any person with the purpose of interfering with any right or privilege secured by section 201 or 202, or (c) punish or attempt to punish any person for exercising or attempting to exercise any right or privilege secured by section 201 or 202.

SEC. 204. (a) Whenever any person has engaged or there are reasonable grounds to believe that any person is about to engage in any act or practice prohibited by section 203, a civil action for preventive relief, including an application for a permanent or temporary injunction, restraining order, or other order, may be instituted by the person aggrieved and, upon timely application, the court may, in its discretion, permit the Attorney General to intervene in such civil action if he certifies that the case is of general public importance. Upon application by the complainant and in such circumstances as the court may deem just, the court may appoint an attorney for such complainant and may authorize the commencement of the civil action without the payment of fees, costs, or security.

(b) In any action commenced pursuant to this title, the court, in its discretion, may allow the prevailing party, other than the United States, a reasonable attorney's fee as part of the costs, and the United States shall be liable for costs the same as a private person.

(c) In the case of an alleged act or practice prohibited by this title which occurs in a State, or political subdivision of a State, which has a State or local law prohibiting such act or practice and establishing or authorizing a State or local authority to grant or seek relief from such practice or to institute criminal proceedings with respect thereto upon receiving notice thereof, no civil action may be brought under subsection (a) before the expiration of thirty days after written notice of such alleged act or practice has been given to the appropriate State or local authority by registered mail or in person, provided that the court may stay proceedings in such civil action pending the termination of State or local enforcement proceedings.

(d) In the case of an alleged act or practice prohibited by this title which occurs in a State, or political subdivision of a State, which has no State or local law prohibiting such act or practice, a civil action may be brought under subsection (a): Provided, That the court may refer the matter to the Community Relations Service established by title X of this Act for as long as the court believes there is a reasonable possibility of obtaining voluntary compliance, but for not more than sixty days: Provided further, That upon expiration of such sixty-day period, the court may extend such period for an additional period, not to exceed a cumulative total of one hundred and twenty days, if it believes there then exists a reasonable possibility of securing voluntary compliance.

SEC. 205. The Service is authorized to make a full investigation of any complaint referred to it by the court under section 204(d) and may hold such hearings with respect thereto as may be necessary. The Service shall conduct any hearings with respect to any such complaint in executive session, and shall not release any testimony given therein except by agreement of all parties involved in the complaint with the permission of the court, and the Service shall endeavor to bring about a voluntary settlement between the parties.

SEC. 206. (a) Whenever the Attorney General has reasonable cause to believe that any person or group of persons is engaged in a pattern or practice of resistance to the full enjoyment of any of the rights secured by this title, and that the pattern or practice is of such a nature and is intended to deny the full exercise of the rights herein described, the Attorney General may bring a civil action in the appropriate district court of the United States by filing with it a complaint (1) signed by him (or in his absence the Acting Attorney General), (2) setting forth facts pertaining to such pattern or practice, and (3) requesting such preventive relief, including an application for a permanent or temporary injunction, restraining order or other order against the person or persons responsible for such pattern or practice, as he deems necessary to insure the full enjoyment of the rights herein described.

(b) In any such proceeding the Attorney General may file with the clerk of such court a request that a court of three judges be convened to hear and determine the case. Such request by the Attorney General shall be accompanied by a certificate that, in his opinion, the case is of general public importance. A copy of the certificate and request for a three-judge court shall be immediately furnished by such clerk to the chief judge of the circuit (or in his absence, the presiding circuit judge of the circuit) in which the case is pending. Upon receipt of the copy of such request it shall be the duty of the chief judge of the circuit or the presiding circuit judge, as the case may be, to designate immediately three judges in such circuit, of whom at least one shall be a circuit judge and another of whom shall be a district judge of the court in which the proceeding was instituted, to hear and determine such case, and it shall be the duty of the judges so designated to assign the case for hearing at the earliest practicable date, to participate in the hearing and determination thereof, and to cause the case to be in every way expedited. An appeal from the final judgment of such court will lie to the Supreme Court.

In the event the Attorney General fails to file such a request in any such proceeding, it shall be the duty of the chief judge of the district (or in his absence, the acting chief judge) in which the case is pending immediately to designate a judge in such district to hear and determine the case. In the event that no judge in the district is available to hear and determine the case, the chief judge of the district, or the acting chief judge, as the case may be, shall certify this fact to the chief judge of the circuit (or in his absence, the acting chief judge) who shall then designate a district or circuit judge of the circuit to hear and determine the case.

It shall be the duty of the judge designated pursuant to this section to assign the case for hearing at the earliest practicable date and to cause the case to be in every way expedited.

SEC. 207. (a) The district courts of the United States shall have jurisdiction of proceedings instituted pursuant to this title and shall exercise the same without regard to whether the aggrieved party shall have exhausted any administrative or other remedies that may be provided by law.

(b) The remedies provided in this title shall be the exclusive means of enforcing the rights based on this title, but nothing in this title shall preclude any individual or any State or local agency from asserting any right based on any other Federal or State law not inconsistent with this title, including any statute or ordinance requiring nondiscrimination in public establishments or accommodations, or from pursuing any remedy, civil or criminal, which may be available for the vindication or enforcement of such right.

Title III—Desegregation of Public Facilities

SEC. 301. (a) Whenever the Attorney General receives a complaint in writing signed by an individual to the effect that he is being deprived of or threatened with the loss of his right to the equal protection of the laws, on account of his race, color, religion, or national origin, by being denied equal utilization of any public facility which is owned, operated, or managed by or on behalf of any State or subdivision thereof, other than a public school or public college as defined in section 401 of title IV hereof, and the Attorney General believes the complaint is meritorious and certifies that the signer or signers of such complaint are unable, in his judgment, to initiate and maintain appropriate legal proceedings for relief and that the institution of an action will materially further the orderly progress of desegregation in public facilities, the Attorney General is authorized to institute for or in the name of the United States a civil action in any appropriate district court of the United States against such parties and for such relief as may be appropriate, and such court shall have and shall exercise jurisdiction of proceedings instituted pursuant to this section. The Attorney General may implead as defendants such additional parties as are or become necessary to the grant of effective relief hereunder.

(b) The Attorney General may deem a person or persons unable to initiate and maintain appropriate legal proceedings within the meaning of subsection

(a) of this section when such person or persons are unable, either directly or through other interested persons or organizations, to bear the expense of the litigation or to obtain effective legal representation; or whenever he is satisfied that the institution of such litigation would jeopardize the personal safety, employment, or economic standing of such person or persons, their families, or their property.

SEC. 302. In any action or proceeding under this title the United States shall be liable for costs, including a reasonable attorney's fee, the same as a private person.

SEC. 303. Nothing in this title shall affect adversely the right of any person to sue for or obtain relief in any court against discrimination in any facility covered by this title.

SEC. 304. A complaint as used in this title is a writing or document within the meaning of section 1001, title 18, United States Code.

Title IV—Desegregation of Public Education
Definitions

SEC. 401. As used in this title—

(a) "Commissioner" means the Commissioner of Education.

(b) "Desegregation" means the assignment of students to public schools and within such schools without regard to their race, color, religion, or national origin, but "desegregation" shall not mean the assignment of students to public schools in order to overcome racial imbalance.

(c) "Public school" means any elementary or secondary educational institution, and "public college" means any institution of higher education or any technical or vocational school above the secondary school level, provided that such public school or public college is operated by a State, subdivision of a State, or governmental agency within a State, or operated wholly or predominantly from or through the use of governmental funds or property, or funds or property derived from a governmental source.

(d) "School board" means any agency or agencies which administer a system of one or more public schools and any other agency which is responsible for the assignment of students to or within such system.

Survey and Report of Educational Opportunities

SEC. 402. The Commissioner shall conduct a survey and make a report to the President and the Congress, within two years of the enactment of this title, concerning the lack of availability of equal educational opportunities for individuals by reason of race, color, religion, or national origin in public educational institutions at all levels in the United States, its territories and possessions, and the District of Columbia.

Technical Assistance

SEC. 403. The Commissioner is authorized, upon the application of any school board, State, municipality, school district, or other governmental unit legally responsible for operating a public school or schools, to render technical assistance to such applicant in the preparation, adoption, and implementation of plans for the desegregation of public schools. Such technical assistance may, among other activities, include making available to such agencies information regarding effective methods of coping with special educational problems occasioned by desegregation, and making available to such agencies personnel of the Office of Education or other persons specially equipped to advise and assist them in coping with such problems.

Training Institutes

SEC. 404. The Commissioner is authorized to arrange, through grants or contracts, with institutions of higher education for the operation of short-term or regular session institutes for special training designed to improve the ability of teachers, supervisors, counselors, and other elementary or secondary school personnel to deal effectively with special educational problems occasioned by desegregation. Individuals who attend such an institute on a full-time basis may be paid stipends for the period of their attendance at such institute in amounts specified by the Commissioner in regulations, including allowances for travel to attend such institute.

Grants

SEC. 405. (a) The Commissioner is authorized, upon application of a school board, to make grants to such board to pay, in whole or in part, the cost of—

(1) giving to teachers and other school personnel inservice training in dealing with problems incident to desegregation, and

(2) employing specialists to advise in problems incident to desegregation.

(b) In determining whether to make a grant, and in fixing the amount thereof and the terms and conditions on which it will be made, the Commissioner shall take into consideration the amount available for grants under this section and the other applications which are pending before him; the financial condition of the applicant and the other resources available to it; the nature, extent, and gravity of its problems incident to desegregation; and such other factors as he finds relevant.

Payments

SEC. 406. Payments pursuant to a grant or contract under this title may be made (after necessary adjustments on account of previously made overpayments or underpayments) in advance or by way of reimbursement, and in such installments, as the Commissioner may determine.

Suits By the Attorney General

SEC. 407. (a) Whenever the Attorney General receives a complaint in writing—

(1) signed by a parent or group of parents to the effect that his or their minor children, as members of a class of persons similarly situated, are being deprived by a school board of the equal protection of the laws, or

(2) signed by an individual, or his parent, to the effect that he has been denied admission to or not permitted to continue in attendance at a public college by reason of race, color, religion, or national origin, and the Attorney General believes the complaint is meritorious and certifies that the signer or signers of such complaint are unable, in his judgment, to initiate and maintain appropriate legal proceedings for relief and that the institution of an action will materially further the orderly achievement of desegregation in public education, the Attorney General is authorized, after giving notice of such complaint to the appropriate school board or college authority and after certifying that he is satisfied that such board or authority has had a reasonable time to adjust the conditions alleged in such complaint, to institute for or in the name of the United States a civil action in any appropriate district court of the United States against such parties and for such relief as may be appropriate, and such court shall have and shall exercise jurisdiction of proceedings instituted pursuant to this section, provided that nothing herein shall empower any official or court of the United States to issue any order seeking to achieve a racial balance in any school by requiring the transportation of pupils or students from one school to another or one school district to another in order to achieve such racial balance, or otherwise enlarge the existing power of the court to insure compliance with constitutional standards. The Attorney General may implead as defendants such additional parties as are or become necessary to the grant of effective relief hereunder.

(b) The Attorney General may deem a person or persons unable to initiate and maintain appropriate legal proceedings within the meaning of subsection

(a) of this section when such person or persons are unable, either directly or through other interested persons or organizations, to bear the expense of the litigation or to obtain effective legal representation; or whenever he is satisfied that the institution of such litigation would jeopardize the personal safety, employment, or economic standing of such person or persons, their families, or their property.

(c) The term "parent" as used in this section includes any person standing in loco parentis. A "complaint" as used in this section is a writing or document within the meaning of section 1001, title 18, United States Code.

SEC. 408. In any action or proceeding under this title the United States shall be liable for costs the same as a private person.

SEC. 409. Nothing in this title shall affect adversely the right of any person to sue for or obtain relief in any court against discrimination in public education.

SEC. 410. Nothing in this title shall prohibit classification and assignment for reasons other than race, color, religion, or national origin.

Title V—Commission On Civil Rights

SEC. 501. Section 102 of the Civil Rights Act of 1957 (42 U.S.C. 1975a; 71 Stat. 634) is amended to read as follows:

"Rules of Procedure of the Commission Hearings"

SEC. 102. (a) At least thirty days prior to the commencement of any hearing, the Commission shall cause to be published in the Federal Register notice of the date on which such hearing is to commence, the place at which it is to be held and the subject of the hearing. The Chairman, or one designated by him to act as Chairman at a hearing of the Commission, shall announce in an opening statement the subject of the hearing.

"(b) A copy of the Commission's rules shall be made available to any witness before the Commission, and a witness compelled to appear before the Commission or required to produce written or other matter shall be served with a copy of the Commission's rules at the time of service of the subpoena.

"(c) Any person compelled to appear in person before the Commission shall be accorded the right to be accompanied and advised by counsel, who shall have the right to subject his client to reasonable examination, and to make objections on the record and to argue briefly the basis for such objections. The Commission shall proceed with reasonable dispatch to conclude any hearing in which it is engaged. Due regard shall be had for the convenience and necessity of witnesses.

"(d) The Chairman or Acting Chairman may punish breaches of order and decorum by censure and exclusion from the hearings.

"(e) If the Commission determines that evidence or testimony at any hearing may tend to defame, degrade, or incriminate any person, it shall receive such evidence or testimony or summary of such evidence o testimony in executive session. The Commission shall afford any person defamed, degraded, or incriminated by such evidence or testimony an opportunity to appear and be heard in executive session, with a reasonable number of additional witnesses requested by him, before deciding to use such evidence or testimony. In the event the Commission determines to release or use such evidence or testimony in such manner as to reveal publicly the identity of the person defamed, degraded, or incriminated, such evidence or testimony, prior to such public release or use, shall be given at a public session, and the Commission shall afford such person an opportunity to appear as a voluntary witness or to file a sworn statement in his behalf and to submit brief and pertinent sworn statements of others. The Commission shall receive and dispose of requests from such person to subpoena additional witnesses.

"(f) Except as provided in sections 102 and 105 (f) of this Act, the Chairman shall receive and the Commission shall dispose of requests to subpoena additional witnesses.

"(g) No evidence or testimony or summary of evidence or testimony taken in executive session may be released or used in public sessions without the consent of the Commission. Whoever releases or uses in public without the consent of the Commission such evidence or testimony taken in executive session shall be fined not more than $1,000, or imprisoned for not more than one year.

"(h) In the discretion of the Commission, witnesses may submit brief and pertinent sworn statements in writing for inclusion in the record. The Commission shall determine the pertinency of testimony and evidence adduced at its hearings.

"(i) Every person who submits data or evidence shall be entitled to retain or, on payment of lawfully prescribed costs, procure a copy or transcript thereof, except that a witness in a hearing held in executive session may for good cause be limited to inspection of the official transcript of his testimony. Transcript copies of public sessions may be obtained by the public upon the payment of the cost thereof. An accurate transcript shall be made of the testimony of all witnesses at all hearings, either public or executive sessions, of the Commission or of any subcommittee thereof.

"(j) A witness attending any session of the Commission shall receive $6 for each day's attendance and for the time necessarily occupied in going to and returning from the same, and 10 cents per mile for going from and returning to his place of residence. Witnesses who attend at points so far removed from their respective residences as to prohibit return thereto from day to day shall be entitled to an additional allowance of $10 per day for expenses of subsistence including the time necessarily occupied in going to and returning from the place of attendance. Mileage payments shall be tendered to the witness upon service of a subpoena issued on behalf of the Commission or any subcommittee thereof.

"(k) The Commission shall not issue any subpoena for the attendance and testimony of witnesses or for the production of written or other matter which would require the presence of the party subpoenaed at a hearing to be held outside of the State wherein the witness is found or resides or is domiciled or transacts business, or has appointed an agent for receipt of service of process except that, in any event, the Commission may issue subpoenas for the attendance and testimony of witnesses and the production of written or other matter at a hearing held within fifty miles of the place where the witness is found or resides or is domiciled or transacts business or has appointed an agent for receipt of service of process.

"(l) The Commission shall separately state and currently publish in the Federal Register (1) descriptions of its central and field organization including the established places at which, and methods whereby, the public may secure information or make requests; (2) statements of the general course and method by which its functions are channeled and determined, and (3) rules adopted as authorized by law. No person shall in any manner be subject to or required to resort to rules, organization, or procedure not so published."

SEC. 502. Section 103(a) of the Civil Rights Act of 1957 (42 U.S.C. 1975b(a); 71 Stat. 634) is amended to read as follows:

"SEC. 103. (a) Each member of the Commission who is not otherwise in the service of the Government of the United States shall receive the sum of $75 per day for each day spent in the work of the Commission, shall be paid actual travel expenses, and per diem in lieu of subsistence expenses when away from his usual place of residence, in accordance with section 5 of the Administrative Expenses Act of 1946, as amended (5 U.S.C 73b-2; 60 Stat. 808)."

SEC. 503. Section 103(b) of the Civil Rights Act of 1957 (42 U.S.C. 1975(b); 71 Stat. 634) is amended to read as follows:

"(b) Each member of the Commission who is otherwise in the service of the Government of the United States shall serve without compensation in addition to that received for such other service, but while engaged in the work of the Commission shall be paid actual travel expenses, and per diem in lieu of subsistence expenses when away from his usual place of residence, in accordance with the provisions of the Travel Expenses Act of 1949, as amended

(5 U.S.C. 835—42; 63 Stat. 166)."

SEC. 504. (a) Section 104(a) of the Civil Rights Act of 1957 (42 U.S.C. 1975c(a); 71 Stat. 635), as amended, is further amended to read as follows:

"Duties of the Commission

"SEC. 104. (a) The Commission shall—

"(1) investigate allegations in writing under oath or affirmation that certain citizens of the United States are being deprived of their right to vote and have that vote counted by reason of their color, race, religion, or national origin; which writing, under oath or affirmation, shall set forth the facts upon which such belief or beliefs are based;

"(2) study and collect information concerning legal developments constituting a denial of equal protection of the laws under the Constitution because of race, color, religion or national origin or in the administration of justice;

"(3) appraise the laws and policies of the Federal Government with respect to denials of equal protection of the laws under the Constitution because of race, color, religion or national origin or in the administration of justice;

"(4) serve as a national clearinghouse for information in respect to denials of equal protection of the laws because of race, color, religion or national origin, including but not limited to the fields of voting, education, housing, employment, the use of public facilities, and transportation, or in the administration of justice;

"(5) investigate allegations, made in writing and under oath or affirmation, that citizens of the United States are unlawfully being accorded or denied the right to vote, or to have their votes properly counted, in any election of presidential electors, Members of the United States Senate, or of the House of Representatives, as a result of any patterns or practice of fraud or discrimination in the conduct of such election; and

"(6) Nothing in this or any other Act shall be construed as authorizing the Commission, its Advisory Committees, or any person under its supervision or control to inquire into or investigate any membership practices or internal operations of any fraternal organization, any college or university fraternity or sorority, any private club or any religious organization."

(b) Section 104(b) of the Civil Rights Act of 1957 (42 U.S.C. 1975c(b); 71 Stat. 635), as amended, is further amended by striking out the present subsection "(b)" and by substituting therefor:

"(b) The Commission shall submit interim reports to the President and to the Congress at such times as the Commission, the Congress or the President shall deem desirable, and shall submit to the President and to the Congress a final report of its activities, findings, and recommendations not later than January 31, 1968."

SEC. 505. Section 105(a) of the Civil Rights Act of 1957 (42 U.S.C. 1975d(a); 71 Stat. 636) is amended by striking out in the last sentence thereof "$50 per diem" and inserting in lieu thereof "$75 per diem."

SEC. 506. Section 105(f) and section 105(g) of the Civil Rights Act of 1957 (42 U.S.C. 1975d (f) and (g); 71 Stat. 636) are amended to read as follows:

"(f) The Commission, or on the authorization of the Commission any subcommittee of two or more members, at least one of whom shall be of each major political party, may, for the purpose of carrying out the provisions of this Act, hold such hearings and act at such times and places as the Commission or such authorized subcommittee may deem advisable. Subpoenas for the attendance and testimony of witnesses or the production of written or other matter may be issued in accordance with the rules of the Commission as contained in section 102 (j) and (k) of this Act, over the signature of the Chairman of the Commission or of such subcommittee, and may be served by any person designated by such Chairman. The holding of hearings by the Commission, or the appointment of a subcommittee to hold hearings pursuant to this subparagraph, must be approved by a majority of the Commission, or by a majority of the members present at a meeting at which at least a quorum of four members is present.

"(g) In case of contumacy or refusal to obey a subpoena, any district court of the United States or the United States court of any territory or possession, or the District Court of the United States for the District of Columbia, within the jurisdiction of which the inquiry is carried on or within the jurisdiction of which said person guilty of contumacy or refusal to obey is found or resides or is domiciled or transacts business, or has appointed an agent for receipt of service of process, upon application by the Attorney General of the United States shall have jurisdiction to issue to such person an order requiring such person to appear before the Commission or a subcommittee thereof, there to produce pertinent, relevant and nonprivileged evidence if so ordered, or there to give testimony touching the matter under investigation; and any failure to obey such order of the court may be punished by said court as a contempt thereof."

SEC. 507. Section 105 of the Civil Rights Act of 1957 (42 U.S.C. 1975d; 71 Stat. 636), as amended by section 401 of the Civil Rights Act of 1960 (42 U.S.C. 1975d(h); 74 Stat. 89), is further amended by adding a new subsection at the end to read as follows:

"(i) The Commission shall have the power to make such rules and regulations as are necessary to carry out the purposes of this Act."

Title VI—Nondiscrimination In Federally Assisted Programs

SEC. 601. No person in the United States shall, on the ground of race, color, or national origin, be excluded from participation in, be denied the benefits of, or be subjected to discrimination under any program or activity receiving Federal financial assistance.

SEC. 602. Each Federal department and agency which is empowered to extend Federal financial assistance to any program or activity, by way of grant, loan, or contract other than a contract of insurance or guaranty, is authorized and directed to effectuate the provisions of section 601 with respect to such program or activity by issuing rules, regulations, or orders of general applicability which shall be consistent with achievement of the objectives of the statute authorizing the financial assistance in connection with which the action is taken. No such rule, regulation, or order shall become effective unless and until approved by the President. Compliance with any requirement adopted pursuant to this section may be effected (1) by the termination of or refusal to grant or to continue assistance under such program or activity to any recipient as to whom there has been an express finding on the record, after opportunity for hearing, of a failure to comply with such requirement, but such termination or refusal shall be limited to the particular political entity, or part thereof, or other recipient as to whom such a finding has been made and, shall be limited in its effect to the particular program, or part thereof, in which such non-compliance has been so found, or (2) by any other means authorized by law: Provided, however, That no such action shall be taken until the department or agency concerned has advised the appropriate person or persons of the failure to comply with the requirement and has determined that compliance cannot be secured by voluntary means. In the case of any action terminating, or refusing to grant or continue, assistance because of failure to comply with a requirement imposed pursuant to this section, the head of the federal department or agency shall file with the committees of the House and Senate having legislative jurisdiction over the program or activity involved a full written report of the circumstances and the grounds for such action. No such action shall become effective until thirty days have elapsed after the filing of such report.

SEC. 603. Any department or agency action taken pursuant to section 602 shall be subject to such judicial review as may otherwise be provided by law for similar action taken by such department or agency on other grounds. In the case of action, not otherwise subject to judicial review, terminating or refusing to grant or to continue financial assistance upon a finding of failure to comply with any requirement imposed pursuant to section 602, any person aggrieved (including any State or political subdivision thereof and any agency of either) may obtain judicial review of such action in accordance with section 10 of the Administrative Procedure Act, and such action shall not be deemed committed to unreviewable agency discretion within the meaning of that section.

SEC. 604. Nothing contained in this title shall be construed to authorize action under this title by any department or agency with respect to any employment practice of any employer, employment agency, or labor organization except where a primary objective of the Federal financial assistance is to provide employment.

SEC. 605. Nothing in this title shall add to or detract from any existing authority with respect to any program or activity under which Federal financial assistance is extended by way of a contract of insurance or guaranty.

Title VII—Equal Employment Opportunity

Definitions

SEC. 701. For the purposes of this title—

(a) The term "person" includes one or more individuals, labor unions, partnerships, associations, corporations, legal representatives, mutual companies, joint-stock companies, trusts, unincorporated organizations, trustees, trustees in bankruptcy, or receivers.

(b) The term "employer" means a person engaged in an industry affecting commerce who has twenty-five or more employees for each working day in each of twenty or more calendar weeks in the current or preceding calendar year, and any agent of such a person, but such term does not include (1) the United States, a corporation wholly owned by the Government of the United States, an Indian tribe, or a State or political subdivision thereof, (2) a bona fide private membership club (other than a labor organization) which is exempt from taxation under section 501(c) of the Internal Revenue Code of 1954: Provided, That during the first year after the effective date prescribed in subsection (a) of section 716, persons having fewer than one hundred employees (and their agents) shall not be considered employers, and, during the second year after such date, persons having fewer than seventy-five employees (and their agents) shall not be considered employers, and, during the third year after such date, persons having fewer than fifty employees (and their agents) shall not be considered employers: Provided further, That it shall be the policy of the United States to insure equal employment opportunities for Federal employees without discrimination because of race, color, religion, sex or national origin and the President shall utilize his existing authority to effectuate this policy.

(c) The term "employment agency" means any person regularly undertaking with or without compensation to procure employees for an employer or to procure for employees opportunities to work for an employer and includes an agent of such a person; but shall not include an agency of the United States, or an agency of a State or political subdivision of a State, except that such term shall include the United States Employment Service and the system of State and local employment services receiving Federal assistance.

(d) The term "labor organization" means a labor organization engaged in an industry affecting commerce, and any agent of such an organization, and includes any organization of any kind, any agency, or employee representation committee, group, association, or plan so engaged in which employees participate and which exists for the purpose, in whole or in part, of dealing with employers concerning grievances, labor disputes, wages, rates of pay, hours, or other terms or conditions of employment, and any conference, general committee, joint or system board, or joint council so engaged which is subordinate to a national or international labor organization.

(e) A labor organization shall be deemed to be engaged in an industry affecting commerce if (1) it maintains or operates a hiring hall or hiring office which procures employees for an employer or procures for employees opportunities to work for an employer, or (2) the number of its members (or, where it is a labor organization composed of other labor organizations or their representatives, if the aggregate number of the members of such other labor organization) is (A) one hundred or more during the first year after the effective date prescribed in subsection (a) of section 716, (B) seventy-five or more during the second year after such date or fifty or more during the third year, or (C) twenty-five or more thereafter, and such labor organization—

(1) is the certified representative of employees under the provisions of the National Labor Relations Act, as amended, or the Railway Labor Act, as amended;

(2) although not certified, is a national or international labor organization or a local labor organization recognized or acting as the representative of employees of an employer or employers engaged in an industry affecting commerce; or

(3) has chartered a local labor organization or subsidiary body which is representing or actively seeking to represent employees of employers within the meaning of paragraph (1) or (2); or

(4) has been chartered by a labor organization representing or actively seeking to represent employees within the meaning of paragraph (1) or (2) as the local or subordinate body through which such employees may enjoy membership or become affiliated with such labor organization; or

(5) is a conference, general committee, joint or system board, or joint council subordinate to a national or international labor organization, which includes a labor organization engaged in an industry affecting commerce within the meaning of any of the preceding paragraphs of this subsection.

(f) The term "employee" means an individual employed by an employer.

(g) The term "commerce" means trade, traffic, commerce, transportation, transmission, or communication among the several States; or between a State and any place outside thereof; or within the District of Columbia, or a possession of the United States; or between points in the same State but through a point outside thereof.

(h) The term "industry affecting commerce" means any activity, business, or industry in commerce or in which a labor dispute would hinder or obstruct commerce or the free flow of commerce and includes any activity or industry "affecting commerce" within the meaning of the Labor-Management Reporting and Disclosure Act of 1959.

(i) The term "State" includes a State of the United States, the District of Columbia, Puerto Rico, the Virgin Islands, American Samoa, Guam, Wake Island, The Canal Zone, and Outer Continental Shelf lands defined in the Outer Continental Shelf Lands Act.

Exemption

SEC. 702. This title shall not apply to an employer with respect to the employment of aliens outside any State, or to a religious corporation, association, or society with respect to the employment of individuals of a particular religion to perform work connected with the carrying on by such corporation, association, or society of its religious activities or to an educational institution with respect to the employment of individuals to perform work connected with the educational activities of such institution.

Discrimination Because of Race, Color, Religion, Sex, or National Origin

SEC. 703. (a) It shall be an unlawful employment practice for an employer—

(1) to fail or refuse to hire or to discharge any individual, or otherwise to discriminate against any individual with respect to his compensation, terms, conditions, or privileges of

employment, because of such individual's race, color, religion, sex, or national origin; or

(2) to limit, segregate, or classify his employees in any way which would deprive or tend to deprive any individual of employment opportunities or otherwise adversely affect his status as an employee, because of such individual's race, color, religion, sex, or national origin.

(b) It shall be an unlawful employment practice for an employment agency to fail or refuse to refer for employment, or otherwise to discriminate against, any individual because of his race, color, religion, sex, or national origin, or to classify or refer for employment any individual on the basis of his race, color, religion, sex, or national origin.

(c) It shall be an unlawful employment practice for a labor organization—

(1) to exclude or to expel from its membership, or otherwise to discriminate against, any individual because of his race, color, religion, sex, or national origin;

(2) to limit, segregate, or classify its membership, or to classify or fail or refuse to refer for employment any individual, in any way which would deprive or tend to deprive any individual of employment opportunities, or would limit such employment opportunities or otherwise adversely affect his status as an employee or as an applicant for employment, because of such individual's race, color, religion, sex, or national origin; or

(3) to cause or attempt to cause an employer to discriminate against an individual in violation of this section.

(d) It shall be an unlawful employment practice for any employer, labor organization, or joint labor-management committee controlling apprenticeship or other training or retraining, including on-the-job training programs to discriminate against any individual because of his race, color, religion, sex, or national origin in admission to, or employment in, any program established to provide apprenticeship or other training.

(e) Notwithstanding any other provision of this title, (1) it shall not be an unlawful employment practice for an employer to hire and employ employees, for an employment agency to classify, or refer for employment any individual, for a labor organization to classify its membership or to classify or refer for employment any individual, or for an employer, labor organization, or joint labor-management committee controlling apprenticeship or other training or retraining programs to admit or employ any individual in any such program, on the basis of his religion, sex, or national origin in those certain instances where religion, sex, or national origin is a bona fide occupational qualification reasonably necessary to the normal operation of that particular business or enterprise, and (2) it shall not be an unlawful employment practice for a school, college, university, or other educational institution or institution of learning to hire and employ employees of a particular religion if such school, college, university, or other educational institution or institution of learning is, in whole or in substantial part, owned, supported, controlled, or managed by a particular religion or by a particular religious corporation, association, or society, or if the curriculum of such school, college, university, or other educational institution or institution of learning is directed toward the propagation of a particular religion.

(f) As used in this title, the phrase "unlawful employment practice" shall not be deemed to include any action or measure taken by an employer, labor organization, joint labor-management committee, or employment agency with respect to an individual who is a member of the Communist Party of the United States or of any other organization required to register as a Communist-action or Communist-front organization by final order of the Subversive Activities Control Board pursuant to the Subversive Activities Control Act of 1950.

(g) Notwithstanding any other provision of this title, it shall not be an unlawful employment practice for an employer to fail or refuse to hire and employ any individual for any position, for an employer to discharge any individual from any position, or for an employment agency to fail or refuse to refer any individual for employment in any position, or for a labor organization to fail or refuse to refer any individual for employment in any position, if—

(1) the occupancy of such position, or access to the premises in or upon which any part of the duties of such position is performed or is to be performed, is subject to any requirement imposed in the interest of the national security of the United States under any security program in effect pursuant to or administered under any statute of the United States or any Executive order of the President; and

(2) such individual has not fulfilled or has ceased to fulfill that requirement.

(h) Notwithstanding any other provision of this title, it shall not be an unlawful employment practice for an employer to apply different standards of compensation, or different terms, conditions, or privileges of employment pursuant to a bona fide seniority or merit system, or a system which measures earnings by quantity or quality of production or to employees who work in different locations, provided that such differences are not the result of an intention to discriminate because of race, color, religion, sex, or national origin, nor shall it be an unlawful employment practice for an employer to give and to act upon the results of any professionally developed ability test provided that such test, its administration or action upon the results is not designed, intended or used to discriminate because of race, color, religion, sex or national origin. It shall not be an unlawful employment practice under this title for any employer to differentiate upon the basis of sex in determining the amount of the wages or compensation paid or to be paid to employees of such employer if such differentiation is authorized by the provisions of section 6(d) of the Fair Labor Standards Act of 1938, as amended (29 U.S.C. 206(d)).

(i) Nothing contained in this title shall apply to any business or enterprise on or near an Indian reservation with respect to any publicly announced employment practice of such business or enterprise under which a preferential treatment is given to any individual because he is an Indian living on or near a reservation.

(j) Nothing contained in this title shall be interpreted to require any employer, employment agency, labor organization, or joint labor-management committee subject to this title to grant preferential treatment to any individual or to any group because of the race, color, religion, sex, or national origin of such individual or group on account of an imbalance which may exist with respect to the total number or percentage of persons of any race, color, religion, sex, or national origin employed by any employer, referred or classified for employment by any employment agency or labor organization, admitted to membership or classified by any labor organization, or admitted to, or employed in, any apprenticeship or other training program, in comparison with the total number or percentage of persons of such race, color, religion, sex, or national origin in any community, State, section, or other area, or in the available work force in any community, State, section, or other area.

Other Unlawful Employment Practices

SEC. 704. (a) It shall be an unlawful employment practice for an employer to discriminate against any of his employees or applicants for employment, for an employment agency to discriminate against any individual, or for a labor organization to discriminate against any member thereof or applicant for membership, because he has opposed, any practice made an unlawful employment practice by this title, or because he has made a charge, testified, assisted, or participated in any manner in an investigation, proceeding, or hearing under this title.

(b) It shall be an unlawful employment practice for an employer, labor organization, or employment agency to print or publish or cause to be printed or published any notice or advertisement relating to employment by such an employer or membership in or any classification or referral for employment by such a labor organization, or relating to any classification or referral for employment by such an employment agency, indicating any preference, limitation, specification, or discrimination, based on race, color, religion, sex, or national origin, except that such a notice or advertisement may indicate a preference, limitation, specification, or discrimination based on religion, sex, or national origin when religion, sex, or national origin is a bona fide occupational qualification for employment.

Equal Employment Opportunity Commission

SEC. 705. (a) There is hereby created a Commission to be known as the Equal Employment Opportunity Commission, which shall be composed of five members, not more than three of whom shall be members of the same political party, who shall be appointed by the President by and with the advice and consent of the Senate. One of the original members shall be appointed for a term of one year, one for a term of two years, one for a term of three years, one for a term of four years, and one for a term of five years, beginning from the date of enactment of this title, but their successors shall be appointed for terms of five years each, except that any individual chosen to fill a vacancy shall be appointed only for the unexpired term of the member whom he shall succeed. The President shall designate one member to serve as Chairman of the Commission, and one member to serve as Vice Chairman. The Chairman shall be responsible on behalf of the Commission for the administrative operations of the Commission, and shall appoint, in accordance with the civil service laws, such officers, agents, attorneys, and employees as it deems necessary to assist it in the performance of its functions and to fix their compensation in accordance with the Classification Act of 1949, as amended. The Vice Chairman shall act as Chairman in the absence or disability of the Chairman or in the event of a vacancy in that office.

(b) A vacancy in the Commission shall not impair the right of the remaining members to exercise all the powers of the Commission and three members thereof shall constitute a quorum.

(c) The Commission shall have an official seal which shall be judicially noticed.

(d) The Commission shall at the close of each fiscal year report to the Congress and to the President concerning the action it has taken; the names, salaries, and duties of all individuals in its employ and the moneys it has disbursed; and shall make such further reports on the cause of and means of eliminating discrimination and such recommendations for further legislation as may appear desirable.

(e) The Federal Executive Pay Act of 1956, as amended (5 U.S.C. 2201-2209), is further amended—

(1) by adding to section 105 thereof (5 U.S.C. 2204) the following clause:

"(32) Chairman, Equal Employment Opportunity Commission"; and

(2) by adding to clause (45) of section 106(a) thereof (5 U.S.C. 2205(a)) the following: "Equal Employment Opportunity Commission (4)."

(f) The principal office of the Commission shall be in or near the District of Columbia, but it may meet or exercise any or all its powers at any other place. The Commission may establish such regional or State offices as it deems necessary to accomplish the purpose of this title.

(g) The Commission shall have power—

(1) to cooperate with and, with their consent, utilize regional, State, local, and other agencies, both public and private, and individuals;

(2) to pay to witnesses whose depositions are taken or who are summoned before the Commission or any of its agents the same witness and mileage fees as are paid to witnesses in the courts of the United States;

(3) to furnish to persons subject to this title such technical assistance as they may request to further their compliance with this title or an order issued thereunder;

(4) upon the request of (i) any employer, whose employees or some of them, or (ii) any labor organization, whose members or some of them, refuse or threaten to refuse to cooperate in effectuating the provisions of this title, to assist in such effectuation by conciliation or such other remedial action as is provided by this title;

(5) to make such technical studies as are appropriate to effectuate the purposes and policies of this title and to make the results of such studies available to the public;

(6) to refer matters to the Attorney General with recommendations for intervention in a civil action brought by an aggrieved party under section 706, or for the institution of a civil action by the Attorney General under section 707, and to advise, consult, and assist the Attorney General on such matters.

(h) Attorneys appointed under this section may, at the direction of the Commission, appear for and represent the Commission in any case in court.

(i) The Commission shall, in any of its educational or promotional activities, cooperate with other departments and agencies in the performance of such educational and promotional activities.

(j) All officers, agents, attorneys, and employees of the Commission shall be subject to the provisions of section 9 of the Act of August 2, 1939, as amended (the Hatch Act), notwithstanding any exemption contained in such section.

Prevention of Unlawful Employment Practices

SEC. 706. (a) Whenever it is charged in writing under oath by a person claiming to be aggrieved, or a written charge has been filed by a member of the Commission where he has reasonable cause to believe a violation of this title has occurred (and such charge sets forth the facts upon which it is based) that an employer, employment agency, or labor organization has engaged in an unlawful employment practice, the Commission shall furnish such employer, employment agency, or labor organization (hereinafter referred to as the "respondent") with a copy of such charge and shall make an investigation of such charge, provided that such charge shall not be made public by the Commission. If the Commission shall determine, after such investigation, that there is reasonable cause to believe that the charge is true, the Commission shall endeavor to eliminate any such alleged unlawful employment practice by informal methods of conference, conciliation, and persuasion. Nothing said or done during and as a part of such endeavors may be made public by the Commission without the written consent of the parties, or used as evidence in a subsequent proceeding. Any officer or employee of the Commission, who shall make public in any manner whatever any information in violation of this subsection shall be deemed guilty of a misdemeanor and upon conviction thereof shall be fined not more than $1,000 or imprisoned not more than one year.

(b) In the case of an alleged unlawful employment practice occurring in a State, or political subdivision of a State, which has a State or local law prohibiting the unlawful employment practice alleged and establishing or authorizing a State or local authority to grant or seek relief from such practice or to institute criminal proceedings with respect thereto upon receiving notice thereof, no charge may be filed under subsection (a) by the person aggrieved before the expiration of sixty days after proceedings have been commenced under the State or local law, unless such proceedings have been earlier terminated, provided that such sixty-day period shall be extended to one hundred and twenty days during the first year after the effective date of such State or local law. If any requirement for the commencement of such proceedings is imposed by a State or local authority other than a requirement of the filing of a written and signed statement of the facts upon which the proceeding is based, the proceeding shall be deemed to have been commenced for the purposes of this subsection at the time such statement is sent by registered mail to the appropriate State or local authority.

(c) In the case of any charge filed by a member of the Commission alleging an unlawful employment practice occurring in a State or political subdivision of a State, which has a State or local law prohibiting the practice alleged and establishing or authorizing a State or local authority to grant or seek relief from such practice or to institute criminal proceedings with respect thereto upon receiving notice thereof, the Commission shall, before taking any action with respect to such charge, notify the appropriate State or local officials and, upon request, afford them a reasonable time, but not less than sixty days (provided that such sixty-day period shall be extended to one hundred and twenty days during the first year after the effective day of such State or local law), unless a shorter period is requested, to act under such State or local law to remedy the practice alleged.

(d) A charge under subsection (a) shall be filed within ninety days after the alleged unlawful employment practice occurred, except that in the case of an unlawful employment practice with respect to which the person aggrieved has followed the procedure set out in subsection (b), such charge shall be filed by the person aggrieved within two hundred and ten days after the alleged unlawful employment practice occurred, or within thirty days after receiving notice that the State or local agency has terminated the proceedings under the State or local, law, whichever is earlier, and a copy of such charge shall be filed by the Commission with the State or local agency.

(e) If within thirty days after a charge is filed with the Commission or within thirty days after expiration of any period of reference under subsection (c) (except that in either case such period may be extended to not more than sixty days upon a determination by the Commission that further efforts to secure voluntary compliance are warranted), the Commission has been unable to obtain voluntary compliance with this title, the Commission shall so notify the person aggrieved and a civil action may, within thirty days thereafter, be brought against the respondent named in the charge (1) by the person claiming to be aggrieved, or (2) if such charge was filed by a member of the Commission, by any person whom the charge alleges was aggrieved by the alleged unlawful employment practice. Upon application by the complainant and in such circumstances as the court may deem just, the court may appoint an attorney for such complainant and may authorize the commencement of the action without the payment of fees, costs, or security. Upon timely application, the court may, in its discretion, permit the Attorney General to intervene in such civil action if he certifies that the case is of general public importance. Upon request, the court may, in its discretion, stay further proceedings for not more than sixty days pending the termination of State or local proceedings described in subsection (b) or the efforts of the Commission to obtain voluntary compliance.

(f) Each United States district court and each United States court of a place subject to the jurisdiction of the United States shall have jurisdiction of actions brought under this title. Such an action may be brought in any judicial district in the State in which the unlawful employment practice is alleged to have been committed, in the judicial district in which the employment records relevant to such practice are maintained and administered, or in the judicial district in which the plaintiff would have worked but for the alleged unlawful employment practice, but if the respondent is not found within any such district, such an action may be brought within the judicial district in which the respondent has his principal office. For purposes of sections 1404 and 1406 of title 28 of the United States Code, the judicial district in which the respondent has his principal office shall in all cases be considered a district in which the action might have been brought.

(g) If the court finds that the respondent has intentionally engaged in or is intentionally engaging in an unlawful employment practice charged in the complaint, the court may enjoin the respondent from engaging in such unlawful employment practice, and order such affirmative action as may be appropriate, which may include reinstatement or hiring of employees, with or without back pay (payable by the employer, employment agency, or labor organization, as the case may be, responsible for the unlawful employment practice). Interim earnings or amounts earnable with reasonable diligence by the person or persons discriminated against shall operate to reduce the back pay otherwise allowable. No order of the court shall require the admission or reinstatement of an individual as a member of a union or the hiring, reinstatement, or promotion of an individual as an employee, or the payment to him of any back pay, if such individual was refused admission, suspended, or expelled or was refused employment or advancement or was suspended or discharged for any reason other than discrimination on account of race, color, religion, sex or national origin or in violation of section 704(a).

(h) The provisions of the Act entitled "An Act to amend the Judicial Code and to define and limit the jurisdiction of courts sitting in equity, and for other purposes," approved

March 23, 1932 (29 U.S.C. 101–115), shall not apply with respect to civil actions brought under this section.

(i) In any case in which an employer, employment agency, or labor organization fails to comply with an order of a court issued in a civil action brought under subsection (e), the Commission may commence proceedings to compel compliance with such order.

(j) Any civil action brought under subsection (e) and any proceedings brought under subsection (i) shall be subject to appeal as provided in sections 1291 and 1292, title 28, United States Code.

(k) In any action or proceeding under this title the court, in its discretion, may allow the prevailing party, other than the Commission or the United States, a reasonable attorney's fee as part of the costs, and the Commission and the United States shall be liable for costs the same as a private person.

SEC. 707. (a) Whenever the Attorney General has reasonable cause to believe that any person or group of persons is engaged in a pattern or practice of resistance to the full enjoyment of any of the rights secured by this title, and that the pattern or practice is of such a nature and is intended to deny the full exercise of the rights herein described, the Attorney General may bring a civil action in the appropriate district court of the United States by filing with it a complaint (1) signed by him (or in his absence the Acting Attorney General), (2) setting forth facts pertaining to such pattern or practice, and (3) requesting such relief, including an application for a permanent or temporary injunction, restraining order or other order against the person or persons responsible for such pattern or practice, as he deems necessary to insure the full enjoyment of the rights herein described.

(b) The district courts of the United States shall have and shall exercise jurisdiction of proceedings instituted pursuant to this section, and in any such proceeding the Attorney General may file with the clerk of such court a request that a court of three judges be convened to hear and determine the case. Such request by the Attorney General shall be accompanied by a certificate that, in his opinion, the case is of general public importance. A copy of the certificate and request for a three-judge court shall be immediately furnished by such clerk to the chief judge of the circuit (or in his absence, the presiding circuit judge of the circuit) in which the case is pending. Upon receipt of such request it shall be the duty of the chief judge of the circuit or the presiding circuit judge, as the case may be, to designate immediately three judges in such circuit, of whom at least one shall be a circuit judge and another of whom shall be a district judge of the court in which the proceeding was instituted, to hear and determine such case, and it shall be the duty of the judges so designated to assign the case for hearing at the earliest practicable date, to participate in the hearing and determination thereof, and to cause the case to be in every way expedited. An appeal from the final judgment of such court will lie to the Supreme Court.

In the event the Attorney General fails to file such a request in any such proceeding, it shall be the duty of the chief judge of the district (or in his absence, the acting chief judge) in which the case is pending immediately to designate a judge in such district to hear and determine the case. In the event that no judge in the district is available to hear and determine the case, the chief judge of the district, or the acting chief judge, as the case may be, shall certify this fact to the chief judge of the circuit (or in his absence, the acting chief judge) who shall then designate a district or circuit judge of the circuit to hear and determine the case.

It shall be the duty of the judge designated pursuant to this section to assign the case for hearing at the earliest practicable date and to cause the case to be in every way expedited.

Effect On State Laws

SEC. 708. Nothing in this title shall be deemed to exempt or relieve any person from any liability, duty, penalty, or punishment provided by any present or future law of any State or political subdivision of a State, other than any such law which purports to require or permit the doing of any act which would be an unlawful employment practice under this title.

Investigations, Inspections, Records, State Agencies

SEC. 709. (a) In connection with any investigation of a charge filed under section 706, the Commission or its designated representative shall at all reasonable times have access to, for the purposes of examination, and the right to copy any evidence of any person being investigated or proceeded against that relates to unlawful employment practices covered by this title and is relevant to the charge under investigation.

(b) The Commission may cooperate with State and local agencies charged with the administration of State fair employment practices laws and, with the consent of such agencies, may for the purpose of carrying out its functions and duties under this title and within the limitation of funds appropriated specifically for such purpose, utilize the services of such agencies and their employees and, notwithstanding any other provision of law, may reimburse such agencies and their employees for services rendered to assist the Commission in carrying out this title. In furtherance of such cooperative efforts, the Commission may enter into written agreements with such State or local agencies and such agreements may include provisions under which the Commission shall refrain from processing a charge in any cases or class of cases specified in such agreements and under which no person may bring a civil action under section 706 in any cases or class of cases so specified, or under which the Commission shall relieve any person or class of persons in such State or locality from requirements imposed under this section. The Commission shall rescind any such agreement whenever it determines that the agreement no longer serves the interest of effective enforcement of this title.

(c) Except as provided in subsection (d), every employer, employment agency, and labor organization subject to this title shall (1) make and keep such records relevant to the determinations of whether unlawful employment practices have been or are being committed, (2) preserve such records for such periods, and (3) make such reports therefrom, as the Commission shall prescribe by regulation or order, after public hearing, as reasonable, necessary, or appropriate for the enforcement of this title or the regulations or orders thereunder. The Commission shall, by regulation, require each employer, labor organization, and joint labor-management committee subject to this title which controls an apprenticeship or other training program to maintain such records as are reasonably necessary to carry out the purpose of this title, including, but not limited to, a list of applicants who wish to participate in such program, including the chronological order in which such applications were received, and shall furnish to the Commission, upon request, a detailed description of the manner in which persons are selected to participate in the apprenticeship or other training program. Any employer, employment agency, labor organization, or joint labor-management committee which believes that the application to it of any regulation or order issued under this section would result in undue hardship may (1) apply to the Commission for an exemption from the application of such regulation or order, or (2) bring a civil action in the United States district court for the district where such records are kept. If the Commission or the court, as the case may be, finds that the application of the regulation or order to the employer, employment agency, or labor organization in question would impose an undue hardship, the Commission or the court, as the case may be, may grant appropriate relief.

(d) The provisions of subsection (c) shall not apply to any employer, employment agency, labor organization, or joint labor-management committee with respect to matters occurring in any State or political subdivision thereof which has a fair employment practice law during any period in which such employer, employment agency, labor organization, or joint labor-management committee is subject to such law, except that the Commission may require such notations on records which such employer, employment agency, labor organization, or joint labor-management committee keeps or is required to keep as are necessary because of differences in coverage or methods of enforcement between the State or local law and the provisions of this title. Where an employer is required by Executive Order 10925, issued March 6, 1961, or by any other Executive order prescribing fair employment practices for Government contractors and subcontractors, or by rules or regulations issued thereunder, to file reports relating to his employment practices with any Federal agency or committee, and he is substantially in compliance with such requirements, the Commission shall not require him to file additional reports pursuant to subsection (c) of this section.

(e) It shall be unlawful for any officer or employee of the Commission to make public in any manner whatever any information obtained by the Commission pursuant to its authority under this section prior to the institution of any proceeding under this title involving such information. Any officer or employee of the Commission who shall make public in any manner whatever any information in violation of this subsection shall be guilty of a misdemeanor and upon conviction thereof, shall be fined not more than $1,000, or imprisoned not more than one year.

Investigatory Powers

SEC. 710. (a) For the purposes of any investigation of a charge filed under the authority contained in section 706, the Commission shall have authority to examine witnesses under oath and to require the production of documentary evidence relevant or material to the charge under investigation.

(b) If the respondent named in a charge filed under section 706 fails or refuses to comply with a demand of the Commission for permission to examine or to copy evidence in conformity with the provisions of section 709(a), or if any person required to comply with the provisions of section 709 (c) or (d) fails or refuses to do so, or if any person fails or refuses to comply with a demand by the Commission to give testimony under oath, the United States district court for the district in which such person is found, resides, or transacts business, shall, upon application of the Commission, have jurisdiction to issue to such person an order requiring him to comply with the provisions of section 709 (c) or (d) or to comply with the demand of the Commission, but the attendance of a witness may not be required outside the State where he is found, resides, or transacts business and the production of evidence may not be required outside the State where such evidence is kept.

(c) Within twenty days after the service upon any person charged under section 706 of a demand by the Commission for the production of documentary evidence or for permission to examine or to copy evidence in conformity with the provisions of section 709(a), such person may file in the district court of the United States for the judicial district in which he resides, is found, or transacts business, and serve upon the Commission a petition for an order of such court modifying or setting aside such demand. The time allowed for compliance with the demand in whole or in part as deemed proper and ordered by the court shall not run during the pendency of such petition in the court. Such petition shall specify each ground upon which the petitioner relies in seeking such relief, and may be based upon any failure of such demand to comply with the provisions of this title or with the limitations generally applicable to compulsory process or upon any constitutional or other legal right or privilege of such person. No objection which is not raised by such a petition may be urged in the defense to a proceeding initiated by the Commission under subsection (b) for enforcement of such a demand unless such proceeding is commenced by the Commission prior to the expiration of the twenty-day period, or unless the court determines that the defendant could not reasonably have been aware of the availability of such ground of objection.

(d) In any proceeding brought by the Commission under subsection (b), except as provided in subsection (c) of this section, the defendant may petition the court for an order modifying or setting aside the demand of the Commission.

SEC. 711. (a) Every employer, employment agency, and labor organization, as the case may be, shall post and keep posted in conspicuous places upon its premises where notices to employees, applicants for employment, and members are customarily posted a notice to be prepared or approved by the Commission setting forth excerpts from or, summaries of, the pertinent provisions of this title and information pertinent to the filing of a complaint.

(b) A willful violation of this section shall be punishable by a fine of not more than $100 for each separate offense.

Veterans' Preference

SEC. 712. Nothing contained in this title shall be construed to repeal or modify any Federal, State, territorial, or local law creating special rights or preference for veterans.

Rules and Regulations

SEC. 713. (a) The Commission shall have authority from time to time to issue, amend, or rescind suitable procedural regulations to carry out the provisions of this title. Regulations issued under this section shall be in conformity with the standards and limitations of the Administrative Procedure Act.

(b) In any action or proceeding based on any alleged unlawful employment practice, no person shall be subject to any liability or punishment for or on account of (1) the commission by such person of an unlawful employment practice if he pleads and proves that the act or omission complained of was in good faith, in conformity with, and in reliance on any written interpretation or opinion of the Commission, or (2) the failure of such person to publish and file any information required by any provision of this title if he pleads and proves that he failed to publish and file such information in good faith, in conformity with the instructions of the Commission issued under this title regarding the filing of such information. Such a defense, if established, shall be a bar to the action or proceeding, notwithstanding that (A) after such act or omission, such interpretation or opinion is modified or rescinded or is determined by judicial authority to be invalid or of no legal effect, or (B) after publishing or filing the description and annual reports, such publication or filing is determined by judicial authority not to be in conformity with the requirements of this title.

Forcibly Resisting the Commission or Its Representatives

SEC. 714. The provisions of section 111, title 18, United States Code, shall apply to officers, agents, and employees of the Commission in the performance of their official duties.

Special Study By Secretary of Labor

SEC. 715. The Secretary of Labor shall make a full and complete study of the factors which might tend to result in discrimination in employment because of age and of the consequences of such discrimination on the economy and individuals affected. The Secretary of Labor shall make a report to the Congress not later than June 30, 1965, containing the results of such study and shall include in such report such recommendations for legislation to prevent arbitrary discrimination in employment because of age as he determines advisable.

Effective Date

SEC. 716. (a) This title shall become effective one year after the date of its enactment.

(b) Notwithstanding subsection (a), sections of this title other than sections 703, 704, 706, and 707 shall become effective immediately.

(c) The President shall, as soon as feasible after the enactment of this title, convene one or more conferences for the purpose of enabling the leaders of groups whose members will be affected by this title to become familiar with the rights afforded and obligations imposed by its provisions, and for the purpose of making plans which will result in the fair and effective administration of this title when all of its provisions become effective. The President shall invite the participation in such conference or conferences of (1) the members of the President's Committee on Equal Employment Opportunity, (2) the members of the Commission on Civil Rights, (3) representatives of State and local agencies engaged in furthering equal employment opportunity, (4) representatives of private agencies engaged in furthering equal employment opportunity, and (5) representatives of employers, labor organizations, and employment agencies who will be subject to this title.

Title VIII—Registration and Voting Statistics

SEC. 801. The Secretary of Commerce shall promptly conduct a survey to compile registration and voting statistics in such geographic areas as may be recommended by the Commission on Civil Rights. Such a survey and compilation shall, to the extent recommended by the Commission on Civil Rights, only include a count of persons of voting age by race, color, and national origin, and determination of the extent to which such persons are registered to vote, and have voted in any statewide primary or general election in which the Members of the United States House of Representatives are nominated or elected, since January 1, 1960. Such information shall also be collected and compiled in connection with the Nineteenth Decennial Census, and at such other times as the Congress may prescribe. The provisions of section 9 and chapter 7 of title 13, United States Code, shall apply to any survey, collection, or compilation of registration and voting statistics carried out under this title: Provided, however, That no person shall be compelled to disclose his race, color, national origin, or questioned about his political party affiliation, how he voted, or the reasons therefore, nor shall any penalty be imposed for his failure or refusal to make such disclosure. Every person interrogated orally, by written survey or questionnaire or by any other means with respect to such information shall be fully advised with respect to his right to fail or refuse to furnish such information.

Title IX—Intervention and Procedure After Removal in Civil Rights Cases

SEC. 901. Title 28 of the United States Code, section 1447(d), is amended to read as follows:

"An order remanding a case to the State court from which it was removed is not reviewable on appeal or otherwise, except that an order remanding a case to the State court from which it was removed pursuant to section 1443 of this title shall be reviewable by appeal or otherwise."

SEC. 902. Whenever an action has been commenced in any court of the United States seeking relief from the denial of equal protection of the laws under the fourteenth amendment to the Constitution on account of race, color, religion, or national origin, the Attorney General for or in the name of the United States may intervene in such action upon timely application if the Attorney General certifies that the case is of general public importance. In such action the United States shall be entitled to the same relief as if it had instituted the action.

Title X—Establishment of Community Relations Service

SEC. 1001. (a) There is hereby established in and as a part of the Department of Commerce a Community Relations Service (hereinafter referred to as the "Service"), which shall be headed by a Director who shall be appointed by the President with the advice and consent of the Senate for a term of four years. The Director is authorized to appoint, subject to the civil service laws and regulations, such other personnel as may be necessary to enable the Service to carry out its functions and duties, and to fix their compensation in accordance with the Classification Act of 1949, as amended. The Director is further authorized to procure services as authorized by section 15 of the Act of August 2, 1946 (60 Stat. 810; 5 U.S.C. 55(a)), but at rates for individuals not in excess of $75 per diem.

(b) Section 106(a) of the Federal Executive Pay Act of 1956, as amended (5 U.S.C. 2205(a)), is further amended by adding the following clause thereto:

"(52) Director, Community Relations Service."

SEC. 1002. It shall be the function of the Service to provide assistance to communities and persons therein in resolving disputes, disagreements, or difficulties relating to discriminatory practices based on race, color, or national origin which impair the rights of persons in such communities under the Constitution or laws of the United States or which affect or may affect interstate commerce. The Service may offer its services in cases of such disputes, disagreements, or difficulties whenever, in its judgment, peaceful relations among the citizens of the community involved are threatened thereby, and it may offer its services either upon its own motion or upon the request of an appropriate State or local official or other interested person.

SEC. 1003. (a) The Service shall, whenever possible, in performing its functions, seek and utilize the cooperation of appropriate State or local, public, or private agencies.

(b) The activities of all officers and employees of the Service in providing conciliation assistance shall be conducted in confidence and without publicity, and the Service shall hold confidential any information acquired in the regular performance of its duties upon the understanding that it would be so held. No officer or employee of the Service shall engage in the performance of investigative or prosecuting functions of any department or agency in any litigation arising out of a dispute in which he acted on behalf of the Service. Any officer or other employee of the Service, who shall make public in any manner whatever any information in violation of this subsection, shall be deemed guilty of a misdemeanor and, upon conviction thereof, shall be fined not more than $1,000 or imprisoned not more than one year.

SEC. 1004. Subject to the provisions of sections 205 and 1003(b), the Director shall, on or before January 31 of each year, submit to the Congress a report of the activities of the Service during the preceding fiscal year.

Title XI—Miscellaneous

SEC. 1101. In any proceeding for criminal contempt arising under title II, III, IV, V, VI, or VII of this Act, the accused, upon demand therefor, shall be entitled to a trial by jury, which shall conform as near as may be to the practice in criminal cases. Upon conviction, the accused shall not be fined more than $1,000 or imprisoned for more than six months.

This section shall not apply to contempts committed in the presence of the court, or so near thereto as to obstruct the administration of justice, nor to the misbehavior, misconduct, or disobedience of any officer of the court in respect to writs, orders, or process of the court. No person shall be convicted of criminal contempt hereunder unless the act or omission constituting such contempt shall have been intentional, as required in other cases of criminal contempt.

Nor shall anything herein be construed to deprive courts of their power, by civil contempt proceedings, without a jury, to secure compliance with or to prevent obstruction of, as distinguished from punishment for violations of, any lawful writ, process, order, rule, decree, or command of the court in accordance with the prevailing usages of law and equity, including the power of detention.

SEC. 1102. No person should be put twice in jeopardy under the laws of the United States for the same act or omission. For this reason, an acquittal or conviction in a prosecution for a specific crime under the laws of the United States shall bar a proceeding for criminal contempt, which is based upon the same act or omission and which arises under the provisions of this Act; and an acquittal or conviction in a proceeding for criminal contempt, which arises under the provisions of this Act, shall bar a prosecution for a specific crime under the laws of the United States based upon the same act or omission.

SEC. 1103. Nothing in this Act shall be construed to deny, impair, or otherwise affect any right or authority of the Attorney General or of the United States or any agency or officer thereof under existing law to institute or intervene in any action or proceeding.

SEC. 1104. Nothing contained in any title of this Act shall be construed as indicating an intent on the part of Congress to occupy the field in which any such title operates to the exclusion of State laws on the same subject matter, nor shall any provision of this Act be construed as invalidating any provision of State law unless such provision is inconsistent with any of the purposes of this Act, or any provision thereof.

SEC. 1105. There are hereby authorized to be appropriated such sums as are necessary to carry out the provisions of this Act.

SEC. 1106. If any provision of this Act or the application thereof to any person or circumstances is held invalid, the remainder of the Act and the application of the provision to other persons not similarly situated or to other circumstances shall not be affected thereby.

Approved July 2, 1964.

37

Voting Rights Act of 1965

AN ACT To enforce the fifteenth amendment to the Constitution of the United States, and for other purposes.

Be it enacted by the Senate and House of Representatives of the United States of America in Congress assembled, That this Act shall be known as the "Voting Rights Act of 1965."

SEC. 2 No voting qualification or prerequisite to voting, or standard, practice, or procedure shall be imposed or applied by any State or political subdivision to deny or abridge the right of any citizen of the United States to vote on account of race or color.

SEC. 3. (a) Whenever the Attorney General institutes a proceeding under any statute to enforce the guarantees of the fifteenth amendment in any State or political subdivision the court shall authorize the appointment of Federal examiners by the United States Civil Service Commission in accordance with section 6 to serve for such period of time and for such political subdivisions as the court shall determine is appropriate to enforce the guarantees of the fifteenth amendment (1) as part of any interlocutory order if the court determines that the appointment of such examiners is necessary to enforce such guarantees or (2) as part of any final judgment if the court finds that violations of the fifteenth amendment justifying equitable relief have occurred in such State or subdivision: Provided, That the court need not authorize the appointment of examiners if any incidents of denial or abridgement of the right to vote on account of race or color (1) have been few in number and have been promptly and effectively corrected by State or local action, (2) the continuing effect of such incidents has been eliminated, and (3) there is no reasonable probability of their recurrence in the future.

(b) If in a proceeding instituted by the Attorney General under any statute to enforce the guarantees of the fifteenth amendment in any State or political subdivision the court finds that a test or device has been used for the purpose or with the effect of denying or abridging the right of any citizen of the United States to vote on account of race or color, it shall suspend the use of tests and devices in such State or political subdivisions as the court shall determine is appropriate and for such period as it deems necessary.

(c) If in any proceeding instituted by the Attorney General under any statute to enforce the guarantees of the fifteenth amendment in any State or political subdivision the court finds that violations of the fifteenth amendment justifying equitable relief have occurred within the territory of such State or political subdivision, the court, in addition to such relief as it may grant, shall retain jurisdiction for such period as it may deem appropriate and during such period no voting qualification or prerequisite to voting, or standard, practice, or procedure with respect to voting different from that in force or effect at the time the proceeding was commenced shall be enforced unless and until the court finds that such qualification, prerequisite, standard, practice, or procedure does not have the purpose and will not have the effect of denying or abridging the right to vote on account of race or color: Provided, That such qualification, prerequisite, standard, practice, or procedure may be enforced if the qualification, prerequisite, standard, practice, or procedure has been submitted by the chief legal officer or other appropriate official of such State or subdivision to the Attorney General and the Attorney General has not interposed an objection within sixty days after such submission, except that neither the court's finding nor the Attorney General's failure to object shall bar a subsequent action to enjoin enforcement of such qualification, prerequisite, standard, practice, or procedure.

SEC. 4. (a) To assure that the right of citizens of the United States to vote is not denied or abridged on account of race or color, no citizen shall be denied the right to vote in any Federal, State, or local election because of his failure to comply with any test or device in any State with respect to which the determinations have been made under subsection **(b)** or in any political subdivision with respect to which such determinations have been made as a separate unit, unless the United States District Court for the District of Columbia in an action for a declaratory judgment brought by such State or subdivision against the United States has determined that no such test or device has been used during the five years preceding the filing of the action for the purpose or with the effect of denying or abridging the right to vote on account of race or color: Provided, That no such declaratory judgment shall issue with respect to any plaintiff for a period of five years after the entry of a final judgment of any court of the United States, other than the denial of a declaratory judgment under this section, whether entered prior to or after the enactment of this Act, determining that denials or abridgments of the right to vote on account of race or color through the use of such tests or devices have occurred anywhere in the territory of such plaintiff. An action pursuant to this subsection shall be heard and determined by a court of three judges in accordance with the provisions of section 2284 of title 28 of the United States Code and any appeal shall lie to the Supreme Court. The court shall retain jurisdiction of any action pursuant to this subsection for five years after judgment and shall reopen the action upon motion of the Attorney General alleging that a test or device has been used for the purpose or with the effect of denying or abridging the right to vote on account of race or color.

If the Attorney General determines that he has no reason to believe that any such test or device has been used during the five years preceding the filing of the action for the purpose or with the effect of denying or abridging the right to vote on account of race or color, he shall consent to the entry of such judgment.

(b) The provisions of subsection (a) shall apply in any State or in any political subdivision of a state which (1) the Attorney General determines maintained on November 1, 1964, any test or device, and with respect to which (2) the Director of the Census determines that less than 50 percentum of the persons of voting age residing therein were registered on November 1, 1964, or that less than 50 percentum of such persons voted in the presidential election of November 1964.

A determination or certification of the Attorney General or of the Director of the Census under this section or under section 6 or section 13 shall not be reviewable in any court and shall be effective upon publication in the Federal Register.

(c) The phrase "test or device" shall mean any requirement that a person as a prerequisite for voting or registration for voting (1) demonstrate the ability to read, write, understand, or interpret any matter, (2) demonstrate any educational achievement or his knowledge of any particular subject, (3) possess good moral character, or (4) prove his qualifications by the voucher of registered voters or members of any other class.

(d) For purposes of this section no State or political subdivision shall be determined to have engaged in the use of tests or devices for the purpose or with the effect of denying or abridging the right to vote on account of race or color if (1) incidents of such use have been few in number and have been promptly and effectively corrected by State or local action, (2) the continuing effect of such incidents has been eliminated, and (3) there is no reasonable probability of their recurrence in the future.

(e)

(1) Congress hereby declares that to secure the rights under the fourteenth amendment of persons educated in American-flag schools in which the predominant classroom language was other than English, it is necessary to prohibit the States from conditioning the right to vote of such persons on ability to read, write, understand, or interpret any matter in the English language.

(2) No person who demonstrates that he has successfully completed the sixth primary grade in a public school in, or a private school accredited by, any State or territory, the District of Columbia, or the Commonwealth of Puerto Rico in which the predominant classroom language was other than English, shall be denied the right to vote in any Federal, State, or local election because of his inability to read, write, understand, or interpret any matter in the English language, except that, in States in which State law provides that a different level of education is presumptive of literacy, he shall demonstrate that he has successfully completed an equivalent level of education in a public school in, or a private school accredited

by, any State or territory, the District of Columbia, or the Commonwealth of Puerto Rico in which the predominant classroom language was other than English.

SEC. 5. Whenever a State or political subdivision with respect to which the prohibitions set forth in section 4(a) are in effect shall enact or seek to administer any voting qualification or prerequisite to voting, or standard, practice, or procedure with respect to voting different from that in force or effect on November 1, 1964, such State or subdivision may institute an action in the United States District Court for the District of Columbia for a declaratory judgment that such qualification, prerequisite, standard, practice, or procedure does not have the purpose and will not have the effect of denying or abridging the right to vote on account of race or color, and unless and until the court enters such judgment no person shall be denied the right to vote for failure to comply with such qualification, prerequisite, standard, practice, or procedure: Provided, That such qualification, prerequisite, standard, practice, or procedure may be enforced without such proceeding if the qualification, prerequisite, standard, practice, or procedure has been submitted by the chief legal officer or other appropriate official of such State or subdivision to the Attorney General and the Attorney General has not interposed an objection within sixty days after such submission, except that neither the Attorney General's failure to object nor a declaratory judgment entered under this section shall bar a subsequent action to enjoin enforcement of such qualification, prerequisite, standard, practice, or procedure. Any action under this section shall be heard and determined by a court of three judges in accordance with the provisions of section 2284 of title 28 of the United States Code and any appeal shall lie to the Supreme Court.

SEC. 6. Whenever (a) a court has authorized the appointment of examiners pursuant to the provisions of section 3(a), or (b) unless a declaratory judgment has been rendered under section 4(a), the Attorney General certifies with respect to any political subdivision named in, or included within the scope of, determinations made under section 4(b) that (1) he has received complaints in writing from twenty or more residents of such political subdivision alleging that they have been denied the right to vote under color of law on account of race or color, and that he believes such complaints to be meritorious, or (2) that, in his judgment (considering, among other factors, whether the ratio of nonwhite persons to white persons registered to vote within such subdivision appears to him to be reasonably attributable to violations of the fifteenth amendment or whether substantial evidence exists that bona fide efforts are being made within such subdivision to comply with the fifteenth amendment), the appointment of examiners is otherwise necessary to enforce the guarantees of the fifteenth amendment, the Civil Service Commission shall appoint as many examiners for such subdivision as it may deem appropriate to prepare and maintain lists of persons eligible to vote in Federal, State, and local elections. Such examiners, hearing officers provided for in section 9(a), and other persons deemed necessary by the Commission to carry out the provisions and purposes of this Act shall be appointed, compensated, and separated without regard to the provisions of any statute administered by the Civil Service Commission, and service under this Act shall not be considered employment for the purposes of any statute administered by the Civil Service Commission, except the provisions of section 9 of the Act of August 2, 1939, as amended (5 U.S.C. 118i), prohibiting partisan political activity: Provided, That the Commission is authorized, after consulting the head of the appropriate department or agency, to designate suitable persons in the official service of the United States, with their consent, to serve in these positions. Examiners and hearing officers shall have the power to administer oaths.

SEC. 7. (a) The examiners for each political subdivision shall, at such places as the Civil Service Commission shall by regulation designate, examine applicants concerning their qualifications for voting. An application to an examiner shall be in such form as the Commission may require and shall contain allegations that the applicant is not otherwise registered to vote.

(b) Any person whom the examiner finds, in accordance with instructions received under section 9(b), to have the qualifications prescribed by State law not inconsistent with the Constitution and laws of the United States shall promptly be placed on a list of eligible voters. A challenge to such listing may be made in accordance with section 9 (a) and shall not be the basis for a prosecution under section 12 of this Act. The examiner shall certify and transmit such list, and any supplements as appropriate, at least once a month, to the offices of the appropriate election officials, with copies to the Attorney General and the attorney general of the State, and any such lists and supplements thereto transmitted during the month shall be available for public inspection on the last business day of the month and, in any event, not later than the forty-fifth day prior to any election. The appropriate State or local election official shall place such names on the official voting list. Any person whose name appears on the examiner's list shall be entitled and allowed to vote in the election district of his residence unless and until the appropriate election officials shall have been notified that such person has been removed from such list in accordance with subsection (d): Provided, That no person shall be entitled to vote in any election by virtue of this Act unless his name shall have been certified and transmitted on such a list to the offices of the appropriate election officials at least forty-five days prior to such election.

(c) The examiner shall issue to each person whose name appears on such a list a certificate evidencing his eligibility to vote.

(d) A person whose name appears on such a list shall be removed therefrom by an examiner if (1) such person has been successfully challenged in accordance with the procedure prescribed in section 9, or (2) he has been determined by an examiner to have lost his eligibility to vote under State law not inconsistent with the Constitution and the laws of the United States.

Sec. 8. Whenever an examiner is serving under this Act in any political subdivision, the Civil Service Commission may assign, at the request of the Attorney General, one or more persons, who may be officers of the United States, (1) to enter and attend at any place for holding an election in such subdivision for the purpose of observing whether persons who are entitled to vote are being permitted to vote, and (2) to enter and attend at any place for tabulating the votes cast at any election held in such subdivision for the purpose of observing whether votes cast by persons entitled to vote are being properly tabulated. Such persons so assigned shall report to an examiner appointed for such political subdivision, to the Attorney General, and if the appointment of examiners has been authorized pursuant to section 3(a), to the court.

SEC. 9.

(a) Any challenge to a listing on an eligibility list prepared by an examiner shall be heard and determined by a hearing officer appointed by and responsible to the Civil Service Commission and under such rules as the Commission shall by regulation prescribe. Such challenge shall be entertained only if filed at such office within the State as the Civil Service Commission shall by regulation designate, and within ten days after the listing of the challenged person is made available for public inspection, and if supported by (1) the affidavits of at least two persons having personal knowledge of the facts constituting grounds for the challenge, and (2) a certification that a copy of the challenge and affidavits have been served by mail or in person upon the person challenged at his place of residence set out in the application. Such challenge shall be determined within fifteen days after it has been filed. A petition for review of the decision of the hearing officer may be filed in the United States court of appeals for the circuit in which the person challenged resides within fifteen days after service of such decision by mail on the person petitioning for review but no decision of a hearing officer shall be reversed unless clearly erroneous. Any person listed shall be entitled and allowed to vote pending final determination by the hearing officer and by the court.

(b) The times, places, procedures, and form for application and listing pursuant to this Act and removals from the eligibility lists shall be prescribed by regulations promulgated by the Civil Service Commission and the Commission shall, after consultation with the Attorney General, instruct examiners concerning applicable State law not inconsistent with the Constitution and laws of the United States with respect to (1) the qualifications required for listing, and (2) loss of eligibility to vote.

(c) Upon the request of the applicant or the challenger or on its own motion the Civil Service Commission shall have the power to require by subpoena the attendance and testimony of witnesses and the production of documentary evidence relating to any matter pending before it under the authority of this section. In case of contumacy or refusal to obey a subpoena, any district court of the United States or the United States court of any territory or possession, or the District Court of the United States for the District of Columbia, within the jurisdiction of which said person guilty of contumacy or refusal to obey is found or resides or is domiciled or transacts business, or has appointed an agent for receipt of service of process, upon application by the Attorney General of the United States shall have jurisdiction to issue to such person an order requiring such person to appear before the Commission or a hearing officer, there to produce pertinent, relevant, and non-privileged documentary evidence if so ordered, or there to give testimony touching the matter under investigation, and any failure to obey such order of the court may be punished by said court as a contempt thereof.

SEC. 10. (a) The Congress finds that the requirement of the payment of a poll tax as a precondition to voting (i) precludes persons of limited means from voting or imposes unreasonable financial hardship upon such persons as a precondition to their exercise of the franchise, (ii) does not bear a reasonable relationship to any legitimate State interest in the conduct of elections, and (iii) in some areas has the purpose or effect of denying persons the right to vote because of race or color. Upon the basis of these findings, Congress declares that the constitutional right of citizens to vote is denied or abridged in some areas by the requirement of the payment of a poll tax as a precondition to voting.

(b) In the exercise of the powers of Congress under section 5 of the fourteenth amendment and section 2 of the fifteenth amendment, the Attorney General is authorized and directed to institute forthwith in the name of the United States such actions, including actions against States or political subdivisions, for declaratory judgment or injunctive relief against the enforcement of any requirement of the payment of a poll tax as a precondition to voting, or substitute therefor enacted after November 1, 1964, as will be necessary to implement the declaration of subsection (a) and the purposes of this section.

(c) The district courts of the United States shall have jurisdiction of such actions which shall be heard and determined by a court of three judges in accordance with the provisions of section 2284 of title 28 of the United States Code and any appeal shall lie to the Supreme Court. It shall be the duty of the judges designated to hear the case to assign the case for hearing at the earliest practicable date, to participate in the hearing and determination thereof, and to cause the case to be in every way expedited.

(d) During the pendency of such actions, and thereafter if the courts, notwithstanding this action by the Congress, should declare the requirement of the payment of a poll tax to be constitutional, no citizen of the United States who is a resident of a State or political subdivision with respect to which determinations have been made under subsection 4(b) and a declaratory judgment has not been entered under subsection 4(a), during the first year he becomes otherwise entitled to vote by reason of registration by State or local officials or listing by an examiner, shall be denied the right to vote for failure to pay a poll tax if he tenders payment of such tax for the current year to an examiner or to the appropriate State or local official at least forty-five days prior to election, whether or not such tender would be timely or adequate under State law. An examiner shall have authority to accept such payment from any person authorized by this Act to make an application for listing, and shall issue a receipt for such payment. The examiner shall transmit promptly any such poll tax payment to the office of the State or local official authorized to receive such payment under State law, together with the name and address of the applicant.

SEC. 11. (a) No person acting under color of law shall fail or refuse to permit any person to vote who is entitled to vote under any provision of this Act or is otherwise qualified to vote, or willfully fail or refuse to tabulate, count, and report such person's vote.

(b) No person, whether acting under color of law or otherwise, shall intimidate, threaten, or coerce, or attempt to intimidate, threaten, or coerce any person for voting or attempting to vote, or intimidate, threaten, or coerce, or attempt to intimidate, threaten, or coerce any person for urging or aiding any person to vote or attempt to vote, or intimidate, threaten, or coerce any person for exercising any powers or duties under section 3(a), 6, 8, 9, 10, or 12(e).

(c) Whoever knowingly or willfully gives false information as to his name, address, or period of residence in the voting district for the purpose of establishing his eligibility to register or vote, or conspires with another individual for the purpose of encouraging his false registration to vote or illegal voting, or pays or offers to pay or accepts payment either for registration to vote or for voting shall be fined not more than $10,000 or imprisoned not more than five years, or both: Provided, however, That this provision shall be applicable only to general, special, or primary elections held solely or in part for the purpose of selecting or electing any candidate for the office of President, Vice President, presidential elector, Member of the United States Senate, Member of the United States House of Representatives, or Delegates or Commissioners from the territories or possessions, or Resident Commissioner of the Commonwealth of Puerto Rico.

(d) Whoever, in any matter within the jurisdiction of an examiner or hearing officer knowingly and willfully falsifies or conceals a material fact, or makes any false, fictitious, or fraudulent statements or representations, or makes or uses any false writing or document knowing the same to contain any false, fictitious, or fraudulent statement or entry, shall be fined not more than $10,000 or imprisoned not more than five years, or both.

SEC. 12. (a) Whoever shall deprive or attempt to deprive any person of any right secured by section 2, 3, 4, 5, 7, or 10 or shall violate section 11(a) or (b), shall be fined not more than $5,000, or imprisoned not more than five years, or both.

(b) Whoever, within a year following an election in a political subdivision in which an examiner has been appointed (1) destroys, defaces, mutilates, or otherwise alters the marking of a paper ballot which has been cast in such election, or (2) alters any official record of voting in such election tabulated from a voting machine or otherwise, shall be fined not more than $5,000, or imprisoned not more than five years, or both.

(c) Whoever conspires to violate the provisions of subsection (a) or (b) of this section, or interferes with any right secured by section 2, 3, 4, 5, 7, 10, or 11(a) or (b) shall be fined not more than $5,000, or imprisoned not more than five years, or both.

(d) Whenever any person has engaged or there are reasonable grounds to believe that any person is about to engage in any act or practice prohibited by section 2, 3, 4, 5, 7, 10, 11, or subsection (b) of this section, the Attorney General may institute for the United States, or in the name of the United States, an action for preventive relief, including an application for a temporary or permanent injunction, restraining order, or other order, and including an order directed to the State and State or local election officials to require them (1) to permit persons listed under this Act to vote and (2) to count such votes.

(e) Whenever in any political subdivision in which there are examiners appointed pursuant to this Act any persons allege to such an examiner within forty-eight hours after the closing of the polls that notwithstanding (1) their listing under this Act or registration by an appropriate election official and (2) their eligibility to vote, they have not been permitted to vote in such election, the examiner shall forthwith notify the Attorney General if such allegations in his opinion appear to be well founded. Upon receipt of such notification, the Attorney General may forthwith file with the district court an application for an order providing for the marking, casting, and counting of the ballots of such persons and requiring the inclusion of their votes in the total vote before the results of such election shall be deemed final and any force or effect given thereto. The district court shall hear and determine such matters immediately after the filing of such application. The remedy provided in this subsection shall not preclude any remedy available under State or Federal law.

(f) The district courts of the United States shall have jurisdiction of proceedings instituted pursuant to this section and shall exercise the same without regard to whether a person asserting rights under the provisions of this Act shall have exhausted any administrative or other remedies that may be provided by law.

SEC. 13. Listing procedures shall be terminated in any political subdivision of any State (a) with respect to examiners appointed pursuant to clause (b) of section 6 whenever the Attorney General notifies the Civil Service Commission, or whenever the District Court for the District of Columbia determines in an action for declaratory judgment brought by any political subdivision with respect to which the Director of the Census has determined that more than 50 percentum of the nonwhite persons of voting age residing therein are registered to vote, (1) that all persons listed by an examiner for such subdivision have been placed on the appropriate voting registration roll, and (2) that there is no longer reasonable cause to believe that persons will be deprived of or denied the right to vote on account of race or color in such subdivision, and (b), with respect to examiners appointed pursuant to section 3(a), upon order of the authorizing court. A political subdivision may petition the Attorney General for the termination of listing procedures under clause (a) of this section, and may petition the Attorney General to request the Director of the Census to take such survey or census as may be appropriate for the making of the determination provided for in this section. The District Court for the District of Columbia shall have jurisdiction to require such survey or census to be made by the Director of the Census and it shall require him to do so if it deems the Attorney General's refusal to request such survey or census to be arbitrary or unreasonable.

SEC. 14.

(a) All cases of criminal contempt arising under the provisions of this Act shall be governed by section 151 of the Civil Rights Act of 1957 (42 U.S.C.1995).

(b) No court other than the District Court for the District of Columbia or a court of appeals in any proceeding under section 9 shall have jurisdiction to issue any declaratory judgment pursuant to section 4 or section 5 or any restraining order or temporary or permanent injunction against the execution or enforcement of any provision of this Act or any action of any Federal officer or employee pursuant hereto.

(c)

(1) The terms "vote" or "voting" shall include all action necessary to make a vote effective in any primary, special, or general election, including, but not limited to, registration, listing pursuant to this Act, or other action required by law prerequisite to voting, casting a ballot, and having such ballot counted properly and included in the appropriate totals of votes cast with respect to candidates for public or party office and propositions for which votes are received in an election.

(2) The term "political subdivision" shall mean any county or parish, except that, where registration for voting is not conducted under the supervision of a county or parish, the term shall include any other subdivision of a State which conducts registration for voting.

(d) In any action for a declaratory judgment brought pursuant to section 4 or section 5 of this Act, subpoenas for witnesses who are required to attend the District Court for the District of Columbia may be served in any judicial district of the United States: Provided, That no writ of subpoena shall issue for witnesses without the District of Columbia at a greater distance than one hundred miles from the place of holding court without the permission of the District Court for the District of Columbia being first had upon proper application and cause shown.

SEC. 15. Section 2004 of the Revised Statutes (42 U.S.C.1971), as amended by section 131 of the Civil Rights Act of 1957 (71 Stat. 637), and amended by section 601 of the Civil Rights Act of 1960 (74 Stat. 90), and as further amended by section 101 of the Civil Rights Act of 1964 (78 Stat. 241), is further amended as follows:

(a) Delete the word "Federal" wherever it appears in subsections (a) and (c);

(b) Repeal subsection (f) and designate the present subsections (g) and (h) as (f) and (g), respectively.

SEC. 16. The Attorney General and the Secretary of Defense, jointly, shall make a full and complete study to determine whether, under the laws or practices of any State or States, there are preconditions to voting, which might tend to result in discrimination against citizens serving in the Armed Forces of the United States seeking to vote. Such officials shall, jointly, make a report to the Congress not later than June 30, 1966, containing the results of such study, together with a list of any States in which such preconditions exist, and shall include in such report such recommendations for legislation as they deem advisable to prevent discrimination in voting against citizens serving in the Armed Forces of the United States.

SEC. 17. Nothing in this Act shall be construed to deny, impair, or otherwise adversely affect the right to vote of any person registered to vote under the law of any State or political subdivision.

SEC. 18. There are hereby authorized to be appropriated such sums as are necessary to carry out the provisions of this Act.

SEC 19. If any provision of this Act or the application thereof to any person or circumstances is held invalid, the remainder of the Act and the application of the provision to other persons not similarly situated or to other circumstances shall not be affected thereby.

Approved August 6, 1965.

SECTION 4

Problems for and Progress Towards a More Perfect Union

38

The Courts Wrestle with Remedies to Racial Inequality: Affirmative Action Revisited

R. L. Raines

Background

Affirmative Action means different things to different people. To conservatives it's a free ride, free lunch, and reverse discrimination. To liberals it is a moral question aimed at rectifying centuries of discrimination. Here are more views about affirmative action:

- It unfairly handicaps whites
- It is reverse discrimination (any program intending to correct the past patterns of discrimination which at the same time harms whites is reverse discrimination)
- It is designed to correct historical patterns of racial discrimination
- It's all about quotas (guaranteeing a certain number of jobs, seats in schools, etc., for racial minorities)
- It allows minorities to get positions for which they are not qualified
- It's only for blacks
- It guarantees equality of outcome rather than equality of opportunity
- It lowers standards
- It allows for unfair preferences
- Without it we can't have diversity in schools, business, military, etc.
- White women have been the dominant benefactor of affirmative action programs

You may think of others. While people will always disagree, the objective here is to provide you with facts that will enable you to have an informed debate rather than simplistic politically-motivated harangues and diatribes about affirmative action.

How it began: Affirmative action began after passage of The Civil Rights Act of 1964 (Title VII), when President Johnson issued Executive Order 11246 requiring federal contractors to develop and implement A/A programs which identified areas of minority and female under representation and set goals and timetables to correct deficiencies. In other words, the white owned businesses getting federal contracts were given incentives to hire minority subcontractors and diversify their workforce.

The legal bases: Title VII prohibits discrimination based on race, color, religion, sex, or national origin. It applies to both public and private institutions. It applies to all colleges and universities with 15 or more employees. The 14th Amendment (Equal Protection Clause) requires the states (therefore there institutions, which include state run colleges and universities) to treat all citizens equally.

Discrimination in education: We have seen that for decades public schools in the south (from grade school to universities) were racially segregated. Many private schools had also, for centuries, discriminated against African-Americans, Jews, women, Hispanics, etc. For example, if you were black, lived in Mississippi and wanted to go to law school or medical school and there was no black educational institution in your state offering such opportunities, you had to leave your home state (where your family pays taxes to support the very educational institutions denying you admission) and go to a black school in another state. While various court victories and passage of the Civil Rights Act of 1964 ended *de jure* (legalized discrimination), centuries of denying African-Americans admission to such schools could not be remedied over night.

> "By the late 1960s, there was recognition of the fact that 'even if all further hostile discrimination were instantly ceased, the momentum of the past—the attitudes, the isolation, and the built-in facially non-discriminatory rules—would continue to exclude blacks and other minorities from the mainstream of opportunity in American life until sometime in the distant future.' The result was what has been termed 'affirmative action', efforts by employers, educational institutions, and government to institute hiring and admissions programs that would help minorities and women compete." (Friendly and Elliot, 215)

By the early 1970's many public and private institutions of higher education wanted to take a very aggressive approach to remedy current and past patterns of discrimination that denied blacks admission to their schools. Many of the administrators saw it as a moral obligation to especially eradicate institutionalized racism in professional schools. The foregoing provides the backdrop for the *Bakke* case.

Bakke v. University of California

Facts: The University of California at Davis Medical School enrolled its first class in 1968; it was a new medical school. There were only two blacks enrolled in the first two years of the school's existence; if you included Asian-Americans and Chicanos, only 3% of the classes were minority. The school's director, after meeting with black community leaders in 1971, promised that the school would guarantee 16 seats to the 'disadvantaged' (out of 100) in the entering class of 1972. He described this as a "guarantee" not a quota. Trying to explain the difference to the courts would later prove problematic. When Bakke applied for the entering class of 1973, the same number of seats had been set aside for the disadvantaged. The problem as Bakke and others saw it, was that these seats were "reserved for minorities" only; whites could apply under the general admissions program while minorities could apply under either or both. Bakke, 32 years old, was denied admissions by UC Davis and 10 other medical schools. He applied again in 1974 and again was denied. Bakke then sues the medical school claiming reverse discrimination in violation of his rights under the *equal protection clause of the 14th Amendment*. Specifically, he argued that he would have been admitted had the school not set aside seats for less qualified candidates.

Legal Issues: Was the UC Davis program constitutional? Or, as the university framed the issue in its oral argument before the Court:

> "This case . . . represents a single vital issue: whether a state university which is forced by limited resources to select a relatively few number of students from a much larger number of well-qualified applicants, is free, voluntarily, to take into account the fact that the applicant is black, Chicano, Asian or native American to increase the number of those minority groups trained for the educational professions and participating in them, professions from which minorities were long excluded because of generations of pervasive racial discrimination."

Court Ruling: (1) The Court upheld affirmative action in the university admissions process stating that the use of race as one of the factors used in determining who to admit did not violate the 14th Amendment, but (2) held that the specific program at UC Davis was unconstitutional (violated the equal protection clause of the 14th Amendment) because the set aside portion of the program (specific number of places reserved for minorities) represented quotas which discriminated against white applicants, thus ordered that Bakke be admitted.

Rationale for the Court's Ruling: This is a case of having your cake and eating it too. A majority of the Court clearly believed that the objectives of affirmative action programs were of value to society, they did not want to slam the door on those wishing to (voluntarily) end and/or correct historical patterns of racism. While at the same time most of the justices did not want to endorse (although well-meaning) affirmative action programs which overtly discriminated against whites, resulting in reverse discrimination.

The answer was to strike down the method used by the university in trying to achieve its laudable goals of diversity, but at the same time uphold the overall constitutionally of affirmative action. The Court ends up by telling the university how to make its program constitutional.

The Court tells the University of California-Davis that it could consider race as *one of* many factors in the admissions process, in the same way undergraduate colleges were already doing. A university could establish a system in which the major weight of the admission decision would be based on meeting the requisite standard for admission. However, other variables could be used to determine the final admission decision. Categories like geography, community service, letters of recommendation, interview, race, gender, legacy, etc.

The Court says that the above approach to affirmative action is constitutional because race is considered like any only factor in the admissions process. It is only one component, not the decisive component, nor does it represent a quota. In the past, if a school needed more athletes or musicians, for example, it would place a greater point value on these categories to replenish in these areas. So now, if the school sees racial diversity as good for the educational experience of its student body, it can weigh ethnicity more heavily, but again, it's just one of many factors in determining who to admit. The irony is that under these scenarios one could have a student be benefitted more by having a parent/grandparent have attended the school than being a racial minority. However, this type of preferential treatment in the admission process is rarely discussed as discriminatory.

In summary, the Court ruled in favor of race-conscience admissions policies but found that quotas were unconstitutional in that they violate the equal protection clause of the 14th Amendment, viz., state laws and practices must be designed and implemented to treat all its citizens equally.

Grutter v. Bollinger

In this recent opinion involving the admissions practices at the University of Michigan School of Law, again the Court followed (affirmed) its ruling in *Bakke* and *upheld race-conscious admissions* in principle but not always as practiced. The Court ruled that while race can be one of the factors in admittance; *it cannot be the determining factor.* The white female applicant who was denied admittance, asserted that there were those (minorities) admitted to the school with lesser qualifications than she. While that may have been the case, the Court denied her petition, stating that the "law school had a compelling interest in enrolling a racially and ethnically diverse student body because of the educational benefits that such diversity provides."

Additional Comments: One of the practices that give affirmative action a bad name is when schools lower these minimum requirements **because** an applicant **is** a **member of a minority group;** the justification being past patterns of discrimination have left these groups educationally disadvantaged. This kind of practice was the impetus for both *Bakke* and *Grutter*; and the Court does not address it head on. But, consider this. These so-called minimum requirements are also waived, and have been since time immemorial, for legacies, highly sought after athletics (black or white), or to obtain any given student for any reason peculiar to the school; the orchestra needs a violinist, for example. How many get into Harvard Business School with a C undergraduate average, as George W. Bush did? Yes, this is complicated, but at least you are now better prepared to discuss, debate, and comment on affirmative action on a more enlightened basis.

Sources

Fred W. Friendly and Martha J. H. Elliott, *The Constitution, That Delicate Balance; Landmark Cases that Shaped the Constitution*, (New York: Random House, 1984).

Constitutional Cases Cited

Bakke v. University of California, 438 U.S. 265 (1978)
Grutter v. Bollinger, 539 U.S. 539 U.S. 306 (2000)

39

Affirmative Reaction: The Courts, the Right and the Race Question

Randall Kennedy

In racial matters, good news from the Supreme Court is generally no news. Since at least the mid-1970s, the Court has been mostly inhospitable to those seeking to advance progressive racial policies through litigation. That is why civil-rights activists often deliberately keep potentially far-reaching cases away from the High Court. In a revealing episode in 1997, for example, the NAACP Legal Defense Fund and other organizations, rather than risk an adverse judgment by the justices, pooled hundreds of thousands of dollars to pay the settlement costs demanded by a white schoolteacher who had initiated a reverse-discrimination lawsuit.

There was a time when Congress could be a counterweight to the Court's rollbacks. In the early 1980s, when the Supreme Court narrowed its previous interpretation of the 15th Amendment's prohibition against racial discrimination in elections, activists pushed successfully for legislation that partially regained what the justices took away. In the late 1980s, Court decisions dramatically weakened protections against racial discrimination at the workplace. Activists again countered, this time with the Civil Rights Act of 1991 (initially vetoed by President George Bush Senior as a "quota bill"). With Congress and the White House now under conservative Republican control, there is even more reason to fear increasingly aggressive action by an emboldened conservative judiciary.

The big racial case this term is, of course, the Michigan affirmative-action one known as *Grutter v. Bollinger*, in which the justices will revisit whether, how and to what extent racial background can be a factor in selecting students for admission to public universities. The Court's last encounter with affirmative action at selective public universities was 25 years ago, in the landmark *Regents of the University of California v. Bakke* case.

In *Bakke*, the Court was closely split, with the decisive opinion rendered by Justice Lewis Powell. On the one hand, Powell ruled against the particular affirmative-action policy under challenge because it set aside a definite number of seats—16 out of every 100—for racial minorities. To Powell it did not matter that the policy aimed to assist historically

Reprinted with permission from Randall Kennedy, "Affirmative Reaction," The American Prospect, Volume 14, Number 3: March 01, 2003. www.prospect.org. The American Prospect, 1710 Rhode Island Avenue, NW, 12th Floor, Washington, DC 20036. All rights reserved.

disadvantaged racial minorities; in his view, racial discrimination to assist minorities should be assessed according to the same standard as racial discrimination aimed at thwarting them. On the other hand, Powell indicated that other, more subtle affirmative-action plans would be permissible. He maintained that while any racial selectivity is presumptively invalid, narrowly tailored plans to advance a compelling justification can pass constitutional muster.

Powell cited Harvard University's admissions policy as a model, noting three features he considered essential. First, the Harvard policy set aside no set number of seats on a racial basis; it therefore allowed all applicants to be considered together and placed in competition against one another. Second, race constituted only one of several "plus" factors. Third, in justifying race as a plus factor, Harvard claimed it was seeking to generate a diverse academic environment from which all students would benefit. Embracing a "diversity" rationale for race-conscious selectivity, Powell posited this exercise of academic freedom as a compelling justification for permitting narrowly drawn affirmative-action plans.

Although no other justice joined Powell's opinion, it became the consensus view, and ever since has been widely relied upon as the authoritative guide to the constitutionality of affirmative action in university admissions. But the status of Powell's opinion may be seriously jeopardized when the Court hears *Grutter*, a suit brought by a disappointed white University of Michigan Law School applicant who charges that the school violated her rights by viewing the racial background of racial minority applicants as a substantial plus in an effort to achieve diversity. Federal District Judge Bernard A. Friedman (a Reagan appointee) refused to be bound by *Bakke*, ruled that the alleged benefits of diversity did not constitute a compelling justification for affirmative action and enjoined the law school from considering race in admissions.

The 6th U.S. Circuit Court of Appeals reversed Friedman, reaffirming the precedential authority of *Bakke* and concluding that the admissions practice of the law school adequately comported with the guidelines set forth by Powell. Affirmative action prevailed by a razor-thin margin. All five votes came from Democrats—four Clinton appointees and one Carter appointee. Three of the four votes to invalidate the affirmative-action plan came from Republican judges—two Bush Senior appointees and one Reagan appointee. In addition, the anti-affirmative-action faction picked up the vote of a Clinton appointee hailing from Memphis, Tenn.

Racial Rollback

A principal reason that *Grutter* is before the Supreme Court is that conservatives on lower courts have created splits within the federal judiciary that would necessitate intervention by the High Court in order to restore some semblance of consistency. Recognizing the significance of lower-court judges in the affirmative-action wars is important, because some commentators assert that Democrats err in vigorously resisting George W. Bush's nomination of right-wing Republicans to courts nominally subordinate to the Supreme Court. These critics contend that such posts are not worth the struggle because lower-court judges basically follow the directives set forth by the Supreme Court. This view is misleading.

Often the directions given by the Supreme Court are sufficiently broad and malleable to permit a range of interpretations. Applying the same Supreme Court precedent, a conservative judge and a liberal judge may and do reach very different results. The Supreme Court reviews a small fraction of the cases decided by lower federal courts; a careful, intelligent, strong-willed judge on a lower court can do much that is beyond the power of the Supreme Court to police. Finally, restive lower-court judges can play an important role by creating divisions that offer opportunities for intervention by their judicial superiors, thus affecting the Supreme Court's agenda.

The right is attacking the affirmative-action status quo on multiple fronts. The most stalwart opponents such as Justices William Rehnquist, Antonin Scalia and Clarence Thomas scornfully dismiss Powell's *Bakke* opinion as a naked, lawless, political compromise that warrants a clear, frank, unapologetic repudiation. Others would also like to uproot affirmative action but feel inhibited from openly saying so. U.S. Solicitor General Theodore Olson is of this sort. In his brief to the Supreme Court on behalf of the federal government, Olson avoids explicitly denouncing *Bakke*. But in various ways the logic of his argument implicitly impugns Powell's compromise. For example, the solicitor general writes disapprovingly that the University of Michigan's affirmative-action program "contains no limit on the scope or duration of its racial preferences and . . . would sanction race-based admissions standards indefinitely." Posited as a narrow complaint about one particular affirmative-action program, the solicitor general's brief is actually a broad attack on virtually all existing affirmative-action programs.

A further line of attack might entail putting new limits on affirmative-action programs while purporting merely to apply Powell's *Bakke* directive. This is an approach likely to find favor with Justices Anthony Kennedy and Sandra Day O'Connor, both of whom are conservative Reagan appointees whose caution frustrates their bolder colleagues on the right. Instead of discarding the Powell opinion, Kennedy and O'Connor might insist that it simply be read more narrowly. This might lead them to strike down the University of Michigan Law School program on the grounds that it gives too much credit to the racial background of minority applicants or that the effort to admit a "critical mass" of minority applicants amounts to the creation of a camouflaged quota.

Is Affirmative Action Defensible?

Racial liberals occupy an awkward position as they face the right's attack on affirmative action. To preserve a policy that has advanced the fortunes of a relatively privileged stratum of historically disadvantaged racial minorities, progressives defend the flawed handiwork of a conservative jurist—Lewis Powell—whose commitment to racial justice was by no means robust. Confronting those who want to stymie even the small bit of reparative justice that affirmative action advances, progressives will be tempted to overlook the deficiencies within Justice Powell's formula. That, however, would be a mistake. Instead, progressives should steel themselves for the difficult task of simultaneously defending the affirmative-action status quo while recognizing the substantial faults of the prevailing doctrine, two of which are especially troubling.

First, under the logic of *Bakke*, all racial distinctions are the same—racial distinctions that assist racial minorities as well as those that keep racial minorities in their "place," i.e., inferior to whites. This assertion of equivalence should not be accepted. As Justice John Paul Stevens has noted on several occasions, there is a large difference between signs that read "African Americans Welcome!" and "African Americans Stay Out!" though both draw racial distinctions.

But what about the negative consequences visited upon those "disfavored" by an affirmative-action program? Such consequences, though unfortunate for the affected individuals, are not created for the purpose of thwarting the relatively few whites whose rejection is directly attributable to affirmative action. White "victims" of affirmative action occupy the ranks of the unintentionally injured—a position that is a far cry from the one occupied by racial minorities who have been (and are) intentionally blocked by real, invidious racial impediments. Affirmative-action programs of the sort under challenge in Michigan, moreover, are ultimately under the political control of a white majority that could, if it wanted, repeal the policy, as was done in California. That political reality imposes constraints on affirmative action that ought somewhat to allay concerns about institutions racially mistreating white applicants.

Second, Justice Powell's *Bakke* opinion rejected alternative justifications for affirmative action in university admissions, leaving "diversity" as practically the lone justification he was willing to recognize. Defenders of affirmative action have therefore felt impelled to rally around the "diversity" slogan. This rationale does have certain virtues. It suggests how affirmative action as a policy benefits all students, not only or even mainly racial-minority students. The diversity rationale also transforms racial-minority status from an extenuating circumstance that excuses lesser performance into a credential identifying the individual as the putative possessor of a different voice that will presumptively enrich a school's environment. Nonetheless, it is difficult for me to see why the possibility that a learning environment may be improved by the inclusion of students from a wide range of geographical, cultural, class, ethnic and racial backgrounds is a more acceptable justification for making racial distinctions than the aim to assist those affiliated with groups that have long been oppressed.

Let's be honest: Many who defend affirmative action for the sake of "diversity" are actually motivated by a concern that is considerably more compelling. They are not so much animated by a commitment to what is, after all, only a contingent, pedagogical hypothesis. Rather, they are animated by a commitment to social justice. They would rightly defend affirmative action even if social science demonstrated uncontrovertibly that diversity (or its absence) has no effect (or even a negative effect) on the learning environment.

Refuting the Right

The argument deployed by right-wing enemies of affirmative action is effective, specious and in need of constant refutation. Sometimes they defend making special efforts to recruit racial minorities while bitterly castigating as a betrayal of racial neutrality policies that boost minorities at the final stage of candidate-selection. But if the latter is a violation of racial neutrality, why isn't the former? In both instances, racially selective steps are being taken to assist racial minorities.

The acceptance that right-wingers seemingly offer to affirmative recruitment at present is mainly tactical; if they succeed in broadly invalidating affirmative action in *Grutter*, affirmative recruitment will be the next focus of complaint about so-called reverse discrimination. Sometimes enemies of racial affirmative action assert that while they want to see more racial minorities on the campuses of high-prestige public universities, they favor using nonracial means of accomplishing this end, such as the Texas plan under which a student in the top 10 percent of any graduating public high-school class in the state is automatically eligible for enrollment at the University of Texas. Now, apart from the questionable efficacy of that plan—some observers doubt that it will adequately boost the numbers of racial minorities that matriculate at top state universities—is its questionable legality.

If it is unconstitutional for a state to aid racial minorities purposefully through transparent affirmative action, why is it constitutional for a state to aid racial minorities purposefully through a method of selection that is formally race-neutral but actually race-conscious? The legal system does not allow states to exclude racial minorities purposefully from juries or ballot boxes via race neutral means (recall the old grandfather clauses and literacy tests). So why should the legal system allow states to foster the inclusion of racial minorities through such means? The day after affirmative action is ended, right-wingers who were previously singing the praises of race-neutral alternatives will all of a sudden begin perceiving that these alternatives also "victimize" whites, deviate from meritocratic standards, and so on and so forth.

Some right-wing enemies of affirmative action proclaim their allegiance to the notion that all governmental racial distinctions are presumptively evil. Their tune changes, however, when the subject is law enforcement. Then they defend practices under which police and security officials at airports take race (or ethnicity or apparent national origin) into account in making determination of suspicion. Racial profiling is reasonable, they say. But isn't affirmative action reasonable? Some right-wing enemies of affirmative action claim to abhor all racial discriminations by government. When one takes a look at their records, however, one finds that they almost invariably focus on affirmative actions that adversely affect (a few) whites and not the traditional, racist discriminations that continue to menace large numbers of people of color. Indeed, these same right-wingers scoff at the notion that affirmative action may serve usefully as a prophylactic device to counteract the real but nonetheless hard-to-trace racial resistance that people of color pervasively encounter.

The fight over affirmative action is not the only battle of significance relevant to the fate of racial justice in America. The defense of affirmative action is a battle worth waging, however, because positive discrimination on behalf of racial minorities in higher education is an important, albeit merely partial, way in which our society is attempting to repair the gaping wounds caused by innumerable racist actions and inactions that have fundamentally betrayed America's most noble aspirations. Hopefully the policy will survive the right's grotesque attempt to strangle it judicially in the name of equality.

40

The Problem: Discrimination

U.S. Commission on Civil Rights

Making choices is an essential part of everyday life for individuals and organizations. These choices are shaped in part by social structures that set standards and influence conduct in such areas as education, employment, housing, and government. When these choices limit the opportunities available to people because of their race, sex, or national origin, the problem of discrimination arises.

Historically, discrimination against minorities and women was not only accepted, but was also governmentally required. The doctrine of white supremacy, used to support the institution of slavery, was so much a part of American custom and policy that the Supreme Court of the United States in 1857 approvingly concluded that both the North and the South regarded slaves "as beings of an inferior order, and altogether unfit to associate with the white race, either in social or political relations; and so far inferior, that they had no rights which the white man was bound to respect."[1] White supremacy survived the passage of the Civil War amendments to the Constitution and continued to dominate legal and social institutions in the North as well as the South to disadvantage not only blacks,[2] but other racial and ethnic groups as well—American Indians, Alaskan Natives, Asian and Pacific Islanders, and Hispanics.[3]

While minorities were suffering from white supremacy, women were suffering from male supremacy. Mr. Justice Brennan has summed up the legal disabilities imposed on women this way:

> [Throughout much of the 19th century the position of women in our society was, in many respects, comparable to that of blacks under the pre-Civil War slave codes. Neither slaves nor women could hold office, serve on juries, or bring suit in their own names, and married women traditionally were denied the legal capacity to hold or convey property or to serve as legal guardians of their own children.[4]

In 1873 a member of the Supreme Court proclaimed: "Man is, or should be, woman's protector and defender. The natural and proper timidity and delicacy which belongs to the female sex evidently unfits it for many of the occupations of civil life."[5] Such romantic paternalism has alternated with fixed notions of male superiority to deny women in law and in practice the most fundamental of rights, including the right to vote, which was not granted until 1920;[6] the Equal Rights Amendment has yet to be ratified.[7]

Although beliefs and practices based on white and male supremacy linger, public attitudes toward civil rights have improved noticeably.[8] The blatant racial and sexual discrimination that originated in our often forgotten past, however, continues to affect the present. A steady flow of data reveals persistent and widespread gaps throughout society between the status of white males and various minority groups and women.[9] Because they occur so often and in so many places, such statistically observable inequalities are strong evidence of a systematic denial of equal opportunities. Those inequalities result from a complex interaction of attitudes and actions of individuals, organizations, and the network of social structures that makes up our society.

Individual Discrimination

The most common understanding of discrimination rests at the level of prejudiced individual attitudes and behavior. Although open and intentional prejudice persists, individual discriminatory conduct is often hidden and sometimes unintentional.[10] Some of the following are examples of deliberately discriminatory actions by consciously prejudiced individuals. Some are examples of unintentionally discriminatory actions taken by persons who may not believe themselves to be prejudiced, but whose decisions continue to be guided by deeply ingrained discriminatory customs.

- Personnel officers whose stereotyped beliefs about women and minorities justify hiring them for low level and low paying jobs exclusively, regardless of their potential experience or qualifications for higher level jobs.[11]
- Hiring officials, historically white males, who rely on "word-of-mouth" recruiting among their friends and colleagues, so that only their friends and proteges of the same race and sex learn of potential job openings.[12]
- Employers who hire women for their sexual attractiveness or potential sexual availability rather than their competence, and employers who engage in sexual harassment of their female employees.[13]
- Teachers who interpret linguistic and cultural differences as indications of low potential or lack of academic interest on the part of minority students.[14]
- Guidance counselors and teachers whose low expectations lead them to advise female and minority students to avoid "hard" courses, such as mathematics and science, and to take courses that do not prepare them for higher paying jobs.[15]
- Real estate agents who show fewer homes to minority buyers and steer them to minority or mixed neighborhoods because they believe white residents would oppose the presence of black neighbors.[16]
- Families who assume that property values inevitably decrease when minorities move in and therefore move out of their neighborhoods if minorities do move in.[17]

- Parole officials who assume minority offenders are more dangerous or more unreliable than white offenders and consequently more frequently deny parole to minorities than to whites convicted of equally serious crimes.[18]

These contemporary examples of discrimination need not be motivated by conscious prejudice. The personnel manager is likely to deny believing that minorities and women can only perform satisfactorily in low level jobs even while acting in ways consistent with such beliefs. In some cases the minority or female applicants may not be aware that they have been discriminated against—the personnel manager may inform them that they are deficient in experience while rejecting their applications because of prejudice; the white male hiring official who recruits through his friends or white male work force excludes minorities and women who never learn of the available positions. The discriminatory results these activities cause may not even be desired. The guidance counselor may honestly believe there are no other realistic alternatives for minority and female students.

Whether conscious or not, open or hidden, desired or undesired, these acts build on and support prejudicial stereotypes, deny their victims opportunities provided to others, and perpetuate discrimination, regardless of intent.

Organizational Discrimination

Discrimination, though practiced by individuals, is often reinforced by the well-established rules, policies, and practices of organizations. These procedures may be officially approved, formal parts of organizational decisionmaking, or they may be unarticulated, informal ways of doing business. Whether formal or informal, they are the organization's standard operating procedures and are carried out by individuals as just part of their day's work.

Discrimination at the organizational level takes forms that are similar to those on the individual level. For example:

- Height and weight requirements that are unnecessarily geared to the physical proportions of white males without regard for the actual requirements needed to perform the job, and, therefore, exclude females and some minorities.[19]
- Seniority rules, when applied to jobs historically held only by white males, that make more recently hired minorities and females more subject to layoff—the "last hired, first fired" employee—and less eligible for advancement.[20]
- Nepotism-based membership policies of some referral unions that exclude those who are not relatives of members who, because of past employment practices, are usually white.[21]
- Restrictive employment leave policies, coupled with prohibitions on part-time work or denials of fringe benefits to part-time workers, that make it difficult for the heads of single-parent families, most of whom are women, to get and keep jobs and meet the needs of their families.[22]

- Rules requiring that only English be spoken at the workplace, even when not a business necessity, which result in discriminatory employment practices toward individuals whose primary language is not English.[23]
- Standardized academic tests or criteria, geared to the cultural and educational norms of the middle-class or white males, that are not relevant indicators of successful job performance.[24]
- Preferences shown by law and medical schools in the admission of children of wealthy and influential alumni, nearly all of whom are white.[25]
- Credit policies of banks and lending institutions that prevent the granting of mortgage monies and loans in minority neighborhoods or prevent the granting of credit to married women and others who have previously been denied the opportunity to build good credit histories in their own names.[26]

Superficially "colorblind" or "gender neutral," these organizational practices have an adverse effect on minorities and women. As with individual actions, these organizational actions favor white males. Even when taken with no deliberate intent to affect minorities and women adversely, they protect and promote the status quo arising from the racism and sexism of the past. If, for example, the jobs now protected by "last hired, first fired" provisions had always been integrated, seniority would not operate to disadvantage minorities and women. If many educational systems from kindergarten through college had not historically favored white males, more minorities and women would hold advanced degrees and thereby be included among those involved in deciding what academic tests should test. If minorities had lived in the same neighborhoods as whites, there would be no minority neighborhoods to which mortgage money could be denied on the basis of their being minority neighborhoods.

Such barriers to minorities and women too often do not fulfill legitimate needs of the organization, or these needs can be met through other means that adequately further organizational interests without discriminating. Instead of excluding all women on the assumption that they are too weak or should be protected from strenuous work, the organization can implement a reasonable test that measures the strength actually needed to perform the job or, where possible, develop ways of doing the work that require less physical effort. Admissions to academic and professional schools can be decided not only on the basis of grades, standardized test scores, and the prestige of the high school or college from which the applicant graduates, but also on the basis of community service, work experience, and letters of recommendation. Lending institutions can look at the individual and his or her financial ability rather than the neighborhood or marital status of the prospective borrower.

Some practices that disadvantage minorities and women are readily accepted aspects of everyday behavior. Consider the "old boy" network in business and education built on years of friendship and social contact among white males, or the exchanges of information and corporate strategies by business acquaintances in racially or sexually exclusive private clubs paid for by the employer.[27] These actions, all of which have a discriminatory impact on minorities and women, are not necessarily acts of conscious prejudice. Because such actions are so often considered part of the "normal" way of doing things, people have difficulty recognizing that they are part of a discriminatory process and, therefore, resist abandoning them despite the clearly discriminatory results. Consequently, many decisionmakers have difficulty considering, much less accepting, nondiscriminatory alternatives that may work just as well or better to advance legitimate organizational interests, but without systematically disadvantaging minorities and women.

This is not to suggest that all such discriminatory organizational actions are spurious or arbitrary. Many may serve the actual needs of the organization. Physical size or strength at times may be a legitimate job requirement; sick leave and insurance policies must be reasonably restricted; English proficiency and educational qualifications are needed for many jobs; lending institutions cannot lend to people who cannot reasonably demonstrate an ability to repay loans. Unless carefully examined and then modified or eliminated, however, these apparently neutral rules, policies, and practices will continue to perpetuate age-old discriminatory patterns into the structure of today's society.

Whatever the motivation behind such organizational acts, a process is occurring, the common denominator of which is the denial of equality of opportunity to large numbers of minorities and women.[28] When unequal outcomes are repeated over time and in numerous societal and geographical areas, it is a clear signal that a discriminatory process is at work.

Such discrimination is not a static, one-time phenomenon that has a clearly limited effect. Discrimination can feed on discrimination in self-perpetuating cycles:[29]

- The employer who recruits job applicants by word of mouth within a predominantly one-race, one-sex work force reduces the chances of receiving applications from people of another race or sex. Traditionally, those holding the most desirable jobs in the work force have been white males. If word-of-mouth recruiting is the method used to fill these jobs, minorities and women will have no opportunity to apply, since they will not hear about vacancies. Since they do not apply, they are not hired. Since they are not hired, they cannot recruit other minority or female applicants. Because there are no minority or female employees to recruit others, the employer is left to recruit from among its predominantly white and male work force.[30]
- The teacher who expects poor academic performance from minority and female students may not become greatly concerned when their grades are low. The acceptance of their low grades removes incentives to improve. Without incentives to improve, their grades remain low. Their low grades reduce their expectations, and the teacher has no basis for expecting more of them.[31]
- The realtor who assumes that white homeowners do not want minority neighbors "steers" minorities to minority neighborhoods. Those steered to minority neighborhoods tend to live in minority neighborhoods. White neighborhoods then remain white, and realtors tend to assume that whites do not want minority neighbors.[32]

- Elected officials appoint voting registrars who impose linguistic, geographic, and other barriers to minority voter registration. Lack of minority registration means that fewer minorities vote. Lower minority voting rates lead to the election of fewer unresponsive officials. These elected officials then appoint voting registrars who maintain the same barriers.[33]

Structural Discrimination

Such self-sustaining discriminatory processes occur not only in employment, education, housing, and government, but also between these structural areas. There is a classic cycle of structural discrimination that reproduces itself. Discrimination in education denies the credentials to get good jobs. Discrimination in employment denies the economic resources to buy good housing. Discrimination in housing confines its victims to school districts providing inferior education, closing the cycle in a classic form.[34]

The cycles of discrimination that white women encounter differ from those minorities encounter, but all women face structural discrimination when they compete with men. When white women live with white men, the women share many of the material and educational advantages that the men enjoy. In addition, white males often pass such advantages on to their daughters or wives. But sharing resources is not the same as sharing power. Access to some of the same material resources that white males enjoy does not give white women the ability to obtain these resources independently. In this sense, white women are caught in a discriminatory cycle that neutralizes the advantages derived by relationships with white men. The educational experiences of white women perhaps best illustrate this cycle. Educational programs, most conspicuously vocational and athletic programs,[35] have significantly disadvantaged white females, although not in the same ways or to the same degree as segregated minorities. On the whole, girls tend to perform at least as well as boys in elementary and high school and even in higher educational programs.[36] Nonetheless, females as a group have yet to do as well in the employment market as do similarly or less educated males.[37]

For women who are minorities, discriminatory cycles may have even more devastating effects. Minority women are subject to the same types of discrimination as white women, but cannot draw on the resources available in the white community. For minority women, the cycle of discrimination is as tightly closed and rigidly self-perpetuating as it is for minority men.

Regarding the similarities and differences between the discrimination experienced by women and minorities, one author has aptly stated:

> [W]hen two groups exist in a situation of inequality, it may be self-defeating to become embroiled in a quarrel over which is more unequal or the victim of greater oppression. The more salient question is how a condition of inequality for both is maintained and perpetuated—through what means is it reinforced?[38]

It is far more productive to understand the various forms and dynamics of the discrimination that minorities and women experience than to engage in endless, value-laden debates over who is suffering more. The nature and extent of the processes that cause the suffering should be the focus of analysis, not just the pain and unfairness caused by those processes.

The following are additional examples of the interaction among social structures that affects minorities and women:

- The absence of minorities and women from executive, writing, directing, news reporting, and acting positions in television contributes to unfavorable stereotyping on the screen, which in turn reinforces existing stereotypes among the public and creates psychological roadblocks to progress in employment, education, and housing.[39]
- Living in inner-city high crime areas in disproportionate numbers, minorities, particularly minority youth, are more likely to be arrested and are more likely to go to jail than whites accused of similar offenses, and their arrest and conviction records are then often used as bars to employment.[40]
- Because of past discrimination against minorities and women, female- and minority-headed businesses are often small and relatively new. Further disadvantaged by contemporary credit and lending practices, they are more likely than white-male-owned businesses to remain small and be less able to employ full-time specialists in applying for government contracts. Because they cannot monitor the availability of government contracts, they do not receive such contracts. Because they cannot demonstrate success with government contracts, contracting officers tend to favor other firms that have more experience with government contracts.[41]

Discriminatory actions by individuals and organizations are not only pervasive, occurring in every sector of society, but also cumulative, with effects limited neither to the time nor the particular structural area in which they occur. This process of discrimination, therefore, extends across generations, across organizations, and across social structures in self-reinforcing cycles, passing the disadvantages incurred by one generation in one area to future generations in many related areas.[42]

These interrelated components of the discriminatory process share one basic result: the persistent gaps seen in the status of women and minorities relative to that of white males. These unequal results themselves have real consequences. The employer who wishes to hire more minorities and women may be bewildered by charges of racism and sexism when confronted by a genuine shortage of qualified minority and female applicants. The guidance counselor who sees one promising minority student after another drop out of school or give up in despair may resent allegations of racism when there is little he or she alone can do for the student. The banker who denies a loan to a female single parent may wish to act differently, but believes that prudent fiscal judgment requires taking into account her lack of financial history and inability to prove that she is a good credit risk. These and other decisionmakers see the results of a discriminatory process repeated over and over again, and those results provide a basis for rationalizing their own actions, which then feed into that same process.

When seen outside the context of the interlocking and intertwined effects of discrimination, complaints that many women and minorities are absent from the ranks of qualified job applicants, academically inferior and unmotivated, poor credit risks, and so forth may appear to be justified. Decisionmakers like those described above are reacting to real social problems stemming from the process of discrimination. But many too easily fall prey to stereotyping and consequently disregard those minorities and women who have the necessary skills or qualifications. And they erroneously "blame the victims" of discrimination,[43] instead of examining the past and present context in which their own actions are taken and the multiple consequences of these actions on the lives of minorities and women.

The Process of Discrimination

Although discrimination is maintained through individual actions, neither individual prejudices nor random chance can fully explain the persistent national patterns of inequality and underrepresentation. Nor can these patterns simplistically be blamed on the persons who are at the bottom of our economic, political, and social order. We regard as an age-old canard of bigotry that the victims of discrimination have only themselves to blame for their victimization. Public opinion polls indicate that overt racism and sexism based on attitudes of white and male supremacy have been widely repudiated, but our history of discrimination based on race, sex, and national origin has not been readily put aside. Past discrimination continues to have present effects. The task today is to identify those effects and the forms and dynamics of the discrimination that reproduce them.

Discrimination against minorities and women should now be viewed as an interlocking process involving the attitudes and actions of individuals and the organizations and social structures that guide individual behavior. That process, started by past events, now routinely bestows privileges, favors, and advantages on white males and imposes disadvantages and penalties on minorities and women. This process is also self-perpetuating. Many normal, seemingly neutral, operations of our society create stereotyped expectations that justify unequal results; unequal results in one area foster inequalities in opportunity and accomplishment in others; the lack of opportunity and accomplishment confirms the original prejudices or engenders new ones that fuel the normal operations generating unequal results.

As we have shown, the process of discrimination involves many aspects of our society. No single factor sufficiently explains discrimination, and no single means will suffice to eliminate it. We must continuously examine such elements of our society as our history of *de jure* discrimination, deeply ingrained prejudices,[44] inequities based on economic and social class,[45] and the structure and function of all our economic, social, and political institutions[46] in order to understand their part in maintaining or countering discriminatory processes.

It may be difficult to identify precisely all aspects of discriminatory processes and assign those parts their appropriate weight. But understanding how discrimination works starts with an awareness that it is a process, and that to avoid perpetuating it, we must carefully assess the context and consequences of our everyday actions.

The Commission believes that a more productive and pragmatic approach toward eliminating discrimination starts with an informed awareness of the forms, dynamics, and subtleties of the process of discrimination. Decisionmakers are then better able to develop programs utilizing the tools of administration to change an organization's practices to those that promote equality instead of support continued inequality. The problem-remedy approach advanced in this statement is intended as an aid toward moving in that direction.

Endnotes

1. Dred Scott v. Sandford, 60 U.S. (19 How.) 393,408 (1857).
2. For a concise summary of this history that refers to numerous other sources, see U.S., Commission on Civil Rights, *Civil Rights: A National, Not a Special Interest* (1981), pp. 1–33; *Twenty Years After Brown* (1975), pp. 4–29; *Freedom to the Free: Century of Emancipation 1863–1963* (1963).
3. The discriminatory conditions experienced by these minority groups have been documented in the following publications by the U.S. Commission on Civil Rights: *Indian Tribes: A Continuing Quest for Survival* (1981); *The Navajo Nation: An American Colony* (1975); *The Southwest Indian Report* (1973); *Success of Asian Americans. Fact or Fiction?* (1980); *The Forgotten Minority: Asian Americans in New York City* (New York State Advisory Committee, 1977); *Stranger in One's Land* (1970); *Toward Quality Education for Mexican Americans* (1974); *Puerto Ricans in the Continental United States: An Uncertain Future* (1976).
4. Frontiero v. Richardson, 411 U.S. 677, 685 (1973), *citing* Leo Kanowitz, *Women and the Law: The Unfinished Revolution* (Albuquerque: University of New Mexico Press, 1969), pp. 5–6, and Gunnar Myrdal, *An American Dilemma* (20th Anniversary ed., 1962), p. 1073. Justice Brennan wrote the opinion of the Court, joined by Justices Douglas, White, and Marshall. Justice Stewart concurred in the judgment. Justice Powell, joined by Chief Justice Burger and Justice Blackmun, wrote a separate concurring opinion. Justice Rehnquist dissented. See also H.M. Hacker, "Women as a Minority Group," *Social Forces* vol. 30 (1951), pp. 60–69; W. Chafe, *Women and Equality: Changing Patterns in American Culture* (New York: Oxford University Press, 1977).
5. Bradwell v. State, 83 U.S. (16 Wall) 130, 141 (1873) (Bradley, J., concurring), *quoted in* Frontiero v. Richardson, 411 U.S 677, 684 (1973).
6. U.S., Const. amend. XIX.
7. See U.S., Commission on Civil Rights, *The Equal Rights Amendment: Guaranteeing Equal Rights for Women Under the Constitution* (1981); *Statement on the Equal Rights Amendment* (1978).

8. Public opinion polls reveal that the expression of prejudiced attitudes toward blacks and women have continued to decline, particularly in the last decade, although such prejudice persists in a significant percentage of the public. A 1978 Gallup poll showed a decline in the expression of prejudice in issues related to housing and politics. Between 1965 and 1978, the number of whites who said they would move out of their neighborhoods if blacks moved in declined from 35 percent to 16 percent. Between 1969 and 1978, the number of whites who said they would vote for a qualified black Presidential candidate of their own party increased from 67 to 77 percent. *Gallup Poll*, Aug. 27, 1978. Another poll found that between 1971 and 1978 a declining number of whites said they believed blacks to be inferior (from 22 percent to 15 percent) or of less native intelligence than whites (from 37 percent to 25 percent). Poll by Louis Harris and Associates for the National Conference on Christians and Jews, *Newsweek*, Feb. 26, 1979, p. 48.

    Although blacks continue to see racial prejudice as an important cause of many of their social and economic problems, whites are now less often seen as standing in the way of black progress compared to a decade ago. In 1969 a *Newsweek* poll found a plurality of blacks (46 percent) feeling that most whites wanted to keep them down. The February 1981 *Newsweek* poll showed fewer (32 percent) supporting this view. *Gallup Poll Watch*, May 18, 1981.

    With regard to women, the findings are ambiguous. A recent Gallup poll shows public support for the Equal Rights Amendment at a new high with 63 percent of Americans who have heard or read about the ERA favoring it and 32 percent opposed. In surveys conducted regularly by the Gallup Poll since 1975, support for the ERA had never exceeded 58 percent. *Gallup Poll*, Aug. 9, 1981. Another poll conducted by the Roper Organization showed a decline in support for the ERA (from 55 percent of women and 68 percent of men in 1975 to 51 percent of women and 52 percent of men in 1980). However, the same poll indicated that support for efforts to strengthen the status of women had increased (from 40 percent of women and 44 percent of men in 1970 to 60 percent of women and 64 percent of men in 1980). *Virginia Slims American Women's Opinion Poll* (Roper Organization, 1980).

9. The Commission has issued a report evaluating the Nation's progress toward equality by systematically comparing the social conditions of the minority and female population to those of the white male population, *Social Indicators of Equality for Minorities and Women* (1978). Separately analyzed by sex were statistics on American Indians and Alaskan Natives, blacks, Mexican Americans, Japanese Americans, Chinese Americans, Filipino Americans, Puerto Ricans, and the majority population. According to the report, minorities and women are less likely to have completed as many years of high school or have a high school or college education than white males. If not undereducated, they tend to be educationally overqualified for the work they do and earn less than comparably educated white males. As of 1976, among those persons 25–29 years of age, 34 of every 100 white males were college educated, while only 11 out of every 100 minorities were college educated. Ibid., p. 26.

Women and minorities are more likely to be unemployed, to have less prestigious occupations than white men, and to be concentrated in different occupations. From 1970 to 1976, when unemployment rates were rising for all groups, the disparity between minority and female rates and the majority male rate generally increased; blacks, Mexican Americans, and Puerto Ricans of both sexes moved from having approximately twice the unemployment of majority males in 1970 to nearly three times the majority male rate in 1976. Ibid., p. 29. In 1976, 47.8 percent of black male teenagers, 51.3 percent of black female teenagers, and 55.2 percent of Puerto Rican male teenagers were unemployed, compared to 15.0 percent unemployment among majority male teenagers. Ibid., p. 32. Occupational segregation is also intense: One-third of the jobs held by minority men and two-thirds to three-fourths of the jobs held by women in 1976 would have to be changed to match the occupational patterns of white males. Ibid., p. 45. Minorities and women have less per capita household income and a greater likelihood of being in poverty. "The indicator values for median household per capita income for 1959, 1969, and 1975 show that most minority and female-headed households have only half the income that is available to majority households." Ibid., p. 65. Relative to the income of white males, the incomes available to Mexican Americans and Puerto Ricans in 1975 were the same as or less than they were in 1965 and 1970. In addition, minority-headed families, regardless of the sex of the family head, are twice as likely to be in poverty as majority-headed families, and minority female-headed families are over five times as likely to be in poverty as majority-headed families. Ibid., pp. 65–66. Finally, minority and female-headed households are more likely to be located in central cities than in the suburbs where majority-headed households are located. Between 1960 and 1970 most minority households were only about one-half to two-thirds as likely as white households to be situated outside a central city. Minorities and women are less likely to be homeowners, more likely to live in overcrowded conditions, and more likely to spend more than a quarter of their family income on rent. American Indian, Alaskan Native, black, Chinese American, Filipino American, and Puerto Rican rental households were all more than two, with Mexican American households almost six, times as likely to be overcrowded as white households in 1970. In 1976 minority and female-headed households were, at best, two-thirds as likely to be owner occupied as majority-headed households. Ibid., pp. 75, 84–85.

10. *See e.g.*, R. K. Merton, "Discrimination and the American Creed," in R. K. Merton, *Sociological Ambivalence and Other Essays* (New York: The Free Press, 1976), pp. 189–216. In this essay on racism, published for the first time more than 30 years ago, Merton presented a typology which introduced the idea that discriminatory actions are not always directly related to individual attitudes of prejudice. Merton's typology consisted of the following: Type I—the unprejudiced nondiscriminator; Type II—the unprejudiced discriminator; Type III—the prejudiced nondiscriminator; Type IV—the prejudiced discriminator. In the present context, Type II is crucial in its observation that discrimination is often practiced by persons who are not themselves prejudiced, but

who respond to, or do not oppose, the actions of those who discriminate because of prejudiced attitudes (Type IV). See also D. C. Reitzes, "Prejudice and Discrimination: A Study in Contradictions," in *Racial and Ethnic Relations*, ed. H. M. Hughes (Boston: Allyn and Bacon, 1970), pp. 56–65.

11. See R. M. Kanter and B. A. Stein, "Making a Life at the Bottom," in *Life in Organizations, Workplaces as People Experience Them*, ed. R. M. Kanter and B. A. Stein (New York: Basic Books, 1976), pp. 176–90; also, L. K. Howe, "Retail Sales Worker," ibid., pp. 248–51; also, R. M. Kanter, *Men and Women of the Corporation* (New York: Basic Books, 1977).

12. See M. S. Granovetter, *Getting A Job: A Study of Contract and Careers* (Cambridge: Harvard University Press, 1974), pp. 6–11; also, A. W. Blumrosen, *Black Employment and the Law* (New Brunswick, NJ.: Rutgers University Press, 1971), pp. 232–34. *See also* EEOC v. Detroit Edison Co., 515 F.2d 301, 313 (6th Cir. 1975), *vacated on other grounds*, 431 U.S. 951 (1977) (practice of relying on referrals by a predominantly white work force rather than seeking out new employees in the marketplace for jobs was found to be discriminatory); EEOC v. Ford Motor Co., 645 F.2d 183, 198 (4th Cir. 1981) (a policy of favoring job applicants who were friends of current workers, where current work force was exclusively male, plus statistical data showing bias in hiring practices, established discrimination under Title VII).

13. *See* U.S., Equal Employment Opportunity Commission (EEOC), "Guidelines on Discrimination Because of Sex," 29 C.F.R. §1604.4 (1979); L. Farley, *Sexual Shakedown: The Sexual Harassment of Women on the Job* (New York: McGraw Hill, 1978), pp. 92–96, 176–79; C.A. Mackinnon, *Sexual Harassment of Working Women* (New Haven: Yale University Press, 1979), pp. 25–55.

14. *See* R. Rosenthal and L. F. Jacobson, "Teacher Expectations for the Disadvantaged," *Scientific American*, 1968 (b), pp. 218, 219–23; also, D. Bar Tal, "Interactions of Teachers and Pupils," in *New Approaches to Social Problem* ed. I. H. Frieze, D. Bar Tal, and J. S. Carrol (San Francisco: Jossey Bass, 1979), pp. 337–58; also, U.S., Commission on Civil Rights, *Teachers and Students, Report V: Mexican American Education Study, Differences in Teacher Interaction With Mexican American and Anglo Students* (1973), pp. 22–23.

15. Ibid.

16. U.S., Department of Housing and Urban Development, *Measuring Racial Discrimination in American Housing Markets: The Housing Market Practices Survey* (1979); D. M. Pearce, "Gatekeepers and Home Seekers: Institutional Patterns in Racial Steering," in *Social Problems*, vol. 26 (1979), pp. 325–42; "Benign Steering and Benign Quotas: The Validity of Race Conscious Government Policies to Promote Residential Integration," *Harvard Law Review*, vol. 93 (1980), pp. 938, 944.

17. See M. N. Danielson, *The Politics of Exclusion* (New York: Columbia University Press, 1976), pp. 11–12; U.S., Commission on Civil Rights, *Equal Opportunity in Suburbia* (1974).

18. *See* L. L. Knowles and K. Prewitt, eds., *Institutional Racism in America* (Englewood Cliffs, NJ.: Prentice Hall, 1969) pp. 58–77, and E. D. Wright, *The Politics of Punishment* (New York: Harper and Row, 1973). Also, S. V. Brown, "Race and Parole Hearing Outcomes," in *Discrimination in Organizations*, ed. R. Alvarez and K. G. Lutterman (San Francisco: Jossey Bass, 1979), pp. 355–74.

19. Height and weight minimums that disproportionately exclude women without a showing of legitimate job requirement constitute unlawful sex discrimination. *See* Dothard v. Rawlinson, 433 U.S. 321 (1977); Bowe v. Colgate Palmolive Co., 416 F.2d 711 (7th Cir. 1969). Minimum height requirements used in screening applicants for employment have also been held to be unlawful where such a requirement excludes a significantly higher percentage of Hispanics than other national origin groups in the labor market and no job relatedness is shown. *See* Smith v. City of East Cleveland, 520 F.2d 492 (6th Cir. 1975).

20. U.S., Commission on Civil Rights, *Last Hired, First Fired* (1976); Tangren v. Wackenhut Servs., Inc., 480 F. Supp. 539 (D. Nev. 1979), *notice of appeal filed* (9th Cir. Dec. 4, 1979).

21. U.S., Commission on Civil Rights, *The Challenge Ahead, Equal Opportunity in Referral Unions* (1977), pp. 84–89.

22. A. Pifer, "Women Working: Toward a New Society," pp. 13–34, and D. Pearce, "Women, Work and Welfare: The Feminization of Poverty," pp. 103–24, both in K. A. Feinstein, ed., *Working Women and Families* (Beverly Hills: Sage Publications, 1979). *See also*, U.S., Commission on Civil Rights, *Child Care and Equal Opportunity for Women* (1981), pp. 44–49. Disproportionate numbers of single-parent families are minorities. *See* U.S., Department of Commerce, Bureau of the Census, *Families Maintained by Female Householders 1970–79* (1980), p. 5.

23. See EEOC, "Guidelines on Discrimination Because of National Origin," §1606.7, 45 Fed. Reg. 85635 (1980) (to be codified in 29 C.F.R. Part 1606).

24. *See* Griggs v. Duke Power Co., 401 U.S. 424 (1971); U.S., Commission on Civil Rights, *Toward Equal Educational Opportunity: Affirmative Admissions Programs at Law and Medical Schools* (1978), pp. 10–12; I. Berg, *Education and Jobs: The Great Training Robbery* (Boston: Beacon Press, 1971), pp. 58–60.

25. *See* U.S., Commission on Civil Rights, *Toward Equal Educational Opportunity*, pp. 14–15.

26. *See* U.S., Commission on Civil Rights, *Mortgage Money: Who Gets It? A Case Study in Mortgage Lending Discrimination in Hanford Conn.* (1974); J. Feagin and C. B. Feagin, *Discrimination American Style, Institutional Racism and Sexism* (Englewood Cliffs, NJ.: Prentice Hall, 1976), pp. 78–79.

27. *See Club Membership Practices by Financial Institutions: Hearing Before the Committee on Banking Housing and Urban Affairs, United States Senate*, 96th Cong., 1st sess. (1979). Pursuant to President Reagan's directive, the Office of Federal Contract Compliance Programs has withdrawn a rule it earlier proposed (45 Fed. Reg. 4954, 1980) that would

have made the payment or reimbursement of membership fees in a private club that accepts or rejects persons on the basis of race, color, sex, religion, or national origin a prohibited discriminatory practice if such membership enhances employment opportunities. 46 Fed. Reg. 19004 (Mar. 27, 1981). It is the position of the Labor Department, however, that the Executive order provisions prohibiting discrimination and requiring affirmative action are "adequate to prevent an employer from using such memberships to structure the conduct of its businesses in a manner which creates employment discrimination." *Id.*

28. *See* discussion of the courts' use of numerical evidence of unequal results in Part B of this statement, "Civil Rights Law and the Problem."

29. *See* U.S., Commission on Civil Rights, *For All the People . . . By All the People* (1969), pp. 122–23.

30. *See* note 12.

31. *See* note 14. Non-English-speaking students may suffer a similar fate. *See, e.g.,* Dexter Waugh and Bruce Koon, "Breakthrough for Bilingual Education: *Lau v. Nichols* and the San Francisco School System," *Civil Rights Digest,* vol. 6, no. 4 (1974), pp. 18–26.

32. *See* notes 16 and 17.

33. *See* Arthur S. Flemming, Chairman, U.S. Commission on Civil Rights, statement before the Subcommittee on Constitutional Rights, Committee on the Judiciary, U.S. Senate, on S.407, S.903, and S.1279, Apr. 9, 1975, pp. 15–18, based on U.S., Commission on Civil Rights, *The Voting Rights Act: Ten Years After* (January 1975).

34. *See, e.g.,* U.S., Commission on Civil Rights, *Equal Opportunity in Suburbia* (1974).

35. *See generally* U.S., Commission on Civil Rights, *More Hurdles to Clear: Women and Girls in Competitive Athletics* (1980).

36. Ruth Bader Ginsburg, "Realizing The Equality Principle," in *Social Justice and Preferential Treatment,* ed. William Blackstone and Robert Heslep (Athens: University of Georgia Press, 1977), pp. 136–37.

37. Elizabeth McTaggart Almquist, *Minorities, Gender, and Work* (Lexington, Mass.: Lexington Books, 1979), p. 181.

38. Chafe, *Women and Equality,* p. 78.

39. U.S., Commission on Civil Rights, *Window Dressing on the Set* (1977).

40. *See* note 18; Gregory v. Litton Systems, Inc., 472 F.2d 631 (9th Cir. 1972); Green v. Mo.-Pac. R.R., 523 F.2d 1290 (8th Cir. 1975).

41. *See* U.S., Commission on Civil Rights, *Minorities and Women as Government Contractors* (1975), pp. 20, 27, 125.

42. *See e.g.,* A. Downs, *Racism in America and How to Combat It* (prepared for the U.S. Commission on Civil Rights, 1970); "The Web of Urban Racism," in *Institutional Racism in America,* ed. Knowles and Prewitt, pp. 134–76. Other factors in addition to race, sex, and national origin may contribute to these interlocking institutional patterns. In *Equal Opportunity in Suburbia* (1974), this Commission documented what it termed "the cycle of urban poverty" that confines minorities in central cities with

declining tax bases, soaring educational and other public needs, and dwindling employment opportunities, surrounded by largely white, affluent suburbs. This cycle of poverty, however, started with and is fueled by discrimination against minorities. *See also* W. Taylor, *Hanging Together, Equality in an Urban Nation* (New York: Simon & Schuster, 1971).

43. The "self-fulfilling prophecy" is a well-known phenomenon. "Blaming the victim" occurs when responses to discrimination are treated as though they were the causes rather than the results of discrimination. *See* Chafe, *Women and Equality*, pp. 76–78; W. Ryan, *Blaming the Victim* (New York: Pantheon Books, 1971).

44. *See, e.g.,* J. E. Simpson and J. M. Yinger, *Racial and Cultural Minorities* (New York: Harper and Row, 1965), pp. 49–79; J. M. Jones, *Prejudice and Racism* (Reading, Mass.: Addison Wesley, 1972), pp. 60–111; M. M. Tumin, "Who Is Against Desegregation?" in *Racial and Ethnic Relations,* ed. H. Hughes (Boston: Allyn & Bacon, 1970), pp. 76–85; D. M. Wellman, *Portraits of White Racism* (Cambridge: Cambridge University Press, 1977).

45. *See, e.g.,* D. C. Cox, *Caste, Class and Race: A Study in Social Dynamics* (Garden City, N.Y.: Doubleday, 1948); W. J. Wilson, *Power, Racism and Privilege* (New York: MacMillan, 1973).

46. H. Hacker, "Women as a Minority Group," *Social Forces,* vol. 30 (1951), pp. 60–69; J. Feagin and C. B. Feagin, *Discrimination American Style*; Chafe, *Women and Equality*; J. Feagin, "Indirect Institutionalized Discrimination," *American Politics Quarterly,* vol. 5 (1977), pp. 177–200; M. A. Chester, "Contemporary Sociological Theories of Racism," in *Towards the Elimination of Racism,* ed. P. Katz (New York: Pergamion Press, 1976); P. Van den Berghe, *Race and Racism: A Comparative Perspective* (New York: Wiley, 1967); S. Carmichael and C. Hamilton, *Black Power* (New York: Random House, 1967); Knowles and Prewitt, *Institutional Racism in America:* Downs, *Racism in America and How to Combat It.*

41

"Savage Inequalities" Revisited

Richer, whiter school districts are still getting more public funds, while the federal government looks the other way.

Bob Feldman

In the late 1980s, I taught health and social studies in a New York City public school. My students came largely from African-American and Caribbean families, and the school was located in a high-poverty district. Because funding was so tight, we had no textbooks for a required eighth-grade health class, no classroom maps for seventh- and eighth-grade history classes, and no photocopying machines that teachers or students could use for free. There was also no school newspaper or yearbook, and the school band had fewer than twenty instruments.

The conditions in this school illustrated a crisis of funding inequality in the U.S. public school system. In his 1991 book *Savage Inequalities*, Jonathan Kozol, a long-time critic of unequal education, famously exposed this crisis. He noted, for instance, that schools in the rich suburbs of New York City spent more than $11,000 per pupil in 1987, while those in the city itself spent only $5,500. The story was the same throughout the country: per-capita spending for poor students and students of color in urban areas was a fraction of that in richer, whiter suburbs just miles away.

Over ten years after *Savage Inequalities* was first published, how close has the U.S. public school system come to providing equitable funding for all students—funding that is at least equal between districts, or better yet, higher in poorer areas that have greater needs?

Not very far, according to a new report by the Washington, D.C.-based Education Trust. Entitled "The Funding Gap: Low-Income and Minority Students Receive Fewer Dollars," the report examines state and local expenditures in 15,000 school districts during 1999–2000. Since federal funds account for only 7% of public school resources, this study of state and local spending zeroes in on the source of funding inequality.

According to the Education Trust study, the poorest 25% of school districts in each state receive an average of $966 less in state and local funds per pupil than the richest 25%. This gap has narrowed by $173 since 1997, but it does not reflect uniform progress: in nine of

47 states examined, the gap widened by at least $100. In states like New York and Illinois, spending differences remain staggering, totaling $2,152 and $2,060 per student, respectively. These figures, like all those in the study, are adjusted to account for the greater expense of educating students in poor districts and areas with a high cost of living. (See Chart 1.)

Funding inequality puts students of color at a special disadvantage. In two-thirds of states in the Education Trust study, the quarter of school districts with the highest percentage of students of color received at least $100 less in state and local funding than the quarter of districts with the lowest percentage of students of color. New York topped the charts for racial inequality: the quarter of districts with the highest percentage of students of color received $2,034 less in state and local funds per student than the quarter of districts enrolling the smallest percentage. (See Chart 2.)

Between 1997 and 2000, 30 of the 47 states studied did move toward providing equal or greater funding for students in poorer districts—and some states made significant progress. Why did this happen? According to Michael Rebell, executive director of the Campaign for Fiscal Equity, lawsuits have produced some changes. New Jersey, for instance, began channeling funds to its poorest districts after a court challenge; as of 2000, the state government provided roughly three times as much per-capita funding to the poorest quarter of districts as it did to the richest quarter. While the state government's targeted funds are counterbalanced by wildly unequal local resources, students in the poorest quarter of districts now receive a net of $324 more per capita than those in the richest quarter. States like Oregon have achieved similar results not by targeting poorer districts, but by assuming a greater share of responsibility for school funding state-wide. Strategies like New Jersey's and Oregon's help explain the narrowing funding gap, and could be models for other states.

Chart 1: Poor Students Get Less

States with Largest Per-Student Funding Gaps, and U.S. Average

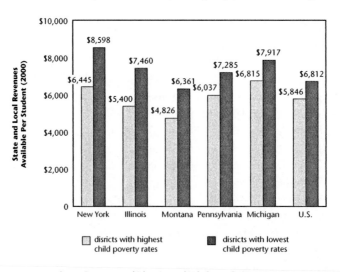

Source: Department of Education and U.S. Census Bureau

Chart 2: Students of Color Get Less

States with Largest Per-Student Funding Gaps, and U.S. Average

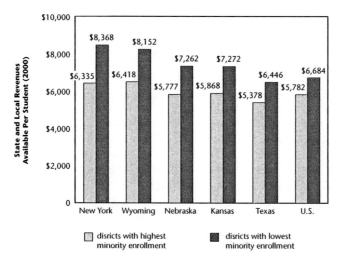

Source: Department of Education and U.S. Census Bureau

Rebell notes, however, that state-level remedies arc fundamentally limited: among states, they are "complex and uneven," and nationally, they leave millions of students unaffected. A more powerful solution might be for the federal government to fund the public school system directly, as governments do in Canada, Japan, and most social democratic countries of Western Europe. Today, the U.S. government does channel money to poor districts through Title I, the largest single federal investment in education. But Title I funds are not intended to equalize funding within states: the federal government leaves that responsibility to state and local authorities, who plainly do not comply.

The needs of students would be justly served by federally guaranteed funding, but current state and federal policies guarantee something very different. As Jonathan Kozol explained a decade ago, "The present system guarantees that those who can buy a $1 million home in an affluent suburb will also be able to provide their children with superior schools." The U.S. public school system is still rigged in favor of students from richer, whiter districts; and as Rebell remarks, the United States remains "the only major developed country in the world that exhibits this shameful pattern of educational inequity."

Resources

Jonathan Kozol, *Savage Inequalities: Children in America's Schools* (Crown Publishers, 1991).
Educational Leadership, December 1, 1993 interview with Jonathan Kozol.
<www. ACCESSednetwork.org>.
"The Funding Gap: Low-Income and Minority Students Receive Fewer Dollars," The Education Trust, Inc., <www.edtrust.org>.

42

The Segregated Classrooms of a Proudly Diverse School

Jeffrey Gettleman

MAPLEWOOD, N. J., April 1—Columbia High School seems to have it all—great sports teams, great academics, famous alumni and an impressive campus with Gothic buildings. But no one boasts about one aspect of this blue-ribbon school, that its classrooms are largely segregated.

Though the school is majority black, white students make up the bulk of the advanced classes, while black students far outnumber whites in lower-level classes, statistics show.

"It's kind of sad," said Ugochi Opara, a senior who is president of the student council. "You can tell right away, just by looking into a classroom, what level it is."

This is a reality at many high schools coast to coast and one of the side effects of aggressive leveling, the increasingly popular practice of dividing students into ability groups.

But at Columbia High, the students nearly revolted. Two weeks ago, a black organization on campus planned a walkout to protest the leveling system. Word soon spread to the principal, who pleaded with the students not to go. The student leaders decided to hold an assembly instead, in which they lashed out at the racial gap.

The student uproar is now forcing district officials to take a hard look at the leveling system and decide how to strike a balance between their two main goals—celebrating diversity and pushing academic achievement.

Educators say that leveling allows smarter students to be challenged while giving struggling ones the special instruction they need. But many students, especially those in the lower levels, which often carry a stigma, say such stratification makes the rocky adolescent years only harder. And at Columbia High, there is no dispute that it is precisely the leveling system that has led to racial segregation.

Anthony Paolini, a senior at Columbia, is one of the few white students in a lower level math class. The fact that most of his classmates are black does not bother him, he said. But the low expectations do.

"It makes you feel like you're in a hole," he said.

From *The New York Times*, Metropolitan Section, 4/3/2005 Issue, Pages 1–31. Copyright © 2005 *The New York Times*. Reprinted with permission.

The school, about 15 minutes from downtown Newark, draws from the cosmopolitan towns of Maplewood and South Orange. Some students live in million-dollar homes. Others rely on government lunches. Of 2,024 students, 58 percent are black, 35 percent white, 4 percent Hispanic and 3 percent Asian. The public school sends more than 90 percent of graduates to college, has a dropout rate of less than half a percent and won a national Blue Ribbon award from the federal government for its academic excellence during the 1992–93 school year. Notable alumni include the actor Zach Braff and the singer Lauryn Hill, and the fact that the two stars, one white, one black, graduated in the same class is seen as a symbol of the diversity Columbia strives to project.

But racial tension is becoming more of an issue. In recent years, the number of black students in the school district has eclipsed the number of white students even though Maplewood and South Orange still are majority white. In the past year, the district has been sued twice for discrimination: once by two former black students who said they were mistreated by teachers after a food-fight in the cafeteria, and also by a group of teachers, mostly black, who accused the principal, who is white, of racial bias.

The superintendent of the district, Peter P. Horoschak, acknowledged that there were, in a sense, two Columbias. The de facto segregation is most visible at the extremes. Statistics for this year show that while a Level 5 math class, the highest, had 79 percent white students, a Level 2 math class, the lowest, had 88 percent black students. Levels 3 and 4 tend to be more mixed, though a school board member, Mila M. Jasey, said, "Some white parents tell me that they know their kid belongs in a Level 3 class but they don't want them to be the only white kid in the class."

Though parents and students are granted some input, students are supposed to be placed in levels primarily based on grades and test scores. Many black students complain that they are unfairly relegated to the lower levels and unable to move up.

Quentin Williams, the 17-year-old leader of the Martin Luther King Association at the school, calls it "contemporary segregation." He said that his organization, one of the largest on campus, had tried to meet with the administration over the issue several times but "got the runaround."

So in mid-March his group planned to walk out of school. They even had the backing of several parents, who volunteered to help. As the date approached, Quentin, a senior, said he felt "a lot of pressure coming in from a lot of different angles."

Student leaders eventually decided that holding an assembly would give them a better opportunity to publicly confront administrators, especially the principal, Renee Pollack. At the assembly, which was mandatory for all students, she stood in front of the student body and apologized for saying anything that might have been construed as insensitive.

Ms. Pollack said later that complaints about her were being spread by teachers on her own staff.

"They were trying to manipulate the kids in order to get at me," said Ms. Pollack, who has been the principal for three years and is up for tenure this month.

The flashpoint of the assembly came when Nathan Winkler, a skinny, intense senior who says he wants to be governor some day, grabbed the microphone and announced that he had no sympathy for people in lower levels because all it took was hard work to move up.

His short outburst was like a cleaver, splitting the student body in two. Many blacks booed him. Many whites cheered. He was then accused of using the term "you people" in his speech—though he did not, according to a videotape of the assembly. After the assembly, he said, he was stalked in the hallways.

He now admits that he spoke out of fear.

"I felt extremely isolated during that assembly," he said. "For the first time I was aware of being part of the minority. White kids are outnumbered at Columbia. I knew that, but I hadn't really felt it before."

Student leaders and administrators are now discussing ways to narrow the so-called achievement gap, like granting students more say in which level they are in; better identifying which level students belong in; expanding a summer school program for students who want to take upper level classes. Administrators say they had been working on all this before the walkout threat.

"But the students forced the issue," Ms. Pollack acknowledged.

Ms. Pollack also pointed out that this year, more students of color from Columbia have been accepted into Ivy League universities than white students, with two Hispanic, three black and two white students gaining early admission.

The debate over leveling here boils down to fairness. Is it fair just to ensure equal access to upper level classes? Or does fairness go farther than that and require administrators to truly level the playing field so that the racial makeup of upper classes better resembles the racial makeup of the school?

Stewart Hendricks, a senior whose father is from Guyana and whose mother is Swiss, said that some teachers do seem to have lower expectations for black students but that he did not let them get him down.

"The purpose of high school is to prepare you for the real world," he said. "And in the real world, you can't listen to other peoples expectations, because in the real world, people are just waiting for you to fail."

Because of his mixed racial heritage, he said, "I guess you can say I'm in the middle of all this."

And in a way, that is why he sympathizes with the principal.

"She's got an entire black population that wants to get rid of the leveling system and an entire white population who would leave this town if they did that," he said. "What's she supposed to do?"

43

A Case of Equity and Justice in Education

Tyna D. Davis

In a perfect world, the issue of equity and justice would not need to be addressed. However, we do not live in a perfect world. Therefore, individuals in a caring society must be vigilant to insure that the issues of inequities and injustices are addressed and resolved. An educated citizenry is necessary for a healthy democracy. However, there has been historically uneven access to this important public service.

There have many attempts to bring about equity and justice in American education. Best known is the landmark case of *Brown v. Board of Education of Topeka*, 347 U.S. 483 (1954). This case was pivotal in dismantling segregation in schools. It is after this case that the state of Alabama began their journey to address educational inequality. The genesis of Alabama's foray to address equity and justice in education was through the Alabama Supreme Court case of *Lee v. MACON COUNTY BOARD OF EDUCATION (1963)*. The litigation was an attempt to bring about equity and justice in education through the integration of Alabama's public schools. Specifically, this case sought to resolve the issue of disparities in facilities and resources.

While *Brown v. Topeka Board of Education*, 1954 brought an end to segregation of public schools in the United States of America, Macon County, Alabama, and many other school systems in the State of Alabama remained virtually segregated. The challenge in Alabama began in August 1963, with the attempt to desegregate schools in Macon County, Alabama. It was Detroit Lee, parent of Anthony T. Lee, who served as the primary named plaintiff in the landmark desegregation lawsuit to integrate public schools in Macon County, Alabama. By his action in this case, Detroit Lee was a "pioneer and giant in the Civil Rights Movement" stated Jerome Gray, field director for the Alabama Democratic Conference, a major voice for Blacks in the Alabama Democratic Party, when interviewed by the *Montgomery Advertiser*. Fred D. Gray noted civil rights attorney and lead counsel in the Lee v. Macon case also lauded Lee's contributions. (Benn 2001).

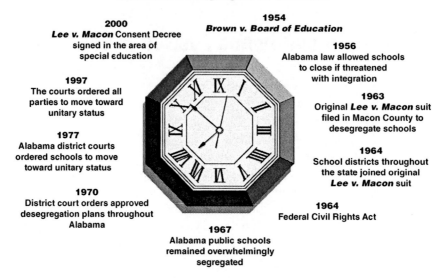

Alabama Desegregation Timeline

2000
Lee v. Macon Consent Decree
signed in the area of
special education

1997
The courts ordered all
parties to move toward
unitary status

1977
Alabama district courts
ordered schools to move
toward unitary status

1970
District court orders approved
desegregation plans throughout
Alabama

1954
Brown v. Board of Education

1956
Alabama law allowed schools
to close if threatened
with integration

1963
Original *Lee v. Macon* suit
filed in Macon County to
desegregate schools

1964
School districts throughout
the state joined original
Lee v. Macon suit

1964
Federal Civil Rights Act

1967
Alabama public schools
remained overwhelmingly
segregated

FIGURE 1

Source: Alabama Department of Education

In the Lee v. Macon litigation, parents and children were seeking an injunction to prevent the Macon County School Board from continuing to run segregated schools. In 1964, school districts throughout Alabama were joined to the original case. *Lee v. Macon,* had riveting effects throughout the state of Alabama. A timeline of desegregation in Alabama is captured in figure 1.

On August 22, 1963, after a hearing, the court granted the relief sought by the plaintiffs, *Lee v. Macon County Bd. of Educ.*, 221 F. Supp. 297 (M.D. Ala. 1963). Acting pursuant to an executive order of the Governor of Alabama, Alabama State Troopers physically prevented African-American pupils from entering one of the county's all-white high schools. On September 24, 1963, the court responded with an order temporarily restraining implementation of the executive order and prohibiting any interference with compliance with court orders, *United States v. Wallace,* 222 F. Supp. 485 (M.D. Ala. 1963) (five-judge court) (per curiam).

In February 1964, the plaintiffs filed an amended and supplemental complaint alleging that State Officials, including the State Board of Education, its members, the State Superintendent, and the Governor as President of the State Board, had asserted general control and supervision over all the public schools throughout the state of Alabama in order to continue the operation of a racially segregated school system. These State officials were made defendants in the *Lee v. Macon* litigation (Anthony T. Lee 1964).

As counsel for the plaintiffs in Alabama's school desegregation litigation, the noted civil rights attorney, Fred Gray, was a pivotal force in dismantling segregated public schools in the state of Alabama. The *Lee v. Macon* case resulted in the desegregation of all trade and junior colleges, the integration of all public elementary and secondary schools in Alabama, the desegregation of all institutions of higher learning and the merger of the Alabama Athletic Association (Caucasian) and the Alabama Interscholastic Athletic Association (African-American) (1967).

Lee v. Macon Applies to Special Education

Disproportionate representation of culturally and linguistically diverse (CLD) students in special education programs has been a national concern for nearly four decades. By mislabeling minority students and placing them in special education, they are deprived of a fair and equitable education because of the limiting nature of special education to a broader base and more rigorous curriculum. In 1968, the United States Office of Civil Rights began sampling school districts to discern if there were problems in this area. It found that African American students were *overrepresented* in special education programs, particularly in the categories of mental retardation and emotional disturbance (National Education Association, 2007).

According to the Education Commission of the States, "federal law mandates data collection and examination to determine race-based disproportionality in special education; no specific remedies are suggested to correct disparities once they are identified. While policy development and implementation are not yet widespread, states are currently employing a variety of methods to address the overrepresentation of minorities in special education" (Education Commission of the States 2003).

A *consent decree* is an agreement between the parties to address the identified legal issue before the courts. This chapter focuses on a case, *Lee v. Macon Special Education Consent Decree*, which sought to bring about equity and justice for African American students in Alabama, who were disproportionately represented in certain special education categories or exceptionalities. It extended the ruling of the original Lee vs. Macon case that dealt explicitly with school desegregation. This *consent decree* addressed disparities in learning opportunities for African American students who were inappropriately placed in special education programs that denied them access to a broader based educational system. Specifically, it sought to remedy the *de facto* segregation that was occurring by segregating disproportionate numbers of African American children in special education classes.

In 1997, United States District Court Judge Myron Thompson, Middle District of Alabama, through a judicial review of consent decrees, called up 12 cases against local school districts. Judge Thompson, on his own, determined that it was time to move forward toward closure and a declaration on unitary status for twelve local education agencies in school districts in the state of Alabama geographically located within the middle district of Alabama. Unitary status has a technical definition but simply it means that the school district has shown significant improvement in evaluating students for "exceptionality".

On February 3, 1998, the Court ordered the parties to report to the Court the status of all statewide issues. On July 31, 1998, the parties submitted their findings. The parties identified two statewide issues. The areas identified were: (1) special education—the overrepresentation of African American students in the mentally retarded exceptionality and emotional disturbance special education classification; and (2) underrepresentation of African Americans in the learning disabled and gifted and talented exceptionalities (Lee v. Macon Consent Decree 2000). The Consent Decree set out procedures to address the appropriate placement of all students. The procedures to be followed included: Steps to be incorporated in the prereferral process, referral process, evaluation procedures, eligibility criteria and awareness training (Lee v. Macon 2000).

The court declared the statewide issues identified in the *Lee v. Macon* judicial review unacceptable and according to Milloy, "this rural Black Belt state took the lead in mapping out an attack plan. Significantly, it was geared as much to improving how teachers taught and assessed all students as it was to how they taught and assessed Blacks" (Milloy 2003).

According to Devine, Dr. Stanley Trent from the University of Virginia assisted in fashioning remedies in the pre-referral stage and in focusing on teacher training. "The State, for its part, came to the table not just willing to talk but committed to addressing and attacking these issues in a meaningful way" (Devine).

In August 2000, the parties in the statewide litigation agreed upon a course of action to address the disproportionality issues. The *Lee v. Macon* Consent Decree was signed in the area of special education. The implications for educators, students, and social policy are profound, says Gary Orfield, professor of education and social policy at Harvard University. This is one of the far-reaching effects of the *Lee v. Macon* case. The nation has taken note at the progress of Alabama in this area. The National Education Association (NEA) published a full story on this issue in the *NEA Today*, January 2003. The article stated: "The statistics tell the tale: Nationally, African-American students show up in certain special education categories—the ones where the diagnosis is largely subjective—in numbers that so exceed their proportion in the general population, that some experts are now calling it a crisis" (National Education Association 2003).

"Blacks are nearly three times more likely than whites to be labeled mentally retarded (up to five times more in some states) and twice as likely to be labeled emotionally disturbed. Across the board the risks are higher for Black males than Black females. Even when accounting for the often-debilitating effects of poverty on early cognitive development, the overrepresentation is still there—and glaringly, according to researchers at the Civil Rights Project at Harvard University. In fact, the odds of being labeled "mentally retarded" actually increase for African-American boys in middle and upper income school districts" (National Education Association 2003).

According to Gary Orfield, "Black students in special education are far more likely than their white peers to be isolated from mainstream classes, stigmatized, and suspended from school, then become drop-outs, face unemployment, and go to jail" (National Education Association 2003).

The Alabama consent decree was entered into for the purpose of ensuring that students are appropriately placed and receiving appropriate services. While the *Lee v. Macon* litigation was initiated on behalf of African American students, the Consent Decree benefits all students by putting into place a uniform process and procedure that document the efforts of teachers in general education and in special education to ascertain the educational needs of students. Specifically, its goal is to rectify the overrepresentation of African American students in Mental Retardation (MR) and Emotional Disturbance (ED) Programs and the under representation of African American students in Specific Learning Disabilities (SLD) and Gifted and Talented (GT) Programs. As part of the *Lee v. Macon* Consent Decree, many changes have been made to carry out the provisions. Specifically, the Alabama State Department of Education (ALSDE), hereinafter referred to as SDE, required *Awareness Training* and made changes in the Pre-Referral Process, Referral Process, Evaluation Procedures and Eligibility Criteria, and Oversight/Reporting/Monitoring.

The Consent Decree requires the implementation of policies and practices that are designed to improve instruction, with the goal of improving student achievement. An area of focus was providing professional development activities related to awareness, instructional strategies, and behavioral interventions related to the over and underrepresentation issues.

As a result of the *Lee v. Macon* Consent Decree, the SDE trained all general education and special education teachers in the areas of instructional strategies and management of behavior. The decree also requires ongoing training and training for new professional employees. Training is provided by the local education agency. (Davis 2001).

"It was not meant to be a quick fix, nor an end in and of itself. But after more than a year of effort, state officials have charted small, encouraging signs of progress. The number of special education students overall has dropped; and the number of Black students identified for mental retardation decreased 2 percent (1,700 were re-identified as having specific learning disabilities and 400 "tested out" of special ed altogether). In addition, 500 fewer Black students were identified as emotionally disturbed" (Milloy 2003).

According to Milloy, "Indeed, in places where pieces of the reform had begun before the consent decree was even official, teachers say the results have been eye opening, even empowering. And, they add, at-risk kids are learning and succeeding" (Milloy 2003).

The great challenge was to allay the fears of more than 47,000 public school teachers who had to implement the mandates of the Consent Decree. The Alabama Education Association worked in partnership with the SDE to accomplish the overall goal. This was accomplished through intensive awareness training programs, the writing of articles in the *Alabama School Journal,* and answering a myriad of questions via telephone and e-mails from members of the Alabama Education Association (AEA).

The Alabama Education Association, through the Education Policy and Professional Practice (EPPP) Division, served as a pivotal force in assuring the teachers of the need to positively carry out the mandates of the Consent Decree. After the intensive involvement

TABLE 1 Total Population of Students in Special Education Based on Child Count 2000–2005 By Exceptionality and Race/Ethnicity

	Emotional Disturbance		Mental Retardation		Specific Learning Disabilities		Gifted	
	African American	White	African American	White	African American	White	African American	White
2000	1,959	2,851	13,368	6,704	15,106	26,232	2,870	18,076
2001	1,741	2,423	10,697	5,964	15,678	24,727	3,549	21,414
2002	1,519	2,101	9,351	5,271	16,316	23,238	4,480	24,217
2003	1,194	1,807	7,807	4,692	17,332	22,261	5,164	24,809
2004	1,007	1,540	6,337	4,265	18,782	21,738	5,751	25,282
2005	867	1,297	5,328	3,968	19,465	21,007	6,030	25,881

of the Alabama Education Association, professionals are successfully implementing the intent of the *Lee v. Macon Consent Decree*.

Successful Implementation

The successful implementation of the plans in the Consent Decree is evidenced by the results. In the area of *Mental Retardation*, the African American number count was reduced from 13,368 to 5,328 in comparison to the Whites whose number count was 6,704 and was reduced to 3,968. In the area of *Emotionally Disturbed*, the African American number count was reduced from 1,959 to 867 in comparison to the Whites whose number count was 2,851 and was reduced to 1,297. In the area of *Specific Learning Disabilities*, the African American number count was increased from 15,106 to 19,465 in comparison to the Whites whose number count was 26,232 and was reduced to 21,007. In the area of *Gifted*, the African American number count was increased from 2,870 to 6,030 in comparison to the Whites whose number count was 18,076 and was increased to 25,881 (The Alabama Department of Education—Special Education Services 2006). (See Table 1)

Summary

In the Sixth Annual Report of the SDE on the Implementation of the *Lee V. Macon Special Education Consent Decree*, it summarizes its success as follows:

> The DOE is encouraged by the successes of this state. Alabama has experienced a shift; not only in the numbers of students identified with SLD, ED, MR, and GT, but in the attitudes, beliefs, and practices regarding students with disabilities. The DOE is committed to continue compliance monitoring and providing professional development in order to continue the positive trends that have proven to reduce

disproportionality in SLD, ED, MR, and GT (The Alabama Department of Education—Special Education Services 2006).

Because significant progress was made, the state of Alabama was dismissed from the Special Component of the *Lee v. Macon* on March 8, 2007. The Alabama case is a model of justice in education. An injustice was recognized and addressed through the courts. The relief sought and given is a testament to the commitment of the *teaching profession* in Alabama. Not only was justice served in an area that was greatly needed but all of Alabama's children benefited from the measures taken by teachers and administrators. Alabama is a testament to what can be done when people of good faith work together to improve the lives of all citizens.

Bibliography

(1954). Brown v. Board of Education of Topeka, Supreme Court of the United States. **347 U.S. 483, 74 S. Ct. 686.**

(1964). Anthony T. Lee and Henry A. Lee, by Detroit Lee and Hattie M. Lee, their parents and next friends, et al., Plaintiffs, United States of America, Plaintiff and Amicus Curiae, v. Macon County Board of Education (Harry D. Raymond, Chairman, Madison Davis, John M. Davis, B. O. Dukes and F. E. Guthrie) and C. A. Pruitt, Superintendent of Schools of Macon County, Alabama, Defendants,. *LEXIS*, United States District Court for the Middle District of Alabama, Eastern Division. **1964 U. S. Dist. LEXIS 6653 231 F. Supp.743:** 231 F. Supp.743.

(1964). Anthony T. Lee and Henry A. Lee, by Detroit Lee and Hattie M. Lee, their parents and next friends, et al., Plantiffs, United States of America, Plantiff and Amicus Curiae, v. Macon County Board of Education (Harry D. Raymond, Chairman, Madison Davis, John M. Davis, B. O. Dukes and F. E. Guthrie) and C. A. Pruitt, Superintendent of Schools of Macon County, Alabama, Defendants. *LEXIS 6653*, United States District Court for the Middle District of Alabama, Eastern Division. **231 F. Supp.743;1964 U. S. Dist. LEXIS 6653:** 231 F. Supp.743.

(1967). Anthony T. Lee and Henry A. Lee, by Detroit Lee and Hattie M. Lee, their parents and next friends, et al., Plaintiffs, United States of America, Plaintiff and Amicus Curiae, v. Macon County Board of Education Defendants. *LEXIS*, United States District Court for the Middle District of Alabama, Eastern Division. **267 F. Supp. 458; 1967 U. S. Dist. LEXIS 8330:** 267 F. Supp. 458.

(1977). Anthony T. Lee et. al., Plaintiffs, United States of America, Plaintiff-Intervenor-Appellant, National Education Association, Inc., Plaintiff-Intervenor, v. Demopolis City School System et al., Defendants-Appellees, United States Court of Appeals, Fifth Circuit.

(1997). Anthony T. Lee, et al. plaintiffs, United States of America, plaintiff-intervenor and amicus curiae, National Education Association, Inc., plaintiff-intervenor, v. Phenix City Board of Education, et al., defendants-consent decree, District Court of the United States for the Middle District of Alabama, Eastern Division. **Civil Action No. 70-T 854.**

(2000). Anthony T. Lee, et. al Plaintiffs, United States of America, Plaintiff-Intervenor and Amicus Curiae, Nationalk Education Association, Plaintiff-Intervenor v Lee County Board of Education, Crenshaw County Board of Education, Middle District of Alabama, Northern Division. **C. A. No. 2455-N; Civil Action Nos. 845-E, 848-E through 855-E, 3099 - N, 3102 - N, 3103-N.**

(2006). Individuals with Disabilities Education Improvement Act of 2004 (IDEA),— Part II Department of Education 34 CFR Parts 300 and 301 Assistance to States for the Education of Children with Disabilities and Preschool Grants for Children With Disabilities; Final Rule: 46845.

Benn, A. (2001). Man Whose suit integrated schools buried. *Montgomery Advertiser.* Montgomery, AL.

Davis, T. D. (2001). "The Lee v. Macon Consent Decree." *Alabama School Journal:* 15.

Devine, K. S. *Alabama state-wide special education agreement: Presented at the minority issues in special education.* Conference Sponsored by the Civil Rights Project of Harvard University.

Education Commission of the States (2003). Addressing the Disproportionate Number of Minority Students in Special Education. Denver, CO, Education Commission of the States.

Milloy, M. (2003). "Truth in labeling." *NEA Today* **21:** 8–9.

National Education Association (2003). "Truth in Labeling." *NEA Today* (January, 2003).

National Education Association (2007). Truth in Labeling: Disproportionality in Special Education. Washington, DC: 48.

The Alabama Department of Education—Special Education Services (2006). The Sixth Annual Report on the implementation of the Lee v. Macon Special Education Consent Decree. Montgomery, Alabama: 7.

44

Majority-Minority Districts: A Reflection on the Merits of an Equal Protection Remedy

Arnold C. Lewis Jr.

> Are distinguishing patterns of political participation by race something govern-
> ment should aim to eliminate, sustain or do something about? Dianne Pinder-
> hughes (1995)

Race conscious policy historically has been very instrumental in the expansion of rights
and privileges to minorities in the United States. The thirteenth amendment abolishment
of slavery, the extension of citizenship via the fourteenth amendment, the fifteenth amendment granting of suffrage to African-Americans, and the civil rights legislation of the 1960s
are all generally viewed as successful examples of race conscious policy achieving several
desired goals. However, each of these attempts to empower African-Americans was followed by counter insurgent tactics by white opponents who feared an erosion of white privilege.[1] Thus, progressive policies designed to eliminate discriminatory behaviors and
outcomes often produce counter-productive racial behaviors as a consequence. The
endurance and severity of racial conservative backlash depends on how much behavioral
change is required by the affected parties and whether the policy inherently and overtly
stimulates racial division. Thus, every time we seek to address racial conflict in the polity
we must confront the question of whether race conscious public policies designed to miti-
gate a current conflict do not have the unintended consequence of making the existing
problem worse.

As the opening quote by Dianne Pinderhughes implies, the pursuit of equal protection
requires a measured and calculated assessment of the immediate and long-term consequences of state intervention. The following analysis will highlight the need for policy makers to be more deliberative in their efforts to address race-based equal protection violations.
The essay examines the consequences of the Justice Department's and civil rights leaders'
zealous and universal pursuit of equal protection in the political arena via the construction
of single member Majority-Minority Districts (MMDs). This equal protection strategy may
have proven to be an example when both common sense and legal precedent were ignored.

Thornburg and MMDs

The revision of section 2 of the Voting Rights Act of 1965 and the Supreme Court's decision in *Thornburg v Gingles* (1986) set the stage for increased consideration of race in the redistricting process. Thus, the Justice Department aggressively supported a policy that mandated states engage in race-based gerrymandering when they were found guilty of using electoral processes in racially polarized political contexts which violated the equal protection and voting rights of protected classes under the fourteenth and fifteenth amendments. In the *Thornburg* case, the equal protection violation was the result of the state of North Carolina utilizing multi-member district electoral processes to select some members to the state legislature. Voters in these districts elected multiple members to the statehouse via at-large (i.e., district wide) elections in accordance with the number of seats that had been allocated to their district. In the absence of racial group conflict this process seems fairly equitable; however, this process produced systematic dilution of black votes given the prevalence of racially polarized voting patterns during this time in many areas of the South. Thus, black voters would consistently vote as a bloc to elect a black candidate but because the white majority in the district also voted in bloc only for white candidates the process systematically impaired the ability of black voters to have an equal opportunity to elect candidates of their choice. In *Thornburg,* the Supreme Court ruled that when these districts produce systematic vote dilution based on race they should be considered unconstitutional violations of the equal protection clause of the fourteenth amendment.

The dilutive redistricting practices highlighted in *Thornburg* clearly and systematically submerged the political preferences and power of the protected class of minority voters to the will of the white majority via the disguise of democratic elections. Thus, it was clear to the judges in this case that when historical circumstances prompt voters to vote in racially polarized patterns the one man—one vote philosophy of equal protection (see *Baker v Carr 1962; Reynolds v. Sims 1964*) had to be modified to approximate one group—one vote (i.e., semi-proportional representation). Hence, the remedy imposed in this case was that North Carolina had to convert these large multi-member districts into smaller single-member districts in which the majority of voters in each district would elect one representative to serve in the state legislature. The equal protection value of this remedy is that it required the state to convert parts of the former multi-member districts into majority-minority single-member districts (MMDs) which would guarantee that black voters in these districts would have an equal opportunity to elect candidates of their choice. Although this decision seemed to imply that context matters when assessing claims of vote dilution, by 1992 this remedial policy became normal practice even in the absence of a state being found guilty of such violations because many states and the Justice Department interpreted the *Thornburg Decision* as a goal instead of a remedy. Thus, by the mid-1990s several states in the South[2] had created numerous majority minority districts to secure the election of minority candidates to their state legislatures or to the U.S. House of Representatives in an effort to "comply" with the *Thornburg Decision*. For example, during the 1980s the number of MMDs at the state level in the South increased to 233 from 126 in the 1970s (Grofman and Handley 1991). Similarly, in the wake of *Thornburg,* after the 1992 redistricting process was complete the South contained 18 congressional MMDs (a net increase of 13 from the 1980s). Thus, this policy led to a substantial increase in the "descriptive" representation[3] of African-Americans. For example, after 1992 there were 18 black representatives in Congress from the South and over 260 black state representatives serving in the region.[4]

The Supreme Court eventually declared some racial gerrymanders unconstitutional and placed significant restrictions on state ability to use this as a goal oriented policy to advance race equity in the electoral process (see *Shaw v Reno 1993*), but the overwhelming majority of these districts were not affected by these decisions.[5] Thus, given that racial gerrymanders are part of the contemporary U.S. political landscape (particularly in the South), this raises the question of whether this was an effective approach to achieve equal protection in the political process?

The Substantive Effects of Racial Gerrymanders

When evaluating the effectiveness of the racial redistricting strategy, one must be cognizant of the fact that representation and power are determined by context. Just as Hrebenar and Thomas (1990) state in their study of interest group influence that you can not equate presence with power, this rule applies in the legislative process as well. Thus, how is substantive influence determined? I contend that substantive influence is shaped by the legislative environment representatives confront. The nature and disposition of the participants in the legislative institution shape the opportunities for cooperation and shape the agenda that a majority of the participants are willing to consider. The agenda shaping majority that emerges is largely a function of coalition building among legislators who share common political and ideological interests. The probability that a representative's interests coincide with other members increases if his/her district shares similar constituent characteristics. However, if a representative comes from a district with atypical constituent characteristics, that lessens his/her chances of being a major partner in the agenda setting coalition.

Implicit in this view of legislator influence is the notion that a legislator's behavior is shaped by constituent composition, but his/her role in the legislative process is structured by the number of colleagues who represent similar constituencies.[6] Thus, representing an atypical district may lead to an alienating experience in the legislative process whereby your district's substantive interests are ignored because they are not "shared" interests. That has been the fear of many opponents of MMDs. The possible "ghettoization"[7] of black interests via the drawing of racially homogeneous districts prompted Guinier (1994) to speak of "legislative racism" being a probable outcome of the MMD policy.

Opponent fears of the outcomes of the MMD strategy begged the question of whether white legislators could be just as representative of black interests as black legislators. Several proponents of MMDs (Grofman 1995; Handley et al. 1994; and Walters 1992) cite that these districts empower minority groups and provide them with a more equitable voice in the political arena. The assumption here is that black interests are best represented by black officials and that the minority candidate's chances of being elected markedly increase in a MMD. This position has found substantial support in the literature.

David Lublin (1997) in a study of the impact of district racial composition on legislator liberalism, found district racial composition was the major determinant of electing black officials. Their probability of electoral success increased markedly as the black population moved from 40 to 55% of the district population. Also, Handley et al. (1994) found that all of the new black congresspersons from the South in 1992 were elected from newly drawn MMDs. This naturally challenged Swain (1993) and Thernstrom's (1987) claims that black candidates can get elected from predominantly white districts. Swain (1993) contends that forty percent of black members of the 102nd Congress were elected from predominantly white congressional districts. However, she failed to note the regional biases imbedded in her data: the districts she cited were mostly outside of the South.

Lublin's research also supported the claim that district racial composition affected legislator behavior. He found that Southern Democrats are more sensitive to minority interests as the minority population increases and they are surprisingly more responsive to district racial composition than their northern counterparts. Also, Southern Republicans assume more moderate positions in the legislature as the minority presence in their districts increases. It appears that race is a more salient factor in the electoral politics of the South than the rest of the nation. However, prior scholarship generally supported the notion that district racial composition had marginal to no affects on legislator voting behavior. For example, Whitby (1987) found the percentage of blacks in the electorate had no individual impact on legislator behavior, but may be spuriously influential via urban areas in the election of Democrats. Whitby and Gilliam (1991) and Fleisher (1993) also concluded that as of the 1980s the percentage of blacks in a district held little systematic influence on a representative's voting behavior. Related claims were forwarded by Grofman, Griffin and Glazer (1992) who found district racial composition may affect the election of Democrats, but did not have a consistent relationship with an elected representative's ideology. Later research by Whitby (1997) cautioned that district racial composition appears to affect black legislators only.

Overall, the generally marginal or bleak evidence in the literature regarding the influence of district racial composition on the voting behavior of white representatives serves as a spring board for supporting the MMD policy as an appropriate remedial strategy for equal protection violations in the electoral system. One of the key components of substantive representation is how responsive the representative is to his/her constituents' interests. The common finding in the literature is that black legislators are most sensitive to district racial composition. Furthermore, they assume policy positions that are more congruent with the black community than their white colleagues. This validates several assumptions of "Black Electoral Success Theory" about the authenticity of black candidates relative to white candidates campaigning for black votes. Lublin (1997) and Whitby (1997) find black representatives are more representative of black interests than even liberal/ progressive white representatives. Swain (1993) argues otherwise, that white progressives are just as representative of black interests as black officials. Yet, even at the state level several scholars have found that black state legislators are more responsive to black interests than their white colleagues (Herring 1990; Nelson 1991; Bratton and Haynie 1992; Button and Hedge 1996).

Thus, the question of whether whites can represent black interests has been answered with a tentative "yes" in favor of Swain (1993) and others. However if the question becomes are white legislators equally representative of black interests as black legislators, the literature leads one consistently to an answer of "no." Hence, the MMD policy may be the most appropriate tool for enhancing minority substantive representation given that MMDs lead to the election of the most authentic representatives of minority interests. This need to elect black officials to truly "maximize" the substantive interests of the minority community poses an interesting paradox for the minority community. The problem with the MMD policy is that there is evidence that a trade-off exists between the goals of maximizing the electoral fortunes of black and white Democrats (the predominant non-black supporters of black interests) in the redistricting process.

Racial Gerrymanders—A Solution with a Problem

Does the MMD policy sacrifice the electoral fortunes of white Democrats in favor of Republicans? White Democrats are essential coalition partners for black officials because they are more inclined to support black interests than Republicans. Lublin (1997) gave a word of caution concerning this endeavor when he stated that creating a new Republican opportunity reduces black substantive representation more than an MMD can enhance it. This referral to the importance of the partisan composition of the legislature was not lost on Swain (1993), Grofman et al (1992) and Grofman (1997). They all cited that black interests relied heavily on Democratic legislative majorities. Research in the area of racial redistricting offers some interesting conclusions about the influence of redistricting on partisan advantages. The creation of MMDs may have some conservative and partisan externalities that may have proven to be formidable obstacles to the newly empowered black electorate. Several scholars have concluded that creating MMDs led to Republican gains in the South at both the state and congressional level (Brace et al. 1987; Hill 1995). Republicans gain from this strategy because white Democratic candidates cannot effectively compete with Republican candidates in the overwhelmingly white, conservative, homogeneous districts that emerge when black voters are taken out of formerly biracial and more diverse districts and packed into newly created MMDs to promote the election of black candidates. White Republicans can run far more conservative campaigns than white Democrats and conservative voters have greater confidence in the conservative credentials of the contemporary Republican Party. Thus, whiter districts increase Republican electoral opportunities. Grofman (1997) argued that this partisan effect was the most important unintended consequence of the MMD strategy. Today the South serves as the strongest base of electoral support and representation for the Republican Party.

Critics of this policy contend that Republicans were quite aware of this paradox and in some instances closely allied themselves with black legislators in support of MMDs (Brace et al. 1987). Additionally, claims have been made that Republican control of the Justice Department during the 1980s and early 1990s was instrumental in the department's aggressiveness in this matter (Grofman 1995; Peterson 1995). Although Grofman (1995) found no evidence of a Republican plot; Guinier (1994) found some evidence of an ad hoc aggressive posture in the department's voting rights enforcement procedures. Guinier cites that the Republican Justice Department had no consistent policy on voting rights enforcement. She found one case where the department failed to deny preclearance to a Louisiana redistricting proposal clearly designed to maximize Republican interests at the expense of creating a MMD.[8] The Louisiana case is seemingly at odds with the normally supportive posture of Republicans when drawing MMDs. Yet, context played a significant role in the Louisiana position. It appears that Republicans like white Democrats are wary of creating MMDs when they are likely to harm incumbent partisans' district boundaries and electoral chances. The Republican Governor of Louisiana feared that the drawing of a second MMD would severely alter an incumbent Republican congressional district. However, in most cases because Demo-crats were in a posture of incumbency protection, Republicans saw an advantage in supporting the creation of MMDs to break the Democratic monopoly on congressional seats. Thus, Republicans have had a consistent position on MMDs. Republicans have been strategically supportive of this policy, not because of its intent to promote black interests, but because of the possible implications it would have on enhancing Republican interests. This partisan result obstructs the influence of newly elected black legislators because of the divergent interests and constituencies of the Republican Party (Brown 1995; Button and Hedge 1996).

Conclusion: Equal Protection or Apartheid?

The Democratic Party has long been the central institution in the practice of Southern politics. However, the role and influence of today's Democratic Party is vastly different from its historic role. The Southern Democratic Party was initially a white man's party. By eliminating its opposition (Republicans and Blacks) during the post-civil war era from the political process, it was able to develop a "so-called democratic country without an opposition party, a country in which, for practical purposes, there has been but one (dominant) party from that day to this" (Black and Black 1987:p.232).

The advent of the Civil Rights movement prompted the emergence of a new southern democracy. This era of social change had a dual effect on the Democratic Party in the South. First, white southerners' loyalty to the Democratic Party began to decline because of the national party's emerging progressive position on race (Lamis 1988; Carmine and Stimson 1989; Huckfeldt and Kohfeld 1989; Edsall and Edsall 1992). Secondly, the electoral reforms of the Civil Rights movement promoted a massive influx of southern blacks into the party. The combination of these forces led to changes in the Southern Democratic Party's position on race and moderation of its extreme conservative views.

The impact of these forces can be seen in the changes in the campaign practices of Democrats in the region. In general, Democratic candidates no longer run campaigns of fear on the importance of maintaining white supremacy. The typical platform consists of conservative aspects of fiscal restraint, low taxes, school prayer, and pro-death penalty; while promoting some progressive themes such as equal opportunity, educational advancement and environmental protection. Thus in the "New South" the campaigns of white Democrats can generally be characterized as a fusion of a progressive agenda with the traditional conservative agenda (Black and Black 1987; Glaser 1996). This fusion is needed in order to secure the core support of blacks and forty to forty five percent of the white vote to win elections. Thus, the Democratic Party has gone from an extreme position of promoting racial exclusion to being dependent on racial inclusion to win electoral office.

Southern Democrats are essentially engaged in the building of biracial political coalitions symbolic of a high wire act. In the post-civil rights era southern democracy has essentially become a politics of balance and compromise. These seemingly fragile coalitions have allowed the party to maintain an increasingly threatened plurality status in the region, but it is no longer the party of the South. The importance of these fragile biracial coalitions to the survival of the Southern Democratic Party indicates the importance of constituent characteristics to any analysis of legislative behavior. The dual importance of these two groups to the electoral fortunes of white Democrats is reflected in the dual platform of the party. These factors indicate that any changes or variations in the need/opportunity to secure the support of one of the groups should alter a specific legislator's commitment to the dual platform accordingly. Specifically, changing the racial composition of the district should alter a white Democratic candidate's commitment to the dual platform in favor of the group whose share of the electorate has increased within the district.

James Glaser's (1996) analysis of campaign politics in the South validates this position. Glaser asserted that the racial context of the district determined the electoral strategies pursued by Democratic and Republican candidates alike. Thus, if candidates shape their campaign strategies based on a district's racial composition, it is not incredulous to conceive of district racial composition shaping legislators governing strategies. Hence, maximizing the number of white Democrats elected in biracial contexts and committed to the dual platform is equally important to minority substantive representation as the goal to maximize the number of black elected officials.

Which representative of this biracial coalition is most desirable should not be the question of civil rights activists and proponents of the MMD policy. The literature clearly indicates blacks represent blacks better than whites. However, at the same time scholarship and reality have shown that only a limited number MMDs can be drawn (due to geographic and legal constraints) and each one comes at potentially great cost to building and maximizing the size of the biracial legislative coalition within the ranks of the Democratic Party. Thus, the more substantive question is when should we value the election of a black official more than the costs to the potential viability of the Democratic coalition?

The answer to this question requires one to engage in case specific contextual evaluations of the merits of having a black versus a white representative. Context should determine the scope of implementing the MMD policy. Similar sentiment has taken root in the courts as they have overturned racial gerrymanders that were not designed as remedial strategies in cases of flagrant violations of the spirit and provisions of the Voting Rights Act (VRA). The broad sweeping implementation efforts of the Republican Justice Dept. in the early nineties regardless of concrete violations of the VRA placed the integrity of the Act at risk along with long term black political influence. Given the dual utility of black and white Democrats, securing the election of a black official should only become the predominant objective in racially hostile contexts.

Racially hostile environments are an overall threat to minority interests given, white representatives (both Democratic and Republican) from these areas are less likely to be responsive to minority groups. In such contexts where the potential for biracial coalition building in the electorate is virtually non-existent, the interests of the embattled minority may only be promoted and protected via a MMD. The elected minority official may find little collegial support among fellow members of his/her delegation, but they are capable of nurturing coalitional ties with fellow partisans external to their state. This represents a case were the minority group's substantive influence within a given state's congressional delegation is maximized at virtually no costs. The possibility of losing white Democrats in successive congressional elections in such contexts is a minimal cost due to the lack of support the community received from white Democrats in those areas.

Racially moderate or neutral contexts represent environments whereby racial gerrymanders may be quite costly to black interests. Although there may be an absence of minority officials in these areas, this does not necessarily mean minority political power is marginalized in such contexts. That power may be channeled through highly responsive white Democrats that rely on biracial coalitions for electoral success. Even if one wanted to secure the election of black candidates, MMDs may be unnecessary given that minority influence districts (MIDs) are effective at electing blacks and are less costly to the overall electoral fortunes of Democrats.[9] Thus, minority substantive representation in such contexts is maximized by drawing several influence districts which have the potential to elect white as well as black candidates who are jointly responsive to minority interests in the legislature.

The key point here is that I believe MMDs should be utilized to maximize the overall substantive influence of minorities and not merely to secure the presence of minority officials. The policy's utility is limited to contexts where minority political influence is descriptively, symbolically and substantively suppressed within the current political context. Therefore, the implementation of the policy should be limited to these circumstances. It is in such cases that an MMD is warranted to promote democratic ideals of equal participation and access that serve to protect the rights and interests of electorally disenfranchised groups. It is in such contexts I believe, contrary to Hrebenar and Thomas (1990), that presence becomes power.

Bibliography

Alt, James E. 1994. "The Impact of the Voting Rights Act on Black and White Voter Registration in the South." In *Quiet Revolution: The Impact of the Voting Rights Act 1965–1990, ed.* Chandler Davidson and Bernard Grofman. Princeton, NJ: Princeton University Press.

Black, Earl and Merle Black. 1987. *Politics and Society in the South.* Cambridge, MA: Harvard University Press.

Black, Earl and Merle Black. 1992. *The Vital South: How Presidents are Elected.* Cambridge, Mass: Harvard University Press.

Brace, Kimball, Bernard Grofman and Lisa Handley. 1987. "Does Redistricting Aimed to Help Blacks Necessarily Help Republicans?" *Journal of Politics* 49:169–85.

Bratton, Kathleen and Kerry L. Haynie. 1992. "Do differences Matter? A Study of Race and Gender in State Legislatures." Presented at the Annual Meeting of American Political Science Association, Chicago, IL.

Brown, Robert T. 1995. "Party Cleavages and Welfare Effort In The American States." *American Political Science Review* 89:23–33.

Button, James and David Hedge. 1996. "Legislative Life in the 1990s: A Comparison of Black and White State Legislators." *Legislative Studies Quarterly* 21(2):199–218.

Carmines, Edward G. and James A. Stimson. 1989. *Issue Evolution: Race and the Transformation of American Politics.* Princeton, NJ: Princeton University Press.

Davidson, Roger H. and Walter J.Oleszek. 1998. *Congress and Its Members 6th ed.* Washington, DC.: CQ Press.

Edsall, Thomas Byrne and Mary D. Edsall. 1992. *Chain Reaction: The Impact of Race, Rights, and Taxes on American Politics.* New York: W.W. Norton & Company.

Fleisher, Richard. 1993. "Explaining the Change in Roll-Call Voting Behavior of Southern Democrats." *Journal of Politics* 55(2):327–341.

Gimpel, James G. 1996. *Legislating the Revolution: The Contract with America in its First 100 Days.* Boston: Allyn and Bacon.

Glaser, James M. 1996. *Race, Campaign Politics, and the Realignment in the South.* New Haven: Yale University Press.

Grofman, Bernard. 1995. "Shaw v Reno and The Future of Voting Rights." *Political Science* 28(1):27–36.

Grofman, Bernard. 1997. *Race and Redistricting in the 1990s.* New York: Agathon Press.

Grofman, Bernard and Lisa Handley. 1991. "The Impact of the Voting Rights Act On Black Representation In Southern State Legislatures." *Legislative Studies Quarterly* 26:111–129.

Grofman, Bernard, Robert Griffin and Amihai Glazer. 1992. "The Effect of Black Population On Electing Democrats and Liberals To the House of Representatives." *Legislative Studies Quarterly* 17(3):365–379.

Guinier, Lani. 1994. *Tyranny of the Majority: Fundamental Fairness in Representative Democracy.* New York: The Free Press.

Handley, Lisa and Bernard Grofman. 1994. "The Impact of the VRA on Minority Representation: Black Officeholding in Southern State Legislatures and Congressional Delegations." In *Quiet Revolution: The Impact of the Voting Rights Act 1965–1990,* ed. Chandler Davidson and Bernard Grofman. Princeton, NJ: Princeton University Press.

Herring, Mary. 1990. "Legislative Responsiveness to Black Constituents in Three Deep South States." *Journal of Politics* 52(3):740–58.

Hill, Kevin A. 1995. "Does the Creation of Majority Black Districts Aid Republicans? An Analysis of the 1992 Congressional Elections in Eight Southern States." *Journal of Politics* 57:384–401.

Hinckley, Barbara. 1988. *Stability and Change in 4th ed.* New York: Harper & Row Publishers, Inc.

Hrebenar, Ronald J. and Clive S. Thomas. 1990. "Interest Groups in the States." In *Politics in the American States 5th ed.* Virginia Gray, Herbert Jacob and Robert B. Albritton. Glenview, IL: Scott, Foresman and Co.

Huckfeldt, Robert and Carol Kohfeld. 1989. *Race and the Decline of Class in American Politics.* Chicago: University of Illinois Press.

Koetzle, William. 1998. "The Impact of Constituency Diversity Upon the Competitiveness of U.S. House Elections, 1962–96." Legislative Studies Quarterly 23(4):562–573.

Lamis, Alexander. 1988. *The Two-Party South.* New York: Oxford University Press.

Lublin, David. 1997. *The Paradox of Representation: Racial Gerrymandering and Minority Interests in Congress.* Princeton, NJ: Princeton University Press.

Nelson, Albert J. 1991. *Emerging Influentials in State Legislatures: Women, Blacks, and Hispanics.* New York: Praeger.

Peterson, Paul. 1995. *Classifying By Race.* Princeton, NJ: Princeton University Press.

Pinderhughes, Dianne M. 1995. "The Voting Rights Act-Whither History?" *Political Science* 28(1): 55–56.

Pitkin, Hanna. 1967. *The Concept of Representation.* Berkeley: University of California Press.

Swain, Carol. 1993. *Black Faces, Black Interests.* Cambridge: Harvard University Press.

Thernstrom, Abigail. 1987. *Whose Votes Count: Affirmative Action and Minority Voting Rights.* Cambridge: Harvard University Press.

Walters, Ronald. 1992. "Two Political Traditions: Black Politics in the 1990s." In *Ethnic Politics and Civil Liberties, ed.* Lucius Barker. New Brunswick, NJ: Transactions Publishers.

Whitby, Kenny J. 1997. *The Color of Representation: Congressional Behavior and Black Interests.* Ann Arbor: University of Michigan Press.

Whitby, Kenny and Franklin D. Gilliam. 1991."A Longitudinal Analysis of Competing Explanations for the Transformation of Southern Congressional Politics." *Journal of Politics* 53(2): 504–518.

Court Cases

Baker v. Carr. 1962. 369 U.S. 186.
Hayes v. Louisiana. 1996. 936 F. Supp. 369. W.D. La.
Johnson v. Mortham. 1996. 926 F. Supp. 1460. N.D. Fla.
Major v. Treen. 1983. 582 F. Supp. 325. E.D. La.
Miller v. Johnson. 1995. 115 S. Ct. 2475, 2504.
Reynolds v Simms. 1964. 377 U.S. 533.
Shaw v. Hunt. 1996. 116 S. Ct 1894.
Shaw v. Reno. 1993. 509 U.S. 630.
Thornburg v. Gingles. 1986. 478 U.S. 30
Vera v. Bush. 1996. 933 F. Supp. 1341 S.D. Tex.

Endnotes

1. See Whitby (1997) for a complete discussion of how the Supreme Court's restrictive interpretation of the civil was amendments and civil rights acts (of which the Civil Rights Act of 1875 was declared unconstitutional) undermined the intentions of their advocates. Also, several scholars such as Huckfeldt and Kohfeld (1989), Carmines and Stimson (1989) and Black and Black (1987, 1992) reveal how the 1960s Civil Rights agenda dealigned the party system due to white conservative dissatisfaction with the Democratic Party. This defection created the emerging partisan conflict that overlaps the racial divide in modern American politics. Furthermore, James Alt (1994) reveals that the Voting Rights Act's black voter registration efforts initiated a counter registration drive among white voters opposed to black enfranchisement.

2. In this study, the South is defined as the eleven states comprising the old confederacy: Alabama, Arkansas, Florida, Georgia, Louisiana, Mississippi, N. Carolina, S. Carolina, Tennessee, Texas, and Virginia.

3. Descriptive representation is simply that a true representative of a group is one who shares similar descriptive traits with the group (i.e., looks like the group). See Pitkin (1967).

4. Source: Table No. 452 U.S. Statistical Abstracts (1994).

5. Due to further litigation in the wake of the *Shaw v. Reno* (1993) decision, several Southern states have redrawn their districts during the mid to late 1990s. North Carolina redrew its districts for the 1998 elections (*Shaw v Hunt* 1996). However the following states redrew their districts by 1996: FL (*Johnson v Mortham* 1996); GA (*Miller v Johnson* 1995); LA (*Hayes v Louisiana* 1996); and TX (*Vera v Bush* 1996). *Miller v Johnson* (1995) declared that drawing districts solely on the basis of race that are not narrowly tailored to meet the compelling interests of VRA compliance was unconstitutional. Thus, all race based districts are not unconstitutional.

6. See (Hinckley 1988; Davidson and Oleszek 1998; Koetzle 1998; Gimpel 1996) for general discussion of how district constituent factors such as race, urbanization and income can determine legislator voting behavior.

7. Term utilized by Carol Swain in her book: *Black Faces Black Interests,* to describe the possible alienation of minority interests in the legislative process when those interests are solely articulated by minority representatives from a limited number of MMDs.

8. See the case of *Major v. Treen* (1983).

9. Minority influence districts are characterized as districts where minority voters are not a majority, but are present in sufficient numbers to influence electoral outcomes. See Lublin (1997) for his discussion of the probability of electing blacks increasing as the racial composition of the district goes from the 40% threshold to 55%. He notes that at 45% to 50% black, a black candidate's chances range from 28% to 60%. Hence excessively black districts waste black political power.

45

The Rise and Stall of the Voting Rights Revolution

Arnold C. Lewis Jr.

Since the late 1960s, U.S. civil rights leaders with the support of the Department of Justice have sought vigorous enforcement of the Voting Rights Act of 1965. Their combined efforts to regulate voter registration, voter education, and the electoral process has given rise to a substantial minority presence in national, state, and local political institutions in the United States. One could say that the regulation of our electoral system has conferred the full rights to petition and participate in government upon African-Americans and other minority groups that have long been available to white citizens. However, the substantive value of this recently acquired civic equity is still questionable.

For many persons involved in the civil rights movement, the passage of the Voting Rights Act (i.e., VRA) represented more than a validation of the Fifteenth Amendment right to vote. It was more than a moment of opportunity to redistribute civic rights in a more equitable manner reflective of the United States's classical liberal creed. The passage of this legislation had a more substantive meaning: the opportunity to transform the governance (i.e., the discourse and operation of the public square) in not only the South, but the United States at large via the election of black officials that would have the power to enact the progressive ideas of the civil rights movement.

Lani Guinier (1994) contends that this transformational view of black electoral empowerment is rooted in a "Black Electoral Success Theory" that posits four general assumptions:

1. Black officials are authentic representatives of blacks and black interests because of their common cultural experiences. Thus there is some value in descriptive representation.
2. The creation of MMDs promotes greater electoral participation from minority groups because of the genuine possibility that they can elect a candidate of their choice.
3. The creation of MMDs promotes the election of black officials; thus breaking the racial barriers of the electoral process caused by racially polarized voting. This process helps integrate black interests into the legislative process. The increase in black participation in decision making over time begins to lessen white fears of black empowerment.

4. Black officials are more responsive to the needs and concerns of black constituents. This responsiveness will ultimately lead to policy reform because of the strong and cohesive civil rights, redistributive and community based agendas of black officials.

(Guinier 1994:58–60)[1]

It has been 43 years since the passage and implementation of this legislation; thus, a historic reflection on the degree to which this more progressive transformational vision was or has been realized is warranted. Thus, what follows is a brief review of the legal-historic record of the VRA. That record seems to indicate that the transformational legacy of the act is a mixed bag. As outlined in the following sections of this essay, the VRA historically has enjoyed substantial support from the Department of Justice and federal courts in instances where legal controversies focus on procedurally transformative questions (i.e., election rules/laws, election administration, voter registration, etc.). However, in the early 1990s when the Department of Justice sought to unleash the substantive transformational potential of the act via aggressive (egregious in some cases) racial gerrymandering and arguments that the act covered changes in the distribution of powers amongst elected officials, the federal courts began to object to what they viewed as "expansive" interpretations of the law. One might conclude that Supreme Court opposition to egregious racially gerrymandered legislative districts was based on a reasonable standard of equity under the Equal Protection Clause. However, its opposition to apply the VRA to instances where local officials reallocate power among their respective offices to dilute the influence of newly elected minority colleagues (i.e., legislative racism) violates the progressive intent and legacy of the act. Hence, the transformational momentum of the Voting Rights Revolution that began in 1965 has stalled in the wake of the Court's refusal to allow the substantive spirit of the law to prevail when members of the protected classes under the act (i.e., racial and language minorities) seek to confront legislative racism.

The Rise of the VRA as a Transformational Force

The VRA of 1965 was an extension of two landmark cases on representation in American constitutional history: namely *Baker v. Carr* (1962) and *Reynolds v. Sims* (1964). Both of these cases dealt with the achievement of fair and equal representation by promoting the implementation of the one person one vote philosophy on the American electoral landscape. Most of the electoral systems in the South were at odds with this objective because of their over-representation of rural areas and suppression of black political participation. However, with the passage of the VRA of 1965 by an overwhelming majority in Congress, southern electoral politics went through some revolutionary changes triggered by the Justice department. The VRA originally had 3 goals it sought to achieve:

1. The VRA sought to abolish the use of literacy tests as a barrier to voting. This barrier was customarily enforced via a double standard for whites and blacks.

2. The legislation called for the Justice Department to dispatch federal marshals as observers to end the denial of voting rights to blacks in certain areas of the South.
3. The VRA included provisions requiring jurisdictions covered by section 5 to submit any proposed changes in their electoral systems, regardless of the level of government involved, to the Justice Department for "preclearance", to ensure that the proposed changes do not undermine minority voting rights.[2]

(Grofman 1990:p9–10)

Although the VRA passed Congress with an overwhelming majority, the legislation received no support from southern Democrats in congress or in the state legislatures. Southern elites increasingly began to rely on other methods to maintain political control primarily via the redistricting and apportionment processes. Thus, one could observe an increased usage of multi-member districts and at-large elections.[3] These structures were designed to dilute the potential influence of the "new" black electorate. A classic case of such resistance was the Mississippi State Legislature's efforts to enact retaliatory legislation to undermine the VRA. The Mississippi legislature in 1966 responded to the VRA by passing what Frank Parker (1990) calls "massive resistance legislation." The legislation achieved the following objectives:

1. The state's congressional districts were racially gerrymandered to break up potential concentrated populations of black influence.
2. The legislation changed the methods of election and electoral rules for local level offices (i.e., increased the use of at-large elections and appointed officials).
3. The legislation also increased the number of state legislative seats that were elected via the combination of multi-member districts and at-large elections.

(Parker 1990)

These changes were subsequently challenged by black candidates and voters and eventually adjudicated by the Supreme Court in *Allen v State Board of Elections* (1969). The Court ruled in favor of the plaintiffs by stating that such changes in election law were subject to the Justice Department's section 5 preclearance screening. This established the grounds for future challenges of the intensified usage of disfranchisement devices in response to the expansion of black voting strength. Several cases such as *Connor v. Johnson* (1971) in Mississippi; *United States v Georgia* (1973); *White v Register* (1973) and *Graves v Barnes* (1974) in Texas were challenges to increased usage of at-large elections and multi-member districts to dilute black voting strength. All of these cases were decided in favor of the plaintiffs and paved the way for the extension of the VRA in 1970 and beyond.

Subsequent revisions of the VRA in 1975 and 1982 allowed for the expansion of the scope and power of the legislation. Each expansive effort has been designed to achieve a more equitable distribution of political rights. The 1975 revisions allowed Hispanics and other minority groups to seek protection under its provisions. However, the most important reforms were the 1982 revisions of section 2 that "prohibited the use of any electoral device that would have the purpose or effect of diluting minority voting strength" (Grofman 1990). This new language made it easier for minority groups to enhance their electoral position because no longer were they required to show discriminatory intent, but merely a discriminatory effect for an electoral system/practice to be in violation of the law.[4]

In conjunction with the section 2 revisions, the Supreme Court's ruling in *Thornburg v. Gingles* (1986) replaced the "totality of circumstances" test for proving the case of minority vote dilution with a simple three pronged test under section 2:

1. Can a majority-minority single member district be drawn?
2. Is voting racially polarized?
3. Is the level of white crossover voting so low that minority candidates usually lose?

(Grofman 1990:p20)

These events paved the way for the creation of majority-minority districts (MMDs) which have been viewed as the best policy for increasing African-American representation within southern communities, statehouses and congressional delegations in the 1980s and 1990s. Thus, ironically the redistricting process continued to serve as the main instrument of managing the potential of the African-American electorate to influence southern politics. Initially redistricting was used to minimize African-American influence via various vote dilution tactics, but after 1982 the process was being used as a tool by the Justice Department to maximize African-American influence.

The Results of the Revolution

The passage and enforcement of the VRA of 1965 has been the key to the rise of biracial democracy in the South. For example, in 1964 only 43.1% of the eligible African-American population was registered to vote, but by 1985 that number had increased to 60.8% (Alt 1994). Thus, the scope of participation was widened by this landmark example of race conscious public policy. Similarly, the section 2 revision by Congress in 1982 sought to further revolutionize southern politics by focusing on the outcomes of this widened participation. The Justice Department began to implement the new interpretation of section 2 during the mid 1980s. The new interpretation called for the creation of Majority-Minority Districts (i.e., MMDs) in areas where there was a large minority population such that redistricting goals of compactness and contiguity would not be violated.

MMDs were designed to increase the ability of minority groups to elect "their preferred candidate" by assuring that they comprise the majority of the electorate within the district. This became the Justice Department's solution for minority group charges of vote diluting practices in the construction of single-member districts. Vote dilution was principally the result of racial bloc voting in majority white districts that undermined the electoral power of minority constituents. This policy secured immediate increases in "nominal" representation for minority groups. African-American representation in southern statehouses increased from 3 in 1965 to 176 in 1985 (Grofman and Handley 1991). This was largely due to the growth in registered African-American voters coupled with an increase in the number of MMDs at the state level from 126 in the 1970s to 233 in the 1980s (Grofman and Handley 1991). The same policy produced similar results on the congressional level in the 1990s. Prior to 1992 there were 5 MMDs in the South, but after the redistricting proceedings there were 18. Thus, the southern congressional delegations that contained only 4 African-American members prior to 1992, swelled to 18 immediately following the 1992 elections.

Overall, as a result of these revolutionary actions, the number of African-American elected officials in the South[5] increased from 565 in 1970 to 5,620 by 2001 (see Table 1)[6] Each of the southern states experienced a significant rate of change in the racial composition of their political and administrative institutions. However, some states in the region have been affected more than other states by this revolution. For example, in several states such as GA, LA, MS, SC, and TX the change in the number of black elected officials from 1970 to 2001 has been about twelve-fold (on average). Even in the remaining states, the average change has been about six-fold.

TABLE 1 Black Elected Officials in the South by State 1970, 2001			
State	**1970**	**2001**	**% Change**
Alabama	86	756	779%
Arkansas	55	502	813%
Florida	36	243	575%
Georgia	40	611	1428%
Louisiana	64	705	1002%
Mississippi	81	892	1001%
N. Carolina	62	491	692%
S. Carolina	38	534	1305%
Tennessee	38	180	374%
Texas	29	460	1486%
Virginia	36	246	583%
Total	565	5620	895%

Source: Data derived from the Statistical Abstracts of the U.S. and the Joint Center for Political and Economic Studies.

This growth in African-American officials at the sub-national level has primarily been the result of the revolution in political participation, in terms of voting and office-holding, in places traditionally most hostile to African-American empowerment: the small cities, towns and rural counties of the Black Belt. Bernard Grofman and Chandler Davidson

(1994) clearly established that the change in municipal election structures from at-large to single-member districts systems was instrumental to the rise of African-American elected officials. Furthermore, the greatest impact was felt in the majority-black cities and counties of the region (i.e., the Black Belt).[7]

The rise in African-American voter participation and subsequently in the number of African-American elected officials has led to a moderation of the traditionally racial conservative politics of the region (see Herring 1990; Lublin 1997; Whitby 1997; Whitby and Gilliam 1991). However, it would be misguided to conclude that moderation has produced substantial transformation in the operation and results of southern political institutions (i.e., particularly at the local level). For example, in areas where African-Americans are not the majority of the population very little has changed since 1965. Grofman and Davidson (1994) found that majority white cities under 10,000 (many within the Black Belt) were far less likely to have eliminated the use of at-large electoral schemes. They specifically observed that African-American representation was abysmally low in hundreds of very small majority-white jurisdictions in North Carolina and Mississippi. However, they noted African-American representational equity began to increase in cities of 10,000 or more. This evidence clearly indicates that in some states and communities, voting rights legislation and litigation has had a limited (if any) effect on dismantling the barriers to African-American access to political power in rural areas.[8] Thus, as Grofman and Davidson contend:

> The dearth of black representation in the smaller cities of the South is particularly noteworthy because these communities, especially the very small ones, may be those where conditions of life for blacks have changed the least since 1965. If so, the absence of black participation in governance may be especially critical. (Grofman and Davidson 1994, 316)

This possibility becomes especially noteworthy when one realizes that the number of African-Americans still living in small communities is considerable. Arnold Lewis (2008) illuminated this phenomenon when he found that only 47.4% of the South's African-American residents live in communities of at least 25,000 persons. Furthermore, this number drops substantially to only 39.2% if you focus on the states that were initially subjected to the preclearance provisions of the VRA.[9] Thus, given the transformational goals of the Voting Rights Movement this data reveals that the revolution is far from complete.

The Stall

Despite the nominal explosion in black representation, the substantive transformational tenets of "Black Electoral Success Theory" have been quite elusive. Several decisions of the Supreme Court in the nineties have made the achievement of these goals even more difficult. For example, in the case of *Shaw v. Reno 1993*, the Court (in a 5–4 ruling) made it clear that it was becoming increasingly uncomfortable with substantive transformational objectives of the Voting Rights Revolution. In this case, white constituents from North Carolina challenged the constitutionality of the twelfth congressional district in their state. The district was designed to be the state's second MMD, but was easily one of the most egregious racial gerrymanders ever drawn. This district stretched over 160 miles across the state and at many points it was no wider than the freeway it draped (I-85). The white plaintiffs argued that this racial gerrymander disenfranchised white voters in the district by violating the principle of one-man one-vote. The district was designed with intentions to increase the power of African-American voters. The lower courts in North Carolina felt the white constituents had no standing; however, the Supreme Court ruled otherwise.

The Supreme Court ruled that the white citizens could challenge the districting process via the "equal protection clause" of the Fourteenth Amendment on grounds of questioning the propriety of race based state legislation (Grofman 1995). Justice O'Connor clearly articulated the opinion of the court in *Shaw v Reno* (1993) when she stated:

> Any policies that are grounded in race classification can be challenged constitutionally.

The Court concluded that redistricting practices that created bizarrely shaped districts which are not the result of any other motivation but race demands the same strict scrutiny given to other state laws that classify citizens by race (*Shaw v Reno* 1993). The Court viewed this as racial gerrymandering and reminded the actors in the redistricting process that the appearance/shape of a district was just as important as who was in it (McClain and Stewart 1995). As a result, several districts drawn during the 1991 and 1992 rounds of redistricting were struck down and reconstructed.[10] However, in most cases the newer districts still were constructed with the intent of increasing minority representation to maintain compliance with the desires of the Justice Department.

Although the *Shaw* decision became an obstacle toward assured implementation of the MMD policy, it did not declare MMDs unconstitutional nor overturn *Thornburg v Gingles* (1986). However, *Shaw* narrowed the discretion available to actors in the redistricting process by prompting officials to pursue this objective in the context of narrowly tailoring the districts to fulfill a compelling state interest (*Shaw v. Hunt* 1995). The compelling state interest in this case is compliance with the Justice Department's desire to enforce section 5 and 2 of the VRA.[11]

It is apparent that none of the adversaries of MMDs shared the Justice Department's concern with the possible impacts that such districts may have on the policy making process and representative government. The extensive criticism of MMDs by the courts made them vulnerable and subject to a lengthy debate over their necessity and consequences. Grofman (1995) argues that much of this controversy could have been avoided had the courts not used the racial component of these districts as the basis for challenging their legality. These districts could have easily been questioned solely on the basis of geographic compactness and contiguity. Grofman (1995) also contends that the racial criticism is inconsistent with the Thornburg test that seeks to resolve the ills of racial bloc voting via race based remedies (i.e., MMDs). However, the debate over the necessity of this race based remedy of enhancing minority representation, although constitutionally resolved in *Miller v Johnson* (1995),[12] still raises some interesting concerns. These concerns not only question the assumption that creating MMDs enhances the political influence of blacks, but also the propriety of race based policies when seeking to resolve racial problems.

A more troubling example of the stalling of the revolution can be found in the case of *Presley v. Etowah County Commission* (1992). The Supreme Court, in a 6-3 ruling that affirmed the District Court's decision but discredited its argument, gave more freedom to local governments covered by the Voting Rights Act to make changes in the allocation of power among officials within their political structure without requiring pre-clearance from the Attorney General. The controversy surrounded actions taken by two Alabama counties to change the responsibilities of county commissioners after or prior to the implementation of consent decrees imposed under the Voting Rights Act that led to the election of African-Americans to their respective commissions. The effect of the changes was to prevent the newly elected African-American commissioners from exercising the same powers/influence historically afforded members of each commission in areas of road construction, maintenance, and the budgeting for these operations. These changes were considered intolerable efforts to dilute the influence of African-American voters and their newly elected representatives because historically the primary responsibilities of the county commissioners were "to supervise and control the maintenance, repair, and construction of county roads" (*Pressley v. Etowah*).

These dilutive efforts were pursued in similar ways. In the case of Etowah County, after coming to terms with a prior voting rights law suit, the all white five member county commission agreed to expand to a six member commission. Each member of the council was to be elected at-large but live in and represent one of the six districts in the county. Thus, once these changes were precleared by the Department of Justice and elections were held, the new commission contained four holdovers from the all white commission and two newly elected members (i.e., Commissioner Williams—white and Commissioner Presley—black). Upon taking their seats on the commission, Mr. White and Mr. Presley were disenfranchised in the areas of road maintenance by the white incumbent majority. The white incumbent majority passed the Road Supervisor Resolution and the Common Fund Resolution on August 25th, 1987. Under the Road Supervisor Resolution, they were stripped of their authority to supervise road work within their respective districts and given distinctly inferior responsibilities (e.g., Mr. White was granted authority over the County Engineering Department and Mr. Presley was granted supervision over the maintenance and operations of the County Courthouse. Under the Common Fund Resolution, decisions about the expenditure of funds out of the county road maintenance budget in particular were no longer solely decided by the commissioner from that district, but were subject to a commission-wide vote.

Thus, as Presley saw it, he had been elected to serve his district in the area of public works (just like the white majority) but was being denied equal enjoyment of the historic privileges of being a commissioner because of his race/constituency. So he challenged these actions in federal district court (with the support of the Department of Justice) on the grounds that these changes were violations of the section 5 preclearance provisions of the VRA. Section 5 of the Voting Rights Act of 1965 requires a covered jurisdiction to obtain either judicial or administrative preclearance before enforcing any new "voting qualification or prerequisite to voting, or standard, practice, or procedure with respect to voting. He argued that these changes which weakened his position as commissioner (relative to the white incumbents) were effectively changes in voting because his constituents' votes had been diluted because their commissioner did not exercise equal influence over the most important affairs of the commission. Thus, in the absence of preclearance these changes were illegal. The District Court supported Presley's position in regards to the Road Supervision Resolution, but allowed the Common Fund Resolution to stand. Thus, Presley filed an appeal concerning the latter decision that was accepted for hearing by the Supreme Court.

A companion case that was subsumed under Presley's appeal was the case of *Mack et al. v. Russell County*. In accordance with the history of county government in Alabama, the commission's major functions of road/public works maintenance and construction were divided amongst each of the five members and they exercised sole authority over these matters within their respective districts. Only non-routine expenditures were subject to a commission wide vote. However, following an indictment of a fellow commissioner in 1979 the commission passed a resolution granting road maintenance authority to the County Engineer (i.e., an appointed official). Thus, county roads would be managed as a unit (this became known as the Unit System). However, this decision was never vetted via the preclearance process. Additional VRA related litigation in 1986 led to the expansion of the size of the commission to seven members and eventually to the election of two new African-American commissioners. These new commissioners eventually filed suit arguing that the Unit System was never vetted via the preclearance process and thus it was an illegal change with respect to the meaning of citizens' votes.

In both instances (i.e., the Etowah and Russell county cases), the plaintiffs based their lawsuits on claims of racial discrimination in the legislative process that were in violation of prior court orders, the Constitution, Title VI of the Civil Rights Act of 1964, and sections 2 and 5 of the Voting Rights Act. However, the section 5 claim is the only claim that was adjudicated via this joint appeal. Upon reviewing both of these cases, the Supreme Court rejected the appeals. The Court ruled that section 5 of the VRA only applied to the physical act of voting. Thus, section 5 pre-clearance can only be enforced in instances when the physical act of voting is subject to dilution or obstruction. Section 5 does not apply to instances of dilution in the actual process of governing except in instances where local officials attempt to create or abolish an existing elective office. As Justice Kennedy (author of the Majority Opinion) states in the specific case of *Presley v. Etowah County*:

A simple example shows the inadequacy of the line proffered by appellants and the United States. Under appellants' view, every time a covered jurisdiction passed a budget that differed from the previous year's budget it would be required to obtain preclearance. The amount of funds available to an elected official has a profound effect on the power exercised. A vote for an ill-funded official is less valuable than a vote for a well-funded one.

No doubt in recognition of the unacceptable consequences of their views, appellants take the position that while "some budget changes may affect the right to vote and, under particular circumstances, would be subject to preclearance," most budget changes would not. . . . Under their interpretation of § 5, however, appellants fail to give any workable standard to determine when preclearance is required. And were we to acknowledge that a budget adjustment is a voting change in even some instances, the likely consequence is that every budget change would be covered, for it is well settled that every voting change with a "potential for discrimination" must be precleared.

Confronting this difficulty, at oral argument the United States suggested that we draw an arbitrary line distinguishing between budget changes and other changes. There is no principled basis for the distinction, and it would be a marked departure from the statutory category of voting. If a diminution or increase in an elected official's powers is a change with respect to voting, then whether it is accomplished through an enactment or a budget shift should not matter. Even if we were willing to draw an unprincipled line excluding budgetary changes but not other changes in an elected official's decisionmaking authority, the result would expand the coverage of § 5 well beyond the statutory language and the intention of Congress.

Under the view advanced by appellants and the United States, every time a state legislature acts to diminish or increase the power of local officials, preclearance would be required. Governmental action decreasing the power of local officials could carry with it a potential for discrimination against those who represent racial minorities at the local level. At the same time, increasing the power of local officials will entail a relative decrease in the power of state officials, and that too could carry with it a potential for discrimination against state officials who represent racial minorities at the state level. The all but limitless minor changes in the allocation of power among officials and the constant adjustments required for the efficient governance of every covered State illustrate the necessity for us to formulate workable rules to confine the coverage of § 5 to its legitimate sphere: voting.

Changes which affect only the distribution of power among officials are not subject to § 5 because such changes have no direct relation to, or impact on, voting.

In the specific case of *Mack v Russell County*, Justice Kennedy writes:

> It is a routine part of governmental administration for appointive positions to be created or eliminated and for their powers to be altered. Each time this occurs the relative balance of authority is altered in some way. The making or unmaking of an appointive post often will result in the erosion or accretion of the powers of some official responsible to the electorate, but it does not follow that those changes are covered by § 5. By requiring preclearance of changes with respect to voting, Congress did not mean to subject such routine matters of governance to federal supervision. Were the rule otherwise, neither state nor local governments could exercise power in a responsible manner within a federal system.

This decision held significant implications for the future of the Voting Rights Revolution. Although the Court's logic about the untenable nature of the Department of Justice's position regarding regulating changes with respect to governing is sound, the refusal to even try to conceive of a "totality of circumstances" test as the only basis for such action revealed the general position of the Court in regards to the status of the Voting Rights Revolution at that time. The history of voting rights jurisprudence revealed that the Court fully endorsed the procedural focus of the revolution and under extreme circumstances viewed regulations that facilitated the election of minority officials as within the realm of that procedurally focused revolution. However, the substantive transformational vision of the revolution that sought to subject issues of governance (particularly legislative racism) under section 5 was far beyond the mission of procedural equity the Court felt was at the core of the VRA. James Button and David Hedge's (1996) survey of black and white state legislators reveals the problem of limiting the VRA to procedural questions. Their research indicated that:

> Black officials [primarily in the South] are more likely than whites to report experiencing or observing discrimination within the legislature, to perceive such discrimination in the party and committee system, and to believe that black issues do not receive a fair hearing in the legislature. In addition, black lawmakers view black political progress over the last decade in the state in much more pessimistic ways than do white lawmakers." (Button and Hedge 1996, 214)

Thus, this decision even more so than the *Shaw* decision, can be looked upon as the moment when the Voting Rights Revolution began to lose momentum and the quest for substantive as opposed to nominal justice stalled.

Endnotes

1. See Guinier (1994, 44). She states that "Robert Moses and other black voter registration activists . . . defended their work as the most promising response to indigenous efforts to transform local reality."

2. The initial southern states (or parts thereof) that were subjected to VRA preclearance authority are: Alabama, Georgia, Louisiana, Mississippi, N. Carolina, S. Carolina, and Virginia. Texas was added to the list in 1975.

3. At-large electoral systems require candidates for local legislative office (i.e., councils/ commissions, etc.) to compete in city-wide (county-wide) elections to secure the desired office. Thus, in racially polarized communities (or counties) dominated by a white majority, any minority candidate preferred by the minority residents of that community (county) would easily be defeated by the majority white electorate. This prevented African-Americans in many southern communities from gaining access to local governing institutions even if they voted in substantial numbers to support one candidate.

4. Section two was revised in response to a Supreme Court decision in the case of The City of Mobile v. Bolden (1980). The court ruled that plaintiffs needed to secure evidence of discriminatory intent, not effect, in order for the city's at-large electoral system to be challenged as unconstitutional.

5. In this study, the South is defined as the eleven states comprising the old confederacy: Alabama, Arkansas, Florida, Georgia, Louisiana, Mississippi, N. Carolina, S. Carolina, Tennessee, Texas, and Virginia.

6. Also, this region contained 68.2% of all black elected officials nation-wide. Sources: The Joint Center for Political and Economic Studies, *National Roster of Black Elected Officials* (Washington, DC: JCPES, 1971) and The Joint Center for Political and Economic Studies, *Black Elected Officials: A Statistical Summary* (Washington, DC: JCPES, 2003).

7. Also, it is important to add that majority black cities in 1970 were likely to be the bastions of mass resistance (white bloc voting especially high and black registration low). Furthermore many of the majority black cities at this time were likely not majority black in terms of voter registration and/or turnout. Also some were only slightly more than 50% black and may have not had black voting age majorities in the early 1970s. See Grofman and Davidson (1994, 308).

8. Overall, according to Grofman and Davidson's research, NC and MS were the poorest performers in terms of black representation in at-large settings and at-large components of mixed cities as well (Grofman and Davidson 1994, 312).

9. See Table 3 in Lewis (2008). Even Grofman and Davidson (1994, 316) note that in 1980 the proportion of blacks living in small cities less than 25,000 in North Carolina was more than two-thirds.

10. Due to further litigation in the wake of the *Shaw v. Reno* (1993) decision, several Southern states have redrawn their districts during the mid to late 1990s. North Carolina redrew its districts for the 1998 elections (*Shaw v Hunt* 1996). However the following states redrew their districts by 1996: FL (*Johnson v Mortham* 1996); GA (*Miller v Johnson* 1995); LA (*Hayes v Louisiana* 1996); and TX (*Vera v Bush* 1996).

11. Section 5 of the VRA mandates that there be no retrogression in minority political influence (i.e., minority power in terms of elected officials should not decrease due to successive changes in the electoral system). Section 2 mandated that changes in the electoral system cannot have discriminatory effects.

12. *Miller v Johnson* (1995) declared that drawing districts solely on the basis of race that are not narrowly tailored to meet the compelling interests of VRA compliance was unconstitutional. Thus, all race based districts are not unconstitutional.

Bibliography

Alt, James E. 1994. "The Impact of the Voting Rights Act on Black and White Voter Registration in the South." In *Quiet Revolution in The South: The Impact of the Voting Rights Act 1965–1990*, ed. Chandler Davidson and Bernard Grofman. Princeton, NJ: Princeton University Press.

Button, James and David Hedge. 1996. "Legislative Life in the 1990s: A Comparison of Black and White State Legislators." *Legislative Studies Quarterly* 21(2): 199–218.

County and City Data Book. 2000. Washington, D.C.: U.S. Census Bureau.

Grofman, Bernard. 1990. *Voting Rights, Voting Wrongs: The Legacy of Baker v. Carr*. New York: Priority Press.

Grofman, Bernard. 1995. "Shaw v Reno and The Future of Voting Rights." *Political Science* 28(1): 27–36.

Grofman, Bernard and Chandler Davidson. 1992. *Controversies in Minority Voting: The Voting Rights Act in Perspective*, ed. Washington, DC: The Brookings Institution.

Grofman, Bernard and Lisa Handley. 1991. "The Impact of the Voting Rights Act On Black Representation In Southern State Legislatures." *Legislative Studies Quarterly* 26: 111–129.

Grofman, Bernard and Chandler Davidson. 1994. "The Effect of Municipal Election Structure on Black Representation in Eight Southern States." In *Quiet Revolution in The: The Impact of the Voting Rights Act 1965–1990*, ed. Chandler Davidson and Bernard Grofman. Princeton, NJ: Princeton University Press.

Guinier, Lani. 1994. *Tyranny of the Majority: Fundamental Fairness in Representative Democracy*. New York: The Free Press.

Hamilton, Alexander, James Madison and John Jay. 2003. *The Federalist Papers*. New York: Bantam Classic Publishing.

Herring, Mary. 1990. "Legislative Responsiveness to Black Constituents in Three Deep South States." *Journal of Politics* 52(3): 740–58.

Key Jr., V. O. 1949. *Southern Politics.* New York: Vintage Books.

Lewis, Arnold C. 2008. "Has the Revolution Been Specified? A Critical Assessment of the Status of Research on the Voting Rights Act and Black Politics." *Western Journal of Black Studies* 32(1): 53–61.

Lublin, David. 1997. *The Paradox of Representation: Racial Gerrymandering and Minority Interests in Congress.* Princeton, NJ: Princeton University Press.

McClain, Paula D. and Joseph Stewart Jr. 1995. " W(h)ither the Voting Rights Act After Shaw v. Reno: Advancing to the Past?" *Political Science* 28(1): 24–26.

Parker, Frank. 1990. *Black Votes Count.* Chapel Hill, NC: University of North Carolina Press.

Schattschneider, E. E. 1960. *The Semisovereign People: A Realist's View of Democracy in America.* New York: Holt, Rinehart and Winston.

The Joint Center for Political and Economic Studies. 1971. *National Roster of Black Elected Officials.* Washington, DC: JCPES.

The Joint Center for Political and Economic Studies. 2003. *Black Elected Officials: A Statistical Summary.* Washington, DC: JCPES.

Whitby, Kenny J. and Franklin D. Gilliam. 1991. "A Longitudinal Analysis of Competing Explanations for the Transformation of Southern Congressional Politics." *Journal of Politics* 53(2): 504–518.

Whitby, Kenny J. 1997. *The Color of Representation: Congressional Behavior and Black Interests.* Ann Arbor: University of Michigan Press.

Court Cases

Allen v. State Board of Elections. 1969. 393 U.S. 544.

Baker v. Carr. 1962. 369 U.S. 186.

City of Mobile v. Bolden. 1980. 446 U.S. 55.

Connor v. Johnson. 1971. 402 U.S. 690.

Graves v. Barnes. 1972. 343 F.Supp. 704 W.D. Texas.

Georgia v. United States. 1973. 411 U.S. 526.

Hayes v. Louisiana. 1996. 936 F. Supp. 369. W.D. La.

Mack etal. v Russell County Commission. 1991. 111 S. Ct.2007

Miller v. Johnson. 1995. 515. U.S. 900.

Presley v. Etowah County Commission. 1992. 502. U.S. 491.

Reynolds v Simms. 1964. 377 U.S. 533.

Shaw v. Hunt. 1996. 517 U.S. 899.

Shaw v. Reno. 1993. 509 U.S. 630.

Thornburg v. Gingles. 1986. 478 U.S. 30.

Vera v. Bush. 1996. 933 F. Supp. 1341 S.D. Tex.

White v. Regester. 1973. 412 U.S. 755.

46

The Myth of the Model Minority

Noy Thrupkaew

Southeast Asians were stereotyped as bolstered by strong values. But when immigrants face grim economic and social conditions, values are not enough.

Mali Keo fled Cambodia with her husband and four children in 1992. Several years later, she was still haunted by searing memories of "the killing fields," the forced-labor camps where millions of Cambodians died, victims of Communist despot Pol Pot's quest for a perfect agrarian society. Because of the brutal beatings she suffered at the hands of Pol Pot's Khmer Rouge, she was still wracked with physical pain as well. Traumatized and ailing, uneducated, unskilled, and speaking very little English, Mali Keo (a pseudonym assigned by researchers) could barely support her children after her husband abandoned the family.

And now she may not even have public assistance to fall back on, because the 1996 welfare-reform act cut off most federal benefits to immigrants and subsequent amendments have not entirely restored them. In what was supposed to be the land of her salvation, Mali Keo today is severely impoverished. Living in a hard-pressed neighborhood of Philadelphia, she struggles with only mixed success to keep her children out of trouble and in school.

The Southeast Asia Resource Action Center (SEARAC), an advocacy group in Washington, estimates that more than 2.2 million Southeast Asians now live in the United States. They are the largest group of refugees in the country and the fastest-growing minority. Yet for most policy makers, the plight of the many Mali Keos has been overshadowed by the well-known success of the Asian immigrants who came before and engendered the myth of the "model minority." Indeed, conservatives have exploited this racial stereotype— arguing that Asians fare well in the United States because of their strong "family values" and work ethic. These values, they say, and not government assistance, are what all minorities need in order to get ahead.

Paradoxically, Southeast Asians—supposedly part of the model minority—may be suffering most from the resulting public policies. They have been left in the hands of underfunded community-assistance programs and government agencies that, in one example of well-intentioned incompetence, churn out forms in Khmer and Lao for often illiterate populations. But fueled by outrage over bad services and a fraying social safety-net, Southeast Asian immigrants have started to embrace that most American of activities, political protest—by pushing for research on their communities, advocating for their rights, and harnessing their political power.

The model-minority myth has persisted in large part because political conservatives are so attached to it. "Asian Americans have become the darlings of the right," said Frank Wu, a law professor at Howard University and the author of *Yellow: Race beyond Black and White*. "The model-minority myth and its depiction of Asian-American success tells a reassuring story about our society working."

The flip side is also appealing to the right. Because Asian Americans' success stems from their strong families and their dedication to education and hard work, conservatives say, then the poverty of Latinos and African Americans must be explained by their own "values": They are poor because of their nonmarrying, school-skipping, and generally lazy and irresponsible behavior, which government handouts only encourage.

The model-minority myth's "racist love," as author Frank Chin terms it, took hold at a sensitive point in U.S. history: after the 1965 Watts riots and the immigration reforms of that year, which selectively allowed large numbers of educated immigrants into the United States. Highly skilled South and East Asian nurses, doctors, and engineers from countries like India and China began pouring into the United States just as racial tensions were at a fever pitch.

Shortly thereafter, articles like "Success Story of One Minority in the U.S.," published by *U.S. News & World Report* in 1966, trumpeted: "At a time when it is being proposed that hundreds of billions be spent to uplift Negroes and other minorities, the nation's 300,000 Chinese Americans are moving ahead on their own, with no help from anyone else." *Newsweek* in 1971 had Asian Americans "outwhiting the whites." And *Fortune* in 1986 dubbed them a "superminority." As Wu caricatures the model-minority myth in his book:

> Asian Americans vindicate the American Dream. . . . They are living proof of the power of the free market and the absence of racial discrimination. Their good fortune flows from individual self-reliance and community self-sufficiency, not civil-rights activism or government welfare benefits.

A closer look at the data paints another picture, however. If Asian-American households earn more than whites, statistics suggest, it's not because their individual earnings are higher but because Asian Americans live in larger households, with more working adults. In fact, a recent University of Hawaii study found that "most Asian Americans are overeducated compared to whites for the incomes they earn"—evidence that suggests not "family values" but market discrimination.

What most dramatically skews the data, though, is the fact that about half the population of Asian (or, more precisely, Asian-Pacific Islander) Americans is made up of the highly educated immigrants who began arriving with their families in the 1960s. The plight of refugees from Cambodia, Laos, and Vietnam, who make up less than 14 percent of Asian Americans, gets lost in the averaging. Yet these refugees, who started arriving in the United States after 1975, differ markedly from the professional-class Chinese and Indian immigrants who started coming 10 years earlier. The Southeast Asians were fleeing wartime persecution and had few resources. And those disadvantages have had devastating effects on their lives in the United States. The most recent census data available show that 47 percent of Cambodians, 66 percent of Hmong (an ethnic group that lived in the mountains of Laos), 67 percent of Laotians, and 34 percent of Vietnamese were impoverished in 1990—compared with 10 percent of all Americans and 14 percent of all Asian Americans. Significantly, poverty rates among Southeast Asian Americans were much higher than those of even the "nonmodel" minorities: 21 percent of African Americans and 23 percent of Latinos were poor.

Yet despite the clear inaccuracies created by lumping populations together, the federal government still groups Southeast Asian refugees under the overbroad category of "Asian" for research and funding purposes. "We've labored under the shadow of this model myth for so long," said KaYing Yang, SEARAC's executive director. "There's so little research on us, or we're lumped in with all other Asians, so people don't know the specific needs and contributions of our communities."

To get a sense of those needs, one has to go back to the beginning of the Southeast Asian refugees' story and the circumstances that forced their migration. In 1975, the fall of Saigon sent shock waves throughout Southeast Asia, as communist insurgents toppled U.S.-supported governments in Vietnam and Cambodia. In Laos, where the CIA had trained and funded the Hmong to fight Laotian and Vietnamese communists as U.S. proxies, the communists who took over vowed to purge the country of ethnic Hmong and punish all others who had worked with the U.S. government.

The first refugees to leave Southeast Asia tended to be the most educated and urban, English-speakers with close connections to the U.S. government. One of them was a man who wishes to be identified by the pseudonym John Askulraskul. He spent two years in a Laotian re-education camp—punishment for his ability to speak English, his having been educated, and, most of all, his status as a former employee of the United States Agency for International Development (USAID).

"They tried to brainwash you, to subdue you psychologically, to work you to death on two bowls of rice a day," Askulraskul told me recently.

After being released, he decided to flee the country. He, his sister, and his eldest daughter, five and a half years old, slipped into the Mekong River with a few others. Clinging to an inflated garbage bag, Askulraskul swam alongside their boat out of fear that his weight would sink it.

After they arrived on the shores of Thailand, Askulraskul and his daughter were placed in a refugee camp, where they waited to be reunited with his wife and his two other daughters.

It was not to be.

"My wife tried to escape with two small children. But my daughters couldn't make it"—he paused, drawing a ragged breath—"because the boat sank."

Askulraskul's wife was swept back to Laos, where she was arrested and placed in jail for a month. She succeeded in her next escape attempt, rejoining her suddenly diminished family.

Eventually, with the help of his former boss at USAID, they moved to Connecticut, where Askulraskul found work helping to resettle other refugees. His wife, who had been an elementary-school teacher, took up teaching English as a second language (ESL) to Laotian refugee children. His daughter adjusted quickly and went to school without incident.

Askulraskul now manages a project that provides services for at-risk Southeast Asian children and their families. "The job I am doing now is not only a job," he said. "It is part of my life and my sacrifice. My daughter is 29 now, and I know raising kids in America is not easy. I cannot save everybody, but there is still something I can do."

Like others among the first wave of refugees, Askulraskul considers himself one of the lucky ones. His education, U.S. ties, and English-language ability—everything that set off the tragic chain of events that culminated in his daughters' deaths—proved enormously helpful once he was in the United States.

But the majority of refugees from Southeast Asia had no such advantages. Subsequent waves frequently hailed from rural areas and lacked both financial resources and formal schooling. Their psychological scars were even deeper than the first group's, from their longer years in squalid refugee camps or the killing fields. The ethnic Chinese who began arriving from Vietnam had faced harsh discrimination as well, and the Amerasians—the children of Vietnamese women and U.S. soldiers—had lived for years as pariahs.

Once here, these refugees often found themselves trapped in poverty, providing low-cost labor, and receiving no health or other benefits, while their lack of schooling made decent jobs almost impossible to come by. In 1990, two-thirds of Cambodian, Laotian, and Hmong adults in America had less than a high-school education—compared with 14 percent of whites, 25 percent of African Americans, 45 percent of Latinos, and 15 percent of the general Asian-American population. Before the welfare-reform law cut many of them off, nearly 30 percent of Southeast Asian Americans were on welfare—the highest participation rate of any ethnic group. And having such meager incomes, they usually lived in the worst neighborhoods, with the attendant crime, gang problems, and poor schools.

But shouldn't the touted Asian dedication to schooling have overcome these disadvantages, lifting the refugees' children out of poverty and keeping them off the streets? Unfortunately, it didn't. "There is still a high number of dropouts for Southeast Asians," Yang said. "And if they do graduate, there is a low number going on to higher education."

Their parents' difficulty in navigating American school systems may contribute to the problem. "The parents' lack of education leads to a lack of role models and guidance. Without those things, youth can turn to delinquent behavior and in some very extreme cases, gangs, instead of devoting themselves to education," said Narin Sihavong, director of

SEARAC's Successful New Americans Project, which interviewed Mali Keo. "This underscores the need for Southeast Asian school administrators or counselors who can be role models, ease the cultural barrier, and serve as a bridge to their parents."

"Sometimes families have to choose between education and employment, especially when money is tight," said Porthira Chimm, a former SEARAC project director. "And unfortunately, immediate money concerns often win out."

The picture that emerges—of high welfare participation and dropout rates, low levels of education and income—is startlingly similar to the situation of the poorest members of "nonmodel" minority groups. Southeast Asians, Latinos, and African Americans also have in common significant numbers of single-parent families. Largely as a result of the killing fields, nearly a quarter of Cambodian households are headed by single women. Other Southeast Asian families have similar stories. Sihavong's mother, for example, raised him and his five siblings on her own while his father was imprisoned in a Laotian re-education camp.

No matter how "traditional" Southeast Asians may be, they share the fate of other people of color when they are denied access to good education, safe neighborhoods, and jobs that provide a living wage and benefits. But for the sake of preserving the model-minority myth, conservative policy makers have largely ignored the needs of Southeast Asian communities.

One such need is for psychological care. Wartime trauma and "lack of English proficiency, acculturative stress, prejudice, discrimination, and racial hate crimes" place Southeast Asians "at risk for emotional and behavioral problems," according to the U.S. surgeon general's 2001 report on race and mental health. One random sample of Cambodian adults found that 45 percent had post-traumatic stress disorder and 51 percent suffered from depression.

John Askulraskul's past reflects trauma as well, but his education, English-language ability, and U.S. connections helped level the playing field. Less fortunate refugees need literacy training and language assistance. They also need social supports like welfare and strong community-assistance groups. But misled by the model-minority myth, many government agencies seem to be unaware that Southeast Asians require their services, and officials have done little to find these needy refugees or accommodate them. Considering that nearly two-thirds of Southeast Asians say they do not speak English very well and more than 50 percent live in linguistically isolated ethnic enclaves, the lack of outreach and translators effectively denies them many public services.

The problem extends beyond antipoverty programs, as Mali Keo's story illustrates. After her husband left her, she formed a relationship with another man and had two more children. But he beat the family for years, until she asked an organization that served Cambodian refugees to help her file a restraining order. If she had known that a shelter was available, she told her interviewer, even one without Khmer-speaking counselors, she would have escaped much earlier.

Where the government hasn't turned a blind eye, it has often wielded an iron fist. The welfare-reform law of 1996, which cut off welfare, SSI, and food-stamp benefits for most noncitizens—even those who are legal permanent residents—sent Southeast Asian communities into an uproar. Several elderly Hmong in California committed suicide, fearing that they would become burdens to their families. Meanwhile, the lack of literacy programs prevented (and still does prevent) many refugees from passing the written test that would gain them citizenship and the right to public assistance.

"We achieved welfare reform on the backs of newcomers," Frank Wu said. "People said that 'outsiders' don't have a claim to the body politic, and even liberals say we should care for 'our own' first." Few seemed to ask the question posed by sociologist Donald Hernandez: "What responsibility do we have to ensure a basic standard of living for immigrants who have fled their countries as a result of the American government's economic, military, and political involvement there?"

But welfare reform also had a second effect. "It was such a shocking event, it completely galvanized the Southeast Asian community," said Karen Narasaki, executive director of the National Asian Pacific American Legal Consortium. "In different Asian cultures, you have 'the crab who crawls out of the bucket gets pulled back' [and] 'the nail that sticks out gets pounded down.' But in the United States, 'the squeaky wheel gets the grease,' and people had to learn that."

The learning process has been a difficult one. At first, because of their past negative experiences with the United States and their homeland governments, many Southeast Asians feared political involvement. Many saw themselves as noncitizens and second-class "outsiders" with a precarious standing in the United States. But as they have grown more familiar with this country, even noncitizens have started to think of themselves less as refugees in a temporary home and more as "new Americans" who are entitled to shape their destinies through political engagement.

The energy for this new activism grew out of the mutual-assistance associations (MAAs) that have taken root in various Southeast Asian communities. Primarily staffed by people like Askulraskul—the more successful members of the ethnic groups they serve—MAAs form the backbone of support for Southeast Asians, providing, among many other things, child care, job training, school liaisons, and assistance with navigating government bureaucracies.

But the MAAs are facing problems of their own. The funding they used to get from the federal Office of Refugee Resettlement is dwindling. In 1996 new federal guidelines mandated that these funds go exclusively to organizations serving the most recent refugees. (In response, several Southeast Asian MAAs have tried to stay afloat by offering their services to newer refugees from places like Ethiopia and Iraq.) As for outside funding, only 0.3 percent of all philanthropic aid goes to groups that work specifically with Asian-American populations, according to the 1998 edition of *Foundation Giving*. "A lot of people in philanthropy think [that Asians] are doing so well, they don't need help," Narasaki said.

Despite these problems, MAAs and national advocacy organizations like SEARAC have won limited restorations of benefits and food stamps for immigrants. And a significant victory came in 2000, when legislation sponsored by Minnesota Senator Paul Wellstone was adopted: It will allow Hmong veterans—or their widows—from America's "secret war" in Laos to take the U.S. citizenship test in Hmong, with a translator.

One key to the MAAs' success is their networking with other minority-advocacy groups, says Sandy Dang, executive director of Asian American LEAD, an organization based in Washington, that provides a range of services for Vietnamese Americans, including ESL classes, youth mentoring, and parent-support groups.

When Dang founded the organization, she didn't know how to write grant proposals, so she asked the director of a nearby youth center for Latin Americans to provide guidance. "The Latino organizations have a lot of empathy for people starting out," she said. "They understand the refugee-immigrant experience.

"Disadvantaged people share a lot in common," Dang continued, "and we have to help each other. People who are empowered in this country like to play us off each other, like with the model-minority myth. They need the poor and disadvantaged to fight each other. Because if we unite, we can make it difficult for them."

Southeast Asians are disproving the model-minority myth not just with their difficult lives but with their growing insistence that it takes more than "traditional values" and "personal responsibility" to survive in this country. It takes social supports and participation in the legacy of civil rights activism as well.

The refugees and their children are forging their identities as new Americans and are starting to emerge as a political force. At first, Yang said, "we had no time to think about anything else but our communities—and no one was thinking about us. But now we know that what we were grappling with [affects both] me and my neighbor, who might be poor black, Latino, or Asian. We are no longer refugees, we are Americans. And we know what being 'successful' is: It's being someone who is truly aware of the meaning of freedom to speak out."

47

Wealth Gap Among Races Widens

Genaro C. Armas

WASHINGTON—The enormous wealth gap between white families and blacks and Hispanics grew larger after the most recent recession, a private analysis of government data finds.

White households had a median net worth of greater than $88,000 in 2002, 11 times more than Hispanics and more than 14 times that of blacks, the Pew Hispanic Center said in a study being released Monday.

Blacks were slowest to emerge from the economic downturn that started in 2000 and ended in late 2001, the report found.

Net worth accounts for the values of items such as a home and car, checking and savings accounts, and stocks, minus debts such as mortgage, car loans and credit card bills.

Greater wealth means a greater ability to weather a job loss, emergency home repairs, illness and other unexpected costs, as well as being able to save for retirement or a child's college tuition.

According to the group's analysis of Census Bureau data, nearly one-third of black families and 26 percent of Hispanic families were in debt or had no net assets, compared with 11 percent of white families.

"Wealth is a measure of cumulative advantage or disadvantage," said Roderick Harrison, a researcher at the Joint Center for Political and Economic Studies, a Washington think tank that focuses on black issues. "The fact that black and Hispanic wealth is a fraction of white wealth also reflects a history of discrimination."

After accounting for inflation, net worth for white households increased 17 percent between 1996 and 2002 and rose for Hispanic homes by 14 percent to about $7,900. It decreased for blacks by 16 percent, to roughly $6,000.

Regardless of race and ethnicity, the median net worth for all U.S. households was $59,700 in 2002, a 12 percent gain from 1996.

Only white homes recouped all their losses between 2001 and 2002. Both Hispanics and blacks lost nearly 27 percent of net worth between 1999 and 2001; the next year Latinos had gained almost all back (26 percent) though blacks were up only about 5 percent.

Roberto Suro, director of the Pew Hispanic Center, said the accumulation of wealth allows low-income families to rise into the middle class and "have some kind of assets beyond next week's paychecks."

"Having more assets enabled whites to ride out the jobless recovery better," he said.

Harrison says Hispanics were more insulated from the downturn than blacks, so they took less of a hit. For example, Hispanics made employment gains in lower-paid, lower-skilled areas such as the service and construction sectors.

Blacks were hit hard by job losses in the manufacturing industry and in professional fields, where they were victims of "last hired, first fired" policies, he said.

Only relatively recently were large numbers of blacks and Hispanics able to make investments and accumulate wealth. They were slower to enter the stock market during the 1990s rush and then had less of a cushion when the market began its decline in 2000.

Another factor affecting disparities is that whites are far more likely to own their homes; homeownership is among the most common ways to build wealth.

Census figures released in August showed the national median household income remained basically flat between 2002 and 2003 at $43,318. Median incomes for whites ($47,800) and blacks ($29,600) also were stagnant, while the median income for Hispanics fell about 2 percent to $33,000.

48

Women's Earnings—GAO Analysis of Women's Workplace Decisions

. . . analysis of data from the PSID identified factors that contribute to the earnings difference between men and women, but cannot fully explain the underlying reasons why these factors differ. For example, the model results indicated that earnings differ, in part, because men and women tend to have different work patterns (such as women are more likely to work part time) and often work in different occupations. However, the model could not explain *why* (emphasis added) women worked part time more often or took jobs in certain occupations. In addition, the analysis could not explain why a remaining earnings difference existed after accounting for a range of demographic, family, and work-related factors. To gain perspective on these issues, we conducted additional work to gather information on why individuals make certain decisions about work and how those decisions may affect their earnings.

Summary of Results

According to experts and the literature, women are more likely than men to have primary responsibility for family, and as a result, working women with family responsibilities must make a variety of decisions to manage these responsibilities. For example, these decisions

---

Editor's note: There has been extensive research documenting inequity between men and women with regard to earnings. It is a well founded conclusion that women earn less than men. What has been debated is the magnitude of that difference. The United States General Accounting Office (GAO) in late 2003 released the results of its study. They found that women earned 44 percent less than men. Their research looked at several explanatory factors but found that work patterns were critical in explaining half of the difference in earning. Women have fewer years of work experience, work fewer hours, more often take leaves of absence and are more likely to work part-time. Once these factors are included the GAO found that the difference was reduced to 21 percent. They were unable to make a conclusive statement about what factors explained the remaining difference. The following excerpt addresses some possible explanations for the difference in workplace decisions and discusses the possibility of discriminatory practices.

may include what types of jobs women choose as well as decisions they make about how, when, and where they do their work. These decisions may have specific consequences for their career advancement or earnings. However, debate exists whether these decisions are freely made or influenced by discrimination in society or in the workplace.

Background

The tremendous growth in the number of women in the labor force in recent decades has dramatically changed the world of work. The number of women—particularly married women with children—who work has increased, in many cases leaving no one at home to handle family and other responsibilities. Single-headed households, in which only one parent is available to handle both work and home responsibilities, are also increasingly common. As a result, an increasing number of workers face the challenge of trying to simultaneously manage responsibilities both inside and outside the workplace. At the same time, however, many employers continue to have certain expectations about how much priority workers should give to work in relation to responsibilities outside the workplace. While workplace culture varies from one workplace to another, research indicates that in some cases an "ideal worker" perception exists. According to this perception, an ideal worker places highest priority on work, working a full-time 9–to–5 schedule throughout their working years, and often working overtime. Ideal workers take little or no time off for childbearing or childrearing, and they appear—whether true or not—to have few responsibilities outside of work. While this perception applies to all workers, most experts and literature agree that it disproportionately affects women because they often have or take primary responsibility for home and family, such as caring for children, even when they are employed outside of the home. However, some research indicates that men are now more likely than in the past to participate in childcare, eldercare, and housework and are beginning to adjust their work in response to family obligations.

Some employers, however, have taken note of the multiple needs of workers and have begun to offer alternative work arrangements to help workers manage both work and other life responsibilities. These arrangements can benefit workers by providing them with flexibility in how, when, and where they do their work. One type of alternative work arrangement allows workers to reduce their work hours from the traditional 40 hours per week, such as part-time work or job sharing.[1] Similarly, some employers offer workers the opportunity to take leave from work for a variety of reasons, such as childbirth, care for elderly relatives, or other personal reasons. Some arrangements, such as flextime, allow employees to begin and end their workday outside the traditional 9–to–5 work hours. Other arrangements, such as telecommuting from home, allow employees to work in an alternative location. Childcare facilities are also available at some workplaces to help workers with their caregiving responsibilities. In addition to benefiting workers, these arrangements may also benefit employers by helping them recruit and retain workers. For example, according to an industry group for attorneys, law firms may lose new attorneys—particularly women who plan to have children—if they do not offer workplace flexibility. This is costly to firms due to substantial training investments they make in new attorneys, which they may not recoup if workers quit early on.

Nonetheless, research suggests that many workplaces still maintain the same policies, practices, and structures that existed when most workers were men who worked full time, 40-hours per week. As a result, there may be a "mismatch" between the needs of workers with family responsibilities and the structure of the workplace.

Working Women Make a Variety of Decisions to Manage Work and Family Responsibilities

Working women make a variety of decisions to manage both their work and home or family responsibilities. According to some experts and literature, some women work in jobs that are more compatible with their home and family responsibilities. In addition, some women use alternative work arrangements such as working a part-time schedule or taking leave from work. Experts indicate that these decisions may result in women as a group earning less than men. However, debate exists about whether women's work-related decisions are freely made or influenced by discrimination. Some experts believe that women and men generally have different life priorities—women choose to place higher priority on home and family, while men choose to place higher priority on career and earnings. These women may voluntarily give up potential for higher earnings to focus on home and family. However, other experts believe that men and women have similar life priorities, and instead indicate that women as a group earn less because of underlying discrimination in society or in the workplace.

Certain Jobs May Offer Flexibility but May Also Affect Earnings

According to some experts and literature, some women choose to work in jobs that are compatible with their home or family responsibilities, and may trade off career advancement or higher earnings for these jobs. Some experts and literature indicate that jobs that offer flexibility tend to be lower paying and offer less career advancement.[2]

Women choose jobs with different kinds of flexibility based on their needs. According to some researchers, some jobs are less demanding or less stressful than others, which may allow women who choose these jobs to have more time and energy for responsibilities outside of work. For example, a woman may work in an off-line, staff position, such as a human resources job, because it requires less travel and less time in the office than an online position in the company. Off-line positions may offer flexibility, but less opportunity for advancement and higher earnings. One expert also indicated that, within a certain field, some women are more likely to choose jobs that allow them more flexibility but lower earnings potential. For example, according to this expert, within the medical field, the family practice specialty is typically more accommodating to home and family responsibilities than the surgical specialty, which offers relatively higher earnings. Surgeons' work is generally less predictable because surgeons are often called in the middle of the night to treat emergencies. . .

According to some experts and literature, women may choose jobs that allow them to quit (for example, to care for a child) and easily reenter the labor force with minimal earnings loss when they return to work. Given that job skills affect earnings, some suggest that certain women may choose jobs in which skills deteriorate or become outdated less quickly. As a result, this may allow women to leave and return to work while minimizing any effect on their earnings.

Alternative Work Arrangements Offer Flexibility but Some May Affect Earnings

Another way that women manage work and family responsibilities is by choosing to use alternative work arrangements, which may affect their career advancement and earnings.[3] For example, some women choose to work a part-time schedule, take leave from work, or use flextime. While some research indicates that certain arrangements may help women maintain their careers during times when they need flexibility, other research suggests that there may be negative effects.

No single, national data source exists that provides information about all workers who use alternative work arrangements. However, some data exist from narrowly scoped studies that focus on particular types of work arrangements, types of employees, or individual companies. Even when employers offer alternative arrangements to all workers, some research and the companies we interviewed indicate that women are more likely than men to use certain arrangements, while both men and women use others in similar proportions. Specifically, women are more likely than men to take leave from work for family reasons and to work part time for family reasons even when these options are available to both men and women. According to our interviews and some literature, some workers—particularly men—are reluctant to use alternative arrangements because they perceive that their advancement and earnings will be negatively affected. This may help to explain why men tend to use personal days, sick days, or vacation time instead of taking family leave. On the other hand, similar proportions of men and women use flextime and telecommuting when these options are available. However, according to some research, men are more likely than women to work in the jobs, organizations, or high-level, high-paying positions that have these options available.

Comprehensive, national data are lacking on how career advancement and earnings may be affected by using alternative work arrangements, but some limited research does exist. Certain researchers indicate that using certain work arrangements may have some beneficial career effects if they help workers maintain career linkages or skills that they might otherwise lose. For example, for women who would have left the workforce or changed jobs if they did not have access to alternative arrangements that could help them manage work and family, part-time work[4] may allow them to maintain job skills, knowledge, or career momentum. In addition, women who can take leave with the guarantee of returning to a similar job benefit because they maintain links with an employer where they have built up specific job-related skills.

Other research indicates that using certain alternative work arrangements may have negative effects on career advancement and earnings. Specifically, employers may view these workers as not conforming to the ideal worker norm because they are not at work as much or during the same work hours as their managers or co-workers. Research indicates that some arrangements, such as leave, part-time work, and telecommuting, reduce workers' "face time"—the amount of time spent in the workplace.[5]

Given that some employers use face time as an indicator of workers' productivity, those who lack face time may experience negative career effects. According to some experts and literature, some employers may view women who use alternative arrangements as less available, less valuable, or less committed to their work. This may result in less challenging work, fewer career opportunities, fewer promotions, and less pay. However, one company representative that we interviewed told us that workers using these arrangements are not necessarily less committed and that, in some cases, they work harder. For example, several of the women we interviewed who were scheduled to work less than full time noted that they sometimes came into the office or worked at home on their scheduled days off. . . .

Managerial support for use of alternative work arrangements is important when considering any effects on advancement and earnings. According to our company interviews, some managers do not support use of these arrangements because they are seen as accommodations to certain workers—even though the company's leadership views them as part of the overall business strategy. Workers who use these arrangements may experience negative effects if managers place limits on the types of work and responsibilities they receive. For example, one worker we interviewed noted that she has not been assigned a high-profile project because she works a part-time schedule. Most of the companies we interviewed noted the importance of managers in implementing alternative work arrangements, and as a result, many train managers on this topic. For example, several companies train managers to focus on the quality of an individual's work rather than on when (i.e., what time of day) or where (i.e., at home or at the workplace) they do their work. One company also revised managers' performance criteria to include their response to flexible work arrangements.

On the other hand, some workers do not have the option to use alternative work arrangements for several reasons. For example, some managers do not allow workers to use alternative arrangements because they want to directly monitor their workers, they fear that too many others will also request these arrangements, or they do not understand how it relates to the company's bottom line. In addition, some workers—often those who are lower paid—do not have the option to use alternative arrangements because the nature of their job does not allow it. For example, telecommuting may not be feasible for administrative assistants because they must be in the office to support their bosses. Furthermore, low-paid workers often cannot afford to choose a work arrangement that reduces their pay.

For example, some women in lower-paying jobs cannot afford to take any unpaid maternity leave, or to take it for an extended period of time, because of their financial situation.

Potential for Direct or Indirect Discrimination

Debate exists whether decisions that women make to manage work and family responsibilities are freely made or influenced by underlying discrimination. Some experts believe that women are free to make choices about work and family, and willingly accept the earnings consequences.

Specifically, certain experts believe that some women place higher priority on home and family, and voluntarily trade off career advancement and earnings to focus on these responsibilities. Other experts believe that some women place similar priority on family and career. Alternatively, other women place higher priority on career and may delay or decide not to have children. However, other experts believe that underlying discrimination exists in the presumption that women have primary responsibility for home and family, and as a result, women are forced to make decisions to accommodate these responsibilities. One example of this is a woman who must work part time for childcare reasons, but would have preferred to work full time if she did not have this family responsibility. In addition, some experts also suggest that women face other societal and workplace discrimination that may result in lower earnings. However, according to other experts, although women may still face discrimination in the workplace, it is not a systematic problem and legal remedies are already in place. For example, Title VII of the Civil Rights Act of 1964 prohibits employment discrimination based on gender.

According to some experts and literature, women face societal discrimination that may affect their career advancement and earnings. Some research suggests that the career aspirations of men and women may be influenced by societal norms about gender roles. For example, parents, peers, or institutions (such as schools or the media) may teach them that certain occupations—such as nursing or teaching, which tend to be relatively lower-paying—are identified with women while others are identified with men. As a result, men and women may view different fields or occupations as valuable or socially acceptable. According to some experts, societal discrimination may help explain why men and women tend to be concentrated in different occupations. For example, some research has found that women tend to be over-represented in clerical and service jobs, while men are disproportionately employed in blue-collar craft and laborer jobs.[6] Other research suggests that gender differences exist even among those who are college educated. For example, men tend to be concentrated in majors such as engineering and mathematics, while women are typically concentrated in majors such as social work and education. Research indicates that men and women who work in female dominated occupations earn less than comparable workers in other occupations.

Additionally, some experts and literature suggest that women face discrimination in the workplace. This type of discrimination may affect what type of jobs women are hired into or whether they are promoted. In some cases, employers or clients may underestimate women's abilities or male co-workers may resist working with women, particularly if women are in higher-level positions. Employers may also discriminate based on their presumptions about women as a group in terms of family responsibilities—rather than considering each woman's individual situation. For example, employers may be less likely to hire or promote women because they assume that women may be less committed or may be more likely to quit for home and family reasons. To the extent that employers who offer higher-paying jobs discriminate against women in this way, women may not have the same earnings opportunities as men.

Finally, other experts suggest that both men and women who are parents face discrimination in the workplace due to their family responsibilities in terms of hiring, promotions, and terminations on the job. According to some literature, discrimination may occur if employers enact policies or practices that have a disproportionately negative impact on one group of workers, such as women with children. For example, if an employer has a policy that excludes part-time workers from promotions, this could have a significant effect on women because they are more likely to work part time. Other experts suggest that workplace practices reflecting ideal worker norms—such as requiring routine overtime for promotion—could be considered discrimination. This could impact women more (particularly mothers) and may result in a disproportionate number of men in high-level positions.

Endnotes

1. Part-time work schedules allow employees to reduce their work hours from the traditional 40 hours per week in exchange for a reduced salary and possibly pro-rated benefits. Job sharing—a form of part-time work—allows two employees to share job responsibilities, salary, and benefits of one full-time position.

2. In contrast, other experts indicate that flexibility is often available in higher paying jobs, particularly those where workers have more authority and autonomy.

3. Since women are more likely than men to use certain alternative work arrangements, any effects apply disproportionately to women in these cases.

4. Research indicates that different types of part-time work exist. Some part-time jobs require relatively low skills, and offer low pay and little opportunity for advancement. In contrast, other part-time jobs are work schedules that employers create to retain or attract workers who cannot or do not want to work full time. These jobs are often higher skilled and higher paying with advancement potential.

5. The idea of "face time" may apply primarily to certain types of jobs, such as professional, white-collar jobs or those that require contact with clients or customers.

6. Notably, research indicates that women tend to be concentrated in service-producing occupations, such as retail trade and government, which lose relatively few jobs or actually gain jobs during recessions. However, men tend to be concentrated in goods-producing industries, such as construction and manufacturing, which often lose jobs during recessions.

49

Cause of Death: Inequality

Alejandro Reuss

Inequality Kills

You won't see inequality on a medical chart or a coroner's report under "cause of death." You won't see it listed among the top killers in the United States each year. All too often, however, it is social inequality that lurks behind a more immediate cause of death, be it heart disease or diabetes, accidental injury or homicide. Few of the top causes of death are "equal opportunity killers." Instead, they tend to strike poor people more than rich people, the less educated more than the highly educated, people lower on the occupational ladder more than those higher up, or people of color more than white people.

Statistics on mortality and life expectancy do not provide a perfect map of social inequality. For example, the life expectancy for women in the United States is about six years longer than the life expectancy for men, despite the many ways in which women are subordinated to men. Take most indicators of socioeconomic status, however, and most causes of death, and it's a strong bet that you'll find illness and injury (or "morbidity") and mortality increasing as status decreases.

Men with less than 12 years of education are more than twice as likely to die of chronic diseases (e.g., heart disease), more than three times as likely to die as a result of injury, and nearly twice as likely to die of communicable diseases, compared to those with 13 or more years of education. Women with family incomes below $10,000 are more than three times as likely to die of heart disease and nearly three times as likely to die of diabetes, compared to those with family incomes above $25,000. African Americans are more likely than whites to die of heart disease; stroke; lung, colon, prostate, and breast cancer, as well as all cancers combined; liver disease; diabetes; AIDS; accidental injury; and homicide. In all, the lower you are in a social hierarchy, the worse your health the shorter your life are likely to be.

Reprinted by permission of Dollars & Sense, a progressive economics magazine (www.dollarsandsense.org).

The Worse Off In the United States Are Not Well Off by World Standards

You often hear it said that even poor people in rich countries like the United States are rich compared to ordinary people in poor countries. While that may be true when it comes to consumer goods like televisions or telephones, which are widely available even to poor people in the United States, it's completely wrong when it comes to health.

In a 1996 study published in the *New England Journal of Medicine,* University of Michigan researchers found that African-American females living to age 15 in Harlem had a 65% chance of surviving to age 65, about the same as women in India. Meanwhile, Harlem's African-American males had only a 37% chance of surviving to age 65, about the same as men in Angola or the Democratic Republic of Congo. Among both African-American men and women, infectious diseases and diseases of the circulatory system were the prime causes of high mortality.

It takes more income to achieve a given life expectancy in a rich country like the United States than it does to achieve the same life expectancy in a less affluent country. So the higher money income of a low-income person in the United States, compared to a middle-income person in a poor country, does not necessarily translate into a longer life span. The average income per person in African-American families, for example, is more than five times the per capita income of El Salvador. The life expectancy for African American men in the United States, however, is only about 67 years, the same as the average life expectancy for men in El Salvador.

Health Inequalities In the United States Are Not Just About Access to Health Care

Nearly one sixth of the U.S. population lacks health insurance, including about 44% of poor people. A poor adult with a health problem is only half as likely to see a doctor as a high-income adult. Adults living in low-income areas are more than twice as likely to be hospitalized for a health problem that could have been effectively treated with timely out-patient care, compared with adults living in high-income areas. Obviously, lack of access to health care is a major health problem.

But so are environmental and occupational hazards; communicable diseases; homicide and firearm-related injuries; and smoking, alcohol consumption, lack of exercise, and other risk factors. These dangers all tend to affect lower-income people more than higher-income, less-educated people more than more-educated, and people of color more than whites. African-American children are more than twice as likely as white children to be hospitalizes for asthma, which is linked to air pollution. Poor men are nearly six times as likely as high-income men to have elevated blood-lead levels, which reflect both residential and workplace environmental hazards. African-American men are more than seven times as likely to fall victim to homicide as white men; African-American women, more than four times as likely as white women. The less education someone has, the more likely they are to smoke or to drink heavily. The lower someone's income, the less likely they are to get regular exercise.

Michael Marmot, a pioneer in the study of social inequality and health, notes that so-called diseases of affluence—disorders, like heart disease, associated with high-calorie and high-fat diets, lack of physical activity, etc.—are most prevalent among the *least affluent* people in rich societies. While recognizing the role of such "behavioral" risk factors as smoking in producing poor health, he argues, "It is not sufficient . . . to ask what contribution smoking makes to generating the social gradient in ill health, but we must ask, why is there a social gradient in smoking?" What appear to be individual "lifestyle" decisions often reflect a broader social epidemiology.

Greater Income Inequality Goes Hand In Hand with Poorer Health

Numerous studies suggest that the more unequal the income distribution in a country, state, or city, the lower the life expectancies for people at all income levels. One study published in the *American Journal of Public Health*, for example, shows that U.S. metropolitan areas with low per capita incomes and low levels of income inequality have lower mortality rates than areas with high median incomes and high levels of income inequality. Meanwhile, for a given per capita income range, mortality rates always decline as inequality declines.

R. G. Wilkinson, perhaps the researcher most responsible for relating health outcomes to overall levels of inequality (rather than individual income levels), argues that greater income inequality causes worse health outcomes independent of its effects on poverty. Wilkinson and his associates suggest several explanations for this relationship. First, the bigger the income gap between rich and poor, the less inclined the well off are to pay taxes for public services they either do not use or use in low proportion to the taxes they pay. Lower spending on public hospitals, schools, and other basic services does not affect wealthy people's life expectancies very much, but it affects poor people's life expectancies a great deal. Second, the bigger the income gap, the lower the overall level of social cohesion. High levels of social cohesion are associated with good health outcomes for several reasons. For example, people in highly cohesive societies are more likely to be active in their communities, reducing social isolation, a known health risk factor. (See Thad Williamson, "Social Movements are Good for Your Health," p. 7.)

Numerous researchers have criticized Wilkinson's conclusions, arguing that the real reason income inequality tends to be associated with worse health outcomes is that it is associated with higher rates of poverty. But even if they are right and income inequality causes worse health *simply by bringing about greater poverty*, that hardly makes for a defense of inequality. Poverty and inequality are like partners in crime. "[W]hether public policy focuses primarily on the elimination of poverty or on reduction in income disparity," argue Wilkinson critics Kevin Fiscella and Peter Franks, "neither goal is likely to be achieved in the absence of the other."

Differences In Status May Be Just As Important As Income Levels

Even after accounting for differences in income, education, and other factors, the life expectancy for African Americans is less than that for whites. U.S. researchers are beginning to explore the relationship between high blood pressure among African Americans and the racism of the surrounding society. African Americans tend to suffer from high blood pressure, a risk factor for circulatory disease, more often than whites. Moreover, studies have found that, when confronted with racism, African Americans suffer larger and longer-lasting increases in blood pressure than when faced with other stressful situations. Broader surveys relating blood pressure in African Americans to perceived instances of racial discrimination have yielded complex results, depending on social class, gender, and other factors.

Stresses cascade down social hierarchies and accumulate among the least empowered. Even researchers focusing on social inequality and health, however, have been surprised by the large effects on mortality. Over 30 years ago, Michael Marmot and his associates undertook a landmark study, known as Whitehall I, of health among British civil servants. Since the civil servants shared many characteristics regardless of job classification—an office work environment, a high degree of job security, etc.—the researchers expected to find only modest health differences among them. To their surprise, the study revealed a sharp increase in mortality with each step down the job hierarchy—even from the highest grade to the second highest. Over ten years, employees in the lowest grade were three times as likely to die as those in the highest grade. One factor was that people in lower grades showed a higher incidence of many "lifestyle" risk factors, like smoking, poor diet, and lack of exercise. Even when the researchers controlled for such factors, however, more than half the mortality gap remained.

Marmot noted that people in the lower job grades were less likely to describe themselves as having "control over their working lives" or being "satisfied with their work situation," compared to those higher up. While people in higher job grades were more likely to report "having to work at a fast pace," lower-level civil servants were more likely to report feelings of hostility, the main stress-related risk factor for heart disease. Marmot concluded that "psycho-social" factors—the psychological costs of being lower in the hierarchy—played an important role in the unexplained mortality gap. Many of us have probably said to ourselves, after a trying day on the job, "They're killing me." Turns out it's not just a figure of speech. Inequality kills—and it starts at the bottom.

Resources: Lisa Berkman, "Social Inequalities and Health: Five Key Points for Policy-Makers to Know," February 5, 2001, Kennedy School of Government, Harvard University; *Health, United States, 1998, with Socioeconomic Status and Health Chartbook,* National Center for Health Statistics < www.cdc.gov/nchs>; Ichiro Kawachi, Bruce P. Kennedy, and Richard G. Wilkinson, eds., *The Society and Population Health Reader, Volume I Income Inequality and Health,* 1999; Michael Marmot, "Social Differences in Mortality: The Whitehall Studies," *Adult Mortality in Developed Countries: From Description to Explanation,* Alan D. Lopez, Graziella Caselli, and Tapani Valkonen, eds., 1995;

Michael Marmot, "The Social Pattern of Health and Disease," *Health and Social Organization: Towards a Health Policy for the Twenty-First Century,* David Blanc, Eric Brunner, and Richard Wilkinson, eds., 1996; Arline T. Geronimus, et al., "Excess Mortality Among Blacks and Whites in the United States," *The New England Journal of Medicine* 335 (21), November 21, 1996; Nancy Krieger, Ph.D., and Stephen Sidney, M.D., "Racial Discrimination and Blood Pressure: The CARDIA Study of Young Black and White Adults," *American Journal of Public Health* 86 (10). October 1996; *Human Development Report 2000,* UN Development Programme; *World Development Indicators 2000,* World Bank.

50

Injustice Anywhere

Arlene Holpp Scala

Injustice anywhere is a threat to justice everywhere.
—Martin Luther King Jr., Letter from Birmingham Jail, April 16, 1963

Injustices that capture media attention can lead to justice. The widely publicized tragic killing of Matthew Shepard, a White, gay middle-class college student, in Laramie, Wyoming, in 1998 led to a heightened awareness of the dangers faced by gay youth. Artistic and educational programs were developed in response to his murder. Although this attention did not bring justice in terms of hate crime legislation, it did advance the cause of lesbian, gay, bisexual, and transgender (LGBT) rights, especially for youth. Unfortunately, the 2003 killing of a Black, lesbian, 15-year-old high school student, Sakia Gunn, in Newark, New Jersey, did not get the media coverage that might have also advanced the cause of just treatment for lesbian and gay young people. At a Newark vigil a year after the killing, Councilman Cory Booker, who was later elected mayor of Newark, asked why there had not been a "national outcry" in response to the crime (Chan, 2009). I contend that the answer rests with the imbedded issues of racism, sexism, and classism in U.S. society.

LGBT rights are about justice and fairness! I always argue that these rights are human rights, but in this chapter I will focus on the issues of justice and the law. LGBT people are members of a minority group that has been denied basic civil rights. We learn about the absence of a right when there is no recourse for justice. The lack of justice for LGBT people exists throughout the United States and abroad.

Some gay activists have always argued that negative attention is better than invisibility. Society cannot hope for justice unless the existence of injustice is made evident. When Bill Clinton was elected president of the United States in 1992, and establishing the right for "out" gay people to serve in the military was one of his campaign promises. He did address the issue, but failed to bring justice to the lesbian and gay people in the military. His "Don't Ask, Don't Tell" compromise policy fell short of justice. However, the controversy around this issue brought the terms "lesbian" and "gay" to the dinner table as news programs and print news gave widespread coverage to the military policy.

Imagine how deflationary the peroration of Martin Luther King Jr.'s "I Have a Dream" speech would have been if it had ended: "Equal at last! Equal at last! Thank God Almighty we are equal at last!" Yet it was chiefly equality, not liberty, that King was after.—Richard D. Mohr, *The Long Arc of Justice*

In the United States, lesbian and gay marriage is a leading issue of social justice. The fight for lesbian and gay marriage goes back to 1972 when the National Coalition of Gay Organizations (NCGO) demanded equal marriage rights for all citizens (Tadlock, Gordon, & Pop, 2007, pp. 193–194). When this demand failed in all of the states, NCGO set it sights on municipal governments and sought domestic partnership rights rather than marriage rights. In 1982, San Francisco, under the leadership of Mayor Dianne Feinstein, became the first city to recognize domestic partnership rights. In 1996, the federal government passed the Defense of Marriage Act (DOMA) in order to deny lesbian and gay people the right to marry by defining marriage as a union between a man and a woman. Forty-one states followed by passing their own DOMA laws (Deakin, Greer, & Skinner, 2009). In 1999, the Vermont Supreme Court ruled that same-sex couples were entitled to the same benefits and protections as heterosexual married couples, and the nation's first civil union law was created (Tadlock et al., 2007, p. 194).

The U.S. Supreme Court's 2003 decision in *Lawrence v. Texas* set the stage for the same-sex marriage debate by throwing out the sodomy laws in Texas and with it all sodomy laws nationwide (Tadlock et al., 2007, p. 195). This decision overturned the 1986 *Bowers v. Hardwick* decision, which had upheld gay-specific sodomy laws against privacy challenges (Mohr, 2005, p. 7). In 2003, Massachusetts legalized same-sex marriage; California and Connecticut followed. In 2004, President George W. Bush called for a constitutional amendment barring same-sex marriage (Mohr, 2005), but it did not lead to an amendment that would have denied a specific right to a portion of the U.S. population. Lesbian and gay people won the right to marry in California in 2007. Then in 2008, California put the state's new right-to-marry law before the voters in the November election as Proposition 8. The proposition was approved by 52% of the electorate, and lesbians and gay men had their right to marry taken away (Deakin et al., 2009). In 2009, there are continuing legal challenges to the loss this civil right.

In Florida, where gay marriage was already illegal, 62% of the voters in the November 2008 approved the "Marriage Protection Amendment" (Deakin et al., 2009), which banned any union similar to marriage as well as any recognition of and/or benefits for unmarried couples, both straight and gay. In Arizona, another state where gay marriage was already illegal, 52% of the voters in 2008 passed Proposition 102, which amended the state constitution so that it defined marriage as between a man and a woman (Deakins et al., 2009). The purpose of the amendment was to prevent future court rulings from allowing same-sex marriage.

Although this trend is disheartening there have been some states willing to expand protections of lesbian and gays. New Hampshire and New Jersey allow civil unions. One common misunderstanding is that civil unions provide lesbian and gay couples with the same rights as marriage. However, a study by the State of New Jersey Civil Union Review Commission (2008) has documented lesbian and gay couples who have civil unions and continue to suffer discrimination when their unions are not recognized by employers and others.

Five states currently allow same-sex marriage, Massachusetts, Vermont, Connecticut, Maine and Iowa. A few other states are considering extending Marriage equality, Hawaii, New York and New Jersey, (NGLTF,2009; Hawaii debates, 2009).

For people who want to argue that marriage has always meant the same thing, we can look to history to see the changing face of marriage. The law used to dole out marital responsibilities based on the sex of the partner, and consequently, the husband had a legal obligation to take care of his wife's material needs without his wife having any corresponding obligation (Mohr, 2005, p. 65). In the past, the law permitted a husband to legally sell his wife's property without her consent. This is no longer the case. As a result of the women's movement, today there is more justice in the institution of marriage, and traditional gender roles are being replaced by a more equitable distribution of responsibilities. It used to be that a husband, by definition, could not rape his wife anymore than he could be seen as raping himself. As a society, we no longer accept this reasoning. In a similar way our evolving understanding of equality and justice makes it unacceptable to deny same-sex couples the right to marriage.

The right of lesbian and gay people to adopt children is another justice issue. Initially children of lesbian and gay parents were typically born to them during earlier heterosexual relationships before one or both parents came out as lesbian or gay. Today, more and more lesbian and gay couples are parenting. The National Center for Lesbian Rights (NCLR) (2004), has reported that over six million children in the United States are being raised in families headed by same-sex parents. Before lesbian and gay adoptions could become an issue, however, child custody and visitation rights for lesbian and gay parents needed to be treated as justice issues. In the 21st century, an increasing number of states are taking a neutral stance regarding a parent's sexual orientation when determining custody and visitation rights (Rimmerman & Wilcox, 2007, p. 24).

Many states now allow second-parent and joint adoptions by same-sex partners. In a second-parent adoption a partner adopts the child of her or his partner (September, 2003, p. 144). In most adoption cases, when someone adopts a child, another person loses parental rights; however, in the typical second-parent adoption case, one lesbian parent bears the child, and the second parent adopts the child, but the biological parent does not lose any parental rights. States must honor second-parent adoptions from other states (National Gay & Lesbian Task Force [NGLTF], 2008).

According to the 2000 federal census, 594,000 households were headed by same-sex couples; this figure is generally assumed to be a low because many couples probably did not want their same-sex relationship reported to the government (Mohr, 2005, p. 59). Although marriage has not yet been legalized in all of the states permitting second-parent adoption, courts in 26 states and the District of Columbia have acknowledged same-sex families by allowing second-parent adoption (NGLTF, 2008). In 17 states it is unclear whether the state adoption law permits second-parent adoptions, and in 7 states second-parent adoption is not permitted (NGLTF, 2008). In some states resistance to adoption and foster-parenting by same-sex couples is fierce. In November 2008, 57% of Arkansas voters passed the "Unmarried Couple Adoption Ban," making it illegal for any unmarried couple living together in the state to adopt or to serve as foster parents for children (Deakin et al., 2009).

With second-parent adoption, both parents are entitled to be treated equally by the law (NCLR, 2008). For example, if a heterosexual couple were to separate, each parent would have equal custody rights, and these rights would be determined by a court without giving an automatic advantage to either parent. Because unmarried couples do not have the parental rights of the legally married, the NCLR urges non-biological and non-adopting parents to obtain an adoption or parentage judgment. Justice cannot be assumed for same-sex parents without all of the available legal protection and documentation, including medical authorization, guardianship agreements, and wills (NCLR, 2008).

The last justice issue that I will address in this article is education. In a country that claims to value children, LGBT students are often not guaranteed the right to an education in an affirming and safe environment. Harassment is often accepted by educators and school administrators. This is documented in *Hatred in the Hallways: Violence and Discrimination against Lesbian, Gay, Bisexual, and Transgender Students in U.S. Schools*, an important book published by Human Rights Watch in 2001. Since that comprehensive study, however, the situation has changed little in most schools. According to the 2007 National School Climate Survey of 6,209 middle and high school students in all 50 states and the District of Columbia Gay, Lesbian, & Straight Education Network [GLSEN], 2008), 9 out of 10 LGBT students (86.2%) experienced harassment at school. Out of this group, 44.1% reported being physically harassed and 22.1% reported being physically assaulted at school during a one-year period because of their sexual orientation or gender expression. Another 60.8% felt unsafe at school because of their sexual orientation or gender expression, and 32.7% skipped a day of school during a one-month period as a result of feeling unsafe. The latter figure compares with 4.5 % of a national sample of secondary school students of all sexual orientations and gender expressions who skipped a day of school because they felt unsafe (GLSEN, 2008).

In schools where fairness and justice are educational values there are Gay-Straight Alliances, supportive staff, and a "safe school policy" (GLSEN, 2008). Gay-Straight Alliances are student organizations that advocate for the rights of students for all sexual orientations and gender expressions and many host educational and social events. In schools where these alliances exist, students report hearing fewer homophobic remarks, suffer fewer assaults, and experience less sexual harassment because of their sexual orientation and gender expression. Also, more were likely to report incidents of harassment and assault to school staff and were less likely to feel unsafe. As a result, LGBT students reported feeling more of a sense of belonging to their school community, and were less likely to miss school because of safety concerns. Supportive staff contributed to a positive school experience and an overall feeling of safety, as did a "safe school policy" that included written protections based on sexual orientation and gender expressions. With these interventions in place, academic achievement and aspirations were higher among LGBT students than for LGBT students in schools where the staff was not supportive (GLSEN, 2008).

Looking at the statistics for schools with the interventions in place, it is clear that the rights of LGBT students are not acknowledged in most schools in the United States. Only one-third of students reported having a Gay-Straight Alliance, and only one-third could identify six or more supportive educators, and only a fifth attend a school that had a comprehensive safe school policy (GLSEN, 2008). In addition, laws fall short of protecting LGBT students. Only 11 states and the District of Columbia protect students from bullying and harassment based on sexual orientation, and only 7 states and the District of Columbia protect students on the basis of gender expression.

As with other justice issues, the rights of LGBT students often depend on legal actions. One of the first legal cases involved Aaron Fricke, a gay high school student in Rhode Island, who petitioned the court in 1980 for the right to bring a same-sex date to his high school prom. In the U.S. District Court decision, *Fricke v. Lynch,* the couple was granted the right to attend the prom (Schwartz, 1994). Aaron Fricke's story appears in his memoir *Reflections of a Rock Lobster.* As a result of a lawsuit won in 1996 by Jamie Nabozny, a gay student from Ashland, Wisconsin, for the first time a school administration was held liable for failing to deal with the anti-gay hatred (Religious Tolerance, 1999). When he was a high school student, Jamie suffered taunts, threats, a simulated rape, and a beating that resulted in the need for abdominal surgery. When first notified about the abuse, school administrators told him and his parents that he would have to learn to expect abuse because he is gay. Later, they responded by placing him in a special education class, and made him travel to school on a bus with elementary school children so that his peers could not attack him. Eventually, he dropped out of school and later obtained his GED (Religious Tolerance, 1999).

As the justice struggle continues for LGBT people, there are many victories and signs of movement toward human and civil rights for people of all sexual orientations and gender expressions. In 2009, *The New York Times* reported that Chance Malley, a public school teacher, invited his entire seventh grade class to his ceremony celebrating his commitment to another man (Dominus, 2009). Malley, who had come out to his students during a diversity workshop earlier in the school year, invited his students in response to the request of some students to attend his celebration. There were a few raised eyebrows and negative murmurs by some parents, but the overall response was affirming. There is another reason to anticipate justice for lesbians and gay men. Fifteen years after "Don't Ask, Don't Tell" became military policy, President Barack Obama, who picked gay Anglican Bishop Gene Robinson to offer an inaugural prayer at the Lincoln Memorial, has promised to revisit the discriminatory policy. According to polls, in 2009, three-quarters of Americans now believe gays and lesbians should serve openly in the military, compared with fewer than half in 1993 (Bronstein, 2009).

Finally, there are signs of justice internationally. In 2008, the United Nations issued a statement calling for the worldwide decriminalization of homosexuality. Currently, 70 UN members outlaw homosexuality (in several countries homosexual acts can be punished by execution (Lee, 2009). The Bush administration refused to sign the UN declaration, but the Obama administration reversed the U.S. stance and formally endorsed it, joining 66 other UN members. Although a UN declaration has no legal power, it is an important signal to the world that lesbian and gay rights are human rights.

References

Bronstein, P. (2009). "Don't Ask, Don't Tell" switch makes "Gay" the new civil rights issue. Retrieved March 5, 2009, from http://www.huffingtonpost.com/phil-bronstein/dont-tell-switch_b_157947.html.

Chan, S. (2009). Film examines a Newark hate crime. *The New York Times*, February 18, (page unknown).

Deakin, M. B., Greer, J., & Skinner, D. E. (2009). Elections brought UUs joy and sorrow. *UU World*, 23(Spring), 48.

Dominus, S. (2009). Most of the seventh grade will be at the commitment ceremony. *The New York Times*, March 23, p. A13.

Fricke, A. (1981). Reflections of a rock lobster: a story about growing up gay. Boston, Alyson Publications.

Gay, Lesbian & Straight Education Network [GLSEN]. (2008). 2007 National school climate survey: Nearly 9 out of 10 LGBT students harassed. Retrieved on March 1, 2009, from http://www.glsen.org/cgi-bin/iowa/all/news/record2340.html.

Hawaii debates same-sex unions. (2009). *The New York Times*, February 23, p. A17.

Human Rights Watch. (2009, February 19). Jamaica: Condemn homophobic remarks. Retrieved February 21, 2009, from http://www.hrw.org/en/news/2009/02/19.

Lee, M. (2009). US endorses UN gay rights text. Retrieved on March 23, 2009, from http://www.google.com/hostednews/ap/article/ALeqM5hMYVcXoZR7YRqBU-8kZ09.

Mohr, R. D. (2005). *The long arc of justice: Lesbian and gay marriage, equality and rights*. New York: Columbia University Press.

National Center for Lesbian Rights [NCLR]. (2004). Adoption by lesbian, gay and bisexual parents: An overview of current law. Retrieved March 13, 2009, from http://www.ndrights.org/site/DocServer/adptn0204.pdf?ID=1221.

National Center for Lesbian Rights [NCLR]. (2008). Legal recognition of LGBT families. Retrieved March 13, 2009, from http://ndrights.or/site/DocServer/Legal_Recognition_of_LGBT_Families_04_2008.pdf?docJD=2861.

National Gay & Lesbian Task Force [NGLTF]. (2009). Relationship Recognition for Same-Sex Couples in the U.S. map. Retrieved May 10, 2009, from http://www.thetaskforce.org/downloads/reports/issue_maps/relationship_recognition_05_09_color.pdf.

National Gay & Lesbian Task Force [NGLTF]. (2008). Second-parent adoption laws map. Retrieved March 23, 2009, from http://www.thetaskforce.org/reports_and_research/second_parent_adoption_laws.

New Jersey Department of Law and Public Safety. New Jersey Civil Union Review Commission. (2008). The Legal, Medical, Economic & Social Consequences of New Jersey's Civil Union Law. Trenton. The Department.

Religious Tolerance. (1999). Protection of les/gay students from harassment. Retrieved March 1, 2009, from http://www.religioustolerance.org/hom_stud.htm.

Rimmerman, C. A., & Wilcox, C. (Eds.). (2007). *The politics of same-sex marriage*. Chicago: University of Chicago Press.

Schwartz, W. (1994). Improving the school experience for gay, lesbian, and bisexual students. ERIC Digest No. 101. Retrieved March 1, 2009, from *http://www.ericdigests.org/1995-2/gay.htm*.

Sember, B. M. (2003). *Gay & lesbian rights: A guide for GLBT singles, couples, and families*. Naperville, IL: Sphinx.

Sullivan, E. (2008). Candidates face off. *The Advocate*, 1018, 18.

Tadlock, B. L., Gordon, C. A., & Popp, E. (2007). Framing the issue of same-sex marriage: Traditional values versus equal rights. In C.A. Rimmerman & C. Wilcox (eds.), *The politics of same-sex marriage* (pp. 193–214). Chicago: University of Chicago Press.

SECTION 5

Where Do We Go from Here? The Nexus of Citizenship and Justice

51

The Education Experience of Immigrants in the United States

Martha Thomas

Introduction

Over the last few decades, the United States has witnessed a surge in immigration unseen since the turn of the century. Between 1990 and 2000, the foreign-born population increased by 57 percent, from 19.8 million to 31.1 million, compared with an increase of 9.3 percent for the native population and 13 percent for the total U.S. population (U.S. Census Bureau, 2003). These new immigrants hail from countries as diverse as Mexico, China, South Korea, and El Salvador. A consequence of this increase in size and diversity of immigrants has been a rise in the number of children from immigrant families attending school in the United States. The Federation for American Immigration Reform has shown that the share of students in the U.S. who are immigrants or the children of immigrants has tripled in the past 30 years; in 1970, they were only 6.5 percent of the student body. Today, one in five students has at least one foreign-born parent (The Federation for American Immigration Reform 2002).

Immigrant students are an ever increasing presence in the classroom[1]. What are the experiences of these immigrant students in the American educational system? Have the education system been able to meet the needs of these students? Have these students been able to enjoy the same level of educational success as their native born (American) counterparts? Does the level of educational achievement vary by class of immigrant or country of origin? Are there resources available to meet the specific needs of those immigrants who are struggling to adjust?

Extant literature has drawn mixed conclusions on the educational experience of immigrants in the United States. On the one hand, are those who argue that immigrant students attending American schools have a positive and rewarding experience, while on the other hand are those who postulate that the American system is wholly incapable of managing the challenges faced by immigrant students. The first group of scholars point to factors such as the superior academic performance of some immigrant groups while the latter group focuses on issues such as the dropout statistics and the quality of education in reaching their conclusion (Hood 2003; Johnson 2008; Crosnoe 2009).

In this chapter I survey these two groups of literature dissecting the explanations provided and offering my view on how immigrants can be better served in the education system. First I discuss why this analysis is important and what broad contributions it makes to our understanding of education in America. Then I survey the scholarship, first presenting the arguments offered by those who postulate that immigrants enjoy significant achievements within the current American education system. This is followed by a survey of the work done by those who offer the opposite view. I then reconcile these contrasting views by offering a lens through which these contributions can be analyzed. I conclude by making some suggestions about how the obvious challenges facing the new 'type' of immigrant to the United States can be addressed.

The Contribution

This analysis is important for several reasons. For one many immigrant populations have numerous socioeconomic disadvantages that hinder economic mobility, and so its fortunes are tied to the American educational system. In the past, immigrants could gain financial security by accessing the large manufacturing sector of the American economy, which allowed entry into secure job trajectories without formal education (Crosnoe 2005). This sector however, has drastically declined, leaving education as the main path to a better quality of life (Pastor, 2001; Wilson, 1991). Given this, it is important to analyze whether and to what extent the American system of education is facilitating the upward mobility of these immigrant groups.

The second reason is motivated by an interest in understanding the academic performance of immigrant students. Without question there are some immigrant groups whose academic achievements are superior to even that of their American counterparts. The Public Policy Institute of California reported that immigrants from East Asia tends to outperform all other students and are actually more likely to obtain a bachelors or even masters degree (Johnson, 2008). At the same time the study also points out that immigrants from Latin America tend to be less educated than all other groups (Johnson 2008). Understanding why this is the case will allow us to better meet the needs of those that are struggling.

The Superior Academic Achievement of Immigrants in the United States

There is a wealth of empirical evidence that immigrant youth do comparatively well in elementary and secondary school. After reviewing the transcript of 745 students enrolled in Los Angeles elementary, middle and high schools, McDonnell and Hill (1993) found that immigrants were just as or even more likely to take college courses for admission into four year colleges. Similarly Kao and Tienda (1995) found that immigrant children tended to earn higher grades than native students after controlling for socioeconomic characteristics.

Studies suggest several reasons that may contribute to these findings. One factor is that immigrant students are more motivated and are willing to work harder than other students (Duran and Weffer 1992). In fact, some studies even assert that teachers prefer teaching immigrants because they tend to be brighter than native born students. In sum, the argument here is that immigrants are institutionally favored by the educational system.

Another reason may be the choices immigrants make. Immigrant students may be faster at adapting to their new school environment. Some have argued that they are more likely to do whatever it takes to achieve upward economic mobility (Duran and Weffer 1992). Thus they tend to be less affected by hostile social and constrained economic environments. They are less reactive to problematic circumstances and better able to "shut-out" the atmosphere and situation in which they live.

Beyond the choices of immigrant students, the attitude of their parents is also cited as another factor for their superior academic performance (Kao and Tienda 1995). The parents of immigrant students tend to have high expectations of their children. They place a high normative value on education and continuously instill the importance of and value of a good education as an important tool for mobility and assimilation into American society. To this end they set aside time for homework and continuously monitor their children's performance in school (Rumbaut 1994). A related argument made by some studies is that the educational attainment of the parents of immigrants also predisposes immigrant students to higher levels of achievement than the average native born student (Fulingi 1997). According to Filingi, the parents of immigrant students on average tend to have received high levels of education in their home country and thus are better able to instill the value of a good education in their children. For example over 40% of the Filipino born immigrants have received a bachelor's degree and over one quarter of them are employed in professional managerial or technical jobs. These parents offer their experience and their attainment of upward mobility as an example that their children can follow.

The general conclusion of these studies is that there is no need to develop policies targeted uniquely to immigrants given that they tend to benefit the most from the American system of education and also tend to outperform their American born counterparts.

The Challenges Faced by Immigrants

In theory, the educational system is intended to alleviate social and economic inequalities by providing opportunities to all children that allows them to make their own way in life. But, some argue that this ideal does not always bear out in reality, largely because the opportunities for different populations of children vary widely in quality and quantity.

One recent study that has empirically demonstrated this lack of connection between the ideal and the reality of American education is Crosnoe (2009). Crosnoe focuses on the experience of Mexican immigrants in elementary school. He uses data from the Early Childhood Longitudinal Study—Kindergarten Cohort for this study. This data is unique in that, in addition to focusing on the immigrant student, it also surveys the parents and teachers of these students. Beyond that, this Longitudinal Study also tracks these students over time—the study started in 1998 and participants have been surveyed four times thus far—following their progress and identifying areas in which immigrant students could be better served.

Crosnoe in his contribution notes that "children from Mexican immigrant families have a good deal to gain from American schools, but their entry points into the educational system differ so sharply from those of their peers that they probably start off on an uneven footing, with lasting repercussions for themselves, their families, and the Mexican American population as a whole" (Crosnoe, 2009, 295). He finds that characteristics of the education environment, that is to say factors beyond the student's socioeconomic status, can be attributed to this lack of achievement in school.

For one, Crosnoe finds that children from Mexican immigrant families attend much larger elementary schools than their peers from other racial/ethnic groups, even net of family background characteristics. This he shows has a negative effect on these students since they tend to rely heavily on social relations and closely knit networks. The impersonal environment of a large school tends to be daunting to Mexican students and this impacts their performance. Second, Crosnoe finds that the schools in which children from Mexican immigrant families were concentrated were characterized by lower levels of teacher experience than those attended by other children. The survey shows that their teachers had been in the profession, and at their current grade level, for shorter periods of time. Thus they lack the experience and skills necessary to adequately support, assist, and nurture these students.

Beyond this, Crosnoe finds that the children of Mexican immigrant families experience hyper-segregation, which has been associated with lower math achievement and mental health problems. "Children from Mexican immigrant families attended schools with higher percentages of minority students than their White peers. More surprisingly, they also attended schools with higher percentages of minority students than their peers from other minority populations" (Crosnoe, 2009, 296). Thus they have according to Crosnoe, replaced African-American children in terms of social isolation. Given this, they suffer from the pitfalls associated with minority over-representation—namely low funding and lack of community support. This tends to have far reaching effects not just on their performance in the classroom but also on their mental stability since they may be frustrated by the academic side of their school.

While Crosnoe (2009) is one of the most recent studies to find a negative effect of education on immigrant students, other earlier studies have also reached the same conclusion. These include (1) Kao (1999) who assessed the relationship between immigrant students and educational achievement using demographic patterns from national datasets; (2) Valenzuela (1999) who unpacked the effects of being foreign–born with more intensive ethnographic work in schools; and (3) Stanton-Salazar, 2001; Suarez-Orozco & Suarez-Orozco, 2001 who utilize multi-method approaches in their studies to show that immigrants from Latin American countries tend to be severely disadvantaged in American schools.

Is it Left, is it Right or is it Both: Reconciling the Contradictory Conclusions

As can be seen above, the literature on immigrants and education provides two conflicting conclusions. On the one hand are those who believe that immigrants are the greatest benefactors in the American education system, while on the other hand are those who believe that immigrants are double-disadvantaged by the current system of American education. Is there a way to reconcile this contradiction? I argue that dissecting immigrants into appropriate types and classes allows us to put these seemingly contrasting conclusions in context.

Separating Immigrant Students into their Appropriate Types

From the studies discussed above, a pattern emerges. Studies touting immigrant students as superior academic achievers tend to focus on the immigrants of Asian origin, while studies bemoaning the difficulties of their education experience tend to focus and speak to the difficulties faced by students of Latin American or Hispanic origin. Understanding the differences between these two groups may shed some light on why both sides present valid arguments about the educational experience of immigrants in the United States. The Latin American experience in the United States has been a very different and comparatively more difficult experience than that of Asian immigrants in the United States.

Two key differences can be readily observed. The first is the educational attainment of their parents. Native Asians with immigrant parents on average, have at least one parent with a college education. They also have a mean family income of more than $60,000 (Kao 1999). This is in contrast with other immigrant groups whose parents have an average annual income in the mid $30,000 range. This difference contributes significantly to the parents' willingness to prioritize their children's educational endeavors and lead by example. Because of higher earnings and more education, immigrant families from Asian backgrounds will be willing to invest in and support their children's education by ensuring that they are placed in better schools and get the support they need.

The differences between both groups also emerge with respect to their acclimatization to American society. Hispanic families as an immigrant group are distinct in their use of Spanish at home. Approximately 83% of immigrant Hispanic youth use their native language exclusively at home, while the comparable figure for Asian immigrants is 65%. The trend is similar for native born immigrant families. Almost 82% of Asian native-born families speak English at home compared to 70% of Hispanic native born children (Cosnoe 2009). The greater effort made by Asians to assimilate into the United States makes the transition easier for this group and this has a profound effort on their performance in the classroom. It means that the learning curve is shorter for these families as there is greater consistency between the home and school environment.

Meeting the Challenges Ahead

The disparity in the educational attainment between Hispanics and other immigrant ethnic groups is cause for concern. Hispanics are not only the largest immigrant group in the United States but also represents the fastest growing minority group. Thus, the educational attainment that Hispanics eventually reach will in large determine the quality of the future labor force of the United States.

Enhancing the educational achievement of this at risk immigrant group will require policies that go beyond the classroom. For one, measures that provide income assistance or various forms of financial assistance to this group will be helpful in alleviating some of the hardships that increase the likelihood of school drop-out among this ethnic immigrant group. While these financial incentives do not have to be specifically targeted to Hispanics they can be aimed at households that fall into the same low income economic-strata as recent Hispanic immigrants.

In addition, special effort should be made to aggressively educate immigrant parents. This will allow them to increase their educational expectations for their children. These parents will be more likely to become more involved in their children's achievement and progress. At the same time, the education of parents increases their own chances for economic mobility, which in turn has a trickle down effect on their children.

And finally, targeted programs and initiatives intended to encourage immigrants to participate in mainstream American society should be pursued. This includes, community programs that acclimatize immigrants to American culture as well as initiates that desensitizes the rest of the community to the stigmas that may permeate about immigrants in the United States. Such programs may go a long way in making immigrants feel a part of the American dream, which ultimately will have a positive impact on the efforts in the classroom.

Endnote

1. In this study, immigrant students refer to those students who were either born in another country but currently reside in the United States, or those who were born in the United States but whose parents are immigrants from another country. I include the latter group since statistics have shown that American born students whose parents are not natives tend to experience many of the same challenges as those students who were not born in the United States (Suarez-Orozco & Suarez-Orozco, 2001).

References

Crosnoe, Robert. 2009. "Family-school connections and the transitions of low-income youths and English language learners from middle school to high school." Development Psychology 45(4).

Crosnoe, Robert. 2005. Double Disadvantage or Signs of Resilience? The Elementary School Contexts of Children from Mexican Immigrant Families. American Educational Research Journal 42(2) 269–303.

Duran, Bernadine and Rafeala Weffer. 1992. "Immigrants' Aspirations, High School Process, and Academic Outcomes." American Educational Research Journal, 29(1):163–181.

Fuligini, Andrew. 1997. The Academic Achievement of Adolescents from Immigrant Families Child Development 68(2): 351–363.

Hood, Lucy. 2003. "Immigrant Students Urban High Schools: The Challenge Continues." Carnegie Corporation of New York. Retrieved from the World Wide Web on August 8, 2009, at: *http://www.carnegie.org/pdf/immigrantstudents.pdf*.

Johnson, Hans. 2008. "Just the Facts: Immigrants and Education." Public Policy Institute of California.

Kao, G. 1999. "Psychological Well-Being and Educational Achievement among Immigrant Youth", in Hernandez Donald J., ed., Children of Immigrants: Health, Adjustment, and Public Assistances, National Academy Press, Washington D.C.

Kao, G., and M. Tienda. 1995. "Optimism and Achievement: The Educational Performance of Immigrant Youth." Social Science Quarterly 76(1).

McDonell, Lorraine, and Hill, Paul. "Newcomers in American Schools: Meeting the Educational Needs of Immigrant Youth." The Rand Corporation.

Rumbaut, R. 1994. "The crucible within: Ethnic identity, self-esteem, and segmented assimilation among children of immigrants." International Migration Review 28(4): 748–794.

Stanton-Salazar, R. D. (2001). *Manufacturing hope and despair: The school and kin support networks of U.S.-Mexican youth.* New York: Teachers College Press.

Suarez-Orozco, C., & Suarez-Orozco, M. (1995). *Transformations: Immigration, family life, and achievement motivation among Latino adolescents.* Stanford, CA: Stanford University Press.

Suarez-Orozco, C., & Suarez-Orozco, M. (2001). *Children of immigration.* Cambridge, MA: Harvard University Press.

The Federation for American Immigration Reform. 2002. "Immigration and School Overcrowding. "Retrieved from the World Wide Web on August 8, 2009, at: *http://www.fairus.org/site/News2?page=NewsArticle*.

U.S. Census Bureau. 2003. "The Foreign-born Population: Census Brief 2000." Retrieved from the World Wide Web on August 9, 2009, at: *http://www.census.gov/prod/2003pubs/c2kbr-34.pdf*.

Valenzuela, A. 1999. *Subtractive Schooling: U.S.- Mexican youth and the politics of caring.* New York: State University of New York Press.

52

On the Duty of Civil Disobedience

Henry David Thoreau

I heartily accept the motto, "That government is best which governs least"; and I should like to see it acted up to more rapidly and systematically. Carried out, it finally amounts to this, which also I believe—"That government is best which governs not at all"; and when men are prepared for it, that will be the kind of government *which the will have*. Government is at best but an expedient; but most governments are usually, and all governments are sometimes, inexpedient. The objections which have been brought against a standing army, and they are many and weighty, and deserve to prevail, may also at last be brought against a standing government. The standing army is only an arm of the standing government. The government itself, which is only the mode which the people have chosen to execute their will, is equally liable to be abused and perverted before the people can act through it. Witness the present Mexican war, the work of comparatively a few individuals using the standing government as their tool; for in the outset, the people would not have consented to this measure.

This American government—what is it but a tradition, though a recent one, endeavoring to transmit itself unimpaired to posterity, but each instant losing some of its integrity? It has not the vitality and force of a single living man; for a single man can bend it to his will. It is a sort of wooden gun to the people themselves. But it is not the less necessary for this; for the people must have some complicated machinery or other, and hear its din, to satisfy that idea of government which they have. Governments show thus how successfully men can be imposed upon, even impose on themselves, for their own advantage. It is excellent, we must all allow. Yet this government never of itself furthered any enterprise, but by the alacrity with which it got out of its way. It does not keep the country free. It does not settle the West. It does not educate. The character inherent in the American people has done all that has been accomplished; and it would have done somewhat more, if the government had not sometimes got in its way. For government is an expedient, by which men would fain succeed in letting one another alone; and, as has been said, when it is most expedient, the governed are most let alone by it. Trade and commerce, if they were not made of india-rubber, would never manage to bounce over obstacles which legislators are continually putting in their way; and if one were to judge these men wholly by the effects of their actions and not partly by their intentions, they would deserve to be classed and punished with those mischievous persons who put obstructions on the railroads.

But, to speak practically and as a citizen, unlike those who call themselves no-government men, I ask for, not at one no government, but at once a better government. Let every man make known what kind of government would command his respect, and that will be one step toward obtaining it.

After all, the practical reason why, when the power is once in the hands of the people, a majority are permitted, and for a long period continue, to rule is not because they are most likely to be in the right, nor because this seems fairest to the minority, but because they are physically the strongest. But a government in which the majority rule in all cases can not be based on justice, even as far as men understand it. Can there not be a government in which the majorities do not virtually decide right and wrong, but conscience?—in which majorities decide only those questions to which the rule of expediency is applicable? Must the citizen ever for a moment, or in the least degree, resign his conscience to the legislator? Why has every man a conscience then? I think that we should be men first, and subjects afterward. It is not desirable to cultivate a respect for the law, so much as for the right. The only obligation which I have a right to assume is to do at any time what I think right. It is truly enough said that a corporation has no conscience; but a corporation on conscientious men is a corporation with a conscience. Law never made men a whit more just; and, by means of their respect for it, even the well-disposed are daily made the agents on injustice. A common and natural result of an undue respect for the law is, that you may see a file of soldiers, colonel, captain, corporal, privates, powder-monkeys, and all, marching in admirable order over hill and dale to the wars, against their wills, ay, against their common sense and consciences, which makes it very steep marching indeed, and produces a palpitation of the heart. They have no doubt that it is a damnable business in which they are concerned; they are all peaceably inclined. Now, what are they? Men at all? or small movable forts and magazines, at the service of some unscrupulous man in power?

The mass of men serve the state thus, not as men mainly, but as machines, with their bodies. They are the standing army, and the militia, jailers, constables, posse comitatus, etc. In most cases there is no free exercise whatever of the judgment or of the moral sense; but they put themselves on a level with wood and earth and stones; and wooden men can perhaps be manufactured that will serve the purpose as well. Such command no more respect than men of straw or a lump of dirt. They have the same sort of worth only as horses and dogs. Yet such as these even are commonly esteemed good citizens. Others—as most legislators, politicians, lawyers, ministers, and office-holders—serve the state chiefly with their heads; and, as they rarely make any moral distinctions, they are as likely to serve the devil, without intending it, as God. A very few—as heroes, patriots, martyrs, reformers in the great sense, and men—serve the state with their consciences also, and so necessarily resist it for the most part; and they are commonly treated as enemies by it.

He who gives himself entirely to his fellow men appears to them useless and selfish; but he who gives himself partially to them in pronounced a benefactor and philanthropist.

How does it become a man to behave toward the American government today? I answer, that he cannot without disgrace be associated with it. I cannot for an instant recognize that political organization as my government which is the slave's government also.

All men recognize the right of revolution; that is, the right to refuse allegiance to, and to resist, the government, when its tyranny or its inefficiency are great and unendurable. But almost all say that such is not the case now. But such was the case, they think, in the Revolution of '75. If one were to tell me that this was a bad government because it taxed certain foreign commodities brought to its ports, it is most probable that I should not make an ado about it, for I can do without them. All machines have their friction; and possibly this does enough good to counter-balance the evil. At any rate, it is a great evil to make a stir about it. But when the friction comes to have its machine, and oppression and robbery are organized, I say, let us not have such a machine any longer. In other words, when a sixth of the population of a nation which has undertaken to be the refuge of liberty are slaves, and a whole country is unjustly overrun and conquered by a foreign army, and subjected to military law, I think that it is not too soon for honest men to rebel and revolutionize. What makes this duty the more urgent is that fact that the country so overrun is not our own, but ours is the invading army.

Unjust laws exist: shall we be content to obey them, or shall we endeavor to amend them, and obey them until we have succeeded, or shall we transgress them at once? Men, generally, under such a government as this, think that they ought to wait until they have persuaded the majority to alter them. They think that, if they should resist, the remedy would be worse than the evil. But it is the fault of the government itself that the remedy is worse than the evil. It makes it worse. Why is it not more apt to anticipate and provide for reform? Why does it not cherish its wise minority? Why does it cry and resist before it is hurt? Why does it not encourage its citizens to put out its faults, and do better than it would have them? Why does it always crucify Christ and excommunicate Copernicus and Luther, and pronounce Washington and Franklin rebels?

One would think, that a deliberate and practical denial of its authority was the only offense never contemplated by its government; else, why has it not assigned its definite, its suitable and proportionate, penalty? If a man who has no property refuses but once to earn nine shillings for the State, he is put in prison for a period unlimited by any law that I know, and determined only by the discretion of those who put him there; but if he should steal ninety times nine shillings from the State, he is soon permitted to go at large again.

If the injustice is part of the necessary friction of the machine of government, let it go, let it go: perchance it will wear smooth—certainly the machine will wear out. If the injustice has a spring, or a pulley, or a rope, or a crank, exclusively for itself, then perhaps you may consider whether the remedy will not be worse than the evil; but if it is of such a nature that it requires you to be the agent of injustice to another, then I say, break the law. Let your life be a counter-friction to stop the machine. What I have to do is to see, at any rate, that I do not lend myself to the wrong which I condemn.

As for adopting the ways of the State has provided for remedying the evil, I know not of such ways. They take too much time, and a man's life will be gone. I have other affairs to attend to.

I came into this world, not chiefly to make this a good place to live in, but to live in it, be it good or bad. A man has not everything to do, but something; and because he cannot do everything, it is not necessary that he should be petitioning the Governor or the Legislature any more than it is theirs to petition me; and if they should not hear my petition, what should I do then? But in this case the State has provided no way: its very Constitution is the evil. This may seem to be harsh and stubborn and unconcilliatory; but it is to treat with the utmost kindness and consideration the only spirit that can appreciate or deserves it. So is all change for the better, like birth and death, which convulse the body.

I do not hesitate to say, that those who call themselves Abolitionists should at once effectually withdraw their support, both in person and property, from the government of Massachusetts, and not wait till they constitute a majority of one, before they suffer the right to prevail through them I think that it is enough if they have God on their side, without waiting for that other one. Moreover, any man more right than his neighbors constitutes a majority of one already.

I meet this American government, or its representative, the State government, directly, and face to face, once a year—no more—in the person of its tax-gatherer, this is the only mode in which a man situated as I am necessarily meets it; and it then says distinctly, Recognize me; and the simplest, the most effectual, and, in the present posture of affairs, the indispensablest mode of treating with it on this head, of expressing your little satisfaction with and love for it, is to deny it then. My civil neighbor, the tax-gatherer, is the very man I have to deal with—for it is, after all, with men and not with parchment that I quarrel— and he has voluntarily chosen to be an agent of the government. How shall he ever know well that he is and does as an officer of the government, or as a man, until he is obliged to consider whether he will treat me, his neighbor, for whom he has respect, as a neighbor and well-disposed man, or as a maniac and disturber of the peace, and see if he can get over this obstruction to his neighborlines without a ruder and more impetuous thought or speech corresponding with his action. I know this well, that if one thousand, if one hundred, if ten men whom I could name—if ten honest men only—ay, if one HONEST man, in this State of Massachusetts, ceasing to hold slaves, were actually to withdraw from this co-partnership, and be locked up in the county jail therefor, it would be the abolition of slavery in America. For it matters not how small the beginning may seem to be: what is once well done is done forever. But we love better to talk about it: that we say is our mission. Reform keeps many scores of newspapers in its service, but not one man If my esteemed neighbor, the State's ambassador, who will devote his days to the settlement of the question of human rights in the Council Chamber, instead of being threatened with the prisons of Carolina, were to sit down the prisoner of Massachusetts, that State which is so anxious to foist the sin of slavery upon her sister—though at present she can discover only an act of inhospitality to be the ground of a quarrel with her—the Legislature would not wholly waive the subject of the following winter.

Under a government which imprisons unjustly, the true place for a just man is also a prison. The proper place today, the only place which Massachusetts has provided for her freer and less despondent spirits, is in her prisons, to be put out and locked out of the State by her own act, as they have already put themselves out by their principles. It is there that the fugitive slave, and the Mexican prisoner on parole, and the Indian come to plead the wrongs of his race should find them; on that separate but more free and honorable ground, where the State places those who are not with her, but against her—the only house in a slave State in which a free man can abide with honor. If any think that their influence would be lost there, and their voices no longer afflict the ear of the State, that they would not be as an enemy within its walls, they do not know by how much truth is stronger than error, nor how much more eloquently and effectively he can combat injustice who has experienced a little in his own person. Cast your whole vote, not a strip of paper merely, but your whole influence. A minority is powerless while it conforms to the majority; it is not even a minority then; but it is irresistible when it clogs by its whole weight. If the alternative is to keep all just men in prison, or give up war and slavery, the State will not hesitate which to choose. If a thousand men were not to pay their tax bills this year, that would not be a violent and bloody measure, as it would be to pay them, and enable the State to commit violence and shed innocent blood. This is, in fact, the definition of a peaceable revolution, if any such is possible. If the tax-gatherer, or any other public officer, asks me, as one has done, "But what shall I do?" my answer is, "If you really wish to do anything, resign your office." When the subject has refused allegiance, and the officer has resigned from office, then the revolution is accomplished. But even suppose blood shed when the conscience is wounded? Through this wound a man's real manhood and immortality flow out, and he bleeds to an everlasting death. I see this blood flowing now.

I have contemplated the imprisonment of the offender, rather than the seizure of his goods—though both will serve the same purpose—because they who assert the purest right, and consequently are most dangerous to a corrupt State, commonly have not spent much time in accumulating property. To such the State renders comparatively small service, and a slight tax is wont to appear exorbitant, particularly if they are obliged to earn it by special labor with their hands. If there were one who lived wholly without the use of money, the State itself would hesitate to demand it of him. But the rich man—not to make any invidious comparison—is always sold to the institution which makes him rich. Absolutely speaking, the more money, the less virtue; for money comes between a man and his objects, and obtains them for him; it was certainly no great virtue to obtain it. It puts to rest many questions which he would otherwise be taxed to answer, while the only new question which it puts is the hard but superfluous one, how to spend it. Thus his moral ground is taken from under his feet. The opportunities of living are diminished in proportion as that are called the "means" are increased. The best thing a man can do for his culture when he is rich is to endeavor to carry out those schemes which he entertained when he was poor. Christ answered the Herodians according to their condition. "Show me the tribute-money," said he—and one took a penny out of his pocket—if you use money which has the image of Caesar on it, and which he has made current and valuable, that is, if you are men of the State, and gladly enjoy the advantages of Caesar's government, then pay him back some of his own when he demands it. "Render therefore to Caesar that which is Caesar's and to God those things which are God's"—leaving them no wiser than before as to which was which; for they did not wish to know.

I have paid no poll tax for six years. I was put into a jail once on this account, for one night; and, as I stood considering the walls of solid stone, two or three feet thick, the door of wood and iron, a foot thick, and the iron grating which strained the light, I could not help being struck with the foolishness of that institution which treated my as if I were mere flesh and blood and bones, to be locked up. I wondered that it should have concluded at length that this was the best use it could put me to, and had never thought to avail itself of my services in some way. I saw that, if there was a wall of stone between me and my townsmen, there was a still more difficult one to climb or break through before they could get to be as free as I was. I did nor for a moment feel confined, and the walls seemed a great waste of stone and mortar. I felt as if I alone of all my townsmen had paid my tax. They plainly did not know how to treat me, but behaved like persons who are underbred. In every threat and in every compliment there was a blunder; for they thought that my chief desire was to stand on the other side of that stone wall. I could not but smile to see how industriously they locked the door on my meditations, which followed them out again without let or hindrance, and they were really all that was dangerous. As they could not reach me, they had resolved to punish my body; just as boys, if they cannot come at some person against whom they have a spite, will abuse his dog. I saw that the State was half-witted, that it was timid as a lone woman with her silver spoons, and that it did not know its friends from its foes, and I lost all my remaining respect for it, and pitied it.

Thus the state never intentionally confronts a man's sense, intellectual or moral, but only his body, his senses. It is not armed with superior wit or honesty, but with superior physical strength. I was not born to be forced. I will breathe after my own fashion. Let us see who is the strongest. What force has a multitude? They only can force me who obey a higher law than I. They force me to become like themselves. I do not hear of men being forced to live this way or that by masses of men. What sort of life were that to live? When I meet a government which says to me, "Your money or your life," why should I be in haste to give it my money? It may be in a great strait, and not know what to do: I cannot help that. It must help itself; do as I do. It is not worth the while to snivel about it. I am not responsible for the successful working of the machinery of society. I am not the son of the engineer. I perceive that, when an acorn and a chestnut fall side by side, the one does not remain inert to make way for the other, but both obey their own laws, and spring and grow and flourish as best they can, till one, perchance, overshadows and destroys the other. If a plant cannot live according to nature, it dies; and so a man.

The authority of government, even such as I am willing to submit to—for I will cheerfully obey those who know and can do better than I, and in many things even those who neither know nor can do so well—is still an impure one: to be strictly just, it must have the sanction and consent of the governed. It can have no pure right over my person and property but what I concede to it. The progress from an absolute to a limited monarchy, from a limited monarchy to a democracy, is a progress toward a true respect for the individual. Even the Chinese philosopher was wise enough to regard the individual as the basis of the empire. Is a democracy, such as we know it, the last improvement possible in government? Is it not possible to take a step further towards recognizing and organizing the rights of man? There will never be a really free and enlightened State until the State comes to recognize the individual as a higher and independent power, from which all its own power and authority are derived, and treats him accordingly. I please myself with imagining a State at last which can afford to be just to all men, and to treat the individual with respect as a neighbor; which even would not think it inconsistent with its own repose if a few were to live aloof from it, not meddling with it, nor embraced by it, who fulfilled all the duties of neighbors and fellow men. A State which bore this kind of fruit, and suffered it to drop off as fast as it ripened, would prepare the way for a still more perfect and glorious State, which I have also imagined, but not yet anywhere seen.

53

Looking for the Perfect Beat

Kendra A. King

Concrete jungles filled with the likes of you and me
I aint trippin just sippin on chocolate-mocha-caramel realities
Can of mase sprayed in ya face
People gentrifying other peoples lives and space
But still . . .
I AM

Looking for the Perfect Beat

Concrete jungles filled with the likes of you and me
No Justice, No Peace—
In the name of equality some get fleeced
While others act like beasts
And we wonder why the dream is a nightmare and not a reality
Remember the check "stamped insufficient funds"
Dr. King said it best and I still believe—
"We Shall Overcome"
Still . . .
Until then,
I AM

Looking for the Perfect Beat

Concrete jungles filled with the likes of you and me
Temporary environmental asylums of freedom
And, dominion

Dominion over the opinions of those who seek to put you in a box
Perhaps even a FOX (hole)
No holds bar
You are star of the KINGDOM
Alpha and Omega
The Beginning and End
Until then
Selah
For the Perfect Beat is found in **P-E-A-C-E.**

Shalom~

54

For Us, By Us: Marginalized Groups Need to Take Back Hip Hop

Kendra A. King and Renee S. King

Is Hip-hop dead, on life support, or paralyzed by the bling of the "Get Money" mantra of Junior Mafia? Clearly, the health status of Hip Hop is a significant question amongst its connoisseurs and business partners. Why? In the day and age of "Change" and "Yes We Can" it is curious to consider how long the new era of Hip Hop can thrive without life support given it's over saturation of "she lick me like a lollipop" and "blame it on the alcohol." In spite of all of the technological genius and electronic voices thanks to T-Pain, one thing is certain. Modernized Hip Hop with all of its slick beats and catchy phrases will never be the same as [or as good as from a socially conscious perspective the Golden Age of Hip Hop].

I Used to Love H.E.R.

Back in the day—where it began—Hip Hop was an art. It was an art with attitude and art as a form of expression from the culture and environment that young blacks and browns from around the way and via the Islands were experiencing. Since the good ole days of music with a message and a mission to warn against "Self Destruction, ya' headed for Self Destruction," Hip Hop has been over-saturated and co-opted by puffed up nihilists, vitamin rich misogynists, and wheezed out addicts who refuse to take personal responsibility for polluting concrete jungles via "get rich" personal and corporate greed schemes of manipulation in the name of freedom of expression. The only way for Hip Hop to survive this mainstream meltdown is to flip the script and go back to its roots: real MC's, real lyrics, and real life stories that, like "The Message," were designed to "speak the truth to young black [brown, latte, and vanilla] youth."

The unraveling love story of Hip Hop is well documented and has not come as a surprise to its vanguard audience, supporters, and critics. As Jeff Chang detailed in his groundbreaking book *Can't Stop, Won't Stop*, "As the 1970s gave way to the '80s, popular culture still largely depended on the decisions of a small, centralized few who dictated the seasonal tastes of the masses (191)." While the faces of the "centralized few" have diversified to include some of the "get money" generation ground crew, the decision making as it relates to *who* becomes "famous" and *what* songs receive heavy rotation has not experienced such

411

diversification. As such, artistic freedom and freedom of expression still remains a mountain of justice and equality to be climbed and conquered. The battle is not modern but has been a historic issue in the Hip Hop community. Let's take Afrika Bambaataa and "Planet Rock," for example. After the success of the single, "Planet Rock" Afrika Bambaataa got into a creative battle with Tommy Boy label head Tom Silverman. As Chang wrote, "When he started, Silverman had planned on releasing only twelve-inch singles. But Bambaataa's success demanded an album. Silverman and Bambaataa began to argue. 'He likes rock and calypso and reggae. He wanted every song different. And people wanted more 'Planet Rock',' Silverman says" (Chang 190). So, even back then decision making (based upon ownership) was concentrated and artistic freedom versus business interests was a burgeoning problem. Needless to say, Baambaataa and many artists after him (in all genres) did not win the battle for creativity. Today, the battle looms and as conglomeration and internationalization in the music business as a whole is the norm, it continues to infringe on artistic freedom, creativity, and continues to make it increasingly difficult to "love" Hip Hop. Moreover, in this day and age of political and social consciousness, increasingly, Hip Hop music has become about the bottom line profitability of the artist/art form and not messages of uplift, empowerment, and economic, political, and socio-cultural equality.

Profit Over Personal Responsibility

Hip Hop, in the early days, was self-contained. It was "for us, by us." Moreover, the target audience was the community; and, the expression came from the community. However, in 1981, when Afrika Bambaataa took Hip Hop to the masses, he opened wide the flood gates of consumerism and carnivorous behavior which has morphed the art into a survival of the fittest [illest] MC mode. Although "He [Bambaatta] was taking the music and culture of the Black and brown Bronx into the white art-crowd and the punk-rock clubs of lower Manhattan," (Chang 92) the cancerous capital gains lens of corporate giants overshadowed the unintended integration that was the real success of Hip Hop. As Chang further states, "the iron doors of segregation that the previous generation had started to unlock were battered down by the pioneers of the Hip Hop generation." However, with the good, comes the bad. Soon Hip Hop was being exploited from all sides by people just wanting to make a buck and not caring about the quality. Industry executives know Hip Hop is a moneymaker; this is why with Billboard reporting on October 1st, 2008, that record sales are down 28.8% from the year-earlier period, many executives have pressured their hottest Hip Hop artists to drop more sales worthy (mainstream appealing) albums. By pushing profit over artistry the industry has treated Hip Hop like trash and rappers like 50 Cent, Lil Wayne, Diddy, and Soldier Boy, among others work in tandem with them. An often-used example is Busta Rhymes' and Diddy's "Pass the Courvoisier" song. The ode helped increase the liquor's sales and was a cross-marketing dream, everyone got a piece. Soon, many followed suit or began the upswing of the trend. Nelly stomped in his Air Force One's, 50 Cent and Jay Z worked with Reebok, and even Rev. Run still has his Adidas. Even late night television icon

Ed McMahon is in the mix rapping in a commercial complete with scantily dressed women, gold, bling, and lots of 'tude.

A Change is Gonna' Come

What can Hip Hop culture do to get off of life support? Will it ever be reflective of the genuine and authentic change? Will its representatives continue to misuse its power and influence and end up "Dead and Gone" or will Hip Hop be resuscitated in a new birth of social responsibility, political involvement, and cultural relevance? If Hip Hop is going to take its position as a responsible shaper of thought and culture, it must do three things. First, Hip Hop must make a space and place for socially conscious artists and lyricists such as Dead Prez, the Roots, Lupe Fiasco, and others to receive both heavy rotation, thrive, and shine. In this regard, the Hip Hop community must work to bring balance to its genre by pumping up and promoting the conscious lyrics of popular artists as well. It does not seem too much to bring balance and promote Young Jeezy's "It's a Crazy World" just as much if not more than his "I Put On For My City."

Secondly, the Hip Hop community must reincorporate and empower female MCs, executives, and consumers. Clearly, the invisibility of the female MC has become tantamount in the last five to ten years and given rise to the popularity and increasing profitability of the video "model." With women allowing themselves to be objectified and the media setting them up as the sexualized other, women in Hip Hop have lost their central position— talent, intelligence, opinion, and femininity. In effect, the whole package of the Golden Age Hip Hop female has been reduced to hyper-sexed rhymes and gratuitous nudity. There must be another Lauryn Hill, MC Lyte, or Queen Latifah out there waiting their turn at the mic. How do we get them on?

According to Yvonne Bynoe women in Hip Hop must create a place of voice and visibility. "Women have not become visible, insofar that they have not staked out spaces that allow their stories and complex realities to be heard by the masses. Whether it is fear of access to capital or some combination of the two, Hip Hop generation women have not created our version of the Lilith Fair to support female rap artists(2)." Bynoe's idea of a hip-hop Lilith Fair is brilliant. The creator of the original Lilith Fair, Sarah McLachlan detailed her frustration at the male-dominated recording industry that shut out intelligent female artists. So she sought sponsorship and Lilith Fair was born—even though many said a female-driven, all-female festival would fail. The fair became a movement among women and feminists, it was successful, it launched careers, and record labels scrambled to fill the niche of the intelligent, female musician. Women in hip-hop must do the same to be heard.

Finally, Hip Hop must look to the context clues of the 2008 Presidential election and make holistic lifestyle changes that will trickle down into the underprivileged and impoverished communities that know more about them and their lyrics than they do about globalization, global warming, and what is going on around the globe. Undoubtedly, music as a whole is in a sad state right now; Hip Hop is in even worse shape. As such, women and men that truly love and appreciate the culture need to put aside lust for money and power and come together to save the integrity of the art form. As Ayanna's article on "The Exploitation of Women in Hip-hop Culture" states, "Censorship of hip-hop music is not the solution. Instead, the solution is to change the culture, system, and ideology . . ." (4). Until hip-hop returns to its roots and back into the hands of the marginalized groups that created it, it will continue on its headlong crash course into extinction and its thirty plus years of existence will continue to spiral out of control as "lollipops," "lambos" and the "last train to London" intoxicate the masses 'til the next go 'round of Michael Richards' and Don Imus' use of the interchangeable "N" word.

Works Cited

AlterNet. 16 May 2007. Bynoe, Yvonne. "Hip-hop's Still Invisible Women." 07 October 2008. *http://www.alternet.org/mediaculture/51933*

Baran, Stanley J. *Introduction to Mass Communication*. 5th ed. New York, NY: McGraw Hill, 2008.

Chang, Jeff. *Can't Stop Won't Stop*. New York, NY: Picador, 2005.

King, Kendra. African American Politics. United Kingdom: Polity Press, 2009.

My Sistah: A Project from Advocates for Youth. Ayanna. "The Exploitation of Women in Hip-Hop Culture." 07 October 2008. *http://www.mysistahs.org/features/hiphop.htm*.

55

Having Ubuntu! Examining Cultural Perceptions to Better Practice Citizenship and Community in the Classroom and Beyond

Darlene Russell

Introduction

Values, principles, beliefs and ideals govern how one lives life and views the world. These values, principles, beliefs, and ideals contour certain perceptions one has of others. The old adage: *Don't say anything if you don't have anything nice to say* and the Golden Rule are akin to Ubuntu. Ubuntu, pronounced "oo-boon-too" according to *Your Life Manual: Practical Steps to Genuine Happiness,* is an African principle revolving around humanity that generated from the Bantu languages of South Africa. This ancient African principle, practice, and philosophy is rooted in the belief that are all connected and knitted together in the family of humanity. Ubuntu beckons one to feel joy when another feels joy, and to feel pain when another feels pain. Through the emphasis on achieving community and unity with all humanity, the practice of Ubuntu promotes social justice, equality, and philanthropy.

Ubuntu is described by South African Archbishop Desmond Tutu as:

> *It is the essence of being human. It speaks of the fact that my humanity is caught up and is inextricably bound up in yours. I am human because I belong. It speaks about wholeness, it speaks about compassion. A person with Ubuntu is welcoming, hospitable, warm and generous, willing to share. Such people are open and available to others, willing to be vulnerable, affirming of others, do not feel threatened that others are able and good, for they have a proper self-assurance that comes from knowing that they belong in a greater whole. They know that they are diminished when others are humiliated, diminished when others are oppressed, diminished when others are treated as if they were less than who they are. The quality of Ubuntu gives people resilience, enabling them to survive and emerge still human despite all efforts to dehumanize them (Tutu, 2005).*

This essay intends to reveal some of my beliefs and perceptions, and a part of my journey as a practitioner of Ubuntu. Additionally, this piece calls for the classroom players—

the students and instructor—to consider the dichotomous relationships between citizenship and humanity, and the manifestations of such in the classroom and beyond.

Words and a Drumming Heartbeat

On my return plane trip from Arkansas, I was flanked by a female volleyball team from an Arkansas college; they were seated behind me, in front of me and to my right. A few of them found solace in ear buds streaming from i-Pods. While others chatted incessantly, and rather loudly, about what they were going to do when they arrived to New York City. I tried to rest my eyes and replay how I felt standing in front of Little Rock Central High School (LRCHS) in Little Rock, Arkansas. I beckoned my brain to remember my time in front of the "castle," as the writer Melba Pattillo Beals describes. I recalled the porcelain, fair, tan, and brown faces that passed by as I climbed the steps to the main entrance of LRCHS along with every smell that whirled up my nostrils, and the summer sounds that sailed through the August air.

My reflective journey was interrupted by another message from the flight attendant who had a pronounced Chinese accent. I closed my eyes after she finished speaking on the PA and taxied my mind right back to Little Rock. I began thinking about more teaching ideas for *Warriors Don't Cry*, a memoir about the historical desegregation of Little Rock High School, to pile into my packed black marble composition notebook. A marathon of ideas sprinted through my mind and I began to smile. Just then, the same Asian female flight attendant made another announcement over the PA system. Like the other times, she was hard to understand, but this announcement was borderline unclear. I was able to make out most of the words and fill in the blanks. Besides, the message was not terribly important, and I wondered how many people really even listen to the in-flight announcements. Almost immediately, I began to get really tense. I thought about the prevailing negative attitudes in this country toward people who speak English with an accent of their native country's tongue wrapped around their words. It made me think about being the "other" and the incredible loneliness attached to it. It was so easy for me to slip into the shoes of the flight attendant because of my own experiences of being the "other" in school, vacation excursions, and some workplace settings. Unbeknownst to the flight attendant, I felt compelled to come to her defense if she was verbally attacked.

I was surrounded by female volleyball players who seemed self-absorbed by the nature of their conversations and gestures. They were all White. And I could not help wonder—especially given my trip to Little Rock, thoughts of the Little Rock Nine, and the upcoming 50th Anniversary of the desegregation of LRCHS—how many authentic exchanges and relationships did these young women have with people who look like the flight attendant or me. I was not sure of the answer, and I could not ignore the longstanding history of the South that polarized folks across racial lines. The two volleyball players seated behind me were talking without cease before the extremely nebulous announcement. However, their conversation quickly halted. They were silent and I my heart was beating like a

Madinka's warrior drum. I did not know what was going to exit their mouths. Were they going to mock the Asian woman's accent? Would I hear a "go back to your country" remark? Were they going to discuss how could someone get a job as a flight attendant without speaking "good" English? These questions stampeded through my cranium like a caravan of lions smelling fresh raw flesh. I waited as I scooted to the edge of my seat with my spine straight.

The silence broke when one of the females in her Southern drawl squealed, "Wow, what did she say? That was a littl' hard to understand."

I created and rehearsed my response right after the silence fell, so I was ready to verbally pounce.

"I'm not sure . . . I guess New York people would be like 'huh' when they hear us talk," the other female explained.

I exhaled and reclined in my seat. I was relieved that these two female athletes did not say anything racist or insensitive. If so, I was certainly ready to respond knowing fully that it would have produced discomfort for all three of us. Given my experiences as an African-American woman in the United States and how these experiences are parallel to other historically marginalized groups, I would have been obligated, as a citizen and someone who tries to work for social change and justice inside and outside of the classroom, to say something.

Teaching Citizenship & Community through Ubuntu

For those few minutes on the airplane, I practiced Ubuntu by feeling the bond or connection to the flight attendant. I use this anecdote to introduce students to the philosophical orientation of Ubuntu to establish classroom community. As I share this episode from my life, I pause at the point where I began to grow tense, and I ask students: *Why do you think I felt tense?* Without fail students are able to answer the question. This is important for a few reasons. The most salient is that this kind of behavior has deeply permeated American culture where it is routinely practiced, recognized, and accepted. This, of course, is the entry point for what type of class and group of citizens we want to be. Some of the questions I pose that orbit around Ubuntu are: *How will we embrace each other even when we do not agree with one another's politics? How will we affirm each other and how will it look like? How do we share— ourselves, our knowledge, our notes—with someone who is seemingly so different from us?* As a collective, we discuss and decide on the ground rules for class discussions, expectations for assignments, and responsibility to self and the class community. It also prefaces the course content on acting and teaching for change using print and non-print literature.

In my teaching, I gingerly demand students to deconstruct and reconstruct their thinking and challenge mainstream ideologies. In the airplane anecdote, my assumptions and preconceived notions are revealed, which can stymie Ubuntu. These assumptions sprout from my experiences and are largely justified given the history and pernicious treatment of tan and brown people in this country. In my zeal to put Ubuntu to practice, I hoisted the cultural assumptions and preconceived notions that were deep within as I anticipated how the White girls were going to respond. One of the take-aways is that Ubuntu celebrates the spirit of togetherness, which counters ethnocentrism, assumptions [founded or unfounded], and separateness. Ubuntu is about humanity having one heartbeat.

The practiced Ubuntu philosophy can teach citizenship and community in the classroom. Recently, one of my students explained to me that his dream is to become a chef and how he was offered a full-time position in the kitchen of a top-notch restaurant in New York City. This meant that he would have to suspend his college education. I asked him how many classes he is taking. He said two. I asked him if he consulted with his family. He said that he did. I told him that I hear the passion in his voice, and did not want to become between him and his passion. I congratulated him and gave him my blessings. I told him that he must not forget about his schooling, and he assured me that he fully intends to return. I asked him to share his good news with the class. Comments like "that's cool" and "congratulations, man" and "that's hot" floated about the room following his descriptive share. The students affirmed him and celebrated with him in his accomplishment. This is Ubuntu in practice. I seek out ways for students to affirm and celebrate each other in order to further "seed" their connection to humanity. Ubuntu is evinced in the way one communicates and interacts with others, verbally and non-verbally. Ubuntu is nestled in soothing and respectful words and the cadence that is produced, and made visible in warm facial expressions. Ubuntu is a way of life.

Practicing Ubuntu in the Classroom and Beyond

*   **Seeing yourself in others**
    I heard something very poignant one day when I was watching a show about the accomplishments of a man who was the director of a community center that helped men in the margins to improve themselves socially, economically, and educationally. The director said that he sees his face on every one of the men in his center . . . and it is easy to help yourself. When people begin to see themselves in others, an automatic connection occurs. This connection can certainly assist in reducing ethnocentrism, racism, inequities, and the rest of the "-ism" family.

*   **Speaking up**
    It is not so easy to take a stand against something that is wrong especially when you are the only one willing to do so in your group of family, friends, or fellow teammates. However, it is necessary. Speaking up against hateful behavior or injustice can be done in a manner that appeals to human emotions. Dr. Martin Luther King, Jr. once said that "injustice anywhere is a threat to justice everywhere." In other words, if one is at danger, so is another. Taking a stand and speaking up helps to enlighten others and remind them of the link to humanity that connects us all.

*   **Busting your bubble**
    People who look alike, live near each other, and share similar values usually fellowship

with each other. This kind of interaction can certainly form a bubble around one and those of the same ilk. This bubble traps some in and keeps others out. It creates limitations and fosters isolation. Busting your bubble allows more space for those who are different from and similar to you to enter your life. Having people who do not all look, act, talk, and think the same in your life can strengthen your bond to humanity.

- **Benevolent affirmations**
  I have always been fascinated with the power of words, and how one word can take on so many meanings, and engender a host of reactions. I think people are caretakers of words. We have the power to affirm, insult, or enrage someone with our words. Our connectedness to humanity is showcased in benevolent affirmations. These affirmations can include complimenting someone, who you may not regularly interact with, on their attire, athleticism, talents, or thinking. It can also be simply practiced in opening the door for someone who has their hands full or someone who may be a little short at the cash register. Benevolent affirmations supports the saying, *it's nice to be nice*.

Conclusion

I have always wanted to be a conscious educator who challenges herself, questions, and ponder ways to teach for change. Ubuntu serves as the foundation for teaching for change because of its intrinsic appeal to the oneness of humanity. This African principle can be used to reshape how we see ourselves and the world. Ubuntu can add a new dimension on how we study art, history, literature, language, mathematics, religion, and science, and move us toward exploring more non-Western philosophies. There is a reflective texture present in the fabric of Ubuntu, which calls us to think about how we have and will relate to others, and how to contribute to improving the human condition. Ubuntu is the blood that flows to the heart of humanity and the soft hand that cradles the soul.

References

Ambrose, D. (2006). Your life manual: Practical steps to genuine happiness. Canada: Revolution Mind Publishing.

Panse, S. (2006, July 22). Ubuntu—African philosophy. Message posted to *http://www.buzzle.com/editorials/7-22-2006-103206.asp*

Pattillo Beals, M. (2007). *Warriors Don't Cry*. New York: Simon & Schuster.

Tutu, D. (2005). God has a dream: A vision of hope for our time. New York: Bantam Books.

Tutu Foundation UK. (2007) Ubuntu: Putting ourselves back together. Retrieved May 18, 2009, from *http://www.tutufoundationuk.org/ubuntu.html*

56

Lessons from School

Frank Wu

As a law professor at Howard University in Washington, D.C., I am reminded of the importance of race every morning when I walk to work.[1] In the leisurely stroll down five blocks between my home and my office in the nation's capital, I move from a mostly white residential neighborhood that is quite affluent to a predominantly black institution that is economically mixed. The switch is more than physical, but it cannot be reduced to easy terms.

Howard University has been for more than a century the leading school in the nation for the training of black lawyers. Its legendary dean of the World War II period, Charles Hamilton Houston, as quoted in the epigraph to this chapter,[2] once said that every lawyer was either a social engineer or a parasite on society. A perfectionist who concurred with Supreme Court Justice Oliver Wendell Holmes Jr., that the law was "a jealous mistress," Houston devoted himself to preparing the social engineers. Graduates during his watch included such giants as Thurgood Marshall, who would use the law to produce racial desegregation by achieving the moral victory of *Brown v. Board of Education* before the Supreme Court in 1954. The tradition they started continues to this day, giving the school a mission that most others cannot claim.

I am privileged to be the first Asian American on the Howard law faculty, and yet there seems to be something remarkable about a person of Asian heritage being associated with a historically black college. Strangers may not be sure what it is that is so surprising to them, but their uncertainty induces them to wonder aloud. Since becoming a member of the academy, I have lost count of the number of times people have asked, "Why are you at Howard?" or been impressed because they thought I taught at Harvard. They ask, "What is it like to be a minority among minorities? How does it feel?" Sometimes, "Do black people accept you? Or do they discriminate against you?" They ask, "What are they like? Are they good students?" Or, "Are you trying to make an ideological statement? Are you rebelling?" They add, "Couldn't you find a job anywhere else? Do you want to stay?" Even, "Did you grow up in a black neighborhood?" On more than one occasion, a person has looked me over carefully, paused, and then stammered, "Are you—are you actually black?"

The people who ask these questions casually but constantly in various combinations are almost all good-hearted. Most are white, some are black, and a few are Asian American themselves. Despite their diverse backgrounds, they share the same curiosity. Within a moment of meeting me and finding out what I do—or more precisely, where I do what I do—whether it is during a professional conference, while I am at a television station appearing as a guest, visiting a campus to speak, at a social gathering such as a dinner party, or in striking up a new acquaintance through an introduction by friends, they pull me aside to confide their surprise. It doesn't matter what I may have been doing or talking about—trying to learn to play tennis or chatting about politics—and I need not make any effort to provoke any racial issue. People raise their eyebrows when I mention my employer.

After awhile, the questions started me mulling over race itself. Speculating about an Asian American teacher with mainly African American students is not offensive, although I admit I am exhausted by the tedious interrogations. I toyed with having a sarcastic retort printed on the back of my business cards, but they are looking for more than cursory answers. They are looking for something, they know not what, but it is directly in front of them. More than might be intended by the people who are inquiring, their inquisitiveness reveals the invisible influence of racial judgments on our everyday perceptions. All of us see race inevitably, without even being awake to what is on our minds. Race is the elephant in the room, in the exercise of trying not to think about the elephant in the room; the harder we try to pay no attention to race, like the elephant, the larger it looms.

When I was pondering where to embark on my life as a scholar, nobody thought to ask, "Well, what will it be like to be the only Asian American at a white school? How does it feel?" or "What are whites like? Are they good students?" I am bemused that Asian Americans now and then suggest that I have taken a position to curry favor with blacks, because I work at a predominantly black institution. They don't seem to realize that if such an assumption can be made about me without any other basis, they must be ingratiating themselves to whites by the same reasoning. Nobody ever bothers my wife, an Asian American who happens to teach at another fine but predominantly white law school across town, about why she has chosen that place of employment or expects her to be an expert on whiteness.

Becoming the only Asian American at a white school was an option available to me. I was fortunate enough to have been invited to interview with many law schools. I would have ended up every bit as much the minority at any of them. None of the law schools with which I interviewed had ever had an Asian American professor. The majority of the 175 accredited law schools in this country did not then and had never had a person of Asian descent in a tenured position teaching any subject. After they hire one, who knows whether they will hire another. There is no place where my wife and I could be among a majority of Asian Americans; even in Asia, we would be out of place as Asian Americans.

Even so, I suspect that not many people who are white—or for that matter Asian American—consider as a "white" law school one that boasts an overwhelmingly white enrollment, a totally white alumni until recently, a mostly white faculty, or an all-white administration; or where the framed photographs of judges and lawyers displayed with pride on the walls include no black faces (or needless to say, Asian faces), where a lone person of color has recently become a professor while a corps of racial minorities have always been janitors. Those African Americans who call a school "white" are likely to be chided for having imagined a problem for themselves. I doubt that anybody would suppose that joining the faculty at such a white law school represents a political choice as much as a politic one.

My hypothesis is that many of us are afflicted with a partial color blindness. We cannot see clearly, and our would-be color blindness conceals the subjectivity of our own vantage point from ourselves. Through this filter, Asian Americans see that being in the company of white Americans is accepted as assimilating into the mainstream, a sign of upward mobility. Someone who is neither black nor white observes that given a choice, it would be smart to try to become white because that status brings tangible benefits. Asian Americans follow whites, not blacks, in trying to become American, and we disregard the dictum that it is blacks who are the most authentic Americans. The alternative, intentionally associating with African Americans, is weird, some sort of naïve error or purposeful subversion. As soon as Asian Americans deviate from the rule that we should prefer to be white rather than black, we will be gently corrected.[3]

Perhaps all of us regardless of race have an unconscious tendency to accept white culture as the majority culture as well as the favored culture. White is normal. Whiteness is desirable. Our world has more than racial categories, so transparent as to be invisible. It has racial hierarchies, both blatant and subtle.

Many whites and Asian Americans do not have enough contact with African Americans to have formed a sense of any individual African American as a human being. For them, I am an interpreter, I can expound on my experience as pompously as John Howard Griffin did poignantly in his 1961 book, *Black Like Me,* in which he recounted his travels throughout the Deep South as a white man disguised through chemicals to look like a black man. As much as I try to resist it, by talking to whites about African Americans I sometimes suspect that I become more white to them. It is as if I am a nineteenth-century adventurer who has explored the Dark Continent and returned as an authority to regale my audience. Or I am an outsider between worlds and thus momentarily an insider in each world. For the same reason, I am a more credible source for a letter of recommendation than an African American colleague, with the authority of independence. I seem to be vouching for students as if I can say that they can fit into a white environment, without racial allegiance toward them.

So I am not sure whether to be flattered or insulted that people consider my current position a form of personal charity or an experimental phase of life. They do not see that, even acting solely out of calculating self-interest, being at Howard has been good for my career. Thanks to them, there probably is a certain cachet to being the Asian guy at the black school. An Asian American law professor is rare enough, to be sure; an Asian American law professor in a black school is *suis generis.*

Every autumn, as the year begins with another set of students on the far side of the podium, I realize again how race is in the details of our daily lives. Race is unyielding and manifests itself in the discrepancy in our respective power to discount its effects. In one of the best articles on whiteness, Wellesley college professor Peggy McIntosh gave a personal account of grasping the advantages of her own skin color. Writing in 1988 from a feminist standpoint, she listed more than fifty conditions of her life she could count on, unlike people of color. They ranged from "I can go shopping alone . . . pretty well assured that I will not be followed or harassed" and "I can talk with my mouth full and not have people put this down to my color" to "I can worry about racism without being seen as self-interested or self-seeking" and "I can chose blemish cover or bandages in 'flesh' color and have them more or less match my skin," "I can talk about the social events of a weekend without fearing most listener's reactions," and "I will feel welcomed and 'normal' in the usual walks of public life, institutional and social."[4] Washington University law professor Barbara Flagg, a critical race theorist, borrowed the lines from the hymn *Amazing Grace* to illustrate how whiteness envelopes: "was blind, but now I see."[5] As anti-affirmative action activist Clint Bolick has said, "I almost never think about my 'whiteness.'"[6] White Americans can choose to stop thinking about race (or to never start), unless they are trapped and cannot avoid an altercation or if they had decided that they will join with Asian Americans or become a scholar studying Asian Americans.[7] Their erstwhile ethnicity is for the St. Patrick's Day parade.[8]

Comic Eddie Murphy spoofed white privilege as a member of the cast of the *Saturday Night Live* television show in 1984. He showed himself being made up in whiteface, donning a suit, and learning how to walk. He says as he rehearses, "their butts are real tight . . . I gotta remember to keep my butt real tight when I walk." He reads Hallmark greeting cards out loud to learn clichés and practices his enunciation. With his camouflage and his new name, "Mr. White," he learns that, when only white people are around, everything is free; once the last black man exits the bus, a party breaks out; loan officers at banks give out money without requiring collateral or even identification. He closes the skit by saying, "I've got a lot of friends, and we've got a lot of makeup." So he warns whites the next time they meet a fellow white, "don't be too sure."

African Americans cannot disregard race, except when they are among a crowd of African Americans. The very act of congregating in a group, which allows them such an escape, only provides white Americans with another negative visual cue. Paradoxically, it takes the race conscious act of forming a group to beget the color blind ideal of being judged on one's merits. When people of color are numerous enough, we form a critical mass. We cease to bear the burden of being representative, and we can relax as our race recedes into latency. We do not generate a stereotype with our every action, because we are uniform except in the superficial sense of skin color. Yet when African Americans come together, they risk the accusation of self-segregation, as if African Americans could be segregated without whites also being segregated.[9]

Although the means and the ends may contradict, race can be eliminated as an element in decision making. The race conscious act of presenting a list of finalists for a job, all of whom were African American, would ensure that an employer behaved in a color blind fashion in hiring one of them. When the same list of finalists for a job has several whites and a single African American, no selection whether of a white or an African American can be free of reservations that it is tainted by some prejudice.

Ambitious Africa Americans must leave behind their background, but ambitious white Americans only become more fixed in theirs. The same career path leads them to divergent lives. African American professionals almost certainly always will be the only people of their racial background in the room at meetings at their law firm, investment bank, major corporation, or university department, becoming more isolated from other people of color as they become more successful, unless they make a deliberate and costly choice to work within minority communities.[10] They must become intimately familiar with the details of WASP culture: wearing clothes ordered from the Abercrombie & Fitch catalog is not enough if they are invited to Thanksgiving dinner and do not recognize aspic. When in public, they must speak with the diction, enunciation, and accent of white people.

Conversely, white professionals equally certainly never will be the only ones of their racial background in the room at meetings at their law firm, investment bank, major corporation, or university department, and even if they do not try to avoid African Americans they will encounter few African Americans who are their social and economic peers or betters. They can consume black culture as radical chic; buying the latest hip-hop album at the mall outlet suffices without any need for knowledge of the origins of jazz. They need never adopt the speech patterns of blacks and in private can even ridicule the sophisticated verbal play on the street corner—a bard's facility with words that converts "salty" into a synonym for "sad" as an allusion to tears, before it is replaced in a few months by another coinage—as ignorant and boorish.

Even white professionals who work among Asians and Asian Americans are not likely to live among Asians and Asian Americans. They have an ability to exit. They may answer to an Asian American boss at a high-tech company, but after business hours they can return home to a suburb that is white. They will not be ostracized if they cannot use chopsticks; they are not expected to study Japanese or Korean. They are held to a standard so low and unlike that applied when the roles are reversed that Asians are charmed when their Caucasian friend knows how properly to proffer a business card with both hands and a slight bow and delighted if they can mutter, "Hello, how are you?" in an Asian language. Few white American expatriates living in Asia would be pleased to see their children "go native."

Asian Americans are deceived if we believe we escape these effects. We all must make choices.

I was no different. Until I started at Howard, I would not have been accustomed to finding myself the only Asian American in a room of African Americans. Growing up in what I did not know was the most segregated major metropolitan area in the country,[11] I knew only whites and no blacks. I attended a suburban high school that shared a campus with another high school. The two schools together had an enrollment of more than 4,000, among which was one African American. Scarcely less rare were Asian Americans. There were no faculty, no administrators, and no staff who were African American, and not more than one or two who were Asian American. There may have been a few Latinos as. There were only a few Jews.

Since coming to Howard, I have become so used to being there that I am startled to be the only Asian American in a roomful of whites—or, for that matter, an Asian American among other Asian Americans.

Here is a thought experiment about the minor symbols of racial double standards. When I began teaching, a street vendor who had set up operations near the Howard University Law School was selling fake leather goods. Likely manufactured in Asia, his bargain wares were emblazoned with the logo Eurosport. Many incoming students bought his backpacks to carry their heavy loads of casebooks back and forth. If a sizable number of first-year students at Harvard Law School passed by advertising Afrosport with their bookbags, it would prompt a double-take. Eurosport on blacks is fashionable; Afrosport on whites would be puzzling.

In many ways, Howard's law school resembles Harvard's. Students are similarly apprehensive about whether they have made a terrible choice in volunteering themselves for the Socratic method. They have the same delusions about legal practice, gleaned from television shows such as *Ally McBeal* and *Judge Judy*. They undergo the same pre-exam panic over distinguishing hypothetical fact patterns from the relevant precedent. They aspire to comparable professional goals of lucre and rank. The field of law has its own culture, with specialized jargon; elaborate ceremonies; and methods of delineating insiders, outsiders, and the ranks of the bar and bench. For this reason, it would be a mistake to treat the law schools at Howard and Harvard as representative of black culture or white culture, respectively. Non-lawyers of any sort would object with good reason if they were measured against lawyers. Some Howard students, even if they come from backgrounds that are not especially privileged, are socialized just as other students from backgrounds of privilege are socialized into having contempt for their clients as unworthy if they are indigent.

In other ways, however, Howard is quite unlike Harvard. Howard students agree that racism still affects their lives, but they disagree on what to do about it. They have first-hand experience with gun violence and economic despair, even if they come from a middle-class upbringing. A relatively high proportion of students have to testify at criminal trials or cope with the day-to-day exertions of being a single mother. The cafeteria has grits for breakfast and greens at lunch. There is an active choir that gives concerts in our chapel. Many students say "sir" and "ma'am," and some staff call me Mister Frank.

Howard is no more perfect than Harvard. There is some grumbling about the number of non-blacks and acceptance of discrimination by black as the "flip side" of white racism elsewhere. An excessive number of students want to become sports or entertainment lawyers. An occasional poster announces a boycott of an Asian American-owned business in derogatory racial terms. I am saddened that, from time to time, when students are under-standably frustrated at the seeming Catch-22 ineptitude of the institution that manifests itself here and there, they will remark, "What do you expect from black folks?"

Black schools and white schools are not mirror images. Their origins, their purposes, and their meaning to society are not alike. Black institutions of higher learning came about because blacks were denied the chance to study elsewhere. White institutions barred blacks by law or by custom.

Black institutions are one of the complicated legacies of racial segregation, which ended only during the lifetimes of people alive today. They have a specific function of ingather-ing, which creates a special community without insinuating that others are inferior. Black students seek out black schools because they are welcoming. White students self-select themselves away from black schools with only a few exceptions. They are absent because they believe the schools are beneath them, not vice versa. Black schools seem immune from the backlash against affirmative action, even though black schools are undeniably not color blind but institutions that are wholly color conscious. The implications are that color consciousness is acceptable if it tends toward racial segregation but not if it is aimed at racial integration, and black institutions either are too important or too inconsequential to be subjected to a stern edict of color blindness. In contrast, many white schools tend to be faceless way stations leading toward a coveted credential. Students matriculate anony-mously at the best school that has accepted them, without any connection to it.

Black schools enhance diversity. They do so at another level than is conventional. They ensure that even as institutions become integrated internally, so that African Amer-icans fit in as equals at Stanford University or the University of Michigan—where I taught as a fellow and graduated from law school, respectively—institutions continue to differ from each other. African Americans ought to have a choice to be more than a token or an anom-aly, even if white Americans are not eager to gain first-hand knowledge of minority status. If every place were identically integrated, African Americans (not to mention Asian Amer-icans) would end up always alone among whites. Whites might feel differently about the allure of color blindness if they knew that each individual white person would be alone among African Americans in order to satisfy the goal. A white person might not feel quite as reassured by a solemn pledge of color blindness if she were the only white person in a roomful of African Americans.

An institution perceived as wholly black can be more integrated than institutions that are thought to be quite ordinary. Howard University, which has always opened its doors to everyone, has had its share of deans, professors, and students who were white.[12] Established after the Civil War, it is named for a white Union general who became the director of the Freedman's Bureau. (This is not to suggest, as sometimes seems to be implied, that a pre-dominantly black institution is only as good as the number of whites it can attract.) It has an annual enrollment of more than 10,000 students, serving as a Mecca for black intellect spanning cultures and transcending politics, drawing to it an African diaspora from well beyond American borders. Its openness has been the basis for a rooted cosmopolitanism rather than an immutable parochialism.

When I looked out at my classroom during my first year, looking back at me were a half-dozen white faces among the fifty students. When I showed up for faculty meetings, around the table sat that same number of whites among my two dozen or so colleagues. These numbers of whites are equal to if not greater than the representation of blacks at other schools. Our faculty is more diverse than that of other law schools. The professors display a range of opinions that matches that found at any other school.

Nor am I unique. Two generations ago, many Asian immigrants could be found teaching at historically black colleges. After they received their doctorates, they found it easier to obtain employment there than at segregated white campuses. They staffed the math, science, and engineering departments of the dozens of historically black colleges. Many of them have retired, but some are still there as the senior faculty.

I have become convinced that there is a value, and not for African Americans alone, to having a place where people of color can be in the overall majority and hold most of the leadership positions. The cumulative effect of being a permanent minority is a demoralizing stress. It is only from the outside—or if the state of affairs is reversed to the extent possible—that the identity of whites as a group is even discernible. Paul Igasaki, the first Asian American to serve as chair of the United States Equal Employment Opportunity Commission, is fond of noting that a white male manager whose team consists of only other white men, who may be unmindful of the message he conveys just by introducing his colleagues at a meeting, cannot help but take notice if Igasaki were to do the same and surround himself with Asian American men. It wouldn't be right if Igasaki's office included only Asian Americans, even if each was eminently qualified.

Nor can the pernicious effects of being in a racial minority be rationalized as a byproduct of numbers. People of color cannot be a minority in any substantial sense, unless their status as people of color is perceptible as a means of differentiating them from the majority. Left-handers are a minority, but not a minority group. The 90 percent of us who are right-handed have historically discriminated against left-handers, and we have built the world to suit us. Southpaws were literally "sinister." They were cured forcibly. A major study, *The Left-Hander Syndrome: The Causes and Consequences of Left-Handedness*,[13] by University of British Columbia psychologist Stanley Coren, documents continuing statistical disparities in everything from life expectancy to mental illness rates based on handedness. According to Coren, left-handedness may be a consequence of prenatal trauma. However, handedness is not a basis for organizing society. Left-handed products may exist, both serious and novelty, and left-handed third basemen may be exceptional on the baseball diamond, but left-handedness is neither used for purposes of segregation and subjugation nor does it divide people. Skin color and handedness are not the same because they do not have the same effects.

On issues of race, I have learned as much as I have taught. My personal opinions on race have been transformed through a series of events, which have in common that I have defied my own as well as others' expectations. All of these events required the purposeful decision on my part to insert myself into places where I would never have found myself by chance. But they also required that I overcome my own confines of identity.

I am convinced that this approach is more generally applicable: By becoming more conscious of our own perceptions, as a society we will be able to neutralize racial prejudice. The necessary but not sufficient threshold is acknowledging that race operates in our lives, relentlessly and pervasively. Working in multiracial coalitions of equal members, united by shared principles, we can create communities that are diverse and just. Together, we can reinvent the civil rights movement.

And that possibility is why I teach at Howard.

Endnotes

1. For the perspective of a white professor at a predominantly black university, *see* Karl Henzy, "Finding Connections: A White Professor at a Black University," *Chronicle of Higher Education*, October 10, 1997, B6.
2. Genna Rae McNeil, *Groundwork: Charles Hamilton Houston and the Struggle for Civil Rights* (Philadelphia: University of Pennsylvania Press, 1983), 84.
3. *See, e.g.,* Tamar Jacoby, "In Asian America." *Commentary* (July–August 2000): 21–28.
4. Peggy McIntosh, "White Privilege and Male Privilege: A Personal Account of Coming to See Correspondences through Work in Women's Studies," in Richard Delgado and Jean Stefancic, eds., *Critical White Studies: Looking Behind the Mirror* (Philadelphia: Temple University Press, 1997), 291–99.
5. Barbara J. Flagg, *Was Blind, But Now I See: White Race Consciousness and the Law* (New York: New York University Press, 1998).
6. Clint Bolick, *The Affirmative Action Fraud: Can We Restore the American Civil Rights Vision?* (Washington, D.C.: Cato Institute, 1996), 20.
7. This is a central claim of critical race theory and its allied field of whiteness studies. I have relied on several anthologies for an overview of the research: Karen Brodkin, *How Did Jews Become White Folks and What Does That Say About Race in America?* (New Brunswick, NJ.: Rutgers University Press, 1998); Kimberle Crenshaw et al., eds., *Critical Race Theory: The Key Writings That Formed the Movement* (New York: The New Press, 1995); Delgado and Stefancic, *Critical White Studies*; Richard Delgado and Jean Stefancic, eds., *Critical Race Theory: The Cutting Edge*, 2d ed. (Philadelphia: Temple University Press, 2000). I also have found the following studies especially helpful: Theodore W. Allen, *The Invention of the White Race: The Origin of Racial Oppression in Anglo-America*, vol. 2 (London: Verso, 1997); Ian F. Haney Lopez, *White by Law: The Legal Construction of Race* (New York: New York University Press, 1996); Grace Eliza-

beth Hale, *Making Whiteness: The Culture of Segregation in the South, 1890–1940* (New York: Vintage Books, 1998); Matthew Frye Jacobson, *Whiteness of a Different Color: European Immigrants and the Alchemy of Race* (Cambridge: Harvard University Press, 1998); Noel Ignatiev, *How the Irish Became White* (New York: Routledge: 1995); Noel Ignatiev and John Garvey, eds., *Race Traitor* (New York: Routledge, 1996); George Lipsitz, *The Possessive Investment in Whiteness: How White People Profit from Identity Politics* (Philadelphia: Temple University Press, 1998); Michael Omi and Howard Winant, *Racial Formation in the United States: From the 1960s to the 1990s*, 2d ed. (New York: Routledge, 1994); David R. Roediger, *Black on White: Black Writers on What It Means to Be White* (New York: Schocken, 1998); David R. Roediger, *The Wages of Whiteness: Race and the Making of the American Working Class*, rev. ed. (London: Verso, 1991); Alexander Saxton, *The Rise and Fall of the White Republic: Class Politics and Mass Culture in Nineteenth-Century America* (London: Verso, 1990).

8. *See* Herbert J. Gans, "Symbolic Ethnicity: The Future of Ethnic Groups and Cultures in America," *Ethnic and Racial Studies* 2 no. 1 (1979): 1.

9. Beverely Daniel Tatum, *Why Are All the Black Kids Sitting Together in the Cafeteria: And Other Conversations About Race*, rev. ed. (New York: Basic, 1999).

10. *See* U.S. Department of Labor, Federal Glass Ceiling Commission. *A Solid Investment: Making Full Use of the Nation's Human Capital* (Washington, D.C.: U.S. Printing Office, 1995) and Federal Glass Ceiling Commission. *Good for Business: Making Full Use of the Nation's Human Capital* (Washington. D.C.: U.S. Printing Office, 1995). *See* Richard L. Zweigenhaft and C. William Domhoff, *Diversity in the Power Elite: Have Women and Minorities Reached the Top?* (New Haven, Conn.: Yale University Press, 1998). The effects continue to this day. *See* Johnathan U. Glater, "Law Firms Are Slow in Promoting Minority Lawyers to Partnerships," *New York Times*, August 7, 2001, A1. A well-known case study concerning an African American attorney at an elite law firm who failed to make partner, who was not only well-qualified but also politically conservative, is Paul M. Barrett. *The Good Black: A True Story of Race in America* (New York: Dutton, 1999).

11. Once the fourth largest city in the country, Detroit has declined to become one of the poorest. Continuing to experience population loss, the number of white residents dropped from more than 1.5 million in 1950 to fewer than 225,000 in 1990. Despite modest integration elsewhere, over time segregation has become more pronounced in Detroit. *See generally* Reynold Farley et al., *Detroit Divided* (New York: Russell Sage Foundation, 2000) and Thomas J. Sugrue, *The Origins of the Urban Crisis: Race and Inequality in Postwar Detroit* (Princeton, N.J.: Princeton University Press, 1996). (Gary, Indiana, is as segregated, or more segregated, but does not compare in scale to Detroit and its metropolitan area.)

12. Among its first students were the white children of the white trustees. It did not have a black president until Mordecai Johnson took the helm in 1926.

13. Stanley Coren, *The Left-Hander Syndrome: The Causes and Consequences of Left-Handedness* (New York: Free Press, 1992). Nor are other means of discriminating among people, some of which we still accept, the same as discriminating by race. Birth order discrimination, which was once severe, does not carry with it the same stigma as racial discrimination. Age discrimination, which continues against both the young and the old, cannot have the same permanence as racial discrimination, for the simple reason that everyone ages at the same rate and passes through each phase of life.

APPENDICES

Appendix A

Declaration of Independence, July 4, 1776

The unanimous Declaration of the thirteen United States of America

When in the Course of human events, it becomes necessary for one people to dissolve the political bands which have connected them with another, and to assume among the powers of the earth, the separate and equal station to which the Laws of Nature and of Nature's God entitle them, a decent respect to the opinions of mankind requires that they should declare the causes which impel them to the separation.

We hold these truths to be self-evident:

That all men are created equal, that they are endowed by their Creator with certain unalienable Rights; that among these are Life, Liberty, and the pursuit of Happiness. That, to secure these rights, Governments are instituted among Men, deriving their just powers from the consent of the governed, that whenever any Form of Government becomes destructive of these ends, it is the Right of the People to alter or to abolish it, and to institute new Government, laying its foundation on such principles and organizing its powers in such form, as to them shall seem most likely to effect their Safety and Happiness. Prudence, indeed, will dictate that Governments long established should not be changed for light and transient causes; and accordingly all experience hath shewn, that mankind are more disposed to suffer, while evils are sufferable, than to right themselves by abolishing the forms to which they are accustomed. But when a long train of abuses and usurpations, pursuing invariably the same Object evinces a design to reduce them under absolute Despotism, it is their right, it is their duty, to throw off such Government, and to provide new Guards for their future security. Such has been the patient sufferance of these Colonies; and such is now the necessity which constrains them to alter their former sSystems of Government. The history of the present King of Great Britain is a history of repeated injuries and usurpations, all having in direct object the establishment of an absolute Tyranny over these States. To prove this, let Facts be submitted to a candid world.

He has refused his Assent to Laws, the most wholesome and necessary for the public good.

He has forbidden his Governors to pass Laws of immediate and pressing importance, unless suspended in their operation till his Assent should be obtained; and, when so suspended, he has utterly neglected to attend to them.

He has refused to pass other Laws for the accommodation of large districts of people, unless those people would relinquish the right of Representation in the Legislature, a right inestimable to them and formidable to tyrants only.

He has called together legislative bodies at places unusual, uncomfortable, and distant from the depository of their public Records, for the sole purpose of fatiguing them into compliance with his measures.

He has dissolved Representative Houses repeatedly, for opposing, with manly firmness, his invasions on the rights of the people.

He has refused for a long time, after such dissolutions, to cause others to be elected; whereby the Legislative powers, incapable of Annihilation, have returned to the People at large for their exercise; the State remaining in the mean time exposed to all the dangers of invasions from without, and convulsions within.

He has endeavored to prevent the population of these States; for that purpose obstructing the Laws for Naturalization of Foreigners; refusing to pass others to encourage their migration hither, and raising the conditions of new Appropriations of Lands.

He has obstructed the Administration of Justice, by refusing his Assent to Laws for establishing judiciary powers.

He has made Judges dependent on his Will alone, for the tenure of their offices, and the amount and payment of their salaries.

He has erected a multitude of New Offices, and sent hither swarms of Officers to harass our people, and eat out their substance.

He has kept among us, in times of peace, Standing Armies without the Consent of our legislatures.

He has affected to render the mMilitary independent of and superior to the Civil power.

He has combined with others to subject us to a jurisdiction foreign to our constitution and unacknowledged by our laws giving his Assent to their Acts of pretended Legislation:

For Quartering large bodies of armed troops among us:

For protecting them, by a mock Trial, from punishment for any Murders which they should commit on the Inhabitants of these States;

For cutting off our Trade with all parts of the world:

For imposing Taxes on us without our Consent:

For depriving us in many cases, of the benefits of Trial by Jury;

For transporting us beyond Seas to be tried for pretended offenses:

For abolishing the free System of English Laws in a neighboring Province, establishing therein an Arbitrary government, and enlarging its Boundaries so as to render it at once an example and fit instrument for introducing the same absolute rule into these Colonies:

For taking away our Charters, abolishing our most valuable Laws, and altering fundamentally the forms of our Governments:

For suspending our own legislatures, and declaring themselves invested with power to legislate for us in all cases whatsoever.

He has abdicated Government here, by declaring us out of his Protection and waging War against us.

He has plundered our seas, ravaged our Coasts, burned our towns, and destroyed the lives of our people.

He is at this time transporting large Armies of foreign Mercenaries to compleat the works of death, desolation and tyranny, already begun with circumstances of Cruelty perfidy scarcely paralleled in the most barbarous ages, and totally unworthy the Head of a civilized nation.

He has constrained our fellow Citizens taken Captive on the high Seas to bear Arms against their Country, to become the executioners of their friends and Brethren, or to fall themselves by their Hands.

He has excited domestic insurrection among us, and has endeavoured to bring on the inhabitants of our frontiers,the merciless Indian Savages, whose known rule of warfare,s an undistinguished destruction of all ages, sexes and conditions.

In every stage of these Oppressions We have Petitioned for Redress in the most humble terms: Our repeated Petitions have been answered only by repeated injury. A Prince whose character is thus marked by every act which may define a Tyrant, is unfit to be the ruler of a free people.

Nor have We been wanting in our attentions to our British brethren. We have warned them from time to time of attempts by their legislature to extend an unwarrantable jurisdiction over us. We have reminded them of the circumstances of our emigration and settlement here. We have appealed to their native justice and magnanimity, and we have conjured them by the ties of our common kindred to disavow these usurpations, which, would inevitably interrupt our connections and correspondence. They too have been deaf to the voice of justice and of consanguinity. We must, therefore, acquiesce in the necessity, which denounces our Separation, and hold them, as we hold the rest of mankind, Enemies in War, in Peace Friends.

We, therefore, the Representatives of the United States of America, in General Congress, Assembled, appealing to the Supreme Judge of the world for the rectitude of our intentions, do, in the Name, and by the Authority of the good People of these Colonies, solemnly publish and declare, That these United Colonies are, and of Right ought to be Free and Independent States; that they are Absolved from all Allegiance to the British Crown, and that all political connection between them and the State of Great Britain, is and ought to be totally dissolved; and that, as Free and Independent States, they have full Power to levy War, conclude Peace, contract Alliances, establish Commerce, and do all other Acts and Things which Independent States may of right do. And for the support of this Declaration, with a firm reliance on the protection of divine Providence, we mutually pledge to each other our Lives, our Fortunes and our sacred Honor.

Appendix B

Constitution of the United States

We the People of the United States, in Order to form a more perfect Union, establish Justice, insure domestic Tranquility, provide for the common defence, promote the general Welfare, and secure the Blessings of Liberty to ourselves and our Posterity, do ordain and establish this Constitution for the United States of America.

Article I

Section 1

All legislative Powers herein granted shall be vested in a Congress of the United States, which shall consist of a Senate and House of Representatives.

Section 2

The House of Representatives shall be composed of Members chosen every second Year by the People of the several States, and the Electors in each State shall have the Qualifications requisite for Electors of the most numerous Branch of the State Legislature.

No Person shall be a Representative who shall not have attained to the Age of twenty five Years, and been seven Years a Citizen of the United States, and who shall not, when elected, be an Inhabitant of that State in which he shall be chosen.

Representatives and direct Taxes shall be apportioned among the several States which may be included within this Union, according to their respective Numbers, which shall be determined by adding to the whole Number of free Persons, including those bound to Service for a Term of Years, and excluding Indians not taxed, three fifths of all other Persons. The actual Enumeration shall be made within three Years after the first Meeting of the Congress of the United States, and within every subsequent Term of ten Years, in such Manner as they shall by Law direct. The Number of Representatives shall not exceed one for every thirty Thousand, but each State shall have at Least one Representative; and until such enumeration shall be made, the State of New Hampshire shall be entitled to chuse three, Massachusetts eight, Rhode-Island and Providence Plantations one, Connecticut five,

New-York six, New Jersey four, Pennsylvania eight, Delaware one, Maryland six, Virginia ten, North Carolina five, South Carolina five, and Georgia three.

When vacancies happen in the Representation from any State, the Executive Authority thereof shall issue Writs of Election to fill such Vacancies.

The House of Representatives shall chuse their Speaker and other Officers; and shall have the sole Power of Impeachment.

Section 3

The Senate of the United States shall be composed of two Senators from each State, chosen by the Legislature thereof for six Years; and each Senator shall have one Vote.

Immediately after they shall be assembled in Consequence of the first Election, they shall be divided as equally as may be into three Classes. The Seats of the Senators of the first Class shall be vacated at the Expiration of the second Year, of the second Class at the Expiration of the fourth Year, and of the third Class at the Expiration of the sixth Year, so that one third may be chosen every second Year; and if Vacancies happen by Resignation, or otherwise, during the Recess of the Legislature of any State, the Executive thereof may make temporary Appointments until the next Meeting of the Legislature, which shall then fill such Vacancies.

No Person shall be a Senator who shall not have attained to the Age of thirty Years, and been nine Years a Citizen of the United States, and who shall not, when elected, be an Inhabitant of that State for which he shall be chosen.

The Vice President of the United States shall be President of the Senate, but shall have no Vote, unless they be equally divided.

The Senate shall chuse their other Officers, and also a President pro tempore, in the Absence of the Vice President, or when he shall exercise the Office of President of the United States.

The Senate shall have the sole Power to try all Impeachments. When sitting for that Purpose, they shall be on Oath or Affirmation. When the President of the United States is tried, the Chief Justice shall preside: And no Person shall be convicted without the Concurrence of two thirds of the Members present.

Judgment in Cases of Impeachment shall not extend further than to removal from Office, and disqualification to hold and enjoy any Office of honor, Trust or Profit under the United

States: but the Party convicted shall nevertheless be liable and subject to Indictment, Trial, Judgment and Punishment, according to Law.

Section 4

The Times, Places and Manner of holding Elections for Senators and Representatives, shall be prescribed in each State by the Legislature thereof; but the Congress may at any time by Law make or alter such Regulations, except as to the Places of chusing Senators.

The Congress shall assemble at least once in every Year, and such Meeting shall be on the first Monday in December, unless they shall by Law appoint a different Day.

Section 5

Each House shall be the Judge of the Elections, Returns and Qualifications of its own Members, and a Majority of each shall constitute a Quorum to do Business; but a smaller Number may adjourn from day to day, and may be authorized to compel the Attendance of absent Members, in such Manner, and under such Penalties as each House may provide.

Each House may determine the Rules of its Proceedings, punish its Members for disorderly Behaviour, and, with the Concurrence of two thirds, expel a Member.

Each House shall keep a Journal of its Proceedings, and from time to time publish the same, excepting such Parts as may in their Judgment require Secrecy; and the Yeas and Nays of the Members of either House on any question shall, at the Desire of one fifth of those Present, be entered on the Journal.

Neither House, during the Session of Congress, shall, without the Consent of the other, adjourn for more than three days, nor to any other Place than that in which the two Houses shall be sitting.

Section 6

The Senators and Representatives shall receive a Compensation for their Services, to be ascertained by Law, and paid out of the Treasury of the United States. They shall in all Cases, except Treason, Felony and Breach of the Peace, be privileged from Arrest during their Attendance at the Session of their respective Houses, and in going to and returning from the same; and for any Speech or Debate in either House, they shall not be questioned in any other Place.

No Senator or Representative shall, during the Time for which he was elected, be appointed to any civil Office under the Authority of the United States, which shall have been created, or the Emoluments whereof shall have been encreased during such time; and no Person holding any Office under the United States, shall be a Member of either House during his Continuance in Office.

Section 7

All Bills for raising Revenue shall originate in the House of Representatives; but the Senate may propose or concur with Amendments as on other Bills.

Every Bill which shall have passed the House of Representatives and the Senate, shall, before it become a Law, be presented to the President of the United States: If he approve he shall sign it, but if not he shall return it, with his Objections to that House in which it shall have originated, who shall enter the Objections at large on their Journal, and proceed to reconsider it. If after such Reconsideration two thirds of that House shall agree to pass the Bill, it shall be sent, together with the Objections, to the other House, by which it shall likewise be reconsidered, and if approved by two thirds of that House, it shall become a Law. But in all such Cases the Votes of both Houses shall be determined by yeas and Nays, and the Names of the Persons voting for and against the Bill shall be entered on the Journal of each House respectively. If any Bill shall not be returned by the President within ten Days (Sundays excepted) after it shall have been presented to him, the Same shall be a Law, in like Manner as if he had signed it, unless the Congress by their Adjournment prevent its Return, in which Case it shall not be a Law.

Every Order, Resolution, or Vote to which the Concurrence of the Senate and House of Representatives may be necessary (except on a question of Adjournment) shall be presented to the President of the United States; and before the Same shall take Effect, shall be approved by him, or being disapproved by him, shall be repassed by two thirds of the Senate and House of Representatives, according to the Rules and Limitations prescribed in the Case of a Bill.

Section 8

The Congress shall have Power To lay and collect Taxes, Duties, Imposts and Excises, to pay the Debts and provide for the common Defence and general Welfare of the United States; but all Duties, Imposts and Excises shall be uniform throughout the United States;

To borrow Money on the credit of the United States;

To regulate Commerce with foreign Nations, and among the several States, and with the Indian Tribes;

To establish an uniform Rule of Naturalization, and uniform Laws on the subject of Bankruptcies throughout the United States;

To coin Money, regulate the Value thereof, and of foreign Coin, and fix the Standard of Weights and Measures;

To provide for the Punishment of counterfeiting the Securities and current Coin of the United States;

To establish Post Offices and post Roads;

To promote the Progress of Science and useful Arts, by securing for limited Times to Authors and Inventors the exclusive Right to their respective Writings and Discoveries;

To constitute Tribunals inferior to the supreme Court;

To define and punish Piracies and Felonies committed on the high Seas, and Offences against the Law of Nations;

To declare War, grant Letters of Marque and Reprisal, and make Rules concerning Captures on Land and Water;

To raise and support Armies, but no Appropriation of Money to that Use shall be for a longer Term than two Years;

To provide and maintain a Navy;

To make Rules for the Government and Regulation of the land and naval Forces;

To provide for calling forth the Militia to execute the Laws of the Union, suppress Insurrections and repel Invasions;

To provide for organizing, arming, and disciplining, the Militia, and for governing such Part of them as may be employed in the Service of the United States, reserving to the States respectively, the Appointment of the Officers, and the Authority of training the Militia according to the discipline prescribed by Congress;

To exercise exclusive Legislation in all Cases whatsoever, over such District (not exceeding ten Miles square) as may, by Cession of particular States, and the Acceptance of Congress, become the Seat of the Government of the United States, and to exercise like Authority over all Places purchased by the Consent of the Legislature of the State in which the Same shall be, for the Erection of Forts, Magazines, Arsenals, dock-Yards, and other needful Buildings;—And

To make all Laws which shall be necessary and proper for carrying into Execution the foregoing Powers, and all other Powers vested by this Constitution in the Government of the United States, or in any Department or Officer thereof.

Section 9

The Migration or Importation of such Persons as any of the States now existing shall think proper to admit, shall not be prohibited by the Congress prior to the Year one thousand eight hundred and eight, but a Tax or duty may be imposed on such Importation, not exceeding ten dollars for each Person.

The Privilege of the Writ of Habeas Corpus shall not be suspended, unless when in Cases of Rebellion or Invasion the public Safety may require it.

No Bill of Attainder or ex post facto Law shall be passed.

No Capitation, or other direct, Tax shall be laid, unless in Proportion to the Census or enumeration herein before directed to be taken.

No Tax or Duty shall be laid on Articles exported from any State.

No Preference shall be given by any Regulation of Commerce or Revenue to the Ports of one State over those of another; nor shall Vessels bound to, or from, one State, be obliged to enter, clear, or pay Duties in another.

No Money shall be drawn from the Treasury, but in Consequence of Appropriations made by Law; and a regular Statement and Account of the Receipts and Expenditures of all public Money shall be published from time to time.

No Title of Nobility shall be granted by the United States: And no Person holding any Office of Profit or Trust under them, shall, without the Consent of the Congress, accept of any present, Emolument, Office, or Title, of any kind whatever, from any King, Prince, or foreign State.

Section 10

No State shall enter into any Treaty, Alliance, or Confederation; grant Letters of Marque and Reprisal; coin Money; emit Bills of Credit; make any Thing but gold and silver Coin a Tender in Payment of Debts; pass any Bill of Attainder, ex post facto Law, or Law impairing the Obligation of Contracts, or grant any Title of Nobility.

No State shall, without the Consent of the Congress, lay any Imposts or Duties on Imports or Exports, except what may be absolutely necessary for executing it's inspection Laws: and the net Produce of all Duties and Imposts, laid by any State on Imports or Exports, shall be for the Use of the Treasury of the United States; and all such Laws shall be subject to the Revision and Controul of the Congress.

No State shall, without the Consent of Congress, lay any Duty of Tonnage, keep Troops, or Ships of War in time of Peace, enter into any Agreement or Compact with another State, or with a foreign Power, or engage in War, unless actually invaded, or in such imminent Danger as will not admit of delay.

Article II

Section 1

The executive Power shall be vested in a President of the United States of America. He shall hold his Office during the Term of four Years, and, together with the Vice President, chosen for the same Term, be elected, as follows:

Each State shall appoint, in such Manner as the Legislature thereof may direct, a Number of Electors, equal to the whole Number of Senators and Representatives to which the State may be entitled in the Congress: but no Senator or Representative, or Person holding an Office of Trust or Profit under the United States, shall be appointed an Elector.

The Electors shall meet in their respective States, and vote by Ballot for two Persons, of whom one at least shall not be an Inhabitant of the same State with themselves. And they shall make a List of all the Persons voted for, and of the Number of Votes for each; which List they shall sign and certify, and transmit sealed to the Seat of the Government of the United States, directed to the President of the Senate. The President of the Senate shall, in the Presence of the Senate and House of Representatives, open all the Certificates, and the Votes shall then be counted. The Person having the greatest Number of Votes shall be the President, if such Number be a Majority of the whole Number of Electors appointed; and if there be more than one who have such Majority, and have an equal Number of Votes, then the House of Representatives shall immediately chuse by Ballot one of them for President; and if no Person have a Majority, then from the five highest on the List the said House shall in like Manner chuse the President. But in chusing the President, the Votes shall be taken by States, the Representation from each State having one Vote; A quorum for this purpose shall consist of a Member or Members from two thirds of the States, and a Majority of all the States shall be necessary to a Choice. In every Case, after the Choice of the President, the Person having the greatest Number of Votes of the Electors shall be the Vice President. But if there should remain two or more who have equal Votes, the Senate shall chuse from them by Ballot the Vice President.

The Congress may determine the Time of chusing the Electors, and the Day on which they shall give their Votes; which Day shall be the same throughout the United States.

No Person except a natural born Citizen, or a Citizen of the United States, at the time of the Adoption of this Constitution, shall be eligible to the Office of President; neither shall any Person be eligible to that Office who shall not have attained to the Age of thirty five Years, and been fourteen Years a Resident within the United States.

In Case of the Removal of the President from Office, or of his Death, Resignation, or Inability to discharge the Powers and Duties of the said Office, the Same shall devolve on the Vice President, and the Congress may by Law provide for the Case of Removal, Death, Resignation or Inability, both of the President and Vice President, declaring what Officer shall then act as President, and such Officer shall act accordingly, until the Disability be removed, or a President shall be elected.

The President shall, at stated Times, receive for his Services, a Compensation, which shall neither be increased nor diminished during the Period for which he shall have been elected, and he shall not receive within that Period any other Emolument from the United States, or any of them.

Before he enter on the Execution of his Office, he shall take the following Oath or Affirmation:—"I do solemnly swear (or affirm) that I will faithfully execute the Office of President of the United States, and will to the best of my Ability, preserve, protect and defend the Constitution of the United States."

Section 2

The President shall be Commander in Chief of the Army and Navy of the United States, and of the Militia of the several States, when called into the actual Service of the United States; he may require the Opinion, in writing, of the principal Officer in each of the executive Departments, upon any Subject relating to the Duties of their respective Offices, and he shall have Power to grant Reprieves and Pardons for Offences against the United States, except in Cases of Impeachment.

He shall have Power, by and with the Advice and Consent of the Senate, to make Treaties, provided two thirds of the Senators present concur; and he shall nominate, and by and with the Advice and Consent of the Senate, shall appoint Ambassadors, other public Ministers and Consuls, Judges of the supreme Court, and all other Officers of the United States, whose Appointments are not herein otherwise provided for, and which shall be established by Law: but the Congress may by Law vest the Appointment of such inferior Officers, as they think proper, in the President alone, in the Courts of Law, or in the Heads of Departments.

The President shall have Power to fill up all Vacancies that may happen during the Recess of the Senate, by granting Commissions which shall expire at the End of their next Session.

Section 3

He shall from time to time give to the Congress Information of the State of the Union, and recommend to their Consideration such Measures as he shall judge necessary and expedient; he may, on extraordinary Occasions, convene both Houses, or either of them, and in Case of Disagreement between them, with Respect to the Time of Adjournment, he may adjourn them to such Time as he shall think proper; he shall receive Ambassadors and other public Ministers; he shall take Care that the Laws be faithfully executed, and shall Commission all the Officers of the United States.

Section 4

The President, Vice President and all civil Officers of the United States, shall be removed from Office on Impeachment for, and Conviction of, Treason, Bribery, or other high Crimes and Misdemeanors.

Article III

Section 1

The judicial Power of the United States shall be vested in one supreme Court, and in such inferior Courts as the Congress may from time to time ordain and establish. The Judges, both of the supreme and inferior Courts, shall hold their Offices during good Behaviour, and shall, at stated Times, receive for their Services a Compensation, which shall not be diminished during their Continuance in Office.

Section 2

The judicial Power shall extend to all Cases, in Law and Equity, arising under this Constitution, the Laws of the United States, and Treaties made, or which shall be made, under their Authority;—to all Cases affecting Ambassadors, other public Ministers and Consuls;—to all Cases of admiralty and maritime Jurisdiction;—to Controversies to which the United States shall be a Party;—to Controversies between two or more States;—between a State and Citizens of another State,—between Citizens of different States,—between Citizens of the same State claiming Lands under Grants of different States, and between a State, or the Citizens thereof, and foreign States, Citizens or Subjects.

In all Cases affecting Ambassadors, other public Ministers and Consuls, and those in which a State shall be Party, the supreme Court shall have original Jurisdiction. In all the other

Cases before mentioned, the supreme Court shall have appellate Jurisdiction, both as to Law and Fact, with such Exceptions, and under such Regulations as the Congress shall make.

The Trial of all Crimes, except in Cases of Impeachment, shall be by Jury; and such Trial shall be held in the State where the said Crimes shall have been committed; but when not committed within any State, the Trial shall be at such Place or Places as the Congress may by Law have directed.

Section 3

Treason against the United States, shall consist only in levying War against them, or in adhering to their Enemies, giving them Aid and Comfort. No Person shall be convicted of Treason unless on the Testimony of two Witnesses to the same overt Act, or on Confession in open Court.

The Congress shall have Power to declare the Punishment of Treason, but no Attainder of Treason shall work Corruption of Blood, or Forfeiture except during the Life of the Person attainted.

Article IV

Section 1

Full Faith and Credit shall be given in each State to the public Acts, Records, and judicial Proceedings of every other State. And the Congress may by general Laws prescribe the Manner in which such Acts, Records and Proceedings shall be proved, and the Effect thereof.

Section 2

The Citizens of each State shall be entitled to all Privileges and Immunities of Citizens in the several States.

A Person charged in any State with Treason, Felony, or other Crime, who shall flee from Justice, and be found in another State, shall on Demand of the executive Authority of the State from which he fled, be delivered up, to be removed to the State having Jurisdiction of the Crime.

No Person held to Service or Labour in one State, under the Laws thereof, escaping into another, shall, in Consequence of any Law or Regulation therein, be discharged from such Service or Labour, but shall be delivered up on Claim of the Party to whom such Service or Labour may be due.

Section 3

New States may be admitted by the Congress into this Union; but no new State shall be formed or erected within the Jurisdiction of any other State; nor any State be formed by the Junction of two or more States, or Parts of States, without the Consent of the Legislatures of the States concerned as well as of the Congress.

The Congress shall have Power to dispose of and make all needful Rules and Regulations respecting the Territory or other Property belonging to the United States; and nothing in this Constitution shall be so construed as to Prejudice any Claims of the United States, or of any particular State.

Section 4

The United States shall guarantee to every State in this Union a Republican Form of Government, and shall protect each of them against Invasion; and on Application of the Legislature, or of the Executive (when the Legislature cannot be convened), against domestic Violence.

Article V

The Congress, whenever two thirds of both Houses shall deem it necessary, shall propose Amendments to this Constitution, or, on the Application of the Legislatures of two thirds of the several States, shall call a Convention for proposing Amendments, which, in either Case, shall be valid to all Intents and Purposes, as Part of this Constitution, when ratified by the Legislatures of three fourths of the several States, or by Conventions in three fourths thereof, as the one or the other Mode of Ratification may be proposed by the Congress; Provided that no Amendment which may be made prior to the Year One thousand eight hundred and eight shall in any Manner affect the first and fourth Clauses in the Ninth Section of the first Article; and that no State, without its Consent, shall be deprived of its equal Suffrage in the Senate.

Article VI

All Debts contracted and Engagements entered into, before the Adoption of this Constitution, shall be as valid against the United States under this Constitution, as under the Confederation.

This Constitution, and the Laws of the United States which shall be made in Pursuance thereof; and all Treaties made, or which shall be made, under the Authority of the United States, shall be the supreme Law of the Land; and the Judges in every State shall be bound thereby, any Thing in the Constitution or Laws of any State to the Contrary notwithstanding.

The Senators and Representatives before mentioned, and the Members of the several State Legislatures, and all executive and judicial Officers, both of the United States and of the several States, shall be bound by Oath or Affirmation, to support this Constitution; but no religious Test shall ever be required as a Qualification to any Office or public Trust under the United States.

Article VII

The Ratification of the Conventions of nine States, shall be sufficient for the Establishment of this Constitution between the States so ratifying the Same.

Appendix C

Amendments

The first ten amendments were ratified December 15, 1791, and form what is known as the "Bill of Rights."

AMENDMENT I

Congress shall make no law respecting an establishment of religion, or prohibiting the free exercise thereof; or abridging the freedom of speech, or of the press; or the right of the people peaceably to assemble, and to petition the Government for a redress of grievances.

AMENDMENT II

A well regulated Militia, being necessary to the security of a free State, the right of the people to keep and bear Arms, shall not be infringed.

AMENDMENT III

No Soldier shall, in time of peace be quartered in any house, without the consent of the Owner, nor in time of war, but in a manner to be prescribed by law.

AMENDMENT IV

The right of the people to be secure in their persons, houses, papers, and effects, against unreasonable searches and seizures, shall not be violated, and no Warrants shall issue, but upon probable cause, supported by Oath or affirmation, and particularly describing the place to be searched, and the persons or things to be seized.

AMENDMENT V

No person shall be held to answer for a capital, or otherwise infamous crime, unless on a presentment or indictment of a Grand Jury, except in cases arising in the land or naval forces, or in the Militia, when in actual service in time of War or public danger; nor shall any person be subject for the same offence to be twice put in jeopardy of life or limb; nor shall be compelled in any criminal case to be a witness against himself, nor be deprived of life, liberty, or property, without due process of law; nor shall private property be taken for public use, without just compensation.

AMENDMENT VI

In all criminal prosecutions, the accused shall enjoy the right to a speedy and public trial, by an impartial jury of the State and district wherein the crime shall have been committed, which district shall have been previously ascertained by law, and to be informed of the nature and cause of the accusation; to be confronted with the witnesses against him; to have compulsory process for obtaining witnesses in his favor, and to have the Assistance of Counsel for his defence.

AMENDMENT VII

In Suits at common law, where the value in controversy shall exceed twenty dollars, the right of trial by jury shall be preserved, and no fact tried by a jury, shall be otherwise re-examined in any Court of the United States, than according to the rules of the common law.

AMENDMENT VIII

Excessive bail shall not be required, nor excessive fines imposed, nor cruel and unusual punishments inflicted.

AMENDMENT IX

The enumeration in the Constitution, of certain rights, shall not be construed to deny or disparage others retained by the people.

AMENDMENT X

The powers not delegated to the United States by the Constitution, nor prohibited by it to the States, are reserved to the States respectively, or to the people.

AMENDMENT XI

Passed by Congress March 4, 1794. Ratified February 7, 1795.

Note: Article III, section 2, of the Constitution was modified by amendment 11.

The Judicial power of the United States shall not be construed to extend to any suit in law or equity, commenced or prosecuted against one of the United States by Citizens of another State, or by Citizens or Subjects of any Foreign State.

AMENDMENT XII

Passed by Congress December 9, 1803. Ratified June 15, 1804.

Note: A portion of Article II, section 1 of the Constitution was superseded by the 12th amendment.

The Electors shall meet in their respective states and vote by ballot for President and Vice-President, one of whom, at least, shall not be an inhabitant of the same state with themselves; they shall name in their ballots the person voted for as President, and in distinct ballots the person voted for as Vice-President, and they shall make distinct lists of all persons voted for as President, and of all persons voted for as Vice-President, and of the number of votes for each, which lists they shall sign and certify, and transmit sealed to the seat of the government of the United States, directed to the President of the Senate;—the President of the Senate shall, in the presence of the Senate and House of Representatives, open all the certificates and the votes shall then be counted;—The person having the greatest number of votes for President, shall be the President, if such number be a majority of the whole number of Electors appointed; and if no person have such majority, then from the persons having the highest numbers not exceeding three on the list of those voted for as President, the House of Representatives shall choose immediately, by ballot, the President. But in choosing the President, the votes shall be taken by states, the representation from each state having one vote; a quorum for this purpose shall consist of a member or members from two-thirds of the states, and a majority of all the states shall be necessary to a choice. [And if the House of Representatives shall not choose a President whenever the right of choice shall devolve upon them, before the fourth day of March next following, then the Vice-President shall act as President, as in case of the death or other constitutional disability of the President.—]* The person having the greatest number of votes as Vice-President, shall be the Vice-President, if such number be a majority of the whole number of Electors appointed, and if no person have a majority, then from the two highest numbers on the list, the Senate shall choose the Vice-President; a quorum for the purpose shall consist of two-thirds of the whole number of Senators, and a majority of the whole number shall be necessary to a choice. But no person constitutionally ineligible to the office of President shall be eligible to that of Vice-President of the United States.

*Superseded by section 3 of the 20th amendment.

AMENDMENT XIII

Passed by Congress January 31, 1865. Ratified December 6, 1865.

Note: A portion of Article IV, section 2, of the Constitution was superseded by the 13th amendment.

Section 1

Neither slavery nor involuntary servitude, except as a punishment for crime whereof the party shall have been duly convicted, shall exist within the United States, or any place subject to their jurisdiction.

Section 2

Congress shall have power to enforce this article by appropriate legislation.

AMENDMENT XIV

Passed by Congress June 13, 1866. Ratified July 9, 1868.

Note: Article I, section 2, of the Constitution was modified by section 2 of the 14th amendment.

Section 1

All persons born or naturalized in the United States, and subject to the jurisdiction thereof, are citizens of the United States and of the State wherein they reside. No State shall make or enforce any law which shall abridge the privileges or immunities of citizens of the United States; nor shall any State deprive any person of life, liberty, or property, without due process of law; nor deny to any person within its jurisdiction the equal protection of the laws.

Section 2

Representatives shall be apportioned among the several States according to their respective numbers, counting the whole number of persons in each State, excluding Indians not taxed. But when the right to vote at any election for the choice of electors for President and Vice-President of the United States, Representatives in Congress, the Executive and Judicial officers of a State, or the members of the Legislature thereof, is denied to any of the male inhabitants of such State, being twenty-one years of age,* and citizens of the United States, or in any way abridged, except for participation in rebellion, or other crime, the basis of representation therein shall be reduced in the proportion which the number of such male citizens shall bear to the whole number of male citizens twenty-one years of age in such State.

Changed by section 1 of the 26th amendment.

Section 3

No person shall be a Senator or Representative in Congress, or elector of President and Vice-President, or hold any office, civil or military, under the United States, or under any State, who, having previously taken an oath, as a member of Congress, or as an officer of the United States, or as a member of any State legislature, or as an executive or judicial officer of any State, to support the Constitution of the United States, shall have engaged in insurrection or rebellion against the same, or given aid or comfort to the enemies thereof. But Congress may by a vote of two-thirds of each House, remove such disability.

Section 4

The validity of the public debt of the United States, authorized by law, including debts incurred for payment of pensions and bounties for services in suppressing insurrection or rebellion, shall not be questioned. But neither the United States nor any State shall assume or pay any debt or obligation incurred in aid of insurrection or rebellion against the United States, or any claim for the loss or emancipation of any slave; but all such debts, obligations and claims shall be held illegal and void.

Section 5

The Congress shall have the power to enforce, by appropriate legislation, the provisions of this article.

AMENDMENT XV

Passed by Congress February 26, 1869. Ratified February 3, 1870.

Section 1

The right of citizens of the United States to vote shall not be denied or abridged by the United States or by any State on account of race, color, or previous condition of servitude—

Section 2

The Congress shall have the power to enforce this article by appropriate legislation.

AMENDMENT XVI

Passed by Congress July 2, 1909. Ratified February 3, 1913.

Note: Article I, section 9, of the Constitution was modified by amendment 16.

The Congress shall have power to lay and collect taxes on incomes, from whatever source derived, without apportionment among the several States, and without regard to any census or enumeration.

AMENDMENT XVII

Passed by Congress May 13, 1912. Ratified April 8, 1913.

Note: Article I, section 3, of the Constitution was modified by the 17th amendment.

The Senate of the United States shall be composed of two Senators from each State, elected by the people thereof, for six years; and each Senator shall have one vote. The electors in each State shall have the qualifications requisite for electors of the most numerous branch of the State legislatures.

When vacancies happen in the representation of any State in the Senate, the executive authority of such State shall issue writs of election to fill such vacancies: Provided, That the legislature of any State may empower the executive thereof to make temporary appointments until the people fill the vacancies by election as the legislature may direct.

This amendment shall not be so construed as to affect the election or term of any Senator chosen before it becomes valid as part of the Constitution.

AMENDMENT XVIII

Passed by Congress December 18, 1917. Ratified January 16, 1919. Repealed by amendment 21.

Section 1

After one year from the ratification of this article the manufacture, sale, or transportation of intoxicating liquors within, the importation thereof into, or the exportation thereof from the United States and all territory subject to the jurisdiction thereof for beverage purposes is hereby prohibited.

Section 2

The Congress and the several States shall have concurrent power to enforce this article by appropriate legislation.

Section 3

This article shall be inoperative unless it shall have been ratified as an amendment to the Constitution by the legislatures of the several States, as provided in the Constitution, within seven years from the date of the submission hereof to the States by the Congress.

AMENDMENT XIX

Passed by Congress June 4, 1919. Ratified August 18, 1920.

The right of citizens of the United States to vote shall not be denied or abridged by the United States or by any State on account of sex.

Congress shall have power to enforce this article by appropriate legislation.

AMENDMENT XX

Passed by Congress March 2, 1932. Ratified January 23, 1933.

Note: Article I, section 4, of the Constitution was modified by section 2 of this amendment. In addition, a portion of the 12th amendment was superseded by section 3.

Section 1

The terms of the President and the Vice President shall end at noon on the 20th day of January, and the terms of Senators and Representatives at noon on the 3d day of January, of the years in which such terms would have ended if this article had not been ratified; and the terms of their successors shall then begin.

Section 2

The Congress shall assemble at least once in every year, and such meeting shall begin at noon on the 3d day of January, unless they shall by law appoint a different day.

Section 3

If, at the time fixed for the beginning of the term of the President, the President elect shall have died, the Vice President elect shall become President. If a President shall not have been chosen before the time fixed for the beginning of his term, or if the President elect shall have failed to qualify, then the Vice President elect shall act as President until a President shall have qualified; and the Congress may by law provide for the case wherein neither a President elect nor a Vice President shall have qualified, declaring who shall then act as President, or the manner in which one who is to act shall be selected, and such person shall act accordingly until a President or Vice President shall have qualified.

Section 4

The Congress may by law provide for the case of the death of any of the persons from whom the House of Representatives may choose a President whenever the right of choice shall have devolved upon them, and for the case of the death of any of the persons from whom the Senate may choose a Vice President whenever the right of choice shall have devolved upon them.

Section 5

Sections 1 and 2 shall take effect on the 15th day of October following the ratification of this article.

Section 6

This article shall be inoperative unless it shall have been ratified as an amendment to the Constitution by the legislatures of three-fourths of the several States within seven years from the date of its submission.

AMENDMENT XXI

Passed by Congress February 20, 1933. Ratified December 5, 1933.

Section 1

The eighteenth article of amendment to the Constitution of the United States is hereby repealed.

Section 2

The transportation or importation into any State, Territory, or Possession of the United States for delivery or use therein of intoxicating liquors, in violation of the laws thereof, is hereby prohibited.

Section 3

This article shall be inoperative unless it shall have been ratified as an amendment to the Constitution by conventions in the several States, as provided in the Constitution, within seven years from the date of the submission hereof to the States by the Congress.

AMENDMENT XXII

Passed by Congress March 21, 1947. Ratified February 27, 1951.

Section 1

No person shall be elected to the office of the President more than twice, and no person who has held the office of President, or acted as President, for more than two years of a term to which some other person was elected President shall be elected to the office of President more than once. But this Article shall not apply to any person holding the office of President when this Article was proposed by Congress, and shall not prevent any person who may be holding the office of President, or acting as President, during the term within which this Article becomes operative from holding the office of President or acting as President during the remainder of such term.

Section 2

This article shall be inoperative unless it shall have been ratified as an amendment to the Constitution by the legislatures of three-fourths of the several States within seven years from the date of its submission to the States by the Congress.

AMENDMENT XXIII

Passed by Congress June 16, 1960. Ratified March 29, 1961.

Section 1

The District constituting the seat of Government of the United States shall appoint in such manner as Congress may direct:

A number of electors of President and Vice President equal to the whole number of Senators and Representatives in Congress to which the District would be entitled if it were a State, but in no event more than the least populous State; they shall be in addition to those appointed by the States, but they shall be considered, for the purposes of the election of President and Vice President, to be electors appointed by a State; and they shall meet in the District and perform such duties as provided by the twelfth article of amendment.

Section 2

The Congress shall have power to enforce this article by appropriate legislation.

AMENDMENT XXIV

Passed by Congress August 27, 1962. Ratified January 23, 1964.

Section 1

The right of citizens of the United States to vote in any primary or other election for President or Vice President, for electors for President or Vice President, or for Senator or Representative in Congress, shall not be denied or abridged by the United States or any State by reason of failure to pay poll tax or other tax.

Section 2

The Congress shall have power to enforce this article by appropriate legislation.

AMENDMENT XXV

Passed by Congress July 6, 1965. Ratified February 10, 1967.

Note: Article II, section 1, of the Constitution was affected by the 25th amendment.

Section 1

In case of the removal of the President from office or of his death or resignation, the Vice President shall become President.

Section 2

Whenever there is a vacancy in the office of the Vice President, the President shall nominate a Vice President who shall take office upon confirmation by a majority vote of both Houses of Congress.

Section 3

Whenever the President transmits to the President pro tempore of the Senate and the Speaker of the House of Representatives his written declaration that he is unable to discharge the powers and duties of his office, and until he transmits to them a written declaration to the contrary, such powers and duties shall be discharged by the Vice President as Acting President.

Section 4

Whenever the Vice President and a majority of either the principal officers of the executive departments or of such other body as Congress may by law provide, transmit to the President pro tempore of the Senate and the Speaker of the House of Representatives their written declaration that the President is unable to discharge the powers and duties of his office, the Vice President shall immediately assume the powers and duties of the office as Acting President.

Thereafter, when the President transmits to the President pro tempore of the Senate and the Speaker of the House of Representatives his written declaration that no inability exists, he shall resume the powers and duties of his office unless the Vice President and a majority of either the principal officers of the executive department or of such other body as Congress may by law provide, transmit within four days to the President pro tempore of the Senate and the Speaker of the House of Representatives their written declaration that the President is unable to discharge the powers and duties of his office. Thereupon Congress shall decide the issue, assembling within forty-eight hours for that purpose if not in session. If the Congress, within twenty-one days after receipt of the latter written declaration, or, if Congress is not in session, within twenty-one days after Congress is required to assemble, determines by two-thirds vote of both Houses that the President is unable to discharge the powers and duties of his office, the Vice President shall continue to discharge the same as Acting President; otherwise, the President shall resume the powers and duties of his office.

AMENDMENT XXVI

Passed by Congress March 23, 1971. Ratified July 1, 1971.

Note: Amendment 14, section 2, of the Constitution was modified by section 1 of the 26th amendment.

Section 1

The right of citizens of the United States, who are eighteen years of age or older, to vote shall not be denied or abridged by the United States or by any State on account of age.

Section 2

The Congress shall have power to enforce this article by appropriate legislation.

AMENDMENT XXVII

Originally proposed Sept. 25, 1789. Ratified May 7, 1992.

No law, varying the compensation for the services of the Senators and Representatives, shall take effect, until an election of representatives shall have intervened.